W9-AXC-557

A MORE PERFECT UNION

A MORE PERFECT UNION

Advancing New American Rights

JESSE L. JACKSON, JR.

WITH FRANK E. WATKINS

Welcome Rain Publishers / *New York*

A MORE PERFECT UNION

Copyright © 2001 by Jesse L. Jackson, Jr. and Frank E. Watkins

Introduction copyright © 2001 by Dr. Susan Brooks Thistlethwaite

All rights reserved.

Library of Congress Cataloging-in-Publication data
available from the Publisher.

Direct any inquiries to
Welcome Rain Publishers LLC,
532 Laguardia Place, box 473
New York, NY 10012.

ISBN 1-56649-186-X
Manufactured in the United States of America
by Hamilton Printing Company

First Edition: September 2001
1 3 5 7 9 10 8 6 4 2

We the People of the United States,

In Order to form a *more perfect Union*,

establish Justice,

insure domestic Tranquility,

provide for the common defense,

promote the general Welfare,

and

secure the Blessings of Liberty to ourselves

and our Posterity,

do ordain and establish this Constitution

for the United States of America.

**—PREAMBLE TO THE CONSTITUTION
OF THE UNITED STATES OF AMERICA**
(emphasis added)

CONTENTS

Acknowledgments...11

Foreword by Susan Brooks Thistlethwaite.................................13

Introduction...15

CHAPTER 1   Public Servant...19

CHAPTER 2   Born in the Struggle to Vote 27

CHAPTER 3   A Capitol Tour..41

CHAPTER 4   The Denial..54

CHAPTER 5   States' Rights or a More Perfect Union? 72

CHAPTER 6   Race Is Central—Tremors (1619–1861)................................89

CHAPTER 7   Race Is Central—The Great Quake (1861–1865)..............119

CHAPTER 8   Race Is Central—Aftershocks (1865–Present)..................162

CHAPTER 9   A More Perfect Union—Equal Opportunity.....................214

CHAPTER 10   A More Perfect Union—Human Rights..............................241

CHAPTER 11   A More Perfect Union—Full Employment.......................252

CHAPTER 12   A More Perfect Union—Universal and Comprehensive Health Care 285

CHAPTER 13   A More Perfect Union—Affordable Housing 300

CHAPTER 14   A More Perfect Union—A Quality Public Education 329

CHAPTER 15   A More Perfect Union—Equality for Women....................350

CHAPTER 16   A More Perfect Union—The Environment........................370

CHAPTER 17   A More Perfect Union—Fair Taxes 384

CHAPTER 18   A More Perfect Union—Foreign Policy..............................404

CHAPTER 19   Politics..425

CHAPTER 20   God Through Us 473

Epilogue 496

APPENDIX I   Chronology of Key Dates in Forming the U.S. Constitution.................500

APPENDIX II   Gettysburg Address 501

APPENDIX III Universal Declaration of Human Rights 502

APPENDIX IV The Earth Charter 507

Endnotes 513

Bibliography...521

The sweeping conservative victory in the elections of 1994 returned control of Congress to Republicans, repudiated what was left of liberal government, and dramatized the tragic failure of racial integration in America.

Race, as it always is in a modern American election, was the underlying issue. In the autumn of 1994 that issue was a prime determinant of the outcome, as white voters everywhere expressed unmistakable yearning for a lost time, before "they" forced themselves into the nation's consciousness.

White animosity toward and fear of African-Americans—seen largely as criminals and welfare cheats—gave emotional edge and added energy to the election's ostensible issues, and the campaign was fought out in code words and symbolism that disclosed rather than disguised its racial character:

> Fierce denunciations of crime and welfare, in white eyes the most prominent products of the black underclass.
> Withering blasts at liberals and liberalism as the "social engineers" behind the "big government" that tried to force racial integration and brought higher taxes.
> Diatribes against "spending" and "the redistribution of wealth" to the poor, a euphemism for social programs believed primarily to aid African-Americans.
> Loud promises to extend the death penalty, from which African-Americans suffer proportionally far more than whites.
> Overwrought demands for a return to "family values" (a term of many meanings, one of which is the sexual restraint that blacks are supposed by whites to disdain).

—Tom Wicker, *Racial Integration in America*

ACKNOWLEDGMENTS

When I left on a ten-day tour of Civil War battle sites in August 1997, I had no thought of writing a book. However, in light of what I experienced and learned on the trip (in addition to my congressional experiences), upon my return the seeds of one had been planted in my mind. As a result, with fervid resolve, Frank and I spent the next three and a half years reading, reflecting, discussing, debating, and writing *A More Perfect Union*. But it literally could not have been done without the help of hundreds of people, most of whom were anonymous but kind enough to share their views forthrightly with us along the way. We acknowledge with gratitude their enormous contribution to this work.

There were also specific resources and people without which this book would not have been possible. I was more interested in being factually accurate than being creative in the chapter on states' rights and the three "earthquake" chapters dealing with the history of slavery, the Civil War, and the legacies of both. Therefore, *The Oxford Companion to the Supreme Court* became the primary resource for "States' Rights." Peter Kolchin's *American Slavery* helped provide the basic conceptual and informational framework for much of the "Tremors" chapter, and James McPherson's *Battle Cry of Freedom* served a similar purpose for the "Great Quake" chapter. Eric Foner's *Reconstruction* and Lou Falkner Williams's *The Great South Carolina Ku Klux Klan Trials of 1871–1872* were most helpful in "Aftershocks." *Nixon's Piano* by Kenneth O'Reilly was also an influential book and full of important information.

Thomas I. Palley's *Plenty of Nothing* and Frank's previous discussions with Sheila D. Collins and the Jobs For All organization provided many helpful conceptual tools for the "Full Employment" chapter. Peter Dreier had numerous useful suggestions for, and my former legislative director Hilary Weinstein helped rewrite, the "Affordable Housing" chapter. Jan Erickson and Twiss Butler from the National Organization for Women aided in re-working "Equality for Women." John Nowak of the University of Illinois Law School and Jamin Raskin, dean of the American University Law School, were very helpful with the proposed voting rights amendment. Rob Richie, executive director of the Center for Voting and Democracy, and independent political consultant Steve Cobble gave invaluable input and assistance on various aspects of the "Politics" chapter. A special word of thanks is also due former Congressman Augustus Hawkins for reading and giving encouraging words for the full employment and education chapters. George Seymore especially, but also Charles Dujon and Sona Virdi, were masterful in converting the book's amendment "ideas" into concrete legislation. Rick Bryant's weekends and evenings were often spent reading and editing various chapters, and Theresa Caldwell, Will Davis, Annette deCaussin, Ken Edmonds, Prima Garcia, Thomas Gary, Terri Harris, Mimi Mesirow, Jeffery Mingo, DeBorah Posey, and LaToya Price-Perry also made useful contributions. Two groups of summer interns— Uzo Asonye, DeAndre Forney, Shanti Hubbard, Areto Imoukhuede, Nadine Lindsey, Reagan McGuire, Aaron McLeod, Alexis Parent, Sandi Pessin, Raul Rohatgi, Doug Thistlethwaite, Ayanna Williams, Jocelyn Yin, and Mary-Margaret Zogby—all took it home and offered helpful critiques and observations.

A special word of thanks is due a former seminary professor of mine, and now president of the Chicago Theological Seminary, Dr. Susan Brooks Thistlethwaite, for writing the foreword. The Reverend Jerry Falwell, Bert and Belle Lance, and Sonny Cauthen were all hospitable and helpful with their information, insights, comments, and cooperation during our Civil War battle sites tour. Bob Sutton, National Park Service superintendent at the Manassas National Battlefield, was especially helpful and supportive from our earliest visit through completion of the book.

We got varying degrees of feedback and critiques by sending first-draft renditions of the book to Dr. Joyce Baugh, Warren Beatty, Dr. Lerone Bennett, Harlan Berk, Dr. Mary Frances Berry, Robert Borosage, Tami Brent, Patricia Bryant, Clayborne Carson, Farai Chideya, Steve Cobble, Michigan Representative John Conyers, Camille Cosby, Patricia Crayton, Stanley Crouch, Connecticut Senator Christopher Dodd, Dr. Michael Eric and Marcia Dyson, Phillip Edmonds, Licia Green, Gail Gross, Dr. Lani Guinier, Dr. Roger Hatch, Dr. John Hope Franklin, Arianna Huffington, Connie Jackson, Lisa Jones, Marty King, Kit Kinports, California Representative Barbara Lee, Dr. Julianne Malveaux, Derrick McGinty, Ralph Neas, John Nichols, Dr. John Nowak, Dr. Charles Ogletree, Gwendolyn R. Payton, Mary A. Pollock, Richard Rabinowitz, Jerome Rowan, Carol Shields, Elaine Shoben, Tavis Smiley, Tina Tindall, Dr. Ronald Walters, Jim and Nadine Walton, Frank's mother Ruby Watkins, North Carolina Representative Mel Watt, Dr. Cornel West, and Dr. Roger Wilkins.

My brothers Jonathan and Yusef, sisters Santita and Jacqueline, Jr., and my mother all read some portions of the book and definitely gave me feedback. My father, the Reverend Jesse L. Jackson, read the book entirely and offered his usual wisdom; he was extremely helpful and generous with his input. My wife, Sandi, offered her own unique critiques but was always supportive, positive, tolerant, and loving throughout the four-year ordeal. My pastor, the Reverend James T. Meeks, and his wife, Jamell, were emotionally and spiritually supportive of Sandi and I, and without their prayers and mentoring we would not have made it—we lost our first child, Lee Louis Jackson, in the middle of writing the book. Grand Master Jhoon Rhee kept me in good physical shape throughout with private Tae Kwon Do lessons.

My deep gratitude goes to Michael Lynch for the creative cover design. The picture credit is due Richard Ellis of *Meet the Press*. Also, a special appreciation goes to those with the courage to assume the risk of endorsing this book with statements on the back cover.

Publisher John Weber, editor Chuck Kim, and editorial manager Karyn Slutsky were all extremely understanding, helpful, supportive, and generally terrific from conception to the completion of this project. It would be hard to overrate how a hard-hitting content editor, Marian Holmes, and a creative copyeditor and proofreader, Laura Jorstad, turned our original rough prose into a readable book.

I would also like to thank my 539 colleagues (including delegates) in the House and Senate, and the thousands of publicly elected and appointed officials, their staffs, and their advisers—who often sacrifice their and their families' privacy, and much of their personal life and security, to toil daily in the various public vineyards of politics and government as they, too, try to bring to fruition their own understanding of a more perfect Union.

As always, however, the final responsibility for this book remains mine and mine alone.

FOREWORD

DR. SUSAN BROOKS THISTLETHWAITE
President, Chicago Theological Seminary

Andersonville: For anyone acquainted with Civil War history, this name should evoke images of a death camp, for a death camp it was. In the blistering sun of August, it was not unusual for a hundred men a day to die from the heat and disease. Of the forty-five thousand imprisoned there, thirteen thousand died. But it is from this book, *A More Perfect Union*, that I learned for the first time that at the height of the civil rights struggles in the late 1960s, segregationist Democratic senators from Georgia persuaded President Lyndon Johnson to convert this notorious southern prisoner-of-war camp into a monument honoring all prisoners of war. And at the same time the law that brought this new monument into being made it illegal for the National Park Service guides to discuss slavery. Two decades ago, before the fall of the Berlin Wall, I was in East Germany for a peace meeting and visited the infamous German death camp Buchenwald, along with former members of the Confessing Church. The Confessing Church broke off from the German Christian churches when Hitler declared himself the second coming of Christ. Many members of the Confessing Church were executed at Buchenwald. I had been to Auschwitz and to Dachau before; I thought I knew what a concentration camp memorial would be. But at that time you could visit Buchenwald and nowhere in the camp or the museum be told that any Jews died there. I can hardly remember a time when I have been as shocked. That was until I read about the law that forbade National Park personnel to mention slavery. I was reminded of Buchenwald and its lying by omission.

Chicago Tribune columnist Clarence Page, in discussing the controversies surrounding a memorial to slavery proposed for the mall in our nation's capital, quotes a white southern friend: "The Civil War's not over to southerners. It's just intermission."

Page is correct to point out the fact that the Civil War still rips at the fabric and heart of American life. But I disagree with him in that I don't think it's an intermission. And neither do Jackson and Watkins. I just think the battlefields have shifted. The battles today are not in fields and on hills; they are in chambers and hallways. They animate the deliberations and decisions of our highest national institutions. They still divide our nation.

The Civil War is not just about memory, but motive; not just about archives, but current actions; not just about yesterday, but today and tomorrow and beyond. Absent the cannons, bayonets, or mortar fire, the Civil War is still being fought. And there are still American casualties. This intense struggle is over the basic question of whether we will be one nation. Will we aspire to be "a more perfect Union," or will states' rights politics continue to subvert the possibility of union? Do we seek a balkanized version of the country, with each state a separate enclave unto itself, or a union "of the people, by the people, for the people"? The term *to balkanize* should be instructive. Do we want a country in which small, mutually hostile political units, as the Balkan states represent, render us socially paralyzed, or do we want to try to realize the vision of our nation's founders of a genuinely more perfect Union? It is the argument of this work that the racial politics of the United States is an excellent lens for viewing the ways in which the promise of a Union is consistently subverted and denied. A "divide and conquer" politics, rooted in the states' rights ideology of proslavery ideologues, consistently sabotages efforts to get people to recognize their common political agendas across the European-African divide. Why do poor and working-class folks so consistently vote against their economic best interests? It is because they are seduced by fears of racial difference that are callously generated to keep people of different races from discovering and celebrating their common interests. Just as "states' rights" has often overtaken "slavery" as the reason for the Civil War, today new "states' rights" language and policy also overtake the possibility of a union of citizens along the lines of their real interests.

It is clear that no genuinely multicultural America will emerge as long as the stranglehold of racism prevents the celebration of both commonality and diversity. As Audre Lorde has written, "Certainly there are very real differences between us of race, age, and sex. But it is not those differences between us that are separating us. It is rather our refusal to recognize those differences, and to examine the distortions which result from our misnaming them and their effects upon human behavior and expectation." Similarly, it is states' rights ideologies that undermine efforts to form political coalitions that will address the actual needs and concerns of most Americans.

This is as true in the arena of gender and gender preference as it is in the case of racial difference. States' rights ideologies defeated the Equal Rights Amendment, just as the current struggle for justice for sexual minorities is being fought town to town, county to county, state to state. No political consensus is allowed to emerge for the very reason that people might discover their capacity for respect and tolerance of their neighbors. *A More Perfect Union* proposes a bold way to get across the quicksand of states' rights. Eight new constitutional amendments! I was struck by the incredible simplicity of it all. Don't play by the states' rights rules. Change the playing field altogether; move it onto a higher ground, a constitutional ground. It is the Constitution itself that has guided the country, as far as we have been able, toward Union. It is the amendments to the Constitution that have changed the country substantially. We were literally a different place before and after the Thirteenth Amendment. A slaveholding country before, and a free country after. Likewise, we were literally a different place before and after the Nineteenth Amendment. Before the Nineteenth Amendment women were chattel. After the Nineteenth Amendment we were human beings. That's a fairly substantial change.

So why not try the same thing with (1) voting rights; (2) full employment; (3) universal comprehensive health care; (4) affordable housing; (5) a quality public education; (6) equality for women; (7) the environment; and (8) fair taxes? If we succeeded, it would have radical foreign policy implications. Polls show that most Americans want these eight rights as national priorities. It is the proposal of *A More Perfect Union* that we pursue a political course that makes these eight a national priority-and mean it.

I'd like to warn the reader that this is not your typical book written by a politician, a loosely collected group of speeches that are about an inch deep. This is a serious and lengthy work, well researched and detailed. It is not easy reading. Some parts are shocking, as I described above regarding Andersonville. But it is substantive reading. Congressman Jackson is taking a risk. He clearly thinks that American citizens take their country seriously. I'm betting he's right about that.

---

1. Clarence Page, "What America Wants to Forget," *Chicago Tribune* (13 June 2001), A27.
2. Audre Lorde, *Sister Outsider* (Freedom, Calif.: The Crossing Press, 1984), 115.

INTRODUCTION

Although I grew up in a home that was very politically conscious and active, my own political philosophy was not all that well developed when I was elected to Congress in a special election on December 12, 1995. That was when my real political awakening began. Through a series of experiences in the last few years, I have come to believe that politics in Congress, and in some parts of the country, often have less to do with Democrats and Republicans, liberals and conservatives, left and right, and more to do with North and South—members who were elected from either northern or southern states.

My experiences in Congress sparked my desire to try to understand this dynamic: Why was this? What did it mean? What were the political consequences and implications? The North-versus-South political dynamic in Congress must be fully understood because it underlies most of our fiscal policies, legislative initiatives, policy and platform positions, and even the rhetoric of our lawmakers.

I began to study our history closely and to observe my fellow congressmen, along with the symbols and surroundings of the Capitol and other historic buildings that I frequented every day. What I discovered, on a much deeper and broader level than I had ever been taught or understood before, is that race—and, unless otherwise indicated, in this book I use the term "race" in reference to African Americans specifically, not to people of color generally—is not merely a recent or peripheral issue in America; it is the most protracted and central factor in all American history. Arriving at this conclusion enabled me to begin to understand the North–South political schism in Congress.

As a public servant and elected official in America, I felt it was my duty to explore this racial dynamic in depth if I was going to make significant contributions as a legislator. Thus, in August and December 1997, and again in the spring of 1998, my press secretary Frank Watkins and I, and my wife on the 1998 trip, toured several of the American Civil War battle sites, mainly the eastern battlefields in the South.

As a result of these visits and extensive research, I've concluded that in addition to race, another central theme has been pervasive in our country's founding and history and continues to be so. That recurring issue is the relationship between the federal government and the states, an ongoing precarious balancing of power—more palatably referred to nowadays as "federalism" versus "localism" or "local control." Even more significant is the fact that states' rights, local control, and race are, for the most part, inextricably bound. Our history shows that a discourse on one invariably insinuates the other.

Even though the states' rights philosophy and its local practice have been the primary means of perpetuating racial injustice in America, it is clear from the reading of our history that both states' rights and federal government advocates have used their respective arguments and authority to establish and maintain the institution of slavery, segregation, discrimination, and inequality between the races in this country.

Race is a linear thread woven into the very fiber of American life and history. In this regard—and this is critically important to understanding my arguments in this book—I am looking at race in a very specific way. I am considering it apart from any of the emotional meanings or attachments that are so often made by both black and white Americans. I am using race simply as a lens through which to view all of American history.

Long-simmering feuds, frictions, and full-blown catastrophes stemming from race issues are not unlike the three phases of an earthquake—tremor, quake, and aftershocks. With this earthquake analogy, I do not mean to imply that racism is a natural event and that Americans had no choices in the matter, in the past or in the future. Simply put, the events of American history from 1619 to 1861 can be compared to the tremors prior to an earthquake. The Civil War, of course, would be analogous to a catastrophic great quake. Everything from 1865 through the present, I see as aftershocks.

The Civil War was initially fought to preserve the Union, which was split apart over the question of slavery, but ultimately it was fought both to preserve the Union and to end slavery. These two factors were so intertwined that scholars still debate the import of each or whether or not they are indeed the same. Supporters of slavery euphemistically referred to their cause as the right to "maintain God's ordained order," to "preserve a region's way of life," to protect "property rights," and to maintain "states' rights." States' rights thus became identified with slavery and racism—a state had the power (superseding the federal government's) to protect the right of whites to privately own property in the form of black slaves and, thereby, preserve southern values and ways of life.

While the Civil War and the Thirteenth Amendment legally ended slavery in 1865, the question of how to bring the former slaves into the economic mainstream has to this day never been fully addressed, despite the addition of the Fourteenth Amendment and the efforts at Reconstruction. And even though the Fifteenth Amendment extended voting rights to former slaves, securing these rights in reality is an ongoing struggle.

Therefore, from this perspective, the 1954 desegregation decision, the 1964 Civil Rights Act, the 1968 Open Housing Act, affirmative action, and economic set-asides are all part of the unfinished task of Reconstruction after the Civil War. So, too, are the 1965 Voting Rights Act, majority-minority districts, and motor voter legislation. But even more efforts will be necessary to achieve the full political enfranchisement of all Americans. Such legislation and court decisions stem from efforts to correct inequities often rooted in the legacy of slavery and Jim Crowism.

A More Perfect Union seeks to trace the history of race in America, and to show how the philosophy and practice of states' rights still dominates our politics and prevents us from building a more perfect Union. I argue that we must attack the states' rights ideology—and its close relative, localism—head-on and dramatically modify our understanding of it if we are to achieve a more just and equitable society.

This book attempts to create a new political paradigm for those who truly wish to build a better nation, in contrast to those who are committed to states' rights and the devolution of the only entity capable of bringing about that more perfect Union—the federal government.

A More Perfect Union offers a policy and program that will gradually provide economic security for all, a plan that will help more whites than people of color; as the majority race, there are more whites than blacks who are poor. The plan, however, would indeed help African Americans, other people of color, and women catch up—because we are farther behind, are disproportionately poor, and have a higher percentage of economic needs. In the end, my economic program will bring about greater equality of opportunity under the law between and among the races, sexes, and classes of people in America.

While I see race as the *lens* through which to view all of American history, I also recognize that economic issues are the *hearing aid* through which the majority of Americans will hear most political discourse and dialogue. Thus, I must speak to the majority with an economic program that appeals not just to African Americans but to all Americans. If we can create unprecedented economic security for all, then our nation will be in a better position to make progress on the central issue of race and racism in our society.

This book grows mainly out of my experience. I came to Congress to serve the people of the Second District of Illinois without any overwhelming ideological, theoretical, or political agenda. Within broad practical political parameters, I am prepared, regardless of political party or philosophy, to work with anyone who will help me better serve the people of my district and the American people in general.

A More Perfect Union is structured in four major parts. The first four chapters are autobiographical, the content coming mainly from my personal experiences, current reading, study, discussions, and observations since I was elected. I write about my first few days in Congress, share some of my experiences growing up in a very public family, and discuss my tour of Civil War battle sites, a journey that was personally illuminating and illustrative of many of the ideas I espouse in this book.

The next four chapters deal with the interconnectedness of states' rights and race—the historical, legal, constitutional, and theoretical aspects of these issues. Applying my earthquake analogy, I then review and discuss pertinent historical events.

In the third section of this book, I set forth an economic program that incorporates new American rights—based primarily on the Universal Declaration of Human Rights as applied to a broad or "living" (versus a narrow or "strict constructionist") interpretation of the U.S. Constitution—and will provide unprecedented economic security for all Americans.

I propose and enumerate eight new amendments to the U.S. Constitution. These include seven new social and economic rights: the rights to work, comprehensive and universal health care, safe and affordable housing, a high-quality public education, equality for women, a safe and clean environment, and fair taxes. And in chapter 19 I also propose a new civil and political right, an eighth constitutional amendment providing Americans with suffrage—which, contrary to what most of us think, is not now a fundamental right in our Constitution. Additionally, I outline a set of principles, based on America's highest and best ideals, to guide our foreign policy.

These proposed amendments reflect what I consider the primary challenges facing politicians today. With the ideological confusion of economic and social liberalism, moderation, and conservatism on the one hand, and the political conflict of Democrats and Republicans on the other, these new rights represent broad and general goals shared by all—legislators and citizens alike. Overall, *A More Perfect Union* advocates a political program that has the greatest possibility of providing racial reconciliation, healing, and relative social and political harmony—indeed, a second American Bill of Rights .

The book's final section deals with how we can achieve these goals and new rights: through politics, and through seeing ourselves as working in the larger context of a higher purpose for our lives and the greater good of others.

Finally, while I have set no time frame for reaching these goals and adding these amendments—the political consciousness and activism of the American people will determine that—I sense that they will be achieved in the long term rather than the short term. Even so, my goal, if I may be so immodest, is to try to put forth a book similar to Dr. Martin

Luther King, Jr.'s, *Where Do We Go From Here?* Like his book, I hope *A More Perfect Union* will inspire millions and give them something meaningful and concrete to organize around and work toward for a very long time.

1

PUBLIC SERVANT

It was near the end of the first year of the 104th Congress, the first Republican-controlled Congress in nearly four decades. Illinois's senior member, Representative Sidney Yates, had just formally introduced me, and House Speaker Newt Gingrich had officially sworn me in as a member of the U.S. Congress representing the Second Congressional District of Illinois. I stood nervously on the floor in the well of the House and made a brief speech ending the official ceremony. Now members were coming over to shake my hand and welcome me as the newest member of their illustrious club.

About a minute into this very warm, welcoming ritual—it couldn't have been more than the seventh or eighth hand I shook—Representative Bill Lipinski, my neighboring colleague from the Third Congressional District of Illinois and a very important member of the House Transportation Committee, stepped forward, shook my hand, and said, "Young man, I want you to know that I can be very helpful to you during your stay here in Congress, but you're never going to get that new airport you spoke about during your campaign."

I had been a member of Congress for all of two minutes and already somebody was telling me how he could help me—and in the same breath vowing to hurt me. I thought: "Welcome to hardball politics."

All of this occurred on Thursday morning, December 14, 1995. Just two and a half weeks earlier, having taken a leave from my position as national field director of my father's progressive political organization, the Rainbow Coalition, I had been a Democratic candidate in a specially called election. The congressman I was replacing, Mel Reynolds, had resigned about two months earlier over a scandal involving sex with a sixteen-year-old campaign worker, and Illinois Governor Jim Edgar had called the special primary and general elections to be held on November 28 and December 12, respectively. I won the primary—to many, unexpectedly—with 48 percent of the vote in a hotly and closely contested seven-person race. On December 12 I won the special general election rather easily with 76 percent of the vote in a heavily Democratic district.

Both Bill Lipinski and I are Democrats, and though we sometimes represent polar opposites of the political spectrum within the Democratic Party, I have come to hold a great deal of respect for him professionally. After all, he was only protecting the legitimate economic interests of his constituents embodied in Chicago's Midway Airport. In fact, to a certain extent *because* of his sometimes brutal honesty and candid approach to politics—a throwback to old-time Chicago ethnic and machine politics—I have even come to like him personally. I certainly now consider him a friend, and I think the feeling is mutual. In casual private conversations he often refers to my very good friend Rod Blagojevich as "salt" and to me as "pepper," his humorous way of pointing out our racial differences. But despite our friendship, I've also continued to fight hard for a new airport that would benefit the people of my district, yet not hurt him or his constituents' interests.

Bill Lipinski aside, one of the many lessons I have learned since coming to Congress is that there are members in the Democratic Party with whom I almost always agree on the issues, but don't particularly care for personally. On the other hand, there are Republicans with whom I almost never agree when it comes to ideas, programs, and legislation, but whom I like and enjoy being around personally. For instance, Henry Hyde and I disagree on almost everything politically—the one exception is an economic partnership we formed to build the new airport for the suburbs south of Chicago—but I enjoy his company personally and love to give him his favorite cigars. Dick Armey and I are on completely opposite political wings, but we have gone fishing together and had a terrific time. During a trip to Asia in the middle of the late-1990s financial crisis, I not only learned to appreciate Jim Leach as a learned congressman, but also came to really like him as a person. I often give my friend David Drier his favorite cigars as well, and I was among the first in the cloakroom urging former member Bob Livingston to reconsider his resignation. I've come to realize that such odd couples, and the mixture of personal friendship and professionalism, are part of Capitol Hill politics.

Just two days had elapsed between my victory and my swearing-in. Usually, members are elected during the first part of November in one year and take office nearly two months later at the beginning of the next year. The new members and their chiefs of staff go through freshman orientation at Harvard's Kennedy School of Government and are briefed by their party's leaders and others. They assemble a staff and become acquainted with legislation and other issues expected to come immediately before Congress. They also learn the mechanics of the legislative process by studying House rules and procedures, all contained in very thick and imposing books. For new members, just getting to know where the buildings and offices on the Hill are is a major task.

On December 14, 1995, I came into office without any such orientation, and the House was in full swing. Congress was nearing the end of a frenetic first session of the 104th, in which Speaker Gingrich and his new band of Republican conservatives had led an ideologically driven crusade throughout most of the year, the result of an overwhelming takeover of Congress through electoral victories in November 1994. Basking in their majority, they aggressively pushed to get the ten items of their Contract with America enacted into law.

On the morning of my swearing-in, I learned the location of my office—Room 312 in the Cannon House Office Building, just across the street from the Capitol. I didn't yet have the key. I had no staff. Just that day I had received my small plastic voting card—but I didn't know how to use it to vote. The General Services Administration had closed two previous district offices in Illinois. Even though Paul Simon, the senior senator from my state, had been extremely kind and helpful leading up to my swearing-in ceremony, I was now essentially on my own.

After the afternoon whirlwind of photo ops, press interviews, receptions, and congratulations had subsided, reality set in. I was now a full-fledged member of Congress, fully responsible and accountable as a government official to nearly six hundred thousand people in my district, to the Constitution, and to laws of the United States. Moreover, I was a new standard-bearer for the sacrifice, service, expectations, and good name that my family had given me. But I would have to make my own way. Suddenly, the task before me seemed overwhelming. I said to myself, "What in the world have I gotten myself into now?"

That same night about 6 PM, my father; his longtime aide and my co–campaign manager, Frank Watkins; my wife, Sandi; my brother Jonathan; Lorraine Westbrook, a friend and former coworker at the Rainbow Coalition; and I met in my office to brainstorm for candidates for chief of staff. After my father expressed his pride in me and offered words of encouragement, we got down to business. Sandi suggested Licia Green, who had experience working on Capitol Hill and was known and respected by each of us because she had worked with us in my father's presidential campaign of 1988. We decided to approach her.

It turned out that Licia had been offered and was considering a job at the White House, but with prayer and persuasion, she was in my office Monday morning heading up my staff. It was one of the best moves I have ever made.

Lorraine and Myra Outlaw, both former Rainbow staff members, also came aboard to temporarily tide us over.

As Licia began to assemble a staff, I instructed her to retain no holdovers from Representative Reynolds's staff and to create a diverse office, reflecting both genders and the races and religions in my district. Licia, who had worked with the late Representative Mickey Leland (D-TX) and had become chief of staff to his replacement, Craig Washington, began reaching out to friends and colleagues. Lorraine became the scheduler and executive assistant and Myra the receptionist and office manager.

Representative Ike Skelton (D-MO) showed me how to use my voting card. The day after I was sworn in, I cast my first three votes, including one against building more B-2 bombers. But with a sparse staff and little time to acquaint myself with the issues, a big mistake was almost unavoidable. The next week, I voted for a piece of legislation that I should have voted against—the Securities Litigation Reform Act. It was the wrong vote, a vote against the interests of my constituents and consumers.

Being the good newspaperman that he is, *Chicago Sun-Times* reporter Basil Talbott called Reverend Jackson at the Rainbow to get a comment from him on my voting counter to his position on the issue. About a year earlier, my father had joined in signing a letter to members of Congress written by Ralph Nader's Public Citizen against the legislation. Ralph Nader immediately made the letter public, put my "yes" vote on the Internet, and accompanied it with scathing criticism of my departure from my father's more progressive and more consumer-oriented position. It's not that I haven't taken positions different from my father's—though we usually agree on the substance of most issues—but in this instance I had taken the wrong position and deserved to be criticized. It was a learning experience.

I realized that as a congressman I needed help in clarifying issues and positions and creating continuity in regard to my father and the Rainbow Coalition. I pleaded my case to Reverend Jackson—that's how I refer to him when he's my boss, not just my father—and asked if I could hire one of his key staff members, Hilary Weinstein, as my legislative director. He obliged. Hilary had gained some legislative experience through working on the Rainbow's "DC Statehood" campaign, and she knew the progressive Rainbow position on most issues. She immediately joined my staff. An old law school friend, Rodney Emery, subsequently joined Hilary, and weeks later, Tariq Ahmed, formerly a staff member of Congressman Craig Washington, completed the legislative team.

I also opened two new offices in my district, two-thirds of which is in the suburbs and one-third in Chicago. In terms of population, however, two-thirds of the voters reside in Chicago. Slowly, Licia put the district team in place.

Back on Capitol Hill, I had found the quickest route from my office to the House floor, and I no longer got completely lost when journeying to caucus rooms and other offices. I had also mastered the most fundamental of the House rules and floor procedures. Overall, things were beginning to take shape.

My choice for press secretary, however, had not worked out, and I needed to hire a replacement. Lacking solid advice and training in dealing with the press, I was still hesitant to give public speeches and press interviews. I wanted Frank Watkins, my father's press secretary, speechwriter, and political adviser for nearly twenty-seven years, to join me. Frank and I had worked closely together at the Rainbow. Frank had planned and, along with Alice Tregay, co-managed my congressional campaign. And we had a good personal relationship. Frank had chosen to return to the Rainbow after the campaign but agreed to join me if I could work it out. I knew that this was going to be a really tough one with my father, but I asked him anyway. Let's just say that in time he was gracious enough to allow it to happen with his blessing, and so on March 25, 1996, Frank came on board.

Not long after, I gave my first floor speech—one of the opening "one-minute" speeches that usually start each legislative day. Any member can speak about anything for one minute. Frank and I had prepared a statement attacking Republicans who were cutting federal funds for education. In the middle of my minute, I began to feel a little too comfortable, departed from my text, and launched into a personal attack on the likely Republican presidential nominee, Senate Majority Leader Bob Dole, calling him by name as one of the major leaders and culprits in this anti-public-education campaign.

At the time, I had read some of the general House guidelines for floor speeches, but I didn't know enough of the details. Calling a person's name is considered a personal attack on the House floor, especially a member of the Senate who isn't there to defend himself; it's completely out of order and against congressional rules. As I stepped away from the podium, I noticed out of the corner of my eye some initial movement toward the microphone by a couple of Republicans, but I didn't know why. Then they quickly went back to their seats. I suspect it was because they remembered that I was new, and they apparently also noticed that Representative Ike Skelton was calling me over. He immediately sat me down and patiently explained the rule and the protocol. I was grateful to those Republicans for not embarrassing me after my first floor speech and to Ike Skelton for his concern for me and for the decorum of the House.

I knew some of the pitfalls that a young Jesse Jackson, Jr., would experience both inside and outside Congress. I also knew that there would be both positive and negative expectations of me. Many times during the campaign and since, I have been asked by reporters to explain the advantages and disadvantages of being the son of the Reverend Jesse L. Jackson—a two-time presidential candidate, a longtime national and international human rights leader, and a world icon. My stock reply: "I inherited both his friends and his detractors, neither of whom I had earned. Thus, I must work hard and, on my own merit, earn the respect of his friends." But I also hoped that his detractors would at least give me a fair hearing and a fair chance. If they did, maybe, just maybe, they would also gain a greater respect for, appreciation of, and understanding of my father.

Since my dad has a national and international reputation and travels the world speaking and helping people, there were many who thought I would immediately follow in his footsteps. They assumed I'd travel the country speaking, marching, and trying to build my own national reputation. They thought I'd be a young man in a hurry.

I am young, thirty-six, but I'm not in a hurry—except to fix some things in my district. I'm also in a hurry to see the unemployed get jobs; the uninsured get health insurance; the homeless find shelter. But I'm not in a personal hurry. I am willing to take my time, pay my dues, learn my craft—which I see as public service—and earn my seniority. Because I am relatively young in the national political arena, I have the time to grow, to learn, and to develop.

I do not see myself as a politician engaged in public service. I see myself as a public servant engaged in politics. That's an important distinction. For a politician engaged in public service, the thrill is in the politics, the party, the ideology, and the next election. For a public servant, partisanship and ideology become the necessary means to achieving good public policy. Politicians will allow politics, party, and ideology to stand between them and the public good. Public servants owe reasonable loyalty to their party and its beliefs, but ultimately they should not allow that allegiance to supersede doing what is necessary to pass legislation that best serves the interest of the public good.

As long as the people of the Second District of Illinois will have me, I would like to continue to represent them to the best of my ability. If there comes a time, later in my life, for greater national service, I hope to be both knowledgeable and experienced enough to perform the job with dignity, integrity, and excellence.

Looking far ahead in politics, however, is seldom wise, usually risky, and often foolish and dangerous. When I beat Mayor Richard M. Daley's candidate and his machine in the special primary election in 1995, there was immediate press speculation about my challenging Daley and running for mayor of Chicago. It's a fine job, but I have no interest in being the mayor of Chicago.

In 1996, when I criticized Senator Carol Moseley Braun for taking a private trip to Nigeria and becoming too friendly with its dictatorial leadership, the press immediately speculated that I was interested in her job and would challenge her in the 1998 Democratic primary. Nothing could have been farther from my mind.

I think the best approach is to focus on the present, do the best job you can do today for your constituents and the country, and the future will take care of itself. That's why I have done relatively little speaking around the country. My constituents sent me to Congress to represent them, and I do. I've missed only one vote since coming to Congress. I go home to my district virtually every weekend. I accept speaking engagements in my district and hold regular town hall meetings to get input and feedback. If I've been criticized for anything, it's been for focusing too much on my district.

Ford Heights, a city of five thousand just twenty-five minutes from downtown Chicago, had water the color of strong tea. The smelly, polluted water was unfit for bathing, cooking, drinking, or washing clothes. A common sight was children carrying bottled water home from the store. The water was so bad that neighboring fire departments refused to run it through their trucks, because it quickly corroded their equipment. The foul water prevented businesses from locating in this impoverished town—no beauty shops, barber shops, or restaurants. From my first days in the House, I worked to get federal money for a new water tower and infrastructure so that fresh water could finally flow in Ford Heights. Even with a "hurried-up" funding process, I still was not able to get the community safe, fresh water until the summer of 2001—my proudest moment as a congressman.

Ford Heights also has a flooding problem. Every time it rains, and sometimes when it doesn't, Deer Creek floods much of the eastern side of the city, destroying homeowners' furniture and eroding house foundations. Water, sometimes eight inches to a foot deep in the streets, prevents children from going to school or outside to play. The streets are impassable even for cars; workers cannot get to their jobs. Because the town has no money for regular garbage pickup, Deer Creek itself becomes the dump. Adding to this grim picture is the fact that more than three-quarters of Ford Heights residents receive some form of government assistance. Most people cannot fathom such Third World conditions just a stone's throw from a large modern metropolis like Chicago. Improving the lives of the people of Ford Heights remains a top priority of my tenure.

You may have heard of Ford Heights when the story of the "Ford Heights Four" was aired by NBC-TV's *Dateline* and other TV programs. Four young African American men from Ford Heights—Dennis Williams, Kenneth Adams, Verneal Jimerson, and Willie Rainge—were arrested for allegedly murdering a young white man and his fiancée. They were tried, found guilty, incarcerated, and served eighteen years in prison—including two who served eleven years on death row—only to have a Northwestern University professor and three of his students prove their total innocence through DNA testing in a six-month investigation. The students' investigation turned up shoddy police work, possible criminal misconduct by the local police, and a failure of the Cook County state's attorney to examine police procedures. As yet, no official or office has been held accountable for these wrongful incarcerations.

Other municipalities in my district are nearly as bad off as Ford Heights. In Harvey, the old Dixie Square Mall has stood vacant and falling down since Jake and Elwood, in the movie *The Blues Brothers*, crashed their way through it on the way to downtown Chicago "on a mission from God." That was the last thing to happen there that generated any revenue. For over twenty-five years, that deteriorating mall has stood as a symbol that our booming economy is not booming for everyone. Industry and workers have fled the area. Consequently, jobs, wages, taxpayers, consumers, schools, and city services have all declined. Today, the abandoned mall is a prime site for rapes, robberies, and drug dealing. The homeless, gangs, and stray dogs often congregate there. And the city of Harvey is so poor that it cannot afford to demolish the unsafe eyesore. Ironically, on one corner of the mall's parking lot rests a brand-new police station with the latest and finest equipment to apprehend the unfortunate young men of Harvey. Getting that mall torn down and working with the people of Harvey and the private sector to build something positive and economically beneficial to the community is another one of my top goals.

Another site that has the potential for economic growth is the 570 acres in southeast Chicago on Lake Michigan that used to be the home of United States Steel. Built in 1881, the huge mill employed almost twenty thousand people in its heyday. Down the street from the site is Bowen High School, which features a large mural in the principal's office depicting the diverse workers—male and female, black, brown, and white—who worked at the U.S. Steel plant for more than a century. The mural seems to be making a statement to students: You, too, can get a good job at the steel plant if you stay in school and do reasonably well. You, too, can raise and provide for your family in this very community if you're willing to work hard. Unfortunately, the mural's message today is as outdated as the old mill's blast furnaces. Since the plant closed in 1992, there have been no comparable jobs available for local students.

Tragically, the mostly African American and Latino student body is not being prepared for the information age and service-based high-tech global economy that is now upon us. With armed police controlling the halls and metal detectors at the entrance, Bowen is hardly an atmosphere conducive to learning.

As for the sprawling steel-mill site, with a mile and a half of shoreline on Lake Michigan and a spectacular view of downtown Chicago, it may be one of the most valuable pieces of urban real estate in America. The old mill works were demolished, and the land has been remediated and given a clean bill of health by city, state, and federal environmental agencies. The site is primed for redevelopment. Yet despite my aggressive marketing of the area, as well as efforts by the steel company and the city, there has been little interest. Nevertheless, I am committed to redeveloping this community and others in my district, so that the South Side of Chicago and its suburbs begin to look like the more prosperous North Side and northern suburbs.

On Chicago's North Side and in the northwestern suburbs, the economy is growing rapidly. There are more jobs than available workers. In Elk Grove Village, for example, with a population of just thirty-five thousand, there are more than one hundred thousand jobs—three jobs for every one person. On the South Side and in the southern suburbs, however, the economy is experiencing a negative "growth" rate—a surplus of workers for available positions. In my district, jobs and opportunities are shrinking. With just under six hundred thousand people, the largest eleven businesses employ a mere eleven thousand people—one job for every sixty people. To get to work, South Siders must travel north and northwest, which adds to the traffic and pollution problems in the Chicago metropolitan area. A study published by *Illinois Politics* said that the Second District of Illinois had the longest commute times to work in America.

The strength of the economy to the north of downtown Chicago is the result of one factor and one factor only—Chicago's O'Hare Airport. It is a giant economic magnet, a pole around which the flags of prosperity fly—mainly high employment, good schools, successful businesses, and attractive communities.

When O'Hare was built in 1962, it nearly put Midway Airport out of business and thus destabilized much of the economic community on the southwest side of Chicago near Midway. The economic downturn resulted in escalated racial tensions in that part of the city, remembers Representative Bill Lipinski, who represents the area. Therefore, I completely understand that the congressman was protecting his district's interests when he said to me within a few minutes of my swearing-in that he would never allow a third airport to be built in the Chicago metropolitan area.

In my 1995 campaign I promoted the necessity of building a new south suburban airport as the economic linchpin in the rejuvenation of my community. It would create 236,000 new jobs—up to 500,000 given the multiplier effect—and generate ten billion dollars annually for the Illinois economy. The airport would be good not only for my district, but also for Chicago, Illinois, and the region. It has the additional advantage of reflecting balanced growth in the region—O'Hare north, Midway west, and a third airport south—so that all in the metropolitan area could share equitably in the prosperity. Most important, a third airport is needed to meet new capacity demands.

The Federal Aviation Administration has said that air travel is expected to nearly double in the next ten years—to one billion passengers annually by 2010. O'Hare is already operating at capacity, and the landlocked Midway Airport will soon reach operational capacity. A new airport in south suburban Peotone, about thirty-five miles southwest of downtown Chicago, would put the jobs and economic development where they are most needed. As proposed, it would be built in stages to accommodate future air travel needs and, therefore, not damage the economic viability of O'Hare or Midway. In fact, most of the communities around O'Hare are asking for relief from air and automobile traffic, noise and air pollution; they're also raising questions of air safety.

Despite the need for additional aviation capacity and the logic behind balanced growth, this airport has become a political hot potato. None of my Democratic primary opponents supported the airport. Some were willing to "study it" to avoid having to take a position on the issue, but none was willing to support it outright. They said it was the Republican governor's airport, and he would control it. They were unwilling to oppose Chicago's Mayor Richard Daley and the leader of the Democratic Party—who opposed the airport because it would be outside his jurisdiction and control—for the higher goal of the public good. Politically, my support of the airport also took away the only major issue my Republican opponent had in the general election. I have since formed a coalition with Representative Henry Hyde, a conservative Republican who represents a district impacted by O'Hare, and whom I almost never agree with on the issues. But together we are working on the third airport—me, because I want jobs; Henry, because he opposes O'Hare expansion.

I believe, of course, that a new airport can be built without jeopardizing another community's well-being. Balanced growth is, in fact, the key to a prolonged strong economy, to easing racial, gender, and generational tensions, to improving public education, to having safer communities and less crime, to improving the quality of life of all Americans, and ultimately to greater peace and stability in the world.

2

BORN IN THE STRUGGLE TO VOTE

I was born in the context of the struggle to vote in two senses. First, I was born in Greenville, South Carolina, the southern state that started the American Civil War at Fort Sumter in 1861 and the most rebellious of the rebel states in the Confederacy. This is also the region where, just over one hundred years ago, blacks had virtually no rights, but especially no right to vote.

I was also born directly in the context of the modern struggle for the right to vote, in 1965 —the height of the black civil rights rebellion and the middle of the fight for voting rights.

On March 7, 1965, John Lewis and others were beaten and bloodied by state troopers as they marched across the Edmund Pettus Bridge in Selma, Alabama, fighting for a basic democratic right—the right to vote. It is known in the annals of American history as Bloody Sunday.

Two days after Bloody Sunday, March 9, the Reverend James Reeb, a Unitarian minister and civil rights worker from Boston, was badly beaten and bloodied about the head by a small group of angry white men. On Thursday he died.

That same day, March 11, 1965, I was born the first son of Jesse and Jacqueline Jackson. My sister, Santita, had arrived about two years earlier in Chicago. My dad had sent his pregnant wife to stay with his mother in Greenville, South Carolina, for my birth and first few days of life so that the two of us would be in quiet, loving, comfortable surroundings. He was then a senior at the Chicago Theological Seminary (CTS) but, because of the crisis in Selma, Alabama, had left school to become involved in the movement for the right to vote.

The situation in Selma was tense. Local and state police viewed civil rights workers as outside agitators who'd come to Selma to cause trouble. As a result, they would stop, harass, and arrest civil rights workers without cause. On March 11 Jesse Jackson had just avoided such an encounter with the Alabama State Police. Outside Selma, he stopped at a pay phone along the roadside to call Greenville and talk with my mother. That was when he learned of my birth. My father was so emotionally caught up in the struggle for the right to vote that he wanted to name me Selma. Thank God, my mother had better judgment.

Just two weeks after Bloody Sunday, on March 21, the historic march from Selma to Montgomery began, led by Dr. Martin Luther King, Jr. It ended on Thursday, March 25, with a throng of nearly fifty thousand gathered in the Cradle of the Confederacy to make a witness for democracy. That same day, Viola Gregg Liuzzo, an Italian American housewife and mother of five from Detroit, Michigan, was shot to death on Highway 80 while driving civil rights workers home after the march.

Later that year Congress passed the 1965 Voting Rights Act, and President Lyndon B. Johnson signed it into law on August 6. This law, the most important piece of social legislation of the twentieth century, is now under attack by members of Congress and the Supreme Court, including Associate Justice Clarence Thomas. Sin, I've learned, is deeper than skin.

Thirty years after my father marched for the right to vote, I was sworn into office as the ninety-first African American—out of a total of 11,639 people—ever to serve in Congress. There have been only 107 African Americans elected to Congress, 103 of them in the House. Four were elected to the Senate, two in the nineteenth century and two in the twentieth—including the only Democrat and only woman, Senator Carol Moseley Braun of Illinois.

Thirty-six years ago my father cast his bread on the water. Thirty years later it came back to him in the form of a son in Congress. Thirty-six years ago, a young John Lewis was bloodied fighting for the right to vote. Today a seasoned Representative John Lewis and a young Jesse Jackson, Jr., are colleagues in the U.S. House of Representatives. As Don King would say, "Only in America."

My earliest recollections are of my mother dropping off my brother Jonathan and me at the Union Church Nursery School on the campus of the University of Chicago. This school was just a block from where my parents lived, in McGiffert Hall. There I received my first multicultural and multiracial education. Obviously, I had no idea that twenty-seven years later I would be graduating from the Chicago Theological Seminary, that my father would be the commencement speaker, or that the graduation ceremony would take place in Union Church.

When I was around three years old, I vaguely remember my parents moving into an apartment on South Ridgeland Avenue in a community on the South Side known as South Shore. I found out at a later age that it was owned by a well-known and politically active funeral director in Chicago named A. R. Leak.

I attended the John J. Pershing Public Elementary School from 1970 to 1976. My first-grade teacher was Mrs. Smith, my third-grade teacher, a Mrs. Miller, and my fifth-grade teacher, another Mrs. Smith. These three were unique in that they taught all five of the Jackson children at Pershing. Each of them expected and demanded more of me than I did of myself. And my fourth-grade teacher, Mrs. Okereafor, a big woman, loomed even larger as a disciplinarian.

I didn't know at the time that Pershing was just a couple of blocks from the former site of Camp Douglas, the North's infamous Civil War prison, or that my elementary school was within eyesight of Illinois Senator Stephen Douglas's tomb and monument. Douglas, of course, was a key Democratic player in events leading up to the Civil War. I discovered these things only as the result of experiences in Congress, which led to my interest in studying more about the Civil War.

During my early years, close friends and family gave me the nickname "Fella." I've never exactly understood why they called me that, but some have told me it's because, as a kid, I was the "baddest fella" they ever knew. To this day, I don't honestly know what they were talking about.

One of the first things I became conscious of was that many of my classmates knew me before I knew them. I had this name—Jesse Jackson—that was very familiar to all my peers. It belonged to the guy who was constantly on television and radio and in the newspaper going to jail, fighting the school board, challenging Mayor Richard J. Daley, leading voter registration drives, and expressing general discontent with the status quo.

My classmates' parents were mostly working-class or newly professional people. Some worked in the post office, for city government, or as schoolteachers, while a few were doctors, lawyers, or preachers. But there I was, the child of the newsmaking agitator. Some of my friends liked him and some didn't—probably reflecting their parents' attitudes—but I didn't understand enough of what my daddy did to adequately explain it to them. That situation was often hard to deal with. Sometimes my lack of knowledge frustrated me and made me uncomfortable. At other times my inadequacy just embarrassed me.

My most lasting memory of Pershing occurred around a sixth-grade classroom project—a drama. I was to play the husband in a mock wedding with a young lady named Florence. Over the preceding several weeks I experienced a lot of uneasiness, because I was expected to kiss Florence—in front of the class—at the end of the play. I had never kissed a girl, and my nerves were getting the best of me. One day just before the play, with my discomfort at its peak, instead of getting "married" Florence and I got into a fight and I beat her up—resulting in a suspension from school. Maybe that was the "Fella" coming out in me.

During this period, my father was traveling extensively, leading boycotts and engaging in political activity. His influence in Chicago and around the nation was growing rapidly. Sometimes he came home and shared his experiences with me. Occasionally, when our schedules permitted, he took us with him to share these experiences. When I was about ten years old, he came home late one night, and we all gave him our traditional hug and a kiss. We then went to bed. About 3:15 that morning he woke me and Jonathan and asked us to stand on a chair and look out the window. We could see through the window of our white neighbors, and there our friends Peter and David Fozzard were studying their lessons. "As African Americans," my father told us, "we have to study harder and longer just to be equal in this society." It was a frequent theme for him; I remember him giving a speech and telling young African American high school students, "In our society, we must be superior just to be equal."

One of my mother's friends had a son who attended a Catholic military school in Rolling Prairie, Indiana—LeMans Military Academy—which was run by the Brothers of Holy Cross. My mother and I visited LeMans. Rolling Prairie, Indiana, is a rural community outside South Bend. I was very excited about going there. The idea of wearing a uniform, getting promoted, and being in charge of something was a big thrill. I went first, and my younger brother Jonathan joined me the following year. At LeMans I played basketball and learned archery, fencing, wrestling, and sharpshooting. But "Fella" kept showing up. I received numerous demerits and became a regular visitor to the principal's office—often to be paddled for conduct unbecoming a cadet.

Still, it was at LeMans that I began to acquire the discipline and order that remain currently a part of my personal and professional life. I owe thanks to Brother John, Brother Peter, Brother Shaun, Mr. Wolfang, and Mrs. Kessler. Each of them, and LeMans as a whole, played a critical role in shaping my personality; I will never be able to thank them enough. "Fella" wasn't finished with me yet, but he was gradually being overcome.

LeMans had closed weekends, which meant we couldn't leave campus, as well as open weekends when we could go home. My mother would drive from Chicago to visit on closed weekends; on open weekends, she'd pick up Jonathan, me, and our friends and take us home. We brought home friends from Mexico, Thailand, and elsewhere.

When my friends came home with me, my father's Saturday community meeting was a regular part of our schedule. Every Saturday for more than thirty-five years, my father's organizations—Operation Breadbasket, Operation PUSH, and Rainbow/PUSH Coalition—

have conducted a community forum with, at times, up to three thousand people in attendance. The meeting includes inspiration, information, and often a call for direct action: picketing against police brutality; boycotting a store selling bad meat in the community or supporting a black-owned store by shopping there; protesting a local issue at city hall; staging a sit-in over employment discrimination. The meeting itself is a spirit-filled, African American–based, Christian-oriented, wake-up-and-liberate-the-people political rally.

Imagine, if you can, my schoolmates from many different countries, cultures, and religions coming to this meeting. They didn't understand the noise, emotion, or purpose of the action. They had not been taught the history of Africans in America, so they would often ask me, "Why are blacks always complaining?" As an adolescent I still couldn't adequately explain it to them. I also sometimes felt inadequate and lacked appreciation for what it meant to have my increasingly famous name. I was happy to have the name, but I didn't really know what it meant.

By the time I graduated from the eighth grade at LeMans Military Academy, I had achieved the rank of staff sergeant. When I returned for the ninth grade, I was promoted to captain. My brother Jonathan, a very gifted musician, played the piano and drums. But my parents noticed that while I was working my way through the ranks, Jonathan was not receiving similar accolades and promotions. He had more than enough talent and skill to be promoted to drum major in the drum corps. But when my parents expressed concern, the response was that they should be content with my promotions. My parents objected, of course, insisting that both their children needed self-esteem. This is when my mother shared with me two valuable lessons in child rearing.

She said, "If a mother has two pork chops and five children, does she conclude that she has three excess children? Or should she make gravy, add some rice and some succotash, and watch as two pork chops magically feed five children?"

Then she asked me a rather adult and challenging question: "Do you think good parents love each of their children equally?" Rather automatically, I said, "Yes." She said, "No, that's not true. Like most people, even good parents, you have it wrong. Even good parents don't love all their children equally. They love them adequately. Some children need more time and attention than others. You can't just fit all of them in an equal-time box, an equal-care box, an equal-love box. You must love them until that little light of self-esteem and self-identity comes on and catches hold."

When I was twelve and in the seventh grade at LeMans, a friend of mine from Pershing Elementary School had accidentally shot and killed his brother while playing with his father's gun during a lunch break. I'd learned of my friend's death when I returned home to Chicago one weekend. It was my first experience confronting guns, violence, and death. This first brush with mortality left me numb. I knew old people died, but to know that a young friend of mine was dead left my mind confused and my emotions very messed up.

The next year my mother came to LeMans to tell Jonathan and me that our grandfather, Charles Jackson, had died. Charles Jackson was actually my father's stepdad, but he was the only grandfather I knew. He was the one who'd taught me one of my favorite hobbies—fishing.

We flew to South Carolina for the funeral. I was thirteen and in the eighth grade, but it was really only during his funeral that I realized I had two grandfathers on my father's side.

My dad always called Noah Robinson his father, but my name wasn't Robinson, it was Jackson. So I always recognized Charles Jackson as my grandfather. Noah Robinson was just someone who, when I occasionally saw him, would say, "Come here, grandson. I'm your granddaddy." After Grandpa Jackson's death, I would say to myself, "You're not my granddaddy. My granddaddy's dead." But I always went along and never made a fuss over it.

However, one day my mother sat me down and explained the very complicated nature of my father's origins. In short, he was born out of wedlock to a poor sixteen-year-old mother who had gotten pregnant by a married man, a much older neighbor, by the name of Noah Robinson. The pregnancy had brought shame and humiliation on her through the local church and community. She was forced to confess her sin before the entire congregation. My father had grown up being called a bastard by some of his "friends," and this had left deep scars on his psyche.

His grandmother—we called her Mama Tibby—couldn't read or write, but she was a "great" grandmother in both senses of the term. She had a great spirit about her and was always so proud of her family, but especially her great-grandsons and great-granddaughters. My father's mother was Helen Jackson, a beautician. She, too, was a wonderful person, and I visited her almost every summer. She and her husband, Charles, would take us to visit our relatives in Pickens and Easley, South Carolina, especially Uncle Foster and Shorty Bub, both mill workers.

After I was thoroughly confused about my father, my mother took the time to explain her own origins, which were similarly complicated. She never met her natural father. Her mother, Gertrude Brown, is a fascinating lady. She had five children and put all of them through college. After they got their degrees—she was in her fifties—she enrolled at the Thomas Nelson Community College and graduated with an associate's degree even as she worked full time for the Veterans Administration in Hampton, Virginia. Then, at sixty, she earned a bachelor's degree in social work from Hampton University. Still not satisfied, she went on to complete a master's degree in social work at Norfolk State University at age sixty-five. My mother's stepfather, Julius Brown—whom I had always known as just Grandpa—became one of my great fishing buddies and best friends during my high school and college years.

Toward the end of my schooling at LeMans, when I was about fourteen, my father took me to Washington to meet Jimmy Carter and Walter Mondale. As I entered the big white house I had only seen on television, I was impressed by the dapper marine opening the door in his full military regalia. I had no idea why we were there. I was sitting in the lobby, sucking on a lollipop, when a lady came out and ushered us into a room. Just minutes later President Carter and Vice President Mondale entered the Oval Office together. A picture was taken and, if you can imagine, there I am shaking hands with the vice president of the United States with my right hand and a lollipop in my left.

We lived in the Jackson Park Highland community of South Shore. Our house was always busy, and often we had exciting guests. Sammy Davis, Jr. visited us once and left his bracelet on the couch. I found it and returned it to him. Donny Hathaway and Roberta Flack were friends of the family. They gave my sister an expensive piano. Just a few weeks later, however, Donny jumped out of a window in a New York hotel and killed himself. My father preached and gave a eulogy at his funeral in St. Louis.

President Daniel Ortega of Nicaragua once visited our house, and my father hosted a reception for him. He also invited one of his top congressional nemeses, Representative Bob "B-1 Bomber" Dornan. They sat in our backyard discussing the issues involved in Nicaragua. I remember only that President Ortega tore his argument to pieces.

Other high-profile people—entertainers like the Brothers Johnson, Quincy Jones, Stevie Wonder, Bill and Camille Cosby, and the Spinners; boxers Joe Lewis and Muhammad Ali; baseball players Jackie Robinson, Ralph Garr, and Dusty Baker; countless African ambassadors, governors, senators, congressmen, aldermen, and more—passed through our home.

My mother determined that her boys needed to spend more time with their father, and increasingly his work was taking him to Washington, D.C. She wanted to send my brother and me to St. Albans, a very good private Episcopalian high school in the nation's capital. Jonathan decided that he didn't want to leave Chicago. I had generally enjoyed my LeMans experience and didn't mind leaving home to go to school. I was used to living away from home and I looked forward to going to school in Washington.

My first experience at St. Albans, however, was a disaster. It was late spring of 1980, and I had already completed the ninth grade at LeMans. But St. Albans has a four-year language requirement. If I wanted to be admitted to the tenth grade, I would have to complete a language class in summer school. Rather than give up my summer, I decided to repeat the ninth grade. At the time I saw it as a personal disaster—now I was a year behind all my friends. In the end, however, it was the best decision.

St. Albans proved to be so challenging that I now believe I would have been ill equipped to meet its academic standards if I hadn't spent a full four years there. The hallmarks of St. Albans are its small classrooms, its teachers—many of whom could have taught in college, and some at the graduate level—and its high expectations. It is a who's who of the Washington political elite. It has a reputation as one of the most prestigious high schools in America.

But my academic career at St. Albans didn't reflect this. I did just enough to get by and to get out. Now that I look back on the experience, my real education at the school came from being around people who knew more and had been exposed to more than I had. Of course, my impulse to be "Fella" could not be denied just because this was St. Albans. My brother Yusef, who later attended the school, recently told me that virtually all of the rules in the dorm for the students who boarded at St. Albans had been rewritten. And the dorm master asked Yusef, "Do you want to know why? Because of your brother Jesse." I was suspended from St. Albans twice: once for bringing a girl into the dorm, and a second time for preparing crib sheets for a calculus exam. St. Albans proved to be the most academically challenging and least academically applied period of my life. It was also the most fulfilling athletically.

I went out for the football team. I wanted to play wide receiver, but on the first day of practice I told Coach Allanson I wanted to play running back—at the time, I didn't know the difference between the two. So early on I found myself on the bottom of a lot of piles, but the rest, as they say, is history.

As St. Albans running back I achieved areawide media recognition for some of my accomplishments. In the first three games of my senior year, I rushed for nearly five hundred yards and scored two touchdowns. Then I sprained my ankle, which put me out of action for several weeks. In the end, I was recruited and offered scholarships by several majority-white universities to play football, including some Ivy League schools. Ultimately, however, I decided to accept a football scholarship to North Carolina A&T State University (NCA&T), my father's alma mater and the place where my parents met.

My brother Jonathan had attended and played football at Chicago's Whitney Young High School, one of the better academic and athletic public high schools in Chicago. The relationship between Jonathan and me, however, was beginning to reflect our vastly different high school experiences. So we decided to close that gap by going to college together at NCA&T.

It was also during my last season of football at St. Albans that on November 3, 1983, my father announced his first presidential candidacy. At the time I had little historical understanding or appreciation for what his candidacy would actually mean to African Americans, America, and the world.

My father always told his children that leadership is bred in a majority experience. I didn't understand what he meant until I got to NCA&T. There, really for the first time, I saw an *institution* being run by an African American chancellor, and other top administrators. I was taught by black professors with doctorates and master's degrees, sitting beside some of the most intellectually gifted black students I've ever met; they may have looked and acted average, but they were brilliant. I saw black lawyers, accountants, and other professionals doing their jobs with skill and dedication. I also saw African American head football coaches, assistant coaches, and quarterbacks. Jonathan and I decided to play football for the Aggies. During our formative years at NCA&T, my brother and I didn't have to fight the power; we were the power.

While in Greensboro, I was one of the original organizers of Students United for a Free South Africa. We launched protests against entertainers who came into North Carolina after having performed in Sun City.

A&T was also very challenging academically, but I had changed. I decided to apply myself. "Fella" was gone, and I went to school every summer. In the end, I graduated magna cum laude in just three years with a bachelor of science degree in business management.

After the civil rights movement of the 1960s had broken down barriers to public accommodations and taken the lock off the ballot box, I had pretty much concluded that that was all that was necessary for change to occur in the United States. But college introduced me to the need for change in ways I hadn't previously considered. And I concluded that I and my generation had a role to play in bringing about that change—and some obligation to do so. My concern, however, was that although my generation was just one removed from the civil rights struggle, already we seemed uninterested in pursuing new challenges for change.

After my father's first campaign and while still a student at A&T, I developed a determination to get more young people involved in the political process. There were forty-five hundred students on campus, so I organized a voter registration drive and registered thirty-five hundred new voters. We decided to target a local congressman, Howard Coble (R-NC), who had consistently voted against divestment in South Africa and student loans beneficial to A&T students. He was being challenged by a man named Robin Britt.

On election day I got my first lesson in how southern Democrats play their politics. We worked hard to get all Aggies to the polls. Senator Terry Sanford even flew to the University of North Carolina at Greensboro (UNCG) in a helicopter to create enthusiasm and stimulate voter turnout. The only problem? Of the sixteen thousand students at UNCG, fewer than one thousand were registered to vote. Rather than come to a historically black college, where more than three-quarters of the student body was registered and solidly in Britt's corner, Senator Sanford chose to go to UNCG where registration was low and the choice of candidate uncertain. Democrat Robin Britt lost the election by sixty votes.

Howard Coble is still in Congress, and we are cordial toward each other. He calls me a scalawag—someone born in the South but identified with the northern cause—and I still do everything I can to defeat him. Because that election was so close, in the 1991 redistricting Coble insisted that his friends draw NCA&T out of his district. The university is now represented by Mel Watt, who was first elected in 1992.

Three NCA&T professors influenced me greatly: Dr. Dong Quen Jeong, Dr. Wayman B. McLaughlin, and Dr. Hattie Liston. From the beginning Dr. Jeong encouraged me to achieve on my own so I would not always live in my father's shadow. Even today when I talk with him, he challenges me to "achieve a great destiny for mankind." He was ecstatic when in 1995 I launched my campaign for Congress. He supported and followed it with great enthusiasm. In 1997, while still in North Carolina, he read in a newspaper that I had gone to South Korea to meet with President Kim Dae Jung during the 1997 Asian financial crisis. When I returned to Washington, he called me with great joy in his voice. I got the feeling that in a small way, I was beginning to fulfill some of the great expectations he had for me.

Dr. McLaughlin—Dr. Mac for short—was my philosophy professor. A Hegelian throughout, he would often tell me, "Jesse, the truth cannot be found in either the thesis or the antithesis, but in the emerging synthesis that reconciles the two." This was Dr. Mac's favorite quote. Whenever I bump into one of my former classmates, the Reverend Mark Anthony Middleton from New York, we ask each other: "Are you in the synthesis?"

Dr. Liston, a professor of psychology, was especially memorable for her lessons on Dr. Abraham Maslow's hierarchy of needs theory. Maslow argued that human beings are motivated by unsatisfied needs, and that certain lower needs must be met before higher needs can be satisfied. He outlined five needs—from lowest to highest, our physiological needs, followed by the needs for safety, love, esteem, and self-actualization. This theory was key in helping me formulate my thoughts about the new American rights and new constitutional amendments that I advocate later in this book. Coincidentally, Dr. Liston taught both my mother and father when they were at NCA&T, and then me, Jonathan, and my younger sister Jacqueline.

After graduating from NCA&T in 1987, I worked as a southern regional director for the 1988 Jackson for President campaign. Along with Dr. Ron Daniels, one of the former executive directors of the Rainbow Coalition, and the late Lewis "Lou" Carter, a longtime civil rights activist, I traveled to more than one hundred churches, registering thousands of people to vote on Super Tuesday, mid-March 1988. I always recognized that there was something different about the South—its language, food, religion, slower lifestyle, and more—but I didn't fully realize what it was until I came to Congress. I have finally concluded that it's economic and social conservatism.

In many ways, my father's 1988 campaign was even more historic than his first one, in 1984. In 1984 what got attention was the uniqueness of an African American running for president of the United States. In 1988, at one point—after my father won Michigan by beating Governor Michael Dukakis by a two-to-one margin—there appeared to be the possibility that he might actually win the nomination. That, of course, sent the Democratic Party into shock. While he didn't win the nomination, he did win thirteen of fifty-four contested races, and finished second in another thirty-three. He also accumulated more delegates (1,218.5) than any second-place finisher in history, yet the natural choice was not put on the ticket.

When my father had all five of his children introduce him before a national television audience at the Atlanta Democratic Convention, it was the first time that most Americans had seen him as a family man. They knew him first as a religious and civil rights protester and economic agitator, then as an educational innovator and a motivational speaker to struggling inner-city students, and finally as a liberator of captives and a presidential candidate. My speech in Atlanta had a fringe benefit for me: It put me in demand as a speaker on college campuses and elsewhere around the country.

After the 1988 presidential campaign, I embarked on a short career as vice president of Operation PUSH, working with its new president, the young and dynamic Reverend Tyrone Crider, who is a great orator and motivational speaker. Operation PUSH was founded in 1971, but since 1984 my father had been devoting most of his time to developing a new D.C.-based political organization, the National Rainbow Coalition. He brought Tyrone and me into PUSH to grow and develop as young leaders, but also to bring new life and more young people into the organization and movement for social justice.

With longtimers Francis Davis and the Reverend Mrs. Willie Taplin Barrow, we set about rejuvenating PUSH. Our efforts met with varying success. While I respect the gifts and role of charismatic leaders like my father, this experience further convinced me that the social justice movement must also develop stronger institutions around such spirit-filled leaders in order to protect past gains and advance social justice even farther. I was always arguing that we needed to apply new, more sophisticated technology and techniques to the movement and to political organizing. This mostly fell on deaf ears—including my father's.

Still, one of the great things that came out of this experience, in addition to my friendship and a good working relationship with Reverend Crider, was a profound respect for the abilities and leadership of Reverend Barrow. I began spending a lot of time with her, having tea together, taking early-morning walks, talking, picking her brain and spirit, discussing generational differences, and trying my best to soak up her knowledge and wisdom, and integrate her experiences into my own. She shared with me the problems of ego as it relates to leadership. She spoke candidly about the unmet psychological needs and insecurities of those who tried to compete with Reverend Jackson. She shared her knowledge and experience about raising money and balancing budgets. She contributed mightily to my development as a leader, and I shall always be extremely grateful for her help and guidance. Today, Reverend Barrow is nearly eighty, but she is vibrant and chairwoman of the newly joined Rainbow/PUSH Coalition. I suspect she will be there as long as she wishes.

I wanted to attend seminary, not because I felt a traditional calling to preach or to the parish ministry, but because I wanted the chance to develop, explore, think, feel, and reflect upon the possible contributions I might make with my life. My father had told me on several occasions that a seminary education would be one of the most challenging and broadest learning experiences I'd ever have.

I remember clearly a meeting I had with Dr. Kenneth Smith, president of CTS. He asked me if I had been called to the ministry. I told him, "If you're asking me whether I've had the deep emotional experience that some people might interpret as their 'calling,' then the answer is no. I haven't experienced that. But," I continued, "if you're asking whether I'm interested in exploring how I might help bring social change or make a difference in the world, then yes, that's what I'm interested in."

He asked me one final question. He said, "Son, if I let you in this seminary, will you finish what you start?" I assumed he was referring to my father going to Selma and then never returning to finish his academic work. I told Dr. Smith, "I finish everything I start."

So I began an exploration of God, the world, and how I might find my place in it. I learned that God is omniscient, all-knowing, and that there are no new inventions or discoveries, only new revelations of God's nature and manifestation. God is omnipotent, all-powerful, and God's power is found in all things and all people—the strong as well as the weak. God is omnipresent, always present, which was the most difficult concept for me to understand, partly because of its revolutionary implications. If you genuinely believe God is always present, then you must accept that there is no moment in history when God has left us alone. That is a truly revolutionary concept, because it means that God is always active and working with and through us for the good. As my dad often says, God plus one is a majority.

Although it's difficult to see God's presence in our day-to-day lives, it can be seen in history through the freeing of the Egyptian slaves—as well as the freeing of the American slaves. History can be seen as the story of irresistible forces advancing evil's cause only to be checked by the forces of justice. There is a moral law in the world—silent and invisible—but akin to the laws of nature. The Hitlers and Mussolinis—and, I might add, the George Wallaces and Bull Connors—may have their day, but they will soon be cut down like grass and rotten timber.

Dr. Martin Luther King, Jr., told us in his book *Strength to Love* (1963) that Victor Hugo, in his graphic account of the battle of Waterloo in *Les Misérables*, wrote: "Was it possible that Napoleon should win this battle? We answer no. Why? Because of Wellington? Because of Blucher? No. Because of God." Napoleon had been negated by the Infinite, and his fall was inevitable. Dr. King wrote, "In a real sense, Waterloo symbolizes the doom of every Napoleon and is an eternal reminder to a generation drunk with military power that in the long run of history might does not make right and the power of the sword cannot conquer the power of the spirit."

It is always difficult to see God in ourselves and others because there is so much wrong in us and evil in the world. But if God is genuinely present in our lives, it also means that God is present in history.

Seminary was full of such thoughts, and of mystery, history, religion, philosophy, theology, Old Testament, New Testament, applied ethics, psychology, worship, and more. So my dad was right: Seminary was both broad and challenging. And I kept my word to Dr. Smith and finished my work with a master of arts in theology in 1990, a year early, though I have never been ordained as a minister.

Now I'm a member of the board of trustees of Chicago Theological Seminary. When in April 2000 Dr. Susan Thistlethwaite and the board of directors determined that Reverend Jackson had satisfactorily met the requirements for a master of divinity degree, I was very excited to be the board member who hooded him and, along with my mother, presented him his degree.

During the 1988 presidential campaign, I met Sandi Stevens at a Congressional Black Caucus gathering hosted by Representative Mickey Leland. Sandi was his press secretary. I'm not sure she even saw me, but I know she paid me no attention whatsoever. She was very busy, clearly in charge, and in control of a lot of important issues for a very important person. But she more than caught my eye. I found out later she was quite intelligent, but what got my attention that day was her beautiful face and smile, lovely figure, and effervescent personality. Now all I had to do was apply that "ol' Aggie wit."

I initially pursued only a friendship. I sensed something unexplainable and very special about Sandi. Part of it was her personality and smile, which lights up the whole room when she enters, as well as her considerable intellect. I often called her in Representative Leland's office just to stay in touch. However, it wasn't until the Atlanta Democratic Convention in 1988 that I finally got her home number and we agreed to keep in touch. Within a few months Sandi and I were communicating regularly. She was very articulate, smart, and politically active. After the Atlanta convention, she began working for the Dukakis campaign out of Austin, Texas. One day I sent her five dozen roses at the campaign headquarters. She told me later, "That's what really won me over." I always add, "From which she has never recovered."

As our relationship grew more serious, she expressed some concern about my interest in seminary. She didn't foresee a long-term relationship with a preacher. She told me of her own desire to pursue a legal degree. She applied and was admitted to Georgetown University Law School. I too applied and was accepted, but we agreed after her first year that the tuition—sixteen thousand dollars a year, each—would amass such a debt that it would burden our future together. So together we agreed to enroll in the University of Illinois College of Law at Champaign-Urbana. She transferred from Georgetown after one year and I enrolled there as a first-year student.

While in law school, Sandi and I decided to get married. On June 1, 1991, after a year and a half of postponements, we tied the knot. I asked my best friend at the time, a young Nigerian named Pius Aileman, to be my best man. He had befriended me at a 1988 California campaign fund-raising event attended by such Hollywood notables as Elizabeth Montgomery, Quincy Jones, and Margo Kidder, had visited my parents' home, and planned to attend NCA&T's homecoming. He told me I would never meet a woman quite like Sandi again, so I should never let her go. Unfortunately, however, when our wedding day came my best man called to tell us he wouldn't be able to attend.

We were perplexed until we visited him in San Francisco during part of our honeymoon. He told us he had been in jail over a passport violation. But that wasn't the end or the worst of it. Pius had told Sandi and me that he was the son of a Nigerian transportation official and had been educated in England and Amsterdam. It was very believable and, to the best of my knowledge, is true. But we soon learned that this very likable, urbane, multilingual, religious young man living in a very modest apartment—my best friend—was actually an international narcotics kingpin. My picture and name first appeared in a San Francisco newspaper article regarding his arrest, the result of an FBI wiretape and sting operation that had recorded many of our conversations. Later the Chicago media picked up the story.

After several years of investigation and a trial in which Mr. Aileman was convicted and sent to jail for many years, I was finally cleared of any knowledge of wrongdoing or involvement in his business. I was indeed totally innocent, but my family's good name had been publicly besmirched. Mr. Aileman had been exploiting the Jesse Jackson name and connection as credible cover for what he was actually doing—trafficking in drugs. It was a bitter lesson about the vulnerability of high-profile people and their families.

When this came to light, Sandi and I had already moved to Washington and we were both working for my father. I was the national field director of the Rainbow Coalition; she was the director of the Citizenship Education Fund. Still preoccupied with technology and institution building, I started to bring that interest to bear on the Rainbow. I installed a high-tech computer system—Monarch, a California-based system originally designed to run congressional campaigns—which was networked to every employee in the office. We had the name, address, phone number, congressional district, state representative and senator district, ward, precinct, and county of nearly three hundred thousand people, and we could code them for political targeting in ten thousand different ways. The names had been gathered from my father's work—PUSH, Rainbow, and two presidential campaigns—but each was on a separate tape and was not being utilized by the organization until I installed Monarch.

Next I created JaxFax, a technologically sophisticated weekly targeted sheet faxed to more than five thousand key leaders of our organization. Usually written by Frank Watkins, its purpose was to inform, educate, and interpret important issues or current events from a progressive perspective. It was sent to more than three hundred clergy, who copied and distributed it to their congregations through church bulletins each Sunday; to college professors, who often used it as a classroom discussion piece; and to key radio stations, which sometimes used it as a topic of discussion on public affairs or current events programs. I also came up with the "Fax Tree" concept. The idea was for those who received JaxFax to create their own smaller targeted list and fax it on for an even wider distribution.

Frank and I created a five-hundred-page organization and teaching manual that could be sent to anyone wanting to become a part of the Rainbow Coalition. It showed how to organize a Rainbow chapter or affiliate, from the precinct level all the way up to a state organization. We also included how-to lesson plans for organizing issue forums, voter registration drives, or lobbying campaigns; for using the media around a local issue; for raising funds; and more.

It became increasingly clear, however, that this more politically structured effort was not the desired direction of the Rainbow, so Sandi and I moved back to Chicago and bought a house in the South Shore community. Sandi was the first to mention the idea of my running for Congress one day. Shortly thereafter I raised the possibility with Frank. He thought it was feasible, and we began to do some research—studying Mel Reynolds's voting record and running some numbers on his past primary and general election campaigns. I was considering running against Mel in the March 1996 primary when news surfaced in mid-1995 of his legal problems. He soon announced his resignation. I was not prepared mentally or financially to run as early as the November 28 special primary election, but Frank insisted that this was my best chance: It would be difficult to unseat a newly elected incumbent. So ready or not, on September 9, 1995, I announced that I was running for Congress.

My dad would have preferred that I gain political experience by running for a local office first—alderman, state representative, or state senator. Other friends said I was just too young to go to Congress. I told my dad and others that if a twenty-six-year-old Patrick Kennedy could be in Congress, then a thirty-year-old Jesse Jackson, Jr., could be there, too. I said, "I'm just going to take my chances. If I win, I win. If I lose, I lose. Maybe then I'll try again, but maybe not." It wasn't a life-or-death thing with me then, and while I love serving the people of the Second District, being a congressman isn't the only way to serve. If the people in my district vote me out of office, I'll find something else to do that is meaningful to me and will make a difference in the world. Elected office is not the only meaningful way to render public service. My father's life and work are testimony to that fact.

There were six other Democrats in the race besides me. Three of them were heavyweights—State Senator and Minority Leader Emil Jones, the most powerful African American in Illinois; State Senator Alice Palmer; and State Representative Monique Davis. They were all good people, with generally progressive views and records and lots of experience. But I plunged into the race.

My district is fifteen to twenty miles wide and twenty to twenty-five miles long at points, and contains nearly 600,000 people, including 372,000 registered voters. I had only seventy-five days to campaign, with the special election to be held on the first Tuesday after Thanksgiving—when nobody would be thinking about voting. I had to ask, "What is the most effective way to campaign under these conditions?"

My father and Jonathan—the treasurer of my campaign—were upset when I spent the first thirty-six thousand dollars I raised on computers, the Monarch system. But this system held the names of all the registered voters in my district and told me whether they had voted in the 1992 and 1994 primary and general elections. So the first thing I was able to do was analyze specifically who and where the registered and most likely voters were. I discovered that there were 45,000 individuals in the Second District who had voted in all four past elections. I also found 58,000 who had voted in the last two Democratic primaries, but they resided in just 44,000 households. So out of 372,000 potential voters, I was able to narrow my target to 44,000 households. Frank then organized a map with all 572 precincts on it and color-coded it, which painted a picture for me "in quarters" showing roughly how many votes I would need to win and where they would come from based on voter registration and past voting patterns. The top quarter, he showed me, would come from only seventy-eight precincts, but the bottom quarter would take 272 precincts. These two facts alone showed me specifically who to target direct mail and phone calls to—the 44,000 households—and where to spend most of my time campaigning—in the precincts with the most people likely to vote.

I won by just five thousand votes in a very tough campaign. I received no newspaper support from the downtown dailies, including the black daily newspaper, the *Chicago Defender*, though I did receive the endorsement of an important African American community newspaper, the *Citizen*, and a significant south suburban newspaper, the *Daily Southtown*. The only politician to endorse me was Mayor Evans Miller of Markham, and the only labor endorsement I received was from the local Markham American Federation of State, County and Municipal Employees. The local progressive political organization, IVI-IPO, supported one of my opponents. The women's organizations supported Alice Palmer. The clergy was split among several different candidates. It may sound like a cliché, but in the end, I was truly elected by the people.

One incident of the campaign stands out in my mind. One televised debate was held with both the Republican and Democratic candidates participating. Emil Jones was my main competitor, and he had pretty much stacked the audience with his supporters. He was also campaigning on his experience, as someone who knew how to get things done. At the end of the debate, we each gave our closing statement. I was next to last. In his closing statement, Senator Jones said, "Being a congressman requires more than just attracting large crowds, giving a good speech, and rhyming"—actually a reference more appropriately directed to my father than to me, but he was targeting me. He went on, "I am someone who has the experience, the connections, and the knowledge of how things work. I know how to deliver. I know how to get things done."

My argument throughout the campaign had been that Senator Jones's years of experience, seniority, and leadership in Springfield meant that he could best help the people of Illinois by staying in Springfield. The Second District needed to send someone to Congress who was young enough and could stay there long enough to gain seniority and eventually bring home the bacon—like Dan Rostenkowski had done for the North Side as chairman of the Ways and Means Committee.

Now, at the time, the Chicago Bulls were the hottest thing in Chicago, but they had just traded a popular player named B. J. Armstrong. Michael Jordan (M. J.) was playing minor-league baseball. So as I began my closing remarks—and immediately after Senator Jones had finished his statement about getting things done and not rhyming—I quipped: "I am not running against Emil Jones. I am trying to build a stronger team. B. J. should have never been traded; M. J. should have stayed in basketball; E. J. [Emil Jones] should stay in Springfield; and J. J. should be sent to Congress." The audience—which Jones had largely organized—broke out in laughter and applause that seemed to last a minute or more. The moderator lost control of the show and forgot that there was still one more closing statement to go. The next day, people on the street stopped me and repeated my line. That one line of rhyme was the most memorable and, for me, effective communication that took place in the entire campaign.

Since my election in 1995, I have tried to conduct myself in public life with a level of humility that is born of the knowledge that many people paid a substantial price for my ability to serve in Congress. Sometimes I asked myself, "Why me?" And knowing both my large dreams for the country and my human limitations, I also often ask myself, "Is it possible that from someone so imperfect, something perfect can come?" The answer that constantly comes to me is contained in the words of a Gospel song that my good friend Wintley Phipps sings and made famous, "Ordinary People." It goes, in part: "Little becomes much when you place it in the Master's hand."

A CAPITOL TOUR

Whether it's your first visit to the nation's Capitol, you're taking a repeat trip, or you work there every day, being in and around this historic building is always an awe-inspiring experience. The beauty. The grandeur. The ideals. The tradition. The personalities. The pictures, documents, and statues. This place lives and breathes old struggles and new ideological battles.

Begun in 1793, and built, burned, and rebuilt on Jenkins' Hill, the nation's Capitol covers about four acres and is reflective of nineteenth-century neoclassical Greek and Roman architecture. Beyond its function as the legislative center for the nation, the Capitol is also a museum of American art and history.

As I became accustomed to my role as a congressman, I began to think more seriously about my presence in this special place.

One day I sat alone on the House floor wondering, "What is this congressional thing? Where do I fit?" About that time, Elijah Cummings, a good friend and a congressman from Baltimore, strolled over. Apparently sensing my pensive mood, he took a seat next to me. Like me, Cummings had been elected in a special Maryland election—his to fill the unexpired term of Kweisi Mfume, who had resigned to become president and CEO of the NAACP. I often refer to Representative Cummings as number 93, and he calls me number 91, because those of us elected in special elections know exactly where we fall in the chronology of African Americans who have served in Congress. An experienced Maryland state legislator, his words penetrated to the very heart and core of some of what I was thinking.

"You know," number 93 said, "there are three stages that every legislator must go through. The first is, 'I'm just glad to be here.' The second is finessing the institution . . . learning its rules, procedures, and protocols. The third stage is actualization. Being able to take an idea, translate it into legislation, maneuver it through various subcommittees and committees, win support from at least 218 representatives and fifty-one senators, and have the president sign it into law. The tragedy is," Cummings continued, "too many legislators never get past phase one, 'Just happy to be here.'"

So I began to study the institution of Congress of which I am a part, and the people here, as well as the symbols that tell and remind us of our nation's history. I knew the basics, of course, from my high school courses in American history, but being on Capitol Hill gave these dry facts an immediacy I had never experienced before.

Every day as I walked to and from my office, I began to observe the statues, the documents, and the paintings around me, and I began to read and ask questions. From my days at the Rainbow Coalition working on a campaign for "New Columbia"—the proposed name of the new state for the nearly six hundred thousand politically disenfranchised citizens living in the nation's capital—I knew that the selection of the original one-hundred-square-mile site of Washington, D.C. (now sixty-seven square miles), had been, in part, like many chapters in our history, a racial compromise between North and South.

In the early days of the Republic, Congress made several cities its home—Philadelphia, Baltimore, Lancaster, York, Princeton, Annapolis, Trenton, and New York City. In June 1783 the Continental Congress was meeting in Philadelphia when a band of drunken and mutinous soldiers, angry with Congress's failure to pay them for their military service during the Revolutionary War, surrounded the legislators in the meeting hall and held them hostage for their back pay.

The legislators sent an urgent message to the governor of Pennsylvania, asking him to send the state militia to protect them. He refused, and Congress remained under siege for two days. Outraged, the legislators swore never again to rely on a "host" state to provide security for them while in session.

As a result of this incident, four years later when the Founding Fathers were drafting what would become the U.S. Constitution, they resolved in Article One, Section Eight: "The Congress shall have power . . . to exercise legislation in all cases whatsoever over such District (not exceeding ten miles square) as may by the cession of particular states, and the acceptance of Congress, become the seat of government of the United States."

The question of where to locate the new federal government sparked intense rivalries. Sectional jealousies, fears that one section of the country might gain economically or politically over another, and the question of whether slavery would exist in the new capital were all influential factors. After various compromises, Congress voted thirty-two to twenty on July 16, 1790, to authorize George Washington to make the final selection of where to establish a new capital district. The current location was Washington's choice.

Maryland and Virginia ceded to the federal government a ten-mile-square piece of largely swampland along the Potomac River. Sparsely populated, it was home to about five thousand people, mostly black slaves working on small rural plots of land.

Between 1790 and 1801, the few eligible white male landowning residents living in this area voted in Maryland and Virginia. On February 27, 1801, when Congress assumed legal jurisdiction over the District, the lawmakers intended to clarify the political rights of District citizens at some future time. To this day, Congress has never gotten around to addressing the question of full political representation, so the more than half a million current residents of the District are still denied the same political rights that other Americans enjoy—that is, two U.S. senators and representation in the House based on population.

By 1846, most of the development in the nation's capital had taken place on the territory donated by Maryland. Residents in some of the areas that had been part of Virginia agitated for political representation, but more important, this section had a thriving slave trade. Local businesses feared that the nation's capital would soon outlaw slavery—which it did on April 16, 1862. Virginia asked for the return of its land, and on September 7, 1846, Congress obliged, thus reducing the size of the District to the land contributed by Maryland.

One of the most famous racial compromises, of course, occurred in the drafting of the U.S. Constitution. Delegates at the Philadelphia Constitutional Convention agreed on September 17, 1787, that for purposes of taxation and representation, the slaveholding states could count their slaves, their "property," as three-fifths "human"—that is, five black slaves would equal three white persons.

Another constitutional compromise concerned the issue of the slave trade. The Founding Fathers resolved that the federal government would end the slave trade with foreign governments in 1808, but that the slave trade within and between the states could continue. The moral question about the institution of slavery itself was postponed until a later day.

I often take visitors to National Statuary Hall, one of our nation's most historic rooms as home to the House of Representatives for nearly fifty years. This semicircular two-story room is located just south of the Rotunda—the center of the Capitol that connects the House and Senate—and is also known as the Old Hall of the House. Since 1864, Congress has invited each state to place two statues of prominent citizens in the Capitol. It now serves as the main room for the nation's statuary collection, housing more than three dozen. It may be best remembered by visitors for its remarkable acoustics. If you stand toward the front of the hall, just to the left or right of the center, and speak softly, even in a whisper, you can be heard plainly nearly sixty feet away. This always brings oohs, aahs, and laughter. The old House chamber is also where the Massachusetts militia was quartered during the Civil War.

Once I visited Statuary Hall with the late congressman Walter Capp, who pointed out to me a small statue of Clio, a female figure holding a pen and pad in hand and positioned just over the back entrance of the old House chamber. In the past, she would have been looking over the shoulders of the legislators as they debated the issues of their day. Symbolically, Clio was recording the words, proceedings, and laws for posterity, Capp told me. He then made the observation that the significance of Clio was lost on current House members, who were often busy playing to the live C-SPAN cameras, campaigning to their own constituents, or pandering to particular interest groups rather than dealing with the long-term interests of the American people.

In the front of Statuary Hall, where the Speaker's chair would have been in the old House chamber, stands a statue larger than Clio, of a woman, symbolizing America's commitment to the ideals of freedom and liberty—even though, at the time it was sculpted, freedom and liberty were largely limited to white male landowners.

I once attended an awards ceremony in Statuary Hall at which a well-educated and urbane clergyman delivered the benediction. As we stood to pray, he intoned on behalf of the group sincere thanks to God for the great leaders America has had throughout its history, many of whom, he said, were represented by the statues we see today in this great hall.

I opened my eyes and scanned the gallery of marble and bronze figures. Immediately in front of me was the statue of Alexander Hamilton Stephens of Georgia, vice president of the Confederacy. To my right stood a statue of Brigham Young, who moved the Mormon Church from Missouri westward because his followers were persecuted, but whose religion excluded African Americans until two decades ago. I turned to my left and there was Henry Clay of Kentucky, the Great Compromiser, who oversaw the slavery compromises of 1820 through 1850. A little farther left, I glimpsed a statue of General Robert E. Lee, the Confederate general of the Army of Northern Virginia, who fought to preserve the institution of slavery in the South during the Civil War. As I continued perusing the hall, I discovered Commander Joseph Wheeler of Alabama proudly wearing his Confederate States of America uniform and belt buckle. And just a few statues away stood Jefferson Davis of Mississippi, the president of the Confederacy. The statues appeared to be all white men, but I later discovered that there is one woman and one person of color in Statuary Hall. Frances E. Willard of Illinois was active in the woman's temperance and education movements, and King Kamehameha of Hawaii was a courageous warrior who unified all of the inhabited islands of Hawaii under one flag.

I always knew that race in America was an issue. But it was becoming increasingly clear to me that the story of African Americans in particular is the central issue in our history—and it is preserved and even honored in many ways in the nation's Capitol.

When the Republicans swept into power in January 1995, they were entitled to become chairs of House committees. Representative Gerald Solomon chaired the Rules Committee. This committee is important because no legislation can come to the floor without first going through the Rules Committee, which sets the dates, times, and rules of debate and voting on every bill before it comes to the floor.

One of the first things Representative Solomon did as chair was remove the painting of the Democratic former chairman of the Rules Committee from the wall of the meeting room. You might expect the Republicans to put up an image of one of their own, but Solomon chose Howard Smith of Virginia, a former Democratic chairman and an arch-segregationist and civil rights foe of the 1950s and 1960s. During his tenure Representative Smith vowed never to allow a piece of civil rights legislation to pass through his committee and come to the House floor for a vote. Forty years after Jim Crow, Representative Solomon was sending a strong signal to his colleagues and the country about the direction the Republicans would be going.

As a young African American in the Capitol, I admit I was looking for symbols that were meaningful to the special circumstances of my people. I was trying to figure out the context and understand my role and where I fit in the scheme of things. More and more I am convinced that workers, women, Native Americans, Asians, Latinos, Jews, the Irish, Polish, Italians, English, and many others should take a similar tour and look at our history through the prism of their ethnicity or from their point of view—not for the purpose of balkanizing America, but to better understand the history of our nation. Most groups, I'm sure, would be shocked at the lack of representation.

From Statuary Hall, I continued my tour of the Senate side of the Capitol. Located in the foyer just outside the Senate chambers is a bust of every vice president through history—the same person who also serves as the president of the Senate.

One floor up, and just outside the Senate gallery, Frank Watkins and I spotted a huge painting depicting the Tilden-Hayes Compromise of 1877. Neither Democrat Samuel J. Tilden nor Republican Rutherford B. Hayes won enough electoral votes to become U.S. president in 1876, so the election was thrown into the House of Representatives in 1877. Hayes eventually became president, but in the process a deal was cut that included removal of the northern troops stationed in the South to protect former slaves. White Republicans joined forces with white Democrats, which led to a weakening of Reconstruction policies favorable to blacks. With no interference from federal troops, these hostile Democrats, former Confederates, could regain control of southern state governments and state legislatures—in other words, a return to the rule of states' rights and local control.

As we looked closer, there appeared to be only two black faces in the Tilden-Hayes painting—Frederick Douglass and one other we could not identify. We asked ourselves where the other black members of Congress were—those elected during Reconstruction? Eventually, the Tilden-Hayes Compromise led to the virtual demise of the black legislator—the original Congressional Black Caucus. But surely they were present to witness the crucifixion!

The current thirty-eight-member Congressional Black Caucus (the only black Republican, J. C. Watts, chooses not to be a member) is the second such organization. The first CBC had twenty-two members between 1870 and 1901—from the appointment of Hiram R. Revels to complete the unexpired term of Senator Jefferson Davis of Mississippi, who had resigned to become president of the Confederacy, to ousted Representative George H.

White of North Carolina, who said in his last congressional speech of the black legislator, "Phoenix-like, he will rise up some day and come again." In 1877, the year depicted in the painting, there were four black congressmen: Blanche K. Bruce of Mississippi in the Senate, and three South Carolinians, Joseph H. Rainey, Richard H. Cain, and Robert Smalls. We have not been able to determine why they are not depicted in the painting.

Throughout the various Senate rooms, there are numerous statues and paintings of Daniel Webster of Massachusetts, John C. Calhoun of South Carolina, and Henry Clay of Kentucky. These men were the principal players in Congress during the first half of the nineteenth century, when lawmakers wrestled almost continuously with the question of slavery. Webster, the great orator, opposed slavery. Calhoun, slavery's most articulate and ardent supporter, actually gave up the vice presidency to devote his time and energies to defending slavery and states' rights. Clay devised compromises from 1820 to 1850 to preserve the Union.

Debates on slavery were almost always heated, and it was not uncommon for members and spectators to bring guns and knives into the Senate and House chambers. Fistfights often broke out. Men were sometimes challenged to step off of the tobacco-juice-soaked floor of Congress and engage in a "duel to the death." When the issue of the Kansas-Nebraska Act came to the floor on May 19 and 20, 1854, tensions were particularly high. Four years earlier, as part of the Compromise of 1850, California was admitted to the Union as a free state, but the agreement left the question of whether the Kansas-Nebraska Territory (and future territories) would be slave or free to be determined by "popular sovereignty"—a vote by locals (in other words, states' rights).

During the heated debates, Senator Sumner of Massachusetts let loose a tirade against the South's institution of slavery: "Murderous robbers from Missouri, hirelings picked from the drunken spew and vomit of an uneasy civilization," had committed a "rape of a virgin territory, compelling it to the hateful embrace of slavery," Sumner railed. Singling out Senator Andrew P. Butler of South Carolina for a personal attack, Sumner charged that the South had prostituted itself to the institution of slavery. "Don Quixote, who had chosen a mistress to whom he has made his vows, and who . . . though polluted in the sight of the world, is chaste in his sight—I mean the harlot, Slavery."

Senator Butler's nephew, Preston Brooks, a congressman from South Carolina who happened to be in the Senate gallery that day, took offense at Sumner's words. A few days later, he confronted Sumner on the Senate floor and demanded an apology. When Sumner refused, Brooks beat him about the head with a gold-topped cane until he collapsed in a bloody heap at his desk. The *Richmond Enquirer* praised the attack as an "act good in conception, better in execution, and best of all in consequence." "Bleeding Sumner" had joined "Bleeding Kansas" in the nation's struggle over slavery.

The House tried to expel Representative Brooks, but the southern bloc prevented them from securing the necessary two-thirds vote. Brooks eventually resigned. In South Carolina he was feted as a hero and sent back to Congress the very next election. Southerners from everywhere sent Brooks dozens of canes, urging him to finish the job. Senator Sumner never fully recovered from his injuries, but he continued to fight against slavery and on behalf of blacks until his death. The desk in the old Senate chambers at which Senator Sumner was sitting when he was beaten is today identified with a single book lying on it. Capitol tour guides and employees in the chamber usually tell this story and answer questions from visitors.

It was out of these heated and ugly debates over slavery that Congress wrote the basic rules of protocol and decorum for conduct on the floor of the House and Senate that apply even today. Addressing the chair, instead of individuals, and referring to colleagues as "my good friend from Alabama," "the honorable gentleman from Maine," or "my distinguished colleague from Missouri" blossomed forth from this history.

Jefferson Davis's Senate desk also has a prickly history. During the Civil War, the Capitol was used as a Union military barracks, hospital, and bakery. When a northern soldier there learned which desk had belonged to Davis—who was by then, of course, the president of the Confederate States—he flew into a rage and began using his bayonet to stab the desk. Senate authorities finally halted the attack, but not before damage was done. Visitors today can still see where carpenters tried to repair the scars left by the soldier's bayonet.

To this day the desks in the Capitol, like its paintings or speeches, are used by some members to send not-so-subtle racist messages. Davis's desk was occupied by Mississippi's Democratic segregationist Senator John Stennis from 1951 to 1989. Mississippi's Republican Senators Thad Cochran and Trent Lott sponsored a 1995 resolution that permanently assigned this desk, which once belonged to the greatest traitor in history, to a senior senator from Mississippi. The Senate passed this resolution on a voice vote without opposition.

It is this kind of symbolism, sometimes highly visible, often not, that plays itself out in the politics of race nearly every day in the nation's Capitol.

It was in this context that on June 11, 1996, I watched Majority Leader Bob Dole deliver his farewell address to Senate colleagues after deciding to devote himself to running full time for president. He reminisced and talked about how much he cared for his fellow senators on both sides of the aisle. He said he even liked the Senate's unique rules of debate, including the filibuster. At that point, Dole turned to Senator Thurmond, sitting behind him, and remarked that the senator held the record for the longest filibuster. But when Senator Dole mistakenly got the length wrong, Senator Thurmond jumped right into the middle of his speech and proudly corrected him: "It was twenty-four hours and eighteen minutes." The entire Senate, press gallery, and balcony erupted in laughter.

I didn't laugh. Why? Because the record filibuster was to block the 1957 Civil Rights Bill, the first piece of civil rights legislation to reach the floor of the Senate since Reconstruction nearly a hundred years earlier. I did not see a single mention of what the filibuster was about in the press coverage that followed Senator Dole's speech. Given the way the current crop of Republicans almost always (and the Democrats sometimes) use racially coded messages, I wasn't sure whether Dole was making an innocent remark or sending a deeper message about his presidential campaign. Such signals, I have learned, are not uncommon.

Three weeks after Ronald Reagan launched his 1980 presidential campaign in the South from Philadelphia, Mississippi, my father confronted the candidate at Chicago's Operation PUSH about the fact that the Ku Klux Klan had attended Reagan's rally and endorsed his candidacy. My father pointed out to me that Philadelphia, Mississippi, was known for only one thing: It was the site of the gruesome deaths of three civil rights workers, Michael Schwerner, Andrew Goodman, and James Cheney, in the summer of 1964. Clearly, Reagan's purpose was to send a political signal to his conservative southern racist supporters!

I have since discovered that the person who had invited Reagan to Philadelphia, Mississippi, and promised him that if he started his campaign there it would assure him of being one of the few Republicans to win the state of Mississippi since Reconstruction, was none other than that area's then congressman, Trent Lott, the recent Senate majority leader. I also found that in 1981 Lott had written a letter to President Reagan urging him to grant tax-exempt status to Bob Jones University of Greenville, South Carolina, even though the school had a clear and open policy of racial exclusion. According to Kenneth O'Reilly in *Nixon's Piano*, "This grew out of a 1980 Republican platform plank promising to 'halt the unconstitutional regulatory vendetta launched by Mr. [Jimmy] Carter's IRS commissioner against independent schools.'"

As I continued to dig deeper into Senator Lott's history, someone shared with me an interview from a 1984 issue of *Southern Partisan*. When asked about a statement he had made at the convention of the Sons of Confederate Veterans in Biloxi, Mississippi—that "the spirit of Jefferson Davis lives in the 1984 Republican Platform"—Trent Lott responded:

> I think that a lot of the fundamental principles that Jefferson Davis believed in are very important to people across the country, and they apply to the Republican Party. . . . After the War between the States, a lot of Southerners identified with the Democrat Party because of the radical Republicans we had at that time, particularly in the Senate. The South was wedded to that party for years and years and years. But we have seen the Republican party become more conservative and more oriented toward the traditional family values, the religious values that we hold dear in the South. And the Democratic party is going in the other direction. As a result, more and more of The South's sons, Jefferson Davis' descendants, direct or indirect, are becoming involved with the Republican party. The platform we had in Dallas, the 1984 Republican platform, all the ideals we supported there—from tax policy, to foreign policy, from individual rights, to neighborhood security —are things that Jefferson Davis and his people believed in.

The rest of the article detailed how southerners, like himself, were becoming more influential in the Republican Party. He also stated his opposition to civil rights legislation—for being unfair to the South—and his opposition to another hot issue at that time, the holiday honoring Dr. Martin Luther King, Jr.

One of Trent Lott's major political activities has been the support and promotion of Jefferson Davis. He was awarded the Jefferson Davis medal by the United Daughters of the Confederacy (UDC) for his successful efforts to get Jefferson Davis's citizenship restored. Davis's last residence was located in Lott's district when he was a congressman. In a speech to the UDC at the Confederate Monument at Arlington National Cemetery on June 3, 1979, Lott detailed his view of Jefferson Davis as a great American.

Even though this restoration of Davis's citizenship required a two-thirds vote in both houses under the Fourteenth Amendment, the measure passed by overwhelming majorities in both cases. In the House fewer than fifteen members opposed it, and President Jimmy Carter signed it into law October 17, 1978. There was some public mumbling, but both Democrats and Republicans seeking southern electoral votes supported the measure nearly unanimously. Unfortunately, most Democratic liberals and progressives don't realize that historical memory is especially important and is rehearsed in a variety of ways in many of the eleven former Confederate States.

Senator Lott is reportedly considered by many southern conservatives to be a leading figure in the neo-Confederate movement. For several years he had a regular column in the

Citizen Informer, a publication of the Council of Conservative Citizens (CCC), a neo-Confederate national organization active in defending Confederate flags across the South and promoting Confederate activities. When his connection to the CCC was exposed in several *Washington Post* articles in 1999, he backed away from them, even as relatives and friends identified him as a strong CCC supporter.

Senator Phil Gramm of Texas, Senator Jesse Helms of North Carolina, Senator Thad Cochran of Mississippi, Senator John Ashcroft of Missouri (now attorney general of the United States), and Representative Dick Armey of Texas have all granted interviews to the *Southern Partisan* and spoken at CCC events.

In observing and studying the nuances of Congress, I have concluded that the Civil War is still going on in Congress. It is just being fought politically, instead of militarily, using different terms. A new language among Republicans and conservative Democrats has emerged in the 1980s and 1990s. African Americans are no longer referred to openly as "niggers" but as "urban"—as in, "Urban programs should be cut or done away with." Whites with a humane agenda are no longer called "nigger lovers" but "liberals"—and most cut and run from the label.

Conservative Republicans and Democrats, with the cooperation of the media, have successfully painted "welfare" and "crime" as code words for African Americans. As a result, the southern-oriented and conservative Democratic Leadership Council and its executive director, Al From, argue that the only way Democrats can become a permanent majority party is to show "responsibility on the fundamentals"—be fiscally conservative and tough on crime and welfare—and recruit suburbanites, the middle class, the more affluent and independent swing voters (whites implied on most counts). A further translation is: Let's move away from the traditional Democratic base and the "special interests" of people of color, women, and labor.

Conservatives today openly talk about "block grants" and "local flexibility and control," the new catchphrases replacing "states' rights," which, of course, was the old code word for protecting slavery, Jim Crow segregation, and racial discrimination.

As I learn more about the legislative process, I am becoming increasingly aware of code words and coded messages. The Confederates of the conservative southern Democratic Party were famous for their interposition and nullification tendencies. "Interposition" refers to the action of a state that places its sovereignty between its citizens and the federal government; "nullification" is an action of a state that impedes or prevents the execution and enforcement of a federal law. Today nullification has been redefined as "unfunded mandates," laws or regulations that the state will not follow or enforce unless they are federally funded, which, of course, is opposed and attacked as a "big government" program or a "liberal tax and spend" policy.

In 1997 I engaged in a floor debate on H.R. 2, the Housing Opportunity and Responsibility Act of 1997, an attempt to rewrite our nation's housing laws. Over a period of several weeks, we debated the voluntary work section of the bill for many hours. This part of the legislation required public housing residents to work "voluntarily" for eight hours a month or be evicted. Such a rule, I felt, was blatantly unfair. No one else in America receiving federal aid or tax breaks was required to do any "voluntary" work in exchange for their benefit.

During the course of the debate of H.R. 2, I carefully avoided using the term "slavery." But a rose by any other name is still a rose. At one point, I asked Chairman Jim Leach (R-IA) if he knew of any other time in our nation's history since December 18, 1865—that's when the Thirteenth Amendment to the Constitution outlawed slavery and involuntary servitude—that such a requirement had been enacted. He said, "No. It was unique."

I noted in my mind at the time that he carefully chose to use the word "unique" instead of "peculiar" in response to my question. If he had used "peculiar," it would have triggered in my mind recollections of the "peculiar institution" of slavery.

Code words aren't the exclusive property of conservatives. Democrats use them as well. For example, the new benevolent party line among Democratic leaders is, "Be a good Democrat." Even if something makes no moral, political, or economic sense, just support it— "Be a good Democrat."

I experienced this when I chose to remain neutral in the Illinois governor's race in 1998 because the Democratic nominee, Glen Poshard, would not support the new suburban airport that would substantially aid my district. Not only would he not support it, he tried to embarrass and humiliate me by inviting the mayor of Gary, Indiana, to Peotone—the site of the proposed airport—to an anti-airport rally. Poshard also endorsed Mayor Daley's plan to use Illinois taxpayer money to improve the Gary Airport. In principle, I support the improvement of the Gary Airport, but I oppose shipping Illinois money and jobs to Gary, Indiana. As an elected public official, I have an obligation to protect the interests of my constituents and Illinois.

While I was officially neutral in the Poshard campaign, I did urge the people in my district to vote their economic interests. As a result, 65 percent of Poshard's margin of loss came from my district. While Poshard was still courting me for my endorsement, he commended me for encouraging my constituents to vote but criticized my advice to make their own economic interests a priority. In essence, he was telling me: I want you to help get the African American vote out, but don't obligate me. I don't want to deal with the real issues of the community—"just be a good Democrat."

I was similarly advised to toe the party line during the debate over President Clinton's impeachment hearings. On October 8, 1998, the morning the House of Representatives was to vote on separate Democratic and Republican proposals to begin a formal impeachment, my guest column, which appeared in *USA Today*, outlined a dual political strategy—the White House was singularly focused on protecting the president—that would have increased the president's poll numbers while also increasing the possibility of Democrats regaining control of Congress, especially the House. Before turning the column in to *USA Today*, I submitted it to the White House. The response was defensive and aggressive. Within a matter of hours I received a call from President Clinton, one from Vice President Gore, and two from Chief of Staff Erskine Bowles. Later, I had an hour-and-a-half personal visit from then Deputy Chief of Staff John Podesta about the article.

In essence, my article said that the president had confessed to the sinfulness of the Monica Lewinsky affair, had showed contrition, and said he had been converted. But the one thing that was missing was a willingness to accept the possible consequences of his actions— yes, possible House impeachment, Senate conviction, and legal action. I argued that if he would say he was willing to accept the potential consequences—and I never believed he would be convicted in the Senate or found guilty in a court of law—he would then be free to take his case directly to the American people before the midterm elections. I believed that the American people would support him, that Democrats would win back control of the House, and, as a result, that he would have avoided even a House impeachment. They didn't buy my argument.

Their message was essentially: We've already got the black vote. Just be a good Democrat and go along with *our* strategy—which was focused solely on keeping the president's numbers high with little regard for the fact that those high numbers were not translating into Democratic gains in Congress.

The subliminal message? African Americans aren't supposed to have independent thoughts, especially about how to attract or win back *white* votes. Both Massachusetts liberal Democrat Barney Frank and Texas conservative Democrat Charlie Stenholm had read my piece and told me the strategy laid out was morally and politically sound and would be helpful to both the president and congressional Democrats. In the end, I ran it without White House approval.

After being in Congress for a while, I noticed that southerners held a disproportionate number of key power positions in the federal government. At first I wasn't concerned, but as I continued to scrutinize the process and the players it became clear that it did make a difference, because the political history and social dynamic of the former Confederate States *is* unique and different from the rest of the country.

Indeed, by January 3, 1995, the South had risen again. President Bill Clinton was from Arkansas; Vice President Al Gore was from Tennessee; and White House Chief Erskine Bowles was from North Carolina.

In the House, on the Republican side, Speaker Newt Gingrich was from Georgia; House Majority Leader Richard Armey was from Texas; Chairman of the Appropriations Committee Bob Livingston, from Louisiana; Chairman of National Security Floyd Spence, from South Carolina; Chairman of the Ways and Means Committee Bill Archer, from Texas; Chairman of the Commerce Committee Thomas Bliley, from Virginia; and Chairman of the Permanent Select Committee on Intelligence Porter Goss, from Florida.

In the Senate, the chairman of the Armed Services Committee and the president pro tem—thus third in line to the presidency—was Strom Thurmond of South Carolina. As already discussed, Majority Leader Trent Lott is a conservative neo-Confederate from Mississippi. The chairman of the Foreign Relations Committee, ultraconservative Jesse Helms, hails from North Carolina; Chairman of the Rules Committee John Warner is from Virginia; and Chairman of the Select Committee on Intelligence Richard Shelby is another converted "Dixiecrat" from Alabama.

At this writing, only two of the nine Supreme Court justices are from the South, Sandra Day O'Connor—who was born in Texas and later became a resident of conservative Arizona—and Clarence Thomas from Georgia. This is fewer than it's had for most of its history.

Clearly, there are many other power centers in Washington, but it would be difficult to assemble a *cumulative* list that is more homogenous or powerful than this one. These men and women are generally representative of their region and reflective of its conservative economics and politics. They tend to prefer states' rights over "big federal government" solutions that set minimum and uniform national standards, which would lead to a more perfect Union for all Americans.

For more than thirty years, and especially since President Ronald Reagan in the early 1980s, the prevailing rhetoric and conservative political climate has fostered radical individuality (libertarianism), privatization, and states' rights. There has been an ideological and a systematic attempt on the part of the Republican Party to discredit and to tear down the federal government—actually government generally—as well as a prevalence of corporate over national interests (for instance, the North American Free Trade Agreement, the World Trade Organization, the Africa Growth and Opportunity Act, and permanent normal trading relations with China). This philosophy extended in part to the Clinton administration, which, under an assignment given to Vice President Gore, downsized ("reinvented") the federal workforce by more than 250,000 jobs and overhauled many programs in conjunction with conservative Republican congressional leaders.

I am *for* individuality. I am also *for* individual responsibility. I know that individual initiative is necessary to succeed in any field of endeavor or even to bring about political change—including creating a more perfect Union. I am a strong supporter of personal liberties and civil rights. And I respect and find necessary the role of the private economic sector in our society. But to truly bring about greater equality of the races and the classes in our society, to establish minimum standards of human decency and civil rights protection, to improve the overall quantity and quality of all Americans' lives, and to move individual Americans from economic need to economic security with greater human, religious, and spiritual development, the federal government must play a significant role.

Nothing could have brought this general point home more clearly than the 2000 election and the attention it focused on the various voting systems, procedures, and standards used by thousands of different counties and local municipalities. If our educational, health, and housing systems were given the same degree of national scrutiny and exposure as our voting system was in 2000, we would find the same convolutions and disparities.

Even as I say this, I also argue that we must experiment with ways to make the political process and the federal government—indeed, all government—more efficient, less wasteful, more democratic, more responsive, fairer, and more accountable to all Americans. There must be no tolerance of waste, fraud, or abuse in any area of our government. Inefficient, arrogant, and unaccountable governmental systems or people must be challenged and changed. And yes, if programs are no longer necessary, they must be done away with altogether.

The Preamble to our Constitution begins with the proposition that "we the people" are to build a more perfect "Union." Lincoln, the first Republican president, preserved the Union and improved it by using a strong central federal government against southern states committed to states' rights and local control. The conservative southern Democratic-controlled states of Lincoln's day, of course, wanted the "Big Federal Government" off their backs—in order to preserve the institution of slavery and protect their economic interests.

Today, however, the party situation has nearly been reversed: It's the Republicans who mostly are the conservative advocates of states' rights and local control. Of course, they don't say they're opposed to the national public good or to building a more perfect Union—one with full employment, safe streets, health care, affordable housing, a quality education, and fair taxes *for all Americans,* or federal laws and minimum standards outlawing discrimination, environmental pollution, unsafe and unhealthy working conditions, and unsafe foods or medicines. No, they just say they are opposed to the "Big Federal Government," the same position the conservative Democratic slaveholding party and states maintained more than a century ago. I suspect, however, their opposition to the federal government is for essentially the same reason—to protect their privileged economic interests.

Today's Republicans and Democratic conservatives insist that they are simply opposed to a big, centralized, bureaucratic federal government. They seem to be unaware that the biggest and most centralized federal government program, Social Security, is also the most popular among the American people. And the same conservative opponents of the "Big Federal Government" are opposed to reasonably cutting the biggest, most wasteful, and most fraud-ridden federal government bureaucracy—the Pentagon and the military budget. In fact, conservatives advocate increasing the Pentagon's bloated and wasteful budget.

As I continued to analyze these situations and similar ones I have researched and reflected upon during my tenure in the House, two fundamental conclusions reverberated. First, that race is not a peripheral issue in America, but has been central throughout our history and continues to be so. And second, that the political divisions in Congress are not about liberal versus conservative, and certainly not about Democrat versus Republican; they are more consistently about North versus South.

When faced with many of its important decisions—committee assignments, legislative programs, politics—Congress seems to divide itself into factions closely aligned to the pre–Civil War schisms: North and South; those who believe in strengthening the Union and those who support localism or states' rights.

Certainly not all southerners are proponents of states' rights and local control, but most are. Nor are all congressional members outside the eleven former Confederate States guided by the principles of improving our Union by working for the betterment of the general good. But in my experience, the "more perfect Union versus states' rights" paradigm is a very apt description of what goes on in Congress.

I have heard some of my more senior colleagues in the House say that the country has not had a real Democrat in the White House since Lyndon B. Johnson left in 1969. Johnson himself was a traditional southern Democrat until he became president. While I'm too young to remember LBJ, I do recall that during one of the Democratic debates in 1988, the candidates were asked whom they thought was the greatest American president of the twentieth century. All the others named FDR or JFK, but my father, while acknowledging the travesty of Vietnam, cited LBJ as the best president in terms of helping improve the lives of the majority of Americans.

As I was growing up, I noticed some important differences between Democratic and Republican presidents. But as an adult, and now as a member of Congress, I don't see the significant differences that I anticipated would be part of a vibrant two-party system in which there were real choices. The Democratic Leadership Council (DLC), the New Democratic Coalition, the Democratic "Blue Dogs"—including President Clinton and Vice President Gore while in office—seemed more in harmony with traditional Republicans than they were with the real needs of the vast majority of the *people* and the prime constituents of the Democratic Party. Presidents Jimmy Carter and Bill Clinton, along with candidate Al Gore, were more like moderate Republicans, especially with regard to their economic policies. They may be perceived by many as *social* liberals—there are some who question even this— but certainly they are not *economic* liberals in the tradition of FDR, Truman, or LBJ. I do not advocate for policies that merely clone those of past presidents and times; I'd like to see revised and new policies that have the same goals, programs that build on the solid progressive economic foundation those leaders laid.

After LBJ signed the Voting Rights Act on August 6, 1965—which affected most southern states and some nonsouthern states—he said privately that the new law probably meant the loss of the South by Democrats for the next quarter century.

The old FDR coalition was always a strange coalition of voters—liberals, intellectuals, blacks, white Dixiecrats, northern white ethnic Catholics, and labor. But with the Voting Rights Act enfranchising the black majority in one region—more than 50 percent of all

African Americans still live in the South—the Republicans began to court the white conservative constituents formerly known as Dixiecrats, now known as Reagan Democrats, who historically are descended from the old slaveholding southern states' rights and local control Democrats.

That was the political basis for the "southern [read *racist*] strategy" for Barry Goldwater's 1964 "conservative" and Richard Nixon's 1968 "law and order" campaign that Republicans have applied and exploited in various forms ever since—and Democrats have attempted to counter using similar tactics. Now conservative Republican leaders see countering claims that they are a racist or intolerant (read *choice for women*) party as key to controlling the increasingly northern-populated and socially moderate southern states. Conservative Democratic leaders and the Democratic Leadership Council see not dealing with issues pertaining to race—except in the coded language of being fiscally responsible, fighting crime, and ending welfare as we know it—as the key to their controlling the South. Ultimately both groups want to influence the South, because the South is crucial to protecting the interests of the small national economic elite who pay for and perpetuate a conservative economic agenda.

With more questions than answers, I wanted to better understand the North-versus-South, "Union versus states' rights" dynamic. I wanted to learn more about the people and the politics in the South, especially the leadership—historic and current.

So I went on the road. In 1997 and 1998 I took three tours of the South, visiting some of its most important Civil War battle sites.

THE DENIAL

And now General Lee is to have a monument erected to his memory! His admirers will spare no expense to make it one of the grandest in the country. It will recite his virtues in long chapters, and laud him, immaculate, the only wise and great of the sons of America. But they forget that the future will look to history, and by its lessons will be formed opinions of the merits of the great butchery inaugurated by politicians in behalf of slavery and against free government. They forget that this monument will keep prominent in the eye of the world the one great fact of Lee's life, namely, his treason. The recital of his virtues will be forgotten in the keen remembrance of this enormous wrong.

—*Methodist Advocate*, Atlanta, Georgia, published 1869–1883

Oh, I say and I say it again—you've been had, you've been took, you've been hoodwinked, BAMBOOZLED, led astray, run amok.

—Malcolm X
Speech at Unity Rally in Harlem, April 1960

A house divided against itself cannot stand [quoting Jesus]. I believe this government cannot endure, permanently half slave and half free.

—Abraham Lincoln
June 16, 1858, Springfield, Illinois,
after Illinois Republicans nominated him to run for the
U.S. Senate against Democrat Stephen Douglas

As I set out on my tour of Civil War battlefields in August 1997, I wasn't sure what I would find. Because the Civil War was such a pivotal point for race relations in this country, I tentatively concluded that a better understanding of the war and of the southern mentality was critical to understanding the role that race had played—and continues to play—in American history and politics.

Frank Watkins and I traveled together touring some of the eastern Civil War battlefields. During the four years of the war some ten thousand different battles were fought—a few in the North and more in the West, which was then Tennessee, Kentucky, Mississippi, Missouri, Louisiana, and Texas. Most of the major battles, however, were fought in the South and Southeast—Virginia, North Carolina, South Carolina, Georgia, eastern Tennessee, Alabama, Pennsylvania, Maryland—known as the Eastern Theater of the Civil War. We visited most of the more significant sites.

Our first stop was Gettysburg, Pennsylvania, about an hour and a half's drive from Washington, D.C. As we left the main highway and drove the smaller roads to get to Gettysburg, the first thing we noticed were the monuments. They were everywhere—more than fourteen hundred monuments, markers, and memorials. It seems that every state and every fighting unit had returned and marked the exact spot of its participation in the three-day battle, July 1–3, 1863.

Some 1.7 million people visit the Gettysburg National Military Park each year. Like many of them, we started our tour with a stop at the visitor center. Inside we found an impressive array of Civil War books, a museum of Civil War artifacts—rifles, cannon, uniforms, medical equipment, tents, cooking and sleeping gear—facts about the battle, and an electronic light-and-sound show that tells the story of the battle at Gettysburg. We were reminded that this was where General George Pickett led his men to slaughter in a foolhardy maneuver that became known as Pickett's Charge.

Across the street from the visitor center is the Gettysburg National Soldiers Cemetery, where on November 19, 1863, President Abraham Lincoln gave his stirring Gettysburg Address honoring the fifty-one thousand soldiers who had been killed, wounded, or captured in the battle, the largest and bloodiest of the Civil War. We read again the inspiring words of this brief two-minute speech.

The victory at Gettysburg—and a similar one at Vicksburg, Mississippi—is considered the turnaround point in the war. Both victories were celebrated on July 4, 1863. The historian and author Garry Wills wrote that the Gettysburg Address reinterpreted what it meant to be an American. Lincoln deliberately avoided mentioning the Constitution—because it defended the institution of slavery—and instead referred directly to the Declaration of Independence. The Declaration's theme that "all men are created equal" better fulfilled Lincoln's purpose. Thus, today, every July 4 is actually more a celebration of what Lincoln said at Gettysburg than what the revolutionaries did at Lexington and Concord, or what the founders wrote in 1787.

A National Park Service guide, attired in period clothing, recalled the day and described the setting. Visitors played along by asking questions as if we were alive then.

Not very far from the visitor center was a tower that offered a panoramic view of the entire battlefield, complete with an audio presentation from all angles. In the summer of 2000 the tower was torn down, because Civil War enthusiasts said it interfered with the preservation and sanctity of the original battlefield. We also took an auto tour of the battlefield, stopping often to read the words chiseled on the monuments. We couldn't help but be impressed, indeed overwhelmed, by the size of the battlefield at Gettysburg—nearly six thousand acres, with twenty-six miles of park roads.

Frank and I were also very moved by what we saw. We noticed, however, that the battle of Gettysburg was not discussed in the context of the overall war, and virtually nothing was said about why the war was being fought in the first place.

Fortunately, we had an expert along to help fill in the blanks. A U.S. Army historian met us at Gettysburg and accompanied us to Antietam, Manassas, and Harpers Ferry. A native Virginian, he shared with us some personal experiences and memories of his early schooling that were enlightening.

For example, he told us that in Virginia schools, Confederate Generals Robert E. Lee and Thomas J. "Stonewall" Jackson were discussed in a way that made them heroes to the children. Indeed, many of the schools were named for Confederates. Students learned that the cause of the Civil War was primarily state sovereignty, not slavery. As an adult, our guide had come to a different conclusion.

On occasion, he continued, he had participated in Civil War reenactments—sometimes as a Union soldier and at others as a Confederate. Participating in reenactments can be expensive, he said. Some people do it just to experience history close up, to get a taste of what the Civil War was like. But there are other "hard-core" actors who take it all very seriously. Once, he said, the Ku Klux Klan visited the Confederate camp the night before the battle to recruit members, which led to actual fights between Union and Confederate "soldiers" before the reenactment. During the battle the next day, the American flag was accidentally knocked to the ground during one of the skirmishes. When it was over, the local sheriff noted the downed flag and praised the Confederate soldiers: "Y'all boys done good today."

From Gettysburg, we went to the Antietam battlefield in northern Maryland. Antietam is a particularly moving experience because on September 17, 1862, more men lost their lives here than on any other single day of fighting throughout the Civil War. By nightfall, six thousand men lay dead and another seventeen thousand wounded.

Here, as at many battlefields, visiting families came to see where their ancestors had fought and, in some cases, died. The vast majority of southerners—and even a few northerners—we talked to at Gettysburg and elsewhere said their relatives had fought the war over the issue of states' rights, not slavery. They offered as evidence the fact that 75 percent of white southerners didn't own slaves.

At Antietam, too, we found the complete story of the battle, but the absence of the context or the cause of the war.

Of the major Civil War battlefields we visited, only Gettysburg in Pennsylvania, a northern state, and Antietam in Maryland, a border state, were won by the North. Most of the major battles during the Civil War took place in the South. Although the North won the war and many of the battles, most of the Civil War battlefields are located in the South and are monuments to southern victories. At these battle sites, we saw no statues or monuments to President Abraham Lincoln, General Ulysses S. Grant, or other Union military heroes. Only Confederate leaders and heroes were preserved for posterity.

In effect, the federal government, through the National Park Service, is funding and giving moral standing and credence to Confederate victories that were fought in the name of a states' rights ideology that was really a political stance to preserve the institution of slavery. Taxpayers fund these National Park Service battlefields, which are essentially propaganda machines for the legacy of the Confederacy.

The deeper irony is that the federal government itself is perpetuating the ideology of states' rights. The presence of these battle sites, absent the context and cause of the Civil War, makes building a more perfect Union all the more difficult, because improving the lives of all Americans is going to require money and planning from the federal government.

Another conclusion we came to as a result of our tour of Civil War battle sites is that the denial of the underlying cause of the war—slavery—and the propaganda that the war was really about states' rights both have conservative political consequences. Obviously, if the war was about states' rights and not about slavery, then national reconstruction efforts—such as the First Reconstruction (1865–1877) and the Second Reconstruction beginning with the *Brown* Supreme Court decision in 1954 and continuing with the 1964 Civil Rights Act, 1965 Voting Rights Act, 1968 Open Housing Act, attempt at a Great Society, launching of a national War on Poverty, affirmative action, and economic set-asides and other forms of compensation, including reparations—make no sense. If, on the other hand, the war was over slavery and its legacy, then they make perfect sense.

I support the presence of Civil War battle sites as national treasures and as a vital part of our history. We found the directors and employees of the National Park Service to be very dedicated and well informed; they often knew more than they were permitted to explain about the sites because of the conservative politics of the local areas. Yes, neo-Confederate organizations are often quite active in many of these communities.

But on the whole, there is no overall focus among the memorials on examining the battles in the context of the politics and events leading up to the war. The most glaring omission is a candid discussion of the cause of the war, slavery. By its absence, the real cause of the war is denied. I believe that visitors to the battle sites should have the benefit of the whole truth when the facts are indisputable. On controversial issues, they should be made aware of diverse interpretations, allowing them to draw their own conclusions.

It was after these experiences, and in this context, that in the 106th Congress I introduced language in an Interior Department bill calling for a description of the historical, social, economic, legal, cultural, and political forces and events that originally led to the larger war and eventually manifested themselves in specific battles.

From Antietam we drove to Harpers Ferry, West Virginia. Before the Civil War, Harpers Ferry was in Virginia. But with the outbreak of war, the western section of Virginia, which had less of a stake in slavery than the tobacco-rich plantations of the eastern part, voted against secession and in 1863 was admitted to the Union as the free state of West Virginia, thus relocating Harpers Ferry.

It was here at Harpers Ferry that a firebrand white religious leader named John Brown seized a U.S. arsenal in 1859 in an attempt to foment a slave uprising. Brown first got involved in the abolitionist movement in Springfield, Massachusetts, in 1850, where he created the Gileadites, a black self-defense group organized to thwart the Fugitive Slave Law, which required slaves escaping North to be caught and returned to their southern slave masters. Though many abolitionists were advocates of nonviolence—and some, like William Lloyd Garrison, even pacifists—John Brown set out to free slaves by any means possible.

Earlier, in 1855, in a violent struggle over territory created by the 1854 Kansas-Nebraska Act, a group of Missouri Ruffians (supporters of slavery) attacked Lawrence, Kansas (a center of abolitionist sympathy and activity), and sacked the town, killing numerous people. John Brown had been on his way to Kansas to join his abolitionist sons in protecting Lawrence from the proslavery forces when the attack occurred.

As John Brown was en route to Lawrence, he learned of Congressman Preston Brooks's vicious attack on abolitionist sympathizer Senator Charles Sumner of Massachusetts. The pillage of Lawrence, Kansas, and the caning of Senator Sumner drove John Brown into a fury for revenge. With a fanatical eye-for-an-eye sense of justice, he plotted a counterraid in Kansas, exhorting his followers to "fight fire with fire" in order to strike terror into the hearts of the proslavery people. Brown, his sons, and three other men launched an attack on a group of proslavery settlers near Pottawatomie Creek, even though none of them had been involved in the Lawrence killings. In a night raid on May 24, 1855, they kidnapped five people and brutally murdered them by splitting their skulls with a broadsword.[1] Brown was never arrested or punished for this act of violence.

With religious zealotry and moral indignation burning in his breast, John Brown soon hatched another violent scheme to free slaves. His plan was to raid the munitions factory in Harpers Ferry, steal more than one hundred thousand rifles along with ammunition, then move eastward through Virginia's plantations, arming slaves so they could fight for their own freedom.

The October 16, 1859, raid on Harpers Ferry failed. A group of U.S. Marines, headed by Colonel Robert E. Lee and Lieutenant J. E. B. Stuart—future Confederate military leaders and heroes—was sent to Harpers Ferry from Washington to put down the rebellion. They succeeded, killing two of Brown's band of revolutionaries and capturing the rest in the local firehouse, including Brown himself. Political leaders in Virginia were incensed and demanded a quick trial to forestall a vigilante lynching of Brown. After a week's trial and forty-five minutes of deliberation, Brown was convicted November 2 and executed December 2, 1859.

As rumors circulated that Brown's supporters were plotting to rescue him at the hanging, Virginia authorities called for military assistance. Among the militiamen present that day was none other than a man from Richmond, John Wilkes Booth, the man who six years later would assassinate President Abraham Lincoln just five days after General Robert E. Lee surrendered to end the Civil War.

Sites and buildings from the Harpers Ferry seizure have been preserved or reconstructed by the National Park Service. The spectacular beauty of the converging Potomac and Shenandoah Rivers, which separate the Blue Ridge Mountains and three states—Virginia, West Virginia, and Maryland—is in itself worth a trip. In addition, the Harpers Ferry site gives visitors an in-depth and accurate history of the events that took place there. Through videos, wall displays, and text, you can also follow the political and legal context, plus the role that slavery played leading up to Brown's raid and ultimately to the war itself. It was clearly one of the most enlightening sites we visited.

An observation we noted after exploring Harpers Ferry was that John Brown was tried for three crimes: murder, for which he received a life sentence; treason, for which he received a life sentence; and inciting a slave rebellion, for which he got the death penalty even though he actually failed to bring about an uprising. For actual murder and treason, his life was spared, but for an unsuccessful attempt to stir up a slave insurrection, he was hanged. The verdict reveals the fear and resulting judicial schizophrenia of the South at that time.

According to historian James McPherson, "Reaction in the South to Brown's raid brought to the surface a paradox that lay near the heart of slavery. On the one hand, many whites lived in fear of slave insurrections. On the other, southern whites insisted that slaves were well treated and cheerful in their bondage."[2]

John Brown has been called the Meteor of the War because in this one daring act at Harpers Ferry, he probably sparked in death what he had hoped to trigger in life—the violent confrontation of slavery. More than any other single event, John Brown's raid on Harpers Ferry made an eventual Civil War almost inevitable, by dramatically escalating southerners' rage and paranoia, posing a threat to their economic self-interest and escalating secessionist tendencies. Lincoln's election a year later meant that southern slavery and state sovereignty would soon be met with northern determination to preserve the Union and to gradually eliminate slavery.

Our next stop was Manassas, Virginia. Manassas Junction was critical as a railroad center because in the Civil War, for the first time in history, railroads became important to military activity—moving troops and supplies quickly. Known as Bull Run by northerners, because the fighting took place near a small stream of that name, it was the site of the first major battle of the Civil War on Sunday, July 21, 1861; later, on August 28–30, 1862, it hosted a second battle. Both were won by the South.

In the early months of the war, neither the North nor the South thought that it would be a protracted one. Each side expected a quick victory with little bloodshed. Neither side had experienced war close up. Their armies consisted of ragtag groups of undisciplined soldiers who marched off gaily, thinking the war a bit of a lark.

When the Civil War started, Union forces totaled about sixteen thousand men, most of whom were assigned to the West to protect settlers and land conquered from the Indians. To meet the new demand, Lincoln issued a call for seventy-five thousand volunteers to enroll in the military for three months only.

To the Confederacy, a victory at Manassas was only one step away from conquering Washington and soon winning the war. For the North, it was a direct route to Richmond, the Confederate capital; taking Manassas would also quickly put down the revolt and send the upstart Confederates home with their tails between their legs. In the end, the battle of Manassas gave both sides the surprise of their lives.

On Sunday, July 21, members of Congress and other Washington elites packed picnic lunches, put their wives in horse-drawn carriages, and rode off toward Manassas for an afternoon of fun and entertainment—an exciting battle, full of fireworks, with an anticipated Union victory.

The first shots were fired in a large field in front of the home of a Confederate sympathizer, Wilmer McLean. At first, the North seemed to be routing the South. But as the day wore on, fortunes turned, mainly due to General Thomas Jackson, who was leading a brigade from Virginia. As General Bernard Lee of South Carolina attempted to rally his flagging troops, he spied Jackson's men returning fire and standing tall. "There is Jackson standing like a stone wall!" he shouted. "Rally behind the Virginians!"[3] Thus was born the legend of "Stonewall" Jackson. As a result, there is a huge muscular statue of Stonewall Jackson sitting on his horse right in the middle of the battlefield. While the real-life Thomas Jonathan "Stonewall" Jackson was not a particularly large man, this statue makes him out to be a superhero with rippling muscles.

By late afternoon the Confederate soldiers were able to turn back the Union forces, a moment that gave rise to the infamous "rebel yell," a piercing repetitive guttural sound uttered by charging soldiers.

The advancing onslaught and the rebel yell struck fear into the hearts of the tired and confused Union troops as they hastily retreated. Scurrying across a creek over Stone Bridge, the soldiers became entangled with the picnicking spectators, including members of Congress. The first battle of the Civil War had turned into a humiliating loss for the Union.

To avoid getting caught again in a military crossfire, Wilmer McLean moved his family to a small Virginia town far south of Manassas, called Appomattox Court House, the next historical site on our itinerary. The irony of the McLeans' move never fails to impress the visitors at Appomattox.

Before going on to Appomattox, however, we were told an astonishing story. James Ricketts, a northern artillery captain in the regular army, was severely wounded, captured, and taken to a nearby hospital in Portici during the first battle at Manassas. His wife, Fanny, armed only with the knowledge that her husband was wounded, journeyed by wagon—driven by a free elderly black man—and talked her way through both Union and Confederate lines to be reunited with her husband in Portici. However, once Fanny was delivered to her destination, the black man (whose name is unknown) was seized by the Confederates and sold into slavery.

En route to Appomattox, we stopped in Lynchburg, Virginia, to see old friends—the Reverend Jerry Falwell and his family. A dozen years ago, one of the reverend's sons, Jonathan Falwell, and I appeared together on *The Oprah Winfrey Show*. Prior to that, in 1985, my father and Reverend Falwell also debated the issue of applying economic sanctions to South Africa on ABC-TV's *Nightline* with Ted Koppel.

Though we seldom agree on things political, I have developed a lasting friendship with the Falwell family. Over breakfast at our hotel, I quizzed Reverend Falwell about his views on the Civil War. He was candid and knowledgeable. He clearly understood that slavery was the underlying cause of the war. During the Second Great Awakening, a religious revival in the first half of the 1800s, northern evangelicals had been key activists in the abolitionist movement, he said, whereas most southern clergy defended the institution of slavery. To Reverend Falwell, abortion is the modern-day moral equivalent of the slavery question.

We asked his opinion of an unusual practice at Virginian Military Institute (VMI) that a waiter had informed us of the previous evening. Apparently, as part of freshmen initiation, the cadets have to salute the campus statue of General Stonewall Jackson. Falwell said he wasn't aware of the practice but didn't find it objectionable. "Do you think African American students should be forced to salute General Stonewall Jackson?" I asked him.

"Well, the probable reason VMI is insisting on saluting him is because he was a great general, not because he fought to preserve slavery, " he responded.

"Do you really think you can separate his 'general-ness' from the cause for which he was fighting?"

"I think you can," Reverend Falwell said.

"So you think that if there was a statue of Lieutenant General Erwin Rommel"—Germany's Desert Fox—"on some university or college campus in this country, it would be all right for Jewish and other students to be made to salute him—and that they would—because he knew military tactics and strategy and was, in that sense, considered a great military general? You think the administration, the faculty, the students, and the broader community would distinguish between his 'general-ness' and the cause for which he fought—Fascism and Nazism?"

"I see what you mean," the reverend said thoughtfully. "I don't think so. I didn't know about the statue and the practice at VMI."

After breakfast we continued on to Appomattox, about twenty-five miles outside Lynchburg. An electronic display at the site tells the final chapter of the war. General Ulysses S. Grant's forces had sparred off and on with General Robert E. Lee and the Confederate Army of Northern Virginia during the winter and spring of 1865. By April, Grant had driven Lee westward, cornering him. Finally, at the town of Appomattox Court House, the North succeeded in forcing Lee to surrender.

The surrender took place on April 9, 1865, in the home of Wilmer McLean. After nearly four years, the final act lasted only thirty minutes. The war was over. Thus, Wilmer McLean could rightfully claim that the war had virtually started in his front yard and ended in his living room.

Standing in the parlor where the official document of surrender was signed and hearing the story of the respect that each side accorded the other was a particularly moving experience for me. The terms of surrender were generous—some have even referred to it as a "Gentlemen's Agreement"—written by Grant to Lee in the form of a letter. The terms stated that Confederate officers and enlisted men would be paroled and allowed to keep their horses or mules, but Confederate military equipment had to be turned over. Grant then sent twenty-five thousand rations to Lee's hungry Confederates. A formal ceremony of surrender was held on April 12, exactly four years after the start of the war at Fort Sumter, with the Union army symbolically recognizing Lee's army in a way that allowed his soldiers to go home feeling that they had been treated with respect and dignity.

Two college students attired in Confederate and Union uniforms played their respective roles, and visitors asked questions in the manner of the era. Having researched their actual characters thoroughly, the young men delivered impressive performances.

Even though I praise the Appomattox site for its emotional impact, I found it intellectually flawed because it did not emphasize the true cause of the war in its narrative for visitors. Everything we saw and experienced seemed designed to say "forgive and forget," although it was unclear from the exhibitions what exactly it was we were supposed to forgive and forget. The emphasis was overwhelmingly on reconciliation: All war is terrible and creates a lot of bad feeling and, therefore, we should be about the business of binding up the wounds of war.

There was no explanation that the war had anything to do with slavery. The reconciliation theme thus seems to be concerned with white folks forgiving each other for getting into this silly but ugly, protracted, and costly family feud. Now we need to get back together and "get on" with the business of reconciling the family.

Politically, such a conservative interpretation puts no emphasis on binding up the wounds from the legacy of slavery or reconciling the broken relationships between black slaves and white slave masters—which, I maintain, is what the Civil War was all about. This forgiveness and reconciliation didn't take place at Appomattox; they are still unfinished tasks that lie before us.

The tour gave us a hint as to just how big these tasks would be.

By the time we arrived at Appomattox, it had become abundantly clear that southerners were in deep denial over the cause of the Civil War. This denial—that the war was fought over states' rights, not slavery—was not limited to battlefields, but indeed permeated southern culture, and apparently had for generations.

This southern mentality was never so evident as at a bed-and-breakfast near Appomattox, where Frank and I bunked for the night. The B&B was a huge whitewashed, two-story antebellum home, complete with pillared portico and a wraparound second-floor balcony. Inside, the decor was predictably "southern": In the vestibule hung an ensemble print of Confederate generals gathered around a make-believe table, portraits of Generals Lee and Jackson stood sentry in the parlor, and prints of southern leaders or battlefields graced the walls in practically every other room. But the lasting impressions were not the mementos. It was our hostesses.

The innkeepers were two semiretired women. One made the beds, the other the breakfast. The cook, it turned out, had in a previous life taught American history to a couple of generations of young adults at the local public high school. So of course, we couldn't resist asking her opinion about the cause of the war.

Not surprisingly, the former history teacher responded unflinchingly that the Civil War was about states' rights, southern sovereignty, and political independence. When we asked her if slavery was part of the equation, she was unequivocal. "The war was about states' rights," she insisted.

The Appomattox history teacher's response made me flash back to the army historian we'd met at Gettysburg, who'd told us that, as a schoolchild in Virginia, he'd been taught the war was over state sovereignty, not slavery. So there it was: In two days, we'd met both the teacher and the student whose personal stories were testimonials to generations of southern institutional denial.

Many Americans will not acknowledge such an interpretation, because they have never been taught American history in a way that would logically lead them to it. They do not see the question of race and the legacy of slavery—the reason the Civil War was fought—as central to America or American history. They see the question of race as a peripheral or side issue, not to mention a nuisance, and something that happened in the far distant past that has no impact and little meaning for today. And most of the Civil War battle sites, our classrooms, the mass media, and popular culture all reinforce this conservative interpretation of race. It is why the ongoing structures and problems associated with the legacy of slavery are consistently denied by the American people.

Our visits to Appomattox and Harpers Ferry prompted a comparison of the treatment of traitors during the Civil War era. John Brown was convicted of treason, murder, and fomenting rebellion, and subsequently hanged. The Confederates, too, committed treason and instigated a rebellion that led to the "murder" of more than 620,000 war dead. Yet unlike John Brown's speedy trial and hanging, after the Civil War there were no "Nuremberg trials" or executions—except for the scapegoat trial and execution of Henry Wirz, commandant of a Confederate prisoner-of-war camp in Andersonville, Georgia. In fact, the treasonous ones became southern heroes, presidents of universities, and accepted business and political leaders.

Even more important, the ideological causes for which the Confederates fought—states' rights, the perpetuation of slavery and an economic and political elite—were defeated in war but not discredited in fact. Thus, the Confederate legacy lives on today in the form of a states' rights mentality and a political culture that perpetrates racism and discrimination against African Americans and many other groups, and which also continues to foster an economic and political elite that comes mostly (not exclusively, but mostly) in the form of Republicans and southern conservative Democrats. As long as such a mentality exists, it will be difficult, if not impossible, to build a more perfect Union for all Americans.

An example of the miseducation about the Civil War is the film we saw at the Kennesaw National Battlefield, northwest of Atlanta. The Cobb County site, which is partly located in the congressional districts of both former Speaker Newt Gingrich and Congressman Bob Barr, featured a movie that was modern in terms of filmmaking techniques, but in content sorely antiquated. A voice-over, accompanying a map illustrating how our nation had developed, intoned: "The country, North and South, developed in two different ways." That was it—"two different ways"! There was no attempt to explain that one developed industrially and the other agriculturally, and no hint that one economic system was based on free labor and the other slave labor.

We also noticed a change in the tone and style of language used in the film as both northern and southern soldiers described their experiences and told why they were fighting, bleeding, and dying in the war. The language used by the northern soldiers seemed cold, calculating, indifferent, matter-of-fact, aloof, and devoid of feeling. For example, one Sergeant Sam M. Pyles of the Fifty-second Ohio Volunteer Infantry is quoted as follows: "Charles Parker, a twenty-seven-year-old West Pointer, takes his brigade to within fifteen yards of the southern works before it is stopped. Parker was killed. To Parker's right the brigades of Daniel Cook and John Jean Mitchell strike the small hill which marks the dead angle of Cheatham's defensive position. . . ."—and so forth.

On the other hand, the film quoted Confederate Private Sam Watkins, First Tennessee, using passionate language and speaking with great feeling. "Still the Yankees came. It seemed impossible to check their onslaught. A solid line of blazing fire from the muzzles of the Yankee guns being aimed at our very faces, singeing our hair and clothes. The hot blood of our dead and wounded is partly on us. The blinding smoke and stifling atmosphere put in our eyes and mouths the awful confusion, causing the blood to gush out of our noses and ears. And above all, the roar of battle made it perfect pandemonium."

One young Confederate soldier in the film explained why he was fighting: "'Cause y'all are down here." As if the war was being fought because the North, for no reason, had invaded the South. That may have been the way this soldier felt, but it was not historically accurate. In our questions and discussion afterward, the park service interpreters insisted on telling us, "Well, that is the reason that young man was fighting." We said, "No, he cannot be the interpreter of why this particular battle and the war were being fought. This battle and the war were being fought over what Abraham Lincoln and Jefferson Davis said, not over what he and other soldiers in the field were saying, North or South."

We gave the park rangers the example of the Vietnam War. You couldn't ask individual soldiers why a particular battle or the war was being fought, we argued; young men and women were in Vietnam for all kinds of reasons. Some couldn't find a civilian job. Others wanted to get away from home and see the world. Still others wanted to use their G.I. benefits to get a college education after the war. Most were just drafted. We contended that you had to look to the political leaders and their policies, their explanations of why the war was being fought, in order to understand its actual causes. I'm not sure that we ever got through to them, but it was certainly a passionate and interesting conversation.

We also noted the credits at the end of the film and later asked the park staff about the researcher and writer. It turned out that he was not a historian at all, but a Texas lawyer who'd been hired as a consultant, chosen by a local Kennesaw Battlefield support group. That surprised us, because the military facts and interpretation at these National Park Service sites are usually so meticulous, but it also gave us a clue as to why it had been written the way it was.

One of the most significant monuments to the Civil War, though not a federally supported historic site, is Stone Mountain, a huge monadnock of granite, some two hundred million years old—sometimes referred to as the Eighth Wonder of the World—in the town of Stone Mountain, Georgia. Dr. Martin Luther King, Jr., mentioned Stone Mountain in his August 28, 1963, March on Washington speech: "Let freedom ring from Stone Mountain of Georgia! Let freedom ring from Lookout Mountain of Tennessee! Let freedom ring from every hill and every molehill of Mississippi. From every mountainside, let freedom ring."

The park surrounding the mountain is a beautiful setting, with a lake, trees, a golf course, bicycle trails, and hiking and jogging paths. It has a hotel and retreat center, boats, quaint little shops, fishing and camping sites, and a full-sized train to ferry visitors through its thirty-two hundred acres. It looks like a Disney World for outdoors lovers, but with some unusual differences.

For example, all of the streets are named for Confederate heroes. And on the northern face of the 1,683-foot-high granite mountain are the carved figures of Confederate President Jefferson Davis and Generals Stonewall Jackson and Robert E. Lee. The world's largest piece of sculpture is 90 feet tall, 190 feet wide, and 11 feet deep. Every summer night at nine o'clock, these three gentlemen are memorialized in a spectacular laser show, complete with rebel yells, to the cheers of a hillside of spectators. Stone Mountain's Internet site crows, "Choreographed to music in surround sound, the colorful laser beams and pyrotechnics recreate dramatic stories, historic tales and create comical characters and images." Nowhere is Georgia's Stone Mountain Park publicly promoted as a monument to the Confederacy—which is what it is.

One morning as we stood looking at the carvings of the Confederate heroes looming above the paper- and cup-strewn hillside, we noticed some prisoners, mostly black, working on the hillside, cleaning up the mess from the previous night's celebration of the Confederacy. After a brief conversation with them, we discovered they were inmates brought every morning to work for free.

Apparently, the KKK or other extreme groups occasionally use the park to exercise their First Amendment right of free speech. Near the train station, we saw a hand-painted sign that read: WE ARE NOT RESPONSIBLE FOR ANY FREE SPEECH THAT MAY TAKE PLACE HERE.

In one section of the park are several antebellum plantation houses, complete with slave quarters. There is also a Confederate Museum, quite a good one actually, with a huge floor display of the state of Georgia complete with an audio presentation describing Georgia's involvement in the Civil War. The museum definitely has a Confederate slant. For example, on its generally excellent historical wall display, it prominently displays the Douglas Prisoner of War Camp in Chicago, but fails to acknowledge Andersonville in the South.

The deeper we delved into the history and creation of Stone Mountain, Georgia, the clearer today's North-versus-South, "more perfect Union versus more perfect states' rights" politics became to me. This Confederate stuff runs deep in underground reservoirs.

Defying the Supreme Court's federal authority, President Andrew Jackson cooperated with the state of Georgia in essentially allowing white Georgians to "legally" steal Creek, Muskogee, and Cherokee Indian land, including the land upon which Stoney or Rock Mountain rested—as it was then variously called. In 1847, however, the small town at the bottom of the mountain changed its name from New Gibralter to Stone Mountain, then the more common name and the name both have had ever since. Stone Mountain was first used for recreation and romance by well-to-do families and their children, who would travel there from Atlanta, first by stagecoach and then by train, to picnic and court.

Confederate General Nathan Bedford Forrest founded the Ku Klux Klan in 1866 out of his resentment (shared by many white southerners) of northern military occupation—which humiliated their southern honor and pride. They viewed the northern presence as Yankee oppression. However, shortly thereafter, in 1869, Forrest ordered the KKK disbanded because he could not control its rabid violence against blacks. But it was the resurrection of the Klan in the twentieth century that identified the KKK with Stone Mountain.

The event that most identifies Stone Mountain in the mind of the nation occurred during the Thanksgiving season of 1915. A native of Alabama, "Colonel" and former minister and organizer of fraternal associations, William J. Simmons, grew up listening to his father's stories about the Civil War and the Ku Klux Klan. America's first feature film, *The Birth of a Nation*, which idealized and glorified the Old South and the original Klan, had just been released and was having quite an impact on the nation, but especially the South. Simmons deliberately linked the creation of his new Knights of the Ku Klux Klan with the movie's premiere in Atlanta. He took a group of men, including owner Samuel H. Venable, to Stone Mountain on Thanksgiving eve, November 25, 1915, for a formal induction ceremony.

> Under Simmons' direction, the fifteen shivering men gathered stones to build a base for the cross of pine boards he had brought up earlier that day, and a crude alter upon which he laid an American flag, an open Bible, an unsheathed sword, and a canteen of water. They put on the bed-sheet robes and pointed masked caps and then gathered around in a semi-circle as Simmons touched a match to the kerosene-soaked cross, the dancing light of the wind-blown flames creating an eerie backdrop for the ceremony. With practiced oratory he then called forth the Invisible Empire from its slumber of nearly half the century.[4]

KKK rallies were held atop Stone Mountain for more than forty years. In 1923 Sam Venable even granted a license to the Atlanta Klavern for such rallies. Not until 1958, when the state of Georgia took control of Stone Mountain and canceled the contract, did such rallies stop.

Turning Stone Mountain into a Confederate memorial was originally the idea of a nineteenth-century poet, Francis Tichnor. But an Atlanta attorney, William H. Terrell, the son of a Confederate veteran, and Helen Plane of the United Daughters of the Confederacy were the modern organizers of the idea. In 1915 Terrell met with Gutzon Borglum, an admirer of Lincoln whose sculpture of him ironically was on display in the Capitol's Rotunda.

He was nevertheless hired by the UDC. With the planning done and his models created, Borglum, a self-promoter, declared the day the work was to begin, June 18, 1923, Virginia Day. Since Robert E. Lee was to be the first figure carved, he decided to invite Virginia Governor E. Lee Trinkle to attend the opening-day ceremonies of the carving and to give the dedicatory address. Governor Trinkle's words summarized the essence and institutional nature, goal, and purpose of this monument:

> We shall have erected a monument which will outlive the centuries and which will carry the history of our Southern War to a future so distant that the mind of man is not gifted to grasp it. . . . Centuries will be born to die—age will follow age down the unending pathway of the years; cities, government, people will change and perish—while yet, our heroes carved in stone, will stand on guard—the custodians of imperishable glory, the sentinels of time.[5]

The federal government contributed no money for the project, but it did receive the personal endorsement of President Warren G. Harding. On January 19, 1924, the first phase of the unveiling General Lee's head was witnessed by more than five thousand people, including the six governors of Alabama, Texas, Virginia, Georgia, and South and North Carolina; President Calvin Coolidge sent his official representative. In other words, it was a day of regional and national political significance.

However, the project was developing in fits and starts. Tensions over money and between Borglum and members of the Memorial Committee grew. Borglum was soon fired, his work on Lee destroyed, and a new sculptor, Augustus Lukeman, hired, with the work to begin anew. Shortly, there were new problems over money and between the committee and Lukeman, and the project essentially lay idle for forty years. With the rise of civil rights activism, however, in January 1963 the project was revived. Walker Kirtland Hancock was awarded the new contract, and actual work began again on July 11, 1964—just nine days after the signing into law of the 1964 Civil Rights Act.

Work on the Confederate Memorial was completed and formally dedicated on May 9, 1970. The Reverend Billy Graham had agreed to give the invocation, and Georgia's Democratic Senator Herman Talmadge had secured the services of President Richard M. Nixon as keynote speaker. However, at the last minute, due to ill health, Reverend Graham notified the committee that he would be unable to attend. President Nixon, preoccupied with the Vietnam War, also canceled, sending Vice President Spiro T. Agnew as his representative.

Many were displeased over Agnew's selection because, at the time, he was under a legal cloud for income tax evasion and taking bribes as governor of Maryland. Also, the Imperial Wizard of the Ku Klux Klan, James R. Venable, boycotted the ceremonies because the committee selected the Reverend William Holmes Borders, a well-known African American pastor of Atlanta's Wheat Street Baptist Church, as Reverend Graham's fill-in.

What could Vice President Spiro Agnew say in tribute to these Confederate heroes— and the greatest traitors in history to the government that he now represented, the United States of America? In a speech full of praise and lofty words, he told the audience that "Jackson's life exemplified loyalty, that Davis illustrated dignity, and that Lee set the highest example of honor." He called these three principals "the bedrock of idealism that underlies our hopes for future generations."[6] The "states' rights" politics in Georgia and the South in general, of course, would not have allowed him to tell the truth even if he had had an inkling to do so.

In March 1992 Stone Mountain became the backdrop for a photograph with a questionable message. On the Monday before the Super Tuesday primary in the South, Democratic candidate Bill Clinton had posed with Georgia's Senator Sam Nunn at Stone Mountain with a group of young black prisoners in the background, similar to the cleanup crew we had seen and talked with. Not only was the image meant to convey a "get tough on black crime" message to whites, but the fact that it was taken at Stone Mountain subliminally sent an even deeper racial message throughout the South.

With my visit to Stone Mountain, Dr. King's 1963 speech had been driven home to me in both an emotional and an intellectual sense. Dr. King was saying that if America can only have faith and a commitment to fairness and justice for all Americans, God can transform even this monument to the Confederacy into a new human reality. Even Stone Mountain can experience a new burst of freedom, a new content of justice, and a new spirit of human reconciliation.

I have a number of "mature" friends like Reverend Falwell, whom I mentioned earlier. Among them are Bert Lance and his wife, Belle. Lance was President Jimmy Carter's director of the Office of Management and Budget (OMB) in the 1970s, a former chairman of the Georgia Democratic Party, and a former chairman of the Democratic National Committee. He has been a good friend to my father and our whole family, and has given each of us good political advice. Naturally, I sought a meeting with him to get his views on the Civil War.

Frank and I met Mr. Lance at a restaurant near his home in Calhoun, Georgia. He had invited two of his close and knowledgeable friends to come along and join us in the dialogue. After breakfast he took us to an old Confederate cemetery a few miles away. Frank and I had visited a lot of cemeteries on our trip, but the location of this one struck a chord. It was surrounded by mobile trailer homes—the domiciles of scores of poor whites.

Here was a well-kept cemetery commemorating the Confederates who had fought and died in a war to preserve states' right to own slaves—a system that set poor whites above all blacks. Yet almost 150 years later, the ancestors of those whites were still at the bottom of the rung. They still couldn't afford decent housing; their children were probably attending inferior schools with college only a remote possibility. My guess was that many of the families had insufficient or no health care at all. I thought, "How can they even bear to hear a conversation on affirmative action or voting rights for others?"

It was here that an insight that had been evolving in my mind finally took shape. If we are ever going to have a chance to make progress on the race question, we must first make every American as economically secure as possible—job security through full employment, comprehensive and universal health care, affordable housing, a quality public education for all Americans. Then, maybe—just maybe—we can make more rapid progress on the race question and racial reconciliation.

After our visit to the cemetery, Mr. Lance and his friends took us to visit some old Indian sites in the area. It was from in and around Calhoun, Georgia, that the Cherokee were forcibly transplanted in the Trail of Tears march to Indian Territory in Oklahoma in 1838.

Finally we got around to asking all of them to comment on our central Civil War question: "What was the cause of the war?" We went through what, by now, had become some fairly standard dialogue about the interplay between states' rights and slavery.

Suddenly one of Mr. Lance's friends asked me a question not directly related to the war. "Do you equate conservatism with racism?"

I replied, "Well that depends on what you mean by 'conservatism' and what you understand about racism."

Most of the time, when I have discussions with people who claim to be conservative they are referring to "conservative social or moral values"—dressing properly, being courteous, respectful of others, honorable, honest, loyal, and so forth. I don't consider sound ethical behavior, good manners, proper dress, speaking well, and using appropriate language "conservative values." I consider these basic values. They are not right or left, neither liberal nor conservative, Republican nor Democratic. So in that sense, I don't equate conservatism with racism.

But if by "conservative" you mean a laissez-faire economic philosophy, an economic system that is based on private ownership of everything and protecting the "freedom" of the owner, with no public accountability or responsibility, then that's a different question. That was the slave system in the South—and I do equate such conservatism with racism.

Because many African Americans and other people of color start out economically behind and not on an even playing field when it comes to education, capital, or land, there is no way we can end up "equal" in such a "survival of the fittest" environment.

Then I said to him, "I don't know what you understand about racism and the various forms in which it manifests itself." For me racism has at least five forms: First, it is a philosophy. It is a system of thought that holds one race superior and another race inferior, a definition put forth earlier by William Shockley and most recently in Charles Murray's book *The Bell Curve*.

Second, racism is prejudice. It means prejudging an individual member of a group on the basis of a group stereotype (for instance, all members of that group are smart, lazy, shiftless, athletic). Third, it's behavior—the actions of one race, or an individual of one race, against another individual or race (burning churches, putting swastikas on synagogues). Fourth, racism may manifest itself in cultural ignorance. Individuals may be good persons, but uninformed on certain facts and information. In part, this book is intended to eliminate such ignorance of the African American experience.

Finally, racism is institutional. Racism sometimes appears to be the "natural" order or course of things. For example, I read in Stokely Carmichael's and Charles Hamilton's book *Black Power* that Americans were outraged when four little girls were blown up in a Birmingham church in 1963. In part this was because the bombing could be directly attributed to an individual or a small group. However, institutional racism is different matter. The black infant mortality rate in that same county was several times that of whites, but it didn't have the same effect on America. Such institutional racism didn't have the "emotional" appeal for television that the bombing of a church and the killing of four little innocent girls had. Slow or institutional deaths could be more easily dismissed as just the result of some combination of "natural" forces or conditions—for which no one was really responsible. Today, however, there are new studies showing that there is no such thing as de facto segregation. All racism is de jure, because it is based on decisions of power.

Finally, I said to Mr. Lance's friend, "If by 'conservative' you mean keeping things the way they are or turning back the clock to the way they were—and racially unjust is the way things were and are—then, yes, I equate conservatism with racism."

He and his friends also told us about a Georgia holiday called Confederate Heritage Day—April 26. Its equivalent is the nation's celebration of Memorial Day in May. "On that day," Mr. Lance said, "I don't care what else is happening politically or otherwise, I will be with my family." I tried to engage him further, but he told me over and over, "Now Jesse, just let that alone. Stay on your economic message. Just let that alone." I got the distinct impression that Mr. Lance was more impressed with my economic insights than with my Civil War and racial observations.

From the home of Bert Lance we drove to Montgomery, Alabama, the original capital of the Confederacy. It was here that Jeff Davis was inaugurated president of the provisional government of the Confederate States of America on February 16, 1861. Montgomery was known as the Cradle of the Confederacy because the Confederate States of America were born here. But about two months later the capital was moved to Richmond, Virginia. It was one way of luring Virginia away from the Union and enticing it to become a part of the Confederacy. On April 17 Virginia seceded from the Union.

In Montgomery I explored the subject of the Civil War with a Democratic friend of mine who lives in Montgomery, Sonny Cauthen. "The war was fundamentally about states' rights and not about slavery—although slavery may have been part of it," he said. "The fundamental problem in the South is not race. We just like to handle things down here quietly and locally, and we don't like the federal government always trying to tell us what to do."

Suddenly, tears welled up in his eyes, and he stammered, "I need your help. I don't know what to tell my twelve-year-old daughter."

"What do you mean?" I asked. "How can we help?"

Apparently *The George Wallace Story* had had its first airing on TNT the night before. My friend had watched this movie with his daughter. She was very upset and had been crying. Over the years, my friend told me, he had been very good friends with George Wallace. In fact, he had worked to get him elected governor of Alabama—"ran some of the campaign right out of a back room in my house"—and had also worked for him in his presidential campaigns. His daughter was upset because he had always told her that George Wallace was not a racist politician. The governor, he had taught her, had only campaigned against the big central government, against federal intrusion into local affairs, and for local control—states' rights.

But in the movie she saw Wallace portrayed as a politician pandering to the racial fears of whites. She was upset because, at her tender age, she could not reconcile what her daddy had taught her with what the television docudrama had shown her—and her father did not know what to tell her or how to bridge the gap. He was shaking and on the verge of tears. Finally, Frank said to him, "The Bible says, the truth will set you free."

In other words, the only way he could calm his daughter down, relieve her anxiety, and reconcile his daughter to himself was to now tell her the truth about George Wallace and black people and racial politics. We told him the truth would free both her and him. Shortly thereafter we had prayer, he ran us around to a few key sites, and we had to hit the road again.

In pursuit of more truths we headed to Andersonville, Georgia. Andersonville, the most notorious Confederate prisoner-of-war camp, was a stockade encampment. It was originally sixteen acres designed to hold ten thousand prisoners, but by August 1864 it had expanded to twenty-six acres and held thirty-three thousand captives—an average of just thirty-four square feet per man. In Andersonville prisoners experienced the punishing heat of a Deep South summer with little protection from the sun. In August 1864 it was not unusual for more than a hundred prisoners to die in a single day. In fact, thirteen thousand of the forty-five thousand men imprisoned there did die of disease, exposure, or malnutrition. Many northerners saw Andersonville as a fiendish plot to murder Yankee prisoners.

We saw the size and felt the heat of Andersonville. We saw the remnant of a tunnel the prisoners had dug in an attempt to escape. We were told about the judicial system that was set up among the prisoners, and the story of a miracle spring that finally brought fresh water directly into the camp—which still operates today. The "safe line" was explained to us. Prisoners could get only so close to the outside wall and remain safe—that is, not seen as potential escapees and be shot to death on the spot.

The most moving story, however, was the one we encountered when we visited the cemetery at Andersonville and stopped at the tombstone of Corporal James Henry Gooding. He was a member of the famous Fifty-fourth Massachusetts Volunteer Infantry that fought at Fort Wagner on July 18, 1863—just days after whites exploded in the New York draft riots—and was made famous by the movie *Glory*.

We were told how Corporal Gooding struggled to change a law that provided a double standard in pay for white and black soldiers. In August all volunteers in service were to receive the same pay and rations. But on July 17, 1862, Congress passed the Militia Act. Blacks were to be paid ten dollars per month minus a three-dollar deduction for clothing, while whites were paid ten dollars per month plus a three-dollar clothing allowance.

Gooding, a literate and articulate Union man who was committed to black rights, argued in impressive letters to President Lincoln and other government officials that blacks were staunch Union men and soldiers who volunteered, fought effectively, bled and died just like white soldiers, and should be equally paid. The Massachusetts Fifty-fourth had such pride and were so clear about the issue that they refused to accept the lesser pay of ten dollars even though their families had gone several months without money and were suffering. "Their self-respect demanded equal treatment from the government which had promised it to them."[7]

It was not until mid-June 1864, however, that Congress passed a compromise bill. On September 28–29, three months later, "The United States paymaster distributed $170,000 in back pay to the men of the Fifty-fourth Regiment."[8] Gooding's eloquence had helped persuade Congress to equalize the pay of black and white soldiers, but it was too late for Gooding himself. He died at Andersonville and is buried in its cemetery.

Proudly showing us a new building under construction, the park guides explained that Andersonville was being converted into a memorial honoring all prisoners of war. I said, "Wait a minute. This looks like another part of the denial!"

We learned that Senator Richard Russell, a segregationist Democratic senator from Georgia in the late 1960s, had persuaded President Lyndon Johnson at the height of the civil rights movement to convert the notorious southern prisoner-of-war camp into a monument honoring all prisoners of all wars.

Under that banner, what happens to Corporal Gooding's story in such a National Park Service presentation? Gooding was fighting to preserve the Union and end slavery, and for equitable treatment of all U.S. soldiers—equality being denied by his own government. What does a monument honoring all prisoners of war from the Revolutionary War to the Persian Gulf have to do with Gooding's story, the internal conflict of America's Civil War, and the quest for equality? Will the Gooding story be distorted or lost in a general conversation about all prisoners of war? Wouldn't a monument to all prisoners of war be more appropriate in Washington, D.C., with its twenty million annual visitors? On both counts I think the answer is yes.

We recalled that Stone Mountain was completed in 1970 as a monument to the Confederacy. Now we learned that these same neo-Confederates wanted to eliminate the negative view of them at the very height of the black power movement. They didn't want "Auschwitz" sitting right in the middle of their state every day, reminding them of the shame of Andersonville and the cause of the Civil War. This was consistent with the southern Civil War strategy of denial.

In the final days of our trip we stopped at the Fredericksburg and Spotsylvania National Military Park in Virginia, where the reverence for Stonewall Jackson was almost more than we could bear. Already a Confederate hero by the campaign in Spotsylvania in 1863, Jackson was accidentally wounded in his left arm by his own troops on the night of May 2. He was taken to a field hospital, where his arm was amputated. On May 4, after being transported by ambulance twenty-seven miles to T. C. Chandler's Fairfield Plantation, he caught pneumonia; he died on May 10 in a small fame office building at Guinea Station near Fredericksburg. We were altogether unprepared to deal with the adulation heaped on Jackson around Fredericksburg. We thought we'd find perhaps a grave or crypt, even a mausoleum. But an altar, a holy place, a Stonewall Jackson Shrine! It was too much.

And there was more. After visiting the spot where Jackson was wounded and other related sites, we were taken out into a distant farm field and shown a small area with a fence around it. There a marker identified where Jackson's amputated arm was buried in a box. Sometime between September 26 and October 4, 1921, we were told, President Warren G. Harding had traveled by train to Virginia's nearby Wilderness area to observe U.S. military maneuvers. Traveling with him was a well-known marine, Smedley Butler, who suggested they stop by the site and dig up Jackson's buried arm—just to make sure it was still there. It was. They reburied the arm and put up a stone marker, still there. A train track is still visible from about half a mile down the hill, where it is said Harding arrived and walked up to the site. First a Stonewall Jackson Shrine. Then his amputated arm buried in a box. What a trip we had had!

During our tour we also discovered some other extraneous, but interesting, things. For example, I hadn't known that many of our national holidays have their origin in the Civil

War. In the fall of 1863, as Lincoln was weighing whether to seek a second term in office, he established the national tradition of Thanksgiving Day. The Gettysburg victory had given Lincoln a boost, but within weeks the New York draft riots broke out. It was a mixed bag, but in the fall of 1863 the Union cause "was a brighter day now than any Lincoln had yet seen in the nearly three winters of war. There had been enough good news [that] past summer and fall to cause him . . . to set aside the last Thursday of November as a day of national thanksgiving."[9]

We also encountered the incredible origin of Memorial Day:

> The "First Decoration Day" came to be recognized in some circles in the North when an estimated 10,000 people, most of them former black slaves, gathered at a place called Planter's Race Course in Charleston, South Carolina. The race track was a prison for Union soldiers, of whom at least 257 died. They were buried behind the judge's stand in unmarked graves. The African American citizens of Charleston built a fence around the graves, landscaped the area, and painted a sign which read "Martyrs of the Race Course." On May 1, 1865, the 10,000 blacks marched around the Race Course and formally dedicated the martyr's cemetery. Thus, the first Memorial Day was born.[10]

Finally, during our Civil War battlefields tour, we were also surprised to learn that the word "racism" did not appear in the dictionaries until 1936, and its origin was not in association with African Americans. The term was used to define the Jewish experience in Nazi Germany, and then adapted by African Americans and other people of color in America to describe their own experience. The word "racism" does not appear in any of the works of Abraham Lincoln or Frederick Douglass. Why? Because the "federal versus state" (states' rights) debate over control of slavery, the origin of the Civil War and Reconstruction was more definitve and descriptive of the problem confronting African Americans.

We had observed and learned so much along the way about the South's Civil War mentality and its interpretation of history and related politics. Battle sites—as well as our classrooms, the mass media, and popular culture—too often reinforce a conservative interpretation of race, by teaching that conflict over states' rights was the cause of the Civil War and denying the American people a true understanding of the very deep legacy of slavery. Without a full comprehension and acceptance of our history, we can't progress toward a more perfect Union.

5

STATES' RIGHTS OR A MORE PERFECT UNION?

I cannot conceive of a government in which there can exist two supremes.

—Gouverneur Morris
Pennsylvania delegate to the Philadelphia Convention, 1787

Think of a place that's bitterly antigovernment and fiercely individualistic, where race is a constant subtext to daily life, and God and guns run through public discourse like an electric current. Think of a place where influential scholars market theories of white supremacy, where the word "liberal" is a negative epithet, where hang-'em-high law-and-order justice centered on the death penalty and throw-away-the-key sentencing are politically all but unstoppable. Think of a place obsessed with states' rights, as if it were the 1850s all over again and the Civil War had never been fought. Such characteristics have always described the South. Somehow, they now describe the nation.

—Peter Applebome, *Dixie Rising*[1]

In 3 Cases, High Court Shifts Power to States

—*Washington Post* headline, June 24, 1999

Two central issues have dominated this country from its beginning.

The first is the relationship between the federal government and the states. That question has been with us since before the writing of our Constitution in Philadelphia in 1787, through the Supreme Court's first major decision in 1793 *(Chisholm v. Georgia)*, during the antebellum period of 1800 through 1860, through the Civil War and post–Civil War periods. It remains an active issue today.

The second issue that has plagued the United States is race. It is the central dilemma in our nation's history and has haunted us since 1619.

What is the proper balance between the national and state governments? Are we fifty nation-states that voluntarily participate in a national federation but can ignore or withdraw from that federation at any time? Or are we one nation, with a national common law that is indivisible, with liberty and justice for all? These were perplexing and troublesome questions for the founders and for the first three-quarters of a century of our existence. They still trouble us today.

In a very real sense, it was the Civil War that converted us from a federation of states to a Union. The current common belief is that we are the latter. In practice, too often, we still try to operate more like the former. Clearly, the ideology and legacy of states' rights lingers and continues to disrupt and interfere with our ability to build a more perfect Union.

For some, not building a more perfect Union appears to be the goal. Downsizing the role of the federal government, or the "revolution of devolution" ideology and practice that Speaker Newt Gingrich brought to the national political scene in such a forceful way following the 1994 Republican conquest of the House and Senate, is an obstacle to achieving national goals. It will be impossible to build a more perfect Union until the ideology of states' rights and its legacy of devolution are defeated politically—as well as in the hearts and minds of the American people. It is currently a central part of the belief system of too many Americans.

Unfortunately, the Clinton administration seemed to share much of this Old Democratic and modern Republican conservative ideology and legacy. It was southern Democrat Bill Clinton and a conservative Republican Congress that pulled the floor out from underneath the poor—a sixty-year-old FDR New Deal national safety net—in the name of "welfare reform." The missing floor wasn't much noticed during the Clinton years, because the economy remained relatively good. But wait until the economy takes a turn for the worse!

It was President Clinton, in 1996, a presidential election year, who declared in his State of the Union Address—using southern states' rights code words—that "the era of big government is over." And it was Clinton who assigned his vice president, fellow southerner Al Gore, to downsize the federal government by eliminating 250,000 jobs in the name of "reinventing government."

If Clinton was right, not only is the era of big government over, but so is our nation's ability to achieve full employment, comprehensive and universal health care, affordable housing, a quality public education, and equal opportunity and equal justice under the law for all Americans. In short, if Clinton was right, the possibility of building a more perfect Union is essentially dead.

Decentralizing *essential* questions and decisions about economic security issues such as full employment, health care, housing, public education, and justice is a guarantee of economic injustice for workers and consumers, and inadequate health care, shelter, learning, and justice for all Americans. The fifty states, acting individually or functioning merely in loose cooperation or voluntary association, simply cannot or will not adequately address, policywise, administratively or financially, these basic national needs. Only if these essential questions are addressed in a democratic, centralized, and coordinated way can we even hope to build a better nation.

There is no simple answer to this balance of power issue. The question of the relationship of the states to the federal government is an ongoing one. Times and circumstances change, and if government is to be relevant, responsive, and accountable to the American people's real needs, the relationship, roles, and balance of power between the federal and state governments must adapt and adjust.

This balance of state and federal power is not something that can be settled "by the opinion of any one generation," wrote Woodrow Wilson in 1911. "Changes in the social and economic condition of society, in the electorate's perception of issues needing to be addressed by government, and in the prevailing political values," Wilson declared, "require each successive generation to treat federal-state relationships as 'a new question,' subject to full and searching reappraisal."[2]

Politically, however, that reality or circumstance should not be used as an excuse to pursue an anti-federal-government philosophy of states' rights. The guiding or dominant principle must remain true to the Preamble to our Constitution—to build a more perfect Union, not more perfect states' rights.

The idea of "state rights" in the American colonies preceded the formation of the Constitution and the United States. It rested on the idea of state sovereignty, that ultimate political authority resided in the states individually. A century later, "states' rights" became the means by which state governments defended slavery and perpetuated the peculiar institution with its elitist and perverted economic, political, and social arrangements.

During the colonial period, citizens strongly identified with and were loyal to their individual colonies or states. For example, early frictions among the colonies prevented them from working together to fight against French and Indian antagonists in the mid-1700s. Only their joint hatred of British domination joined them together in the Continental Congress and as states in 1776 to fight and win a revolution. Even then, the hostilities among the states continued, postponing adoption of the Articles of Confederation until 1781.

Thus, internal mistrust among the states and external colonial and revolutionary experiences with England made most Americans suspicious and distrustful of undemocratic centralized power and made these new Americans cautious of anything federal, central, or national. Indeed, when they drew up the Articles of Confederation in 1776 and ratified them in 1781, they made central authority so weak as to be unworkable for the Union.

The Founding Fathers—women and people of color were not included—tried to correct this flaw when they drafted the Constitution in Philadelphia in 1787. Their mixed feelings and the politics surrounding centralized (federal) and decentralized (state) power led them to create a Constitution with divided powers both within (legislative, executive, and judicial branches) and without (federal versus state governments) that were deliberately ambiguous. It was a central issue of debate during the constitutional ratification process as well.

Anti-nationalists, also known as anti-federalists, opposed ratification of the Constitution. Many states ratified the Constitution only because they were given assurances that certain amendments would be added to it to protect individual liberties and states' rights. The new Congress quickly proposed ten amendments that secured these rights, including the key Tenth Amendment, which delegated to the states those powers not authorized or prohibited by the federal government. Despite the Ninth (Americans' rights are not limited to those listed in the Constitution) and Tenth Amendments, and later the Eleventh (limiting federal courts from hearing cases brought by citizens of another state or foreigners), the Constitution was still vague and ambiguous in terms of the balance between national and states' rights.

The dilemma was this: State power was inadequate to meet the needs of the Union, but centralization could not be imposed for fear of disruption or dissolution of the Union by resentful and rebellious states. The U.S. government, still feeling its way, was unsure of its power and trying to determine its proper role and functions.

What needs would a federal government meet? What tasks should a federal government perform when the current state governments were effectively and efficiently fulfilling many needs in a relatively accountable manner? What role should a central government play?

What functions should it perform? What real authority should it have? Those were the questions then. In many respects, they remain questions today.

The issue of southern slavery immensely complicated this question of federal versus state power, which ultimately led to a civil war that only temporarily and partially clarified the issue.

The Founding Fathers believed that a national government stronger than that established under the Articles of Confederation was necessary if the nation was to survive and thrive. One dimension of the debate began with the interpretation of Article III of the Constitution, which defines the judicial branch of government. The framers of the Constitution clearly understood that Article III had implications for state political power. The central question was: Would the U.S. Supreme Court have the power to review decisions made by state courts, including state supreme courts? If so, the federal government would be supreme. If not, the state government would be the superior.

When the Philadelphia Convention convened in May 1787, the words "federal," "national," and "supreme" dominated much of the discussion. Thirty-three-year-old Governor Edmund Randolph of Virginia argued that a union of the states that was "merely federal" would not accomplish the goal that had brought them together. "He therefore proposed a 'national government, consisting of a supreme legislative, executive and judicial.' . . . Silence followed, complete and ominous."[3]

During the nation's infancy, in a speech invoking both general and abstract principles, Chief Justice John Jay in 1790 gave voice to this complicated issue of federalism. If the new Constitution was going to be effective as well as just, Jay said, it was essential to "provide against Discord between national and state jurisdictions, to render them auxiliary instead of hostile to each other; and so to connect both as to leave each sufficiently independent, and yet sufficiently combined."[4] A little something for everyone on both sides of the issue, in other words.

Such a statement of abstract principle has, to this day, been broad enough to allow the Supreme Court to act in different ways at different times. The Court, at times, has rendered broad federal decisions that allowed for national innovation and progressive change. However, it has also mostly been narrow and conservative in its interpretations, using its power to thwart the advance of broad common law and national progressive change.

This is also true largely because the former slave states and their legacy of conservative southern politics have always enjoyed disproportionate power in the nation—on the Supreme Court, in Congress, and with regard to the federal executive branch—and their conservative leaders have almost always used this disproportionate power to prevent the country from building a more perfect Union.

This alternately conservative and progressive role of the Court as constitutional umpire, responding to current political winds and pressures, is part of our history and will be part of our future. Since the Court is a responsive political institution, like the legislative and executive branches of government—it moves more slowly, but its consequences usually last longer—progressive political activists must recognize the influence their actions will have on the Court. Conservatives are not naive about this fact, nor should we be.

The first Congress, under Article III, passed the Judiciary Act of 1789 creating a Supreme Court originally of six judges, along with a three-tiered federal judicial system. Section Twenty-five gave the Supreme Court jurisdiction over federal questions arising in state court litigation. This guarantee of national power was contested from the start and, in one sense, was only partially settled by the Civil War nearly seventy-five years later.

The conservative philosophical concept the founders created with regard to the relationship between the federal and state governments was dual federalism. Dual federalism made each state sovereign, but gave the federal government a limited number of specifically enumerated powers. This was called the "compact theory" of the Constitution. Each state was voluntarily entering into a compact with the other states to form a national government for certain limited purposes.

The origin of the theory was that the royal authority of the British Crown had been transferred to the individual states. "The states could act much as independent nations except respecting powers vested exclusively in the federal government."[5] The interpretive geometric metaphor was that the two dimensions of government were "two separate spheres of dual sovereignty" that contained "mutually exclusive powers" and "concurrent powers."

In practical terms, the "mutually exclusive powers" doctrine meant that if the state could regulate something, the federal government could not. The second "concurrent powers" doctrine meant that if a state's enforcement power and Congress's commerce clause came to the same conclusion, each still had authority even though administratively it was cumbersome. Both doctrines favored the individual states over a national central government.

Dual federalism had two legitimate concerns. On the one hand, the founders did not want the national legislature creating laws that infringed on individual liberties. From their experience with the British monarchy, they had developed a strong, if not always healthy, distrust of centralized power. On the other hand, the founders wanted the Constitution to guard against the destructive nature of excessive claims by the states against the national government. They recognized that they would never be able to build one nation with one set of common laws and rules if the multiple special-interest tentacles of the various states were allowed to dominate or interfere with the general government's laws.

For obvious reasons, proslavery southern states strongly favored and took advantage of this murky concept of dual federalism. The Roger B. Taney Supreme Court—he was chief justice between 1836 and 1854—used the dual federalism concept as a guiding principle in its rulings regarding slavery. Later, as an associate justice writing the majority opinion in the infamous *Dred Scott* decision of 1857, Justice Taney became well known for his white supremacist conclusion that "blacks had no rights that a white must respect."

Not so well known, however, but equally profound, devastating, and even longer lasting—with regard to the legacy of constitutional interpretation—was the fact that the *Dred Scott* decision was based not just on the concept of racial superiority, but also on the constitutional principle of state superiority over federal authority. It was the theory of state superiority—states' rights—that was the second premise in *Dred Scott* upon which the Taney Court also ruled, which forbade Congress from passing legislation to outlaw slavery in any state anywhere in the United States.

Democratic Party founder and theorist Thomas Jefferson and "Father of the Constitution" James Madison were both advocates of this conservative compact constitutional theory of government. In 1798 and 1799 they drafted state constitutional resolutions for Virginia and Kentucky, respectively, denying the Supreme Court's authority to determine whether laws passed by Congress were constitutional.

Jefferson's "strict constructionist" and literal view of the Constitution led him to conclude that granting federal courts the power of judicial review would imbue Court discretion, not the Constitution, with the measure of its power. "He argued that when the federal government assumed a power not granted to it by the Constitution, each state, as a party in the constitutional compact, had a right to declare the law unconstitutional."[6]

In Jefferson's view, each state was a co-equal with the federal government, with the same power and authority to act and decide as the national government in their state "sphere" of "reserved powers"—those powers not specifically given away to the federal government. The threat of a state seceding from the Union was a constant national concern, especially when it was unclear whether the Union had the power—legally or militarily—to keep the Union together.

While slavery was the cause of the Civil War, the nonslavery rationale for the war and the argument that won it broader public support in the South—and almost won it international recognition—was Madison's and Jefferson's interpretation of self-determination as states' rights, and their offshoot political tactics, theoretically based interposition and nullification. These theories and tactics eventually led southern political leaders to commit treason against the government of the United States by leading eleven southern states to secede from the Union in the name of "states' rights"—with the real purpose being to defend the institution of slavery.

The obnoxious Sedition Act, passed by Congress on July 14, 1798, was an early attempt by our second president, John Adams, to stifle dissent and criticism of the federal government. Leading opponents of the Sedition Act were James Madison, who developed a theory of interposition in the Virginia Resolution of 1798, and Thomas Jefferson, who developed the theory of nullification in the Kentucky Resolution of 1799.

In Madison's Virginia Resolution, "interposition" meant that when, in the eyes of the state, the federal government exceeded its constitutional authority, the states "have the right and are duty bound to interpose for arresting the progress of the evil." In short, a state could stop the effectiveness of a law's execution, administration, or interpretation by interposing itself between the people of the state and the federal government.

The idea of interposition was originated to fight the Sedition Act of 1798, but in the 1830s South Carolina applied it against a federal tariff. That so angered President Andrew Jackson that he threatened to use force against the state, and South Carolina backed down. A few years later, John C. Calhoun, by then a senator from South Carolina, used Madison's theory of interposition to try to stop delivery of abolitionist materials through the federal mail.

With passage of the Fugitive Slave Law in 1850, however, northerners used interposition for the exact opposite reason—to enact personal liberty laws and issue court decisions to avoid sending escaped slaves back South to their slave masters. In the most famous state court case involving interposition, abolitionist Sherman Booth was freed by the Wisconsin Supreme Court in 1854 when it declared the slave law unconstitutional.

Five years later, in *Abelman v. Booth* (1859), Roger B. Taney, author of the *Dred Scott* decision just two years earlier, overturned the Wisconsin decision, arguing "that 'such propositions are new in the jurisprudence of the United States' and that the Supreme Court had the final authority to interpret the meaning of the Constitution."[7] As with many people even today, racism made Justice Taney's constitutional interpretations inconsistent.

Of course, secession by eleven southern states and the formation of the Confederate States of America proved to be the most significant use of interposition in American history. After the Brown decision in 1954, several southern states appealed to the theory of interposition when they engaged in "massive resistance" to fight school desegregation.

Thomas Jefferson, writing against the Sedition Act in the Kentucky Resolution of 1799, developed the theory of nullification. Building on the conservative compact constitutional theory of government, he argued that states had the right to nullify all laws that they considered unconstitutional.

Dual federalism and states' rights dominated constitutional interpretation during the first half of the nineteenth century. But Thomas Jefferson's theory of nullification was more systematically developed and became even more elaborate and hardened as Senator John C. Calhoun of South Carolina articulated a response to the increasing moral and political pressure being applied by northern abolitionists in the 1830s and 1840s to end slavery.

In 1828, in his second term as vice president of the United States, Calhoun argued that if a state thought the federal government had overstepped its authority, that state had the right to call a special convention and nullify federal actions by declaring them unconstitutional. He argued further that if the federal government countered the state's action with a constitutional amendment, a state had a right to secede. During the 1830s, 1840s, and 1850s, southern slave states repeatedly threatened nullification in the form of secession from the Union as they defended the institution of slavery on the basis of states' rights.

Calhoun was a late bloomer with regard to states' rights. As a member of Congress, he supported the War of 1812, supported protective tariffs, advocated for state improvements at federal expense, and agreed with Alexander Hamilton's earlier arguments with regard to a national bank. By 1828, however, "he was convinced that a protective tariff was not only harmful to his state, South Carolina, but was also contrary to the Constitution."[8] He resigned from the vice presidency, was elected senator from South Carolina—in order to defend the institution of slavery—and began to work out a system for state resistance to or nullification of "unconstitutional" laws.

He modified and expanded on the earlier compact theories of Jefferson and Madison by basing "his theory on the assumption that the people in each state (not the government) were sovereign and, in their sovereign capacity, had ratified and thus given validity to both the state constitution and the U.S. Constitution."[9] In other words, the people in each state, according to Calhoun, could either "accede" to the Union by ratifying the Constitution or they could "secede" from the Union by repealing the previous ordinance of ratification.

Calhoun soon concluded that with each state acting individually, nullification had not really worked the way he had envisioned. Armed with a new and more comprehensive strategy, he set out to unify all of the southern slave states around the idea of nullification. While it didn't happen in his lifetime, his efforts did eventually culminate in the secession of eleven southern states in the struggle over slavery that became the American Civil War.

As in much of life, American political development produced great ironies. Senator Daniel Webster of Massachusetts, an original states' righter who later converted and became a nationalist, and his foil, Senator John C. Calhoun of South Carolina, a former nationalist who became a states' righter, became the two symbols of the free- and slave-state debates that dominated the often stormy and raucous national debates in the Senate over the issues of slavery and states' rights from the 1820s through the 1850s.

Of course states' rights, as a live political option, all but died at Appomattox on April 9, 1865. It maintained some judicial vitality until the 1930s but thereafter remained weak—to a large extent because of FDR-appointed justices. Dormant, that is, until the Rehnquist-led Supreme Court issued a series of conservative opinions relying on states' rights reasoning, and Republican and southern Democratic presidents attached similar rhetoric to some of their actions and helped revive the idea of states' rights. Thus, the spirit, legacy and politics of states' rights continues even today.

Conservatives, both Republican and Democratic, are often fond of quoting from Dr. Martin Luther King, Jr.'s, famous August 28, 1963, "I Have a Dream" speech. In light of this discussion of interposition and nullification, however, seldom does anyone use the following quote from that same speech: "I have a dream that one day the state of Alabama, whose governor's lips are presently dripping with the words of interposition and nullification, will be transformed into a situation where little black boys and black girls will be able to join hands with little white boys and white girls and walk together as sisters and brothers."

To build a more perfect Union—"one nation, under God, indivisible, with liberty and justice for all"—we need the application and enforcement of a common set of laws, legal standards, and regulations applicable to every state. *Dred Scott* was the negative application of that principle. Progressives need its positive application. Even apart from slavery, the alternative political philosophy of states' rights creates a society with an inherent inability to build a more perfect Union.

The logical conclusion of states' rights theory is anarchy. If a state has the right to secede from the Union, then a county has the right to secede from a state, a city has the right to secede from a county, and an individual has the right to secede from a city—hence anarchy, militias, and Timothy McVeigh. In addition, assuming the best and even without pursuing the states' rights logic, fifty individual states acting separately or "merely as a voluntary federation" cannot create or build a more perfect Union.

Finally, while the issue of slavery will be discussed in much greater detail in later chapters, it should be clear already that the issues of race, racism, and slavery are intimately intertwined with the questions of federalism and states' rights. No discussion relating to the issue of building a more perfect Union can ever escape the fact, in regard to either doctrine or policy, of the political impact of the system of private ownership of slaves, protected by state governments, and this states' rights legacy that continues even today.

In fairness, however, it must be noted that all U.S. politics has been infused by the slavery question, as has all of our constitutional law. Neither states' rights nor federalism is a concept that can be separated from the slave system that was supported by state and federal governments then, or the legacy of race relations that continues today.

Despite the Union victory in the Civil War, a start at Republican Reconstruction, and new constitutional amendments following the Civil War—when the states' rights ideology was in disrepute and building a more perfect Union was a top agenda item of the Radical Republicans—dual federalism still refused to go away and continued to assert itself through Supreme Court decisions designed to limit federal regulatory power. Not until the New Deal years of the Roosevelt administrations in the 1930s and 1940s did the concept of dual federalism virtually disappear as a major guiding legal principle of American jurisprudence.

The Ninth, Tenth, and Eleventh Amendments are the primary amendments applicable to this states' rights versus more perfect Union view of the Constitution, but at the heart of the matter is the Tenth Amendment.

Article VI: "This Constitution, and the Laws of the United States which shall be made in Pursuance thereof; and all Treaties made, or which shall be made, under the Authority of the United States, *shall be the supreme Law of the Land*; and the Judges in every State shall be bound thereby, any Thing in the Constitution or Laws of any State to the Contrary notwithstanding" (italics added).

While Article VI of the Constitution seems to be unequivocally clear about the primacy of federal power, the Tenth Amendment has led history to render a different judgment. It is central to the states' rights advocates of yesterday and today. The Tenth Amendment was ratified in 1791 as part of the Constitution's Bill of Rights. It specifies that "the powers not delegated to the United States by the Constitution, nor prohibited by it to the States, are reserved to the States respectively, or to the people." This is called the reserve powers clause. It reserves for the states and the people powers not enumerated in the Constitution. It has been a key legal weapon of slave owners, states' righters, anti-federalists, and political conservatives generally. The Tenth Amendment is a states' rights tool. Only by overcoming the so-called restrictions that the Tenth Amendment contains can we ever hope to build a more perfect Union.

Anti-federalists wanted an explicit amendment guaranteeing states' control over their internal affairs. They even wanted the word "expressly" used in the amendment, so as to read, ". . . the powers not expressly delegated. . . ." The word "expressly" had been used in the Articles of Confederation. But Congress already knew of the national weakness and resulting states' rights problems that the use of this word would create with regard to building a more perfect Union. Thus, when this language was proposed for the tenth constitutional amendment before Congress, it was soundly defeated, thirty-two to seventeen.

In 1791, when President George Washington asked Jefferson, his secretary of state, for his opinion on the constitutionality of a bill to incorporate the Bank of the United States—a nationalist or federalist question—Jefferson cited the as-yet-unratified Tenth Amendment as the basis for expressing opposition to an act of Congress, and he did so as if the word "expressly" were in the amendment.

Jefferson "described the 10th Amendment as 'the foundation of the Constitution' and added, 'to take a single step beyond the boundaries thus specially drawn . . . is to take possession of a boundless field of power, no longer susceptible of any definition.'"[10] Jefferson's formulation of the conservative doctrine of strict construction was echoed by the champions of states' rights for many decades.

Washington asked his secretary of the treasury, Alexander Hamilton, to address the same question about a national bank, and he received a broader, organic, liberal, and "loose construction" interpretation of the Constitution. Hamilton's opinion thus became the model and point of view for those advocating an extension of congressional power, even though Hamilton's opinion did not conflict with the substance of the Tenth Amendment.

Hamilton chose not to challenge dual federalism directly. In fact, he specifically rejected any claim that Congress could interfere in the internal affairs of a state. He argued that concerns such as the health, morality, education and welfare of the people were totally outside the congressional realm. His argument was not so much against the Tenth Amendment as against its necessity. Chief Justice John Marshall made the same argument. On the other hand, Chief Justice Roger B. Taney, during his reign, was so extreme in protecting the "reserved powers clause of the states" that he went overboard in defending dual federalism.

Thomas Jefferson used the Sedition Act of 1798, and states' rights opposition to it, to defeat the Federalist Party of John Adams and propel himself into the presidency in 1800—after Adams had defeated him in 1796. Thus, from the time of Democratic (actually Democratic-Republican) President Thomas Jefferson (1801–1809), through the antebellum period of American history, until Republican President Abraham Lincoln (1861–1865), a strict construction interpretation of dual federalism, based on the Tenth Amendment, was the dominant constitutional theory.

It must be acknowledged, however, that at one point or another, for one reason or an-other, virtually all of the states appealed to the Tenth Amendment and to this conservative constitutional theory to challenge the role and decisions of one branch or another of the federal government. Opposition to the federal government ran deep before the Civil War. Democratic Party states' rights opposition to the big centralized Republican government of Reconstruction after the Civil War was even more pronounced.

President George Washington and his secretary of the treasury, Alexander Hamilton, were both nationalists and belonged to the Federalist Party. Even though they had supported Washington for president, Jefferson and Madison were anti-federalists. Jefferson soon re-signed his post, and along with Madison, formed an anti-federalist political party called the Republican Party. Running on the Republican Party ticket in 1796, Jefferson lost to John Adams on the Federalist Party ticket.

Jefferson's Republican Party soon became the Democratic-Republican Party, but what it really was, was the beginning of what is known today as the oldest political party in the world, the Democratic Party. Thus the modern Democratic Party has its roots in states' rights theory and practice, a theory and practice that defended private property rights (slav-ery) and in the name of states' rights limited the federal government's ability to build a more perfect Union.

The first great case to come before the Supreme Court was *Chisholm v. Georgia*, which involved the relationship between federal jurisdiction and state sovereignty. The case, de-cided on February 18, 1793, involved a citizen representing a South Carolina merchant who sued the state of Georgia for the value of clothing supplied by the merchant during the American Revolutionary War. The state of Georgia refused to appear in court, claiming im-munity on the basis that it was a "sovereign and independent state."

The Court refused to accept the "no show" defense and entered a default judgment against Georgia. Supreme Court Justices James Wilson and John Jay spoke in "ringing declarations of the nationalist view that sovereignty resided in the people of the United States 'for the pur-poses of Union' and that as to those purposes Georgia was 'not a sovereign state.'"[11]

Anti-federalist, anti-nationalist, anti-Union, and anti-Chisholm sentiments, however, ran so high that when Congress passed the Eleventh Amendment to the Constitution on March 4, 1794, within a year—February, 7, 1795—three-quarters of the states had ratified it. The Eleventh Amendment states: "The Judicial power of the United States shall not be con-strued to extend to any suit in law or equity, commenced or prosecuted against one of the United States by Citizens of another State, or by Citizens or Subjects of any Foreign State." In plain language it restricts the federal judiciary from hearing cases brought by citizens of another state or foreigners. Only the Eleventh and Sixteenth Amendments were passed as direct repudiations of Supreme Court decisions. The Eleventh Amendment was intended to protect the states from federal judicial power. However, it does not explicitly do so; nor does it contain any actual barriers to federal suits to enforce the Constitution and laws of the United States.

Underlying the suspicion and fear of federal authority and antigovernment feeling was the English philosopher John Locke's theory of natural rights. Natural rights theory main-tained that certain basic human rights are inherent in nature and precede the establishment of any government. Roger Sherman said, "The people have certain natural rights which are retained by them when they enter into society."[12] According to Locke's theory, then, con-stitutional rights established and guaranteed by governments were necessary only to make the rights of humankind more public, more visible, and, therefore, more secure than they would be if left purely in the abstract realm of nature.

Not all natural rights could be spelled out, but they were limited only by the imagination and constituted a maximized realm of freedom for every individual. As constitutional framer James Wilson stated: "Enumerate all the rights of men! I am sure, sirs, that no gentleman in the late Convention would have attempted such a thing."[13]

In 1816 the Supreme Court established its authority by saying that it had the power to review state and state supreme court decisions (*Martin v. Hunger's Lessee*). Thus, Martin helped establish the form of government known to us as American federalism. However, during the reactionary period following the Civil War and Reconstruction, and amid the reemergence of states' rights, the Supreme Court said that it would not second-guess state courts' decisions on state law (*Murdock v. Memphis*, 1875). According to *Murdock*, state courts reigned supreme over state laws, while the U.S. Supreme Court was the ultimate authority over federal law. Thus, at the height of Democratic Party resistance to Reconstruction and the presence of the Big Federal Government—meaning Black Republican rule in the South, which was soon to come to an end in the Compromise of 1877—the Court returned to dual federalism.

Yet another decision (*Hans v. Louisiana*, 1890) seemed to seal the fate of federal judicial authority by ruling that "the 11th Amendment bars all unconsented suits brought by citizens against states in federal courts, including suits to enforce the Constitution."[14] Hans proved unworkable, however, because a supreme federal law required a federal enforcement mechanism. Interpretations of the Eleventh Amendment since *Hans* have tried to create and define a series of exceptions to this broad interpretation.

Thus, the court held in *Ex parte Young*, 1908, that the Eleventh Amendment does not bar suits for injunctions against state officials. The court more recently held that the Eleventh Amendment does not apply to suits against the states that are expressly authorized by Congress (*Pennsylvania v. Union Gas Co.*, 1989).

In recent years—since the Warren Court—states' legal authority has undercut federal authority utilizing two conservative legal concepts: equitable discretion and abstention doctrines.

The equitable discretion concept urges the federal courts to abstain on certain kinds of cases until a state court has ruled on relevant state-law issues. The abstention doctrine argues for the efficient use of state and federal courts and against "judicial activism" by lower federal courts.

While the efficient use of federal and state courts is important, and concern about federal judicial overreach is sometimes valid, judicial equitable discretion and abstention doctrines should not supersede the concern for social, economic, and racial justice. I see the reemergence of these doctrines as part of a broader conservative states' rights movement strategy to inhibit and slow the process of building a more perfect Union. These judge-made doctrines may have helped mitigate federal–state disputes, but they have also had the effect of slowing the march toward greater justice and equity in American society.

Through equitable discretion and abstention doctrines, the federal authority of Article III of the Constitution has been weakened and states' rights authority has been strengthened.

The Ninth Amendment to the Constitution provides that "the enumeration in the Constitution, of certain rights, shall not be construed to deny or disparage others retained by the people." This seems to mean that a common law, a "fundamental right," that is not enumerated in the Constitution is nevertheless a right that should be protected.

The Ninth Amendment, linked to the Fourteenth Amendment's equal protection and due process clauses—and progressively interpreted—could be a powerful constitutional instrument for building a more perfect Union. That is how I see seven of the eight constitutional amendments that I later propose.

Again, John Locke's theory of natural rights was a highly influential concept with the Founding Fathers. His philosophy taught that people had certain natural rights even before governments were formed, and the people had these rights whether governments recognized them or not. Governments were formed as a practical matter, more or less to publicly validate these inherent rights—rather than leaving them to be recognized by chance in the subjective realm of nature. But governments were not the source of these rights!

To reiterate, anti-federalists such as James Madison and Thomas Jefferson felt strongly about these natural rights and wanted them written into the Constitution, while federalists, including Alexander Hamilton, thought such assurances were unnecessary.

Hamilton and other federalists were concerned that if the rights were spelled out, future interpreters might conclude that the enumerated rights were the only rights the people had. Believing this to be a legitimate concern, Madison proposed the following amendment: "The exceptions here or elsewhere in the Constitution, made in favor of particular rights, shall not be construed as to diminish the just importance of other rights retained by the people, or as to enlarge the powers delegated by the Constitution; but either as actual limitations of such powers, or as inserted merely for greater caution."[15] Madison's language eventually was transformed and molded into the language of the Ninth Amendment.

For 150 years the Ninth Amendment was essentially ignored by the Supreme Court. The dominance of southern jurists on the Supreme Court, the presence of slavery, and the developed rationale of states' rights to defend the institution of slavery were part of the reason for this neglect.

Over the last fifty years, however, two fundamental interpretations of rights have emerged. The first and more conservative interpretation is that "retained rights and delegated powers are *logically* complementary. Retained rights are those left after powers were delegated to the federal government. To interpret the 9th Amendment, we simply look to see if the federal government has the power it claims; if so, any right that is logically inconsistent with this power cannot be among those retained by the people. . . . Since the 10th Amendment clearly limits the exercise of federal power to powers delegated by the Constitution, this interpretation seems to render the 9th Amendment without any practical function."[16]

In other words, the enumerated powers of the federal government take precedence over any unenumerated rights of the people because of the limits set by the Tenth Amendment. This is circular reasoning that logically leads to a states' rights interpretation of the Constitution and has been the general view of most legal scholars until recently.

The other, more liberal view argues that "retained rights and delegated powers are *functionally* complementary. Even a power actually granted to the government can be constrained by a retained right. For example, when a retained right is infringed, the government might have to offer a more weighty justification for exercising its power than it would when no right is infringed. Moreover, although the 9th Amendment, like the rest of the Bill of Rights, originally applied only to the federal government, this interpretation sees the passage of the 14th Amendment as extending federal protection against state infringement to both enumerated and unenumerated rights."[17]

My more liberal view is that the unenumerated rights in the U.S. Constitution's Ninth

Amendment—whether considered as natural rights, human rights that are evolving with society, or articulated, recognized, and ratified rights, such as the United Nations Universal Declaration of Human Rights—can and should be recognized as legitimate unenumerated constitutional rights, if we also take the Fourteenth Amendment's equal protection and due process rights seriously for all Americans.

Following the Civil War and during Reconstruction, significant changes took place in the balance of power between the victorious Union government and the losing Confederate States. The powers of the federal government were increased enormously during and immediately following the Civil War as the Republican government and its armies directly occupied the states and, with the establishment of the Freedmen's Bureau, exercised the full range of police powers relative to the former Confederate States. Of greater long-range importance, the Fourteenth Amendment opened the door for a broader range of congressional actions and Supreme Court interpretation in areas that would have previously been reserved to the states.

However, this period, so full of hope, was short lived. In 1883 the Supreme Court, having already limited Fourteenth Amendment protections of the rights of the newly freed slaves, declared the Civil Rights Act of 1875 unconstitutional on the grounds that it was offensive to the Tenth Amendment.

A new period of struggle between federal and state power followed. The tension was between the states' rights inherent in the Tenth Amendment on the one hand, and the power of Congress to regulate interstate commerce and to levy taxes on the other. The Supreme Court upheld the Pure Food and Drug Act (1906), the Meat Inspection Acts (1906 and 1907), and the White Slave Traffic Act (1910), but in *Killer v. United States* (1909), the Court used the Tenth Amendment to rule an act protecting alien women from immoral trafficking unconstitutional. Similarly, in the child labor law cases of 1918 *(Hammer v. Dagenhart)* and 1922 *(Bailey v. Drexel Furniture Co.)*, the Court overturned long-standing precedent and ruled against the Keating-Owen Child Labor Act (1916) in support of states' rights with regard to regulating child labor and commerce. Justice Oliver Wendell Holmes, in *Hammer*, wrote one of the Court's most powerful and famous dissents, declaring that "the power to regulate commerce and other constitutional powers could not be cut down or qualified" as a consequence of their "indirect effects."

The bottom line, however, was that the Court was sending mixed and confusing signals to Congress based on the states' rights claims in the Tenth Amendment and the nationalism inherent in the commerce clause.

Then new complications arose. In 1911 Congress passed its first grants program, the Weeks Act, which was designed to prevent forest fires, and in 1921 the Sheppard-Towner Act to provide medical care for expectant mothers. In these instances, it was the states' righters from the North who challenged these federal grants-in-aid programs on the basis that they violated the Tenth Amendment.

In *Massachusetts v. Mellon* (1923), the state of Massachusetts attacked the Maternity Act and the Supreme Court rejected the Tenth Amendment argument, declaring, in essence, that the federal government imposed no obligation and the state yielded no rights unless they voluntarily chose to participate in the program. "Perhaps most important, the Court held that a state could not, in its role of *parens patriae*"—as legal guardian of people who do not have the full legal capacity to act on their own behalf, such as children—"institute judicial proceedings to protect its citizens from operation of otherwise valid federal laws."[18] This was a blow to states' rights.

With the advent of the Great Depression and the need to greatly expand the federal reach through the recovery acts of the New Deal, a conservative Court fought Roosevelt and the new Congress—and initially won. Following FDR's new appointments during his second term, however, this changed, and for all practical purposes the Tenth Amendment was laid to rest—at least for a while.

It is this legacy of slavery and states' rights, however, that makes the Democratic Party and most of its white candidates in the South, even today, so economically and politically conservative. The modern-day essentially white Republican Party has tried (and to date largely succeeded in) building its party in the South on the political legacy of slavery, states' rights, decentralized localism, and anti-tax and anti-federal sentiment. It is no accident that a Republican platform of less government, local control, lower taxes, lax regulation, individualism, personal responsibility, religious charitable choice, and volunteerism comes from a region of the country that established and maintained the institution of slavery with the ideology of states' rights—with the same rhetoric.

It makes no sense morally, economically, or politically for the poorest and most materially needy region of the country, the South, to be economically conservative. The South has the least materially to conserve in terms of good and well-paying jobs, education, health care, affordable housing, wealth, or income—which is part of the legacy of slavery—yet it remains economically and politically conservative. Why?

In part, it's because conservative political leaders use valid conservative religious and social rhetoric—espousing sound moral values, patriotism, good work habits, family responsibility, and staying away from drugs, crime, and other antisocial behavior—to appeal to southern voters. However, they also deliberately confuse and misinform the people by identifying and linking these conservative religious and social values with conservative economics. Thus, good, sincere, and well-intentioned people who "love the Lord" and believe they are "doing God's will" often end up voting against their own material and economic interests.

The South should be the most economically liberal region of the country based on its material needs. Instead, it is led by conservative politicians, mainly white Republicans now, who use the Democratic Party's legacy of slavery, racism, and anti-federal, anti-big-government, and states' rights ideology—with a huge pinch of "Down Home, Good Ol' Time Religion" thrown in for flavor—for the purpose of maintaining the economic status quo. The central effect of southern conservatism in the nineteenth century was a defense of slavery. The central manifestation of southern conservatism in the twenty-first century is the crusade to defend a very unjust economic order.

I have noted the many people who even now believe that the American Civil War was fought over the issue of states' rights versus the big federal government, not over the preservation of slavery. They are wrong, but their states' rights legacy and ideology, politically, continues to play an obstructionist and nullifying role. In the southern region of the country, it plays the dominant role. The South's conservative political leadership, with its antifederal-government ideological and political tentacles, is stifling the nation's ability to build and become a more perfect Union. Economic conservatism's historic roots are in southern slavery, states' rights, and local control. Its current rallying cries are lower taxes, less government, and increased defense spending—all of which would benefit the South economically. But its branches manifest themselves in all parts of the country. George W. Bush's election both symbolizes and nationalizes conservative southern politics.

Despite the Supreme Court's *Gore v. Bush* exception in 2000, the doctrine of states' rights is alive and well today in our highest court. Less than a month after *Gore v. Bush*, in an environmental case involving the 1972 Clean Water Act, the court returned to its old states' rights ways. Writing for the majority in another five-to-four decision, Justice William Rehnquist defended "the states' traditional and primary power over land and water use." In an act of conservative judicial activism, it read language in the statute selectively, dismissing environmental agency expertise and congressional intent with respect to protecting *all* U.S. waters and wetlands. The court effectively rewrote the statute to fit its states' rights views.

The presiding officer at President Clinton's impeachment trial in the Senate was U.S. Supreme Court Chief Justice William Rehnquist, the ultimate conservative states' righter. Nominated to the Court by Nixon and elevated to chief justice by Reagan, this intellectually gifted conservative, while clerking for Justice Robert H. Jackson in 1952 and 1953, wrote a memorandum arguing in favor of upholding the "separate but equal" doctrine of the 1896 *Plessy v. Ferguson* ruling in preparation for the 1954 decision on *Brown*. As a conservative Phoenix lawyer, he appeared as a witness before the Phoenix City Council in opposition to a public accommodations ordinance and took part in a program of challenging African American voters at the polls.

From 1969 until 1971 he served as assistant attorney general for the Office of Legal Counsel. In that capacity, he supported the use of executive authority to conduct wiretaps and surveillance without a court order, a no-knock entry policy by the police, preventive detention, and abolishing the exclusionary rule—that is, he supported the admission of evidence gathered in illegal ways.

> As a member of the Burger Court, Rehnquist played a crucial role in reviving the debate regarding the relationship between the federal government and the states. . . . The consequences of Rehnquist's state-centered federalism surfaced dramatically in the area of individual rights. Since the 1960s, the Court had held that nearly every provision in the Bill of Rights applies to the states through the Due Process Clause of the 14th Amendment. Rehnquist voiced his disagreement with such a method of determining the constitutional requirements of state action, particularly in the context of criminal proceedings, urging a return to an earlier approach whereby the states were not required to comply with the Bill of Rights but only to treat individuals with "fundamental fairness."[19]

Rehnquist holds a strict constructionist view of the Fourteenth Amendment's mandate to the states not to deny individuals equal protection of the laws. He interprets the equal protection clause narrowly, seeing it merely as preventing states from treating black and white citizens differently. He argues that the Fourteenth Amendment should not apply when a state has not *intentionally* discriminated (*Columbus v. Penick*, 1979). It should not be applied to the private sector unless the state is a participant in the discrimination (*Moose Lodge v. Irvis*, 1972). And Rehnquist argues against applying the equal protection clause to protect women from disparate treatment (*Craig v. Boren*, 1976; *Michael M. v. Superior Court of Sonoma County*, 1981).

His states' rights philosophy may have come through most clearly in his 1976 *National League of Cities v. Usery* decision, which deemed unconstitutional a federal statute extending the maximum hours and minimum wage provisions of the federal Fair Labor Standards Act to most employees of state and local governments. Breathing new life into the Tenth

Amendment, the Court held that part of the Fair Labor Standards Act was unconstitutional because it interfered with a state's sovereignty and, thus, violated the Tenth Amendment. It was the first time since the days of FDR's New Deal that the Supreme Court had ruled against a federal law on the basis that Congress had overstepped its federal boundaries.

National League of Cities, like *Hans* before it, proved to be unworkable and was overruled in *Garcia v. San Antonio Metropolitan Transit Authority* in 1985, when Justice Harry Blackmun changed his vote by voting against Chief Justice Rehnquist's states' rights position.

The most important values for Rehnquist are his state-centered federalism, the priority of private property, and individual rights. In other words, his current views are consistent with the core of the states' rights legal philosophy of a century and a half ago, when the individual right to own property (slaves) was to be protected by a states' rights government!

As noted in an earlier chapter, political leaders, strategists, and intellectuals seldom use the term "states' rights" today because it is associated with slavery and tends to set off alarms in African American, liberal, and even some conservative communities. The new, more acceptable terminology includes: block grants; limited, smaller, and more efficient government; local flexibility and control; and similar nonthreatening words. The effect, however, is the same.

Conservatives will probably try to attack me as a liberal ideologue who advocates a "Big Centralized Bureaucratic Government." Nothing could be farther from the truth. I am not ideologically for more and bigger government for the sake of more and bigger government. I am certainly not for a rigid and inefficient bureaucracy that cannot change or is not democratically accountable. Neither, however, am I ideologically for smaller and lesser government because conservatism demands it.

We should be aware of the options of ideology, and we should think through our own political philosophy clearly to reach a personal political direction. But we should not be driven by or rigidly married to an ideology.

We must apply not an ideological test, but a practical one. What kind of government will it take to meet all of the American people's basic material needs such as employment, health care, housing, education, protecting our environment, and equal opportunity? How much government will it take to do that basic job in the most effective and efficient manner?

But can we really achieve national full employment without the government making this its number one priority and democratically building a mixed economy to achieve it? Without government involvement, can we provide health care to the nearly one-third of the American people—approximately ninety million now—who have no health insurance or inadequate health insurance?

Our nation is confronted with an affordable housing crisis. If the private sector alone could have addressed this problem, it would have done so by now. It will obviously take a national government engaged in democratic planning, coordination, and funding to meet the nation's affordable housing needs.

All of the polls show that the American people put public education among their highest priorities. It is conservatively estimated that paying for the physical construction needs of public education in America will alone cost more than a hundred billion dollars. Yet the 105th Congress was unwilling to pay a mere five billion dollars to pass Senator Carol Moseley-Braun's (D-IL) school construction legislation to help America's children. Property taxes in local school districts, combined with state education funds, and a pittance in federal education funds (about 6 percent)—the present formula—will not guarantee all of America's children a world-class public education for the twenty-first century. In a practical sense, only the national government can raise the national educational standards and provide an equal educational opportunity for all of our children.

The national common law of equal opportunity and nondiscrimination must be effectively administered and enforced. That will require adequate federal funding to ensure effective and efficient administration, coordination, and enforcement.

The world's—not just the nation's—environment is one, interconnected and interdependent. Only national—indeed, international—cooperation, coordination, and funding can protect and sustain a clean and safe environment.

There is strong talk among some conservatives in Congress—and a majority of the Republican candidates who ran in the 2000 presidential campaign—not just to reform the Internal Revenue Service (IRS), and make it fairer, simpler, more consumer friendly and efficient, but to eliminate it. They know that this would prohibit the American people from building a more perfect Union. Those who are unwilling to answer the practical questions of how we realistically meet the basic material needs of all American people are, de facto, arguing against building a more perfect Union.

Some are rather open about their conservative views. During the presidential campaign of 2000, Governor George W. Bush stated several times that he would appoint strict constructionists to the Supreme Court in the tradition of Antonin Scalia and Clarence Thomas. And when confronted with the controversy of flying the Confederate flag over the South Carolina Capitol, he said—in typical states' rights fashion—"On issues related to South Carolina, I believe it is important for a presidential candidate to trust the people of South Carolina to make the right decision. . . . In my opinion, the people of South Carolina, the good people of South Carolina, the people of this great state can figure out how to resolve that issue."[20] Bob Peeler, Bush's South Carolina campaign co-chair, said: "It's a South Carolina issue. I believe in the flag flying and moving on to other issues."[21] Texas "recognizes the Confederacy as one of six governments that have ruled" the state, "but it doesn't fly the rebel flag" over the statehouse in Austin. Instead, the seal of the Confederacy "is incorporated in two places on the Statehouse building."[22]

Others may not as openly identify with or call themselves states' righters, but the conservative economic and political forces in both political parties in Congress, in the White House, and on the Supreme Court that prohibit an economic program that would uplift and benefit the vast majority of the American people are unwittingly aiders and abetters of the same.

This antidemocratic and elitist ideological legacy will not go away on its own volition. It must be confronted, challenged, taken on, and defeated. Only then can we get on with the business of building a more perfect Union.

When the "Mother of the Civil Rights Movement," Rosa Parks, refused to give up her seat on a bus in Montgomery, Alabama, in 1955, she was fighting states' rights in the name of building a more perfect Union.

RACE IS CENTRAL—
TREMORS (1619–1861)

When I think about the institution of slavery on the one hand and
I think about God being a just God on the other, I shudder for my
country.

—Thomas Jefferson, Jefferson Memorial, Washington, D.C.

O! had I the ability, and could I reach the nation's ear, I would today
pour out a fiery stream of biting ridicule, blasting reproach, withering sarcasm, and stern rebuke. For it is not light that is needed,
but fire; it is not the gentle shower, but thunder. We need the storm,
the whirlwind, and the earthquake.

—Frederick Douglass
Independence Day speech, Rochester, New York, July 4, 1852

Why was Harriet Beecher Stowe's *Uncle Tom's Cabin* the best-selling book of its day?
Despite his substantial progressive contribution to the nation's economic growth,
why is former Supreme Court Justice Roger B. Taney known for only one thing, *Dred Scott*?
Why did Alex Haley's made-for-television movie, *Roots*, based on his best-selling book, set
a record for viewership? Why did Ken Burns's Civil War documentary on PBS engage the
nation as never before on public television? Why did the Rodney King beating and its aftermath, and the O. J. Simpson murder trial and its verdict, so grip the country? There are
a variety of reasons, I'm sure. But central to all of these is one issue: race.

I am not using race as a club to beat white people over the head. I am not using it to try
to send people on a guilt trip or make them feel ashamed of their ancestors. Neither am I
trying to make African Americans feel sad, ashamed, or inferior by reminding them of their
past. In this book I use race as a pair of tinted sunglasses. If you put on blue sunglasses, the
world looks blue; yellow sunglasses, it takes on a yellow tint. In essence, I am asking you to
put on "African American sunglasses" and look at American history as objectively as you can
through the subjective lens of race. I believe that this view will reveal more about how and
why America is what it is today than any other perspective you may choose. Clarity on this
point is important.

We could view American history through the lens of women's rights—from the denial of
the right to vote, through the struggle for women's suffrage and its successful achievement
in the Constitution, to the current struggles over equal pay for equal work, the ERA, violence against women, and choice. While such a view would be instructive, with all of our
country's pain and deeply rooted discrimination and gender inequality, this is still not the
best prism for seeing the nature of America's problem.

Or we might choose to view American history through the lens of labor's struggles. The issues of economic growth, unemployment, inflation, recession, depression, the need for benefits, minimum wages, the right to organize, and more offer meaningful lessons about capital and labor and the creation of the middle class. And while this is an important prism, it is still not the best one for viewing the nature of our nation's central problem.

The nation often chooses to consider the experience of European immigrants in the nineteenth and early twentieth centuries as central to understanding America and Americans—and clearly this is an important aspect of our history (witness the overwhelming public interest in the opening of Elis Island online in early 2001). But without negating that importance in the least, a focus on the European immigrant experience can actually distort or deny an even deeper and more important understanding of America. Many European immigrants were among the more talented citizens of their countries, which is why they were able to come here in the first place. They generally had high self-esteem, were highly motivated to improve their condition, and often were relatively educated or skilled. They also often lived in relatively poor countries, or under undemocratic or oppressive political leadership, and they were willing to work hard. Thus more often than not, for the European immigrant this country represented exactly what the Statue of Liberty symbolizes—a land of opportunity for those willing to overcome hardship and discrimination and work hard. And this is a valid experienc and perspectives.

However, the immigrants were accepted by and able to become a part of the economic and political structure, arrangements, and attitudes that already existed—white Democrats and Republicans—without necesssarily knowing the underlying racial history and assumptions upon which both parties were built. They could join the political arrangements (mostly Democratic, but also Republican) and work their way up to the privileges. Buth this also meant joining the dominant attitudes toward people of color—and black people in particular—that already existed in the two parties. At a deeper level, then, the European immigrant experience helped maintain the economic and political status quo—at least as far as people of color, but especially blacks, were concerned. The immigrants simply joined the existing political paradigm; they did not fundamentally change or alter it.

Likewise, none of them gives the truest picture of America or most fully reveals the nature of its current dilemma.

The most productive and insightful way to view the nature of America and its problem is the history of African Americans. This prism presents Americans and the world with the best, truest, broadest, and deepest understanding of American history and the nature of its most central problem. And it suggests that dealing with this is the way out of our existing morass.

No other prism shows us as clearly the formation of the federal government; how representation was apportioned in the Senate (two per state) and the House (proportional); why the electoral college was formed; why states were admitted two by two into the Union (to preserve the balance of power between slave and free states); how Supreme Court interpretations have been used (the Constitution as a "living" versus a static "strict constructionist" document); why eleven states seceded and brought on a Civil War; how our current two-party system of Democrats and Republicans was formed. And in its response to America's most fundamental economic and other needs, no other history explains the creation of the social and economic political philosophies currently described as conservative, moderate, and liberal.

Race dominates American history. Race is more central than the state-versus-federal-government arguments, because race predates the founding of a formal nation with laws and institutional relationships. More important, even after government institutions and laws were founded and their relationships were established, race remained our most central issue, because *both* states' rights and central government advocates have used *both* federal and states' rights arguments and power at one time or another to establish and/or maintain the institution of slavery, segregation, discrimination, and inequality between the races (and classes) in this nation.

I am an advocate and a fighter for equality and equal opportunity for all Americans of whatever race, gender, nationality, or religion. My intent here is *not* to pit the arguments of race and gender against each other; both have been shameful and important aspects of American history. But in most instances, if not all, race has been the dominant issue in the formation of American economics, politics, religion, culture, and law. U.S. Civil Rights Chairwoman Dr. Mary Frances Berry gives one example of race over gender when she notes that even though the Fifteenth Amendment was added to the Constitution in 1870—and the Nineteenth Amendment not until 1920—it was not until passage of the 1965 Voting Rights Act that African Americans were allowed to register and vote in significant numbers. While black men had the right to vote after the Fifteenth Amendment, the lack of the *actual ability* to vote was true for both black men and black women, and did not change until 1965.

Even though the states' rights philosophy and practice has been the primary means of perpetuating racial injustice, it will become increasingly clear over the next three chapters that those who have an interest in perpetuating racial division and economic inequality care little, in the end, whether they use states' rights arguments or federal power to maintain the status quo or to turn back the clock on racial and economic equality. While states' rights—and its stepchildren, localism and local control—has been the chief means of enforcing and institutionalizing racial oppression, these perpetrators of injustice and division are primarily concerned about the *end*, not the *means*. They have and are willing to use *any means* that protects the goal of racial and class inequality and white superiority.

It is not an oversimplification to say that from our country's earliest beginnings to its founding, the ratification of our Constitution, and our early growth as a nation, one issue led directly to the Civil War, and that one issue was slavery. Race was an integral part of slavery, which eventually evolved into institutional racism, but the peculiar institution and the resultant war were neither inescapable nor foreordained. Economic circumstances certainly played a significant role, but political choices were even more important on the road to civil upheaval.

In his book *American Slavery*, Peter Kolchin divides slavery into four periods prior to the Civil War: pre-American colonial slavery (1441–1619); American colonial slavery (1619–1770); slavery during the American Revolution (1770–1800); and slavery during the antebellum period (1800–1861).[1] In keeping with my own earthquake analogy, I refer to this entire era as the tremor phase. Still, Kolchin's divisions are a useful tool in examining the era.

It is both important and surprising to note that while race is central to understanding American history, most Americans—regardless of color or education—don't have a thorough understanding of race in general or race in America in particular, even though race, consciously and unconsciously, dominates much of our lives.

President Clinton's call for a dialogue on race in June 1997 was a worthwhile effort to increase the knowledge of Americans about African Americans and other ethnic groups. Unfortunately, we made little progress. Without understanding the history of our long-standing problems, it is hard to design solutions that will be understood or accepted.

It is impossible to truly understand America without understanding that race is central to its very being. Race is not an addendum, an adjunct, or a side issue in America. Though largely ignored until lately, African American history is one and the same with American history—two sides of the same coin. America and race are inseparable.

PRE-AMERICAN COLONIAL SLAVERY (1441–1619)

Nonfreedom is more characteristic of humankind and human history than freedom, and this was the case during the pre-American colonial period. This point is critical: Until the nineteenth century, slavery or involuntary servitude was a more dominant form of social organization than liberty. In its various forms—slavery, serfdom, peonage—nonfreedom has served a variety of purposes and should not be solely identified with commercial agricultural labor or house servants, its dominant manifestation in the United States. Historically, slaves "served as warriors, government officials, wives, concubines, tutors, eunuchs and victims of ritual sacrifice."[2]

Slaves have even enjoyed high status. Kolchin points out, "In many pre-modern societies there were high-status slaves who exercised considerable authority; such elite slaves ranged from stewards who managed vast agricultural estates in China and early-modern Russia to high government officials in Rome and the Ottoman Empire. Throughout much of Asia, Africa and Latin America, slaves served in the armed forces, at times—especially in the Islamic world—achieving high rank and wielding considerable power."[3]

Over the centuries slavery has engulfed both genders, many tribes, and a multiplicity of ethnicities, races, and religions. In the New World the need for strong male labor was a prime motive for slavery, but in Africa and Asia women slaves were prized as wives, concubines, and farmhands. Physical differences such as gender, race, and color were often used to justify why one group "deserved" to be master and the other group "deserved" to be slave, but not always. "Both Muslims and Christians traditionally believed that only heathens (non-Muslims and non-Christians, respectively) could be enslaved."[4] Sociologist Orlando Patterson found that, of the nearly sixty slaveholding societies he studied, about a quarter enslaved some others like themselves.

The European-based African slave trade that manifested itself in the New World was characterized by the need for labor to plant, cultivate, and harvest commercial agricultural products in the colonial territories. In the American South, the plantation system of forced labor was distinctive because of its size and ethnic composition. The southern United States represented the northernmost arena of a plantation system modeled after the large sugar estates of Jamaica, Haiti, Cuba, and other Caribbean colonies.

Labor was the motivating need that led to slavery, and Africans were not the first choice. European colonialists first tried to enslave Native Americans and fellow Europeans. At one time, Native Americans were bought and sold in open slave markets. By 1708 in South Carolina, for example, there were an estimated 1,400 Indian slaves in a population of 12,580.

In time, indentured servitude of other Europeans came to be the most common practice. Most indentured apprenticeship programs lasted from five to seven years and usually involved male children and youths, sometimes adult males, but very rarely women. While most indentured servants in the eighteenth century came voluntarily to America, some were kidnapped, while other troublemakers were forced to immigrate against their will as punishment for criminal behavior. Because men in the American colonies greatly outnumbered women, women often were able to move up the social ladder through marriage after their indenture.

As a rigid and exploitative economic system of labor, American slavery had more in common with Russian serfdom than with the premodern systems mentioned above. Though some indentured whites and Native Americans were slaves, and a small number of Native and African Americans were slaveholders, the slave system as it evolved in the New World was primarily identified as Europeans and their descendants over Africans and their descendants, and as white over black. Over time, this artificially created norm of an aristocratic, unequal labor system, and of a superior–inferior economic and social relationship of white over black, institutionalized itself in culture, law, politics, and religion. This hierarchical, top-down, European over African economic system soon became—and deservedly so—identified with white racism, a systematic race-based ideology and practice of institutional arrangements of white over black.

Although a Dutch boat captain sold twenty Africans into indentured servitude in Jamestown, Virginia, in May 1619, African slavery did not begin there. The Portuguese, under Henry the Navigator, son of John I, were exploring Africa's west coast and in 1441 returned to Lisbon with gold and a handful of African slaves. A thousand slaves were imported over the next few years; by 1448 Portugal had established the first African trading station on the Arguin Island, just off the coast of Mauritania. The Roman Catholic Church, through Pope Nicholas V, implicitly legitimized the slave trade in writings (bulls) sanctioning war against the Moors and the conversion of pagans.

Slaves proved to be of moderate economic value to Portugal, though during the 1500s about ten thousand a year were imported as agricultural laborers by Spain. Spain's colonization of Hispaniola after Columbus's "discovery" of the New World in 1492, however, nearly exterminated the native Arawak Indians and created the need for additional labor in the Caribbean.

The first African slaves were shipped to the Spanish in Hispaniola around 1501. The slave trade grew so rapidly, however, that by 1513 Spain was making a handsome profit from the sale of licenses to import Africans. For the next three hundred years the maritime European powers competed in the lucrative slave market, carrying to the New World a minimum of fifteen million live slaves. Of course, many more lives were lost in the process of securing slaves in Africa and in transit over the ocean.

"America absorbed relatively few of these Africans. The great bulk—more than 85 percent of the total—went to Brazil and the various Caribbean colonies of the British, French, Spanish and Dutch. Others went to the Spanish mainland. The United States, or more accurately, for most of the slave-trade years the colonies that would later become the United States, imported only 600,000 to 650,000 Africans, some 6 percent of all the slaves brought from Africa to the New World."[5] By 1700 the population of black slaves in the English colonies was estimated to be twenty-eight thousand, of whom twenty-three thousand resided in the South.

AMERICAN COLONIAL SLAVERY (1619–1770)

For a variety of reasons—climate, food, absence of certain diseases, crops raised, fertility rate—the population of Africans in the American mainland colonies grew to become, by far, the largest outside Africa, while it declined in the other places where the African slave trade had flourished. Atypically, black population growth in America came mainly through reproduction. Growth elsewhere was mainly dependent on the African slave trade bringing new male slaves. The slave trade in the United States officially ended in 1808, but by 1810 "the 1.1 million slaves in the United States constituted almost twice the total number it had imported from Africa during the preceding two centuries."[6]

War, culture, and European diseases rapidly eliminated Native Americans as a ready supply of slave labor in the new colonies. African slaves continued to be brought to America, but cultural and language barriers made an investment in African slaves uneconomical. Indentured servants from Europe better met the country's basic labor needs. The migration of European indentured servants peaked between 1650 and 1680, and the colonies remained predominantly white.

Beginning in the 1680s, however, because the status of indentured servitude was temporary and the former European white servants were now free in America, the mainland colonies experienced a rapid rise in the white population and a dramatic decline in the numbers of European indentured servants. In 1660 the monarchy had been restored in England, which brought political stability and greater economic opportunity to those who might otherwise have been inclined to come to America as indentured servants. All these factors led to a sudden labor shortage.

To fill this void, American colonialists turned to the African slave trade. Experts estimate that between 1680 and 1750, the proportion of blacks in Virginia increased from 7 percent to 44 percent and in South Carolina from 17 percent to 61 percent.[7] While at this time England transported most African slaves to the Caribbean islands to work in the sugar industry, many also found their way to the agricultural mainland of the American South.

With the switch to African labor, however, came a fundamental shift in the nature of servitude as well. The European indentured servant business was essentially voluntary, with a limited time of service and eventual freedom as a reward. African slave labor was involuntary and without an end reward. While a few Africans experienced indentured servitude, the vast majority experienced slavery—but neither was voluntary. Also, unlike European indentured servants, an initial investment in African slaves had the additional advantage of reproducing itself for a lifetime (and more) of essentially free labor. Finally, when white indentured servants escaped from their masters, they usually blended into the general population and often made it to freedom. The racial distinctiveness of escaping African slaves was a disadvantage virtually impossible to hide or overcome.

The aristocratic English had a rather low opinion of the poorer economic classes generally, treating all of them, including both lower-class whites and blacks, rather rudely and roughly. Despite the differences, however, in the seventeenth-century American colonies from Massachusetts to South Carolina, there was much interaction between poor and working-class blacks and whites, some of it actually based on equality. But even where racial prejudice was present, it was not deep enough to make the enslavement of blacks *inevitable*.

So what was the interplay of race and slavery? Did the enslavement of Africans create prejudice, or did prejudice create slavery? The reality is that both were factors, and they mutually reinforced one another. There was a labor need that, at first, was filled on a color-blind basis. There also was prejudice, based on racial differences, which contributed to a rationale for black enslavement. "First . . . the English saw Africans as black and themselves as white—in both cases inaccurately. Associated with the former term were numerous pejorative meanings ranging from dirty to immoral, whereas the latter carried equally positive connotations of purity, virtue and godliness. Second, they were 'savage' or 'uncivilized.' . . . Third, they were 'heathens.'"[8] As prejudice became further constituted and the racial patterns more pronounced over time, the mixing of the races neither in labor, sexually, through acculturation, nor through conversion to Christianity was able to undercut the institutional establishment of African slavery in America.

Peter Kolchin argues that "more than anything else, it was the involuntary nature of blacks' migration to America that dictated their growing separation from the white labor force."[9] Voluntary indentured servants had to be treated with a certain degree of humanity and given new opportunities if a steady flow of such labor was to continue. The same treatment was not necessary for those who were brought here against their will.

The demographic situation changed again in the eighteenth century. A better-educated and -trained group of European craftsmen and artisans, not just unskilled and indentured servants, arrived in America during the 1700s, lured by greater economic opportunities than in Europe and motivated by the chance to develop their skills and enrich themselves. Few of these new immigrants came as agrarian laborers wishing to immerse themselves in an agricultural economy. Involuntary African slaves had no such choice.

As the economic conditions, opportunities, and positions of white Europeans improved, the reverse occurred for the African slaves. There were no opportunities for them to improve their lot regardless of their talent or motivation. Their only opportunity was survival.

Thus, a clear division between European and African, between black and white, was becoming more apparent, pronounced, and concentrated. Such a division eventually gave rise to a systematic *cultural rationalization* of "superior" and "inferior" races. A century earlier, when the labor of both was needed, when neither white nor black was free, and when non-freedom seemed more the common plight of humankind than liberty, racial superiority theories and practices were harder to justify. By the 1700s, though, the upward mobility of Europeans in America and downward mobility of Africans made it easier for a racial rationale to develop. Laws could be written that institutionalized this economically uneven, socially unjust, and morally unjustifiable arrangement. And once this arrangement was set—in the economy, the social customs, and the law—it was easier to pass the cultural disease of racism along to the next generation. After all, it was now the law!

According to Kolchin, "Whereas the legal status of the few blacks who resided in the colonies remained uncertain prior to the 1660s, a spate of legislation passed during the subsequent century regulated the condition of the growing population of black slaves and set them off from white settlers. These acts established that slaves—and the children of slave women—would serve for life; limited the rights of slaves and even of free blacks (they could not vote, testify in court against whites, or marry whites); prohibited slaves from carrying arms or leaving home without written permission; discouraged masters from freeing slaves . . . ; and mandated severe corporal punishment for those who dared challenge white authority."[10] These new slave laws were not imported from England but homegrown by each of the colonies.

Ironically, while the slave trade that serviced most of the New World was dominated by England, a mass movement in the mid-1700s to abolish slavery also had its roots in that country. The British government and shipping merchants who had made England the world's largest slave-trading nation were suddenly confronted with a shift in popular feeling that also became the world's prime mover behind the ultimately successful suppression of the slave trade.

Slavery was first made legal in the North, not the South, and early laws pertaining to indentured servants and African slaves varied greatly from state to state. Apart from slavery itself, the law was neither *always for* nor *always against* the African slave. African slaves were imported into Connecticut in 1629 and into Maryland and Massachusetts in 1634. Acknowledging the fact of slavery, in 1630 Massachusetts passed a law to protect African slaves from abusive owners—a provision later adopted by all of the New England colonies. Between 1640 and 1699, laws to punish both fugitive indentured servants and black slaves were passed in Connecticut, Maryland, New Jersey, South Carolina, and Virginia. However, in 1643 a New England Confederation laid the groundwork for future fugitive slave laws by declaring that "mere certification by a magistrate is sufficient evidence to convict a runaway slave."[11]

In 1662 Virginia passed a law that said the status of slave or free children would be determined by the lineage of the mother. Maryland, in 1663, passed a law declaring that all imported Africans were slaves, and any white women who married an African man was to be considered a slave herself, as well as their children. In 1681 Maryland revised the law to say that the children of such a relationship were to be considered free citizens.

In 1670 Virginia denied voting rights to both newly freed slaves and former indentured servants, and declared that all non-Christians imported into the colony "by shipping" were to be slaves for life. However, slaves who entered Virginia by land route were to be indentured until the age of thirty if they were children, and for twelve years if they were adults when their period of servitude commenced. Later Virginia law denied Africans many specific rights.

In 1688 in Germantown, Pennsylvania, the Mennonites circulated an antislavery resolution, the first formal protest against slavery in the Western Hemisphere.

Even though legal slavery existed in both the North and the South, slavery's sheer numbers and its relationship to the economy made it more viable in the South. While slavery was growing in the South's agrarian-based economy, it had not yet converted the region into a "slave society," as it would eventually do.

In 1705 the Virginia Assembly declared: "No Negro, mulatto or Indian shall presume to take upon him, act in or exercise any office, ecclesiastic, civil or military." Blacks were also forbidden to serve as witnesses in court cases and condemned to a lifetime of servitude unless they could prove that they had been Christians in their native land or free men in a Christian country. In 1711 the Mennonites and the Quakers pressured the Pennsylvania colonial legislature to outlaw slavery, only to have the British Crown overrule them. In 1723 the colony of Virginia again wrote laws limiting the rights of freed blacks by denying them the right to vote and forbidding them to carry weapons of any sort.

In 1740 South Carolina's colonial legislature passed a law, a slave code, that forbade black slaves from owning or raising livestock and imposed severe penalties on any slave who might make a "false appeal" to the governor on the grounds that blacks had been enslaved illegally. In 1749 Georgia passed a law that allowed the importation of African slaves but attempted to protect them from cruel treatment or from being hired out.

By 1750 the black slave population in the English colonies had reached a little more than 236,000—about 20 percent of the total population in the colonies—with approximately 206,000 of the total living south of Pennsylvania.

Some of the most famous Americans of the day were counted among the early slave owners. In 1752 George Washington acquired his estate in Mount Vernon, Virginia, which at the time had eighteen slaves. Over time, he expanded this number to two hundred. While apparently treating his slaves relatively well for his time and place, he did not hesitate to use them and never advocated for their freedom.

REVOLUTION-ERA SLAVERY (1770–1800)

Despite widespread slavery, African Americans were involved in and contributed significantly to our early American history. In 1770 a black man, Crispus Attucks, was shot and killed during the Boston Massacre, becoming one of the first casualties of the American Revolution. In that same year a Philadelphia Quaker named Anthony Benezet opened a school for blacks. In 1773 in Savannah, Georgia, George Lisle and Andrew Bryan organized the first Baptist church for blacks in the state of Georgia.

In the battle of Bunker Hill, 1775, Peter Salem, Salem Poor, and other blacks fought heroically. Ironically, the very next year, 1775, that same body barred blacks from serving in the army during the American Revolution. At the same time, the first abolitionist society was being organized in Philadelphia, Pennsylvania. Also in 1775, while the great philosophers François-Marie Arouet de Voltaire, David Hume, and others were promoting racial theories that blacks were akin to apes, in Germany Johann Friedrich Blumenbach was publishing *On the Natural Variety of Mankind*, which asserted that the skulls and brains of blacks were the same as those of Europeans. And in 1776, "two blacks, Prince Whipple and Oliver Cromwell, crossed the Delaware with George Washington en route to an attack on the British and their Hessian mercenaries in Trenton, New Jersey."[12]

A black battalion of three hundred former slaves was formed in Rhode Island in 1778. They were compensated the same as whites and were promised freedom after the War for Independence. The battalion killed one thousand Hessians and took part in a battle at Ponts Bridge in New York. Alexander Hamilton supported a plan by Henry Laurens of South Carolina to use southern slaves to fight for independence in the South in 1779.

This period also saw increasing attempts to outlaw or limit slavery. In 1774 Rhode Island banned slavery, except for slaves brought into Rhode Island before 1774. That same year, the Continental Congress demanded the elimination of the slave trade and approved embargoes against countries participating in it.

The amended July 4, 1776, American Declaration of Independence did not include Thomas Jefferson's earlier drafted denunciation of slavery. Jefferson's diatribe in his rough draft of the Declaration of Independence stated that the "King of Great Britain kept open a market where *men* were bought and sold, and prostituted his negative by suppressing Virginia's legislative attempts to restrain this execrable commerce."[13]

By this time the American-born slaves already outnumbered Africans brought here as slaves. By the time of emancipation, at the start of 1863 during the Civil War, the African American population was six times the number originally brought here as slaves, approximately 4.3 million, with roughly 4 million living in the eleven states of the Confederacy, which had a total population of 9 million. Slightly more than a quarter million blacks lived in the North.

In 1780 the Pennsylvania Assembly passed a law to gradually emancipate the slaves. The Massachusetts Supreme Court abolished slavery in 1783 and granted political suffrage to those in taxable categories. By the end of the American Revolution in 1783, ten thousand blacks had served in its armies, including five thousand as regular soldiers. Great Britain officially recognized the thirteen colonies with the signing of the Paris Peace Accord on October 18, 1783. In 1787 the Second Continental Congress passed the Northwest Ordinance forbidding slavery's expansion into the Northwest Territory. At the same time, back in Philadelphia, Richard Allen and Absalom Jones organized the Free African Society. By 1790 the first census reported 757,000 African Americans, 19 percent of the total population, but only 9 percent were free.

On May 14, 1787, fifty-five delegates from twelve states—Rhode Island didn't send any delegates—convened in Philadelphia. It was known as the Constitutional Convention only in hindsight, because its original purpose was to revamp the Articles of Confederation. Two of the central issues facing the convention were the "big states" versus the "little states" and, of course, slavery. The two issues were connected by way of debate over whether slaves would be counted, in terms of political representation, as population or as property. If counted as population, slaves would then be seen as equal to whites. If counted as property, the South would receive much less representation and lose considerable political power.

The argument was posed as to whether states should have power according to population or to wealth. South Carolina's Pierce Butler declared bluntly "that money is power and the states should have weight in the government according to their wealth."[14] The Massachusetts delegate Elbridge Gerry shot back, "Blacks are property and are used to the southward as horses and cattle to the northward. Why then should not horses and cattle have the right of representation in the North?"[15]

At that time and in that context it was a hard and penetrating question, one that arose again and again over the years. In Philadelphia, in 1787, the dilemma was addressed with the first of many compromises in America over the issue of slavery. James Wilson, one of the eight delegates from Pennsylvania, proposed the "three-fifths rule." The idea was taken from an earlier proposal at the Confederation Congress of 1783, which, for purposes of representation, allowed slaves to be counted as three-fifths white—that is, the "whole number of white and other free citizens and three-fifths of all other persons except Indians not paying taxes. . . ." While this "federal ratio" was adopted and remained law until the Reconstruction Amendments were added to the Constitution after the Civil War, the word "slavery" never appeared in the Constitution.

The slave matter in Philadelphia was not just a North and South issue. George Mason of Virginia, an owner of two hundred slaves, was nevertheless openly abolitionist and wanted to be done with the institution. On the other hand, some New England shipowning delegates who had benefited from the African slave trade argued that slavery was an "economic" matter, not a "moral" issue, and should therefore be left to the states. The convention, which began in mid-May, did not fully address and debate the slavery issue until August.

The *direct* question at issue in Philadelphia was not slavery, but proportional representation. This great debate was resolved on July 16. The "Great Compromise" created "proportional" representation in the U.S. House, or one representative for every forty thousand inhabitants, to benefit the big states; and "equal" representation in the U.S. Senate, or two members per state, to benefit the smaller states and slave states. The "big state" versus "little state" issue was thus resolved, while the deeper issue of slavery was submerged.

On August 6 the Convention's Committee of Detail—the group responsible for putting forth a finished constitutional product—offered up the first complete draft. Five weeks of debate followed. James McHenry of Maryland, a slave state with tobacco as its prime staple crop, was concerned about giving Congress the power to pass navigation acts, collect taxes and imposts, and "regulate commerce among the several states." He feared such commerce would be controlled by the four largest states.

These commercial questions would soon be settled with a bargain and a compromise on the slavery question. "The Northern states agreed that Congress should not pass any navigation law by a mere majority, but must have a two-thirds vote of each house; agreed also that the import tax on slaves would not exceed ten dollars a head; that slaves would be counted, for purpose of representation and taxes, in the proportion of five slaves to three free white inhabitants—the 'federal ratio.' In return, the Southern states conceded that the importation of slaves would cease in the year 1808. . . . Roger Sherman of Connecticut said it was better to let the Southern states import slaves than to part with these states, 'if they make that a *sine qua non*'"[16]—that is, if the South made slavery an essential element or condition of its remaining in the Union.

Alexander Hamilton and others later contended that there would have been no Union and no Constitution if the slavery compromise had not been made. "The question before the Convention was not, Shall slavery be abolished? It was rather, Who shall have the power to control it—the states or the national government? As the Constitution now stood, Congress could control the traffic in slaves exactly as it controlled all other trade and commerce."[17]

While the immorality of slavery was not central, moral tirades were launched against the institution. Connecticut's Roger Sherman looked upon it as "iniquitous." Gouverneur Morris of Pennsylvania referred to slavery as a "nefarious institution, the curse of heaven on the states where it prevailed."

But the defenders had their say as well. James Rutledge of South Carolina dismissed concerns about religion, morality, and humanity, stating flatly, "Interest alone is the governing principle of nations," and arguing that the northern traders in slaves and slave goods benefited, too. Charles Pinckney argued plainly that South Carolina would not agree to any government that prohibited the slave trade, but if left to itself South Carolina by degrees would probably "do of herself what is wished"—the perennial solution of voluntarism to end slavery, Jim Crow segregation, and ongoing discrimination.

Only South Carolina delegate Charles Pinckney offered a *moral defense* of slavery. The institution, he argued, was alive and well all over the world. It had existed in ancient Greece and Rome, and was currently sanctioned by France, Holland, and England. "In all ages, one half of mankind have been slaves. If the Southern states were let alone they would probably of themselves stop importation." General Charles Cotesworth Pinckney, his cousin, and a fellow Carolinian, delegate, and later two-time Federalist presidential candidate, argued that their constituents would never accept a government that outlawed slaves, and stated simply, "South Carolina and Georgia cannot do without slaves."[18]

In Philadelphia the big-versus-little-states issue was compromised and essentially resolved, unlike the issue of slavery, which was compromised but not resolved. Had the delegates really tried to end slavery, the Union probably would have never begun. Slavery was that central and critical to one section of the country's economy, and that divisive in the United-States-to-be of 1787. The slavery issue did not go away. It was submerged and pushed underground in Philadelphia, only to constantly reemerge and eventually divide the Union in the Civil War nearly three-quarters of a century later.

On September 17, 1787, the Philadelphia Convention adopted the Constitution of the United States of America. Thirty-nine delegates voted for it, and three voted against it. The ratification process began immediately. Indeed, in Pennsylvania it began that very afternoon. Ratification required three-quarters of the states to approve, which occurred when New Hampshire became the ninth to ratify on June 21, 1788. Prior to New Hampshire came approval by Delaware, Pennsylvania, New Jersey, Georgia, Connecticut, Massachusetts, Maryland, and South Carolina. Five more states quickly followed suit: Virginia, New York, North Carolina, and Rhode Island, along with the new fourteenth state of Vermont, which ratified it on January 10, 1791.

The word "slavery" never explicitly appeared in the Constitution of the United States until the Thirteenth Amendment. Nevertheless, the Constitution explicitly protected the institution of slavery in five clauses: Article I, Section Two, the three-fifths clause; Article I, Section Nine, the capitation tax clause limiting the taxes on slaves to ten dollars a head; Article I, Section Nine, allowing the slave trade to continue until 1808; Article V, giving added protection to the slave trade by prohibiting any amendment of the migration and importation clause before 1808; and Article IV, Section Two, which provided for the return of fugitive slave labor.

Additionally, the "equal" representation of the states in the Senate was later enhanced by maintaining an equal number of slave and free states—which inhibited any antislavery legislation. For example, the balance of power in the Senate was protected after the Missouri Compromise of 1820—when there were twelve slave and twelve free states—by admitting to the Union three slave and three free states over the next thirty years.

Finally, the requirement that two-thirds of both houses and three-quarters of the states assent to any constitutional amendment guaranteed that the South could always block any proposed antislavery amendments. "William Lloyd Garrison, America's most celebrated abolitionist, believed the Constitution's many compromises over slavery created 'a covenant with death' and 'an agreement with Hell.'"[19]

"Major Supreme Court cases involving slavery arose over five areas where slavery came under federal jurisdiction: (1) the African slave trade; (2) interstate commerce and slaves; (3) the return of fugitive slaves; (4) slavery in the federal territories; and (5) the interstate transit or sojourn of slaves through or in free states."[20]

ANTEBELLUM SLAVERY (1800–1861): FROM FOUNDING TO FIGHTING

Growth—population, territorial, and economic—characterized the United States in the early 1800s. Most Americans saw this as "progress." The issue of slavery, however, continued to plague the country. How could a nation founded on "God-given," "natural" and "inalienable rights," "equality," and "liberty" perpetuate slavery?

In broad terms an often self-righteous North, increasingly developed, industrial, and not economically dependent on slavery, began to hound the less developed, rural, and agrarian South, which had become totally dependent on the institution of slavery for its economic livelihood and survival. Compromised at the nation's founding, slavery only escalated the contradictions, tensions, and divisions in American society during the first six decades of the nineteenth century.

Eli Whitney's invention of the cotton gin in 1793 would eventually revolutionize southern commercial agriculture and is probably the most significant milestone in turning the *fact of slavery* into its *peculiar institutionalized form*—with ramifications for every facet of southern life.

The same year that Whitney invented the cotton gin, Congress passed the Fugitive Slave Act, which made it a federal crime to harbor an escaped slave. In 1797 Congress refused to accept the first recorded antislavery petition seeking redress against a North Carolina law that required slaves, although freed by their Quaker masters, to be returned to their former slave masters in North Carolina. In 1801 Congress voted eighty-five to one to reject a petition of "free blacks in Philadelphia to gradually end slavery in the United States."[21]

In 1794 Richard Allen was offended by segregation in his northern church—blacks were required to sit in the balcony—and founded the African American–based Bethel Church. The failure of whites to accept blacks as equals in their institutions led blacks to create their own institutions. Twenty-two years later, in 1816, Allen organized the African Methodist Episcopal Church. Just five years later, James Varick became the first bishop of the newly formed African Methodist Episcopal Zion Church.

By now, too, slave uprisings were increasingly a part of the American landscape. This especially frightened slaveholding southerners. In Louisiana in 1795, fifty blacks were killed or executed after a slave revolt. In 1800 Gabriel Prosser, a Virginia slave insurrectionist, plotted to lead thousands of slaves to attack the state capitol in Richmond. Prosser's plan failed and he, along with fifteen of his fellow rebels, was arrested, tried, and hanged. A precursor to John Brown, George Boxley, a white man, led a slave rebellion in Virginia in 1816. Denmark Vesey planned one of the most elaborate slave revolts in Charleston, South Carolina, in 1822. It too failed and he, along with thirty-six of his cohorts, was hanged. Additionally, 130 blacks and four whites were arrested. Following Vesey's failed plot, all of the slave states adopted more repressive laws.

In what may be the most widely known slave rebellion, Nat Turner, in 1831, led a violent slave revolt in Southampton County, Virginia. This uprising killed sixty whites and sent fear and panic throughout the South. Turner was captured later that year on October 30 and, just twelve days later, was hanged by the neck in Jerusalem, Virginia.

While oppressed slaves sometimes rebelled, some free blacks were trying to assess and build up the African American community. For conservatives who argue now that the African American community ought to stop being so dependent on others, especially the government, and spend more time developing itself internally, the answer is, "We always do and we always have!" The first National Negro Convention met in Philadelphia's Bethel Church on September 20, 1830, in a four-day conference for the purpose of improving the social status of blacks in America.

The first Annual Convention of the People of Color met in Philadelphia a year later, where delegates from five states resolved "to study black conditions, explore settlement possibilities in Canada, and raise money for an industrial college in New Haven."[22] Most African Americans also opposed the American Colonization Society—which advocated sending blacks back to Africa—and recommended that the convention meet annually.

In 1843 Henry Highland Garnet, Samuel R. Ward, and Charles Ray attended the Liberty Party Convention in Buffalo, New York, becoming the first blacks to participate in a national political convention.

However, lifting oneself by one's own bootstraps wasn't easy because most of the laws, the vast majority of the highest political leadership, and almost all of the religious community, even in the North, were actively aligned and organized against such uplift.

Laws were often a hindrance to African Americans lifting themselves by their own bootstraps. In 1816 the state of Louisiana enacted a law prohibiting "slaves from testifying against whites and free blacks, except in cases involving slave uprisings."[23] Mississippi enacted a law in 1823 that prohibited teaching blacks to read or write, and prohibited all blacks from meeting in groups larger than five. An 1834 South Carolina law made it illegal to teach black children, slave or free. In 1835 North Carolina outlawed whites from teaching free blacks. In 1839 the U.S. State Department rejected "a black man's application for a passport on the grounds that blacks are not citizens."[24] In 1841 a South Carolina law forbade "white and black mill hands from looking out of the same window. Whites and blacks in Atlanta were required to swear on different Bibles in court."[25] And in Virginia in 1848, "Postmasters were forced to inform police of the arrival of pro-abolition literature and to turn it over to authorities for burning."[26]

Eighty-five-year-old Benjamin Franklin, in what was probably his last public act, signed and transmitted a Pennsylvania Abolitionist Society petition in early 1790 urging Congress to "step to the very verge of the power vested in you for discouraging every species of traffic in the persons of our fellow men."[27] But he stood almost alone in his antislavery beliefs. While often *morally* opposed to the institution, five of the first seven American presidents were slave owners. And politically they all practiced the "southern strategy"—giving sway and deference to southern leaders by compromising on the slavery question—which made them virtual co-conspirators with the slave owners and the slave states to oppress blacks.

Our first president, General George Washington (1789–1797), showed the true grit of his military background, strength, and leadership ability by remaining officially "neutral" on the question of slavery. "While southerners shook the House and Senate with predictions of 'tumults, seditions, and insurrections,' Washington kept his own council. 'I was not inclined to express my sentiments on the merits of the question,' he explained after a Quaker called to discuss 'the morality—injustice—and impolicy of keeping these people in a state of slavery.'"

From the first person in our highest office came a first and an enduring southern strategy that elevated expedience—for the nation's sake—over morality. President Washington, and those who followed him, did not so much advocate slavery as simply protect it. All were merely men of their time and, like Washington, believed that slavery was wrong. They usually stood and watched in silence, always in the name of order and stability, even as the institution slowly corrupted the nation and eventually split it apart.

Like Virginia Federalist Party President George Washington, the nation's second president, Federalist John Adams (1797–1801) of Massachusetts, remained mostly silent on the subject of slavery. Toward the end of his presidency Adams said he would "'always be ready to cooperate' with the opponents of slavery 'as far as my means and opportunities can reasonably be expected to extend.' No opportunities arose; no means extended. Thirteen years later he warned against abolition while holding that his soul remained anti-slavery."[28]

Despite writing the towering words of freedom and equality in the Declaration of Independence, Virginian Thomas Jefferson's eight years in the White House, 1801–1809, did nothing to disturb the institution of slavery. Additionally, historian Winthrop Jordan observed that Jefferson's *Notes on the State of Virginia* constituted the most "extreme formulation of anti-Negro *thought* offered by any American in the 30 years after the Revolution."[29] Jefferson may have said that God created all men equal, but the science in his *Notes* "proved" blacks inferior to whites. Because of his lofty political position, President Jefferson's unscientific and racially prejudiced words aided and abetted the racist myths that gripped his times and have been transmitted to our own time. Jefferson, a Democratic-Republican and ideological founder of the Democratic Party, died in 1826 having stipulated in his will that only five of his slaves should go free; the rest were to be bequeathed to his heirs.

Democratic-Republican James Madison (1809–1817) of Virginia railed against the three-fifths compromise in Philadelphia on the slavery question in *The Federalist* No. 54, but as president he was mostly silent. In his second message to the Congress, he abided by the rules and southern strategy of his day by condemning the slave trade—which was now constitutionally and legally prohibited—but said nothing about condemning the *institution of slavery itself.*

President James Monroe (1817–1825), also a Democratic-Republican from Virginia, was clear on the slavery question. He preferred "asylum"—his word for colonization, or sending the slaves back to Africa or elsewhere—and supported the organization of the American Colonization Society during his first year as president. He knew the dangers that American slavery could bring—he was governor of Virginia during Gabriel Prosser's slave uprising in 1800. As president, he mainly sat on the sidelines while Henry Clay of Kentucky worked out the Missouri Compromise of 1820.

As religious and political liberals asserted themselves, and the abolitionist movement grew, it began to polarize the country, North and South, over the question of slavery. But the nation continued to compromise the issue. When the country expanded through the purchase of the Louisiana Territory from the French in 1803, it wasn't long before Congress entered into the Missouri Compromise of 1820, which split the country at the latitude of 36°30', allowing slavery in Missouri alone above this Mason-Dixon line but prohibiting it everywhere else below the line.

Maine came into the Union as a free state in 1820 and Missouri as a slave state in 1821, which balanced the national scales at twelve slave and twelve free states. Southerners, joined in Philadelphia by small-state delegates at the writing of the Constitution, had organized a balance of power—with two senators from each state and three-quarters of the states needed for new amendments—so that their institution of slavery would not easily be disturbed or overthrown. To ensure that these scales of injustice and this delicate national balance of power did not tip and force an end to compromising on the slavery issue, new states entered the Union during the next several decades the same way animals entered Noah's Ark, two by two, one free and one slave.

John Quincy Adams (1825–1829) of Massachusetts, another Democratic-Republican, is best known as an abolitionist for defending and winning the case of Joseph Cinque and his followers in the famous *Amistad* trial before the Supreme Court. But that occurred in 1838, *after* he left the presidency and was serving as a Massachusetts congressman. While president, his southern strategy—the ongoing compromise with the South—led him to believe that "slavery in a moral sense is an evil, but as connected with commerce it has its uses,"[30] and it didn't stop him from advocating a "westward ho" expansionist policy of taking Indian land and exterminating Indian people.

As the worldwide demand for cotton rose and the southern economy boomed, the 1830s and 1840s saw a transition occur with regard to slavery. With the moral persuasion and agitation of northern abolitionists growing and increasingly gaining various degrees of political support among both northern Whigs and Democrats, the political ideologists in the South were increasingly moving away from their historic negative defense of slavery and adopting a new offensive strategy—a positive defense of slavery. These apologists increasingly argued that slavery was a positive good for black and white, slave and free alike.

The process of engraving into law the practice and customs of the peculiar institution of slavery, complemented by an aggressive and "positive" ideological advocacy of white racial superiority and black racial inferiority, and accompanied by the solidification of the politics of southern conservatism—individuality, voluntarism, fiscal conservatism, less government, states' rights, and local control—only escalated the sectional tensions North and South as the country marched, inevitably it seemed, toward a head-on confrontation over slavery.

Religion in the South was also a major force of oppression rather than liberation. The personalistic and pietistic religion practiced there did not threaten the legal, economic, and institutional structures of slavery. Those trying to pull themselves up by their bootstraps thus also faced the opposition of religion. It was during the 1820s and 1830s that the Second Great Awakening of Protestantism took place. Evangelicals, primarily in the North but a few in the South as well, preached both a personal and a collective Gospel that called individuals and groups to accountability for their sins, and sought change. Slavery was a sin, these evangelicals said, but sinners could be "born again" and become partners with God to change their individual attitudes as well as the social structures that propped up the institution of slavery.

Not only was this kind of liberating theology and religion the antithesis of the Calvinist doctrine of predestination so deeply rooted in southern religion, but it was also a threat to the southern social order and way of life—which was becoming increasingly conservative as it defended the institution of slavery. In the early days, religious conservatism and social intolerance had been a dominant feature of the rigid Calvinists and Puritans of the North, not representative of the liberal Deists of the South. The political statesmen in the early days of the South generally had been liberals. Indeed, they had produced much of America's revolutionary thought, most of its enlightenment thinking with regard to equal rights—often questioning the morality of slavery, even while practicing it—and argued for the strict separation of church and state.

The South became conservative as slavery grew into the peculiar institution. The South had as its primary defenders the 75 percent of southern state legislators who were slaveholders. They were, therefore, self-interested in making laws to protect their economic investment. Gradually, with the help of legislation, the South's slaveholding political elite converted the region into a conservative and reactionary slave society, not just a society where some people were slaves.

In this conservative social climate, almost every dimension and aspect of southern life was tied to defending the institution of slavery—the economy, religion, education, women, literature, social mores and customs, virtually everything. Thus, while the North was dismantling legal slavery, adopting the liberal economics of "free labor," and being influenced by the public education and antislavery reform movements, the South was moving in exactly the opposite direction. As a result, both southerners and northerners soon came to see slavery and conservatism as inextricably linked. "Challenged by reformers who would remake society, slavery was, its defenders insisted, the bedrock of the true social order."[31]

Even so, there was some southern opposition to slavery, especially in states of the upper South. Some thought colonization might be an answer, including the American Colonization Society, founded in 1816. In this movement to send freed blacks back to their "native country," between 1817 and 1867 about six thousand blacks were transported to Liberia, Africa, a country founded in 1821 by former slaves from the United States. However, most Americans, North and South, recognized that because of the number of people and the cost involved, colonization was not a practical or real solution. As the debate continued in the country, the institution of slavery became more entrenched throughout the South, and the religious, social, and political conservatism of the region became more pronounced.

All was not lost, however, because highly motivated religious reformers were not easily discouraged. The Second Great Awakening among evangelical Protestants, especially Baptists and Methodists, was transforming the North and moving South. Joined by a few political liberals, they were concerned with charitable and benevolent work, establishing Sunday schools and public schools, and establishing morally correct behavior through temperance or abstinence from alcohol.

While northern and southern religionists had much in common, they also had their differences. In the North, the spirit of human perfectibility undergirded northern reformers during the antebellum years. The belief that both the individual *and the society* could be changed for the better was largely absent in the South. Southern evangelicals, far more than their northern counterparts, stressed a personalistic and pietistic religion that had little or nothing to do with altering institutional arrangements. Given the oppressive nature of slavery, and the danger associated with challenging the institution, the few southern political, religious, and intellectual leaders who did resist had little room to operate. It was too dangerous to question such established human arrangements. Even the tamest of reforms in the South came to be seen as conspiracies that threatened time-tested traditions.

While the North was moving ahead with statewide public education in the 1800s, southern slaveholding legislators opposed public education. A formal education was not necessary to till the ground, to grow and harvest the crops—especially not for the slaves. It was this elite political leadership, linked to the legacy of slavery and conservatism, that put—and has kept—the South behind in terms of public education. "More radical reform movements—such as utopian socialism, trade unionism, feminism, pacifism, and of course abolitionism—movements that although never actively supported by the majority of northerners were important features of antebellum northern life, were almost totally absent from the South. Indeed, southern publicists routinely ridiculed such 'isms' as absurd curiosities that both typified the excesses of 'Yankee' culture and revealed the superiority of the conservative, slave-based southern order."[32] It was only after the Civil War, as a practical matter, that public education came to the South. Even then, however, it was never adequately organized or funded.

Because of the political conservatism that slavery wrought, there has always been a certain antidemocratic element to southern social and political life. Openly antidemocratic rhetoric was limited, however, because southern politicians still had to appeal to nonslaveholding whites for their vote. Thus, rather than openly attacking democracy, they more commonly negatively denounced fanatical reformism and positively appealed to conservatism, order, and tradition.

Change, any change, was always seen as a threat to slavery. Reform, any reform, was also always seen as a challenge to the South's peculiar institution. South Carolina's planter-statesman James H. Hammond bluntly declared, "I repudiate, as ridiculously absurd, that much lauded but nowhere accredited dogma of Mr. Jefferson, that all men are born equal." His fellow South Carolinian Henry W. Ravenel lauded the southern "spirit to conservatism," which he attributed to slavery. Ravenel also boasted that the South was "the conservator of law and order—the enemy of innovation and change—the breakwater which is to stay that furious tide of social and political heresies now setting towards us from the shores of the old world."[33]

The new ideas of freedom, change, education, innovation, human betterment, and perfection that had gripped the hearts and minds of northerners had no place in a conservative southern society dominated by the harsh reality of slavery. The human and religious freedom found in a northern anti-Calvinist, anti-Puritan, evangelical Protestantism that focused on individual salvation *and* social change could not be theologically, socially, or politically tolerated in a conservative slave society.

"'Believe us Sir, the fault is not in cities, nor yet in slavery, not in marriage, nor religion,' D. R. Hundley lectured would-be reformers; 'it is in man. . . . Although you were to abolish every institution under the sun, so long as the human race continues mortal and frail as at present there will be no lack of sin and shame, sorrow and suffering.'"[34]

The message was clear: It is useless for reformers to try to use religion to improve the human condition. That is against nature and the human predicament. Christianity can be pure and unadulterated when its only mission is to make every person a new creature in Christ Jesus. Christ's mission was not to abolish or reform institutions. Personal redemption alone, not combined with social justice, was the mission of Jesus.

In the 1830s and 1840s the issue of slavery moved ever more center stage and was so volatile that Congress debated whether it could even be discussed publicly. When a petition drive challenged Congress in 1836 to end slavery in the District of Columbia, Congress responded with a "gag rule" that lasted until 1844. The gag rule prohibited any discussion of slavery in Congress and questioned whether the Constitution's right of petition could include petitioning against human bondage. This rule angered so many Americans who were anxious to preserve their freedom of political expression that its overall effect was to add support to the abolitionist cause.

In 1828, just prior to the gag rule, Andrew Jackson of Tennessee organized the Democratic Party that we know today and ran for the presidency on its ticket using a "common man" theme—hence the proud celebration of Jefferson-Jackson Democratic dinners around the country. Jackson, however, was a conservative southern segregationist Democrat.

The scholar and author Kenneth O'Reilly suggests that President Andrew Jackson, Old Hickory, is probably the only president in American history who did not consider slavery a moral evil. The political movement that Jackson organized into the Democratic Party "sought to structure a political party with no greater goal than protecting slavery forever."[35] Jackson thought abolitionists were "'monsters' sent by moneyed masters to 'stir up amongst the South the horrors of servile war.' They intended to free the Negro and drive him North to drive down working-class wages"[36]—an attempt by Jackson to gain northern white working-class political support through an appeal to fear.

A northern Democrat from New York, Martin Van Buren (1837–1841), soon "went South," showing his support for the southern strategy by supporting the gag rule in Congress and by taking the pledge: "'I must go into the presidential chair the inflexible and uncompromising opponent of any attempt on the part of Congress to abolish slavery in the District of Columbia, against the wishes of the slave holding states; and also with a determination *equally* strong, to resist the slightest interference with the subject in the states'. . . . The first chief executive to use the word 'slavery' in an inaugural address, he promised to veto any bill concerning the institution that the South opposed and to make every abolitionist as a threat to the Union."[37]

After his first term, Democrats unanimously renominated Van Buren as their candidate and came up with a new campaign tool—a national party platform. However, Van Buren's vice president, Richard M. Johnson—a military man and alleged killer of Chief Tecumseh—was not renominated because it was known that he had several black mistresses. He had even taken "a leave of absence" from the vice presidency in 1839 over the issue, going to White Sulphur Springs, Virginia (West Virginia today), to manage a hotel instead of fulfilling his duties as vice president. "No vice-presidential nominee was chosen. In effect, though, Johnson was Van Buren's running mate."[38]

It made little difference, because Van Buren lost the 1840 election to William Henry Harrison, an Ohio resident but a transplanted Virginia aristocrat and the Whig Party's first presidential candidate. The Whig Party—an almost unexplainable mixture of national Democratic-Republicans, southern states' righters, abolitionists, protectionists, and free traders—was formally founded in December 1839 at a Harrisburg, Pennsylvania, convention at which Harrison was nominated for president. Henry Clay of Kentucky, the leader of the Whigs in Congress, led the presidential nominating list in a first unofficial ballot, but he lacked a majority and eventually lost the nomination to Harrison. Harrison, sixty-eight years old, delivered his 8,578-word inaugural address in the cold without a hat or a coat, caught pneumonia, and died a month into his term of office. Vice President John Tyler of Virginia became president.

A former Democrat who had broken with the Jacksonians—among other things over the issue of nullification—the aristocratic Tyler nevertheless sided with the southern slave owners and stood against almost everything the Whig Party officially stood for. Only in 1841 did he address the slavery issue, after nineteen slaves mutinied on the brig *Creole* on their way from Virginia to New Orleans. They made it to Nassau in the British Bahamas, gaining freedom for themselves and 116 other slaves on board. Tyler did his best to get them back—sending his secretary of state, Daniel Webster, to argue his case—but Webster failed to convince British authorities. The former slaves were granted asylum and freedom.[39]

Democrats regained presidential power when James K. Polk (1845–1849) from Tennessee, the sixth presidential slave owner, defeated the Whigs' Clay. Upon entering the White House his wife, Sarah, replaced the paid white servants with unpaid black slaves and turned the basement of the White House into slave quarters.

Polk himself was soon confronted with another of Thomas Jefferson's legacies—an American expansionist ideology. Through the 1803 Louisiana Purchase and other conquests, the U.S. had already added the slave states of Louisiana, Missouri, Arkansas, Florida, and Texas. Later defined by John L. O'Sullivan as "Manifest Destiny"—the belief that America had a God-given right, or destiny, to expand the country's borders from "sea to shining sea," but especially south and west—the country grew rapidly in those directions. But it was now time for the South to cash in on the spoils of war.

Southerners saw the war of conquest with Mexico as an opportunity for the expansion of slavery. Southern pride demanded it, and such pride should not be denied. Northerners saw the same possibility and demand negatively. In the conquest of Mexican territory (1846–1848), the South had furnished most of the soldiers. Now they were outraged at congressional attempts to shut them out of its benefits—to deny the South the right to expand slavery into the new territories. "'When the war-worn soldier returns to his home,' asked an Alabamian, 'is he to be told that he cannot carry his property [slaves] to the country won by his blood? No true Southron,' said scores of them, would submit to such 'social and sectional degradation. . . . Death is preferable to acknowledged inferiority.'"[40]

At the start of the war David Wilmot, a freshman Whig congressman from Pennsylvania, acting on behalf of northern Democrats who were tired of southern domination of the Democratic Party, on August 8, 1846, "rose during the debate on an appropriations bill for the Mexican War and proposed an amendment: 'that, as an express and fundamental condition of the acquisition of any territory from the Republic of Mexico . . . neither slavery nor involuntary servitude shall ever exist in any part of said territory.'"[41]

President Polk, when confronted with the politics of the Wilmot Proviso—which twice passed in a bipartisan House of *northern* Whigs and Democrats, and twice was defeated in the same bipartisan manner in the Senate by *southern* Whigs and Democrats—responded by applying the southern strategy. He called it "a 'mischievous and foolish' product of 'demagogues and ambitious politicians' bent on promoting 'their own prospects.'"[42]

Paranoid Democratic southerners—who feared that the Wilmot Proviso would add ten free states and end their stranglehold on congressional power—called the Wilmot Proviso unconstitutional. This was an interesting twist, since most southerners had signed on to the ordinance outlawing slavery in the Northwest Territories in 1787, and had supported this antislavery policy as it was reiterated in each new territory. They had also supported the Missouri Compromise of 1820, which had outlawed slavery north of the Mason-Dixon line following the Louisiana Purchase in 1803. But now, in 1847, South Carolina's Senator John C. Calhoun was arguing that the new territories of Mexico and California "were the 'common property' of sovereign states."[43]

The Wilmot Proviso not only joined together the lions of war in both parties, but also split the two parties into northern and southern factions. The presidential choice was made to avoid resolving the slavery question, postponing it yet again. But it would not be postponed much longer.

Ailing and aging, James K. Polk declined to run for a second term. His secretary of state, James Buchanan, sought the Democratic Party's nomination on a policy of extending westward the line below which slavery could exist—all the way to the Pacific Ocean. The Democrats rejected Buchanan in 1848 and instead nominated Senator Lewis Cass of Michigan. Cass campaigned for the nomination on a theme of "popular sovereignty"—let each new territory or state (it wasn't clear which) decide its own slavery policy. The idea won enough southern support to win him the nomination. While Cass's idea was not in the Democratic Platform, rejection of the Wilmot Proviso was. The popular sovereignty concept and policy would manifest itself in critical legislation and in the most famous American debates—the 1854 Kansas-Nebraska Act and the 1858 Lincoln-Douglas debates, respectively.

Democrats did something else for the first time. They established a Democratic National Committee and appointed a national chairman to coordinate the presidential campaign and handle party matters between conventions. The Democratic National Committee founded in 1848 is the same one that continues today. Even in 1998, the Democratic National Committee was still passing out literature heralding its 1848 foundation. The pamphlet said that the Democratic Party was founded "to carry out its cause." Its cause in 1848 was the perpetuation of slavery! In 1848, however, the Democrats were defeated by another southerner—this time a Whig from Louisiana, Zachary Taylor, hero of the Mexican War that most Whigs had opposed.

There was much turmoil in the land, and various other political conventions were held in 1848. The most important was the Free Soil or Liberty Party Convention in Buffalo, New York, and attended by abolitionists, free blacks, and members of the Democratic Party's "Barnburners" faction and the "Conscience Whigs," who were dissatisfied with both of their party's nominees over their proslavery stances. The Free Soil Platform pledged "no more slave states and no more slave territory,"[44] and vowed to "fight on, and fight ever" for "Free

Soil, Free Speech, Free Labor, and Free Men." Then "the delegates returned home to battle for the Lord."[45]

Hoping to realign American politics along the lines of free states and slave states, the Free Soilers made the slavery question unavoidable for Democrats and Whigs in the 1848 election. While the two major parties were forced to abandon their traditional strategy of ignoring the question, they instead adopted a strategy of blurring it—making the issue unclear. The nation's highest moral and political leaders were still unable or unwilling to approach the institution of slavery and try to deal with it on a higher plane.

Zachary Taylor, who became the seventh slave-owning president in 1849, was the first to try triangulation. Hoping to have it both ways, he positioned himself as a moderate. He criticized both the North and the South as extremists. In the end, however, moderation meant siding with the South and adopting the southern strategy. While politically he supported bringing into the Union two free states, "he tried to hide from public view his fifteen White House slaves who labored in the family's private quarters upstairs and slept in eight attic rooms."[46]

After the 1848 elections, a Whig controlled the White House; Democrats were in the majority in the Senate but held only a plurality in the House (112 Democrats to 105 Whigs). Twelve Free Soilers held the balance of power and would determine the Speaker—either Democrat Howell Cobb of Georgia or Whig Robert Winthrop of Massachusetts.

After three weeks and sixty-two ballots the House still had no Speaker. "If, by your legislation, you seek to drive us from the territories of California and New Mexico," thundered Robert Toombs of Georgia, "*I am for disunion.*" "We have calculated the value of the Union," warned Albert Gallatin Brown of Mississippi. "We asked you to give us our rights" in California; "if you refuse, I am for taking them by armed occupation." The South's liberty was at stake as much now as in 1776, for "it is clear," according to an Alabama congressman, "that the power to dictate what sort of property the State may allow a citizen to own and work—whether oxen, horses, or negroes . . . is alike despotic and tyrannical."[47] Fistfights between southerners and northerners broke out in the House. In the Senate it is reported that Jefferson Davis challenged an Illinois congressman to a duel. Mississippi's Senator Henry S. Foote drew a loaded revolver during a heated debate. In desperation the House finally adopted a special rule that allowed the Speaker to be elected by a plurality. Cobb was named Speaker on the sixty-third ballot. The mid-decade House session was off to an inauspicious start.

The new territories of California (soon to see the arrival of gold-rush forty-niners) and New Mexico were encouraged by President Taylor to draft state constitutions without slavery and to seek admission directly as states. Both territories were partly below the Mason-Dixon line that was to have perpetually protected slavery. If successful, however, these two new states would increase by four the number of free senators in a slave-state-controlled Senate.

Slave-state representatives in the Senate saw this as a threat to their "property rights"; accused President Taylor of being a closet abolitionist and a traitor to his race and class, as well as of achieving the Wilmot Proviso by other means; and threatened nullification in the form of secession. "'For the first time,' said Senator Jefferson Davis of Mississippi, 'we are about permanently to destroy the balance of power between the sections.'"[48] By admitting California and New Mexico as free states, Taylor also saw the opportunity to attract the Free Soilers in the Liberty Party to the Whig Party.

As the political discourse and sectional division reached a fever pitch, along came old reliable Senator Henry Clay from the border state of Kentucky to work out another compromise, which once more failed to deal with the underlying question of slavery but did again manage to keep the Union together. Clay's compromise was comprised of eight resolutions, the first six grouped in pairs in order to give each side, North and South, something. However, bending to the southern strategy again, the last two resolutions—denying Congress power over the slave trade between the states and a stronger Fugitive Slave Law—clearly tipped the scales in favor of the South.

On every issue but one, antebellum southerners stood for states' rights and a weak federal government. However, as northern abolitionists increasingly gave aid and comfort to slaves escaping North to freedom on the Underground Railroad, the one exception was the Fugitive Slave Law of 1850. This law gave the federal government more power than ever before.

After a seven-month debate in Congress, the various parts of the Compromise of 1850 passed Congress. However, after listening to July 4 speeches all day in the hot sun at an unfinished Washington Monument, and after eating raw vegetables, a monstrous bowl of cherries, and chilled buttermilk, President Taylor became ill and suddenly died five days later on July 9.

New Yorker Millard Fillmore assumed the presidency in 1850. Even though he posed no threat of a presidential veto, it still took another two months for the various pieces of the Compromise of 1850 to work their way through Congress for the new president's signature. There was something for everyone in the compromise. For those who opposed slavery, California would enter the Union as a free state, and the interstate slave trade would end in the District of Columbia. For slavery supporters, there was a tough new Fugitive Slave Law, while the slavery question in the new territories would be decided by applying the concept of popular sovereignty. No one was satisfied. The compromise turned out to be the opening round in a decade of crises that pulled the nation ever closer to war.

Following the Compromise of 1850 were the most famous debates in the history of Congress. They featured three tired and ailing old warriors of nearly three decades of increasingly tense battles over slavery. They were the "Big Three" or the "Immortal Trio"—Henry Clay, a border-state Whig from Kentucky; Daniel Webster, a northern free-state Whig from Massachusetts; and Democrat John C. Calhoun of South Carolina, a slave state. New political stars on the horizon also played key parts: Stephen A. Douglas, a Democrat from Illinois; William H. Seward, a former Whig governor of New York; Jefferson Davis, a Democrat from Mississippi; and one of two Free Soilers in the Senate, Salmon P. Chase of Ohio.

On March 4, 1850, Senator Calhoun had his farewell speech delivered by James Mason of Virginia because he was too weak to give it himself. Gaunt and wrapped in a flannel blanket, a dying Calhoun watched as his speech was read; as Civil War historian James McPherson said, his "prophecies of doom were reflected in the piercing eyes that stared from deep sockets within the shroud."[49] He warned that northern aggression had divided the nation with its discriminatory laws—he failed to mention that he had supported many of them—and that by attacking slavery, the North had split churches, political parties, and other organizations: the very forces that might be the only instrument that could keep the nation together.

Because the North had always been the aggressor, it must cease criticizing slavery, return fugitive slaves, give the South equal rights in the territories, and consent to a constitutional amendment "which will restore to the South, in substance, the power she possessed of protecting herself before the equilibrium between the two sections was destroyed." California was the test case. Admission of this free state would serve notice of a purpose to "destroy irretrievably the equilibrium between the two sections." In such circumstances southern states could not "remain in the Union consistently with their honor and safety."[50]

On March 7 the Whig Party's Daniel Webster disappointed his free state and formerly admiring abolitionists by coming out in favor of the Clay compromise in order to preserve the Union. It was time, Webster said, for northerners "to bury the passions of the past."[51] "The South, in my judgment, is right, and the North is Wrong."[52] While his speech helped pass the 1850 Compromise, it also cost him the Whig Party's presidential nomination two years later, because he could not even win the support of his own state's delegates.

Senator Seward's view of the situation was just the opposite of Calhoun's and Webster's. In a "Higher Law" speech on March 11, Seward spoke out against any compromise along the lines that Clay had outlined and condemned Calhoun's slavery as unjust, saying, "'There is a higher law than the Constitution,' the law of God in whose sight all persons are equal. The present crisis 'embraces the fearful issue whether the Union shall stand, and slavery, under the steady, peaceful action of moral, social, and political causes, be removed by gradual voluntary effort, and with compensation; or whether the Union shall be dissolved and civil war ensue, bringing on violent but complete and immediate emancipation.'"[53]

Clay's compromise legislation was actually defeated on July 31 even as he had warned in an earlier Senate floor speech: "All now is uproar, confusions and menace to the existence of the Union."[54] The seventy-three-year-old Clay left Washington to recuperate from exhaustion over his struggles and failed compromise attempts. In the end it was left to a five-foot-four-inch, hard-drinking, hardworking "Little Giant," Senator Stephen Douglas of Illinois, to organize the votes and assemble the various coalitions to get the compromise legislation through Congress piece by piece.

Each vote on the compromise, however, had been configured along *sectional*, not party, lines. It was becoming increasingly clear that the slavery question was splitting down the middle the two-party system of Whigs and Democrats as well. In fact, in the Capitol's old Senate chamber, at some point during this period of tension over slavery, senators began to sit, not left and right by party, but rather left and right by region. As the presiding officer sat in the president's chair looking out over the U.S. Senate, members representing the southern slave states sat on his right, and those representing the northern free states sat on his left.

Much of the country celebrated, thinking the Compromise of 1850 to be the last word on the slavery question. But the two political movements for and against slavery did not go away. There was a respite; the nation had dodged the slavery bullet again, but not for long.

It was in this general political climate that a self-educated and articulate escaped former slave named Frederick Douglass—whose original last name was Bailey—was invited to speak at an Independence Day celebration in Rochester, New York, on July 4, 1852. He said in his speech:

Fellow citizens, pardon me, allow me to ask, why am I called upon to speak here today? What have I, or those I represent, to do with your national independence? . . . I say it with a sad sense of the disparity between us. I am not included within the pale of this glorious anniversary? Your high independence only reveals the immeasurable distance between us. The blessings in which you, this day, rejoice are not enjoyed in common. The rich inheritance of justice, liberty, prosperity, and independence bequeathed by your fathers is shared by you, not by me. The sunlight that brought light and healing to you has brought stripes and death to me. This Fourth of July is yours, not mine. You may rejoice, I must mourn. . . .

O! had I the ability, and could I reach the nation's ear, I would today pour out a fiery stream of biting ridicule, blasting reproach, withering sarcasm, and stern rebuke. For it is not light that is needed, but fire; it is not the gentle shower, but thunder. We need the storm, the whirlwind, and the earthquake. The feeling of the nation must be quickened; the conscience of the nation must be roused; the propriety of the nation must be startled; the hypocrisy of the nation must be exposed; and its crimes against God and man must be proclaimed and denounced. What to the American slave, is your Fourth of July? I answer: a day that reveals to him, more than all other days in the year, the gross injustice and cruelty to which he is the constant victim. To him, your celebration is a sham; your boasted liberty, an unholy license; your national greatness, swelling vanity; your sounds of rejoicing are empty and heartless; your denunciation of tyrants, brass-fronted impudence; your shouts of liberty and equality, hollow mockery; your prayers and hymns, your sermons and thanksgivings, with all your religious parade and solemnity, are, to Him, more bombast, fraud, deception, impiety, and hypocrisy—a thin veil to cover up crimes which would disgrace a nation of savages.[55]

Slaveholders took their property to Utah where, in 1852, Governor Brigham Young and his state lawmakers quickly legalized slavery (the same year the Saints openly endorsed polygamy). A slave law was also enacted in New Mexico in 1859. According to the census in 1860, however, Utah had only twenty-nine slaves, and New Mexico none. The new state of California sent no radicals to Congress, so the South's concern about throwing the "balance of power" out of kilter was misplaced.

In 1852, President Fillmore's last year in office, a "book bomb" hit the country. A product of the religious Second Great Awakening and abolitionist movements, Harriet Beecher Stowe's *Uncle Tom's Cabin* shook the country's very foundation with anger and outrage in both the North and the South. The book sold more than three hundred thousand copies in its first year in the United States and three million worldwide; proportionate to population, this would be the equivalent of selling nearly twenty-five million copies today. Stowe came from a family of very well-known preachers—father, brother, and husband—and the book was aimed at pricking the conscience of the evangelical North with a depiction of the immorality of slavery. During the Civil War, President Lincoln once met her and greeted her by saying, "So you're the little woman who wrote the book that made this great war."[56]

Referring to a black person today as an "Uncle Tom" is considered offensive. The epithet summons an image of a foot-shuffling, handkerchief-head, race-betraying sellout. But this was neither the message Stowe intended nor the message that northern Protestant, middle-class, family-oriented evangelical Christian Americans received in 1852. While Stowe did hold certain negative perceptions of African Americans in common with the general population—that blacks were "feminine" and childlike people, less assertive and ambitious than whites—she portrayed these qualities as strengths. She depicted blacks as *morally superior.*

In *Drawn with the Sword*, James McPherson points out that for Stowe, "these African traits of childlike simplicity of affection, and facility of forgiveness exhibit the highest form of the peculiarly *Christian* life. For Stowe and many of her readers, Christian virtues were the highest virtues. The meek shall inherit the earth. A little child shall lead them. In the better world to come, the African traits would prove *superior* to those of the Anglo-Saxon. In what really counted for Stowe and the Christian culture of which she was a part, African Americans were a finer race than white Americans, just as women and children had a finer nature than men."

McPherson continues, "In Christian terms, Tom is by far the strongest character in the novel. Indeed, he is a Christ figure. Tom forgives his oppressors; so did Jesus. Tom turns the other cheek to blows; so did Jesus. Tom blesses those who curse him; so did Jesus. Tom prays for those who sin against them; so did Jesus. In Christian theology, Christ gave his life to save humankind; in Stowe's novel, Tom gives his life to save his people. . . . At the climax of the novel, when Legree literally beats Tom to death because he refuses to tell what he knows of Cassy and Emmy's hiding place, the parallel between Christ's crucifixion and Tom's death must be clear to all but the most obtuse reader."[57] Stowe was not writing to touch the mind, but to touch the heart and stir the soul of white northerners over the destruction that slavery was bringing to black families, and the resulting separation of mothers and children.

As volatile and impassioned opinions on the slavery issue poured forth, the two major parties held contentious conventions in 1852. Democrats selected northerner Franklin Pierce of New Hampshire on the forty-ninth ballot—"a Northern man with Southern Principles"[58]—as their party's standard-bearer. To balance the ticket even further, a southerner, Senator William King of Alabama, was added as vice president. Rejecting incumbent President Millard Fillmore, the Whigs took fifty-three ballots to nominate a northerner, General Winfield Scott of New Jersey. To balance their ticket, the Whigs also selected a southerner, Secretary of the Navy William Graham of North Carolina, as their vice presidential candidate, but it wasn't enough to win.

An uneasy peace hovered over the nation. Based on the popular sovereignty principle of the 1850 Compromise, Congress passed the Kansas-Nebraska Act in 1854. But rather than bringing calm, it provoked a mini war, both in Congress and on the plains of Kansas and Missouri.

Violence erupted on the Senate floor with the caning of Charles Sumner, and as pro- and antislavery forces rushed to Kansas to determine its fate, the territory became a battleground. Scores of settlers were killed in the sacking of Lawrence, the bloody revenge raid led by John Brown, and other bloody skirmishes. The territory became known as Bleeding Kansas. These events dramatically intensified the debate over slavery in the country as a whole.

As the crisis escalated, American presidential leadership seemed to get weaker. Democrat Franklin Pierce was handsome and personable, but deficient of any strong moral principles. A Jacksonian and Calhounian on the slavery question, Pierce appointed his friend, ally, and confidant from Mississippi, Jefferson Davis, as secretary of war. Pierce was considered by many to be a northern man with southern principles—such a person at the time was called a "doughface"—who acted against slavery on only two occasions. He first called the Fugitive Slave Act enforceable—if inhumane and immoral. But southerners reacted angrily to his words, which forced Pierce to claim that his remarks had been misinterpreted. His second act of courage came when he backed away from his own administration's policy of acquiring Cuba by any means necessary. The South had always coveted Cuba as a place where to expand its slave power.

Legislatively, Pierce pushed Congress to pass the Kansas-Nebraska Act—which it did in 1854. Following the dictates of the Clay Compromise of 1850, this "popular sovereignty" and "let the states decide" legislative strategy was designed to shove the slavery problem as far away from Washington as possible—out into the countryside. Shortly, the consequences of this strategy and legislation were to be felt.

Democrat James Buchanan of Pennsylvania was elected president after it had become clear that the concept of popular sovereignty as the way for Congress to deal with the slavery question had been an utter failure. Buchanan seemed oblivious, however, and urged the former Bleeding Kansas to be admitted to the Union as a slave state. Ultimately, Kansas came into the Union a free state.

The sectional tensions and hostility leading up to and surrounding the 1854 debate over the Kansas-Nebraska Act had split the Democratic Party North and South, and destroyed the national Whig Party forever. Southern Whigs would soon join the southern Democratic Party to form a solid Democratic South of slaveholders and slave states. Border-state Whiggery hung on for a few more years before it died.

Northern Whigs had hoped to pick up members from the Free Soil and other antislavery forces in the off-year elections of 1854. But the Whig Party's days were numbered. Given their limited political options, the antislavery forces chose to be a movement of principle against slavery rather than supporting any particular political party. As a result, the fall elections of 1856 were imbued with a new spirit of resistance and insistence as antislavery coalitions formed throughout the North. These new coalitions went by a variety of names, but the one that stuck was Republican. The term "Republican" was probably first adopted at an 1854 anti–Kansas-Nebraska Act rally at a church in Ripon, Wisconsin. A short time later, at a meeting of thirty congressmen in Washington on May 9, the name was formally adopted. The modern-day Ripon Society traces its Republican roots to this liberal antislavery Republican Party founding.

Attempting to identify their party with the revolutionary first principles of 1776—a republican (representative) form of government—a Republican Convention in Michigan resolved to be "against the schemes of aristocracy the most revolting and oppressive with which the earth was ever cursed, or man debased, we will co-operate and be known as Republicans."[59]

In nearby Illinois a young lawyer named Abraham Lincoln maintained his credentials in the Whig Party, but nevertheless joined with the antislavery forces in 1854 to campaign for Republican candidates. Positioning himself to run for the U.S. Senate in 1858, Lincoln engaged in two Chicago debates with incumbent Senator Stephen Douglas in October 1856. Even then Lincoln was testing the overall theme that would mark future debates and his presidency: "If the president and the Congress (the federal government) could fence slavery in with the vote, it could thereby stop its westward expansion, and the nation could gradually end it." Lincoln considered the approach of leaving the slavery question to nature, chance, local autonomy, and volunteerism a "lullaby" strategy not grounded in reality. When it was clear that the Whig Party was dead and could not be revived, Lincoln joined the Republican Party in early 1856.

After serving one term in Congress, 1847–1849, as a Whig, Abraham Lincoln had gone into private law practice and distanced himself from politics. But the Kansas-Nebraska Act of 1854, introduced by Senator Stephen A. Douglas of Illinois, had drawn him back, as well as creating a Republican Party dedicated to prohibiting the expansion of slavery westward. Douglas supported westward expansion and the building of a transcontinental railroad, but he knew that in a heterogeneous nation neither goal could be achieved in the middle of a divisive western territorial controversy over slavery. Douglas introduced the Kansas-Nebraska Act to resolve this dilemma legislatively by applying the already failed 1848 Democratic presidential nominee Senator Lewis Cass of Michigan's principle of popular sovereignty—let every new territory decide for itself whether the state would come into the Union slave or free. But his legislation also repealed the Missouri Compromise of 1820, which, with the exception of Missouri, had barred slavery's expansion above the Mason-Dixon line.

After the 1854 elections, the upstart Republicans captured a House plurality and nominated Nathaniel P. Banks to be Speaker. After two months of raucous debate and balloting, Banks was still 118 votes short. This struggle, however, helped bring together and crystallize Banks's antislavery supporters *as Republicans*. When on February 2, 1856, the House, nearing exhaustion, changed its rules to permit a mere plurality to prevail, Banks became the Speaker of the House on the 133rd ballot with 103 votes. This moment, more than any other, marked the birth of the Republican Party.

The newly formed party's first national convention was held in Philadelphia in June 1856 and reflected the North–South split: Delegates came only from northern and four border states. Republicans made no effort to get even one southern vote. Even so, Democrat James Buchanan barely won the presidency. Buchanan, winning all of the southern states, defeated Republican candidate James Fremont of California, who won all but five of the northern states.

Antislavery agitation was gaining political strength in the North and drawing ever stronger reaction in the South. The year 1857 was to be pivotal for both North and South as the Supreme Court stepped front and center.

Born in Virginia, the slave Dred Scott moved with his master to St. Louis, Missouri. His owner, Dr. John Emerson, an army physician, had at one point in his travels taken his slave to the free states of Illinois and Wisconsin. On one visit to Wisconsin, Scott married Harriet Robinson, and her ownership was transferred to Dr. Emerson. Emerson died in 1843, and on April 6, 1846, Dred and Harriet Scott sued his wife Irene Emerson for their freedom. The case was based on a Missouri law that granted freedom to a slave who formerly lived in a free state, but returned to Missouri. Based on *Rachael v. Walker* (1837), the law stated, "Once free, always free." The Scotts won in the circuit court of St. Louis, but the verdict was overturned by the Missouri Supreme Court in 1852. The case went to the federal court, where, given the tenor of the times, it became a national cause célèbre of the antislavery forces, and ended up in the Supreme Court.

In 1852 the Missouri Supreme Court, acting as partisans and defiant against outside antislavery sentiment, overturned precedent and in controversial proslavery rhetoric reversed the "once free, always free" principle in *Rachael*. To test whether a state court could defy a Supreme Court precedent, Scott's lawyers filed a new federal lawsuit, *Dred Scott v. John F. A. Sandford*. Sanford, Mrs. Emerson's brother—through a clerical error his name was misspelled in the court records—was looking after his sister's business affairs. Sanford's attorneys, however, brought other issues into the case, such as whether a black person was a U.S. citizen and even had the right to bring a suit in federal court, and whether the 1820 Missouri Compromise outlawing slavery above the Mason-Dixon line was constitutional, because slaves were private property and protected by the Constitution. Thus the issue was transformed from whether Missouri could make Dred Scott a slave again to whether he had ever been free at all. So controversial was the case that the Court undertook the unusual procedure of hearing oral arguments twice, once in February and again in December 1856.

At first the Court seemed inclined to essentially avoid the issue by affirming that Missouri had the right to interpret its own state law. Justice Samuel Nelson was assigned to write such an opinion. Again, however, historical forces of the time impacted the Court. Five justices, all from southern slave states, accepted a proposal by Justice James M. Wayne of Georgia to finally resolve in the highest federal court of the land what the political forces in Congress had been unable to settle—the fundamental question of slavery. Justice Roger B. Taney was assigned to write the opinion.

Delivered on March 6, 1857, the infamous seven-to-two *Dred Scott* decision—Justices Curtis and McLean dissented—held that Scott was still a slave; the case was thus dismissed, because blacks were not citizens of the United States and had no standing in federal court. Moreover, the high court held that Scott had never been free; that Congress could not abolish slavery in the territories, so the Missouri Compromise of 1820 was unconstitutional and slavery was legal *everywhere* in the United States; that slaves were property protected by the Constitution; and, finally, that the southern principle of states' rights enjoyed primacy. If the Missouri Supreme Court held that Dred Scott was a slave, he was a slave.

Chief Justice Taney's decision was highly southern and polemical. *Dred Scott* expert and historian Don Fehrenbacher argues that Taney's apparent purpose was to negate U.S. citizenship rights for blacks. Taney wrote with the sweeping purpose of launching a militant counterattack against the antislavery movement. If he could separate the Negro race absolutely from federal constitutional protection, southern stability would be restored. To achieve that purpose, however, Taney perverted history, the law, and logic in a flagrant defilement of the facts. The 1857 *Dred Scott* decision is still considered by many the worst Supreme Court decision ever rendered.

The *Dred Scott* decision was issued on March 6, 1857. A Georgia newspaper argued that it "covers every question regarding slavery and settles it in favor of the South. . . . The decision also seemed to undermine Douglas's doctrine of popular sovereignty, for if Congress lacked the power to prohibit slavery in a territory, how could a legislature created by Congress do so? . . . Slavery, announced President Buchanan, henceforth existed in all the territories, including Kansas, 'by virtue of the Constitution.'"[60]

In early 1858 President Buchanan was in agreement with a Kansas Constitution drafted by a prosouthern convention that had never submitted it for ratification to Kansans. But this was a violation of Douglas's principle of popular sovereignty, and he voted against it in Congress. Known as the Lecompton Constitution, it endeared Douglas to northern Democrats but sent a signal to southern Democrats that he could not be trusted to be their ally on the slavery question. His vote cost him a unified Democratic Party presidential nomination in 1860. Thus, by 1858, the year of the Lincoln-Douglas debates, the political climate in the country had been racheted up to a fever pitch over the slavery controversy. As a result of a downturn in the economy in 1857, there were other important issues in the campaign, such as tariffs, but the only issue in the Lincoln-Douglas debates was slavery.

Lincoln challenged Douglas to a series of debates, and they agreed to seven. Part of Lincoln's purpose was to undermine the credibility that Douglas had gained in the North by voting against the Lecompton Constitution. While Lincoln was no abolitionist, he revered the Union and the Constitution, and over a protracted period of time had developed two arguments that would ultimately propel him to the presidency and guide him through the war: first, that slavery was morally wrong; and second, that the way to eventually end this moral wrong was to freeze it in place and stop its further expansion westward. In that manner, it could gradually be ended politically.

Upon accepting his party's nomination for Douglas's Senate seat in June 1858, Lincoln laid out their differences in his "House Divided" speech. He began:

> Mr. President and Gentlemen of the Convention.
>
> If we could first know *where* we are, and *whither* we are tending, we could then better judge *what* to do, and *how* to do it.
>
> We are now far into the *fifth* year, since a policy was initiated, with the *avowed* object, and *confident* promise, of putting an end to slavery agitation.
>
> Under the operation of that policy, that agitation has not only, not ceased, but has *constantly augmented.*
>
> In *my* opinion, it *will* not cease, until a *crisis* shall have been reached, and passed.
>
> "A house divided against itself cannot stand." [Lincoln here is quoting Jesus.]
>
> I believe this government cannot endure, permanently half *slave* and half *free.*
>
> I do not expect the Union to be *dissolved*—I do not expect the house to *fall*—but I do expect it will cease to be divided.
>
> It will become *all* one thing, or *all* the other.
>
> Either the *opponents* of slavery, will arrest the further spread of it, and place it where the public mind shall rest in the belief that it is in course of ultimate extinction; or its *advocates* will push it forward, till it shall become alike lawful in *all* the States, old as well as *new*—*North* as well as *South.*[61]

Still insistent on applying his principle of popular sovereignty, Douglas argued in the debates that he "did not care" whether slavery was voted up or down in the new territories. Lincoln responded to this "care not" policy with a moral argument: "Everything that emanates from [Douglas] or his coadjutors, carefully excludes the thought that there is anything wrong with slavery. . . . If you do admit that it is wrong, Judge Douglas can't logically say that he doesn't care whether a wrong is voted up or down."[62]

While Lincoln believed in local autonomy for most things, he thought slavery was of a different order, one that demanded a national policy and solution instead of a series of local ones. (I view the issues of employment, health care, education, housing, women's rights, the environment, taxes, and the right to vote in the same light. That is why I propose that local entities, municipalities, counties, and states operate within the bounds of national guidelines to solve them—that is, within the context of federal constitutional amendments.) At the Freeport debate Lincoln tried to present Douglas with a predicament by putting him in the crosshairs between the "nationalization" of slavery inherent in *Dred Scott* and the "localization" inherent in his principle of popular sovereignty. Douglas continued to insist that *Dred Scott* and popular sovereignty could live comfortably alongside each other.

Now, however, the southern states' righters were upset at Douglas for not taking the side of *Dred Scott.* "Abandoning the principle of local autonomy that had been one of the bulwarks of the defense of slavery, Southern political leaders demanded that Congress establish and protect the peculiar institution in every territory. It was a logical consequence of the *Dred Scott* decision, they insisted, that if a territory failed to protect slave property Congress had an obligation to do so."[63]

Douglas couldn't win for losing, and lose is what he and both sections of the Democratic Party did. In 1860 southern Democrats refused to support him for president and instead put John C. Breckenridge of Kentucky on their ticket, even as northern Democrats supported Douglas. This sectional split provided the political opening for Lincoln's election.

With all of this background of racial history and conflict, and with the firewood ready to be set aflame in the fireplace of the Union, all that was needed now was for someone to come along and pour kerosene on the logs and strike a match. This pyromaniac's job fell to none other than that zealous religious antislavery crusader, John Brown.

A group of prominent northerners who had supported Brown's work in Kansas and became known as the Secret Six—Gerrit Smith, Thomas Wentworth Higginson, Theodore Parker, Samuel Gridley Howe, George L. Sterns, and Franklin B. Sanborn—decided to financially, intellectually, morally, and politically back John Brown's effort toward violent revolution.

In May 1858 John Brown convened a group of thirty-four blacks and eleven whites in Chatham, Canada, to plot the violent overthrow of American slavery. He was fond of quoting Hebrews 9:22: "Without shedding of blood there is no remission of sin." His plan was to raid the munitions factory in Harpers Ferry, Virginia, and pass out guns and ammunition to Virginia's slaves, who would fight for their freedom. Brown tried to talk Frederick Douglass into accompanying him, but Douglass refused. Before the Fugitive Slave Law he had been a pacifist and staunch advocate of nonviolence. After the act he advocated "forcible resistance." Still, he saw Brown's plan as an unworkable suicide mission.

When Brown finally moved, on October 18, 1859, he launched the raid with twenty-two in his guerrilla force—five black and seventeen white men, including three of his sons. The raid was launched with no previous notice to the slaves he desired to free. His band was without rations, had scouted no escape routes, and apparently had no plan for what to do once they captured the armory at Harpers Ferry. It was almost as if Brown instinctively knew that his failure and martyrdom would do more to set the sparks of rebellion ablaze and achieve his ultimate goal of violently confronting slavery than even the most successful raid he could imagine. In any case, that is exactly what happened.

John Brown's raid tabbed him as the meteor—the star, asteroid, nebula, nova—that launched the American Civil War.

RACE IS CENTRAL—
THE GREAT QUAKE (1861–1865)

Treason against the United States, shall consist only in levying war against them, or in adhering to their enemies, giving them aid and comfort.

—U.S. Constitution, Article III, Section Three

South Carolina is too small for a republic, but too large for an insane asylum.

—James L. Petrigru to Benjamin F. Perry
after Lincoln's election, but before the
shelling of Fort Sumter, December 8, 1860[1]

When the American Civil War erupted, both North and South defended their cause as morally just, legally right, and constitutionally sound. Northerners and southerners saw themselves as the true Americans, following in the tradition and footsteps of the Founding Fathers.

North and South used the Constitution as the source of their moral and legal authority for conducting a war against the other. Both sides saw themselves as standing in the tradition of the American Revolution.

Each side contended that it was fighting for freedom and liberty—though certain facts contradicted the beliefs of both. The South said it was fighting to preserve freedom, while owning slaves. The North said it was fighting for liberty, while not initially fighting to grant liberty to the slaves. President Abraham Lincoln's address to the Sanitary Fair in Baltimore on April 18, 1864, summed up the quandary:

We all declare for liberty; but in using the same word we do not all mean the same thing. With some the word liberty may mean for each man to do as he pleases with himself, and the product of his labor; while with others, the same word may mean for some men to do as they please with other men, and the product of other men's labor. Here are two, not only different, but incompatible things, called by the same name—liberty. And it follows that each of the things is, by the respective parties, called by two different and incompatible names—liberty and tyranny.

The shepherd drives the wolf from the sheep's throat, for which the sheep thanks the shepherd as a liberator, while the wolf denounces him for the same act as the destroyer of liberty, especially as the sheep was a black one. Plainly the sheep and the wolf are not agreed upon a definition of the word liberty; and precisely the same difference prevails to-day among us human creatures, even in the North, and all profess to love liberty.[2]

The North, which had only a small population of African Americans and was not dependent on slave labor to sustain its economy, felt morally superior to the South. It did not, however, hesitate to profit handsomely from the African slave trade, nor shrink from gain by processing and selling products produced from free southern slave labor. But for northerners, industrial capitalism's free-labor economic system was superior to the South's agrarian slave-labor economic system.

The South's economy was almost totally dependent on slave labor, and slaveholders began to rationalize their system as more natural and superior to the North's, because the North's free-labor system was a more impersonal and insidious form of slavery.

To a "free white southern land holder"—a Jeffersonian property owner—wage labor was no different from and just as bad as slave labor, because both made men dependent on others and stripped them of their "liberty." And devoid of such liberty, men could not form a representative government. This "independence" based on the "ownership of property" was the essence of Jefferson's philosophy of republicanism. From the southern viewpoint, then, whites in the North were actually worse off than southern blacks, because wage labor was actually lowering the state of white humanity. On the other hand, because of the "inherent inferiority" of the African, slave labor was actually raising the Negro slave to a higher level.

In this Jeffersonian tradition of farmers and artisans who understood freedom as personal ownership of the means of production and self-sufficiency—resulting in personal independence—the South saw the owners of northern industry as the more impersonal and sinister slave masters, and their northern industrial employees as bigger "slaves" than southern rural ones. The Constitution verified and reinforced this understanding of Jeffersonian representative democracy by limiting the vote to white male property owners. All those whom the Constitution had made dependent in the original economic deal—white male non–property owners, industrial workers, women, and slaves—could not provide the basis of a polity of republican freemen.

In 1860, just prior to the start of the Civil War, the population of the United States was thirty-two million. Twenty-three million people lived in the northern states, while only nine million lived in the South, including four million slaves. A mere 258,000 African Americans lived in the North.

The first half of the nineteenth century was, as I have noted, characterized by rapid growth and dramatic change—growth in terms of population, expansion of territory, and economic productivity. Such growth brought with it dramatic social changes as well. A transportation revolution took place as "modern" and easily traveled roads were built. A water canal system (including the Erie Canal) was dredged that greatly facilitated commerce in the Northeast, and the harnessing of steam power propelled steamships up and down the high seas and inland rivers. A railroad system—the Iron Horse—further revolutionized travel and commerce.

Chicago was becoming more than a cow town: It was emerging as a leading industrial and financial center in the West. By 1860 fifteen railroad lines were based in Chicago, while Cincinnati became the meatpacking capital of the United States.

The invention of the telegraph greatly facilitated communication and transformed the newspaper business. As a result, the Associated Press was founded in 1848, the result of several major newspapers pooling their resources to more efficiently gather and report to more people a broader base of news. The Second Great Awakening religious revival also characterized this period, producing temperance and abolitionist movements.

America was being transformed from a rural, self-sufficient, and craft-oriented society that produced for the family and the immediate community to an urban, industrial, specialized, and interdependent society that produced for commercial profit to a broader community called "the market." Entrepreneurs were creating new inventions and new forms of organization that made mass production more cost efficient and profitable for the owners, but also made a larger variety of goods and services available and affordable to ever more consumers.

This new form of industrial mass production became known as the American system of manufactures, because it mass-produced goods within tolerances that allowed for interchangeable parts. Not unlike the cutting-edge technology of today, this new system first became practiced and useful to the military in the manufacture of small arms. The Springfield rifle was built in a munitions plant in Springfield, Massachusetts; Samuel Colt built military pistols in similar plants in Connecticut and London, England. It was such a munitions plant that John Brown attacked at Harpers Ferry.

In the urban industrial North, a high premium was also placed on education. The Protestant Reformation, of which most of the early settlers were a part, had given rise to a belief in the "priesthood of all believers." The need to read the Bible helped foster mass literacy. The commitment to education also contributed to a more flexible workforce that was adaptable to changing times and conditions of work and, in turn, helped shape those work conditions with creative contributions of their own. This came to be known as Yankee ingenuity.

Industrial capitalism was also undermining traditional republican values, such as the virtue of putting the community's general interests above a person's own narrower individual economic interests, and the virtue of building a commonwealth that benefited all of the people rather than merely an economic elite. Thus, this new mode of mass industrial production was contributing to a growing economic inequality in the land.

It was in this context that a two-party political system emerged in the mid-1800s. Banking was the most important and emotionally charged political issue of the day. By the 1830s, the ideological Republican Party of Thomas Jefferson had become the organizational Democratic Party of Andrew Jackson and was comprised of trade unionists and yeoman farmers—a truly independent lot who were against the banks. Common people often regarded bankers as "bloodsuckers" and "parasites" who grew fat off the hard work and earnings of the laboring class. The Whig Party—the pro-nationalist and, therefore, pro-national-banking party that evolved into the Republican Party in 1854—was now the Democratic Party and localism's principal opponent.

Lincoln came of age at the dawn of this industrial boom. Born on February 12, 1809, in a log cabin near Hodgenville, Kentucky, he was the son of Thomas and Nancy Hanks Lincoln and named for his paternal grandfather. Thomas Lincoln was a carpenter and farmer. Both of Lincoln's parents were Baptists, and their family belonged to a congregation that had split off from another church because the one that Lincoln attended was opposed to slavery.

As Lincoln grew up, his love for reading and learning over working in the fields put a strain on his relationship with his father, who preferred farming to learning. Just past his teen years, in 1830, Abe Lincoln moved to Illinois with his family, settling in New Salem in 1831, where he lived until 1837. While in New Salem he worked at several jobs, including operating a store, surveying, and serving as the local postmaster from 1833 to 1836 through the appointment of a Democratic president, Andrew Jackson. He wrestled the town bully, impressed the residents with his character, and earned the nickname Honest Abe. Lincoln, who stood nearly six feet, four inches, and weighed only about 180 pounds, saw brief service in the Black Hawk War. He studied law in his spare time and became a lawyer in 1836. Lincoln was elected bipartisanly to the Illinois General Assembly in 1834, then elected as a Whig in 1836.

His interest in politics was rejuvenated when Congress passed the Kansas-Nebraska Act in March 1854. Inspired, he began giving speeches on the slavery question. In May 1856 Lincoln gave his famous "Lost Speech," a speech apparently so moving and powerful that not one of the more than three dozen reporters present copied it down. At an Illinois state convention of Republican delegates who had come to Bloomington to help organize and strengthen the newly formed Republican Party, Lincoln spoke extemporaneously for ninety minutes, clearly identifying slavery as the root cause of the nation's problems.

His law partner, William Herndon, who usually took notes but was so caught up in Lincoln's oratory that he stopped writing about fifteen minutes into the speech, concluded, "His speech was full of fire and energy and force. It was logic; it was pathos; it was enthusiasm; it was justice, equity, truth, and right set ablaze by the divine fires of a soul maddened by the wrong; it was hard, heavy, knotty, gnarly, backed with wrath."[3]

Following the speech, the 270 delegates declared in a resolution that Congress had the power to stop the spread of slavery westward, and it ought to do so.

Lincoln also spoke out in opposition to the *Dred Scott* decision in 1857 and gave his "House Divided" speech on June 16, 1858, after receiving the Illinois Republican Party nomination to run for the U.S. Senate against incumbent Democratic Senator Stephen Douglas. In the speech "Lincoln reviewed the process by which Democrats had repealed the Missouri Compromise in 1854 and then declared it unconstitutional in 1857."[4]

He also made reference to the "four carpenters"—by which he meant his Democratic opponent, Senator Stephen Douglas, author of the infamous Kansas-Nebraska Act of 1854; Democratic President Franklin Pierce, who as president signed the bill into law on May 30, 1854; Democratic Supreme Court Chief Justice Roger B. Taney, who had written the *Dred Scott* decision in 1857; and the current Democratic president, James Buchanan, whom Lincoln and many others viewed as a tool of the southern slave power—all of whom had helped build a house divided, splitting North and South between free and slave states, respectively.

Lincoln conceded that he could not prove a slave power conspiracy between the four carpenters. "But when we see a lot of framed timbers . . . which we know have been gotten out at different times and places and by different workmen—Stephen, Franklin, Roger, and James, for instance—and when we see these timbers joined together, and see they exactly make the frame of a house . . . we find it impossible not to believe that Stephen and Franklin and Roger and James . . . all worked upon a common plan."

Following this initial campaign speech, Lincoln engaged in a series of debates with Senator Douglas in the 1858 Illinois contest for a U.S. Senate seat. Lincoln and Douglas each may have scored points and won various rounds in their seven debates across the state, but Douglas won the contest and went back to Washington to represent Illinois as senator. Still, Lincoln's framing of the debates and his opposition to the westward expansion of slavery into the new territories had gained him national recognition, a reputation, and a political following—and doomed Senator Douglas's Democratic presidential nomination and campaign two years later.

During this famous series of debates, Lincoln revealed that he was no political radical or outraged abolitionist. He had a moderate position on the slavery question that generally reflected public opinion in the North in 1860—limit slavery to where it currently exists, stop its westward expansion into the new territories, and the country, over time, will gradually rid itself of the institution.

The Lincoln-Douglas debates, which were followed nationally, gave Lincoln increased recognition in the country. In February 1860—a presidential election year in the state where the leading Republican candidate for president, William Seward, resided—Lincoln gave a speech in New York. Known as the "Cooper Union" speech, Lincoln thoughtfully laid out his constitutional and legal arguments as to why the federal government had a right to limit the expansion of slavery into new territories while showing that there was no constitutional basis for southerners who supported such expansion. But Lincoln argued that whether the original signers of the Constitution were "for" or "against" the expansion of slavery, all agreed that the federal government had a right to control slavery in the territories, and the individual states did not represent a higher law on the subject according to the Constitution. Thus, he argued, the Republican stance was not a revolutionary one, but rather a similar view to that held by the Founding Fathers.

"I defy any man to show that any one of them ever, in his whole life, declared that, in his understanding, any proper division of local from federal authority, or any part of the Constitution, forbade the Federal Government to control as to slavery in the federal territories," Lincoln asserted.

In a word to southerners, he said: "You say you are conservative—eminently conservative—while we are revolutionary, destructive, or something of the sort. What is conservatism? Is it not adherence to the old and tried, against the new and untried? We stick to, contend for, the identical old policy on the point in controversy which was adopted by 'our fathers who framed the Government under which we live;' while you with one accord reject, and scout, and spit upon that old policy. . . . Your purpose, then, plainly stated, is that you will destroy the Government, unless you be allowed to construe and enforce the Constitution as you please, on all points in dispute between you and us. You will rule or ruin in all events. . . ."[5]

To northern New York Republicans, he advocated: "Neither let us be slandered from our duty by false accusations against us, nor frightened from it by menaces of destruction to the Government nor of dungeons to ourselves. LET US HAVE FAITH THAT RIGHT MAKES MIGHT, AND IN THAT FAITH, LET US, TO THE END, DARE TO DO OUR DUTY AS WE UNDERSTAND IT."[6]

Thus, the political scene was set for the party conventions of 1860. When Lincoln was nominated by the Republican Party in 1860 it was a distinctly northern sectional party, known in the South as the Black Republican Party because of its position on slavery. After Lincoln's election they called him "that Black Republican president."

By 1860 the issue of slavery had split the Democratic Party into southern and northern factions. The northern and border-state Democratic delegates nominated Stephen A. Douglas, while the Deep South faction of the party, which was openly in favor of preserving slavery in the new territories, chose John C. Breckinridge of Kentucky as their presidential candidate. Finally, John Bell of Tennessee became the candidate of a fourth party comprised of old Whigs and a conglomerate of other interests on the Constitutional Unionist ticket.

Abraham Lincoln was elected our sixteenth president on November 6, 1860. Hannibal Hamlin of Maine was his vice president. The Republican ticket received 1,865,593 popular votes (39.8 percent) and 180 electoral votes from seventeen of the thirty-three states. The sectional nature of the election is notable for the fact that Lincoln's name did not even appear on the ballot of ten southern states.

If the abolitionists saw slavery as the central moral question of the day, and the Radical Republicans saw it as the central political issue in the land, Lincoln's moderate stance on the slavery question was the main reason the Republicans nominated him and the American people elected him. However, the evolution of Lincoln on this question was not complete.

The 241-year pattern of avoidance, compromise, and denial on the slavery question—the tremor phase—had run its course in America. The tensions between a free-labor industrial North, and a slave-labor agrarian South; between religiously and economically motivated northern abolitionists, and religiously and economically motivated southern slaveholders; and between their political representatives in Washington was now ready to explode. While it didn't necessarily appear that way at the time, the election of Lincoln had, in fact, finally forced the issue of slavery to a head.

Still, neither region thought the other side was serious about turning its fighting words into a fighting war. And even if a war was to be fought, both thought it wouldn't last long or be very costly in terms of treasure or lives. But words continued to be spoken and actions taken that made war virtually inevitable.

Viewing Lincoln as a radical antislavery proponent and his election as a threat to the southern way of life, on December 20, a mere six weeks after Lincoln had been elected president and long before he was inaugurated, the South Carolina legislature called a state convention and voted unanimously to secede from the Union. South Carolina's departure sparked the quick exit of six other southern states in early 1861: Mississippi on January 9; Florida on January 10; Alabama on January 11; Georgia on January 19; Louisiana on January 26; and Texas on February 1. Less than three months after Lincoln was elected, and with more than a month to go before he assumed office, seven states had seceded from the Union. They met in Montgomery on February 4, 1861, to take care of the business of dis-Union and cobble together a new southern government.

Even as Lincoln was putting together an administration and preparing to assume control of an existing government, these seven original Confederate States of America had already voted 160 to 0 to dissolve their ties to the Union, formed an entirely new provisional southern government, established a new provisional national capital in Montgomery, Alabama, written a new provisional Constitution (based on the U.S. Constitution), elected a new provisional president (Jefferson Davis) and vice president (Alexander Hamilton Stephens), and set a November 1861 election date to confirm these provisional actions.

The new Confederate Constitution, written by slaveholding Democrats, was based on the U.S. Constitution, but there were significant differences that are even interesting to look at in light of today's politics. The Confederates made no secret of the fact that their government was to be aristocratic, slaveholding, elite, and state centered. Their preamble omitted the general welfare clause and the phrase "a more perfect union"—a sentiment more reflective of today's conservative Republicans and Democrats. After "we the people," the phrase "each state, acting in its sovereign and independent character" was added to make plain the new government's states' rights philosophy—again, more representative of today's Republicans. Instead of the code words used in the U.S. Constitution, the Confederate Constitution called a slave a slave.

Another clause forbade "government aid for internal improvements"—which was the Democratic Party's philosophy of 1861, but also more closely reflects the Republican philosophy of 2001. After weakening the executive by limiting it to one six-year term, the Confederate Constitution strengthened that branch by giving the president the "line-item veto" for appropriations. While today the line-item veto reflects more a Republican philosophy of government, it was President Bill Clinton—reminding us of the Democratic Party's roots in this Democratic legacy of the Confederacy, along with conservative northern Copper-headism—who finally pushed it through Congress, ironically only to have it overturned as unconstitutional by a predominantly conservative Republican Supreme Court.

President Lincoln's inaugural was not until March 4, yet Confederate President Jefferson Davis was sworn into office three weeks earlier, on February 18. Two days prior, on February 16, William Lowndes Yancey of South Carolina, one of the most ardent and fire-eating secessionists of his day, introduced Jefferson Davis to a wildly enthusiastic crowd in Montgomery. "It was on this occasion that *Dixie* became the unofficial Confederate anthem."[7] Southerners greeted secession with fireworks, parades, and dancing in the street.

Southern leadership was united around a common goal—protecting their southern way of life, which was based on slavery—and divided only over tactics and timing. Some states preferred to lay out a list of demands to Lincoln—"enforcement of the fugitive slave law, repeal of personal liberty laws, guarantees against interference with slavery in the District of Columbia or with the interstate slave trade, and protection of slavery in the territories, at least those south of 36-30"[8]—wait for the new president-elect to reject them, and secede. Others preferred to wait, to give Lincoln a chance to actually govern and see what his policies would be. Then, if they were not to southern liking, they could still secede.

While the North saw secession as unconstitutional and illegal, the South saw it as perfectly constitutional, legal, and historical. Southerners argued that the Revolution of 1776 was an act of secession from Britain. Secession had an ideological and constitutional foundation—dual federalism, states' rights, and the Tenth Amendment—so this was merely an act of state sovereignty over national sovereignty. "Those who could not find in the Constitution such intellectual justification for their secessionist actions appealed to the right of revolution. . . . A Georgia disunionist explained to supporters of these 'go slow' approaches: 'we will go for revolution, and if you . . . oppose us . . . we will brand you as traitors, and chop off your heads.'"[9]

Southerners believed that the Founding Fathers had provided future generations with the paradigm of an eternal struggle between freedom and coercion, and freedom was both good and more important than coercion, even if coercion was necessary to bring about greater justice or equality, either individually or collectively. The paradigm was argued and defended in the high-sounding rhetoric of "constitutional liberty," but the real meaning was that southerners claimed they had the personal liberty to own slaves, and their personal liberty ought be defended by state governments advocating states' rights. Any coercion by the Union or federal government that moved them toward a more inclusive racial justice would not be tolerated. Their personal liberty and state honor had to be protected and preserved against an overbearing and dictatorial federal government.

Today, economic and political conservatives emphasize freedom and liberty over justice for all—rather than promoting a democratic, organic, living, and flexible balance between the two. They prefer volunteerism, depend on localism and state action to bring about justice and greater equality, and resist any legal or coercive means for achieving greater equality for all. This orientation and these priorities are part of the Confederate legacy of "freedom over justice" at all costs. It puts individual liberty, wrongly exercised, and states' rights above justice and equality for all.

The South felt that in the Union, it was rapidly losing its power to maintain and expand its peculiar institution. Through northern aggression and coercion, its freedom was being taken away, and its honor and pride were being violated. Only by forming another counterbalancing coercive force—a Confederate States of America—could it protect its freedom, maintain its way of life, and restore its pride and honor. James McPherson reports that on March 4, 1861, one Georgia secessionist declared, "We are either slaves in the Union or freemen out of it."[10]

Just in case there was some unclarity as to why the Confederacy was being founded, or any thought that Jefferson might have had blacks in mind when he penned the words in the Declaration of Independence, the ninety-pound former Georgia Whig and new vice president of the Confederacy, Alexander Hamilton Stephens—putting the notion of "all men are created equal" to rest—spoke to an enthusiastic crowd in Montgomery, Alabama, on February 18, 1861. Known as the "Cornerstone Speech," in it Stephens said: "Our new government is founded on exactly the opposite idea of the equality of the races; its foundations are laid, its cornerstone rests, upon the great truth that the negro is not equal to the white man; that slavery . . . is his natural and normal condition. This, our new government, is the first in the history of the world based upon this great physical, philosophical, and moral truth."[11]

Defending the right to own slaves was politically problematic, because only a quarter of the southern Democrats actually owned slaves. In all of the secessionist conventions the counties with the most slaves had voted overwhelmingly for secession, and those with few slaves had opposed it. Slaveholders wrestled with the question: Why would the nonslaveholding three-quarters of the citizenry have an interest in protecting their special economic interests?

Slaveholders were fearful that a politically savvy President Lincoln might be able to gradually peel off this majority of nonslaveholding Democrats and win them over to the Republican Party and Unionist cause. What was their solution? White supremacy! Southern Democratic slaveholders undertook a campaign to convince white nonslaveholders that they, too, had a stake in disunion and in the Confederacy. The nonslaveholder was taught that his stake was not primarily economic: His "white over black" interest was instead emotional and psychological. Even though he was poor and struggling economically, the poor white man was still better than the "even lower and sub-human niggers."

Fearful men developed fear-based tactics, promoting fear of racial equality (political and economic) and fear of black amalgamation (sex with his wife or daughters)—an ironic concern, since he was already having sex with black wives and daughters! But if the slaveholders could divert the nonslaveholding white man's attention from his real economic needs and interests, and instead redirect it onto such "social issues"—the same tactic economic conservatives use today—then the nonslaveholding whites could be kept on board the ship of slavery.

Influential clergymen joined with the slaveholders in spreading this message. The Reverend James Furman, a Baptist clergyman, railed, "'If you are tame enough to submit . . . Abolition preachers will be at hand to consummate the marriage of your daughters to black husbands.' No! No! came an answering shout from Alabama. 'Submit to have our wives and daughters choose between death and gratifying the hellish lust of the negro!! . . . Better ten thousand deaths than submission to Black Republicanism.'"[12] Snookered by such diversionary ploys, economically and politically impotent nonslaveholding white men rallied around the flag of white supremacy to protect their wives and daughters.

Such was the irrationality of white supremacy, slavery, and racism in 1861. But it is not unlike today's more sophisticated ploys that keep the wealthy on top and the poor on the bottom. Why else would the most economically needy section of our country be the most conservative?

It was significant, too, that only seven states joined the Confederacy in the first six weeks, and they were generally the poorest and least resourceful. Recognizing some of their predicament, they chose moderates over fire-eaters as their leaders in an attempt to reach out to the other slave states in the upper South, and the border states. The new Confederacy needed their white numbers and their industry to go against the North.

The firestorm and explosion that occurred in the South after Lincoln's election created the greatest threat of a domestic implosion in the Union's brief history. Fearing Black Republican control of the government, slaveholders rushed to protect their peculiar institution as white nonslaveholders rushed to protect their white skin.

President Buchanan, a Democrat sympathetic to the South, surprised his brethren by telling them in a message to Congress on December 3 that, despite their rumblings and threats, they had no moral or constitutional right to secede. But there wasn't universal agreement on secession in the North either. Mayor Fernando Wood of New York proposed that New York City sever its ties with the Union as well.

While Lincoln and others denounced secession, they did recognize that, under certain intolerable conditions, the Constitution granted the right of revolution. Revolution, not secession, was the legacy of the Founding Fathers. But a moral right to revolution could not be exercised for light or frivolous reasons, and Lincoln saw no justified cause in these states' act of disunion. "We must settle this question now," Lincoln said, "whether in a free government the minority have the right to break up the government whenever they choose."[13] Proceeding moderately, Lincoln had no intention of disturbing slavery where it already existed; he planned only to stop its expansion.

The country seemed to be coming apart at the seams as states left the Union and senators and representatives resigned their offices. Having compromised its way out of this dilemma many times, the nation made one more attempt.

A Committee of Thirteen was set up in the Senate and a Committee of Thirty-Three (one representative from each state) was appointed in the House to consider various compromise proposals. Kentuckians, a people proud of their history of mediation on the slavery question, and Kentucky's John J. Crittenden, senatorial inheritor of the legacy of Henry Clay, offered a proposal. Crittenden's plan contained the 1820 Missouri Compromise of permitting slavery South but denying it North; popular sovereignty for new states; enforcement of the Fugitive Slave Law; and compensation to slave owners whose slaves escaped. It also provided that Congress could never amend the Constitution to give Congress power over slavery in any state. Lincoln accepted everything in the Crittenden Compromise except the inclusion of slavery in the territories. He wrote to a Republican associate: "Entertain no proposition for a compromise in regard to the extension of slavery."[14] The plan collapsed.

If the South had not forced the issue with an attack on Fort Sumter about a month and a half later, however, a fourth compromise might have worked. It certainly would have made things more complicated. On February 27 the House passed a bill agreeing to aggressively enforce the Fugitive Slave Law. The next day, February 28, it passed a proposed *thirteenth* constitutional amendment that guaranteed the protection of slavery against any future federal interference. It was sent to the states for ratification. Only disunion and the outbreak of war prevented the possibility of its adoption. Ironically, four years later, a Thirteenth Amendment was added to the Constitution—the amendment outlawing slavery.

While the seven slave states of the lower South were trying to attract other slave and border states to their newly formed Confederacy, the North was also wooing these same states with a moderate stance on the slavery question. Legislation was introduced admitting New Mexico as a free state; the Crittenden Compromise was offered; and a "Peace Convention" convened on February 4, led by a conciliatory New Yorker, William Seward. These efforts contributed to keeping the border states of Kentucky, Missouri, Maryland, and Delaware in the Union.

On February 11, 1861, both presidents-elect left home for their inaugurations. Abraham Lincoln gave a moving farewell address to a thousand well-wishers at the Great Western Station in Springfield, Illinois, on his way to Washington, D.C., and Jefferson Davis said good-bye to his family and plantation slaves from his Brierfield Plantation in Mississippi on his way to Montgomery, Alabama. Abraham Lincoln left by train with his family on a circuitous eleven-day journey that took him to Indianapolis, Cincinnati, Columbus, Pittsburgh, Cleveland, Buffalo, Albany, New York City, Trenton, Philadelphia, Harrisburg, and Baltimore —which was a risky city for Lincoln due to its prosouthern sympathies—before entering the nation's capital on February 23. Davis left by boat to Vicksburg, traveling to Jackson, Mississippi, Chattanooga, and Atlanta before arriving in Montgomery on February 16.

Lincoln was careful not to say anything of a controversial nature when he gave numerous speeches to cheering crowds along the way. It was also a dangerous trip; assassination threats were in the air. In fact, his arrival in the nation's capital was rather inauspicious in that he had to sneak out of Baltimore and into Washington in the wee hours of the morning, arriving at 6 AM because of such a threat. The president-elect was now sporting a new beard that an eleven-year-old girl from New York had suggested he grow. He was to be sworn in on March 4.

How was he to communicate his political intentions to his northern supporters and southern doubters? There were divisions within his own party and even more serious divisions out in the country. The Republican Party was still an amalgam of old Whigs, Know-Nothing nativists, antislavery moderates, militant abolitionists, and more. One channel of communication was through his cabinet appointments. Here, Lincoln did something unprecedented and unparalleled in American history—he appointed his chief political rivals to the four highest cabinet posts in his administration.

His inaugural address would be even more important. As he had worked on it in Springfield nearly two months before, not only had seven states seceded, but they had begun to seize federal properties as well. Again, what to do? Civil War historian James McPherson reports that Lincoln's first draft of his inaugural had one theme and two variations. Lincoln was determined to preserve an undivided Union, but he was willing to use a sword and an olive branch to achieve his goal. The sword, softened in the final version, was to indicate that he would use all means at his disposal to retain—not necessarily to regain, as in the earlier version—all federal properties. His phrases, "hold, occupy and possess" properties and "collect duties and imports," were deliberately ambiguous. The olive branch was to reiterate his oft-repeated promise not to disturb slavery where it was already in place. In the end, the speech was vague enough that all saw in it what they wanted to see. Northern Democrats and upper South Unionists—Lincoln's critically important and prime political targets—saw it as reasonable and moderate. The lower South saw it as a declaration of war.[15]

Fort Sumter, just off the coast of South Carolina—the state that triggered secession— was still in federal possession and had become a symbol of national pride and Union in the North and an irritant and symbol of shame for the Confederacy. A northern immovable object was being met by a southern irresistible force.

Lincoln had hoped that his inaugural address would buy time. Time is what Lincoln needed to gradually reconnect the severed states to the Union body politic. Fort Sumter would give him no such time. The morning after his March 4 address he received a message from Major Robert Anderson that shortly he would need more supplies. Major Anderson had moved his men under the cover of night from Fort Moultrie to Fort Sumter on December 26, 1860, for fear of an attack by Confederate forces. President Buchanan had tried to resupply the men there on January 9, but the supply ship had been forcibly turned back to sea by Confederate forces. Tension on the string holding North and South together increased, but did not break.

In mid-March Jefferson Davis sent representatives to Washington to negotiate the transfer of Fort Sumter and other federal forts to the Confederacy, even as he sent General Pierre G. T. Beauregard of Louisiana to command the men and coordinate the activity around Fort Sumter in the Charleston harbor.

After taking office, Lincoln had only six weeks—that's when supplies would run out—to make some hard choices. It seemed that whatever choice he made would only alienate both his friends and his enemies. While most of the people of the North were urging the new president to defend Fort Sumter at all costs, only one member of his cabinet, Montgomery Blair, had advised him to do so—until March 28. On this critical date he convened an emergency cabinet meeting and read to them a recommendation from U.S. General Winfield Scott urging the surrender of Fort Sumter to the Confederates. The recommendation was based on political, not military, grounds. Lincoln and the cabinet, buoyed by the position of the people, were outraged and supported protecting Fort Sumter.

Secretary of State William Seward was ambitious to be "king of the hill" in Lincoln's cabinet—and maneuvered in strange ways to get there. He had apparently led Davis's representatives to believe that Fort Sumter would be turned over to them. Seward had Lincoln meet with a Virginia Unionist on April 4 in an attempt to dissuade a secessionist vote in the Virginia legislature—the same day that Lincoln finally gave the go-ahead to send in supplies to Fort Sumter—but Lincoln was disappointed with the meeting. Seward had also secretly recommended to Lincoln a bizarre strategy regarding Fort Sumter, a plan that would change the perception of the issue from Union to slavery; Lincoln rejected it, informing Seward privately that the president must make the final decision. Still, he didn't want to lose Seward's services. His cautious approach worked and Seward became one of Lincoln's most loyal and effective cabinet members during the war.

On April 6 Lincoln notified South Carolina Governor Francis Pickens of his peaceful intentions to resupply the men at Fort Sumter with "food for hungry men." While that was his intention, Lincoln was also setting a tactical moral trap. If the Confederates fired on unarmed boats carrying food for hungry men, the South would be accused of initiating a hostile act and could be blamed for starting a war. This would serve two purposes: uniting the North against the South, but also keeping the South divided. If the South let the supplies through, on the other hand, peace would be sustained and the northern Union government could declare a symbolic victory. It was the first sign of the tactical mastery that would mark Lincoln's presidency.

Just as South Carolina had triggered secession by immediate and drastic legislative action on December 20, it now stood poised to start a war by doing the same thing with respect to military action. The South Carolina fire-eater Louis Wigfall, joined by two aggressive Virginia secessionists, Edmund Ruffin and Roger Pryor, promoted an idea to bring reluctant southern slave states into the Confederate fold—start a war by attacking Fort Sumter. "'The shedding of blood,' wrote Ruffin, 'will serve to change many voters in the hesitating states, from the submission or procrastinating ranks, to the zealous for immediate secession.' If you want us to join you, Pryor told Charlestonians, 'Strike a blow!'"[16]

On April 9 Davis ordered General Beauregard to strike Fort Sumter before Lincoln's re-supplies arrived. At four o'clock on Friday morning, April 12, 1861, Confederate forces opened fire on Fort Sumter and the American Civil War was begun. After thirty-three hours of fighting and the expenditure of thousands of rounds of ammunition between the two sides, which set the fort on fire, the Confederates captured Fort Sumter with only one ca-sualty on this first day of the war—a dead horse.

The taking of Sumter rang the alarm in the North, and on April 15 Lincoln issued a call for seventy-five thousand men to volunteer for ninety days to curb the insurrection. The response was overwhelming throughout the North, among both Republicans and Democrats; Senator Douglas supported Lincoln's position in a highly publicized visit to the White House. The South had gone too far. True patriots must crush these traitors.

Earlier, a southerner, reflecting his view of northern manhood and cowardice, suggested that a lady's thimble could hold all the blood that would be shed if a war between the North and the South were to break out. Before it was over much more than a "lady's thimble" of blood would be shed by both sides.

Though thirty-three "United" States had been reduced to twenty-six through disunion, the Union could clearly defeat the seven rebel states. But eight states in the upper South— Virginia, Arkansas, North Carolina, Tennessee, and the border states of Maryland, Missouri, Kentucky, and Delaware—would be crucial in maintaining this favorable tilt. The attack on Fort Sumter and Lincoln's call for volunteer troops immediately tipped the scales toward the Confederacy in the four lower South states of Virginia, Arkansas, North Carolina, and Tennessee. Lincoln's mobilization was seen by southerners as an unconstitutional act of co-ercion directed against their liberty. The Constitutional Unionist candidate for president, Tennessee's John Bell, announced on April 23 in Nashville his support for a "United South." "A North Carolinian stated the popular view: 'The division must be made on the line of slavery. The South must go with the South. . . . Blood is thicker than Water.'"[17]

Virginians were so thrilled by the actions in the Charleston harbor on April 12, and so outraged by Lincoln's actions on April 15, that by April 17 they had organized not one but two secessionist conventions—an official convention that voted eighty-eight to fifty-five to go out and an unofficial "Spontaneous Southern Rights Convention" that was unanimous. A ratification vote on May 23 merely confirmed the already accomplished fact of April 17. The Confederacy now totaled eight.

On April 27 the official Virginia convention invited the government housed in Mont-gomery to take up residence in Richmond. On May 21—just two days before Virginia's ref-erendum—the Confederacy agreed to move its capital out of Alabama and into Virginia.

Virginia brought many pluses with it. It had the respected revolutionary history of Wash-ington, Jefferson, and Madison; a large population; and an industrial capacity greater than the other seven Confederate states combined. The Tredegar Iron Works, the only south-ern plant capable of producing heavy ordnance, was in the state. Robert E. Lee was also part of the Virginia haul. Lincoln had actually offered Lee command of his new volunteer army, but despite Lee's moral opposition to slavery and his political opposition to secession, he remained loyal to Virginia. Lee resigned from the U.S. Army and within five days accepted an appointment as commander in chief of Virginia's military.

On the heels of Virginia, Arkansas on May 6 voted sixty-five to five to secede; North Carolina went out on May 20; and Tennessee followed on June 8 in a referendum vote of 104,913 to 47,238. The Confederate States of America had now grown to eleven.

The principled vote in these four states revealed something else as well. Despite the high-sounding rhetoric and writing about "rights," "constitutional liberty," "honor," and "unconstitutional coercion," the bottom line all along had been slavery. Counties with lots of slaves voted to secede; counties with few slaves voted to stay in the Union. In the final analysis, however, these upper South states, like their Deep South counterparts, voted to go to war to defend the freedom of white men to own slaves and carry them into the new territories at their pleasure rather than submit to the new Republican president, who threatened to deprive them of their freedom.

Delaware's loyalty to the Union was never really in doubt. Slavery in Maryland, Missouri, and Kentucky was only half that of the other eleven Confederate states, and they also remained in the Union. Maryland was strategically important because it bordered Washington on three sides. Had Maryland joined the Confederacy, the capital of the United States would have been completely isolated and encircled by Confederate states, since Virginia was the fourth border. With a significant political constituency for secession and a history of political violence in Baltimore, Maryland seemed ripe for Confederate pickings. It almost happened.

On April 19 the Sixth Massachusetts Regiment was on its way to Washington as the first fully equipped unit to respond to Lincoln's call. As the soldiers left their train on the north side of Baltimore and marched through the city to board a train on the south side for the last leg of their journey, they were confronted and attacked by militant secessionist crowds. By the time they reached the train, nearly half a dozen soldiers and a dozen Baltimoreans were dead, and many more lay in the streets wounded. They were, in fact, the first human casualties of the Civil War.

The passions of Marylanders were inflamed. They crippled northern soldiers' access through Baltimore by burning railroad bridges on Philadelphia and Harrisburg routes. They tore down the telegraph lines between Washington and Maryland, hampering communications between North and South, and created the fear of an imminent attack on the nation's capital by trying to isolate it.

Lincoln visited the officers and wounded of the Sixth Massachusetts when they finally made it to Washington on April 24. He was disheartened by the lack of response to his April 15 call; the very next day, however, the Seventh New York Regiment arrived, with many others arriving in the following days. Though the mood in Baltimore remained volatile, Union military strength along vulnerable railroad tracks and a declaration of martial law on May 13 helped Baltimore residents suppress their southern sympathies.

Lincoln even suspended the writ of habeas corpus as a way of controlling secessionist tendencies in Maryland. The most celebrated civil liberties case growing out of this action involved John Merryman, a wealthy landowning secessionist who had been a leader of the disruptive tactics in Baltimore in April. Justice Taney ruled against Lincoln's suspension of the writ of habeas corpus on May 28, but Lincoln ignored him and justified his actions in a special message to Congress on July 4. Union political forces finally got control of the state in November legislative elections, and Maryland stayed in the Union.

In keeping with its earlier ruffian days against Kansas, the struggle in Missouri was histrionic and violent. The two principal protagonists were a Lyon and a Fox—the newly elected Governor Claiborne Fox Jackson and Captain Nathaniel Lyon, commander of U.S. forces in St. Louis at the largest arsenal in the slave states, along with Unionist Congressman Francis P. Blair, Jr., and secessionist Sterling Price.

Upon assuming office on January 5, 1861, Governor Jackson announced that Missouri had common origins, pursuits, tastes, manners, and customs with the other southern states of the Confederacy. Therefore, he argued, Missouri should join with the slaveholding states in common cause. Confederates even set up a "Camp Jackson" on the outskirts of the city to demonstrate their resolve.

In a June 11 meeting between secessionists Jackson and Price and Unionists Lyon and Blair, the secessionists offered to keep Confederate troops out of Missouri if the Unionists would do the same with regard to federal troops. In another classic confrontation between states' rights and federal rights, Lyon refused.

Straightaway Missouri was set ablaze. William Quantrill, "Bloody Bill" Anderson, and George Todd became notorious Confederate bushwhackers. Their infamous associates, Jesse and Frank James and Cole and Jim Younger, became even better known after the war. Their ongoing guerrilla warfare, long after Appomattox, assured that Missouri would suffer from internecine warfare more than any other state.

Missouri's governor was a Confederate sympathizer; otherwise Union forces controlled the state politically. The legislature was not in session in July, but it reconvened a quorum from the special March convention that had rejected secession on July 22. Members called themselves the "Provisional Government of Missouri," declaring the current offices vacant and the state legislature nonexistent. This provisional government actually ruled Missouri until January 1865, when a new government was chosen under a new free-state Constitution.

Not willing to take his unseating lying down, Governor Jackson convened a proslavery faction of state legislators in Neosho, near the Arkansas border, and, even though a quorum had not shown up, they voted for Missouri to secede from the Union on November 3, 1861. On November 28, the Confederate Congress, now firmly settled in Richmond, voted to admit Missouri as the twelfth Confederate state. This new government actually sent political representatives to serve in the Confederate legislature, but they were driven out of Missouri and "governed" in exile throughout the war. In fact, Missouri never left the Union, and three-quarters of its white men fought on the Union side.

Kentucky, the birthplace of both Abraham Lincoln and Jefferson Davis, was surrounded by three slave states and three free states. It was proud of the nationalist and reconciling tradition of Henry Clay, now occupied by John J. Crittenden, but it also had roots in the southern slave culture and traditions. Torn between these two contending forces, Kentucky chose "strict neutrality." Lincoln understood that when it comes to debating choices and actions, not merely abstract ideas, "strict neutrality" was essentially an alignment with the secessionists. But at the time, official neutrality was better than official secession, so Lincoln told Kentuckians on April 26 that if they remained in the Union, but neutral, he would not pressure them. His patience paid off. By June 20 Unionists had gained control of both the state and federal political delegations in special elections, and an August 5 regular election gave Union forces even more control. Kentucky, too, was now firmly in the Union camp.

In Virginia and Tennessee, there were enough counties voting against secession to spark movements that during the war would call to establish themselves as separate states. The primarily white eastern part of Tennessee did not secede from the heavily black western part, but Virginia split on the issue of slavery. If we remember that three-quarters of whites in the South were nonslaveholders, but three-quarters of state lawmakers in the South were slaveholders, the political dynamics of Virginia become clearer. Nonslaveholding Virginians in the western part of the state had long-standing grievances with slaveholding "tidewater aristocrats" in the eastern part. Eastern state legislators had taxed their slaves at less than one-third of market value, while other property in the state was taxed at full value. Yet when it came time to spend on state internal improvements, the benefits had gone overwhelmingly and disproportionately to the eastern counties. Northwest Virginia shouted out in vain for more roads and railroads.

On June 11 citizens from the western part of the state convened in Wheeling to consider establishing their own separate state. The U.S. Constitution, however, requires consent by the existing state legislature, which was now in Confederate hands. To get around this roadblock, the westerners formed a "restored government" of Virginia. On June 20, even though they only represented the western part of the state, Lincoln immediately recognized them as the state's legitimate government. Two senators and three representatives took their seats in the U.S. Congress on July 13, 1861.

Shortly thereafter, at a constitutional convention, delegates established a new state to be named after a familiar scenic area, the Kanawha Valley. In fact, the new state was first called Kanawha. As in Missouri, an internecine war was going on within the "two Virginias" even as Ole Virginny was waging a war against the Union. The federal government, however, could not send troops to protect this potential new state of Kanawha—its troops were fighting elsewhere. Thus, it was left to the governors of Ohio and Indiana to come to its rescue.

Northern Yankee armies sent from Ohio and Indiana allowed a state referendum to take place on October 24, 1861. A small turnout overwhelmingly voted for the establishment of a new state. In January 1862 a constitutional convention drew state boundaries around fifty counties. The "restored state legislature of Virginia" approved what was now to become not Kanawha but the new state of West Virginia on May 23, 1862. Even though only 4 percent of the population were slaves, Congress insisted on emancipation as a condition of its admission as the thirty-fifth state of the Union (following Kansas). West Virginia's statehood became official on June 20, 1863. Its constitution freed all slaves born after July 4, 1863, and all others following their twenty-fifth birthday. With West Virginia serving as a republican model of how to bring the wayward back into the Union, eastern Tennessee seemed ripe for such an effort as well—but it wasn't to be.

In Tennessee, Unionists held two conventions in 1861. Their leaders were Democratic Senator Andrew Johnson, the only senator from a seceding state to remain loyal to the Union—and because of such loyalty he was selected by Lincoln as his vice president in 1864—and William G. "Parson" Brownlow, a former Methodist clergyman whose profane language against secessionists earned him his nickname. Nearly thirty thousand white Tennesseans fought for the Union cause, which was more than any other Confederate state, but east Tennessee Unionists suffered greatly because of their loyalty.

The first actual battle of the Civil War began at Manassas, Virginia, near a small creek named Bull Run. The Confederates near the creek had been tipped by one of their spies of Union plans to begin a march to Richmond with an attack near Manassas—a critical railroad path to the Confederate capital. Union General Irvin McDowell and Confederate General Joseph E. Johnston stood ready to lead green and untried troops into battle on the morning of July 21, 1861. Union troops had risen early and were leading a surprise attack on the outnumbered Confederate forces. This battle was perceived by both sides to be the first, last, and only clash of the war. It was a winner-take-all confrontation, and both sides were confident of an early and easy victory.

The first battle of Manassas Junction, begun in the front yard of Wilmer McLean's four-teen-hundred-acre plantation, was won by the Confederates. The legend of General Thomas J. "Stonewall" Jackson and his Stonewall Brigade was born.

Both sides had cobbled together military units locally—local people wearing a mixture of local uniforms and carrying locally made flags. In the midst of battle, with noise, bullets, and smoke flying everywhere, confusion reigned supreme. The line between friends and enemies became blurred. Following Manassas, "Generals P. G. T. Beauregard and Joseph E. Johnston modified a design that had been submitted as a national flag by William Porcher Miles of South Carolina. Miles' design consisted of a rectangular red field traversed by a blue St. Andrew's cross edged in white and bearing white stars equal to the number of Confederate states. Beauregard added a border, and Johnston altered the proportions to square."[18] It is this battle flag that most Americans identify as the banner of the Confederacy. However, during its four-year existence the Confederacy actually adopted three official national flags, all different from the Confederate battlefield flag. The first was nicknamed the Stars and Bars, and the second the Stainless Banner. A third flag was adopted on March 4, 1865, just a month before the war's end.

After Manassas, the South erupted in exultation. It was true what they had said about their superiority after all! Northerners, meantime, were now full of self-doubt; they had been beaten badly and sent home with their tails between their legs. Defeat, while disheartening, at a deeper level renewed resolve. The day after the defeat at Bull Run, Lincoln signed into law the enlistment of half a million three-year troops, another law the next day for the same number, and appointed General George B. McClellan to replace McDowell to lead them. Well organized, a good administrator, and a superb motivator, McClellan immediately began to build discipline, pride, and esprit de corps among a rapidly growing band of Union troops gathering in and around Washington. He converted a ragtag group of recruits into a finely tuned fighting machine—the Army of the Potomac. While his troops loved him, his skills at fighting turned out not to match his skills at preparing to fight. This shortcoming led some to question even his commitment to the Union cause. Later, when he was replaced, he became the Democratic candidate for president against Lincoln in 1864.

The first battle of the Civil War, while relatively insignificant in military terms, had a deep and unanticipated psychological impact on both sides. It emboldened southerners with a false pride and power that helped them in future battles by making up in will and determination what they lacked in actual matériel and manpower. Bull Run also made the North more determined to reunite the nation and spurred it to better preparation for future battles. On the other hand, the skirmish made its troops more hesitant to act boldly because of the ferocious courage of these southerners with a cause.

Early in the Civil War, antislavery forces began to emphasize the issue of slavery in the sectional conflict; the battle was not just about keeping the Union together. They contended that the South's actions did not just constitute an internal domestic dispute or insurrection. It was a war! Abolitionists argued that the South, by seceding over slavery, had forfeited its constitutional rights. The U.S. government, therefore, had a legal right to confiscate southerners' property, including their "slave property," charge the rebels with treason, and punish them as traitors. In fact, they argued, Lincoln was treating the conflict as a war with his naval blockades of Confederate ports and by considering captured southern rebels prisoners of war.

The most prominent person to act on this rationale was Benjamin F. Butler, a former Massachusetts Democrat turned Republican and leader of the Eighth Massachusetts. In May three slaves escaped and found refuge with Butler at Fortress Monroe, Virginia. The slaves' owner, a Confederate colonel, appeared the next day under a flag of truce to demand that his property be returned to him under the Fugitive Slave Law. Butler told him that Virginia had seceded and claimed not to be a part of the Union; therefore, the Fugitive Slave Law was not applicable. Butler referred to the escaped slaves as "contraband of war." Northern newspapers picked up on this phrase and thereafter referred to slaves who escaped and found refuge and work on the Union side as contraband. The Lincoln administration approved this policy.

Fort Sumter was April 12, and Manassas July 21. By mid-July, however, almost a thousand contraband slaves had found safety with Butler behind Union lines at Fortress Monroe, but their legal status was cloudy. Butler wrote to the War Department on July 30 seeking to uncloud the issue, simultaneously leaking his letter to the newspapers. Congress was at the time debating a confiscation act (finally passed on August 6) that would allow Union forces to confiscate any property used to directly aid the rebellion. The question was: Could slave property be confiscated under this law?

Out west in Missouri, Lincoln was confronted with another problem. He had placed John C. Frémont in charge of the Western Department of the war effort. In an attempt to crush and punish Confederate forces in Missouri, on August 30, 1861, Frémont had declared martial law, promised the death penalty to any guerrillas he caught operating behind Union lines, and announced the freeing of Confederate slaves.

Worried about the political impact in the border states of such actions—especially the freeing of slaves—Lincoln wrote Frémont, first asking him to reverse the directive regarding slaves. When Frémont insisted he was right, proving himself arrogant and politically tone deaf, Lincoln later publicly ordered him not to implement the "freeing of the slaves" part of his actions. Lincoln wrote to him and explained that such antislavery action, in particular, could alarm the North's southern Unionist friends, causing them to turn against the Union cause, and probably even trigger Kentucky to secede and join the Confederate cause. If Kentucky left, Lincoln thought it would not be long before Maryland and Missouri would also go. Lincoln argued that this had to be a war to preserve the Union, and could not be turned into a war to end slavery.

Legally, however, things were becoming clearer—if not totally clear. Slaves—if shown to be of direct aid to the Confederate cause—could be confiscated as contraband. But then, legally, were they free? That wasn't as clear! While the new law didn't completely satisfy Republicans (who mostly voted for it) and antislavery abolitionists, both groups felt that Congress was at least moving in the right direction. But Congress appeared to be moving in the wrong direction to Democrats and border-state Unionist congressmen, who had mostly voted against the new law. For the first time in Congress there was a rupture of bipartisan support for the Union's war effort. It reinforced in Lincoln's mind the conviction that if, in the public's mind, the conflict became a war to end slavery instead of a war to save the Union, it would irreparably divide the war's political coalition—built around preserving the Union—cause the border states to defect to the Confederacy, and ultimately cost the North victory, which would allow the spread of slavery westward and, therefore, perpetuate the peculiar institution indefinitely into the future.

The compromiser, Senator John J. Crittenden of Kentucky, giving credence to Lincoln's concerns about making ending slavery the war's rationale, argued that if it was unconstitutional to pass antislavery laws in peacetime, it was also unconstitutional to pass antislavery laws in time of war. Republicans agreed, but argued that Congress could punish treason by confiscating property. Such punishment could be interpreted as against the individual slaveholder, but not against the peculiar institution. It was this law, passed by Congress on August 6, that Lincoln first urged and then demanded that Frémont obey in Missouri.

Thus, Butler's situation with contraband slaves in May, the passage of the Confiscation Act in early August, and Lincoln's cancellation of Frémont's August emancipation of slaves in Missouri triggered a response from both ends of the political spectrum. Unionists in the border states of Kentucky, Maryland, and Missouri communicated their concerns to Lincoln and warned him against turning a war over disunion into a war over slavery. They argued that they could not sustain such a rationale in their states. On the other hand, northern Republicans and abolitionists, who had largely given Lincoln the benefit of their doubt and remained silent, now began to speak out and pressure Lincoln publicly to turn the war against secession into a war against slavery.

Feeling the sting of criticism from Republican supporters and friends, Lincoln responded on September 22 in a private letter to his close friend from Illinois, Senator Orville H. Browning—a letter written exactly one year to the day before the revelation of his Preliminary Emancipation Proclamation. In the letter he argued that "Frémont's proclamation, as to confiscation of property, and the liberation of slaves, is purely political, and not within the range of military law, or necessity. If a commanding General finds a necessity to seize the farm of a private owner, for a pasture, an encampment, or a fortification, he has the right to do so, and to so hold it, as along as the necessity lasts; and this is within military law, because [it is] within military necessity. But to say the farm shall no longer belong to the owner, or his heirs forever; and this as well when the farm is not needed for military purposes as when it is, is purely political, without the savor of military law about it. And the same is true of slaves. If the General needs them, he can seize them, and use them; but when the need is past, it is not for him to fix their permanent future condition. That must be settled according to laws made by law-makers, and not by military proclamations."[19] Yet additional pressure came on Lincoln when Secretary of War Simon Cameron sent him a report on December 1, released it to the press, and called on the administration to use contraband slaves as it would use the gunpowder contraband—to make war on the rebel Confederates.

By the end of 1861, Lincoln had witnessed eleven of thirty-three states separate themselves from his government and launch a war against the Union. His own party was increasingly at odds with him. On December 4 congressional Republicans refused to vote again in support of a Crittenden resolution affirming that ending slavery was not a goal of the war. Lincoln was also aware of the growing political uneasiness of Unionists in the border states. To date, there had been few successful naval blockades off the coasts of North Carolina, Alabama, Louisiana, and South Carolina, and Confederates were winning most of the important battles. There was increasing Republican unrest over the military leadership of the politically inept Democratic General George McClellan, and Congress established a Joint Committee on the Conduct of the War to look over Lincoln's shoulder in December.

At this point, Lincoln stood very much alone in the midst of a major civil war. He was caught in the vise of border-state pro-Unionist and northern-state antislavery politics.

Lincoln and the Union's weak and uneasy position in early 1862, however, turned out to be the darkness before the dawn. While many other dark nights would follow over the next three years, military and political prospects turned in the Union's favor in late winter and early spring of 1862.

An attempt by the South to embargo its cotton in an endeavor to blackmail Europe into supporting the Confederacy backfired and actually resulted in better European–American relations. Another incident, the North's capture of Confederate ambassadors to Europe, James Mason of Virginia and John Slidell of Louisiana, strained U.S.–European relations. In response, Britain threatened to withhold Indian saltpeter, the main ingredient of gunpowder, declaring, "No settlement, no saltpeter." Lincoln quickly resolved the dispute. "One war at a time," he said.

The North also achieved several military land victories between February and May of 1862 in the Western Theater of the war. Forced to resign from the army in 1854 because of drunkenness, Ulysses S. Grant repaired his military image in the West and learned valuable military lessons that he would apply throughout the war. As a colonel on his first assignment, Grant led the Twenty-first Illinois Regiment in an attack on a Confederate stronghold in Missouri. Summoning his flagging courage, Grant approached the camp. The enemy had fled their camp, and Grant realized that the Confederates were as afraid as he was. It was a lesson he would never forget and contributed to his military style for the rest of the war. Aggressive offense—worrying about what he planned to do to the enemy rather than what the enemy planned to do to him—characterized Grant's actions from that point to the end of the war, sometimes to the detriment of his men, who often suffered high casualties.

Elected as provisional president in November, Jefferson Davis was officially sworn into his one six-year term of office as president of the Confederacy on February 22, 1862. The very next day the North captured Nashville in the battle of Shiloh, the first Confederate state capital to fall. With a total of twelve thousand battle casualties, it was a foretaste of the huge Civil War battles to come. Both sides realized that the war in the West would not be short or easily won. Corinth, Memphis, Baton Rouge, Natches, and New Orleans followed as Confederate losses and Union victories. Only Vicksburg withstood the North's assault in the West.

The North praised Grant for his victories but criticized him for the massive loss of northern lives. Lincoln agreed with Grant's military strategy of attacking the enemy's army—as opposed to McClellan's tactic of maneuvering to capture places—and defended it by insisting that Grant was willing to fight, in contrast to McClellan, who had to be urged into battle.

Lincoln and Davis also had contrasting personalities. Lincoln was willing to lose an argument in order to win the war; Davis seemed more intent on winning the argument.

Many "firsts" came from the Civil War. On April 16, 1862, the first conscription law in American history was passed by the Confederate Congress. It became the most hated and resisted law of the Confederacy, especially by the governors of Georgia and North Carolina. Southerners had seceded from the Union to preserve their individual liberties, not to have them taken away by the Confederate government. Southern civil libertarians linked conscription and martial law in condemning Davis as a "despot." Full of loopholes, the conscription law could be evaded by the practice of "substitution," paying another to serve for you. The phrase "A rich man's war but a poor man's fight" aptly applied. Davis, like Lincoln, also declared martial law and suspended the writ of habeas corpus.

The South's antipathy toward federal taxes is also rooted in slavery and the Civil War. An agrarian society with more than a third of its population slaves, the 75 percent of the state legislators who were slave owners taxed themselves lightly, if at all, and had little stomach for or interest in paying for public education or public services. The few taxes that the South did collect, except for federal tariffs, were collected by local or state governments. With most of its wealth in a nonliquid form, land and slaves, the new southern government, the Confederacy, had no national mechanism for collecting federal taxes and no constituency with a habit of paying them. The South borrowed, planning to let the next generation pay for the war—not unlike Ronald Reagan's 1981 conservative economic and military policies (or George W. Bush's 2001 tax-cut plan) of borrow from the future, consume, and binge today and let the next generation deal with the deficits and debt.

In the South, inflation was running red-hot. An 1861 dollar was worth only about seventeen cents by 1863; wage increases of 55 percent for skilled and unskilled workers were not keeping pace with price increases of 300 percent. Disproportionately affecting the poor, these disparities increased southern class tensions, causing a growing gap and political alienation between lower-class nonslaveholders and upper-class slaveholders. But as is often the case when people are confronted with miserable economic circumstances beyond their control or understanding, the average poor whites, working class, and small farmers in the South looked for a scapegoat. And they found one in the Jews, who were labeled as "worse extortionists" than the northern Yankees. Jews in business and banking were no more or less exploitative than any other group, yet as a distinct minority they became the target. Thus, southern anti-Semitism too has its roots in and is a by-product of the Civil War.

The North paid for the war through increased taxation by creating the first federal income tax system in American history on August 5, 1861. Secretary of the Treasury Salmon P. Chase also pioneered in selling "war bonds" to ordinary citizens. Also, out of the Civil War came a centralized national currency, paper money called "greenbacks" used as legal tender for all private and public debts—the result of a bill signed into law on February 25, 1862. On July 1, 1862, the Republican Congress passed a comprehensive tax law that was relatively progressive—the more wealth and income you had, the more taxes you paid. Paying for much of the war with taxes, and creating a more rational national monetary and credit system, were among several important reasons why the North eventually won the war.

The American Civil War was a people's war, not a war among professional soldiers, which impacted other dimensions of Americans' lives. In this sense it was even more political than most wars. As the battles in the war ebbed and flowed, so did the nation's politics.

Northern Republicans—minus the southern Democratic Party's slave power representatives in Congress—were able to create a more perfect Union and to act in the longer-term economic interests of the country. The Thirty-seventh Congress (1861–1862) was one of the most progressive in all American history. In addition to financial legislation in 1862, it enacted a series of Hamilton-Whig-Republican "Big Government" measures such as the Homestead Act, the Pacific Railroad Act, and the Morrill Act. This legislation affirmed a widely held public view held then that federal government investment in national economic growth was a benefit to the entire society.

The Homestead Act helped expand and develop the country westward. The federal government gave settlers—male or female—160 acres if they resided on a plot for five years and improved the land. The Homestead Act did not provide "every poor man a farm," as was originally hoped, but half a million families did eventually settle eighty million acres of land.

The Morrill Act, named for its Republican sponsor, Vermont's Justin Morrill, proposed to grant a total of thirty thousand acres of public land per congressional delegation in every state—including the southern ones when they returned to the Union—for the purpose of developing higher education in agriculture and the mechanical arts. Cornell University in Ithica, New York, the University of Illinois in Champaign-Urbana (where my wife and I graduated from law school), the University of Wisconsin at Madison, Michigan State University in East Lansing, the University of Minnesota in Minneapolis, and the University of California at Berkeley were among the universities founded because of the Morrill Act. The Thirty-seventh Congress also created the Department of Agriculture to aid in rural economic development.

The Homestead Act was designed to facilitate the creation of new markets, the Morrill Act to provide educational help to grow them, and the Pacific Railroad Act to link these new markets in a northern route from the East Coast to the West. While there had been agreement on building a transcontinental railroad prior to the Civil War, there was also a congressional war over which route to take—southern or northern. Absent southern legislators, however, the northern Republicans, joined by westerners, passed the Pacific Railroad Act granting government bonds to corporations organized to build a railroad from sixty-four hundred acres of public land per mile, later doubled. It also lent sixteen thousand dollars per mile "for construction on the plains" and forty-eight thousand dollars per mile for construction "in the mountains."

With 2 billion acres of public land, the 225 million acres the federal government finally gave away under these three laws was a mere drop in the bucket. Even though, under these three Republican "Big Government" programs, there was plenty of "waste, fraud, and abuse"—the most celebrated words of conservative Republicans nowadays—they also populated the West, interspersed it with schools, and traversed it with the steel rails of a new transcontinental railroad.

Thus, by passing legislation to create a national Internal Revenue Service to finance the war, federalizing the nation's money ("greenbacks") and credit, creating government war bonds, investing in the nation's public lands for purposes of homesteading, education, and creating a railroad to boost our nation's future economic growth, the Thirty-seventh Congress legislatively probably did more than any other in history to change the course of our national life. In economic terms, it brought about a second American revolution. It could have happened only without southern conservative Democrats in Congress.

Today we need a modern national investment in our future to help bring another economic revolution consisting of full employment, comprehensive and universal health care, affordable housing, a high-quality public education system for all Americans, a clean environment, equal rights for all, and fair taxation. These changes can only occur if the unnaturally conservative South of today is converted or transformed politically. Such modern progressive legislation could pass again if many of the current conservative representatives—Democrats and Republicans alike—of the narrow southern elite economic interests were freed up or replaced by authentic representatives of the real economic interests and needs of the vast majority of southern people, both white and black.

The Civil War was fought prior to the medical discoveries of Louis Pasteur and Joseph Lister in the new science of bacteriology. As a result, dysentery, typhoid, and pneumonia killed twice as many soldiers as were killed or mortally wounded in combat. One by-product of the war was a changing role and respect for women and for the nursing profession. Like Florence Nightingale and her innovative reforms of the British Army Medical Services, women North and South contributed to the war through medical efforts that not only aided the warriors but contributed to liberating women and professionalizing nursing. In response to southern women's care and nursing of the war's wounded and disabled, the Confederate Congress passed a law in September 1862 "giving preference in all cases to females where their services may best subserve the purpose."[20] The medical role of southern women brought them for the first time out of their homes and into the public domain, removing them from the pedestal on which the patriarchal and aristocratic slave culture had placed them. It also gave them a place in southern "lost cause" Civil War history alongside their fighting husbands and sons.

Women in the North, though always more public and active than southern women—in abolition, temperance, and public education causes—made major contributions to the war effort and to their own struggle for liberation. Elizabeth Blackwell, who in 1849 became the first woman in America to earn a medical degree, organized more than three thousand women at New York's Cooper Institute to form the Women's Association for Relief (WAR), a national medical assistance coordinating body. Volunteers of the WAR served as an adjunct to the U.S. Army Medical Bureau. Initially opposed by the army, the group became so popular with soldiers that it grew to be a powerful political force. The WAR, which involved some important and talented men as well, formed the nucleus of the U.S. Sanitary Commission, signed into law on June 13, 1862.

In April 1861 Dorothea Dix, the crusading reformer of insane asylums, was named "Superintendent of Female Nurses" and helped recruit more than three thousand paid female nurses for the North. Clara Barton became a virtual "one-woman soldiers' aid society, gathering medicines and supplies and turning up on several battlefields or at field hospitals to comfort the wounded and goad careless or indifferent surgeons."[21] After the war, her crusading efforts led to the founding of the American Red Cross, an affiliate of the international Red Cross. Engraved atop the American Red Cross's national headquarters paying tribute to such women are the words, IN MEMORY OF THE HEROIC WOMEN OF THE CIVIL WAR. Thus, another contribution of the Civil War was to bring about a qualitative and a perceptual change in nursing, transforming it from a menial service to a genuine profession.

"Quotas" has been a misused and controversial concept in today's fight over affirmative action. It is a term especially offensive among conservative politicians in the South. Part of the subconscious—if not the conscious—negativity toward this word in the South came out of the Civil War experience. While both sides used "conscription" to recruit soldiers for the war, only the North assigned a "quota" to each state. Thus, the quota was another of the factors contributing to the North's victory over the South. Southerners take history much more seriously than northerners. Through the study, constant institutional reminders, and reenactments of the war in the South, especially among its conservative leadership, the concept of "quotas" is seen as almost inherently negative because of the role it played in the Civil War.

But the war effort proceeded both North and South. George McClellan had been ordered by Lincoln toward Richmond, and the general devised an elaborate strategy for conquering the Confederate capital. After battles lost along the Chickahominy River north of Richmond in May and June 1862, Jefferson Davis replaced a wounded Joe Johnston with Robert E. Lee. Lee began immediately to put in place a defensive–offensive strategy. He first dug defensive trenches around Richmond that could be defended with the fewest number of men—which got Lee dubbed King of Spades, after being nicknamed Evacuating Lee for his failure in western Virginia. At the same time, Lee was preparing for a large offensive effort against McClellan's forces to the north.

In the Seven Days' battles, begun on June 5, 1862, thirty thousand participants were either killed or wounded—a foretaste of even larger numbers of casualties to come.

At Mechanicsburg the South endured a tactical defeat, but won strategically because a victorious McClellan unexplainably retreated, giving Lee a psychological edge over McClellan—not unlike the psychological edge Grant had gained over Confederate forces in Missouri, and one that he, too, never relinquished. Lee was a devout Episcopalian and had great personal gentleness, but this trait was accompanied by a daring military style that the North would soon come to know. Assisted by Thomas J. "Stonewall" Jackson, at first a major military failure, Lee put James Longstreet and Jackson in charge of a newly reorganized two-corps Army of Northern Virginia.

As skilled an organizer, trainer, and motivator of men as McClellan was, an aggressive fighter he was not. If he had been more tough minded and aggressive, he might have defeated Lee early on, shortened the war, reduced the number of wounded, and saved many lives. But he also would have preserved slavery and the accompanying institutions of the Old South. The war had escalated into a "total war." Everyone and everything was being mobilized and used to defeat the enemy on the other side.

Even as Lincoln denied McClellan's request to send him fifty thousand more troops on July 2, 1862, the president was calling for three hundred thousand new three-year volunteers. Economic carrots and legal sticks were put in place to achieve the goal. After a year of actual battle, the romanticism of war had waned. The War Department agreed to pay more and earlier bounties (incentives) to those who volunteered. Eighteen governors informed the president that they could meet their quotas on a short-term basis, but would have difficulty doing so on the longer three-year basis. Congress responded by passing a law to create state militias that the federal government could call into action for nine months. Included in this law was a little-noticed provision empowering the president "to enroll 'persons of African descent' for 'any war service for which they may be found competent'—including service as soldiers."[22]

On August 4 the War Department imposed on the states an additional quota of three hundred thousand nine-month volunteers. As an incentive, the states were told that all three-year recruits above the quota would be counted four to one against their nine-month quota. Before the end of 1862, these techniques had successfully signed up 421,000 three-year volunteers and 88,000 in state militias.

As divisions in the country grew, Lincoln tightened the screws on his opponents. On September 24, 1862, he suspended the writ of habeas corpus, resulting mostly in the arrest of conservative northern Democrats known as Copperheads. Some people saw this as strictly political. With the midterm elections coming in November, politics may have been a part of it, but these conservative northern Democrats were also most of the "aiders and abettors . . . discouraging volunteer enlistments, resisting militia drafts . . . affording aid and comfort to Rebels against the authority of the United States."[23] And politically, they were not only resisters to the militia drafts, but also the ones most opposed to the Emancipation Proclamation—whose existence had been made public just two days prior, on September 22—and they had been most opposed to the progressive internal improvement laws passed by Congress (the Homestead, Pacific Railroad, and Morrill Acts).

Through the work of abolitionist radicals like Wendell Phillips and others in the first half of 1862, and because of Lincoln's frustrating and failed efforts to get the border states to buy into a gradual compensated emancipation proposed on July 12, he had decided the timing was right to issue an Emancipation Proclamation. Republicans were gradually coming to see that, politically, the issues of Union, disunion, and slavery were inseparable. So on July 22, 1862, Lincoln announced his intention in a cabinet meeting. The cabinet was in agreement, but Seward counseled Lincoln on its timing. Wait, Seward told the president, until after a northern victory so it would not appear to be an act of desperation or defeat. Lincoln thought this was wise counsel, accepted it, and began looking for such an occasion.

It came in mid-September after the battle of Antietam in Maryland. Antietam was less than a complete victory, and it had certainly been a costly one in terms of casualties, but it had stopped Lee's invasion of the North and sent him back across the Potomac into Virginia. It had also virtually ended any chance of European recognition of the Confederacy as an independent nation, even though on the very day of Antietam, September 17, 1862, Britain's foreign minister, Lord John Russell, had recommended to the prime minister that they offer to mediate this North–South dispute; if the North refused, Russell continued, Britain should recognize the Confederacy. However, five days after Antietam, on September 22, Lincoln formally announced his intention to issue an Emancipation Proclamation to take effect on January 1, 1863, and apply it to the states in rebellion. Attaching the war to the moral cause of antislavery closed the door on the possibility of Britain, France, or any other European country recognizing the Confederacy.

Republicans, while united in opposition to slavery, were divided into three camps on the means for ending it. The radicals wanted an immediate and unconditional emancipation of the slaves. Conservatives wanted the slave states to voluntarily end it. Moderates, of whom Lincoln was one, were strongly opposed to slavery on moral grounds but also politically fearful of the racial consequences of immediate wholesale emancipation. That is why Lincoln proposed on several occasions a compensated gradual emancipation. Before his July 12 effort, in a message to Congress on March 6, Lincoln proposed and on April 10 Congress supported a resolution offering "pecuniary aid" to "any state which may adopt gradual abolishment of slavery."[24] He did so one last time on December 1. Some misread this last overture, wondering whether Lincoln really intended to follow through with his 1863 New Year's resolution. He did.

Over the course of a year, feeling the pressure of northern abolitionists and confronted by the obstinate southern and border slave states, Lincoln had gradually moved from a moderate to a radical position. He became convinced that morally and militarily, emancipation would help the overall effort to save the Union. The two were intertwined. Either the slaves would be freed or the North would be subdued, Lincoln realized. Even though the Emancipation Proclamation applied only in the states where the federal government had no power, the rebelling states, it was still seen as a radical action. The Confiscation Act of July 1862 revealed the dual nature of the conflict as both a domestic insurrection and a war. This act allowed Union forces to seize the property of the rebels as punishment for treason, and also free the slaves, the contraband, as captives of war. The act also increasingly became a symbol of a war effort designed to overthrow an oppressive southern slave society, to be replaced with a more perfect Union.

The proposed Emancipation Proclamation raised several concerns. Would northern white soldiers continue to fight if the emancipation of slaves was also at issue? Would Lincoln's proposal cost the president and the Republican Party public support for the war and political power in the Congress after the November election? And what was the real meaning of the Emancipation Proclamation?

The Democrats of 1862, like most Republicans and some Democrats today, only in a much more subtle and covert manner, wasted little time in trying to unite whites by making race the central issue in the 1862 midterm election. The strategy was clear. Northern Democrats had received 44 percent of the free states' vote in the 1860 election. Add to that the border-state Democratic votes and Lincoln was actually a minority-elected president in the Union states. While some northern Democrats had converted to Republicanism, others had remained loyal to the Union but were just as opposed to the emancipation of the slaves as southerners. Confederate southern Democrats placed a great deal of hope in these northern Copperhead Democrats. If they could just gain enough power in the November election, then maybe a peace and reconciliation could be negotiated that would leave slavery and the southern way of life essentially in place.

Since the founding of the Republican Party, Democrats had always exploited the race issue at election time, and 1862 was to be no different. Democrats feared equality and saw Republicans as fanatics, willing to free millions of "semi-savages" to compete with northern workers and mix with their wives and daughters. It was the usual combination of racist fear and economic diversion. In today's politics the buzzwords "law and order," "antibusing," "ethnic purity," "welfare queen," "Willie Horton," "Sister Souljah," and "crime" all fit the model and are manifestations of the belief that meeting the legitimate economic needs of blacks is a financial and social threat to white interests. Add to them in 2000 "death penalty," "Bob Jones University," the "Confederate flag," a "strong military," "lower taxes," and "less government" from Bush; and "enforcement," a "victims' bill of rights," and "cover America in blue with fifty thousand new police officers on the street" from Gore—all attempts at subliminal communications on race.

To undercut these racist political attacks by Democrats, some Republicans—including Lincoln, who probably used it more as a political tactic to defuse the emancipation issue in the election than actually seeing it as a sound proposal for solving the race issue—dug up the old proposal of colonization (send them out of the country) as an answer to ending slavery. The U.S. government actually resettled 453 blacks on an island near Haiti in 1863, but malnourishment and sickness decimated the colony. Efforts to colonize blacks finally ended in 1864.

In 1862, Lincoln's announced support of colonization, along with his lack of public support for emancipation, was generating sometimes vicious attacks from militant abolitionists, including a "Prayer for Twenty Millions" editorial urging emancipation that appeared in Horace Greeley's *New York Tribune*. On August 22, a month after the private announcement to his cabinet on July 22 that he intended to issue an Emancipation Proclamation, Lincoln replied to Greeley's editorial with a masterfully written open letter:

> If there be those who would not save the Union, unless they could at the same time save slavery, I do not agree with them. If there be those who would not save the Union unless they could at the same time destroy slavery, I do not agree with them. My paramount objective in this struggle is to save the Union, and is not either to save or to destroy slavery. If I could save the Union without freeing any slave I would do it, and if I could save it by freeing all the slaves I would do it; and if I could save it by freeing some and leaving others alone, I would also do that. What I do about slavery, and

the colored race, I do because I believe it helps to save the Union; and what I forbear, I forbear because I do not believe it would help to save the Union. I shall do less whenever I shall believe what I am doing hurts the cause, and I shall do more whenever I shall believe doing more will help the cause.[25]

Lincoln was reiterating his central thesis, that the purpose of the war was preservation of the Union, but in light of the intransigence of the border states, he was publicly hinting that he might have to do something more, including emancipation, to save the Union. In this open letter, Lincoln was saying "if," but he had already concluded in his own mind "that" the only way to save the Union was to free the slaves.

After the emancipation proposal became public, Lincoln was sometimes ridiculed in political oratory and newspaper editorials about his Emancipation Proclamation, which would free the slaves only where the president had no power to do so—in the rebel southern states—but preserve the institution everywhere else. But Lincoln's enemies either misunderstood the president, lacked his understanding of the Constitution, or ignored his politics. On saving the Union, Lincoln had additional flexibility under the Constitution. Politically, he could sometimes get away with violating it by engaging in arbitrary arrests and suspending the writ of habeas corpus. On the question of ending slavery, however, Lincoln saw no such flexibility. His understanding of the Constitution committed him to acting within both it and the law, for neither had yet been changed. Under the Constitution, slavery was still legal in the United States.

Lincoln understood, if others didn't, that issuing the Emancipation Proclamation would convert a struggling Union army, trying to hold a nation together, into a liberation army to free the slaves. The newly freed slaves could help win the struggle by fighting alongside the Union soldiers. Of course, the liberation of slaves would happen only if the North won the war. Militant abolitionists still thought the proclamation weak, southerners thought it an outrage, but most antislavery advocates, both black and white, understood its revolutionary implications. It was the one act that changed the entire character of the war. It gave the war a moral purpose—human freedom—to bolster the political goal of saving the Union. And a purpose with such deep emotional power condemned the Confederacy to sure defeat.

The question now was, having transformed the conflict into a war of liberation, would the northern Union soldiers still fight? Some said no. "An Ohio Democrat amended the party's slogan to proclaim 'the Constitution as it is, the Union as it was, and the Niggers where they are.'"[26] But most said yes! "A Democratic private in the Army of the Potomac whose previous letters had railed against abolitionists and blacks now expressed support for 'putting away any institution if by so doing it will help put down the rebellion, for I hold that nothing should stand in the way of the Union—niggers, nor anything else.'"[27]

What of the election results? Democrats did achieve significant gains in 1862: a New York governorship; a governor and state legislature in New Jersey; similar legislative majorities in Illinois and Indiana; and thirty-four seats in the U.S. House. Fortunately, odd-year (1863) legislative elections were held in several other key states (Ohio and Pennsylvania), and four-year gubernatorial terms in Illinois and Indiana prevented further erosion of Republican power.

While historians differ on how the midterm elections of 1862 should be interpreted—historically they were seen as a disaster for Republicans and a bonanza for Democrats—lately there has been a kinder interpretation for Republicans. After all, they did retain seventeen out of nineteen Union governorships and sixteen of those legislatures. They also made first-time gains in Missouri, picked up five Senate seats, and lost the fewest seats in two decades in an off-year election by maintaining a twenty-five-vote margin in the House.

With substantial Republican majorities in Congress after the 1862 election, Lincoln became even more aggressive and radical. On November 7 he finally fired McClellan. In December the House overwhelmingly voted against a Democratic resolution declaring emancipation "a high crime against the Constitution." Instead, it decisively voted for the Emancipation Proclamation and passed enabling legislation that required West Virginia, as a condition of its admittance, to come into the Union as a free state.

Signing the Emancipation Proclamation into law on January 1, 1863, Lincoln went beyond his moral decree of liberation. He issued a call that former slaves "of suitable condition . . . be received into the armed service of the United States to garrison forts, positions, stations, and other places, and to man vessels of all sorts in said service."[28] Lincoln was arming former slaves against the rebels. This was the South's worst nightmare. It was John Brown incarnate! The North was going for revolution in earnest.

Colored sailors had been used as firemen, coal heavers, and stewards by the U.S. Navy from the inception of the war. One navy man, Robert Smalls—later one of the first blacks to serve in the U.S. House—commandeered a dispatch boat in the Charleston harbor on May 12, 1862, and brought it out to the naval blockade. The organization of black regiments began before January 1, 1863. Such regiments were organized among contraband in South Carolina and Kansas, and among free blacks in Louisiana and Kansas in late 1862. Colored troops from Kansas had seen action as early as October in Missouri, where they lost ten soldiers, the first colored military casualties in the war. In January 1863 Thomas Wentworth Higginson of Massachusetts led his colored First South Carolina Volunteers into battle and wrote a glowing report of their faithful and effective performance under fire, which was leaked and reported in the *New York Tribune*. Governor John Andrew of Massachusetts sought permission from the War Department to organize black regiments. He organized the Fifty-fourth and Fifty-fifth Massachusetts, of which the Fifty-fourth became the most famous, as portrayed in the movie *Glory*.

The southern response to the arming of colored troops growing out of the Confiscation Act and the Emancipation Proclamation was to be anticipated. General Robert E. Lee warned the Confederate secretary of war on January 10, 1863, of the consequences of Lincoln's "savage and brutal policy." Jefferson Davis sent a retaliatory message to his Congress on January 12 characterizing the proclamation as "a measure by which millions of human beings of an inferior race" were being encouraged to assassinate their masters. He recommended severe punishment for captured white officers of black troops. The Confederates did treat white commanders and their colored troops more harshly than whites troops when captured. They sometimes shot black soldiers "while trying to escape." And when the Confederates refused to treat captured colored troops "as legitimate prisoners of war, it contributed to the eventual breakdown in prisoner of war exchanges that had tragic consequences for both sides."[29]

To counter the proclamation's threat, Confederate propagandists issued an "Address to Christians throughout the World" in their June 11, 1863, periodical, the *Index*, in which a number of prominent southern preachers testified that slavery's abolition would "interfere with the plans of Divine Providence."[30]

And still playing the race card, southerners appealed to northern conservative Copperhead "peace" Democrats by charging that the war was no longer aimed at saving the Union, but at bringing about Negro equality.

While the Antietam "victory" had interrupted a series of northern setbacks and given Lincoln the military success he felt he needed to come forth with his Emancipation Proclamation, it also foreshadowed defeats on the battlefield during the winter of 1862–1863. To a certain extent, this winter was a disaster for both sides. Lincoln replaced General McClellan with General Ambrose E. Burnside, a man who thought himself unequal to the task—which soon proved to be true. In the battle at Fredericksburg, Maryland, on December 13, 1862, the North again showed its vulnerability to more determined Confederate fighters. The Union army not only lost the battle, but also suffered twelve thousand casualties in one of its worst defeats.

Following Fredericksburg and the election, Radical Republicans in the Senate grew frustrated at the administration's timidity and plotted to impose themselves on the conduct of the war by reorganizing Lincoln's cabinet. Thanks largely to the efforts of fellow cabinet member Salmon Chase, many Republicans had in particular grown weary of Secretary of State William H. Seward's moderate approach. They were going to get rid of him, but unbeknownst to the senators, Seward got advance notice and offered Lincoln his resignation. Even as the Committee on the Conduct of the War was conducting a field investigation in Fredericksburg on December 19, critical senators, such as Benjamin F. Wade, met with the president in Washington, in essence to demand Seward's ouster. The next day the president invited the senators and his entire cabinet back—minus his secretary of state. Lincoln defended his entire cabinet, indicating that all cabinet members had input into the war policies, but that, in the end, he alone made the final decisions on the conduct of the war—and he confirmed it by polling each cabinet member. An embarrassed Chase corroborated Lincoln's account and the next day offered his resignation. Lincoln refused both resignations, kept his cabinet in place, and thwarted Senate efforts to gain control over the conduct of the war.

Jefferson Davis also had his difficulties. After winning at Fredericksburg, the heaviest casualties of the war in proportion to the total number of troops involved were inflicted in a battle at Stones River, Tennessee. Even though General Braxton Bragg's Confederate Army of Tennessee claimed victory over the North, for the second time in three months the North had forced Bragg to retreat after he had claimed victory. Additionally, there was internecine warfare within the camp of his top generals—Cheatham, Breckinridge, and Bragg.

Union displeasure with Burnside's leadership continued and came to a climax as the general was making his way to Richmond, which turned into a "Mud March" in the winter of 1863. The rains created havoc for his soldiers crossing the Rappahannock River. Amused Confederates watching the enemy bogged down in the mud from the opposite bank held up signs reading THIS WAY TO RICHMOND.

Lincoln soon replaced Burnside with General Joseph Hooker, a move that Hooker had helped orchestrate but one that also surprised almost everyone. General Hooker was better known for his fun-loving lifestyle and the availability of young women in his camp than for his fighting ability. (These women were called "Hooker's girls," hence the origin of the modern "hookers" as applied to prostitutes.) General Hooker, loved by his men, turned out to be a pretty good military organizer as well. Never short on confidence, Hooker told Lincoln that the question was not whether he would take Richmond, but when. Disapproving of Hooker's arrogance and overconfidence, Lincoln replied, "The hen is the wisest of all the animal creation . . . because she never cackles until the egg is laid."[31]

After Fredericksburg, both armies in Virginia during the winter of 1862–1863 were mostly idle, and in Tennessee both sides licked their wounds after the battle at Stones River.

In the West, however, there was plenty of activity, if little progress, in and around Vicksburg, Mississippi. It was in this Republican political crisis and war context that northern Democratic Copperheads came forth with a program of "peace and reconciliation" or "peace without victory."

As a supporter of the Jeffersonian philosophy of limited government, Copperhead Democrat Clement L. Vallandigham of Ohio wasted little time in rubbing raw the issues of black emancipation, the internal improvement legislation passed by the Republican Thirty-seventh Congress, the National Banking Act passed in February, and the conscription law passed in March 1863—all unpopular with conservative Democrats, North and South. Vallandigham linked all of them to "peace." The war, he said, had changed its purpose. It was no longer about saving the Union but about liberating the slaves. "'I see more barbarism and sin, a thousand times, in the continuance of this war . . . and the enslavement of the white race by debt and taxes and arbitrary power' than in Negro slavery. 'In considering terms of settlement we [should] look only to the welfare, peace, and safety of the white race, without reference to the effect that settlement may have on the African.'"[32] Vallandigham's positions became the Peace Platform of northern Copperhead Democrats over the next two years.

The war had disrupted the flow of traffic and commerce along the Mississippi River and elsewhere and had caused economic disruption and hardship to small farmers in the Midwest. The economic grievances of the lower economic classes of these so-called Butternut Democrats—descendants of southern settlers now living on farms and in small midwestern cities in Ohio, Indiana, Illinois, Iowa, and Pennsylvania—and similar economic concerns of Copperhead and Catholic immigrant Democrats living in Northeast cities, were now reinforcing their cultural attitudes against blacks. While national banking, conscription, and internal improvements were all issues of concern to the Butternut and Copperhead Democrats, it was really slave emancipation and the fear that poor southern blacks would come North and take their jobs that united them and drove the politics of mid-1863.

As a result of his political activism, Vallandigham was arrested and convicted of being disloyal to the United States. His trial became the most celebrated civil liberties case of the war. In an attempt to minimize the political damage of his arrest and trial, Lincoln commuted Vallandigham's sentence from imprisonment to banishment, sending him South to reside with the Confederates. Vallandigham first meandered his way through the South to Wilmington, North Carolina, but eventually settled in Windsor, Ontario, Canada, where he conducted a campaign for governor of Ohio and actually won the Democratic nomination.

Apart from emancipation itself, nothing separated Democrats and Republicans in the Congress more clearly than the draft. Republicans voted 100 percent for. Democrats voted 88 percent against. The new conscription law, passed in March 1863 on the heels of the Emancipation Proclamation, brought the war into nearly every northern home. "More than any other Republican wartime legislation, the new draft brought the presence of the federal government into the community, into the waged work place, and into the household—into nearly every corner of working-class life."[33] Ever true to their racial orientation, northern peace Democrats deliberately linked economically difficult times with emancipation and conscription, declaring both unconstitutional. Nowhere was this volatile mix more explosive than in New York, a city and state controlled by Democrats, which had previously enjoyed a close relationship with Democratic administrations in Washington but now was largely left out by the Republican one.

One result of the explosive blend of the draft law, emancipation, economic insecurity, and racially inflammatory speeches—a staple of Democratic Governor Horatio Seymour—was the New York City draft riots on July 13–16. They occurred less than two weeks after major northern victories at Gettysburg and Vicksburg in early July. Anti-Negro violence had occurred in several northern cities around the country. The economic insecurity of poor Irish workers had been fueled as recently as June, when black stevedores, under police protection, were used to break a New York longshoremen's strike.

In addition, corruption was rampant in the draft system. A well-to-do person could avoid the draft by paying a commutation fee of three hundred dollars for a "substitute"; doctors also granted deferments for a fee, and professional bounty jumpers signed up to receive a reward in one place, deserted, and repeated the pattern in other places. Poor Irishmen were particularly resentful of both draft corruption and emancipation. In New York several draft offices had been attacked and enrollment officers killed by draft dodgers and mobs in 1863. Democrats fueled their anger. New York's Governor Seymour said, "Bloody and treasonable and revolutionary doctrine of public necessity can be proclaimed by a mob as well as by a government." On Saturday, July 11, the names of New York City's first draftees appeared in the newspapers next to the names of the soldiers who had died at Gettysburg.[34]

On July 13 four days of the worst rioting in American history commenced in various parts of the city. No black person was safe as rioters sacked and burned draft offices, burned the Colored Orphan Asylum, attacked business establishments that employed blacks, tried to destroy Republican Horace Greeley's *New York Tribune* newspaper, and attacked the homes of other prominent Republicans and abolitionists. Troops from Gettysburg were rushed to New York City to help quell the riot. At least 105 people were killed. Not to be deterred, Lincoln resumed the draft in New York on August 19 under the protective guard of twenty thousand troops in Manhattan.

As the war reached the two-year mark, underlying economic tensions also surfaced in the South. The planter class persuaded the Confederate Congress to exempt from conscription one white man on every plantation that had at least twenty slaves. It became known as the Twenty-Negro Law. But this "special interest" of the minority slave-owning class increased tensions with the majority of nonslaveholders.

Food was also a major problem in the South. Both the soldiers and the civilian population suffered in this regard because of the war. Trading with the enemy to survive was not unusual. Jews, North and South, were sometimes involved. General Grant had issued orders forbidding trade with the enemy unless special permits had been secured. The anti-Semitic prejudices of Grant and other Union generals had previously come to light when they had openly voiced suspicions that Jewish "speculators" loved money more than they loved their country. So when Grant discovered that several highly visible traders who had violated his orders were Jews, and his own father had come to him with three Jewish merchants from Memphis wanting to secure the special permits, his temper exploded. On December 17, 1862, he issued this order: "The Jews, as a class, violating every regulation of trade established by the Treasury Department, and, also Department orders, are hereby expelled from the Department."[35] Democrats in Congress quickly jumped on the issue. Sensing the politics, Lincoln quickly overturned Grant's order, arguing that he had no problem with expelling individual corrupt traders, but that Grant's order was a ban against an entire class of people, some of whom were fighting in Union ranks.

From a strategic standpoint, the Civil War was won in the West even though most of the battles and much of the focus had centered on eastern conflicts. In this regard Vicksburg,

Mississippi, was key. While the North had entered the winter of 1862–1863 with hope and, objectively, with relatively few political losses at the polls in November, it emerged in the spring having to confront several military setbacks, some draws, and a lot of disappointment and frustration—and the Democratic Party was now trying harder than ever to reemerge and take political advantage of these circumstances.

Understanding this, Grant's winter maneuvering catastrophes in Mississippi turned to renewed determination in the spring. Frustrated by his failure to capture Vicksburg the year before, he resumed his efforts against this "Gibraltar of the West" in April 1863. Union troops first captured and then destroyed Jackson to the east on May 14, burning to the ground railroad facilities, foundries, arsenals, factories, other businesses and homes. The torching of the city was so complete that its conquerors referred to Jackson as Chimneyville.

Six months after the Emancipation Proclamation, the top Union command was still divided over the wisdom of arming colored troops to fight in the Union army. For example, William Tecumseh Sherman was against it, while Grant was for it. Frederick Douglass and other abolitionists had fought incessantly since Fort Sumter for the Union to recruit colored troops. "Once let the black man get upon his person the brass letters, 'U.S.,'" said Frederick Douglass, "let him get an eagle on his buttons and a musket on his shoulder and bullets in his pocket, and there is no power on earth which can deny that he has earned the right to citizenship in the United States."[36]

Lincoln supported the position of Douglass and Grant against the opposition. "You say you will not fight to free Negroes. Some of them seem willing to fight for you. [When victory is won] there will be some black men who can remember that, with silent tongue and clenched teeth, and steady eye and well-poised bayonet, they have helped mankind on to this great consummation; while, I fear, there will be some white ones, unable to forget that with malignant heart and deceitful speech, they strove to hinder it."[37]

Lincoln's position was substantiated when the first important test came alongside the Louisiana and Mississippi border. On June 7, a group of fifteen hundred Texas Confederates attacked a smaller Union force of black and white soldiers at Milliken's Bend, Louisiana, just above Vicksburg. "After it was over," a Union officer wrote, "many men were found dead with bayonet stabs, and others with their skulls broken open with butts of muskets. . . . The bravery of the blacks at Milliken's Bend completely revolutionized the sentiment of the army with regard to the employment of Negro troops. I heard prominent officers, who formerly had sneered . . . at the idea of the Negroes fighting, express themselves after that, as heartily in favor of it."[38] The "bottom rail was now on top." Southern troops fighting at Milliken's Bend were so maddened at the sight of armed black troops that they shouted "no quarter" and apparently murdered several captured colored troops.

The most important battle on the way to conquering Vicksburg, Mississippi, took place on May 16 on Champion's Hill, where twenty-nine thousand Union soldiers trounced twenty thousand Confederates. Finally, on July 4, 1863, Grant was able to defeat the Confederates and conquer Vicksburg. Coupled with General Meade's victory at Gettysburg the day before—Meade had replaced General Hooker on June 28, just days before Gettysburg—it was the most memorable Independence Day celebration in American history for northerners. For most southerners, it added symbolic insult to real injury. Grant later asserted that, strategically, the capture of Vicksburg was the most important northern victory of the war. "The fate of the Confederacy was sealed when Vicksburg fell," he said.

That was the West. Back in the East in Virginia, Robert E. Lee was scoring his greatest success in the Wilderness Campaign just nine miles west of Chancellorsville, not long before suffering his greatest defeat at Gettysburg. Lee, outnumbered two to one in Chancellorsville's Wilderness area of thickly bunched trees, nevertheless aggressively took the fight to a cautious "Fighting Joe" Hooker, once again outfoxing Union forces with a series of daring military moves that paid off in victory. Unfortunately, one of the prices Lee paid in his Wilderness Campaign was the loss of his fast-flanking cavalryman, General Thomas J. "Stonewall" Jackson. Jackson had been shot by mistake twice in his left arm by his own nervous Confederate soldiers as he returned after dark from a scouting detail. The arm had to be amputated, following which Jackson caught pneumonia and died eight days later—a permanent and irreparable loss for Lee. However, with regard to this April and May campaign—concluded around a burning Chancellorsville Mansion—it made no difference. Lee had won his greatest military triumph.

But Lee's pride at Chancellorsville went before his destruction at Gettysburg. The victory generated great southern boastfulness and convinced Lee that his troops were invincible, which led him to an arrogant contempt for and underestimation of his northern foes. In the North, despair increased as the defeat at Chancellorsville gave Democrats more political ammunition to use against Lincoln and the Republicans. Democrats talked about a war for emancipation that "Republicans cannot win" and a southern conquest that "they cannot hold."

Lee was still not out of the woods. With Grant on the move in Mississippi, with Union forces making noise in middle Tennessee and with Hooker's army of ninety thousand still poised on the Rappahannock in Virginia, there was no time for Lee to rest on his laurels. It was time for another aggressive and risky maneuver—invasion of the North. At a May 15 meeting in Richmond, Lee laid out before President Davis, his cabinet, and other top generals his vision for such an invasion of Pennsylvania, and persuaded virtually all of them.

Lee's victory at Chancellorsville had also revived southern hope for international recognition and prompted Lincoln's old Whig friend, Confederate Vice President Alexander Stephens, to seek a meeting with him to discuss prisoner-of-war exchanges. These discussions went nowhere, because the Confederate government refused to include blacks in the exchanges.

As Confederate forces moved into Pennsylvania with the idea of cutting off rail, supply, and communications lines to Pennsylvania's state capital in Harrisburg, and possibly moving on to conquer Philadelphia, A. P. Hill, one of Lee's generals, had heard that the well-off community of Gettysburg had a ready supply of shoes. He gave his men permission to go to town and "get those shoes." When the Confederates arrived on the morning of July 1, Union forces were already there. While Lee had issued orders not to engage the enemy until he was ready, the battle started when forces from both sides accidentally ran into each other and started fighting. It escalated into a fight initially involving twenty-four thousand Confederates and nineteen thousand Union soldiers shooting at each other northwest of Gettysburg. A battle that neither side intended to start nevertheless began and, over the next few days, was destined to become the largest and most important battle of the Civil War.

The battle at Gettysburg made places such as Cemetery Hill, Cemetery Ridge, Little Round Top, Big Round Top, and Devil's Den famous, along with the northern names of Colonel Joshua L. Chamberlain and the Twentieth Maine, the First Minnesota, and General Gouverneur K. Warren. For the South, the name of a thirty-eight-year-old general, George Pickett, was forever made infamous when Lee ordered him to conduct "Pickett's Charge," an almost suicidal foray against Union troops. It was a great northern victory, but a total of more than fifty thousand men had given of their blood or lives—as many as twenty-three thousand Union casualties and twenty-eight thousand southern men killed, wounded, or missing, more than a third of Lee's army. The combination of victories at Gettysburg and Vicksburg turned out to be the all-important turning point in the war.

The burial of the Gettysburg dead was originally planned for October 23 but rescheduled to November 19 because the principal orator, Edward Everett of Massachusetts, could not be ready before then. Lincoln, by comparison, was casually invited to attend and make a few remarks. "No insult was intended. Federal responsibility or participation was not assumed, then, in state activities. And Lincoln took no offense. Though specifically invited to deliver only 'a few appropriate remarks' to open the cemetery, he meant to use this opportunity. The partly mythical victory of Gettysburg was important to his administration's war propaganda."[39]

There are mythical accounts that Lincoln wrote his Gettysburg Address on the back of an envelope. Even though the 272-word speech probably took less than three minutes to deliver—interrupted with applause five times by the twenty thousand in attendance—such cavalier preparation would have been totally uncharacteristic of Lincoln, who took such opportunities very seriously.

Lincoln intended to use this occasion and speech to lift the nation's eyes above the death and carnage at Gettysburg "to a level of abstraction that purges it of grosser matter. . . . Lincoln did for the whole Civil War what he accomplished for the single battlefield."[40] He transformed its meaning and in so doing transformed what it meant to be an American.

Lincoln mentioned neither slavery nor Gettysburg. He drained his speech of all particulars in order to lift up an ideal. Lincoln intended to create something good and new out of this tragic and bloody episode. Both North and South strove to interpret Gettysburg to further their own war interests. Lincoln was after an even bigger victory—winning the ideological as well as the military war. And he succeeded. "The Civil War is, to most Americans, what Lincoln wanted it to mean. Words had to complete the work of the guns."[41]

When we wave the flag and celebrate on July 4, Independence Day, we are not so much celebrating our American-ness in terms of our independence from England. We are celebrating the meaning of the flag and America as Lincoln interpreted them in his Gettysburg Address. At Gettysburg, Lincoln reinterpreted the Constitution. Looking past slavery in the Constitution, he appealed to the Declaration of Independence and its claim that "all men are created equal." Conservative political "heirs to this outrage still attack Lincoln for subverting the Constitution at Gettysburg."[42]

Lincoln is here not only to sweeten the air at Gettysburg, but to clear the infected atmosphere of American history itself, tainted with official sins and inherited guilt. He would cleanse the Constitution—not, as William Lloyd Garrison had, by burning an instrument that countenanced slavery. He altered the document from within, by appeal from its letter to the spirit, subtly changing the recalcitrant stuff of that legal compromise, bringing it to its own indictment. By implicitly doing this, he performed one of the most daring acts of open-air sleight-of-hand ever witnessed by the unsuspecting. Everyone in that vast throng of thousands was having his or her intellectual pocket picked. The crowd departed with a new thing in its ideological luggage, that new Constitution Lincoln had substituted for the one they brought there with them. They walked off, from those curving graves on the hillside, under a changed sky, into a different America. Lincoln had revolutionized the Revolution, giving people a new past to live with that would change their future indefinitely.[43]

Lincoln's Gettysburg Address was transforming the United States from a plural to a singular noun—from the United States *are* into the United States *is* a free government. According to Garry Wills, Lincoln, by his words and actions, converted the Union from a mystical hope into a constitutional reality.

Current scholars and politicians call the Gettysburg Address just as authoritative a statement of the American spirit as the Declaration of Independence, perhaps more so because it determines how we read the latter. Wills argues that for most people, the Declaration means what Lincoln told us it means, correcting the Constitution in the process without overthrowing it. This spiritual correction and intellectual revolution makes attempts to go back beyond Lincoln virtually impossible. "The proponents of states' rights may have arguments, but they have lost their force, in courts as well as in the popular mind. By accepting the Gettysburg Address, its concept of a single people dedicated to a proposition, we have been changed. Because of it, we live in a different America."[44]

With the July 4, 1863, victories at Gettysburg and Vicksburg, northern hopes rose as southern spirits sank. Lincoln now wanted to concentrate on Tennessee. He was still pursuing his strategy of a military full-court press that would keep the main Confederate armies divided so they could not reinforce one another. After careful planning, General William S. Rosecrans lead his Army of the Cumberland to quick and bloodless conquests of Knoxville, the center of Unionism in east Tennessee, on September 3, while Bragg and his Confederate Army of Tennessee evacuated Chattanooga on September 8. Chattanooga was a strategic rail center that linked the Confederacy eastward and westward. The North was now on the move toward Georgia.

After a northern loss and temporary setback in a battle at Chickamauga Creek just below Chattanooga on September 19—the bloodiest battle in the West during the Civil War, in which George Thomas became known as the Rock of Chickamauga by assuming a critical leadership role for the North in stifling Bragg's forces from reconquering Chattanooga— the Confederates tried to isolate and starve the Union forces defending (for the first time) a besieged city. With his forces stationed at the top of Lookout Mountain and on the high slopes of Missionary Ridge, Bragg seemed destined to succeed. Lincoln decided to send two units from the Army of the Potomac to aid Chattanooga. The 1,233-mile trek went "through Union-held territory over the Appalachians and across the un-bridged Ohio River twice. Eleven days later more than 20,000 men had arrived at the railhead near Chattanooga with their artillery, horses, and equipment. It was an extraordinary feat of logistics—the longest and fastest movement of such a large body of troops before the twentieth century."[45]

To give some sense of the size that the war had now grown to, in October Lincoln created the Army of the Mississippi, put Grant in charge, and sent him to break the Confederates' stranglehold on Chattanooga. By October 23, Grant had broken the lock on Chattanooga and established the "cracker line" that allowed food to once again flow to the Union bluecoats. By mid-November, Sherman's seventeen thousand troops from the Army of Tennessee and Hooker's twenty thousand men from the Army of the Potomac had reinforced the thirty-five thousand infantrymen of Thomas's Army of the Cumberland. The Confederates now were increasingly in trouble and in tumult. President Davis came to Tennessee to try to resolve a no-confidence vote among his generals over Braxton Bragg's leadership. No substitute could be found. Bragg was retained and little changed.

On the morning of November 24, 1863, Joe Hooker's men to the west conquered Lookout Mountain in a heavy fog that came to be known as the "Battle Above the Clouds." At the other end, Sherman quickly took his assigned eastern hill, Missionary Ridge. Then George Thomas, the Rock of Chickamauga, surprised everyone by leading a perceived suicide charge up the middle of the hill toward the top of Missionary Ridge—a sort of Pickett's Charge in reverse. Shouting "Chickamauga! Chickamauga!" in memory of their recent defeat, the renewed will, determination, energy and excitement of Thomas's men drove the Confederates off the ridge. At the same time, General Longstreet, who had been assigned the task of retaking Knoxville, was turned back by northern forces on November 29. The Union was indeed on the march.

While Lincoln had been pleased with the July military victories in Gettysburg and Vicksburg and the positive September developments in Knoxville and Chattanooga, he was worried about the possibility of political losses in important off-year November gubernatorial elections in Ohio and Pennsylvania. Voicing their usual conservative themes, both states were running conservative Copperhead Democrats, Clement Vallandigham (exiled in Windsor, Canada) in Ohio and George W. Woodward in Pennsylvania, who, along with the Copperhead governor of New York, Horatio Seymour, governed half the people in the North. Military victories would be hollow if Lincoln suffered two significant political losses.

"In Ohio the party portrayed the contest as an 'irrepressible conflict between white and black laborers. . . . Let every vote count in favor of the white man, and against the Abolition hordes, who would place negro children in your schools, negro jurors in your jury boxes, and negro votes in your ballot boxes!' Party orators lampooned the portly Republican gubernatorial candidate, John Brough, as a 'fat Knight of the corps d'Afrique.'"[46] But times had changed. Northerners had seen in the New York draft riots what could happen when politicians played the "race card" in politics—northern cities could explode.

Additionally, while the New York draft riots occurred July 13–16, on July 18, in a failed Union campaign to capture Charleston, South Carolina, two brigades of six hundred men of the all-black Fifty-fourth Massachusetts assaulted Fort Wagner under the leadership of a white colonel, Robert Gould Shaw, who hailed from a prominent abolitionist family.

During the battle at Fort Wagner, the struggle had deteriorated, the soldier carrying the battle flag had been cut down, and an order was given for Shaw's troops to withdraw. Sergeant William Carney seized the flag and carried "it back to his lines despite bullets in the head, chest, right arm, and leg. He was the first of twenty-three blacks to win the Congressional Medal of Honor for the war—although he had to wait thirty-seven years to receive it."[47] One of the most famous monuments of the Civil War is Boston's Shaw Memorial, an idea initiated in 1865 but not completed and dedicated by sculptor Augustus Saint-Gaudens until May 31, 1897. The Shaw family had rejected an earlier clay model of an equestrian statue of Colonel Shaw alone and insisted that the sculptor include some of Shaw's black soldiers. Twenty-three colored troops were ultimately portrayed with Shaw in the memorial. Sergeant William Carney was joined by Booker T. Washington and other dignitaries at the dedication.

In the battle, nearly half of the Fifty-fourth was killed, including Colonel Shaw. "Confederates stripped his body, then threw it into a ditch with those of his men. Shaw's grieving father spoke to the press. 'The poor, benighted wretches thought they were heaping indignities upon his dead body, but the act recoils upon them. . . . They buried him with his brave, devoted followers who fell dead over him and around him. . . . We can imagine no holier place than that in which he is . . . nor wish him better company—what a bodyguard he has.'"[48] It was becoming increasingly clear that whites in the North were gaining more respect for blacks who were fighting for the Union than for white Democrats who were fighting against it.

Lincoln said so in an August 26 letter addressed to a Copperhead peace Democrat, James C. Conkling, about "unconditional Union-men." Acknowledging their dissatisfaction with him for not bringing peace, he told them he saw only three ways to achieve it: win a military victory; give up the Union; or agree to some compromise that was not feasible. Lincoln concluded that Conkling was actually dissatisfied with him over slavery, and while acknowledging a difference of opinion on that issue, he continued his logic:

> I suggested compensated emancipation; to which you replied you wished not to be taxed to buy negroes. But I had not asked you to be taxed to buy negroes, except in such a way, as to save you from greater taxation to save the Union exclusively by other means. . . . Some of the commanders of our armies in the field who have given us our most important successes, believe the emancipation policy, and the use of colored troops, constitute the heaviest blow yet dealt to the rebellion. . . . You say you will not fight to free negroes. Some of them seem willing to fight for you; but, no matter. Fight you, then, exclusively to save the Union. I issued the proclamation on purpose to aid you in saving the Union. Whenever you shall have conquered all resistance to the Union, if I shall urge you to continue fighting, it will be an apt time, then, for you to declare you will not fight to free negroes."[49]

The "race bait" dangled from the Democratic Party's fishing pole was losing its appeal. Emancipation was on the offensive and seen as a positive good both for the war effort and for saving the Union. Republicans won the governors' races in Ohio and Pennsylvania and two-thirds of the New York state legislature in November 1863.

While Lincoln was solidifying his political grip on the North, Davis was losing political ground in the South. The South, with its history and logic of states' rights, gave individual governors, members of the Confederate Congress, and generals the intellectual basis for obstructionist tactics. For example, the "line-item veto" in the Confederate Constitution—the ability to negate part of a bill without losing all of it—was there for the purpose of whipping states in line using the purse strings. This weakened a centralized or unified Confederate effort. Also, the Confederate Constitution's one six-year term for its president meant Davis had no incentive to build party organization for a reelection effort. Thus, opposition candidates ran as individuals. The Confederacy couldn't effectively fight all of these scattered targets.

Davis was losing support in the Confederate Congress. In November 1863, anti-Davis representatives went from 26 to 41 (out of 106), while twelve of twenty-six senators were anti-Davis. Interestingly enough, the strongest support for Davis came from areas under Union occupation. Lincoln's opponents in the North were called Copperheads and Butternuts. In the South, Davis's were called reconstructionists and Tories.

Such political cracks in the Confederate wall encouraged Lincoln to try his gradualist and reconstructive program once again. In a Proclamation of Amnesty and Reconstruction accompanying his annual message to Congress on December 8, 1863, Lincoln proposed pardon and amnesty for all reconstructed southerners—except Confederate officials and high-ranking rebel officers—willing to take an oath of allegiance to the United States, its laws, and its declarations concerning slavery. And if a state could muster just 10 percent of the voters of 1860 to take such an oath, they could form a state government that Lincoln would recognize as legitimate. This was consistent with Lincoln's view that secessionists had acted illegally, and that the southern states had never left the Union but had been taken over by those in rebellion.

There was general agreement in the Republican North about ending slavery and about the illegality of secession, but there were various views of and approaches to the question of reconstruction—which arose long before the war was over. First, there was the question of who should control it, the executive or legislative branch of government. Second, there was the question of substance. Lincoln's offer of amnesty in exchange for reunion and emancipation would leave much of the old southern order in place. The Radical Republicans envisioned a more dramatic reconstruction, a revolutionary change in the South. There was also an emerging view that the only way to reconstruct the South was to create a political counterforce to the Democrats, who could not be trusted. This meant, to some extent, politically enfranchising the newly freed slaves and bringing them in as the foundation of a new Republican Party in the South. Republican radicals generally, and Secretary of the Treasury Salmon P. Chase in particular, felt that there was a growing feeling among many whites in the North that since the former slaves had been willing to fight to help save the Union, they ought to be able to vote to help reconstruct it.

Lincoln privately agreed that blacks should have the right to vote, at least the intelligent ones and those who had served in the military. But he and congressional moderates were nervous about taking such a position publicly. At the time only six northern states had laws permitting black men to vote. Lincoln still felt that granting blacks the right to vote was just about as unpopular among white northerners at the end of 1863 as it was before the Emancipation Proclamation.

The ambiguity contained in Article IV, Section Four of the Constitution, which required a "republican form of government," became the centerpiece for both executive and legislative proposals for reconstruction. While Congress debated the issue, Lincoln acted on his amnesty and 10 percent plan, with Louisiana to serve as the president's first experiment. The Radical Republicans in Congress and Unionists in Louisiana strongly disagreed with Lincoln's approach. In fact, Representative Henry Winter Davis of Maryland ridiculed Lincoln's Louisiana experiment, characterizing it as a "hermaphrodite government, half military, half republican, representing the alligators and frogs of Louisiana."[50] But as various sides approached particular issues before them, a potpourri of distinct topics was on the table: how to resolve the slavery issue; the role of black politics in reconstruction; the definition of loyalty; and how free black labor was to be made to fit in the new and broader southern and national economic order.

On the first question, Lincoln and all Republicans agreed that a Thirteenth Amendment outlawing slavery must be added to the Constitution. The Senate quickly passed such an amendment, but the House—which had gained thirty-four Democrats in the 1862 midterm elections—was opposed. It denied the two-thirds majority by a thirteen-vote and ninety-three-to-sixty-five margin on June 15, 1864.

The primary reconstruction proposal was contained in the Wade-Davis Bill, named for Senator Benjamin Wade of Ohio and Representative Henry Winter Davis of Maryland. Republicans still wanted to ensure that emancipation was part of reconstruction, so on July 2, they included in the Wade-Davis Bill a provision outlawing slavery in the rebelling states as a condition for their readmittance to the Union. Lincoln pocket-vetoed the bill in order to preserve his more moderate executive approach to reconstruction.

The issue of granting voting rights to blacks became central to postwar reconstruction arguments. Radical Republicans continued to agitate for the vote even though it certainly wasn't supported by southern whites and generally not supported by the vast majority of northern whites either. The radicals, abolitionists, and Republicans argued that it was not only immoral but politically ludicrous to allow the white traitors to vote but disallow suffrage to blacks who fought to save the Union. As early as January 1864 the free people of color in New Orleans had petitioned Congress for the right to vote. But political equality, even after emancipation, was too much for Louisiana whites to swallow. The best that a Louisiana convention could do at this point was vote to overturn a resolution forbidding black suffrage and mandate a future legislature to decide the issue.

Union loyalty was also an issue debated before the war's end. Abolitionists and Radical Republicans considered blacks, and whites who had not assisted the rebellious states and remained steadfast, as the only loyal Unionists. Those converted Confederates who had merely taken Lincoln's oath of loyalty—known as "galvanized" rebels—were viewed with suspicion.

Finally, there was a fourth issue of reconstruction. As former star Watergate questioner Senator Howard Baker (R-TN) might have put it: What kinds of assistance do these former slaves need? And how long do they need it? These two questions, stemming from the legacy of nearly two and a half centuries of slavery—with an additional fifty-eight years of Jim Crow and forty-six years of ongoing discrimination—remain alive, unchanged, and unanswered even today.

Eighteen sixty-four was a presidential election year. Copperhead Democrats in the North and Confederate Democrats in the South still saw hope for their conservative cause if they could effectively exploit race in the fall campaign. Trying to alarm the public by charging that Lincoln wanted to bring equality between the races, the *New York World* coined a new word, "miscegenation," meaning the blending of the races. Democrats exploited the term ad nauseam. The Emancipation Proclamation became the Miscegenation Proclamation. Cartoons appeared with thick-lipped, grinning, coarse black men kissing lovely white girls dancing at the Miscegenation Ball following Lincoln's reelection.

Confederate hatred of blacks was also made evident on the battlefield during the 1864 presidential election season. Nathan Bedford Forrest, the future founder of the Ku Klux Klan, led an assault on Fort Pillow on the Mississippi River on April 12, where 557 Union troops, including 262 U.S. Colored Troops, were stationed. After the Confederates overran the Union forces, a startling incident took place. The surrendered and captured black and white troops were killed in a massacre—with special focus put on murdering the colored troops. Recalling this incident, some black units vowed in the future to take matters into their own hands and, with a "take no prisoners" attitude, retaliated by yelling "Remember Fort Pillow" when they went into battle.

With victories at Gettysburg, Vicksburg, and Chattanooga, optimism was also alive in the North in the spring of 1864. The war itself involved two different strategies. The North had to fight, destroy, conquer, and occupy the South in order to win. The South could "win" by holding its own territory with a "strategy of political and psychological attrition—wearing down the other side's will to continue fighting. . . . The crucial turning point of both strategies was the Union presidential election of 1864."[51]

Both Democrats and Republicans wanted to use military strategy to enhance their political position in November. The Democrats' goal was to prolong the war, and the Republicans' was to end it. "The Confederate secret service mounted a simultaneous effort to sway northern opinion. Operating from Canada, southern agents plotted a variety of raids to harass the Union war effort and sabotage the northern economy—including . . . the burning of factories and warehouses; and the subsidization of anti-war Democratic candidates for office in northern states."[52] This disruptive plot was combined with a diplomatic plan of peace overtures—even meeting with Horace Greeley and John Hay, Lincoln's private secretary, on the matter in Niagara Falls, Canada, in July 1864. When Lincoln insisted that the terms were "reunion and emancipation," southern negotiators went public, accusing Lincoln of "inflexibility" on the emancipation question, suggesting if Americans truly desired peace they should vote for Democrats in the fall. If Democrats could offer an "unconditional peace" and play to the frustration and weariness over the war, they thought they could win the White House and gain control of Congress. Such a scenario would return things, to a large degree, to the way they were before the war. By August, when Democrats were meeting at their convention in Chicago, it looked like Lincoln would lose in November.

How had this happened? In Virginia in battles from the Wilderness to Petersburg, Lee's Army of Northern Virginia and Grant's Army of the Potomac had been engaged in a nine-month stalemate in some of the bloodiest fighting of the war. Sherman had left Chattanooga and moved south through Georgia, but now he, too, seemed to be bogged down around Kennesaw Mountain outside Atlanta. On August 23, fully expecting to lose, Lincoln wrote his famous "blind" Memorandum on Probable Failure of Re-election to his cabinet, laying out his transition intentions with respect to the new president-elect. He set forth his duty to "save the Union between the election and the inauguration," knowing full well that the Democratic nominee "will have secured his election on such ground that he cannot possibly save it afterwards."[53]

The Democrats wrote a peace platform but selected a war candidate, the former head of the Union's Army of the Potomac, General George B. McClellan. Democrats North and South were happy until three days after the convention. Sherman had broken through and captured Atlanta. Military gains in the Shenandoah Valley and in the Richmond-Petersburg area soon followed. These northern military victories had transformed Republican politics from an August midnight into a November noon, and convulsed confident Democrats toward doom. By October it looked as though Lincoln was assured of a landslide.

Having conquered Atlanta and burned a third of it, Sherman set off toward Savannah. With sixty-five thousand men and a supply train twenty-five miles long, he destroyed everything in his path. Sherman believed that the only way to defeat the South's army was to wreak havoc on the civilians who sustained it. And that is exactly what he did in his 425-mile "March to the Sea," begun on November 16, 1864, and causing one hundred million dollars' worth of damage. "'We had a gay old campaign,' a private recalled. 'Destroyed all we could not eat, stole their niggers, burned their cotton and gins, spilled their sorghum, burned and twisted their railroads and raised Hell, generally.' . . . 'The whole army of the United States could not restore the institution of slavery in the South,' Sherman wrote. 'They can't get back their slaves, any more than they can get back their dead grandfathers. It is dead.' Twenty-five thousand slaves flocked to his army."[54] Communication between Lincoln and Sherman had been cut off since Sherman left Atlanta, but upon his arrival in Savannah on December 22, 1864, he telegraphed Lincoln, saying, "'I beg to present you, as a Christmas gift, the city of Savannah, with 150 heavy guns and plenty of ammunition; also, about 25,000 bales of cotton.' The President was delighted: 'Grant has the bear by the hind leg,' he said, 'while Sherman takes off its hide.'"[55]

Following his conquest of Savannah, Sherman gave the order and his troops began heading northward through South Carolina on January 19—where his army's wrath was even more destructive. Their two-month goal was Goldsborough, North Carolina. In South Carolina, Sherman fumed and raged, "Here is where treason began," and vowed, "here is where it will end."

Congress passed the Thirteenth Amendment outlawing slavery on January 31, 1865, by a vote of 119 to 56 and sent it to the states for ratification. The next day, February 1, Charles Sumner presented John Rock, a lawyer from Boston, to Salmon P. Chase—after he departed as secretary of the treasury, Lincoln appointed him chief justice of the Supreme Court—to be sworn in to practice law before the Court, the first African American ever to be admitted. The Thirteenth Amendment was added to the Constitution on December 18, 1865, when twenty-seven of thirty-six states ratified it.

On January 16 Sherman issued Special Field Orders No. 15. This order was to provide the freedmen with the sea islands and rich plantation areas for thirty miles inland off the South Carolina coast from Charleston to Jacksonville, Florida. Under this "Forty Acres and a Mule" proposition, Sherman's order temporarily granted each freedman's family forty acres of land, which was to be permanently bestowed to them by Congress later. Forty thousand former slaves were actually settled on the land of former slaveholders for several months. Sherman's military action was part of the larger question of postwar reconstruction. In March 1865 Congress passed the Bureau of Refugees, Freedmen, and Abandoned Lands Act. Its purpose was to aid both blacks and whites in need as a result of the disruption of the war, and to specifically assist former slaves in their transition to freedom. Following up on Sherman's orders, Congress said that individual freedmen "shall be assigned not more than forty acres" of land, which they could rent for three years, with an option to buy after that time, with "such title thereto as the United States can convey." This extension of the federal government into areas of social welfare, land usage, and labor was really the "Big Government" flexing its muscle for the common good.

On February 6 General Robert E. Lee was named general in chief and put in command of what was left of all Confederate armies. Even so, South Carolina's capital, Columbia, fell to Sherman on February 17. It too was trashed and set ablaze.

Lincoln's inauguration occurred on March 4 against the backdrop of the newly finished U.S. Capitol and dome glistening against Washington's cold and windy air. Lincoln had promoted its completion during the war. His inaugural address was both soft and hard as he "vowed to fondly hope, but fervently pray"; "with malice towards none; with charity for all; with firmness in the right as God gives us to see the right," he was determined to finish the work, bind up the nation's wounds, achieve and cherish a just and lasting peace.

On March 13, in a desperate move, General Lee asked and the Confederate Congress granted permission to use colored troops in the Confederate cause. Thus, on March 19, there was a strange sight of white Confederate convalescents from Chimborazo Hospital in Richmond marching up the street toward Capitol Square drilling together with black hospital orderlies to the melodic strains of "Dixie." Many Confederates, even on the eve of disaster, were still resistant to the use of black troops. Georgian Howell Cobb said, "If slaves will make good soldiers our whole theory of slavery is wrong."[56]

In the meantime, Grant's army had forced itself on Richmond on Sunday, April 1—as President Davis rushed from a church service to escape—and the Confederate government evacuated it on April 2. Lincoln visited Richmond on April 4, went to the Confederate

White House, and sat in the president's chair. As he walked the streets of Richmond crowds gathered around, including former slaves, who proclaimed him, among other things, "The Great Messiah." "Overwhelmed by rare emotions, Lincoln said to one black man who fell on his knees in front of him: 'Don't kneel to me. That is not right. You must kneel to God only, and thank Him for the liberty you will enjoy hereafter.'"[57] Describing these events in Richmond from a desk in the Confederate Capitol to the *Philadelphia Press* was its reporter T. Morris Chester, a black man.

On April 2, in addition to capturing Richmond, Union troops had seized a critical Confederate munitions center in Selma, Alabama, and broken the Confederate line protecting Petersburg, Virginia, just a short distance from Richmond. Union armies had stretched Lee's forces thin around the south of Petersburg, finally breaking through, and now Grant's 125,000-man force was tracking down and hounding what was left of Lee's army—about 25,000 dwindling, disheveled, dispirited, and starving men. Lee retreated to a place called Amelia Courthouse where he was expecting to receive rations for his men—none were there. After a Union attack at Sayler's Creek on April 6, Grant sent Lee an offer of surrender on April 7. Trapped on all sides with no way out, Lee met with his commanders on the evening of April 8 still determined to carry the fight to the enemy.

Early the next morning, Lee's forces launched an attack against Union forces, but were swiftly met with an advancing solid blue line. Lee knew it was over. Not only were they outmanned at Appomattox Court House, but overall the Union armies now had one million men under arms to the Confederates' one hundred thousand. A broken man, Lee said to his aides, "There is nothing left for me to do but to go and see General Grant and I would rather die a thousand deaths."[58] Thus, on April 9, 1865, at about noon, a Confederate horseman suddenly appeared waving a white flag—in fact, a white towel. General Robert E. Lee was sending a note of surrender to General Grant at Appomattox. They secured the home of Wilmer McLean for the two men to meet. Grant penned the simple terms of surrender, the document was signed by both men, and the war was officially over.

Earlier, Lincoln had resisted the immoral and politically expedient temptation to accept a Democratic unconditional peace. Instead, he fought through to a moral and political Republican unconditional victory. Through his steadfastness, he had achieved both his goals—preservation of the Union and emancipation for the slaves.

On April 10 Lincoln engaged in light banter in a brief speech at a preliminary celebration with a few citizens, along with several small bands. On April 11 he gave a speech on reconstruction, setting a forgiving tone toward the rebels. Reminiscent of the New Testament's story of the prodigal son, Lincoln said, "Finding themselves safely at home, it would be utterly immaterial whether they had ever been abroad."[59] Also, for the first time he publicly addressed the question of the vote for blacks. "It is also unsatisfactory to some that the elective franchise is not given to the colored man. I would myself prefer that it were now conferred on the very intelligent, and on those who serve our cause as soldiers."[60] Political equality was the last straw for some southerners; an infuriated white supremacist and a southern sympathizer in the audience, John Wilkes Booth, vowed in his heart to take the life of Lincoln.

In Appomattox on April 12 a formal ceremony of surrender took place—four years to the day after the first shots were fired at Fort Sumter. On April 13 Lincoln wrote a letter to Major General Godfrey Weasel in Richmond clarifying previous correspondence involving the former Virginia legislature in rebellion, reiterating that he had only recognized them as an acting body, but not as the rightful legislature of Virginia, in order for them to de facto withdraw their rebel Virginia troops.

On Good Friday, April 14, 1865, Abraham and Mary Todd Lincoln attended a play titled *Our American Cousin* at Ford's Theatre. During the performance, a known actor arrived at the theater, entered the State Box from the rear, and shot the president in the back of his head at about 10:15 PM. Lincoln was carried across the street to the Petersen House, where he died the next morning, April 15, at 7:22—just six days after Lee had surrendered at Appomattox. Lincoln's was the first presidential assassination in American history. The nation mourned its martyred leader. Lincoln's body was taken to Springfield by train, and he was buried in the Oak Ridge Cemetery on May 4, 1865. Reconstruction would take place without Lincoln's guidance and leadership.

Interpreting Lincoln's life and work is extremely important. Recently there have been questions raised as to whether Lincoln should be credited with freeing the slaves. The argument goes: Given some of Lincoln's history, his racial attitudes and statements, his moderate views on the subject, his noninterference with slavery where it already existed, his once proposed solution of colonization, his gradualist approach to ending the institution, his hesitancy with respect to issuing the Emancipation Proclamation and using colored troops in the war, his late conversion to limited voting rights for blacks, and more, why should he be given credit with freeing the slaves? Some have even argued that it was various actions taken by the slaves—including the power given to the Union cause as a result of the moral case for overturning slavery, plus the actual military role of working and fighting in Union campaigns—that actually freed them. By forcing the emancipation issue onto the agenda, first of military officers, then of Congress, and finally of Lincoln, it was their actions that led to freedom.

Clearly, just as the Congress and Lyndon Johnson would not have been able to pass and sign the civil rights and social legislation of the 1960s apart from a modern civil and human rights movement, so too the military commanders, the Congress, and Lincoln would not have been able to achieve what they did without the agitation and movement of the slaves and their allies. On the other hand, the slaves would not have become freedmen apart from what these leaders did. Because historical interpretation has played up the role of white male leaders while playing down the role of mass movements and leaders of color and women, our understanding of history has been skewed. Some of the current "putdown" of traditional historical interpretation is legitimate rejection and reaction to this past limited and distorted understanding and interpretation of our history. The search now, it seems to me, should be for a more balanced interpretation, which includes striving to put many forces and multiple players in proper balance and perspective. That, I think, is what is at issue with regard to the question: Did Lincoln free the slaves?

To answer this question James M. McPherson says in *Drawn with the Sword* that we must first ask: What was "the essential condition, the one thing without which it would not have happened? The clear answer is the war."[61] Slavery had existed for nearly two and a half centuries, it was more deeply entrenched in the South than ever, and every effort at self-emancipation—and there were plenty—had failed. "Without the Civil War there would have been no confiscation act, no Emancipation Proclamation, no Thirteenth Amendment (not to mention the Fourteenth and Fifteenth) . . . and almost certainly no end of slavery for several more decades at least."[62]

As to the first question, what brought on the war, there are two interrelated answers. What brought on the war was slavery. What triggered the war was disunion over the issue of slavery. Disunion resulted because initially seven and ultimately eleven southern states saw Lincoln as an antislavery advocate and candidate, running in an antislavery party on an antislavery platform, who would be an antislavery president. Rather than abide such a "Black President" and "Black Republican Party," southern states led by the Democratic Party severed their ties to the Union. Through secession, which Lincoln and the Union refused to accept, they went to war over preserving the Union. While Lincoln was willing to allow slavery to stand where it stood from 1854 when he reentered politics onward, Lincoln never wavered or compromised on one central issue—extension of slavery into the territories. And while gradualist in approach, Lincoln (and the slave states of the South) knew this would eventually mean the end of slavery. It was Lincoln who brought out and sustained all of these factors.

Thus, while Lincoln's primary emphasis throughout was on saving the Union, the result of saving the Union was emancipation for the slaves. If the Union had not been preserved, slavery would not have been ended and may even have been strengthened. Strategically, Lincoln understood that the Union was a common-ground issue around which he could rally the American people, while slavery and antislavery were divisive. And looked at in perspective, by holding his coalition together around the issue of the Union, enough Unionists eventually saw the connection between the two issues that he could ease into emancipation in the middle of the war—when it gave the North a huge boost.

Even when Lincoln believed he was going to lose the presidency in August 1864, he said, "'There have been men who proposed to me to return to slavery the black warriors' who had fought for the Union. 'I should be damned in time & eternity for so doing. The world shall know that I will keep my faith to friends and enemies, come what will.' . . . In effect, he was saying that he would rather be right than president. . . . As matters turned out . . . he was both right and president."[63]

Clearly, many slaves did self-emancipate through the Underground Railroad before the war, and through flight during the war. Even so, that is not the same as bringing an end to the peculiar institution of slavery, which only the Civil War and Lincoln's leadership did. "By pronouncing slavery a moral evil that must come to an end and then winning the presidency in 1860, provoking the South to secede, by refusing to compromise on the issue of slavery's expansion or on Fort Sumter, by careful leadership and timing that kept a fragile Unionist coalition together in the first year of war and committed it to emancipation in the second, by refusing to compromise this policy once he had adopted it, and by prosecuting the war to unconditional victory as commander in chief of an army of liberation, Abraham Lincoln freed the slaves."[64]

8

RACE IS CENTRAL—
AFTERSHOCKS (1865–PRESENT)

The war is over—the rebels are our countrymen again.

—Ulysses S. Grant, April 9, 1865

In the South, the war is what A.D. is elsewhere; they date from it.

—Mark Twain, *Life on the Mississippi*, 1883

At times history and fate meet at a single time in a single place to shape a turning point in man's unending search for freedom. So it was at Lexington and Concord. So it was a century ago at Appomattox. So it was last week in Selma, Alabama.

—President Lyndon Baines Johnson
responding to police brutality on the
Edmund Pettus Bridge, March 1965

His biggest problem here won't be that he's Jewish. It's that he's a Northerner.

—Jay Kaiman, Southeast regional director,
Anti-Defamation League of B'nai B'rith, on
Al Gore's selection of Senator Joseph Lieberman as
his running mate, *New York Times*, August 10, 2000

As of April 9, 1865, the fighting war—the Great Quake—was essentially over. A mop-up military operation continued for a few months, but the South, the Confederates, slavery, and the southern Democratic Party had all been defeated. Military victory belonged to the North. The Union had defeated the Confederacy. Free labor had prevailed over slave labor. The Republican Party had emerged victorious over the Democratic Party.

That was outward. Inwardly, ideologically, psychologically, and politically, racial resistance continued. The South still saw its culture, religion, and way of life as superior to the North's. It was impossible for the vast majority of southerners, especially the political and economic elite, to accept the former slave as a fellow human being. After all, it had been only eight years since the Supreme Court in *Dred Scott* had declared that black slaves were noncitizens, essentially property, and had no rights that a white was bound to respect. Now whites were expected to consider blacks their equals.

The political reversal of fortunes—"bottom rail on top"—was totally unacceptable to the former slave-owning legislators and influential plantation owners who had grown accustomed to laws that favored their narrow economic interests. The new laws of Reconstruction, which involved a bigger government, more interventions, and higher taxes, were written to meet the economic needs and social interests of others, including the longer-term interests and public good of the nation. But many southerners deemed them too costly, economically inefficient, totally illegitimate, and insulting to southern pride, dignity, and honor—even treasonous. Slaveholders preferred lower taxes, smaller government, local control, and a local police or state militia strong enough to protect their property and put down any racial or labor unrest. "Home rule" became a southern Democratic Party code word for white supremacy.

Also, race, as a central factor in the nation, could continue to be denied or avoided because of the way the war was fought both North and South. Throughout the war, strategically and tactically, President Lincoln argued that the war was about saving the Union, not about ending slavery. For northern consumption and potential international recognition, President Davis argued that the war was about states' rights, not about preserving slavery. Only a small minority of Radical Republicans publicly argued that the war was about slavery. Therefore, after the war, only they saw the need for southern radical reconstruction to overcome the way of life and the institutional legacy of racial, economic, and political inequality that slavery had left in its wake. If the analysis of the antebellum period, the war itself, and its aftermath denied or avoided the central problems—slavery and racism—then how could anyone propose a plan or sustain the political will to solve them? They could not and did not. This unresolved legacy is still playing itself out today.

Race, therefore, continued to remain central in southern and important in northern life. The legacy of slavery was and is cited in circular reasoning as proof that the black race was "inferior," "uncivilized," "barbaric," "criminal in orientation," "lazy," "shiftless," and "incapable of governing."

The North, through war, had politically conquered the South. In peace, however, it was unable to penetrate the South's essence. The soul of the South remained deeply rooted in religiosity, racism, regionalism, classism, and elitism. It resisted progressive racial and economic change, sometimes in cunning ways, but often in militant and even violent ways. In large measure these core political frameworks and structural patterns remain in place today.

If the end of slavery began before the start of the Civil War, the start of Reconstruction began before the Civil War ended. Symbolically, the two roads crossed on January 1, 1863, when President Lincoln signed the Emancipation Proclamation. With the stroke of a pen he put the nation on a long and winding course toward freedom and justice; toward building a more perfect Union for all Americans. Today we are still slowly and awkwardly tramping down that same road.

To better understand the politics during the era of Reconstruction, the basic philosophies of the two major political parties were the reverse of today. The Democratic Party of the late nineteenth century parallels more closely the Republicans of the late twentieth. In the 1860s the Republican Party enjoyed overwhelming black political support, while the Democratic Party consistently appealed to racial fears in its political campaigns. Today, of course, it is the Democratic Party that enjoys overwhelming black support and it is the Republicans who mostly campaign with subtle and sometimes not-so-subtle racial appeals. In the late 1860s it was the southern "Redeemer Democrats"—those who represented and wanted to restore the old order—who were trying to turn back the clock on economic and racial progress. Now we could say it's the southern "Redeemer Republicans." Besides the flip-flopping of party labels, the big difference between then and now is that the racism of the Democrats in the nineteenth century was more blatant and extreme than the more coded racism of the Republicans of the last thirty or forty years.

Just as the grassroots agitation of slaves, northern free black leaders, and white abolitionists triggered a war that ultimately ended slavery in the nineteenth century, so too it was local agitation, marches led by Dr. Martin Luther King, Jr., and other black leaders, and white liberals who joined forces to defeat the Jim Crow laws of southern apartheid in the twentieth century. Just as there were mixed feelings about black people in the Republican Party and a lack of full commitment to their humanity, freedom, and equality in the nineteenth century, there is a similar uneasy state of affairs within the Democratic Party today.

Like most wars, the Civil War was rooted in economics. In the South prior to the war, because of small governments and low taxes, the economic interests of the slave owners did not always openly conflict with the economic interests of the upcountry yeomen. Small white farmers who celebrated their self-sufficiency apart from slavery shared a mutual commitment to ideological egalitarianism (for whites only) and felt a commitment to the Union. However, as the war had progressed and state governments intervened in their lives through conscription, with their young men fighting and dying and their taxes increasing, it became apparent to the yeomen that the big plantation owners' commitment to the institution of slavery was much greater than their commitment to the interests of the small farmer or the Confederacy.

Unfortunately, however, most often white yeomen shared a common negative attitude toward African Americans and a commitment to white supremacy. Thus, when the small white farmer, businessman, or merchant agitated for a fairer economic arrangement, the planter and ruling class manipulated the race question to divert attention from their true economic needs and interests in order to keep the poor white farmers under their conservative Confederate thumb. Gradually, however, the war brought devastation, suffering, and even greater poverty to the South, from which it has never fully recovered.

During the Civil War, the North's system of industrial capitalism proved superior to the slave labor and agrarian feudalism of the South. In the North, industries and individuals tied to the war effort reaped the greatest economic benefits. Agriculture and farm mechanization grew dramatically and westward. Delivering food and transporting soldiers during the war enabled Chicago, with its cattle and railroad industries, to become the commercial center of the Midwest. Cyrus McCormick, inventor of the mechanical reaper, saw war as an opportunity to get rich and gain power. He borrowed lots of money, hoarded raw materials, bought up farmland and urban real estate, and, by 1865, was Chicago's largest landlord. Clothing industries in the Northeast and mid-Atlantic regions were booming as a result of the demand for soldiers' uniforms and blankets.

The war nationalized the country and the economy as never before. The elementary national coordination of many local manufacturers and businesses required to conduct an effective war effort provided a daily reminder of the importance and profitability of organization. For example, during the war instantaneous communication was actually hampered because of the multiplicity of local telegraph companies. As a result, in 1866 the government helped found the nation's first major monopoly, Western Union, to more efficiently facilitate national communication.

Government policies worked disproportionately to the benefit of big industry and against the agricultural sector. They centered capital on Wall Street and industry in the Northeast and, to a lesser extent, the Midwest. Government policy also deprived the West and South of sorely needed investment capital for similar economic development.

The war produced a new American industrial class. Young men like Philip D. Armour and John D. Rockefeller revolutionized industry and earned their first fortunes off the war. Armour made his money supplying beef to the Union armies and, in the process, made Chicago the nation's meatpacking center. Rockefeller, then just twenty-one, gleaned government contracts and began uniting refineries into a petroleum empire. Others, including Thomas Scott, pioneered railroad management and finance.

The war tied this new rich industrial class to the Republican Party, an interventionist government, and a more nationalized economy. The war caused Congress to issue four hundred million dollars in paper money, sell bonds, and create a debt of two billion dollars—all of which required a national banking system. The national government raised funds through tariffs and new taxes at virtually every level of production and consumption. To compensate for a labor shortage, a Republican government encouraged immigration. Through the Homestead Act, the Land Grant College Act, and the Pacific Railroad Act—free gifts of public land and generous financial assistance to private companies—a Republican government created a railroad system that tied the nation together, encouraged westward expansion and growth, and resulted in a national market. Republicans were, as I have mentioned, able to accomplish most of this because of the absence of southern Democrats in Congress.

In a broader sense, however, this unprecedented expansion of public federal power took place within a private deregulated economic system, and was exercised in a defensive, relatively uncoordinated, and fragmented manner in response to critical war needs. Because of the immediate demands of the war, the private sector held the upper hand and could basically demand its own price for its goods and services. This phenomenon created a *private–public* relationship between the private economic sector and the federal government—one in which the democratic public sector operated on an even and mutually beneficial playing field—rather than a *public–private* one. In effect, Republicans laid the foundation for Keynesianism, or the modern American corporate welfare state.

Prior to the war, Americans had looked almost exclusively to their state and local governments for help. Because of the war, the federal budget grew from sixty-three million dollars in 1860 to one billion dollars in 1865, and the federal government became the nation's largest employer. Also, emancipation and the Reconstruction amendments now made all Americans equally subject to the authority of national law.

States outside the South slowly and begrudgingly made some progress in racial justice. For example, California became the first state to allow blacks to testify in criminal cases in 1863. Senator Charles Sumner swore in the first black admitted to the bar of the Supreme Court in February 1865—John S. Rock of Boston. In 1865 Illinois repealed its laws barring blacks from entering the state and Ohio eliminated its "black laws"—laws specifically regulating black movement and behavior. Massachusetts passed America's first public accommodations act in May 1865.

While the South stood alone in terms of slavery, it was not alone with regard to discrimination or the mistreatment of blacks. Only five northern states permitted blacks to vote in the same manner as whites before the war—and none was added during the war. While

Lincoln had articulated the free-labor ideology of the industrial North as the way average workers could raise their status as citizens and become independent producers, the war and industrialization were actually creating a permanent working class dependent on industry. This development helped lead to the rebirth of the labor movement in the North—but labor discriminated against black workers as well.

The Democratic Party, resistant to change, was preeminently the most conservative institution of the day. The Civil War, on the other hand, both symbolized and brought significant change. Thus, politically, the Democratic Party reaped the harvest of these reactionary forces. Eric Foner argues that throughout this period it remained a "party of negations." Its political base could be found in the small farming areas of southern Ohio—the Butternuts—which, politically, was racially akin to the South and had also been bypassed by the northern economic boom created by the war. Urban Catholic immigrants also found a home in the Democratic Party. The Democratic Party united these motley groups with an ideological appeal developed in the 1850s. This ideology identified Republicans as the party of special interests (the freedmen) and political centralization (big government). Democrats argued that this was an abandonment of the Jeffersonian tradition of limited government. The "Elmer" in the "glue" that held the Democratic Party together North and South was the two-sided coin of white racism and white supremacy. "Slavery is dead," the *Cincinnati Enquirer* announced at the end of the war, "the negro is not. There is the misfortune."[1]

Blacks clearly saw themselves as Americans. Appeals for them to leave the shores of the United States largely fell on deaf ears. In the North, "the small black political leadership of ministers, professionals, and members of abolitionist societies, had long searched for a means of improving the condition of Northern blacks while at the same time striking a blow against slavery. Most embraced what one historian calls the Great Tradition—an affirmation of the Americanism that insisted that blacks formed an integral part of the nation and were entitled to the same rights and opportunities white citizens enjoyed. Free blacks were advised to forsake menial occupations, educate themselves and their children, and live unimpeachable moral lives, thus 'elevating' the race, disproving the idea of black inferiority, and demonstrating themselves worthy of citizenship."[2] For example, Frederick Douglass consistently preached support for establishing equality under the law, that emancipation should mean the end of discrimination on the basis of color, and that the freedmen should be fully and completely enfranchised and integrated into the whole "family" of the United States.

This growing sense of nationhood and equality for blacks inevitably created a political backlash from conservative whites. While the war preserved the Union, ended slavery, created a nation, expanded a government, and destroyed the prevailing labor ideology, it did not end the nation's racial ideology. A new counterrevolutionary movement returned to the old political ideology of localism, laissez-faire economics, and racism.

This same ideology, pattern, and manner prevail today, albeit sometimes in more sophisticated ways. Corporations, the rich, and ruling-class interests—and their interpreters, often with contempt for people of color—manipulate race against the white poor and working and middle classes. The propagators in the last century were overwhelmingly Democrats. Today they are mainly Republicans, but they are joined by a significant number of conservative Democrats in the lineage of this southern-based Democratic legacy of the Confederacy.

As difficult and divisive as the war had been, Reconstruction proved no easier. It was like trying to put Humpty Dumpty together again. Even the basic questions were complex. Under what terms would the nation be reunited? Who would determine those terms and timetables, the executive or legislative branch of government? What freedoms would blacks enjoy, and how, and when? And what role would the federal government assume relative to the states, North and South?

Even before he was assured of victory, Lincoln was nevertheless thinking about the postwar period. It was nearly a year after the Emancipation Proclamation, however, before he offered his initial plan of reconstruction, unveiled on December 8, 1863. The plan reflected Lincoln's priority of reunion, not his concern for the slaves or reconstruction. The "10 Percent Plan" allowed a state to reenter the Union if it could find just 10 percent of the white population to take a loyalty oath and agree to accept abolition. The critics had a field day, saying it did too little. One, Wendell Phillips, remarked that Lincoln's plan "frees the slave and ignores the Negro." In state after state, it became clear that the absence of slavery did not mean the presence of land ownership, economic development, social rights, or political suffrage for the former slaves.

The Senate passed the Thirteenth Amendment twice. The first time it failed in the House, but the second time it passed 119 to 56 with the necessary two-thirds majority. Thus, the Thirty-eighth Congress passed the Thirteenth Amendment abolishing slavery and sent it to the states for ratification on January 31, 1865. It was added to our Constitution on December 18, 1865, when three-quarters of the states (twenty-seven of thirty-six) ratified it. Several of the border and new southern state legislatures delayed ratification, fearful that it would open the floodgates to more rights for blacks. In fact, Kentucky did not ratify it until March 18, 1976, and Mississippi until March 10, 1995—130 years after it became part of the Constitution.

Emancipation and the Republican Party were now hand-in-glove, but were the freedmen ready to become full citizens and to compete equally in a deregulated market economy? Conservatives said, "Yes, you're legally free and you're on your own." Radical Republicans, free blacks, and the freedmen themselves insisted on more: Reconstruction for blacks meant reuniting their families, gaining independence from white labor control, labor rights, building up their institutions—churches, schools, and fraternal associations. It also meant equal protection under the law, the guarantee of an education, access to the court, access to land ownership, and an opportunity for self-sufficiency—and, above all, the right to vote.

With freedmen populating nearly half of the former Confederate states, the surest way for the Republican Party to dominate the politics of the South was to politically enfranchise the former slaves and coalesce with white progressive Unionists. That combination would have provided Republicans a broad-based constituency that, together, could have planned and politically sustained an economic program to benefit blacks and whites alike, all across the region and nation. It also would have prevented the former Democratic aristocratic plantation ruling class from regaining political power. Racial and conservative attitudes, however, prohibited that coalition from forming.

For free blacks and the freedmen—if we look only on the surface—Reconstruction and development seemed to mean two opposite or contradictory things. On the one hand, since slavery in the South and discrimination in the North had taken away or limited blacks' freedom and made them dependent on whites, blacks sought freedom in a kind of separation or independence from whites. Blacks' cultural expression had grown out of their human experiences and was different from white society. And because whites did not accept or treat them as full human beings and equal partners—in the church, at work, at school, or in society—they were forced into creating their own separate institutions, organizing their own churches, associations, and schools. In addition, it was necessary for their own self-identity and self-confidence to achieve and build their own institutions.

On the other hand, they viewed the United States as one nation and themselves as full American citizens entitled to all that America had to offer. Thus, at the political level, both the free black and the freedman fought for total integration into America. The central focus of this thrust was equality before the law and the right to vote. The demand for full and total citizenship inclusion was met with general white resistance, including, for a significant segment, pervasive and persistent violence against the black community. Black homes, schools, churches, and mass meetings were often targets.

Twice in 1865, white students from the University of North Carolina violently attacked peaceful black gatherings. A Freedmen's Bureau agent once observed, "Southern whites are quite indignant if they are not treated with the same deference that they were accustomed under slavery, and behavior that departed from the etiquette of antebellum race relations frequently provoked violence. Conduct deemed manly or dignified on the part of whites became examples of 'insolence' and 'insubordination' in the case of blacks."[3]

Freedmen, for the most part, were poor, illiterate, limited in skills, and living in a war-devastated economy. The South was bankrupt, the currency was worthless, personal and institutional savings were gone, debt was high, and investment capital was unavailable. More than a quarter million Confederate men had died in the war, and many more were permanently disabled. In 1865 over one-fifth of Mississippi's budget was spent on artificial limbs. Slavery, which had shaped southern society and benefited the economic interests of a wealthy elite, was now gone; indeed, virtually everything in southern society and culture was destroyed. Aristocratic southerners faced an identity crisis, as they were now masters without slaves, but average whites faced an identity crisis also—blacks were now their equals legally.

A pressing question among southern white leaders was: Will the freedmen work? The northern answer to this question was to introduce a "superior" labor system. The free-labor market ideology of the North, they believed, would show the South how to control and lift the freedmen at the same time. The North also brought a dual motivation: helping as a way to make a profit. Additionally, even among those whites and abolitionists who sincerely wanted to help, in both the South and the North, the dominant attitude was one of paternalism, not equality.

The federal government's vehicle for reconstructing the South was the Bureau of Refugees, Freedmen and Abandoned Lands, more widely known as the Freedmen's Bureau. Conceived as temporary, and initially given no funding by Congress, its overwhelming responsibilities "included introducing a workable system of free labor in the South, establishing schools for freedmen, providing aid to the destitute, aged, ill, and insane, adjudicating disputes among blacks and between the races, and attempting to secure for blacks and white Unionists equal justice from the state and local governments established during Presidential Reconstruction. In turn diplomat, marriage counselor, educator, supervisor of labor contracts, sheriff, judge, and jury, the local Bureau agent was expected to win the confidence of blacks and whites alike in a situation where race and labor relations had been poisoned by mutual distrust and conflicting interests."[4] For a clearer understanding of just how shallow was the federal government's commitment to the Freedmen's Bureau, at its height it employed only nine hundred agents to "uplift" four million freedmen, along with millions of poor and working-class whites, and to reconstruct a totally devastated society.

To the extent that the Freedmen's Bureau could establish order, control labor, and get the freedmen back to work in the fields, the bureau was doing the bidding of the planters. To the extent that it prohibited labor coercion and violence against blacks, helped mediate grievances, promoted black education, provided equal protection under the laws, and otherwise advanced black interests, it was viewed as helpful to the freedmen. Overall, as inadequate as the Freedmen's Bureau was, its greatest achievement was in the area of education. Its contribution was never in the funding of education but in the coordination of northern philanthropy and private donations. It laid the foundation for the first public education system in the South.

Some in both races sought total equality. However, in the hostile racial environment of Reconstruction, most white benefactors emphasized benevolent personal improvement, basic economics, and self-discipline for blacks, while eschewing social equality and voting rights. For example, in 1868 General Samuel C. Armstrong founded Virginia's Hampton Institute as a citadel of industrial education, character development, and economic self-help. Even the most paternalistic of white educators, however, saw themselves as preparing blacks for a future of self-actualization and self-direction devoid of class conflict. White supporters of black education, who included northern leaders of finance and industry such as Sears' Chairman Julius Rosenwald, saw such uplift as helping create an expanded consumer market.

The separation of moral and educational uplift from social and political equality came *after* Reconstruction. This detachment came when one of General Armstrong's pupils, Booker T. Washington, joined hands with the South's white "Redeemers" in the 1890s to give rise to a self-help orientation in southern black education that embraced a "just pick yourself up by your own bootstraps" philosophy, but let politics alone. Prior to this shift in thought, most southern black educators pursued racial uplift as well as equality before the law and black suffrage. Many teachers promoted or were active in black political organizations.

Much is made of the fact that the Republican government "occupied" the South militarily after the war. In fact, there was a northern military presence during Reconstruction, but not a large one. At the war's end there were about one million Union troops in the South. By the end of 1865, however, that number had fallen to 152,000. By the fall of 1866 there were about thirty-eight thousand, and many were stationed on the western Indian frontier. While they were often helpful, and to some degree a deterrent to white intimidation and violence, the idea that northern troops actually provided effective protection for the freedmen and their abolitionist and southern Republican allies has been grossly exaggerated. Nevertheless, in the South, the troops and the bureau's presence served as a resented reminder of Confederate defeat and a barrier to returning to the old days.

If "what to do after the war" was only briefly discussed and legislated by the president and Congress before the war's end, the first phase following the war was known as "Presidential Reconstruction." A brief struggle ensued around what to do and who should do it, which the president won practically by default. With the war and slavery over, most politicians were tired of the racial struggle and wanted to get back to "life as usual." Conservative Democrats wanted to reunite, making as few concessions as possible. Conservative and moderate white Republicans wanted to concentrate on building the party in the South with white Unionists, and on reuniting with the Confederate states. Only the minority of Radical

Republicans in Congress, and the still-disenfranchised freedmen, wanted to build a southern Republican Party around a black and white coalition. Only this progressive coalition saw the end of the war as the beginning of a longer period of Reconstruction.

White southern Democrats knew that their long association and identification with slavery, and their recent military defeat, had left them in a morally and politically weakened position, and their narrow economic interests were vulnerable. Previously, they had been able to protect them with brute economic and political power, and raw military force. Now, however, they had lost control. To get it back over time they knew they had to adopt a more sophisticated strategy, using greater political guile and cunning. In fact, their hearts had not changed, and much of their conduct remained the same.

Most whites could not even conceive of the freedmen as human, much less their equal and deserving of the vote. "Men, who are honorable in their dealings with their white neighbors, will cheat a negro without feeling a single twinge of their honor; to kill a negro they do not deem murder; to debauch a negro woman they do not think fornication; to take property away from a negro they do not deem robbery. . . . They still have the ingrained feeling that the black people at large belong to the whites at large."[5]

As for Lincoln, there is little documentation available concerning his views on Reconstruction. We can only speculate about how far his usual moderate and flexible political approach would have taken him. The selection of a loyal Unionist and Tennessee Democrat, Andrew Johnson, as his vice president in 1864, however, reflected a continuation of this moderate political approach.

As a U.S. senator and later military governor of his former Confederate state, Johnson had developed a reputation as somewhat of a radical on the war. His famous quote, "Treason must be made odious and traitors punished," warmed the heart of every Radical Republican. In fact, however, he had always been and remained a Jeffersonian believer in limited government and a conservative strict constructionist interpreter of the Constitution. In his mind, his strongly held Unionist view that no state had a right to secede in any way conflicted with his firm belief that in almost everything else the Union must respect states' rights. He believed that Congress could not legally and constitutionally impose Reconstruction on the South. It must be left to the states of the South to reconstruct themselves. And even though he was a strong advocate of emancipation as military governor, his speeches often reflected a somewhat neurotic preoccupation with racial miscegenation; he never spoke of social equality or suffrage for the slave.

Johnson also saw no role for the freedmen in Reconstruction. When black leaders met with him in the White House in February 1866, he proposed migration out of the United States as the solution. He had revealed his plan for Reconstruction on May 29, 1865, and it consisted of two parts. First was amnesty, pardon, and the restoration of all property rights (except for slaves) to the former Confederates if they swore loyalty to the Union and accepted emancipation—with the additional caveat that fourteen classes of former Confederate leaders and those with property valued at more than twenty thousand dollars would have to apply individually for a presidential pardon. Second, the vote would be limited to whites. Southern Unionism, whatever its hue—driven by loyalty oaths, rooted in the Whig tradition, or merely anti-Confederate—did not confirm social or political rights for blacks.

Thanks to Presidential Reconstruction, "benevolent liberalism" had finally come to the South. Southern whites appreciated Johnson's liberal terms for reunification with the former Confederate states. Under Johnson, however, not much would change for southern blacks. By 1866 he had liberally granted seven thousand special presidential pardons to former Confederate leaders and prewar elites, appointing several to local political offices. His belief in white supremacy and his growing identification with the South's former economic and political elite made him increasingly popular among southerners. He was basically positioning himself to run in the 1868 presidential campaign. It also meant that his success or failure in 1868 would be closely tied to the success or failure of Presidential Reconstruction.

With the collapse of slavery and new free-labor relations emerging, an obvious question arose: Who will enforce labor discipline? In the absence of the slave master, the state increasingly became the taskmaster. But who was running the state? Johnson had put the prewar economic and political elite back in power! And these southerners did not hesitate to create new state laws, called Black Codes, that restored many of the same social and work conditions of slavery. Mississippi and South Carolina passed the first and most extreme Black Codes in late 1865. Their primary purpose was control over the black labor force, but illegal actions according to Mississippi's Black Codes included preaching the Gospel without a state license. In North Carolina, Black Codes "made 'the intent to steal' a crime and decreed that all attempted thefts, even if unsuccessful, should be prosecuted as larceny."[6] Convict release laws—releasing convicted criminals to work on the plantations for free—were also a central part of the Black Codes, reminding me of the black prisoners we had seen working at Stone Mountain.

The freedmen were not opposed to being taxed. Indeed, they often taxed themselves for educational purposes. The states also sometimes collected taxes from blacks, but the freedmen insisted that they benefit. There was to be "no taxation without representation." The Black Codes also provided the South, in miniature, what would later become the full-blown laws of Jim Crow after the *Plessy v. Ferguson* decision in 1896. While *Plessy* argued for "separate but equal" public facilities, most of the early Black Codes attempted to exclude the freedmen from public institutions completely. When blacks did benefit from state revenue, it was usually a special tax levied only on them, rather than coming out of general state funds. The Black Codes were relatively short lived. By the end of 1866, most southern states had repealed them. Even so, Presidential Reconstruction had profound legal consequences. It limited black options, perpetuated white access and economic privilege, shielded the former slave owners from the full ramifications of emancipation, and limited the development of a free market in land and labor.

Debt divided the white South more than any other part of Johnson's Presidential Reconstruction plan. "Stay laws"—laws prohibiting the collection of debt, which was common among individual white farmers who were suffering the most because of the war—discouraged significant capital investment from the North. The South also was unable to attract white immigrants because of its identification with slavery. Then, too, some white Republicans in the South wanted the impossible: an economic revolution that included a free-labor market but excluded the freedmen.

In less than two years, Presidential Reconstruction proved to be a terrible failure. But northern and southern congressional Democrats supported Johnson's program of states' rights and localism, white supremacy, and reconciliation. Johnson's close Democratic political allies from Missouri, Francis P. and Montgomery Blair—for whom the famed Washington guest quarter near the White House, the Blair House, is named—advised Johnson that for political purposes he needed to shift the nation's focus from slavery to race. The

Blairs argued that while the country supported emancipation, it certainly didn't support social equality or political enfranchisement for blacks. The president needed to change the subject, appeal to white fears. Identify black suffrage with miscegenation—race mixing.

In contrast, the one thing that unified Radical Republicans was support for black suffrage. A later division among Republicans developed as to whether merely granting blacks the right to vote and then saying "you're on your own" was enough—the position of the conservative and moderate majority of Republicans—or whether, as the Radical Republicans thought, the right to vote was just one of the steps down a much longer road of federal assistance and intervention that would be required to reconstruct the South.

As a result of the failure of Presidential Reconstruction, and after the 1866 elections, Republicans controlled more than three-quarters of the seats in both houses of the Thirty-ninth Congress. A unified Republican Party could now put together and pass any Congressional Reconstruction plan it wanted and override any presidential veto. The Radical Republican wing, while still in the minority, had moral authority and disproportionate influence as a result of being in the forefront of the struggle in the nation's battle for abolition. Radical Republican Senator Henry Wilson of Massachusetts roared, "I believe in equality among citizens, equality in the broadest and most comprehensive democratic sense." However, the meaning of the theory of "equality" among most Republicans still reflected an understanding "inherited from the antebellum era, which distinguished sharply between natural, civil, political and social rights. . . . The vote was commonly considered a 'privilege' rather than a right."[7]

Radical Republicans were determined to use their new national power to bring about fundamental change in the South. Senator Charles Sumner of Massachusetts argued that the Declaration of Independence should have an equal footing alongside the Constitution in law. He claimed that the Confederate states had committed "state suicide," were now territories, and should only be resurrected and readmitted to the Union if their new constitutions met stringent congressionally mandated laws of equal opportunity. Increasingly, Radical Republicans used the Constitution's "republican form of government" clause to argue that any southern state that did not grant all of its citizens equal protection under the law, and did not govern with the consent of all of its people, did not meet the criteria for a republican form of government. Their plan was to uproot the plantation system root and branch, and provide the former slaves with everything available to whites, including land. Radical Republicans insisted upon full equal natural, civil, social, political, and economic rights for the freedmen.

Earlier, at a Pennsylvania Republican convention in September 1865, House Republican radical Thaddeus Stevens "called for the seizure of the 400 million acres belonging to the wealthiest 10 percent of southerners. Forty acres would be granted to each adult freedman and the remainder—some 90 percent of the total—sold 'to the highest bidder' in plots, he later added, no larger than 500 acres."[8] It never became law, because even some Radical Republicans were divided over such bold land confiscation and redistribution proposals, citing the sanctity of property other than slaves.

On suffrage, there was no division among the Radical Republicans. Representative James M. Ashley of Ohio said, "If I were a black man, with the chains just stricken from my limbs and you should offer me the ballot, or a cabin and forty acres of cotton land, I would take the ballot."[9] Most Radical Republicans believed that in a free-labor South, if everyone had access to the ballot and all were given the "same chance," blacks and whites would work out their destiny together. The keys were to provide everyone with equal access to the ballot and an equal opportunity in a free-market economy.

President Johnson's emphasis had been on restoration, but Congress formed a Joint Committee on Reconstruction. Conservative and moderate northern Republicans weren't all that supportive of granting blacks the franchise either. They supported civil rights within the context of the free-labor ideology but were unwilling to go much farther. The war had made them weary. Enfranchising blacks would only create more trouble. In the North, black suffrage wouldn't help them build the party and would cost them votes. Enfranchising blacks in the South would be highly controversial and destabilizing. A much safer and easier political course would be to coalesce with similar "forward thinking" whites in the South and create a new Republican Party. This is essentially the same course the current Democratic Leadership Council is choosing for "New Democrats" after the civil rights movement of the 1960s, but especially after Jesse Jackson's 1984 and 1988 presidential campaigns.

Along with the failure of Presidential Reconstruction, there was growing oppression and increased violence in the South. So even Republican conservatives and moderates agreed that blacks needed certain civil rights protections. The problem was that the civil rights they supported had always been the purview of state authority. These Republicans worried that securing such rights—the traditional civil rights operating within the free-labor ideology— through federal legislation would raise the specter of undue centralized power. These Republicans had greater concern over violating the rights of states—even if these states' rights were clearly unjust and violated the rights of free labor—than they had in protecting the individual civil rights of the freedmen.

Lyman Trumbull of New York and Republican moderates proposed two pieces of legislation. One extended the Freedmen's Bureau and funded it, though making clear that it was a very temporary institution. A second, more significant, proposal was a civil rights bill to guarantee certain civil and free-labor rights. With the Black Codes in mind, these were the first pieces of federal legislation passed that attempted to spell out the meaning of the Thirteenth Amendment. These laws mainly benefited the freedmen, though they applied to the North as well. Both laws were moderate, even conservative, and relied on the states for enforcement. The legislation was directed at state laws and public (not private) acts of injustice, with the federal government standing only as a deterrent force in the background. Radical Republicans saw civil rights in broader terms and with stronger enforcement teeth.

These laws were passed with overwhelming Republican support, with the expectation that the president would sign them. Instead, Johnson vetoed them, arguing that the Freedmen's Act was politically motivated, too expensive, and unconstitutional; further, such extravagance had never been visited upon whites. Using the protest of fiscal conservatism and fear of a centralized government treading on citizens' rights, and insisting that individual self-help rather than government dependence provided the best road to economic advancement, Johnson articulated the same general themes that today sustain opposition to federal efforts at improving the social and economic conditions of all Americans.

Johnson went even farther in his presidential message rejecting the Civil Rights Act, taking issue not just with the legislation itself, but with the federalized policy that lay beneath it. First arguing that it did not reflect our nation's history and was unconstitutional, he went on to make the modern-day conservative racist argument of "reverse discrimination"—that the law bestowed special or preferential rights on the freedmen and denied rights to whites. He argued that immigrants understood the constitutional system better than blacks and were more deserving of these rights. Johnson concluded with his usual sex scare—that the legislation would lead to interracial marriage. Additionally, Frederick Douglass pointed out that "no political idea was more deeply rooted in the minds of men of all sections of the country [than] the right of each State to control its own local affairs."[10] However, virtually all Republicans believed that the civil rights bill was right and that Johnson's views would destroy the Democratic Party. Thus, for the first time in American history, Congress overrode a presidential veto. This marked the end of Presidential Reconstruction and the beginning of Congressional or Radical Reconstruction.

What could Congress do that would be beyond the reach of changing political constituencies and presidential vetoes? It could pass constitutional amendments protecting gains achieved during the Civil War and affirm new rights—due process, equal protection under the law, and nondiscrimination in voting on account of race, color, or previous condition of servitude.

Two legal principles central to Radical Republicans were contained in the Fourteenth Amendment that Congress passed and sent to the states for ratification: first, a broad national standard of due process; and second, equality before the law. Radical Republicans tried to add a "right to vote" to the Fourteenth Amendment, but failed. There is still no "explicit fundamental right" to suffrage in the Constitution, only nondiscrimination in voting on the basis of race (Fifteenth Amendment), gender (Nineteenth Amendment), and, for those eighteen and over, age (Twenty-sixth Amendment). In fact, the debate over the proposed voting rights section of the Fourteenth Amendment caused a split between the women's movement and the abolitionist movement. Abolitionists were concerned primarily with race, and were willing to put gender on the back burner. Until then the abolitionist and women's movements had been mutually supportive. This controversy led women to create their own independent movement and organizations to fight for nondiscrimination in voting on the basis of gender.

Violence against blacks was increasing in the South, and the Freedmen's Bureau seemed impotent to stop it. In Memphis, in May 1866, three days of white violence resulted in the death of forty-eight people, all but two of them black. A few weeks later, after former Confederates regained power in New Orleans, a virtual massacre of blacks occurred. Even though Republicans remained divided on the suffrage question, it was clear that blacks needed equal protection under a national law. As a result, in the 1866 midterm elections, Republicans campaigned in support of the Fourteenth Amendment. Democrats and President Johnson campaigned against it. For the first time in American history, civil rights for blacks was a central debate in a national campaign. The country voted overwhelmingly for Republicans and against the president and Democrats, returning a veto-proof Congress to Washington. Still, Johnson and the Democrats persisted on their white course.

Congress proposed the Reconstruction Act of 1867, President Johnson vetoed it, and Congress overrode the veto. It contained two major provisions. The first was martial law in the South. Excluding Tennessee, it divided the remaining ten former Confederate states into five military districts of two states each, with commanders empowered to protect life and property. The second provision set forth a formula for their readmission to the Union, which included ratification of the Fourteenth Amendment and suffrage for blacks written into their state constitutions. The voting provision applied only to the South, not the nation as a whole. However, it created no new federal institutions to enforce these rights.

Thus, in just a few short years—1863 to 1867—blacks had gone from slavery, to emancipation, to protection of civil rights under law, to the right to vote within former Confederate states. This new burst of freedom was accompanied by a new explosion of political activity. One ex-slave clergyman noted that voting was approached with such enthusiasm that politics sometimes got in the way of religious work. Black churches, as well as virtually every other black institution, became obsessed with politics. Some reported that every AME preacher in Georgia was actively engaged in Republican organizing. Political pamphlets were read aloud at "churches, societies, leagues, clubs, balls, picnics, and all other gatherings. One plantation manager summed up the situation: 'You never saw a people more excited on the subject of politics than are the negroes of the south. They are perfectly wild.'"[11]

The old abolitionist Union Leagues and the Republican Party were the greatest beneficiaries of this explosion of southern black political activity. And everywhere blacks went, they engaged in political education—which was not limited merely to electoral politics, but involved the establishment of schools and other self-help associations and institutions. Such political activity also created a new black leadership class that was committed to equality under the law. The party of emancipation, the Republican Party, was as important in the black community as the church and school. When white violence did not interfere, blacks often turned out at the polls at a 90 percent rate. Freedom and voting were seen as synonymous. "'It is the hardest thing in the world to keep a negro away from the polls,' commented an Alabama white, 'that is the one thing he will do, to vote.'"[12] While voting was the freedmen's top priority, owning land was a close second.

Out of this period grew what Princeton historian Nell Irvin Painter describes as the "carpetbagger-scalawag-Negro-era-of-misrule" myth. The "carpetbagger" was supposed to be the lower class or scum of the North who had come South to take advantage of the current southern predicament after passage of the Reconstruction Act of 1867. Because of their poverty, carpetbaggers were alleged to be able to leave the North quickly by putting everything they owned in a carpetbag and moving South. In fact, northerners who went South were the exact opposite: the most educated and economically well off.

The "scalawag" was a native southerner who had thrown his lot with the freedmen. Scalawags were even more reprehensible than carpetbaggers. They had betrayed "their own"; southern Democrats considered them "white niggers" and treated them as lepers.

Scalawag reformers were often upcountry small white independent farmers with grievances against the former slave owners who had brought this terrible war down on their heads. Some southern reformers were even revolutionary, supporting blacks and whites fighting together for land confiscation and seeing the Republican Party as potentially a defender of the poor regardless of color. Southern reformers generally, however, were subject to the same racial prejudices that gripped most whites of that day; they fought mainly for themselves and for the exclusion of blacks as equals. The largest plantation owner in the Mississippi delta, a former Whig and scalawag governor, James L. Alcorn—for whom the historically black Alcorn State University is named—supported the freedmen as long as he could call the shots. However, as soon as the freedmen began to assert themselves, Alcorn parted ways with them. When it came to northern investment and southern economic development, moderate "cooperationists," as they were called, seemed to offer more incentives to outside investors and southern arrangers than actual benefits to upcountry white farmers or the freedmen.

Radical Republicans in the Fortieth Congress, led by Senator Charles Sumner, sought to go even farther by abolishing the "moderate" Democratic and scalawag Republican governments that Johnson had put in place during Presidential Reconstruction, establishing integrated public schools, and granting the freedmen land through homesteading. Few in Congress were supportive. Opponents termed such proposals "class legislation." Republicans remained committed to equal opportunity in the off-year elections of 1867. The results produced Republican losses and Democratic gains, however, and the Republicans' commitment to equality and inclusion began to wane as they began again to emphasize "reunion" and "fiscal conservatism."

Throughout 1867, new constitutions were being drafted and voted on at state conventions. Blacks had significant representation at these conventions, though it did not reflect their percentage in the population, which was more than 50 percent in South Carolina, Louisiana, and Mississippi. However, even as southern Republican conventioneers affirmed in resolutions their belief in equal rights for blacks and renewed their commitment to building a New South, divisions within the Republican Party began to show. On general principles they could agree. On particulars there was division. Republicans could support public education, but not racially integrated public schools. They could agree that blacks should have civil and political rights, but not social equality. Republicans could agree on expanding democracy and including black voters. They could not tolerate black majorities or live with black elected officials ruling over whites in local or state governments. They were supportive of economic modernization, but couldn't mesh the need for outside capital with the up-country farmers' need for debt relief or black demands for land. Conservative Democrats—like conservative Republicans today—used race to embarrass and disrupt the Republican coalition. In every way they could, Democrats put Republicans on the defensive on such questions as integrating black and white students in public schools and interracial marriage.

Talk of integrating public facilities generally caused divisions between black and white Republican delegates. Debt relief also divided black and white delegates. White upcountry farmers and white black-belt planters wanted debt relief to save their farms. Blacks didn't, because debt relief to them meant never having access to the land that might be forfeited to the state for failure to pay taxes. They hoped the government would make such land available to them in some form or fashion. Voting, too, was controversial. North Carolina Governor Jonathan Worth saw universal male suffrage, or democracy, as "government by mere numbers." He considered the privilege of voting a preserve of the landowning aristocracy.

The fate of Reconstruction would still have to wait on the election of 1868. Johnson continued to campaign by courting white voters and opposing Reconstruction. Fed up with Johnson's continuous race baiting and obstructionist ways with Congress, Republicans countered by voting unanimously for eleven highly questionable articles of impeachment. The impeachment pretense was that Johnson had violated the Tenure of Office Act by firing his secretary of war, Edwin M. Stanton, without congressional approval. The Republicans' central reason was nowhere cited—which was to rid themselves of an opponent of Reconstruction. In May, Johnson was acquitted when the Senate fell one vote shy of conviction, aided by seven Republican votes. Both Johnson and the Radical Republicans emerged from the impeachment and trial in a weaker position. That put the Union war hero and Reconstruction moderate Ulysses S. Grant in the strongest position to receive the Republican nomination. Republican business interests also pictured a Democratic victor poised to overturn Reconstruction as politically destabilizing. In contrast, it saw a Grant presidency—his campaign slogan was "let us have peace"—as moderate and fiscally responsible, and as creating southern political stability for northern financial investment. After Grant was nominated, a unified Republican Party moved quickly to readmit seven southern states—without whose electoral votes Grant probably would not have won the presidency.

The Democrats nominated for president New York Governor Horatio Seymour, whose racially taunting rhetoric had contributed gasoline to the draft riots in New York City in 1863, and for vice president Francis (Frank) P. Blair, Jr., of Missouri, a border-state Unionist who had no sympathy for blacks. Blair set the tone for the campaign by advocating in blatant racial terms the restoration white power and end of Reconstruction. In a widely circulated letter on the eve of the Democratic Convention, he wrote of "a semi-barbarous race of blacks who are worshipers of fetishes and polygamists," who would "subject . . . white women to their unbridled lust."[13] The 1868 race for the White House was the last campaign openly conducted on a theme of white supremacy.

The Democratic campaign of 1868 was highlighted by a strategy of economic intimidation and physical violence. Planters threatened southern blacks with homelessness and with wage and job reprisals if they voted for the Republican ticket. A Tennessee social club founded in 1866, the Ku Klux Klan (KKK), was now organizing in every state in the South and unleashing a violent "Christian and Democratic Redeeming" crusade against blacks and Republicans. In some cases, armed KKK Democrats prevented polling places from opening or denied freedmen entrance.

In August, radical House Republican Thaddeus Stevens died. A throng of mourners descended on the Capitol for a funeral second in size only to Lincoln's. Without Lincoln and without Stevens, it was a more moderate Republican Party that was now assuming power, a party primarily focused on social stability and fiscally conservative economic issues rather than full social and political justice for blacks. The freedmen's day had quickly come and gone. The course was modified and the direction was reversing. It was only a matter of time before Democratic Redeemers would be fully back in power.

Confronted with an empty national treasury and the challenge of establishing legal, if not moral, legitimacy, moderate Republicans faced an uphill struggle and almost insurmountable odds as they attempted to build a party in hostile southern territory. Tensions between moderate Republicans, who insisted on maintaining control, and blacks who insisted on participating equally, divided the party even further—to some extent paralleling the struggle that has gone on within the Democratic Party from the 1960s until today. Ironically, the hard-core Redeemer Democrats and former Confederates seemed to be enjoying the economic and political spoils despite losing the war, while the victorious Republicans were losing ground in both areas. While blacks asserted themselves and were elected to many offices, they never held their fair share in proportion to their numbers and, early on, often deferred leadership positions to whites. Black voting and representation at the state level troubled Democrats, but black power at the local level, where most decisions affecting their daily lives were made then, really outraged them.

Southern Democrats elected to office in the antebellum days were usually from the more educated and wealthier classes. They used the law to protect or expand their propertied or economic interests. If they got out of politics, they could usually return full time to their former employment as a source of income. This was generally not true of southern Republicans, especially blacks. As the first elected officials of color, they were usually a propertyless and less educated people; holding office for many of them became a source of livelihood and enrichment. For a few, the shift from plantations to politics as the vehicle for getting things accomplished paved the way for bribery and political corruption.

These Republican Reconstruction governments were faced with many new, controversial, and unprecedented challenges. Education was one of them. Traditionally, southerners, of whatever political persuasion, were accustomed to local control and low taxes. Now, however, Reconstruction Republican governments were establishing a state responsibility for public education, and taxes would have to be raised to pay for it. Public education was complicated further by white parents who did not want to send their children to school with blacks, and black parents who were concerned about their children getting an education anywhere they could. As a result, segregated schools were the rule, if not the law.

There were exceptions. New Orleans had significant integration in its schools in 1874. More typical, however, was separation if not legal segregation. White resistance to integrated education was extremely strong. "South Carolina's School for the Deaf and Blind, initially integrated, established separate classes after the white faculty resigned in protest; thus, 'a color was distinguished where no color was seen.'"[14] Higher education was also generally separate. Alcorn was established, with black trustees and former first black Senator Hiram Revels as its president, to avoid admitting black students to the University of Mississippi. The University of Arkansas admitted black students when it opened in 1872, but they were taught at night, separated from the rest of the white student body. Only the University of South Carolina—historically the center of the most rabid Confederate and elitist thought and action, but now with a black majority in its state legislature—attempted to integrate and democratize its system of higher education.

Free labor over slave labor, political rights over disenfranchisement, and education over ignorance were all new concepts in the South, but none was as challenging as turning the abstract words of "equal citizenship" into concrete social reality. Black and carpetbagger demands to outlaw racial discrimination split the Republican Party more than any other issue. "Should such a law be adopted, declared a White South Carolina legislator, 'I am no longer with the party. I'm willing to give the Negro political and civil rights, but social equality, never.'"[15]

As southern white Republican elected officials became more timid and conservative, and blacks became more powerful and assertive, conflicts arose over equal access to public accommodations. Georgia and Arkansas passed laws that foreshadowed Jim Crow, but Texas, Mississippi, Louisiana, Florida, and South Carolina all passed relatively strong nondiscrimination in public accommodations laws. Even communities like New Orleans, Austin, and Charleston progressed toward integration. While blacks were proud of the independent institutions they were building—churches, schools, aid societies—legally, they insisted on equal citizenship rights in the public domain. And in fact, politics and government were the two most equal institutions in southern life. While the Reconstructed South may not have achieved a fully integrated society, blacks and their allies were able to establish a broad legal framework through the Thirteenth, Fourteenth, and Fifteenth Amendments and state laws, and raise black expectations to the level of demanding equal citizenship rights.

Economic or labor rights also went through dramatic adjustments during Reconstruction. Antebellum planters had constructed laws in their favor, giving workers few rights. If a crop was bad or failed, everyone else had first claim before the worker, who had no recourse in the law. Reconstruction laws moved the worker and small farmer closer to the front of the line. While both upcountry white yeomen and newly freed slaves benefited from these changes in labor and economic law, there were differences. White farmers' principal concern was debt relief. Blacks were primarily concerned with acquiring land. But even if these Reconstruction governments were to make land available, the freedmen had little money with which to purchase it. While most southern Reconstruction governments did little in this area, once again South Carolina was the exception, setting up a land redistribution program and establishing a land commission to oversee it. After initial problems of mismanagement, by 1876 this creative program had settled fourteen thousand black and white families on homesteads.

Economic investment was critical to Reconstruction. But where were the states to get the money? Moderates, rather than using the more direct and progressive method of South Carolina, choose the more indirect method of "tax policy" to bring about the desired social change. Opponents of Reconstruction began to focus on taxation as another political tool to split the tentative black and white Republican coalition in the South.

Many blacks supported this tax policy approach. The South generally was sparsely populated, and much of its land already lay idle and uncultivated. Additionally, blacks were hoping that higher taxes on the economic elite would force them to forfeit much of their land to the state, and the government, in turn, would divide it up and make it available to the freedmen on acceptable economic terms. This approach seemed plausible. In Mississippi, during Reconstruction, nearly one-fifth of all the land in the state, some six million acres, became the property of the state for nonpayment of taxes. However, 95 percent of the land eventually made its way back into the hands of the original owners. Overall, the tax policy approach to economic development during Reconstruction was an utter failure.

The political climate was increasingly negative. Apart from South Carolina, the same political and ideological forces that had kept progress from occurring in the nation, but especially in the South, were still active. The colonial mentality of localism and states' rights was still dominant, and federal Reconstruction was resented. The antebellum South had imposed low or no taxes. Southern landowners, who had largely determined their own taxes prior to the Civil War, resented and resisted having the state imposing them. The evolving moderate and "practical" Republican leaders of Reconstruction, both South and North, were in no mood to stand behind more radical agrarian policies or launch the kind of new "class" programs necessary to lift the freedmen and the region to the social, economic, and political level of the rest of the nation. The free-labor ideology itself—the ideological framework out of which Reconstruction was operating—had no place for democratic governmental intervention and economic participation. And of course, blatant racism, with a violent cast, was also prominent.

Moderate Reconstruction Republicans, South and North, were preaching a "gospel of prosperity" that they thought would develop the South and win it over to the Republican Party. But they had inherited a war-torn and devastated regional economy and society—and the addition of four million former slaves had doubled the workforce. In this scenario— given the increase in public spending to meet new needs and government responsibilities— debt was rising, property values were falling, and, to compensate, taxes were increasing even more.

Republican hopes for reconstructing the South rested heavily on the railroads. In the North, Republican use of government financial incentives for railroad expansion through the Pacific Railroad Act had joined the country into one vast market and, along with the Homestead Act and the Land Grant College Act, had dramatically increased the investment of private capital. Such unregulated investment resulted in unprecedented, if greatly imbalanced, economic growth. This political formula of offering public economic incentives to private corporations opened the door to bribery and government corruption. Corruption was nothing new in American politics, and it was not limited to the South. In 1871, New Yorkers experienced Tammany Hall boss—"As long as I count the votes, what are you going to do about it?"—William Marcy Tweed's embezzlement scandal; and during Grant's second administration his personal secretary was tried as a member of the Whiskey Rings that defrauded the government of millions of dollars in excise taxes. But the South's infancy and limited experience in such private–public partnerships made it particularly susceptible and vulnerable to corruption—and it succumbed.

The attempt to attract capital to the South by priming southern railroad growth with public largesse failed when many railroads went bankrupt. Railroad bankruptcies, in turn, had the reverse snowball effect of discouraging other capital investment, which added to the overall crisis. The saving rope had become an albatross around the South's neck. These economic failures and government corruption were not self-contained. Both issues helped Democratic opponents undermine political support for Reconstruction in both the North and the South. Ironically, Republicans made their greatest political gains among whites in areas with the least capitalist development.

Government and private investment—mainly through the railroad companies—in reconstructing the South was highest between 1869 and 1871. Unfortunately, growing debt, rising taxes, and increasing corruption reached their zenith then as well. The Republicans' free-labor and free-market ideological approach, along with their attempt to build a difficult political coalition with weak and suspect moderate southern whites, and a growing black assertiveness and black disillusionment with white Republicans' failure to fight for their interests and build a more natural political coalition with them, all resulted in meager economic reconstruction and political party building. This left white conservative southern Democrats salivating, because they saw an opening to reenter local, state, and national politics. The whole approach is reminiscent of the Democratic Leadership Council's current approach to coalition building and governing: Play footsie with the Republicans, triangulate and steal their issues, rather than aggressively pursue the legitimate economic interests of your most loyal constituencies with a broad-based national economic appeal of jobs, universal health care, housing, and education for all Americans.

Republicans weren't the only divided party. Some Democrats, discredited morally and politically, felt it was time to put the image of slavery and the "old way of life" behind them. They forged a new "moderate" strategy and called for a "New Departure." They lowered the level of their racial rhetoric and, in 1869, mostly supported disaffected Republicans for elective office. Rather than openly oppose black suffrage, they concentrated their efforts on Confederate re-enfranchisement.

By 1870, with this "new movement" for a "New South," Democrats were picking up steam. Instead of emphasizing race to oppose Reconstruction, they attacked Reconstruction's economic policies. These "moderate" Democrats did not openly convene antiblack conventions and use antiblack rhetoric anymore. Instead, they organized "Taxpayers' Conventions." While the leaders of these conventions were most often the same economic and political elite that had ruled the antebellum South, the issue of taxes cut across white class lines. "Taxes" became the new code word for antiblack opposition to Reconstruction. These Democrats not only resented the new burden of taxes—imposed by a majority of elected Republicans who owned no property and, therefore, paid no taxes—but also objected to the way their taxes were being spent, on black education and other forms of development. Accordingly, new Democrats charged Republican Reconstructionists with spending "their money" on such things as common education and the education of the freedmen. The mission of these new Democrats was to "redeem" the South and save it from the destruction and corruption of Republican Reconstruction.

Fiscal conservatism was the deracialized message these "Redeemer Democrats" wanted to send to the industrialized Republican leaders of the free-labor North. But control of labor behavior, white supremacy, and racial suppression were still their actual goals. They wanted new labor behavior on the plantation—mainly from blacks, but from poor whites as well—rather than a new economic order off the plantation.

The activity that almost drove local whites into a racial frenzy was blacks organizing politically. Beyond the freedmen's new right and ability to vote, emotionally, local white leaders saw this as comparable to a violent revolutionary act and as a threat to "civilized society" itself. They lobbied hard to overturn black voting rights, and locally, Democrats continued to campaign strictly along racial lines and on racial issues.

In Tennessee, Democratic Redeemers disparaged education for common people, repealed the state education law, assigned the decision of "voluntary education" to each county, and destroyed public education for blacks except in Memphis and Nashville. Border-state Redeemers also began to experiment with legal segregation in public accommodations. The Fifteenth Amendment outlawing voter discrimination on the basis of race, color, or former servitude was ratified in 1870, but Redeemers thought of new and creative ways of eliminating, limiting, or reducing the impact of the black vote in elections. These discriminatory practices included: requiring the payment of poll taxes; property ownership qualifications; gerrymandering of districts (to minimize black representation); reducing the number of polling places in black districts; restructuring political boundaries so that single-member districts from which blacks could be elected were replaced with majority white at-large districts where they couldn't; moving black polling places at the last minute without public notification; barring voters convicted of petty larceny; establishing residency and registration requirements; and appointing rather than electing local governments. In one extreme case, Louisiana lawmakers in 1890 enacted the "grandfather clause," which stated that if your grandfather hadn't voted, you couldn't vote. This allowed whites to vote but not blacks. Of course, if all else failed, stringent psychological intimidation, physical violence, and even murder were used. In four years between the late 1860s and early 1870s, black voter registration plummeted from 130,000 to 5,000.

Redeemer Democrats also wanted the importation of cheap immigrant labor, any Irish or Germans who would work "for ten dollars a month. Even more attractive were indentured laborers from China, whose 'natural' docility would bolster plantation discipline and whose arrival, by flooding the labor market, would reduce the wages of blacks. With the coming of the Chinese, said one newspaper, 'the tune . . . will not be 'forty acres and a mule,' but . . . work nigger or starve.'"[16] At the same time, Redeemer Democrats also were keen on modernizing the South's economy through automation. A machine would not only produce more for less and more quickly than the irksome and "lazy" freedmen, but more important, it couldn't vote, they said.

While the Redeemer Democrats were making a rebound in southern society, Republican Reconstruction was failing miserably on many fronts. It was not modernizing the economy. It was not building a political party. It lacked local moral credibility and broad-based white political support. It was not using its military to protect the human rights of the former slaves, nor committed to economic, political, and social justice. Indeed, ideologically, economically, and politically, Reconstruction was on the wrong course. The formula of political localism, a strict construction interpretation of the Constitution, laissez-faire economics, and racism in social relations was a direction that doomed southern Reconstruction from the start.

But if one factor put the final nail in Reconstruction's coffin, it was violence on an unprecedented scale. Between 1868 and 1871, the South experienced white-on-black violence as no former slave society had ever experienced it. The KKK, the Knights of the White Camelia, and similar white supremacy and terrorist organizations were active throughout the South. The violent actions during this period firmly etched the KKK into the minds of blacks. While never highly organized or coordinated, these local groups shared common beliefs and a common agenda. And such terrorism served Democratic Party, planter class, and white supremacists' interests. It was terror with a political purpose in the largest sense: It was intended to affect both the public and private power relations throughout the South. It aimed to undermine and reverse the basic intent of Reconstruction. Its goal was to destroy the Republican Party, to get the federal government off the citizens' backs, to reassert control over black labor, and to restore white supremacy and black subordination throughout southern society. Terrorist groups sought to achieve in violent and extralegal ways what they had been unable to achieve democratically through the law.

While white Republican moderates sought Reconstruction through conciliation, white Democrats sought to overthrow it with violence. It was no contest. Republican resistance could be political suicide. Governor William W. Holden of North Carolina suppressed Klan violence with military force while snubbing his nose at the Constitution. Local voters were so outraged at the governor's actions that they elected a two-thirds Democratic majority in the state legislature. Shortly thereafter Holden became the first governor in American history to be impeached, convicted, and removed from office—for "subverting personal liberty."

The federal government's greatest effort to curb the Klan took place in the famous South Carolina Ku Klux Klan trials of 1871–1872. Prior to the trials, the federal government had ratified the three Reconstruction constitutional amendments (Thirteenth, Fourteenth, and Fifteenth), enacted the Enforcement Act of 1870, and enacted a third enforcement law, quickly labeled the Ku Klux Klan Act of 1871, which was an attempt to curb *private* lawlessness. However, neither the meaning, nor the breadth of the three amendments' interpretation, nor the constitutionality of the laws had been tested in federal courts. Constitutional interpretation, not retributive justice, was primarily at issue in the KKK trials.

The KKK had been active in South Carolina since 1868 when a Klansman from Pulaski, Tennessee, organized a Klan in York County. Humiliated in the election of 1868 by Republican reformers, whites in the county swore, in essence, "never again" and launched a campaign of terror. To counter the violence, President Grant on October 17, 1871, declared nine upcountry South Carolina counties in a "state of rebellion," suspended the right of habeas corpus, arrested hundreds of KKK members outside the usual procedures of due process, and prosecuted them for crimes under the Ku Klux Klan Act. The trial began on November 28, 1871, in Columbia's Fourth Federal Circuit Court with a majority black jury—the same Fourth Circuit that had never had one black federal judge in its courts until Clinton named Judge Roger Gregory to an interim appointment near the end of his second term in office.

In 1857, the Supreme Court had in *Dred Scott* declared African Americans noncitizens. Historically, by law, blacks were not permitted on juries and could not testify in court against whites. Justice was always the exclusive prerogative of white males during the antebellum period. So in 1871, how was it that a black-majority jury was now preparing to hear the KKK trial? Were white defendants actually to be judged by black jurors? Were white jurors really being forced to sit next to black jurors as equals? Were white attorneys really going to have to address black jurors seriously? And respectfully? What had the world come to? The KKK trial symbolized a world turned upside down, and white South Carolinians were outraged by it. Widely watched throughout the nation, the trial served only to increase the South's antagonism toward the North and the federal government.

The pivotal question at hand was: Who is responsible for protecting civil rights—each state or the federal government? The goal for blacks and Radical Republicans was not merely to convict some Klansmen, but to nationalize an interpretation of the Fourteenth and Fifteenth Amendments and the Bill of Rights in order to secure civil and political rights for blacks. In short, they believed civil rights should be a federal issue. On the other hand, defense attorneys, representing the dominant view of the day, argued for the traditional constitutional federal–state relationship with its states' rights interpretation. Civil rights, they countered, were state matters.

In the end, prosecutors hoped to bring the case to the U.S. Supreme Court and get a favorable ruling on the new amendments and Enforcement Acts that would place civil rights law under federal jurisdiction. Their legal goal was to establish the precedent of affirmatively protecting black civil and political rights from either individual discrimination or state action, even though the Fourteenth and Fifteenth Amendments were stated negatively. They wanted to replace the narrow strict construction constitutional theory with a more expansive broad construction.

In pretrial maneuvers designed to pose the legal questions in such a way as to allow the Supreme Court to decide these broader constitutional issues, the prosecution failed. "In seven days of pretrial arguments the prosecuting attorneys saw their major constitutional aims defeated before the first Ku Klux Klan trial ever began. . . . The defense had already attained its goals on the most important constitutional issues involved in the cases. The actual trials, in this sense, were epilogues,"[17] because "the prosecution had failed to convince the judges that the 15th Amendment provided a positive right to vote or that the 14th Amendment had radically altered the federal system, granting the national government authority to protect citizens in their individual rights."[18] In the first Klan trial, *U.S. v. Robert Hayes Mitchell*, government prosecutors successfully convicted an individual KKK member. They failed, however, to secure a judicial interpretation of the Constitution that nationalized black civil rights. Judges in the Fourth Federal Circuit held a traditional dual federalism view of the Constitution's three new Reconstruction amendments and Congress's Enforcement Acts.

The trials continued in the next session of the Fourth Circuit in April 1872. But actions by a new U.S. attorney general less committed to equal rights than his predecessor prevented the Supreme Court from considering the broader constitutional questions. Thus, "the federal government's most sustained effort to provide positive civil and political rights for black citizens ended with no substantial constitutional gains."[19] The South clarified its intentions as early as 1868. Led by white South Carolinians, southerners asserted that they would "never quietly submit to negro rule" but would "keep up this contest until we have regained the *heritage* of political control handed down to us by honored *ancestry.* "[20] Southern whites were determined to resist and outlast the federal government's will to seek equality and justice for blacks. Gradually, Republicans in Congress and the executive branch were losing interest in black rights and were tiring "of dealing with the 'annual autumnal outbursts' of violence. And it [the attempt to federalize black rights] was defeated by a constitutional vision which failed to recognize that the Thirteenth, Fourteenth and Fifteenth Amendments to the United States Constitution could have effected a nationalization of government powers broad enough to establish a 'Second American Constitution.'"[21]

Redeemer Democrats saw any *national* laws or amendments designed to protect the "rights of individuals," in contrast to the "rights of the states," as unconstitutional and a threat to their southern way of life. Benjamin F. Butler asked, "If the Federal Government cannot pass laws to protect the rights, liberty, and lives of citizens of the United States in the States, why were guarantees of those fundamental rights put in the Constitution at all?"[22] States' rights Democrats denounced and stigmatized such legal approaches as "Force Acts." Frederick Douglass said, "The law on the side of freedom is of great advantage only where there is power to make the law respected."[23] Neither federal individual protection of rights nor federal enforcement of individual rights was to be.

Clearly, the narrow, conservative, and strict constructionist interpretation rendered by Judge Hugh Lennox Bond of the Fourth Circuit in the South Carolina KKK cases was a setback for civil rights. But his interpretation was neither legally nor logically required. Nor was it the only judicial interpretation rendered at the time. A few months earlier, in an Alabama case, *U.S. v. Hall,* Federal Judge William B. Woods argued that "'the right of freedom of speech and the other rights enumerated in the first eight articles of the amendment' are the 'privileges and immunities of citizens of the United States' as secured by the 14th Amendment."[24] Judge Woods further argued that the Fourteenth Amendment not only denied states the power to enact laws that discriminated or denied any American equal protection under the law, but in the judge's mind, equal protection also "includes [state] inaction as well as action . . . omission to protect, as well as the omission to pass laws for protection."[25]

Back in Washington, demonstrating that he too, like President Johnson before him, was a true liberal, President Grant, in the summer of 1873, granted clemency to all Klansmen whose cases had not yet gone to trial and pardoned those who had been tried and found guilty. Reading this as a signal of liberal license, Kansas State historian Lou Falkner Williams reports that the pardoned Klansmen returned to the same South Carolina counties to again pummel the area with "the seeds of rebellion, sedition and murder." Williams says the Democrats' target was the election of 1874. Their plan was to return control of the South Carolina government to those considered to be its rightful heirs, "the educated, propertied, taxpaying citizens. Rifle clubs, white leagues, and secret police, organized ostensibly for 'social purposes,' made a show of force in both town and countryside throughout the state."[26] Grant's administration again sent troops in to provide for a relatively peaceful election, but shortly thereafter withdrew them again.

In February 1869 Congress passed the Fifteenth Amendment to the Constitution, and this guarantee of nondiscrimination in voting was ratified by three-quarters of the states in 1870. Most blacks and progressives saw the Fifteenth Amendment as the "crown jewel" of Reconstruction and, in many ways, it was. William Lloyd Garrison hailed it as moving four million blacks from "the auction-block to the ballot-box." However, while giving the appearance of a constitutional guarantee of the right to vote, it said nothing about the right to hold office or establishing a uniform set of national voting requirements, which some Radical Republicans had proposed. For example, nonracial requirements such as the use of literacy, property, or educational tests for voting were not prohibited, yet all of these "tests" would result in repressing and limiting the black vote. Surprisingly, even today, most Americans see the Fifteenth Amendment as the guarantee of a "fundamental right to vote." It is not. The Constitution only provides for *nondiscrimination* in voting on the basis of race. There is no explicit or fundamental right to suffrage in the Constitution.

Unlike the Fourteenth Amendment's universal language of "all citizens," Democrats weren't entirely wrong when they charged that the Fifteenth Amendment seemed to single out the freedmen for special attention and protection. "Congress had rejected a far more sweeping proposal barring discrimination in suffrage and office holding based on 'race, color, nativity, property, education, or religious beliefs.' Nor did the Amendment break decisively with the notion that the vote was a 'privilege' that states could regulate as they saw fit."[27] And of course, there was no mention of suffrage for women in either proposed amendment. Thus, in many ways, the Fifteenth Amendment was more noteworthy for what it did not say and include than for what it did.

Congress rejected voting provisions that were most inclusive, that is, applying to white and black men alike. With Confederates in mind, both Radical Republicans and southern Republicans feared such sweeping language. The North and West had qualifications for voting, which they wanted to retain. For example, literacy was a requirement in Massachusetts and Connecticut. Often nativist prejudice was involved. In California, the Chinese couldn't vote. Nationalist bigotry and partisan advantage allowed many other restrictions to survive because the poor, illiterate, and foreign-born were mainly Democrats. Surprisingly, the North actually reduced the right and ability to vote during Reconstruction more than the South. If "equality under the law for all Americans" is the bedrock concept of American constitutional law, then "it was not a limited commitment to blacks' rights, but the desire to retain other inequalities, affecting whites, that produced a 15th Amendment that opened the door to poll taxes, literacy tests, and property qualifications in the South."[28] Historian and Reconstruction expert Eric Foner also points out that blacks preferred explicit and inclusive language that "guaranteed all male citizens the right to vote." Even though the Fifteenth Amendment did not include women—which, as noted, caused a division between the women's and abolitionist movements—the African American position, not for the first time, still exceeded most Americans' in terms of a desire to reach a more universal and inclusive commitment to the ideal of equal citizenship.

The thinking of a majority of moderate northern and conservative southern Republicans matched the politics of the day. Because they believed black civil rights were assured under the Fourteenth Amendment and black voting rights were guaranteed under the Fifteenth Amendment, most Republicans and Americans believed that blacks had been given an "even playing field" and the 250-year-old "Race Problem" was behind them. The freedmen needed little further assistance from the government. They merely needed to learn the rules of the free market. Beyond that, they were on their own to pursue the dream of American republicanism.

With Democrats always against increased "centralization," and Republicans growing ever more nervous about potential federal expansion of power and economic and political involvement on behalf of the freedmen, many legislative ideas were offered, but few were accepted. The national Weather Bureau was established in 1870, but public education was of little concern at the federal level. Likewise, a national bureau of health, a federal railroad commission to oversee a rapidly growing railroad industry, and the nationalization of the telegraph industry all failed to pass in Congress. "Georgia scalawag Amos T. Akerman observed that while the postwar amendments had made the government 'more national in theory,' he had observed 'even among Republicans, a hesitation to exercise the power to redress wrongs in the states. . . . Unless the people become used to the exercise of these powers now, while the national spirit is still warm with the glow of the late war, . . . the 'state rights' spirit may grow troublesome again."[29]

Corruption under the Grant administration also made a contribution to undermining Reconstruction. Under Republican Reconstruction, new private–public partnerships, with federal and state government largesse heaped on the private sector, resulted in bribery, corruption, and malfeasance. The National Mining Act of 1866 resulted in a free gift of millions of acres of land to the mining industry. Assistance to the railroad industry was especially generous and resulted in the famous "Crédit Mobilier" scandal—a lucrative insider's deal that involved Union Pacific stockholders, the Speaker of the House, and Grant's vice president in 1868, Schuyler Colfax of Indiana. For a decade during and following the war, 1862 to 1872, the federal government conferred more than one hundred million acres and millions of dollars in direct aid to private railroads. The contrast between the government's generosity in land and financial aid to the private sector and its stinginess toward the freedmen was conspicuous.

What followed was what Mark Twain referred to as the "Gilded Age," variously defined, but roughly 1880 to 1915, which stimulated unprecedented economic growth and prosperity for some, while leaving most behind. And as a result of this economic boom's lack of inclusion of American workers, a labor movement arose to reap a larger share of the bounty for itself. While the unprecedented economic inequality of the Gilded Age of capital threw the North's free-labor ideology into question, its discrediting did not run deep enough to alter the view of reform and "cooperationist" labor leaders. Such leaders saw the interests of labor and capital as, if not the same, at least not in fundamental conflict. Promoters of the free-labor ideology did not see—or did not want to see—American workers as a "working class," the way European workers saw themselves. Thus, labor fought for incremental improvements, including the eight-hour day. Yet when labor won, states often refused to abide by the law. Part of the free-labor ideology and argument was that government interference in the "natural laws" of the economy should be shunned.

As support for the freedmen and Reconstruction waned among Republicans, a new "reform" and "liberal" movement arose—uncharted, but in some ways sharing ideological parallels with the Democrats. The twin tensions of race in the South and labor in the North produced a new Republican politics of "cooperation and bipartisanship" that was less ideological, along with new politicians who were more management oriented. This new approach to politics meant that money and organization, rather than ideas, issues, or policy, was ascendant. Additionally, such reform ideology believed that the political world, like the natural world, was governed by knowable laws that could be turned into "scientific legislation." Thus, "classical liberalism supplied the axioms of reformers' 'financial science'—free trade, the law of supply and demand, and the gold standard."[30]

These new liberals also believed in limited government and laissez-faire economics and politics. Laissez-faire economics meant no governmental inference in the economy and a reliance on the market to achieve the general welfare and the public good. Laissez-faire politics was the belief that government should rest on the shoulders of the people with the highest intelligence, vision, and virtue—the best and the brightest. Such an elite class of leaders, it was felt, would not represent any "special class or interests," but, standing above the fray, would look, see, and act on behalf of the common good. The role of such political leaders was to create laws that promoted civic and political equal opportunity, not take government action to promote social equality. This, then, gives us a better understanding of President Clinton's and the DLC's ideological commitment to "equal opportunity" but not "equal results"—to be discussed shortly.

These northern reform liberals wanted to see intelligence in legislation. Of the Grant administration, E. L. Godkin declared that "the government must get out of the 'protective' business and the 'subsidy' business and the 'improvement' business and the 'development' business. . . . It cannot touch them without breeding corruption."[31] Reform liberals feared that a strong central government would be used for the wrong purposes, and they assailed "the fallacy of attempts to benefit humanity by legislation."[32]

Economic and social unrest in the North and the South was drawing Republicans and Democrats closer together politically. With the freedmen making demands in the South and white organized labor increasingly resisting violently in the North, Reconstruction and the free-labor ideology were both failing. In the North, free labor was agitating for a greater share of a thriving, but unjust, capitalism. Both the North and the South, however, believed that the only way out of their dilemma was through an elite leadership class of intelligent property owners. Thus, liberal Republicans were concluding what conservative Democrats had "known" all along—that it was "intelligence" and "capital" that must be relied upon to run the country. The educated, property-owning, taxpaying class must be in charge. That meant Republican capitalists in the North and former Democratic slave owners in the South.

Liberal Republicans articulated their themes for the 1872 national elections—civil service reforms to clean up corruption in government, amnesty for the former Confederates, an end to federal intervention in the economy and military intervention in the South, and a return to laissez-faire control of local government. Northern Democrats sounded similar themes and picked up the support of several high-profile liberal Republicans. A platform of fiscal conservatism in government, lower taxes, political reform, and a new rhetoric of racial tolerance characterized their campaigns—they now referred to the freedmen as "negro" rather than "nigger." By ridding themselves of the racial rhetoric, northern Democrats had positioned themselves well for the coming economic collapse. In the South, the election results discredited moderate cooperationist "New Departure" Democrats; from now on southern Democrats could run as straight-out white supremacy candidates.

In 1873 the economy went into a nosedive that lasted for sixty-five months, still the longest economic contraction in the nation's history. Known as the Great Depression until a similar situation arose in the 1930s, it changed the economic and political landscape. The Republican majority, who had been in power since the southerners had seceded and were now led by an elite group of liberal laissez-faire reformers, felt that the only way out of the recession was to stand back and let the market regulate everything. The result? The election of 1874 resulted in the greatest political reversal of party alignments of the nineteenth century. House Republicans went from a 110-seat majority to a 60-seat minority. Republicans had brought down a political disaster on their heads by putting the Civil War behind them and slowly shifting their focus from a broad radical program of equal rights for blacks (and whites) to a more conservative agenda of economic respectability for a narrower white elite. Rather than Democratic ascendancy, however, the election left behind a political stalemate characterized by a House, Senate, and White House that divided power over the next two decades.

By choosing the undemocratic "top-down" rather than the more democratic "bottom-up" approach, Republicans set into motion a counterrevolution that they could do little to stop politically. They had not sufficiently empowered those on the "bottom rail" to protect themselves, and now the "top rail" was in trouble. The senior abolitionist leaders were old and dying off, and "the era of moral politics," as the *New York Times* described it, was coming to an end.

Therefore, the elite leaders in both sections of the country concluded that democracy was unworkable, and that government by "mere numbers" led only to waste, corruption, and disaster. Mass democratic participation through universal suffrage, concluded Charles Francis Adams, Jr., in 1869—he was the former liberal Massachusetts congressman, reformer, author, son of John Quincy Adams, and grandson of John Adams—"can only mean in plain English the government of ignorance and vice: it means a European, and especially Celtic, proletariat on the Atlantic coast, an African proletariat on the shores of the gulf; and a Chinese proletariat on the Pacific."[33] The freedmen had rising expectations, which were increasingly being met by elitist elected officials with class and racial prejudices who were distancing themselves from the lower classes and losing interest in their cause. Freedom, for these Republican reformers, did not mean using the state, if necessary, to achieve full citizenship equality. Freedom for them meant the freedom to survive, if you can, in the marketplace, and freedom from government, even a government proclaiming to be of, by, and for the people. They had concluded that the government had done all it could do, or could be expected to do, for blacks. The freedmen were now on their own.

Reflecting the traditional conservative strict constructionist view of the Constitution, and recognizing the increasingly conservative and racist political climate of the times, the Supreme Court aided and abetted the counterrevolution in the Slaughterhouse Cases of 1873. These three cases—involving white labor rights, not black rights—were the first opportunities for the Supreme Court to interpret the Fourteenth Amendment. Its five-to-four decisions, written by Justice Samuel F. Miller, severely limited the meaning of the privileges or immunities clause in the amendment's first section. Justice Miller "concluded that 'the one pervading purpose' behind the Civil War Amendments was to secure the freedom of black Americans, not to expand or add protections for the rights of whites."[34] The Court was distinguishing between state citizenship and federal citizenship, and the Fourteenth Amendment was being interpreted as protecting only individual citizenship rights within states, not individual federal rights. This narrow interpretation severely limited the scope of the Fourteenth Amendment.

Justice Miller believed that the "right to labor" was a state right, that states' rights were not to be interfered with by the federal courts or Congress, and that there were few national citizenship rights. The rights defined by Miller were narrow and were of little benefit to the freedmen. "Basically Miller decided that the federal government could protect its citizens on the high seas or in foreign countries, but not in the states where they resided. . . . The dissenting opinions recognized what Miller feared, that the 14th Amendment was meant to transform the federal system. Rights were no longer to be 'separate and exclusive' but 'complementary and concentric,' allowing the long arm of the federal government to reach in to protect the rights of its citizens when the states failed to do so."[35] *Slaughterhouse's* narrow interpretation throttled attempts to implant a broader interpretation of the rights inherent in national citizenship.

The *U.S. v. Cruikshank* decision of 1876 was even more devastating. More than a hundred black Republicans were killed by white Democrats in the Louisiana "Colfax Massacre"—the single bloodiest act during Reconstruction. The massacre erupted from a dispute over the winner of a gubernatorial race in 1873. Three whites were indicted and found guilty of conspiring to deny black citizens their constitutional rights in violation of Section Six of the Enforcement Act of 1870. The case was appealed to the Supreme Court. Resisting congressional efforts to broaden federal power, a conservative Court found that the case was wanting because the prosecutors had not shown that the convicted rioters had a "racial motivation" to deny blacks their civil rights. And the Court further interpreted the Civil War amendments to mean that only states and local governments had the power to protect black rights, not the federal government. If punishment for violence against blacks rested with the states, Redeemer Democrats need only regain control of the states. The *Cruikshank* decision laid the foundation for violence to again play a major role in governing throughout the South.

In the private sector, the Freedmen's Savings and Trust Company, chartered in 1865, collapsed in 1874. It destroyed the trust of the black community in financial institutions for years to come.

In Congress in 1874, the Civil Rights Bill languished until Senator Charles Sumner died in March. Two months later the Senate passed the bill as a tribute to his twenty-three years of fighting for equal rights. However, taking its lead from the Slaughterhouse Cases decision, the House opposed Sumner's bill by arguing that many of the rights included in it lay beyond federal jurisdiction. Reminiscent of antebellum days, the former Confederate Vice President Alexander H. Stephens, now a Georgia congressman, argued in opposition on the House floor that Sumner's legislation would convert our Jeffersonian republic "into a centralized empire."

The South was a society fomenting domestic violence based on deeply ingrained racism, facing internal economic destruction and external economic collapse, looking at a corrupt national government for which it had nothing but utter contempt, and from which it was seriously estranged. Southern Democrats were also clear that a vacillating national government was more preoccupied with pleasing an impatient and increasingly weary and indifferent electorate in the North than in protecting the rights of the freedmen. Following the lead of a successful 1875 "Mississippi Plan" of "white supremacy" redemption, South Carolina Democrats vowed that the 1876 election would be a time of restoring state power to the educated, property-owning, taxpaying citizens of South Carolina. And they kept their vow.

During the gubernatorial campaign, Democratic candidate Wade Hampton's rhetoric was "moderate" by 1876 South Carolina standards. The essence of his message was, "No negroes need fear having their rights taken away; just don't expect to be given special rights." However, the same could not be said of his closest supporters, men like young "Pitchfork" Ben Tillman from Edgefield County, the home of Senator Strom Thurmond. In Edgefield and Aiken Counties, in particular, intimidation and threats against blacks weren't enough. Open violence was the more desired tactic. "Race riots replaced Klan raids as the preferred political statement. Not waiting for cover of darkness, Democratic paramilitary forces attacked black Republicans in the light of day. . . . The riots, according to Tillman, 'were most potent influences in shaping the conflict between the whites and blacks and producing the gratifying result which brought the white man again into control of his inheritance.'"[36]

In 1876 the presidential election featured Republican Rutherford B. Hayes and Democrat Samuel J. Tilden. Hayes had won the governorship of Ohio in 1875 on a "let alone" policy and fiscal conservatism, but his nomination for president by the Republicans in 1876 was a surprise. A platform debate contained a plank opposing the "immigration and importation of Mongolians"—the first time a Republican national platform had reflected racial discrimination. The Democrats nominated Governor Tilden of New York, one of the richest men in America. Because of voter fraud in Florida, Louisiana, and South Carolina, there was still uncertainty after the votes were counted over who had actually won the election, and neither man had enough electoral votes to win. The election ended in controversy and conflict. It was thrown into the House of Representatives for resolution, as mandated by the Constitution.

In congressional negotiations, southern Democratic representatives wanted to be assured that their region would be given kind consideration. Meanwhile, tired of the Reconstruction tussle, northern Republicans were also looking for a way to throw overboard a policy they believed had failed. An omen of the shifting political winds was the repeal of the Southern Homestead Act of 1866 just prior to the 1876 Republican Convention. Here again extreme rhetoric prevailed, with Democrats at one point demanding "Tilden or War." To resolve the impasse, the House approved a series of compromises, including one that set up an Electoral Commission as part of an overall "plan of peace."

The Electoral Commission, created by law in late January, established a fifteen-member body made up of ten congressmen, five from each political party, and five Supreme Court justices. Four of the Supreme Court justices, cited in the law and divided equally between Democrats and Republicans, were given the power to select the final commission member—expected to be Democratic Justice David Davis. Instead, Illinois Democrats surprised everyone by nominating Justice Davis as their candidate for U.S. Senate, and Republican Justice Joseph P. Bradley took his place. Then, in a series of eight-to-seven votes, Hayes finally won enough electoral votes to become president.

Democrats were outraged at this turn of events, but they didn't have the power to put Tilden in the White House. They only had the power to obstruct, which they did with vigor. As a result, it was still unclear whether president-elect Hayes would be sworn into office on his inauguration date of March 4, 1877.

To add insult to injury, the two sides negotiated in the nation's capital at the Wormley Hotel, a respected black-owned hotel—the compromise was originally called the Wormley Compromise—over forgiveness of Civil War debts, aid for southern infrastructure development, and much else, but the central issue for Democrats in the 1877 deal was the preservation of "home rule." Negotiations ended in an agreement in February, and President Hayes was sworn in as scheduled on March 4. Conventional storytelling has it that Hayes then ordered the removal of all federal troops from the South—which is not true. However, within two months, Hayes did order federal troops out of two state capitals, Louisiana and South Carolina, where election results were in dispute and Republicans remained in power only through military force. Their removal from these two states—and all federal troops were soon withdrawn—elevated Democrats to power and sent a signal to the rest of the

South that "home rule" would be the new national policy toward the region. This was a consummate victory for Democratic Redeemers. They were now free to "redeem" the rest of the South.

Removing federal troops from the South was one sign that Reconstruction was finally over. Inheritent in that notice, however, was another message: that the federal government was engaging in a deplorable retreat from protecting blacks rights. The Civil War, which basically created the national government, was now reneging on protecting the fundamental rights of all Americans.

However, just as the South had acted in contradiction to its heritage of states' rights when it insisted that the federal government enforce the Fugitive Slave Law, the federal government too was inconsistent when it came to Indians and property. Even as Reconstruction was ending in the South, federal troops were driving the Nez Perce Indians from Oregon's Wallowa Valley. And as labor-class unrest continued to challenge capital's unjust prerogatives in the North, the federal government did not hesitate to use its power to protect the rights of property, as witnessed by its use of federal troops to put down the "Great Strike" of 1877.

On July 16, in the tradition of free labor and the free market, workers for the Baltimore & Ohio Railroad walked off their jobs in Martinsburg, West Virginia. They were soon joined in sympathy strikes by miners and steelworkers in Pennsylvania, and supported by general strikes in Chicago and St. Louis. The strikes united "skilled and unskilled workers in demands for an eight-hour day, a return to predepression wage levels, an end to child labor, the nationalization of the railroads, and the repeal of 'tramp ordinances' allowing the arrest of unemployed workers."[37] When the local militia in Pittsburgh refused to fight the workers, the militia from Philadelphia was brought in, and when they killed twenty workers, the people of the city rebelled and set on fire the railroad yards of Pittsburgh. The strike paralyzed large parts of the nation.

Frightened governors and frantic leaders of industry called for President Hayes's assistance. Without investigating the facts in the dispute, Hayes sent in federal troops. The troops acted more like strike-breaking agents for the companies than impartial referees in a fight, and by July 29 the Great Strike of 1877 had been crushed. While Hayes had just pulled federal troops out of the South, leaving the freedmen's citizenship rights unprotected, he did not hesitate to send federal troops into the striking communities of the North, keeping them there for a considerable time to protect the property rights of industry. Labor unrest raised questions about the concept of "home rule" in the North and resulted in a greatly expanded National Guard and the building of armories. National Guard troops were used more than one hundred times to put down labor unrest. The Great Strike demonstrated how closely the Civil War had allied the interests of the industrial and middle classes with the interests of the Republican Party and national government.

The Great Strike of 1877 had phenomenal long-term ramifications for both capital and labor. It created a strong class consciousness both within and between these two forces, which led to two decades of labor–capital conflict and created one of the most violent periods in our nation's history. During this period, however, skilled and unskilled, blacks and whites worked together as never before, giving rise in the 1880s to the Knights of Labor. Capitalism created an emerging middle class, but the violent conflicts between labor and capital reinforced both the middle class's elitism and its racial bias—and it also permitted it to retreat from Reconstruction. The *New York Tribune* reported that "the strike demonstrated that the radical spirit of 'communism' was abroad in the land and that only the 'substantial, property-owning' classes could save 'civilized society.'"[38]

Democratic Redeemers were now free to move with "home rule"—which also involved voter fraud and violence—to put into place a new structure of political, labor, and race relations in the South. While the new architects of the South had their economic and political differences, they were unified in legally undermining Reconstruction, maintaining control over labor, reducing black political power, and maintaining white superiority and black subordination. Through the passage of new constitutions, Redeemers proceeded to remove, as one newspaper referred to them, Reconstruction's "instruments of prohibition." This meant being "fiscally responsible" by cutting state budgets and salaries, reducing the length of legislative sessions, cutting taxes on the propertied classes, limiting the ability of government to borrow money, prohibiting aid to railroads and other industries, and in some instances eliminating state boards of education. Most southern Democrats saw education as a "luxury" for the well off; thus, there was no need for states to "tax and spend" to educate common people. Louisiana's educational cutbacks were so horrific that, although blacks suffered the most, it was the only state where the percentage of native white Louisianians unable to read or write actually rose between 1880 and 1890.

The new constitutions quickly reinstated vagrancy laws, stricter criminal codes, and a vastly expanded convict lease system to railroad, mining, and lumber companies; new laws affecting property rights and terms of credit for planters, the essence of rural power, were also put in place. Southern sheriffs and state militias regularly crushed agricultural workers attempting to organize. In 1891, four years after a strike for higher wages on sugar plantations in Louisiana was violently ended by white vigilantes and the state militia, nine of fifteen workers killed in Arkansas were hanged for leading a cotton pickers' strike.

To understand why today's South, the poorest, most illiterate, ill-housed, violent, least educated, most unhealthy, most environmentally degraded, and least organized region in the country—a region that should naturally be progressive—is still economically conservative, we need only recognize the structural seeds of repressive labor relations that Democratic Redeemers planted following Reconstruction. The attempt to integrate a poor and devastated southern colonial economy into a national capitalist market forced the South to create a peculiar and hybrid repressive labor system. So-called right-to-work laws are one manifestation of this legacy. While the South's new upper class of large farmers, businessmen, and industrialists prospered, the vast majority of southern blacks and whites alike sank deeper and deeper into poverty. Even so, the psychic strain of white racial superiority ran so deep in southern society that neither military defeat, the end of slavery, nor continuing abject poverty ever suggested to whites that they might need to reexamine their racial relationships and assumptions.

Even the incentives that attracted industry to the South—low wages, free convict labor, low taxes, weak governments—resulted in both slow and imbalanced economic growth. The southern region never developed because, while the long arm of outside federal legal power and military control represented in Reconstruction was gone, it was replaced with the long arm of outside corporate power and control that dictated its conditions of investment and labor relations, which affected the future of both black and white southerners. Under the rule of Redeemer Democrats, the freedmen found themselves increasingly ensnared in an interrelated web of political, labor, and racial oppression. Unable to make outward economic and political progress, and gripped by fear, the black community often turned inward or away. Unable to live alongside whites as equals, blacks started migrating northward and westward, with the biggest movement at that time centering on "the Exodus" to Kansas in 1879. Some whites were so upset that their former slaves were leaving the South that they threatened to shut down the Mississippi River by blockading its river landings and promising to sink any boats carrying freedmen.

While overall Reconstruction was a failure, it didn't have to be. In particular, if the national political leadership had had stronger convictions, asserted greater leadership, made different choices, more creatively attempted to unite black and white together in a struggle for full equality, and persevered through difficult times, the South and the nation would be very different and much better today. Instead, the death of Reconstruction, with great assistance from the Supreme Court, allowed the caste system of racism, its class legacy of elite economics, and the constitutional doctrine of states' rights to reemerge and again dominate the South. As a result, both white and black people and workers suffered economically and socially. Conditions for African Americans fell to a nadir that lasted for more than half a century. How did it happen?

Congressional Republicans attempted a two-pronged approach to Reconstruction, one positive and one negative. First, they tried to readmit the secessionist states to the Union in such a manner as to allow each former Confederate state, under its state constitution, to provide equal protection under the law for all of its citizens. Second, they wrote national laws and passed constitutional amendments prohibiting states from depriving citizens of certain specified rights. Based on the particular form of the Fourteenth and Fifteenth Amendments, a series of new national laws were written. For the first time, under the Removal Act of 1875, the Constitution authorized parties to move any case originating under the Constitution, laws, or treaties of the United States from state to federal courts. Republican Reconstructionists clearly saw the federal courts as a future ally in strong enforcement.

Federal courts, at first, seemed to sustain a broad interpretation of national legislation designed to protect individual civil and political rights under the Civil War amendments. However, as southern resistance and racist politics again became dominant, the Supreme Court shifted. Even though sitting members of this Court identified with the Republican Party, it worried that Radical Republicans in Congress may have taken federalism and federal legislation too far and, beginning with *Blyew v. United States* (1872), shifted back to the ideology of dual federalism, states' rights, and strict constructionist constitutional interpretations. Following *Blyew*, the Slaughterhouse Cases (1873) arrived at a tortured construction of the privileges or immunities clause of the Fourteenth Amendment that divided rights into two categories: undefined, but limited, rights held by U.S. citizens, which were protected under the Fourteenth Amendment; and a series of broader common rights held by citizens of each state, which were not.

As Reconstruction and national protection of equal citizenship rights continued to wane, the Supreme Court, in the 1883 Civil Rights Cases, declared unconstitutional the Civil Rights Act of 1875, arguing that blacks must give up "the special favor of the laws." In these cases a "state-action" theory and interpretation was manufactured. It said that Congress could not protect national rights directly. It could only act against state action that denied individual civil rights. In a seeming contradiction, however, the Court also said that because Reconstruction laws had not been written specifically to protect black rights, but to protect all Americans' rights, the Enforcement Acts were "unconstitutional because they failed to specify that private individuals could be prosecuted *only* if they deprived people of rights on account of their race or previous condition of servitude."[39] Similarly, the Court illogically ruled invalid any convictions that did not specifically prove racial motivation. The Court's Catch-22 logic—that the laws were written in a color-blind fashion, but you had to prove color-conscious motivation and discrimination in order to win a verdict—was part of the racially charged political climate of the times. Southern officials read these decisions as virtual green lights for violence and for an all-out attack on Reconstruction generally. Thus ended, to this day, the affirmative nationalization of broad individual civil rights protection under the Fourteenth and Fifteenth Amendments to the U.S. Constitution.

It was but another example of the Supreme Court's preoccupation with dual federalism and states' rights taking precedence over, or serving as an excuse for not, claiming and affirming national individual civil rights protection. The logical consequence of these decisions left the country with legal doctrines providing either a narrow "equal and color-blind" interpretation of the Constitution, or a "broad" interpretation that applied politically unacceptable "racial logic." If blacks were not specified in the law, the Court interpreted it in a strict constructionist and universal way in which an "even playing field" was assumed and the law disregarded the particular history and context in which blacks had lived and continued to live in the United States. If, on the other hand, the law did specify blacks, "human rights" opponents on the Court claimed that blacks were getting special treatment—"the special favor of the laws," not equal protection under the law. Thus, legally, racism and its legacy handed African Americans a two-headed coin with the Court always calling tails the winner. It was a legal logic that blacks could never win.

The Court, then as now, does not or chooses not to understand that neither of these two static and narrow forms of constitutional interpretation fits the African American experience and predicament. Then, as now, the Court, the Congress, and presidents seem more preoccupied with not violating the doctrines of dual federalism and states' rights—which leaves the historic injustices and legacy of slavery in place—than with reconciling them in a manner that achieves social, economic, and political justice for every individual American.

Further, it is interesting to note that, historically, the Founding Fathers, but especially the Jeffersonians, insisted on including the first ten amendments, the Bill of Rights, in the Constitution to protect every American against national government violations of individual rights. Because of racism, however, these same Democratic Jeffersonians—and even the nationalist and Republican-oriented Supreme Court of that day—were anxious and more than willing to use dual federalist constitutional theories to insist on protecting states' rights over individual rights. It was just another instance of the Court's willingness to allow the means tail to wag the ends dog.

When Congress in 1890 narrowly failed to pass a strong law to implement the Fifteenth Amendment's guarantee of nondiscrimination in voting—largely because states' rights Court interpretations were prevailing over the protection of national individual rights—and with Democratic racism nationally revived, the Court could openly espouse racist rulings. It did so in *Plessy v. Ferguson*, the "separate but equal" decision of 1896.

Thus, after a period of bright hope and great effort begun by African Americans and Radical Republicans in 1865 after the Civil War, and a strong economy in the North, the country gradually over three decades succumbed to confusing and difficult economic times, narrow and conservative Supreme Court rulings, an aroused and renewed racism, a restless public, and an increasingly moderate Republican and conservative Democratic politics that had grown fatigued of wrestling with racial matters. After the big-government "activism" of

Reconstruction, the educated, economic and political elite in the North *and* the South concluded that it was time for a more moderate leadership, a better-managed economy, and a less centralized government.

If you didn't recognize *today's* politics in that paragraph, let me paraphrase it for you. Thus, after a period of bright hope and great effort begun by African Americans and liberal Democrats in 1954 after the *Brown* decision, and a historically strong economy in the country from 1945 to 1973, the country gradually, after three decades, succumbed to confusing and difficult economic times, narrow and conservative Supreme Court rulings, an aroused and renewed racism, a restless public, and an increasingly moderate Democratic and conservative Republican politics that had grown fatigued of wrestling with racial matters. After the big-government activism of the 1960s, the educated and moderate political elite in both the North and the South concluded that it was time for a better-managed economy and a more decentralized government.

The Democratic Party of today is sounding and acting more and more like the Republican Party of a century ago. Recall candidate Mike Dukakis's statement that the election of 1988 was not about ideology, but about competence—in other words, it was about better management, not human rights, meeting Americans' unmet material needs, or social and economic justice for all. It reflects Clinton's "the era of big government is over" and Gore's "reinventing government"—otherwise known as downsizing the big central government. Or how about the "better management" arguments that it is time to be more "fiscally responsible" by "balancing the budget" and "retiring the national debt"? Obviously, we must be fiscally responsible, but fiscal responsibility means having *proportionate* debt and deficits, in the context of balanced economic growth, as the real goal.

Since 1976, the Democratic Party's tickets have fundamentally represented (with, to some extent, the exception of Mondale in 1984) this conservative century-old Republican Party pattern. In 1992 a moderate southern governor—a conservative Democrat by national standards—picked a southern Tennessee senator more conservative than himself as vice president; then, in 2000, that more conservative vice president picked an even more conservative northern Connecticut Yankee to be his vice presidential running mate. Finally, to complete the political picture, the conservative white Republican Party of 2000, of course, is playing the same role that the white southern Democratic Party played a century ago. And all of these conservative politics are being played mostly because neither party, or the country, has been able to come to grips with the issue of race and the legacy of slavery and racism!

B y 1901, just five years after *Plessy,* the first congressional black caucus was completely gone. It had been comprised of a total of twenty-two blacks elected and serving at different times in Congress between 1870 and 1901. After 1901, no black served in Congress until Oscar DePriest (R-IL) became the first northern black elected in 1928. In 1915, DePriest had been the first black elected to Chicago's City Council. The absence of blacks in public life during this period automatically shifted the political center of American politics decidedly to the right, and complicated the tasks of economic and social progressives for decades. Also, as a result of the political disenfranchisement of blacks, racism rapidly returned from its existence underground to the forefront of American politics. Racism now embedded itself in the nation's culture and politics more deeply perhaps than at any time since the antislavery crusades of the 1830s, 1840s, and 1850s—and maybe in our entire history.

As a result of the Republican Party's failure to coalesce with a black constituency as political partners in the South, and through massive resistance and the reascendance of racism, the South remained a one-party Democratic-dominated region of the country under the control of a white reactionary conservative ruling elite. It used fear and violence to intimidate blacks, engaged in voter sabotage and election fraud to defeat the Republicans and Reconstruction, strangled virtually all internal dissent through policelike repression, imposed racially repressive "Black Codes" and labor laws—and, in the process, subverted the possibility of building a more perfect Union. The white Democratic South behaved this way not because it feared black and biracial democratic *failure*, but because it feared black and biracial democratic *success*. Success would destroy all of their black racial inferiority theories. The enduring consequence of Reconstruction's failure—one that we are still living with and suffering from today—was a narrowly based white conservative solid Democratic South that defined and limited American politics. It has weakened the nation's prospects not simply for improving race relations and achieving racial justice, but also for implementing a much broader social, economic, and political program of progressive change for all Americans.

The African American nadir, which lasted from 1890 through the Great Migration (which reached its zenith in 1960), is more popularly known as the period of Jim Crow segregation. The term "Jim Crow" originated and was popularized by a white minstrel entertainer named Thomas "Daddy" Rice. Applying burned cork to his face and wearing ragged clothes, as in the movie *Bamboozled*, he appeared before white audiences in blackface. While wearing the ill-fitting and tattered garments of a beggar, he would grin broadly and entertain his white audiences by imitating the dancing, singing, and demeanor stereotypically attributed to blacks of the time. Calling his dance Jump Jim Crow, "he based the number on a routine he had seen performed in 1828 by an elderly and crippled Louisville stableman belonging to a Mr. Crow. 'Weel about, and turn about / And do jis so; / Eb'ry time I weel about, / I jump Jim Crow.'"[40]

In the 1830s and 1840s, minstrel shows were one of the white public's favorite forms of entertainment. "Daddy" Rice's caricature of black life allowed the term "Jim Crow" to enter America's mental lexicon. Additionally, many whites, in both the North and the South, allowed minstrel shows to form or reinforce negative images of African American life, character, and aspirations. "But by the 1890s, 'Jim Crow' took on additional force and meaning to denote the subordination and separation of black people in the South, much of it codified, much of it still enforced by custom and habit."[41]

Among many other things, the dawn of the Jim Crow era meant the destruction and disappearance of whole categories of black workers. "Around the turn of the century, Isaac Murphy and other black horse jockeys who had dominated the Kentucky Derby winners' circle since the end of the Civil War found themselves shut out of the major racetracks. Black jockeys then took their place at the back of an employment queue headed by native-born white men."[42]

In the 1890s, with many of the white Radical Republican political leaders and black activists either too old to be effective or deceased, and with the increased stranglehold of racial and economic repression, the cultural emphases on politics and agitation were either waning or dead. It was in this context that a young thirty-nine-year-old Booker T. Washington, on September 18, 1895, gave his famous speech at the Cotton States Exposition, dubbed by black scholar Dr. W. E. B. Du Bois the Atlanta Compromise.

In an era featuring massive violence, regular lynching of blacks—there were 3,175 recorded hangings of blacks between 1882 and 1921—political disenfranchisement, and economic re-enslavement through sharecropping, Washington chose to concede white political domination; to surrender the struggle for a biracial democracy. For "practical" and "realistic" reasons he essentially told blacks to accept and live with their situation, befriend southern whites, make the best of it by trading off an academic education for an industrial education, and pull themselves up by their own bootstraps. "Ignorant and inexperienced," he said, "it is not strange that in the first years of our new life we began at the top instead of at the bottom; that a seat in Congress or the State Legislature was more sought than real estate or industrial skill; that the political convention or stump speaking had more attractions than starting a dairy farm or truck garden. . . . 'Cast down your bucket where you are.' . . . In all things that are purely social we can be separate as the fingers, yet one as the hand in all things essential to mutual progress. . . . The wisest among my race understand that the agitation of questions of social equality is the extremist folly, and that progress in the enjoyment of all the privileges that will come to us must be the result of severe and constant struggle rather than of artificial forcing. No race that has anything to contribute to the markets of the world is long in any degree ostracized."[43] Exclusive white achievers, North and South, made him (with his conservative message) the most prominent African American of his day.

It was the Republican Party's business commitment to the free-labor economic ideology that had led it to fight against slavery and the southern states that perpetrated slavery. In some quarters it was feared that black free labor would come north after emancipation and take white ethnic Catholic Democrats' jobs—both organized labor and big-city Democratic Party political patronage jobs. That economic fear added fuel to Republicans' nurtured racism, contributed to their resistance to biracial labor and political democracy, and sometimes sparked violence in the North. This was true because the Republicans' free-labor ideology was increasingly becoming less dependable as the economy went through peaks of growth and boom, and valleys of depression and bust. The supply of steady jobs secure enough to sustain white families was becoming increasingly uncertain.

Many whites concluded that new black free-labor competition must be eliminated among artisans and factory workers alike. Because of the black push for jobs and equal rights, racism and illogical stereotypes were created to protect white jobs. Blacks were accused both of aggressively pursuing jobs, replacing white workers, contaminating workplaces, and cheapening white labor; *and* of being lazy, shiftless, and slothful. Given the lowest and most menial jobs, they were labeled as intellectually "unsuited" for the more skilled jobs, even as they were barred and denied vocational and industrial education. Most important—because it is still dominant today—whites were fed the notion that social and economic progress must be a zero-sum game, that the development, elevation, progress, and additional material advancement of blacks meant the demise, elimination, or loss of material progress for whites. Whiteness was seen as "a prerequisite if not a guarantee of economic mobility and political power, and too often, 'blackness' represented a liability that could not be overcome through hard work, talent or ambition."[44]

When the free-labor ideology began to lose credibility among white workers in the North, and they began to resist economic injustice and organize unions in response to imbalanced economic growth and failing to reap their fair share of what their labor had produced, Republican free-labor industrialists chose their narrow special economic interests over labor democracy. Republican industrialists began to use the state police and military apparatus against workers in the North, just as the former slaveholders were now using Democratic economic, legal, and state police power primarily against blacks in the South. It was clear that white industrial workers in the North and black (and white) agricultural workers in the South were both being exploited and suppressed by elite economic interests and political ruling forces and classes that were over both of them.

But racism, racial stereotypes, and the political manipulation of race by both Republican and Democratic economic elites were major factors in keeping urban and rural workers from seeing their economic common ground and forming labor and political alliances. Such biracial coalitions *were* formed, but rarely, and because of racism among workers and labor leaders almost never on equal terms.

After the Emancipation Proclamation, there was some black migration north and west, but even as late as 1917 nine out of ten blacks still lived in the South, and 80 percent of them in rural areas. Land ownership among blacks reached its peak in 1915, when approximately one-fifth of all black farmers owned their property. However, the advent of World War I represented a divide and contributed to both southern outmigration and northern job creation. It gave, for the first time, an impetus to half a million rural black southerners to leave the South for jobs in northern industries—still not on an equal basis with whites, of course. "In general, black men and some white women took the unskilled industrial and other blue-collar jobs left by immigrant men who entered the army; white women replaced native-born white men who had served as clerks and other kinds of white-collar workers; and black women took the positions abandoned by white women and boys."[45]

Even as the war gave southern blacks new civilian job opportunities, from 1906 to 1917 Texas congressmen introduced a series of "elimination laws" to deny them the opportunity to serve in the military. After fighting dutifully, effectively, and faithfully in all of America's wars, blacks were still not welcomed in the military. Such efforts were not totally successful, however, and in 1906 two black privates were beaten by whites for taking the inside of a city sidewalk. This violent incident in Brownsville, Texas—known as the Brownsville Raid—led President Theodore Roosevelt, in the usual irrational pattern of racial logic, to dishonorably discharge 167 black soldiers from the army. In 1917, in Houston, whites secretly hanged thirteen black soldiers for challenging the morality and legality of Jim Crow streetcars.

It was in this climate of violence, hangings, job denial, and racial discrimination that black organizations were born, including the NAACP, the National Urban League, and the National Black Business League. Following a conference of black leaders in 1905 convened in Niagara Falls, Canada, by Dr. W. E. B. Du Bois, William Monroe Trotter, and others opposed to the accommodationist policies of Booker T. Washington, the leadership of the Niagara Movement in 1909 founded the National Association for the Advancement of Colored People (NAACP) to combat the lynching of blacks and to fight for equal civil and human rights. As a result of their efforts, there were (only) 304 lynchings between 1922 and 1945. In 1908, twenty-five bishops from the Colored Methodist Episcopal, African Methodist Episcopal Zion, and the African Methodist Episcopal Churches made an appeal to the nation to stop mob violence, end Jim Crow laws, cease free convict labor, and quit general labor repression against blacks.

A 1905 New York organization, the Committee for the Improvement of the Industrial Condition of Negroes, evolved into the National Urban League in 1911 to fight for suffrage and jobs. "In rejecting their ascribed places as field hands and domestics, blacks not only kept alive the spirit of the American Revolution; they also sought to fuse political rights to economic rights, and thus to advance the agenda of freedom in a truly revolutionary way."[46] The Urban League primarily used moral persuasion to break down employment barriers and offer new job opportunities to African Americans. In 1915 the NAACP protested the Atlanta premiere of D. W. Griffith's movie *Birth of a Nation*, which praised the Confederacy and stereotypically and derogatorily portrayed blacks generally, but "Negro rule" during Reconstruction in particular. And a progressive United Negro Improvement Association was founded in 1919 by Maggie Lena Walker and black labor leader A. Philip Randolph to challenge employment practices in workplaces controlled by whites. Walker also founded the St. Luke Penny Savings Bank in Richmond, Virginia, and became the country's first female bank president. Mary McLeod Bethune founded the National Council of Negro Women in 1935.

Massive race riots occurred in East St. Louis, Illinois, in 1917, where hundreds were either killed or wounded and martial law was declared. So much blood was shed as a result of more than twenty-five major race riots in 1919 that the NAACP's James Weldon Johnson characterized it as "Red Summer." One such riot occurred in Chicago where, on July 27, what would be almost a week of violence began when four young African Americans crossed an imaginary line separating black and white swimming beaches along Lake Michigan. There was also the irony that the 1922 dedication of the Abraham Lincoln Memorial was "a segregated ceremony in which African Americans had to use separate washrooms and restaurants and stand in a special section roped off behind the white ticket holders."[47] In 1931, nine black youths were arrested by Scottsboro, Alabama, policemen, accused, tried, and convicted on hearsay evidence of raping two white women who, like them, had hitched a ride on a freight train. A national and international protest ensued, but the "Scottsboro Boys" were not all freed until 1950.

Also active during this time was the antilynching journalist Ida B. Wells, the crusading Robert Abbott's *Chicago Defender* newspaper, the adventuresome New York–based Jamaican Marcus Garvey, who established his Universal Negro Improvement Association, a "Back to Africa" movement, and the Black Star Shipping Line. A forerunner to an organization my father headed, SCLC's Operation Breadbasket, was the Double Duty Dollar Campaign, which urged blacks to shop in black-owned stores. Northern black politicians leveraged their positions for increased patronage. And entire black towns were formed, such as Boley, Oklahoma, founded in 1904, which "employed its own teachers, controlled its own utilities, and elected its own mayor and councilmen."[48]

The Roaring Twenties gave way to the stock market collapse of 1929, and the resulting second Great Depression affected everyone. Everyone on the social, economic, labor, employment, and political totem poles was pushed down onto those below, which meant blacks were routed out first. Although Democratic candidate Franklin Delano Roosevelt had run on a fiscally conservative "balance the budget" platform, when he assumed office and confronted the national economic crisis—25 percent of the American people were out of work—he had to do something quickly. He experimented with a variety of job-creation programs that were only moderately successful and effective.

After the Civil War and the Fifteenth Amendment, blacks had been extremely active politically in the Republican Party. Following the election of 1876, however, blacks were depoliticized through Democratic violence, fear, and voter disenfranchisement, and remained politically impotent in the South. But with migration to the North had come incremental progress in securing and exercising the franchise. Still, because of the 1854 origins of the

Republican Party as an antislavery party and Lincoln's 1863 Emancipation Proclamation, blacks remained loyally and predominantly Republican. They did not vote for Roosevelt in significant numbers in 1932. Even so, he established a "Black Cabinet," whose most famous member was Mary McLeod Bethune. And despite FDR's failure to support a congressional antilynching bill—one was finally passed in the House in 1937, but was killed by a southern Democratic filibuster in the Senate—and being chastised by the NAACP for not proposing other necessary civil rights legislation, between 1932 and 1936 blacks began to make better progress under FDR's New Deal social and economic programs than under nonexistent Republicans in the South or free-labor business- and industry-oriented Republicans in the North. Another sign of the shifting political times occurred in 1934, when Chicago's Arthur W. Mitchell became the first black Democrat elected to the U.S. House.

So when the 1936 election rolled around—and given the continuing migration of blacks from the rural South to the urban centers of the North, a certain increase in sensitivity born of political necessity, and northern urban Democratic machines and the national party having, to some degree, to sheepishly court the black vote—blacks switched their vote to the Democratic Party in substantial numbers. Even so, Senator Ellison "Cotton Ed" DuRant Smith (D-SC) and the mayor of Charleston walked out of the Democrats' Philadelphia convention because a black preacher had delivered the opening prayer. The South Carolina delegation officially protested the presence of blacks at the convention.

This was both a blessing and a curse for the Democratic Party. The party wanted black votes, but there were complications. Since the Civil War, Democrats had been reunited under one party label. But politically, in the South, blacks were now voting with a party led by white segregationists whose fathers and grandfathers were Civil War Confederates, Confederate sympathizers, and slaveholders—Dixiecrats. In the North, they were part of a Democratic Party dominated and led, at the least, by a combination of racially ignorant and insensitive European ethnic Catholic immigrants, workers, and labor leaders—mainly Irish, Italian, Polish, and Eastern European people, and to a lesser extent Jews and liberal intellectuals, many of whom tended to dislike or distrust blacks. Before, during, and after the New York draft riots of 1863 there had been tension, animosity, and violence between black and white northern ethnic workers and politicos. For these white ethnics it meant—among many other things socially, economically, and psychologically—sharing political power, patronage, and perks.

Thus, even when FDR passed progressive new minimum wage legislation, southern white fellow Democrats insisted on excluding agricultural workers from coverage because blacks in the South were mostly poor rural workers. But of course, this excluded poor white rural workers too! So poor workers, white and black, had to stay in the economic hole together. Even when a Democratic-led Congress passed progressive public housing legislation, northern urban Democrats and southern rural Democrats insisted that it be segregated. In the South virtually everything—restaurants, lunch counters, rest rooms, drinking fountains, hotels, motels, trains, buses, schools, churches, businesses, theaters—was either de jure or by custom segregated. Blacks were kept politically impotent through voter registration and electoral shenanigans, and kept out of the Democratic Party. In the North, too, blacks were still mostly resented in workplaces, neighborhoods, and churches, and played largely a token role in the Democratic Party. Nationally, during the seventy-year African American nadir, the U.S. military, Congress, the courts, federal executive branches, businesses, state and local political offices, workplaces, churches, the entertainment industry, and more were all still mostly de facto segregated. So mainly a combination of northern conservative business-oriented Republicans and southern conservative race-oriented Democrats formed a regressive political coalition in Congress that on a wide range of issues stifled progress for all Americans because of how it would affect the black and white social, economic, and political dynamic. While it has been slightly altered—because of an increase in black voter registration, black turnout, and black elected officials—that fundamental regressive alliance is still in place today.

In 1925 Marian Anderson made her debut with the New York Philharmonic. But race was still the dominant factor in American entertainment and life, and black exclusion caused her to perform in Europe from 1930 to 1935. Concert opportunities were greater and racial discrimination was less severe there. Upon her triumphal return to the United States, Sol Hurok signed her to sing at the Town Hall in New York on December 30, 1935. Following this appearance, she annually performed some seventy recitals in various parts of the United States. Four years later Hurok tried to book her into the Daughters of the American Revolution–owned Constitution Hall, but he was told that no dates were available. Shortly thereafter he posed as an agent for a white performer and was told the previously unavailable dates were available. Posthaste he publicly lambasted the DAR, charging them with racial prejudice. First Lady Eleanor Roosevelt was outraged and resigned from the DAR in protest. U.S. Interior Secretary Harold L. Ickes then arranged for Ms. Anderson to sing on the steps of the Lincoln Memorial on Easter Sunday, 1939. More than seventy-five thousand people attended this historic outdoor concert, with millions of other Americans listening on the radio. This event, with the vast visual publicity that followed, became a potent symbol for the soon-to-emerge modern civil rights movement.

Jobwise, even as small progress was being made legally to break down continuing practices of racial discrimination in the workplace, stereotypes, customs, seniority, work rules, and job classifications continued to deny blacks employment opportunities, upward mobility, and substantial careers.

Thus, the stage was being set for the evolution of the modern-day civil rights movement. The Pullman porters' Brotherhood of Sleeping Car Porters (BSCP), the first successful all-black union (founded in 1925 and officially recognized in 1937), took pride in providing first-class personalized service to the more affluent riders of the luxurious Pullman sleeping cars—the historic Pullman community is in my Chicago congressional district—but also developed a strong political consciousness and played an important role in challenging segregated Jim Crow job arrangements all around the country. As early as 1941, A. Philip Randolph, BSCP's founder, saw the need and called for a March on Washington, which finally occurred in 1963. Another of the Sleeping Car Porter's leaders, E. D. Nixon, was instrumental in organizing the legal defense of Rosa Parks in Montgomery that led to the 1955 Montgomery Bus Boycott, directed by Dr. Martin Luther King, Jr. In 1940, in the South, only 5 percent of eligible black voters were registered, and in 1947 only about six hundred thousand blacks were even eligible to register under Jim Crow election laws. In 1942 James Farmer, a student at the University of Chicago, founded the Congress of Racial Equality (CORE) to fight for racial justice using nonviolent protest tactics and Gandhi's principles of passive resistance. CORE led boycott campaigns around the slogan, "Don't eat or shop where you can't work." To test compliance with a 1946 Supreme Court prohibition of segregated interstate buses, CORE led the first bus of black and white "Freedom Riders" on a dangerous trip through the South.

The 1948 Democratic National Convention in Philadelphia was convened in the following political climate: President Harry Truman had urged Congress to pass civil rights legislation, including antilynching, fair employment, and anti-poll-tax legislation; he had signed Executive Order 9981 desegregating the U.S. military and all federal employment; the Supreme Court in *Shelley v. Kraemer* had ruled against segregated housing covenants; a federal district court had opened the way for blacks to join the South Carolina Democratic Party by ruling that it could not require an oath from its members supporting segregation and opposing employment nondiscrimination laws; NAACP President D. V. Carter in Montgomery, Georgia, had been beaten for leading blacks to the polls to vote; Richard Mallard in Vidalia, Georgia, had been lynched for voting; William Bender at Tougaloo College in Mississippi had been held prisoner at gunpoint to keep him from voting; and the newly formed Progressive Party of Henry Wallace was aggressively courting the black vote. Shedding light on the racial politics surrounding today's Confederate flag controversies, when President Harry Truman proposed a set of tougher civil rights laws, Dixiecrats from thirteen southern states began to fly the Confederate flag again under the banner of a states' rights party. It was in this context that Hubert H. Humphrey stepped to the podium at the Democratic National Convention in 1948 and declared forthrightly that it was time for the Democratic Party to step out of the shadow of states' rights and into the sunlight of human rights.

And when the convention adopted a civil rights plank in its platform, delegates from Alabama, Mississippi, and South Carolina—including the current Senator James Strom Thurmond, then the governor of South Carolina—walked out. Three days after the Democratic Convention, the States' Rights Party nominated Thurmond for president and Mississippi's Governor Fielding Wright for vice president—and they won 1,176,125 popular votes, four Deep South states, and a total of thirty-nine electoral votes. Thurmond had run for the U.S. Senate as a Democrat in 1950, but lost. After practicing law in Aiken, he was appointed U.S. senator after the resignation of Charles E. Daniel in 1954. He resigned his office in 1956, because of a promise he had made to voters to stand for election, and ran to fill his own vacancy that fall. He was reelected; served from November 7, 1956, to January 3, 1961; and has ever since been returned to office by South Carolina voters. However, after the successful black struggle for public accommodations, following the July 2 signing of the 1964 Civil Rights Act, he switched parties and became a Republican on September 16, 1964.

The May 17, 1954, *Brown* school desegregation decision gave great legal, moral, and spiritual impetus to the struggle for equal rights. Rosa Parks had just returned home to Montgomery following nonviolence training sessions at the radical Highlander Folk School in Tennessee. She was highly impressed and greatly influenced at the school by Septima Clark, an instructor there. On August 14, 1955, Parks had her first encounter with a bright new young preacher in Montgomery, Dr. Martin Luther King, Jr., at an NAACP meeting at the Metropolitan United Methodist Church. He was teaching about thirty members, mostly women, about the implications of the *Brown* decision, and Parks had been very impressed with his knowledge, analysis, and presentation. The day before, August 13, Emmett Till was abducted and killed by two white men in Mississippi for saying "Bye, baby" to a white woman, Carolyn Bryant. Within a few days "Till's mangled corpse was found in the Tallahatchie River with a crushed skull, an eye gouged out, a bullet in the brain, and a seventy-five-pound cotton-gin fan barbed-wired to the neck."[49] Parks was deeply affected.

On October 21 eighteen-year-old Mary Louise Smith, riding on Montgomery's segregated buses, had refused to give her seat to a white woman and was arrested for disobeying an officer. Her past behavior was less than stellar, and the fact that she had not been charged with violating Jim Crow's segregation laws made her unacceptable for an NAACP test case. However, when Rosa Parks, a woman of impeccable character and reputation, was arrested for refusing to give up her seat to a white man on Thursday, December 1, 1955, E. D. Nixon knew he had found the woman and the case he needed to break the back of segregation. "They've messed with the wrong one now" became Montgomery's rallying cry. Out of her arrest grew the start of the Montgomery Bus Boycott on Monday, December 5, 1956. It lasted for more than a year, until, on November 13, the Supreme Court upheld an earlier federal district court decision in *Browder v. Gayle* destroying Alabama's segregation laws. It became final on December 17 when the Court refused a final appeal of the decision. On December 21 Montgomery's buses were desegregated.

It didn't mean, however, an end to racial discrimination or violence. On December 23 Dr. King's home was the target of a drive-by shotgun blast. On January 10, 1957, Ralph David Abernathy's parsonage and sanctuary were bombed, followed by bombings at three other black Montgomery churches and the home of a white supporter, the Reverend Robert S. Graetz. But things would never be the same again in the South or in America. "Across the street from where Rosa Parks was arrested still stood the Winter Building, where the telegraph was sent granting General P. G. T. Beauregard the discretion to fire on Fort Sumter; nearby were the spots where William L. Yancey delivered his speech presenting Jefferson Davis as president-elect of the Confederacy and the portico of the capitol of Alabama where Davis gave his inaugural address."[50] As history recorded, however, the leader and spokesperson of the bus boycott, Dr. King; his Dexter Avenue Baptist Church, located in the shadow of the former Confederate Capitol; the Holt Street Church, where the Montgomery Bus Boycott was organized; and the street corner on which Rosa Parks was arrested would become even more famous than the Lost Cause, and better define what America was trying to become. Thus was brought into the nation's consciousness the era of the modern civil rights movement.

Most Americans are familiar with at least the broad outlines of the civil rights struggles of the 1950s and 1960s: the 1957 Little Rock Central High School crisis, when President Dwight D. Eisenhower had to send in federal troops to assist in the admission of nine black students—including my good friend Ernie Green; the student sit-ins to desegregate lunch counters in Nashville and Greensboro, North Carolina in 1960 (my father was a leader and went to jail in Greensboro); the Freedom Riders in 1961, who desegregated travel on interstate buses, "whites only" waiting rooms, and restaurants (highlighted when students arriving on those buses in Anniston, Alabama, were trapped inside as the vehicles were firebombed); the Student Nonviolent Coordinating Committee's movement in 1961 and 1962 to desegregate the Jim Crow structures of Albany, Georgia (assisted by Dr. King); the struggle to admit the first black student to the University of Mississippi, James Meredith, in 1962.

On January 14, 1963, speaking in terms consistent with much of the spirit of the South, the new governor of Alabama, Democrat George C. Wallace, announced at his inauguration: "I draw the line in the dust and toss the gauntlet before the feet of tyranny . . . and I say segregation now . . . segregation tomorrow . . . segregation forever." Alabama's largest city, Birmingham, was a blue-collar steel-mill town, and its white hooligans were sometimes referred to as "millbillies." A member of the KKK, Robert Chambliss, was known around town as

Dynamite Bob. "Since the end of World War II, as many as fifty bombings had rocked the city. Many black churches had been targets, and two synagogues. One black section of town was attacked so often people called it Dynamite Hill."[51] This neighborhood was the childhood home of black activist Angela Davis, born in 1944; her family had been the first to move into this formerly all-white community. "The city itself was often referred to as Bombingham. So strong was the segregationist influence that the city had closed down its system of public parks and its professional baseball team rather than admit blacks."[52] The Reverend Fred Shuttlesworth had led a nearly decade-long campaign to desegregate Birmingham and fight its three-tiered segregationist structure: the Klan, the police, and the courts. The most dominant symbols of the 1963 Birmingham struggle were the image of the city's segregationist police commissioner, Eugene "Bull" Connor, releasing dogs and high-powered fire hoses on demonstrators, and the four little girls murdered September 15 in Sunday school when the church in which they were worshiping was bombed—just three weeks after Dr. King had delivered his most famous speech at the Lincoln Memorial, on August 28.

Northern black and white young people came South to assist black Mississippians in an organized voter registration campaign from 1961 through 1963, only to be met with massive and sometimes violent resistance by the police, White Citizens' Councils, the KKK, and state Democratic Party organizations. This was followed by a 1964 "Freedom Summer" voter registration campaign in Mississippi and a seating challenge to the Democratic Party of Mississippi at the Democratic Convention in Atlantic City by Fannie Lou Hamer and the Mississippi Freedom Democratic Party. After Dr. King received the Nobel Peace Prize in December 1964, he headed to Selma, Alabama, seeking national legislation to give legal protection to black people's right to vote. The lingering image of this campaign is the Reverend C. T. Vivian being punched in the face by Sheriff Jim Clark for trying to register black people. The campaign culminated with President Johnson signing the Voting Rights Act on August 6, 1965, and saying privately afterward that this would probably cost Democrats the South for the next quarter century. In 2000 his "word has become flesh" in much of the South: A late-twentieth- and early-twenty-first-century southern white Republican Party has replaced the nineteenth- and early-twentieth-century southern white Democratic Party—and forced most white southern Democrats to become almost as conservative as white southern Republicans to get elected. That's why, in the 2000 Republican primary, conservatives McCain initially and Texan Bush continuously said that the Confederate flag issue in South Carolina was a states' rights issue, and Tennessean Gore felt obligated to argue that the Elian Gonzalez federal immigration case was a states' rights issue and belonged in a state family court—even though the state family court judge had publicly said it was not in her legal domain.

In 1966 James Meredith led a "March Against Fear" from Memphis to Jackson, Mississippi, in which he was shot. During the march Stokely Carmichael (later Kwame Ture), to encourage a growing black militancy, made popular the slogan "Black Power" in a speech in Greenwood, Mississippi, on June 16. Dr. King also went North and led open-housing marches in Chicago in 1966, even as his opposition to the Vietnam War was growing. He spoke out against it in a major speech on April 4, 1967, at New York's Riverside Church and at two anti–Vietnam War rallies at the United Nations and the Pentagon later that year. In 1966 and 1967, the new black militancy in the North caused Huey P. Newton and Bobby Seale to found the Black Panthers in Oakland, California; there were serious riots in Detroit, Michigan; and Carl Stokes was elected the first black mayor of Cleveland.

In 1968 Dr. King was making plans to build a "Resurrection City" to house a massive "Poor People's Campaign" in the nation's capital when he was assassinated in Memphis on April 4. Bobby Kennedy, who had just won the California Democratic primary, was assassinated in Los Angeles on June 5. In August the Democratic National Convention turned into a Chicago "police riot" against anti–Vietnam War protesters. Northern racial tensions increased during struggles over control of education in the Ocean Hill–Brownsville section of New York in 1967 and 1968; in Boston a white antibusing backlash was gaining momentum in the late 1960s and early 1970s; in Philadelphia during this period whites were angry and labor was resisting an affirmative action jobs plan (affirmative action finally came to somewhat of a head in the controversial *Bakke* case in 1978, but it remains a hot racial issue even today); and black prisoners were killed when an Attica riot over prisoners' rights occurred in 1971; while a Black Political Convention was held in Gary, Indiana, in 1972.

As the "civil rights" era successfully came to an end in the late 1960s and early 1970s— blacks won in the law all of the basic civil rights struggles in which they engaged—a new era of "economic rights" was needed. What good did it do to have the right to stay in any hotel or eat in any restaurant if you didn't have a job or the money to pay for it? So in 1971, building on his earlier days as the national director of SCLC's Operation Breadbasket and keeping the economic focus (albeit in the private economy) of Dr. King's Poor People's Campaign, my father formed Operation PUSH (People United to Serve Humanity) to shift the emphasis of the struggle from "civil rights" in the public sector to "silver rights" in the private sector. And after more than a dozen years down this path, it became increasingly clear to him that the laws written in the public political order determined the quantity, quality, and equal (or unequal) distribution of rewards and benefits in the current private–public economic order. Seeking to influence or lead this private–public arrangement as the chief executive of the country, in 1984—after a massive southern voter registration drive through most of 1983—he ran his first campaign for the presidency in 1984 and a second campaign in 1988 to emphasize the issues of racial justice and reconciliation through rebuilding America around a common-ground economic agenda of full employment and national health care for all Americans.

Even so, race continues to dominate and shape our politics today, sometimes openly with Confederate flags in South Carolina, or in ugly ways, such as the dragging death of James Byrd in Texas. But more often race manifests itself through the use of subtle code words and policies within mainstream Republican and Democratic Party politics. Gun politics illustrate the point. According to a May 19, 1999, *Wall Street Journal* article, the Republican Party Platform in 1968 said, "We pledge an all-out federal-state-local crusade against crime, including enactment of legislation to control indiscriminate availability of firearms." That's the time frame of the 1967–1968 urban riots, when the Black Panthers were openly wielding them. But the Republican Party Platform of 1996 stated, "We defend the constitutional right to keep and bear arms." This statement was in the political context of Timothy McVeigh and white militias parading around with guns.

This code language often includes high responsible-sounding words, phrases, policies, and politics: budget priorities of fiscal restraint and responsibility; balancing the budget and eliminating the debt; tight-money monetary policies; conservative constitutional interpretations, such as strict constructionism; and a general political philosophy of conservatism, moderation, and, yes, liberalism. However, none of these mainstream ideas or policies will solve the pressing material needs of the American people regardless of gender or color, and sometimes they even make matters worse. Liberalism takes economics seriously, but not the breadth, depth, and legacy of slavery and racism.

The conscious modern-day conservative political resistance movement began in 1964 when "Mr. Conservative," Barry Goldwater, at the height of the civil rights movement, emphasized states' rights and local control as he won a mere fifty-two electoral votes—all of them from a solidly conservative Deep South. In 1968 conservative southern Democrat George Wallace ran as a third-party candidate on the American Independent Party ticket, making a rather unsophisticated racial appeal, and Richard Nixon's campaign used a slightly more subtle "southern strategy" with the racial code words of "law and order" in response to the 1967 and 1968 black urban uprisings. In 1972 both Nixon and Wallace used the racially charged issue of antibusing, and Wallace was shot and wounded in the middle of the campaign in Laurel, Maryland, which consigned him to a wheelchair for the rest of his life. He tried to run again as a Democrat in 1976 but was defeated by Jimmy Carter in the Florida primary; his quest for the presidency was over. In 1980 Reagan's racial appeal was apparent as he launched his southern campaign from Philadelphia, Mississippi—the same place, as I've noted, where two Jews and a black were murdered in the June 1964 campaign to register blacks—and used the stereotype of a "welfare queen" to appeal to white voters. George Bush and Al Gore used Willie Horton in 1988 and Clinton used "Sister Souljah" in 1992. In 2000 Bush used a straight-out appeal to "conservatism" and "strict constructionism"; Gore's continuing "get tough on crime" appeal reflected the political success that both parties have had in identifying and linking "crime" and "welfare" in the public's mind with black people.

We know from the tremor and great quake phases of American history about racial hostility, callousness, indifference, and political manipulation by presidents and Congresses during the antebellum and Civil War periods. However, a similar pattern continued to exist through the aftershock period from Andrew Johnson in 1865 to Bush and Gore in 2000. What were our honored presidents and Congress doing with regard to the race problem following the Civil War to the present?

> ❭ Andrew Johnson, president from 1865 to 1869, was basically a Democratic Negro-phobe. He claimed that the abolitionists were determined to "place every splay-footed, bandy-shanked, hump-backed, thick-lipped, flat-nosed, woolly-headed, ebon-colored negro in the country upon an equality with the poor white man."[53] While advocating white supremacy, he pardoned former Confederate leaders, restored economic and political power to the former slaveholders, denied all civil rights to the freedmen, fired any Freedmen's Bureau agent who did his job, and used U.S. soldiers to steal land back from blacks and give it to the master class of whites.

> ❭ From 1869 to 1877, Republican President Ulysses S. Grant oversaw the three post–Civil War amendments, as well as the Civil Rights and anti-KKK legislation of 1866, 1870, 1871, and 1875. Even so, this Civil War military hero proposed that blacks have no role in Reconstruction, remained silent with respect to supporting the Fifteenth Amendment, saw colonization as the best answer to the black problem, was lax in civil rights enforcement, and, fearing a race war, finally caved in to white supremacy in 1876. "On a field of battle this human bulldog would not surrender. On matters of race he would not fight."[54]

❭ Another Republican was president from 1877 to 1881. Primarily concerned with reconciling conservative northern Republicans and southern former Confederate Democrats, Rutherford B. Hayes had a states' rights political orientation that led him to a "let alone" race policy on the part of the federal government. Even though (as we saw earlier) he was willing to send federal troops into four states to protect property rights and help industrialists during the Great Strike of 1877, he was at the same time telling workers, blacks, women, farmers, and others that they didn't need the federal government; they should "make it on their own."

❭ James Garfield, a Republican, was elected in 1881. He made strong statements on behalf of black rights, but harbored antiblack sentiments, and early on was assassinated.

❭ Republican Chester A. Arthur (1881–1885) engaged in symbolic gestures—the Fisk University Choir brought him to tears—but he was the first president since the Civil War not to address the race question in his message to Congress.

❭ Grover Cleveland served eight years in two different stints, 1885–1889 and 1893–1897. A Democrat, Cleveland criticized the Reconstruction era's Republican "carpetbag" governments and, while seeing education as the answer to the African American problem, supported separate schools for blacks—getting his wish during his second term when *Plessy* established the "separate but equal" legal principle that lasted for fifty-eight years. He too used the federal government to break the Pullman strike in Chicago but not to assist the freedmen. During his eight years in office there were 728 recorded lynchings of blacks.

❭ Republican Benjamin Harrison served between Cleveland's two terms. The Harrison administration initially seemed promising to blacks and, for the first time in fifteen years, both houses of Congress were controlled by Republicans. They pushed two major pieces of legislation, centered on voting rights and education. However, they were again disappointed when Mississippi blacks met with Harrison, to no avail, to find relief from voting rights violations in their state, and the Republican-led Congress reneged on a promise to support new voting rights legislation. Finally, Harrison disappointed blacks by accommodating a new southern strategy.

❭ The U.S. president between 1897 and 1901, Republican William McKinley, used black federal patronage and advice from Booker T. Washington to relate to African Americans. He also organized two all-black army regiments and sent them to the Philippines to fight on behalf of the "white man's burden" while remaining silent about the grandfather clause adopted in Louisiana and denial of the black vote written into the North Carolina constitution.

❭ "Rough Rider" Theodore Roosevelt served from 1901 to 1909. A "progressive" Republican, Roosevelt was nevertheless shaped by racism and top-down bureaucratic (versus democratic) solutions. He once called the Japanese "lacquered half-monkeys," and he contributed to "a thinking man's racism" by bringing pseudo-science, false social studies, and perverted humanities into the classroom of the university. Roosevelt seemed to be obsessed with race. In his head he preserved a "gene hierarchy," spending countless hours gathering, organizing, and placing the "stronger races" and "weaker races" in order. Blacks, he argued, were the "most utterly underdeveloped" and, not surprisingly, he placed them near the bottom of his list. According to TR: "'Suffering from laziness and shiftlessness' and prone to 'vice and criminality of every kind,' blacks threatened white citizens and 'race purity.' Roosevelt studied the problem scientifically, in the progressive manner, and concluded that Negro 'evils' were 'more potent for harm to the black race than all acts of oppression of white men put together.' '[This] perfectly stupid race can never rise,' he added on another occasion. 'The Negro . . . has been kept down as much by lack of intellectual development as by anything else.'"[55]

> Republican William Howard Taft (1909–1913) called the disenfranchisement of blacks in the South "a turn for the better" and saw nothing wrong with legally barring "an ignorant electorate."

> The son of a southern Virginia Presbyterian minister, a Democrat and Princeton University president, Woodrow Wilson served form 1913 to 1921. Wilson, who benefited from the first slight defection of blacks from the Republican Party, garnering 5 to 7 percent of the black vote. He nevertheless saw segregation as rationally and scientifically sound, and was deeply offended when civil rights leader Monroe Trotter disagreed with his segregationist views and couldn't understand why Trotter didn't talk to him in a "Christian spirit." Wilson also worried about white women working in the same confines with black men and allowed a White House screening of *Birth of a Nation*. In 1913, after Wilson was elected, the Democrat-controlled Sixty-third Congress introduced the most antiblack legislation in American history.

> A few southern Democratic white supremacists actually accused our twenty-ninth president, Republican Warren G. Harding (1921–1923), of being black. The only black issue he saw or understood, however, was black patronage.

> While the prominent influence of the KKK at the Madison Square Garden Democratic Convention in 1924 was not manifest at the Republican Convention in Cleveland, Calvin Coolidge, our thirtieth president (1923–1929), was nominated with black and white delegates separated by chicken wire.

> The *Chicago Tribune* accused thirty-first president, Republican Herbert Hoover (1929–1933), "of turning the GOP into 'a socially acceptable mansion for southern gentlemen.'"[56]

❭ While Franklin D. Roosevelt's (1933–1945) "New Deal" programs proved greatly beneficial to all Americans, including blacks, it wasn't until FDR's second election in 1936 that blacks, out of economic self-interest, switched from the Republican Party and voted, for the first time, in significant numbers for a Democratic president. However, in four terms FDR passed not a single piece of civil rights legislation, let Jim Crow alone, and, according to reports, did not even discuss race privately. In part, as a result of blacks switching their loyalty to the Democratic Party, when FDR called Congress into a special session in late 1937 urging them to pass legislation to continue his economic recovery, "a bipartisan group, dominated by southern Democrats, issued a ten-point 'Conservative Manifesto.' Principally drafted by Senator Josiah Bailey, it denounced the sit-down strikes, demanded lower federal taxes and a balanced budget, defended states' rights as well as the rights of private enterprise against government encroachment, and warned of the dangers of creating a permanently dependent welfare class."[57]

❭ With the end of World War II and the start of the Cold War, conservative Democrats—along with some liberal Democrats—and Republicans appealed to the fear of communism. Spending huge sums of money to maintain a strong military was the excuse for not being able to afford the completion of the unfinished business of economic Reconstruction. Southern Democrats, who had kept Henry Wallace off FDR's ticket in 1944 and put Harry S. Truman (1945–1953) on, were pleased to have him as president after FDR's death because, they reasoned, "The new president knows how to handle the niggers."[58] With Henry Wallace threatening to run as a liberal third-party candidate, Truman did a number of positive things for blacks, including establishing a Fair Employment Practices Commission, desegregating the armed forces, and, on June 29, 1947, becoming the first U.S. president to address an NAACP gathering, at the Lincoln Memorial.

❭ Republican Dwight D. Eisenhower (1953–1961), a World War II military hero, saw no need to be militant on civil rights or the race question. Playing at segregated golf courses never bothered him, but he was uncomfortable around blacks. He preferred to leave such matters as the resolution of the race problem to the approach of volunteerism. He did sign the 1957 Civil Rights Act, the first piece of civil rights legislation since Reconstruction, but only after Senator Strom Thurmond, then a South Carolina Democrat, set a record by conducting the longest fillibuster in the history of the Senate. It was also during Eisenhower's tenure in office that the *Brown* decision came down, and every southern congressman and senator from the former eleven Confederate states—except Lyndon Johnson of Texas and Estes Kefauver and Albert Gore, Sr., of Tennessee—issued a "Southern Manifesto" vowing to resist and overturn it.

❭ "Liberal" northern Democrat John F. Kennedy (1961–1963) made a call during the 1960 presidential campaign to Coretta Scott King during one of Dr. King's southern jailings in Georgia. The call paid off in securing "Daddy" King's endorsement and an even bigger switch from the Republican to the Democratic Party. But upon election, Kennedy felt compelled to "balance" his Democratic politics by appointing five segregationist judges to southern federal benches, including segregationist Senator James Eastland's (D-MS) college roommate, Harold Cox.

> Texas Democrat Lyndon B. Johnson (1963–1968), while, in Dr. King's view, wrongly spending the lives and treasure of Americans in an immoral war in Vietnam instead of a war on poverty at home, nevertheless politically and legislatively overcame much of his segregationist past and did more to make America one, Reconstruction real, and the Union more perfect than any other president since the Civil War.

Thus, it turns out, race and the legacy of slavery and racism is not just a recent and current problem of individual prejudice and personal racial discrimination. Instead, it is a long-standing structural and institutional pattern that is wedded to the two-party system of Republicans and Democrats and manifests itself through both parties' economic, social, and political philosophies and policies. *I call the two-party political arrangement the racial paradigm, and I call the economic, social, and political philosophies of conservatism, moderation, and liberalism the racial matrix.* Both the paradigm and the matrix are aided and abetted by the fourth estate, the media, because this "vigilant institution" does not challenge the underlying assumptions of these basic structural arrangements.

Before the Civil War, white male Americans could express their economic and social philosophies, at various times, primarily through four political parties—Federalists, Democrats, Whigs, and, after 1854, Republicans. They structured an economy to benefit an elite group of white males—in the North industry moguls, in the South slaveholders. These few white males essentially exploited industrial workers and skilled craftsmen in the North, and small white farmers and slaves in the South. By the conclusion of the war, however, race had narrowed their political options to two major political parties, Democrats and Republicans, with three social and economic philosophies, conservatism, moderation, and liberalism. Today these slave-legacy politics (the paradigm), and their philosophies and policies (the matrix), are still playing themselves out.

After the war, Frederick Douglass and Radical Republicans (the economic liberals of that day) argued that the federal government should help the former slaves economically—with education, land, housing, training, and employment—until they got on their feet as full equals with whites. Economic moderates argued that the federal government should pass the Thirteenth, Fourteenth, and Fifteenth Amendments—giving them equal protection under the law—and help the former slaves economically for an unspecified amount of time, but then the former slaves were on their own. Economic conservatives and racists, the Democrats, argued that the former slaves were politically free as a result of the Emancipation Proclamation and the Reconstruction amendments; they should now just pull themselves up economically by their own bootstraps without government assistance.

Social liberals—again the Radical Republicans—argued that the former slaves were free and should be treated under the law as full and equal Americans entitled to every right under the Constitution that any other American had. The entire society should be totally integrated into "one America" with no distinctions, under the law, between the former slaves and whites. Social moderates—politically, a mixture of Democrats and Republicans—argued that the former slaves were free and "equal" human beings, but that equality should express itself with the former slaves establishing their own institutions and not mixing with whites. This was the social forerunner of the "separate but equal" legal philosophy later expressed in *Plessy*. Social conservatives—mainly southern Democrats, but racists generally—argued that the former slaves might be technically free, but they were still inferior to whites. Full integration or "race mixing" in any form was totally unacceptable and out of the question. Today this sometimes takes the public (or more often deeply private) form of "I don't want them in my neighborhood, my church, my golf club, my social club, and certainly not in my family. They're uneducated, untrained, unskilled, unclean, sexually promiscuous, and commit too much crime." These attitudes take various forms, usually deeply subtle.

The race problem today and its legacy, then, is the comfort level that Americans find in the racial paradigm of Democrats and Republicans, and the racial matrix of economic and social conservatism, moderation, and liberalism that our national history has created. Voters often proclaim, "I'm a Republican who's conservative on economic issues, but liberal on social issues." Or, "I'm a Democrat who's liberal on economic issues, but moderate on social issues." Or, "I'm a Republican who's moderate on economic issues, but conservative on social issues." This confusing hodgepodge serves to maintain caste and class distinctions through our politics and our laws.

It is precisely the comfort (or discomfort) level that most Americans feel in this racial paradigm and matrix that is our greatest barrier to building a more perfect Union or accomplishing something for everybody. This two-party economic and social conservatism, moderation, and liberalism is what we're stuck in. Trying to enact a new law through this paradigm and matrix is the *racial gauntlet* through which all political dialogue, action, and legislation must pass. It is this racial/political paradigm, matrix, and gauntlet at work in our intensely personal politics when we label ourselves as Republican, or Democrat, or conservative. This gauntlet creates the opportunities and limitations of our progress as a society.

The race gauntlet is the current structure of political power that is in the hands of both Democrats and Republicans and protects the narrow interests of the economic elite who are really in charge of and primarily responsible for influencing our politics. The race paradigm and matrix have created our history-driven gauntlet that has failed, and will continue to fail, to secure our new American rights.

Since the Civil War, the race question has taken the political form of Democrats and Republicans, and the ideological form of economic and social conservatism, moderation, and liberalism. But the substance of the race question has always been, and remains now, about money and economics—tax policy, fiscal policy, and monetary policy.

First, taxes. How much and who will pay enough taxes to fix this historic problem of caste and class; to provide everyone a genuine equal opportunity throughout their lives? Second, spending. What are our spending priorities? Who should we spend our money on? And for what reason? Are our spending priorities directed toward having an overwhelming military presence in the world in order to maintain an unjust economic order? Or are they directed toward achieving economic justice at home and abroad by having the strongest people as a result of a full-employment peacetime economy, balanced economic growth (not just aggregate growth), the best education, health care, and housing, and the cleanest environment? In short, are our spending priorities truly directed toward achieving social and economic justice at home and around the world? Third, money. Monetary policy is responsible for our economic stability, by balancing full employment and inflation. Should it then be managed with the priority of fighting inflation for the purpose of protecting financial interests first (they don't want their loans paid back with inflated dollars), or should we manage it with the priority of putting people first by creating enough jobs to put everyone to work?

Today, racial politics must be viewed through the eyes of, and measured by, taxes, spending, and monetary policy priorities. The economics and politics of the officials who genuinely want to put people first will be reflected in their views and decisions on taxes, spending, and macro money management. They will be willing to collect enough fair taxes to fix the legacy of race and class disparity in our society. Their spending priorities will be the economic security and human development of all Americans. While managing both within reasonable boundaries, macro money management priorities will "tilt" toward full employment instead of a hurtful preoccupation with inflation.

By the same token—since such economic policies are the only way we can fix our historical race problem and overcome its legacy—those who are opposed to paying enough fair taxes, efficiently and effectively spending enough money, or prioritizing balanced growth in a full-employment peacetime economy must be seen and judged as opponents of racial justice and reconciliation no matter how benevolent is the language used to explain their opposition.

Today's actual opponents of social and economic justice don't often use racially offensive language—they don't blatantly call African Americans "niggers" anymore—and those who do aren't the real enemies of racial justice, they're just ignorant, so we shouldn't get sidetracked. The real opponents of racial justice spare no dime to support a "strong national defense," but pinch pennies on education, housing, and health care for all Americans. They are strong "welfare reformers" and opponents of "crime," want to "blanket America in blue," be known as the "enforcement president" and pass "victims' rights amendments," but those aren't the real solutions. If you show me a community that has full employment, decent health care, affordable housing, and a good educational system for all, I'll show you a community that doesn't have a serious crime problem. Being for welfare reform and being tough on crime, without a willingness to strongly and aggressively address the actual underlying economic causes and solutions, is playing racial politics.

Opponents of racial justice blindly and rhetorically support the death penalty at a time when most of the rest of the world is moving in another direction and international organizations increasingly refer to it as a violation of human rights. We obviously need—and I support—business, free enterprise, and finance; they are critical helpmates on the road toward achieving racial and economic justice. But racial justice adversaries tend to put militarism, financial, and business-oriented priorities ahead of democratically determined people priorities.

And the biggest opponents of racial justice just say they want less or lower taxes, or less or smaller government; are predeterminedly and ideologically opposed to federal solutions and support state and local ones; use overkill and are preoccupied with balancing federal budgets and reducing national debts; and "name-call" using demagoguery against "tax and spend" liberals. Sometimes they just use shorthand and say, "I'm a conservative."

The race problem is so profound that it is unpollable, un-focus-groupable, un-one-lineable, non-soundbitable, and, so far, insurmountable. Politicians must do something that they have failed to do since Lincoln, Roosevelt, and Lyndon Johnson—educate and lead the American people. It is not something that can be covered in a sixty-minute focus group.

Candidates who heavily rely on such tactics do not approach the problem with the strength, courage, or character of the one president who is most responsible for preserving and strengthening our Union, Abraham Lincoln. I believe Americans have been wishing, longing—indeed, waiting, hoping, and praying—for such a moral and political leader to address their unmet material needs.

Accepting the current political gauntlet and rhetorical framework is a dead-end street. It will not lead to a more perfect Union. Thus, if we are to make progress and achieve economic justice for all Americans, we must take the nonideological, nonprogrammatic, and nonpartisan path of human rights, not the current route of the accepted racial paradigm, matrix, and gauntlet of Democratic and Republican economic and social conservatism, moderation, and liberalism. If both parties and our variety of political ideologies agree on the major material goals, then let's turn them into new rights for the American people and codify them in the Constitution in the form of new amendments.

We must now advance the idea that, in our affluent society and under our Constitution, every American should be empowered and have the *individual right* to vote, and to work, health care, housing, education, a clean environment, equal protection under the law, and fair taxes. Which economic, social, and political philosophy, ideology, or legislative program—or what mixture or combination of them all—will be required to take us there, should be a purely secondary question. Our focus must be on the practical goal of making sure that every American has equal access, under the Constitution, to these new American rights. With these new rights, all Americans should be able to achieve—to the best of their ability, while utilizing their best effort—our fullest developmental potential as individual human beings and as a society. Such rights will take us a long way down the path to a more perfect union.

9

A MORE PERFECT UNION—
EQUAL OPPORTUNITY

I believe the promise of America is equal opportunity, not equal outcomes.

—President Bill Clinton, from the Democratic
Leadership Council's New Orleans Declaration, 1990

Differences in outcomes derive from differences in opportunities.

—The Reverend Dr. Samuel DeWitt Proctor

It is not enough just to open the gates of opportunity. All our citizens must have the ability to walk through those gates. This is the next and the more profound stage of the battle for civil rights. We seek not just freedom but opportunity. We seek not just legal equity but human ability, not just equality as a right and a theory, but equality as a fact and equality as a result.

—President Lyndon B. Johnson
Howard University, June 4, 1965

Most Americans abstractly or theoretically believe in equal opportunity. Thomas Jefferson's words in the Declaration of Independence that "all men are created equal" are deeply rooted in American idealism and in the American psyche. Americans also understand "all men are created equal" to mean "equal opportunity" and "equal before the law," not that we are all equal in talent, intellect, motivation, determination, drive, money, or wealth. That's a proper distinction.

Most Americans begin with the idea that we are a land of opportunity, and that our nation stands for equal opportunity. The underlying assumption is that if an individual has essentially the same talent and determination, and he is not discriminated against, he will eventually achieve similar success. That's the American concept of equal opportunity, and it's generally a good one. This belief is part of what it means to be an American. I hope to add a broader and deeper meaning to most Americans' understanding of equal opportunity, but belief in this paradigm is a huge plus for advocates of equality. American ideals are also against discrimination, and we do not favor giving one individual or a group an advantage over others. I hope to clarify some misunderstandings here as well.

In 1990 a relatively new conservative organization, the Democratic Leadership Council (DLC), met in New Orleans, Louisiana. This disproportionately southern-based organization—historically in the lineage of another "DLC," the Democratic Legacy of the Confederacy—was founded to counter the National Rainbow Coalition and the growing influence of blacks, minorities, women, labor, and other progressives in the Democratic Party after my father's two presidential campaigns of 1984 and (especially) 1988.

After 1988, blacks and other progressives were gaining power within the Democratic Party. The democratic reforms of George McGovern in 1972 and the Jackson campaigns had brought the National Democratic Party Ron Brown as its new chair. Ed Cole was the new state party chair in Mississippi. Joel Ferguson occupied a similar post in Michigan. Countless African American men and women, plus new liberal leaders like Paul Wellstone in Minnesota, Donna Shalala in Wisconsin, and other progressives throughout the party structure were assuming leadership positions as a result of the Jackson candidacy. With re-districting in 1991, under a Supreme Court interpretation of the 1965 Voting Rights Act that mandated district lines be drawn to give African and Latino Americans an equal op-portunity to win, it was clear even then that there was going to be a significant increase in African and Latino American legislators at every level of government in the next election.

At the 1990 New Orleans DLC meeting, this corporate-sponsored and -oriented organi-zation passed its platform, called the "New Orleans Declaration." Arkansas Governor Bill Clinton had just been elected the DLC's new chairman, and the phrase opening this chapter was based on this DLC declaration. It was a not-so-subtle attack on affirmative action.

When my father saw the DLC slogan supporting equal opportunity but not equal results in a *USA Today* article, he wrote to then Governor Bill Clinton and expressed his concern about this particular phraseology. It was dangerous rhetoric, my father warned, that could lead to significant misunderstandings, because the language contained an underlying premise of inequality.

In other words, theoretically, if every individual has a genuine equal opportunity, we should expect equal outcomes. If, on the other hand, every individual truly has an equal op-portunity, but there are inherently inferior and superior people, you would expect unequal results. Thus, the phrase is nonsensical, a non sequitur, and has a sexist and racist premise. The implication and logic of President Clinton's statement is that some—racial minorities and women—need something more than a genuine equal opportunity to achieve an equal outcome. In other words, people of color and women are genetically inferior and white males genetically superior!

Clinton did not initially respond to my father's letter. Instead, the governor sent the let-ter to Washington to the DLC, which selectively edited and ran it—without my father's per-mission—as an article in its magazine. Seeing the letter, my father called Governor Clinton asking for a personal response to his original letter. A few weeks later Clinton sent him a one-page response indicating that he thought they were "saying the same thing only using different language." Even though Clinton had been warned of the danger of its underlying racist and sexist premise—and the troubling implications of his words—he continued to use this rhetoric in his two presidential campaigns and even as president of the United States.

Contrary to the public image he projects and the support he receives, Bill Clinton has a mixed history on the question of race. As everyone knows, he is a very gifted politician who is a master of rhetoric, image projection, and spin. As a result, most Americans, including African Americans, see him as a "liberal" on the question of race. I don't!

I see him, as I saw his fellow southerner Jimmy Carter, generally as a social liberal, but an economic moderate and sometimes economic conservative. I would prefer that he be pro-gressive on both, but if the president had to be one or the other, I think I would actually prefer the reverse. If people have economic security, it's easier for them to be social liberals.

However, social liberalism in the context of economic conservatism—which cannot achieve the ideals of social liberalism—is a formula for resentment, frustration, and even violent explosions.

Having said that, clearly, even as a mere social liberal, Clinton is better on the subject of race than any elected Republican I know. While there are many Republicans in Congress whom I like very much personally, every official Republican I know has a pretty poor record on both understanding the problem and recommending realistic and adequate solutions to the equal opportunity and race question—socially and economically.

However, there are official and unofficial Republicans. I use the term "official Republican" because I consider both Bill Clinton and Jimmy Carter—two "southern moderate" Democrats—to be essentially Republicans with regard to their economically conservative policies and approach to government. In fact, from my point of view and study of history, there hasn't been a real Democrat in the White House since President Lyndon B. Johnson. From my reading of American political history, it seems to me that we have been governed by Republican economic policies since Richard Nixon came to power in 1969, and some of his *economic* policies were actually more liberal than either Carter's or Clinton's. In fact, it was Nixon who said, "We are all Keynesians now."

While President Clinton has a liberal image, his substance on the question of equal opportunity and race is very weak. He was governor of Arkansas for twelve years, yet Alabama and Arkansas were the only two states lacking a state civil rights law during that time. In 1991, leading up to his presidential campaign, Governor Clinton actively opposed passing such a law, and used his considerable political skills to get the state's black legislators to go along with him.

My father had been invited and participated in every DLC conference until Governor Clinton became the head of the organization. Clinton snubbed and blocked him from coming to their conference in Cleveland in 1991.

When Clinton got in trouble during the New Hampshire primary over his alleged sexual affair with Gennifer Flowers, he tried to divert attention from her and his problems by returning to Arkansas and putting to death a lobotomized black man named Ricky Ray Rector. In other words, he used a black man to send a political signal to the white community that he was a New Democrat—trying to attract Reagan Democrats back to the party—who was tough on crime and supported the death penalty. The next day, January 25, 1992, he came to the National Rainbow Coalition's presidential forum in Washington, D.C., and tried to explain his actions.

At the Rainbow's presidential forum, all of the candidates were offered an opportunity to spend a day on the campaign trail with Reverend Jackson at a "point of challenge," which meant going with him to an event that focused on those most in need. Senator Tom Harkin chose to have Reverend Jackson go to a point of challenge with him in South Carolina on the day before the South Carolina caucus. While the Clinton campaign had inquired about the nature of the South Carolina visit—whether Jackson was endorsing Harkin (he was not)—the reply did not get back to Clinton. Thus, when Clinton heard about the Harkin-Jackson joint event—during a satellite television interview into Arizona—he exploded and referred to my father as a "dirty, double-crossing, back-stabbing" kind of person. It was all captured on television, because he forgot that the satellite was still operating.

On the Monday before the southern primary on Super Tuesday, candidate Clinton and Senator Sam Nunn, the conservative military hawk from Georgia, went to Stone Mountain and were photographed in front of a group of one hundred black prisoners in their white prison uniforms. The intent was to send a not-so-subtle racial message to conservative white southerners. The political signal? A President Bill Clinton will not be soft on crime (a racial code word), and he knows how to deal with black criminals. The race signal was so strong that Jerry Brown asked Clinton about it at their next debate.

After Clinton won the Illinois primary, he was "discovered" the next day playing golf at a segregated golf course back in Little Rock, Arkansas. Some political pundits have written that this was a "calculated mistake" to reassure his good ol' boy southern political friends not to worry about his cultivation of black voters; nothing much was going to change.

Trying to create Clinton as a New Democrat, not beholden to the old liberal Democratic coalition of "special interests"—minorities, especially African Americans (above all, Jesse Jackson), labor, and women—Paul Begala and Mandy Grunwald, Clinton's image makers, launched what they called a "counterscheduling strategy." The idea was to schedule themselves before traditional Democratic "special-interest" groups—their Democratic base— and say things that would offend them (politically, they had no place else to go) in order to send a signal to the Reagan Democrats that Clinton was no traditional Democrat, bound by liberal special-interest groups.

It was in this context that candidate Clinton came to the National Rainbow Coalition conference in the summer of 1992 and did his little "Sister Souljah" stunt. Sister Souljah is a black rap singer who was reported to have made some inflammatory statements in the press following the Los Angeles uprising after the Rodney King verdict. Reverend Jackson had visited with her privately in New York and cautioned her about such rhetoric, but he also invited her to participate in the youth workshop on voter registration at the Rainbow's annual conference. Clinton came to the conference and publicly singled her out for criticism, without prior consultation, for the sole purpose of scoring political points. The idea was to insult and make Reverend Jackson publicly express his anger. It would look as though Bill Clinton had stood up to Jesse Jackson. Then conservative whites and Reagan Democrats could return to this New Democrat and his new conservative Democratic Party. In other words, just as George Bush had used the Willie Horton incident to play racial politics in 1988, Bill Clinton was playing the race card through the Sister Souljah incident in 1992.

It's partially unfair to link George Bush solely to Willie Horton. Al Gore was actually the first politician to use William R. Horton, Jr. (without naming him), against Michael Dukakis in a Democratic candidates' debate in New York—posturing to show his "tough on crime" and conservative political credentials against Dukakis's "permissive northeastern liberalism." Massachusetts Governor Michael Dukakis had furloughed a black man named William R. Horton, Jr., out of prison on weekends, and during one weekend he raped a white woman in Maryland; the furlough program was actually begun under a previous Republican governor. A Republican researcher, studying the transcript of the Democratic debate, called this item to the attention of Bush's top campaign strategist, Lee Atwater, a southerner who had learned his politics under former Dixiecrat and now Republican Senator Strom Thurmond of South Carolina. Knowing the psycholinguistics of race and recognizing a race opportunity when he saw one, Atwater changed the name to Willie Horton—William R. Horton, Jr., would not rape your wife or daughter, but "Willie" Horton would—and Republicans used Willie Horton in an ad against Dukakis during the general election campaign.

Candidate Clinton went to Houston in 1992 and promised the U.S. Conference of Mayors that he would be an investment president. He laid out for them a plan to invest two hundred billion dollars over four years, eighty billion dollars of it in the cities. Despite the racial antics and distancing stunts, Clinton had actually run his 1992 campaign on economic issues—"It's the economy, stupid"—and as a result had pulled the traditional moderate/liberal Democratic coalition back together for the first time since the 1960s.

However, when Clinton was elected with only 43 percent of the vote (Perot got 19 percent), he took a poll, employed triangulation, and became not the investment president but the deficit reduction president. Minorities, the poor, and working people were hurt the most by that shift in priorities. Any discussion of equal opportunity, then, must be seen in the context of economic substance. In the future, when politicians speak to us about equal opportunity, progressives must demand more than high-sounding, benevolent social rhetoric. The right words and symbolism are important, but economic substance is more so. In the future, we must demand it.

Candidate Clinton criticized the Bush administration for its inhumane policy toward the Haitians, who were escaping an oppressive and violent Haiti in dangerous and rickety boats en masse. A week before he took office he reversed himself and adopted the Bush policy.

Once in office, President Clinton said he wanted his cabinet to look like America, and in some respects it did. It was definitely multicultural and multigender. President Clinton had the most racially diverse cabinet and administration in the history of the country up to that time, though in that regard, the Bush administration is similar. For this, both Clinton and Bush should be highly commended. However, except for Labor Secretary Alexis Herman, almost all people of color in the Clinton administration had a corporate orientation, and that is not the orientation of most Americans. So in an economic sense, Clinton's cabinet did *not* look like America. They mostly fit the Clinton mold and criteria of social liberals and economic conservatives; few had a civil rights or "movement" background. Commerce Secretary Ron Brown, a good and competent man who formerly headed the Washington Urban League, nevertheless later became a corporate lawyer who represented such human rights oppressors as "Baby Doc" Duvalier of Haiti.

On November 13, 1993, Clinton gave a speech to a group of African American clergy at Mason Temple in Memphis, the pulpit from which Dr. Martin Luther King, Jr., had preached his "I've Been to the Mountaintop" speech on the night before he was assassinated. He told them that crime, violence, and black men making babies and not being responsible for helping raise them was not what Dr. King had fought and died for. This is true, of course, but removing a sixty-year-old floor beneath the poor and calling it "ending welfare as we know it," or placing priority on balancing the budget rather than balancing the lives of unemployed and untrained poor people with jobs and adequate training, is not what Dr. King gave his life for either. Clinton made it clear that he knew jobs were the primary antidote to crime, but he offered no economic program of full employment and equal opportunity as a way out. President Clinton, leader of the wealthiest and most powerful government in the world, lectured black people about criminals, moral values, and degenerate behavior. He emotionally attacked the effects, but to correct the underlying economic causes offered only a passionate speech.

Clinton is a talker, and a good one. But providing real economic programs and political equal opportunity for all Americans is going to take a long-term investment of money. Social liberalism alone won't do it! This country cannot overcome the four-hundred-year-old legacy of slavery, apartheid, and discrimination, or America's economic class divisions, without a commitment to foot the real costs of genuine equal opportunity for all Americans.

The Clinton administration was not known for its aggressive and strong enforcement of civil rights laws. Civil rights appointments were late in coming, and their departments were underfunded. Indeed, after Clinton had been in office for more than three years, on February 11, 1996, Gilbert Casellas, chairman of the Equal Employment Opportunity Commission, complained in the *Washington Post* that he had not met privately with the president since his confirmation and the White House never returned his telephone calls. "Nobody gives a crap about us," Casellas said. Clinton is mostly remembered for caving in to the right wing; for turning his back on an old Yale classmate and friend, Lani Guinier, when she was the nominee for the post of assistant attorney general for civil rights at the Justice Department; and for his weak defense of affirmative action—"mend it, don't end it."

Republicans won control of both the House and the Senate in the midterm elections of 1994. Reading it as a conservative message and rebuff to his "liberal" health care plan, Clinton decided to move his presidency even farther to the right. But how to send the signal and who to use? Dr. Joycelyn Elders, an African American physician from his home state of Arkansas and the U.S. surgeon general, had given a frank and straightforward answer to a question about masturbation at a U.N. conference on AIDS shortly after the election. The right wing was outraged by her remarks and Clinton fired her. He had decided to use this black woman as the vehicle for sending a signal that his administration was changing to a more conservative course.

On June 14, 1997, President Clinton spoke at San Diego State University launching a yearlong "dialogue on race." Two things struck me about the speech. About two weeks before, he and the Republicans, supported by mostly conservative southern Democrats, passed and signed legislation calling for a balanced budget by 2002. Liberals and progressives were left out of the deal. This priority guaranteed that there would not be enough money to provide equal economic opportunities to everyone in America, or even to support the commonsense recommendations of Clinton's Race Commission and its chairman, Dr. John Hope Franklin.

The second interesting thing about the speech was that it was a call for a dialogue on *race*, not a dialogue about racism. I call Clinton's overture on the racial question the "Rodney King Approach"—"can't we just all get along?" Obviously, talking to one another, becoming knowledgeable about other races and cultures, and coming to appreciate and celebrate different cultures is all fine and necessary and could help us get along. However, it doesn't confront the central problem of racism and the denial of equal opportunity to all Americans in this country. Race, per se, is not a problem. We are all born into a particular sociological category called "race." This is not a matter of choice, and nothing can be done about it. And biologically speaking, of course, the Human Genome Project has shown conclusively that there is only one race, the human race.

Racism is another matter. It was created by and grew out of human political choices, legal structures, and social and economic institutions. Racism—a product of the African slave trade, slavery, apartheid, and institutionalized discrimination—is the problem, not race. And since human choices created it, different human choices can alter and end it! But that requires courage, skill, knowledge, and political leadership on the question of racism, not merely a discussion of race. And even the president's approach to race was virtually devoid of any economic content. He spelled out his major trust by discussing how California would soon become a "majority-minority" state—that is, the people of color combined—Asian, Latino and African Americans—would soon constitute a majority of the state. On the question of tackling racism, however, President Clinton remained virtually silent and largely inactive, especially if it cost any money.

Ward Connerly, the African American leader of the anti-affirmative-action initiative in California in 1996—and elsewhere later—was in the audience when Clinton gave his San Diego speech. As soon as the president concluded his speech, Connerly held a press conference and attacked it on the basis of affirmative action. Thus, even the limited and intended dialogue on race was immediately reduced and transformed into a dialogue about affirmative action. The next day Connerly appeared on NBC-TV's *Meet the Press* with my father to further press his anti-affirmative-action message, and in the Sunday *New York Times* he and Speaker Newt Gingrich had a long anti-affirmative-action article on the op-ed page. This, of course, was all intentionally orchestrated by a conservative right wing to define and limit even the race debate and any discussion of equal opportunity to the issue of affirmative action.

In 1998 Clinton participated in ESPN's "Racism in Sports" dialogue, but in 1993 he had crossed the picket line at Baltimore's Camden Yards Stadium on baseball's opening day when the National Rainbow Coalition was protesting documented racism in Major League Baseball—clearly revealed that night on ESPN to still be the worst of all the mainline professional sports leagues. But Clinton's actions in Baltimore were never mentioned.

President Bill Clinton's second inauguration happened to fall on Dr. Martin Luther King, Jr.'s, national holiday. As the national media does every year, President Clinton ignored the economic substance of the first three-quarters of Dr. King's August 28, 1963, "I Have a Dream" speech—I call it Dr. King's "Promissory Note" speech—and went to its poetic conclusion. But Dr. King, looking toward the Capitol and speaking to Congress, had started his speech by referencing Lincoln's Emancipation Proclamation of one hundred years earlier. He then challenged Congress on its lack of an economic commitment to all Americans. He said, "America has given the Negro people a bad check which has come back marked 'insufficient funds.' But," Dr. King continued, "we refuse to believe that the bank of justice is bankrupt. We refuse to believe that there are insufficient funds in the great vaults of opportunity of this nation." Finally, he concluded, if we change this policy of ignoring the real needs of all Americans, then "I have a dream. . . ." That's why, symbolically speaking, Dr. King's and President Clinton's speeches collided over the Washington Monument and the friction between them caused sparks to fly; while the American people thought it was exploding fireworks they were watching at Clinton's second inaugural.

The standards and criteria that Dr. King laid out in the economic substance of his address are what every president, every Congress, and every Supreme Court decision should be measured against—not his uplifting conclusion. Dr. King's dream was not about the sweetness of cotton candy, but about overcoming the hard realities that the economic legacy of king cotton left to all Americans, not just African Americans. Yes, poor people can and should dream. But too often poor people don't have the luxury of dreaming because of their economic nightmare!

President Clinton got more support from African Americans, and in return gave less in substance, than was the case with any other ethnic group in American history. A *New York Times* op-ed piece written by the ex-president shortly after he left office was typical of the largely smoke-and-mirrors rhetorical symbolism displayed during his administration. He laid out a lengthy agenda for the Bush administration, challenging them on the race question in such areas as ending mandatory minimum prison sentences, which disproportionately affect blacks. After reading Clinton's challenges to President Bush, however, I couldn't help but ask myself, "Who has been president for the past eight years?" It was the perfect postscript to Clinton's relationship with the black community—talk loud and carry a rubber stick.

America—government at every level, the private sector, religious institutions, foundations, charitable organizations, and volunteers—must contribute to making every American economically secure. We must be that kind of people and create that kind of society for religious, moral, economic, and political reasons. The economy is the hearing aid through which all Americans hear the nation's political dialogue and the lens through which they see their fellow Americans and the world. It will be hard for any American who is not economically secure himself to hear the cry of other Americans in need, not to mention others around the world.

Too often poor and struggling working-class whites can't hear the equal opportunity discussion because of their own circumstances. The public elementary and secondary schools to which they send their own sons and daughters often aren't very good. They can't get their own kids into college. And their personally dire economic situation makes them vulnerable to political manipulation by opportunists. I know because, as I documented earlier, I see their rhetorical manipulation operating in private meetings, in committee hearings, and on the floor of the House and Senate virtually every day, as well as in the media.

The issue that has been the most emotionally charged, and the one conservatives have gotten the most mileage out of, is affirmative action. Anyone who links affirmative action with "reverse discrimination," "preferences," and "quotas" without clarifying each is engaged in political demagoguery and manipulation. Ward Connerly, current and past representatives like Charles Canady, Newt Gingrich, and Richard Armey, and senators such as Trent Lott, John Ashcroft, and others love to perpetuate a series of affirmative action myths—mostly devoid of facts.

They argue that white males are being hurt and discriminated against—reverse discrimination—because of affirmative action. The facts contradict the allegation. Adult white males comprise roughly 33 percent of the population, but 80 percent of tenured professors, 80 percent of the U.S. House, 80 percent of the U.S. Senate, 92 percent of the Forbes 400, 97 percent of school superintendents, 98 percent of professional athletic team owners, and 100 percent of U.S. presidents and vice presidents.

Since the inception of this nation, white men have been given preferential treatment—the rights to vote, to own land, and to attend institutions of higher learning. In the late 1800s, whites were given millions of acres of mineral- and soil-rich land under the Homestead Act as a bonus to go west and replace Native Americans. (White females were included, but constituted a very small percentage of those who actually benefited from the Homestead Act.) Such preferential treatment has carried over to today. White men are still the most educated, the most highly paid, the wealthiest, and the most politically powerful. The issue is not to pit black, brown, and white, male and female, against each other. The issue is to grow the pie large enough, fair and balanced enough, so that all of us can develop to our fullest potential—and no American is left behind.

Conservatives argue that affirmative action creates preferences for women and people of color. After 250 years of slavery, 100 years of apartheid, and untold years of discrimination, this unbroken record of race (and sex) discrimination warrants a conservative remedy—affirmative action. Actually, reparations—repair for damage done—are truer to America's history. That was the type of assistance the United States offered Western Europe and Japan in the Marshall and McArthur Plans and in our aid to Israel. Those who have been locked out through negative action need affirmative action to draw even. Equal opportunity does not demand race neutrality, but race and gender inclusiveness. We should not be color and gender blind; but we need to be color and gender caring.

Conservatives assert that affirmative action has hurt people of color, women, and the nation. In fact, I contend, affirmative action's inclusiveness has benefited the entire nation. We have the strongest and most diversified workforce in the world. Two-wage-earner households are now possible. African Americans, Latinos/Hispanics, Asians and Native Americans, women and the disabled, all can now make a contribution. It has helped create a new middle class.

Conservatives insist that affirmative action is no longer needed. We cannot fall prey to the inane notion that discrimination is an evil of the past. It is a very painful reality today. While affirmative action has diversified and improved the American workforce and its centers of higher learning, the nation still has a long way to go to reflect genuine and full equal opportunity for all Americans.

Despite the controversy and emotion often generated by discussions over affirmative action, the concept is relatively easy to explain and simple to understand. There are two fundamental questions: What is affirmative action? and What is not affirmative action?

What is the history of affirmative action? President John F. Kennedy issued Executive Order 10925 on March 6, 1961, which made the first reference to "affirmative action." It created a Committee on Equal Employment Opportunity and mandated that projects financed with federal funds "take affirmative action" to ensure that hiring and employment practices were free of racial bias. On July 2, 1964, the Civil Rights Act, the most sweeping civil rights legislation since Reconstruction, was signed by President Lyndon Johnson. It prohibited discrimination of all kinds based on race, color, religion, or national origin. On June 4, 1965, President Lyndon Johnson gave an impassioned speech to the graduating class at Howard University defining the premise underlying affirmative action. He said, "You do not take a man who for years has been hobbled by chains, liberate him, bring him to the starting line of a race, saying, 'you are free to compete with all the others,' and still justly believe you have been completely fair. . . . This is the next and more profound stage of the battle for civil rights. We seek not just freedom but opportunity, not just legal equity but human ability, not just equality as a right and a theory, but equality as a fact and as a result."

On September 24, 1965, President Johnson issued Executive Order 11246, which for the first time provided affirmative action with an enforcement mechanism. It required government contractors to "take affirmative action" to include prospective minority employees in all aspects of their hiring and employment practices. Contractors were instructed to take positive steps to ensure equality in hiring and forced to document their efforts. On October 13, 1967, Executive Order 11246 was amended to cover discrimination on the basis of gender. In 1969 President Richard Nixon initiated the "Philadelphia Plan" aimed at the construction industry. Philadelphia was selected as the test case because Assistant Secretary of Labor Arthur Fletcher contended, "The craft unions and the construction industry are among the most egregious offenders against equal opportunity laws. . . . openly hostile toward letting blacks into their closed circle."[1] The Philadelphia Plan also included specific "goals and timetables." President Nixon said at the time, "We would not impose quotas, but would require federal contractors to show 'affirmative action' to meet the goals of increasing minority employment."

Affirmative action *is* equal opportunity! It is a mechanism designed to combat discrimination by defining and creating a level playing field for everyone. It is a conservative legal remedy, growing out of past and present race and gender discrimination, that preserves traditional American values such as equal opportunity based on merit.

Passing laws against discrimination, while an extremely important first step, was neutral at best. "Thou shall not" do certain things was helpful, but it was an inadequate remedy to the overall problem and depth of discrimination. These new laws outlawed the negative, but they did not bring about the positive. Dr. Martin Luther King, Jr., often said that the absence of segregation was not the presence of justice.

The analogy of a track race is often used to explain the legacy of discrimination. If two runners are running a mile race, but one runner has run the first half mile with weights on his ankles, is it really fair merely to remove the weights and continue the race? In order for the race to be considered fair, some plan must be devised that considers the advantage that the lead runner enjoyed for the first half of the race, as well as the disadvantage that the trailing runner endured.

Needless to say, this plan should not be punitive to the first runner, especially if the runner was not personally responsible for putting the weights on his opponent's ankles.

If the track judge does not take into account both factors in the race, the corrective plan will be inadequate. An acceptable remedy must give both runners an equal opportunity to win the race.

The track race analogy parallels the case of racial advantage and disadvantage in our nation. Because of legal slavery and ongoing discrimination against people of color, especially African Americans, we have been running the employment, job promotion, education, voting and political representation, health care, open housing, economic development, and business ownership races with very heavy weights on our ankles.

Additionally, there was also the American legacy of racism and genocide against Native Americans, racism against other ethnic minorities, and sexism or gender discrimination. Later, age and disability were also recognized as areas of discrimination requiring similar, if not always exactly the same, legal remedies. The issue of job, housing, and other forms of secular civic discrimination on the basis of sexual orientation also remains unresolved on the national agenda.

The first step was to recognize the discrimination and barriers to equal opportunity, and outlaw them—to recognize that the trailing runner had weights on his ankles and remove them. In *Brown*, the Civil Rights Act, the Voting Rights Act, and the Open Housing Act, this objective was achieved.

The second step was to recognize that merely removing the weights from the runner's ankles did not transform the contest into a fair race. Maintaining the status quo—continuing to run the race—would not, in the end, be enough to create a fair race. The track judges needed to go out of their way, to take some kind of "affirmative action," in order to overcome the historical negative action, which they now recognized had given one of their contestants an unfair advantage.

The third step was to determine what kind of affirmative action to take. With regard to employment, promotions, admission to school, and economic development opportunities, certain practical steps were recommended that would lead to an increase in the inclusion of those who had previously been locked out—minorities and women and, later, the aged and disabled.

What were the practical steps? So much of how we secure jobs, choose a school, or find economic opportunities is dependent on whom we associate with. Especially in the case of whites and minorities, de facto, if not de jure, segregation was the usual pattern. Thirty years ago, when the idea of affirmative action was being developed, blacks and whites seldom worked or attended school together. We virtually never lived, worshiped, or socialized together. While things have improved incrementally in all of these areas, the fundamental pattern is not dissimilar today.

Whether minorities and women are sought after, and made to feel welcome, often determines whether they will apply for a job or admission to a school or for an economic opportunity. Since this was the reality, the government recognized that companies, governments, and schools needed to take affirmative steps: to advertise where they had not done so previously, and go to new places in order to attract those traditionally left out. Advertising in minority newspapers and on minority radio stations was a good first step. Recruiting employees at historically black colleges and universities or black conventions was another sensible move. Opening up a more public bidding process for minority and female businesses to provide goods and services also made good competitive economic sense. These were some of the broad overtures that constituted what we now call affirmative action. Thus, this initial form of affirmative action was aggressive, not passive or neutral. It was positive and forward-looking.

Affirmative action recruited minorities, women, and others as groups in order to ensure that individuals from these groups, which historically have been excluded on the basis of their group identification, were included in the pool for consideration.

Individuals from discriminated groups now had an equal opportunity to compete on a relatively level playing field. Because they were now in the pool, affirmative action had given them an equal chance of being chosen for a particular job, promotion, or admission on the basis of their individual qualifications and merit. Affirmative action succeeds only in getting the individual from a discriminated group into the pool for consideration. It does not guarantee that an individual will be selected for the opportunity or position.

In addition, you have to be qualified in order to be considered—or qualifiable with reasonable compensatory assistance. It is illegal, under affirmative action laws, to require the hiring, promotion, admission, or granting of a contract to an unqualified person or company.

Proponents of affirmative action policy soon recognized that a fourth step was necessary. If we are really determined to overcome the legacy of discrimination, we must devise a way of objectively measuring whether or not we are making progress. Thus goals and timetables were instituted. It was one way of more objectively measuring the effectiveness of an affirmative action plan. Theoretically, of course, a school or business could advertise and recruit with the utmost of sincerity and devotion, yet still come up empty handed or with only a few new recruits.

With a goal and a timetable, such as "within five years we want to increase the diversity of our company's workforce or our school's enrollment to 15 percent minority representation," a school or company can evaluate and improve its programs. Any business organization that is purposeful accepts planning, setting goals, meeting timelines, evaluating, and adjusting plans so that it can actually reach its target within an allotted time frame. For business, this is standard operating procedure. Profits and jobs usually depend on strict adherence to such goals and timetables. Applying such objective business principles to affirmative action plans and programs should be seen as no different and just as beneficial.

But the press of circumstances and court suits challenging affirmative action demanded that legal guidelines be devised. What is legitimate affirmative action? What are its limits? What is its appropriate goal? How long should an affirmative action plan remain in place? These were just some of the questions raised and adjudicated in court.

In the late 1970s opponents began to attack affirmative action with lawsuits—*Regents of the University of California v. Bakke* (1978), *Fullilove v. Klutznick* (1980), *Wygant v. Jackson Board of Education* (1986), *United States v. Paradise* (1987), *City of Richmond v. Croson* (1989), *Adarand Constructors, Inc., v. Pena* (1995), *Hopwood v. University of Texas Law School* (1996). Affirmative action is still under severe attack, and the terms of judicial relief have been narrowed, but it has survived. *Bakke* preserved affirmative action while outlawing rigid quotas. *Fullilove* even preserved a limited and qualified use of quotas. In a case involving a school board's firing of a white teacher to protect the job of a minority teacher with less seniority, the court ruled against the school board in *Wygant*, saying that affirmative action in hiring may affect some innocents seeking jobs, but firing existing workers was too injurious and burdensome to society. The *Paradise* case, filed in 1970, involved the Alabama State Police, which had never hired a black trooper in its thirty-seven-year history. Twelve years and several lawsuits later, Alabama still had not promoted a single black beyond an entry-level job, nor put a fair hiring plan in place. As a result, the court ordered specific racial quotas. Still, only the courts can establish rigid quota systems after a finding of deliberate discrimination has been proven in court. *Paradise* mandated that for every white hired or promoted, Alabama was required to hire or promote one black until at least 25 percent of the upper ranks of the Alabama State Police was comprised of blacks. The Supreme Court upheld the decision as the only reasonable means of combating obstinate racism.

Croson narrowed the scope of affirmative action, but did not eliminate it. For the first time the courts viewed affirmative action as a "highly suspect tool" unless it met a "strict scrutiny" legal standard of meeting a "compelling governmental interest . . . narrowly tailored" by "smoking out" illegitimate uses of race as a legal remedy of justice. *Adarand* basically applied the state and local standard of *Croson* to federal affirmative action programs. In response, on July 19, 1995, the Clinton administration issued a "mend it, but don't end it" memorandum of legal guidelines that barred the use of quotas, preferences for unqualified individuals, reverse discrimination, or continuing affirmative action programs after the equal opportunity goals have been achieved.

The *Hopwood* decision, involving the University of Texas Law School, was a major blow to affirmative action because it rejected diversity as a legitimate goal, arguing "educational diversity is not recognized as a compelling state interest." The attorney general of Texas announced that "Texas public universities [should] employ race-neutral criteria in the future." In 1997 California passed Proposition 209, the Ward Connerly–led state ban on all forms of affirmative action. Connerly also led the Initiative 200 campaign in Washington State, which in 1998 became the second state to ban affirmative action plans. Connerly began a similar campaign in Florida, but Governor Jeb Bush undercut him with his "One Florida" plan. Bush did not want the affirmative action initiative controversy on the ballot in 2000 during his brother's quest for the presidency.

Out of these court cases came narrower but more sharply drawn legislation, regulations, executive orders, and guidelines. Together, they set forth a general framework for establishing affirmative action, equal opportunity, and nondiscriminatory programs in employment, school admissions, and other areas of society in most states and nationally. Although such programs remain under fire and in retreat in some states, the goal of affirmative action was always to generally reflect the statistical labor market or student pool available in the community from which the company or school drew its employees or students. A university affirmative action policy for admissions obviously drew from a much broader universe of available students, but most schools saw this as part of their broader mission anyway. Academically, universities already espoused the idea that the best education took place in the context of a mixture of ideas growing out of differing experiences and cultural expressions. Most of the intellectual community saw such a mixture of students as academically advantageous.

The time frame for achieving the goals in a business affirmative action program is dependent upon a number of criteria, including the average annual job openings due to retirements and resignations and the annual job growth rate of the company.

As we saw in the *Paradise* case, a fifth step is sometimes necessary when a company or institution is taken to court and found guilty of discrimination because it has not put forth a "good faith effort" to end and correct the discrimination. Again, the courts have set forth the criteria we have shown, and more, for determining whether such a good faith effort by an institution has been made. A court can impose penalties, such as fines and rigid quotas, if it finds that it hasn't.

While affirmative action was originally designed primarily to remedy the problem of discrimination against African Americans, the legal principle of "equal protection under the law" meant universal application. The law must be applied in such a way as to provide equal protection and equal opportunity for all Americans, including blacks, Latinos, Asians, Native Americans, women, the disabled, and whites. It has to provide remedies for individuals within discriminated groups but, at the same time, not discriminate against whites and males. Thus, ensuring that everyone is in the pool, so that everyone has an equal opportunity of being chosen, is the essential goal of affirmative action.

The creation of affirmative action programs also illustrates the law of unintended consequences. The equal opportunity principle of affirmative action forced society and, even more important, the courts to take a closer look at the link between jobs, their functions, and their qualifications. The result of this investigation was a finding that part of the job discrimination experienced by many minorities and women stemmed from job qualifications that were often subjective and not directly related to objective tasks actually performed on the job. While such qualifications may have been intended primarily to exclude minorities and women, they had a broader impact: They sometimes worked against whites, including white men.

For example, NAACP Legal Defense Fund Director Elaine Jones notes that prior to the courts' linking of job qualifications with actual job performance, all onboard airline passenger help had to be "attractive" women weighing no more than a hundred pounds; they were called stewardesses. After successful equal opportunity lawsuits, anyone, male or female, able to do the job could be hired as a "flight attendant." As another example, prior to affirmative action, many state statutes set forth varying height restrictions on who could become a state trooper. Thus, for example, Mississippi state troopers may have to be six feet tall to qualify for the job. If you were under six feet, you need not apply. But once the courts established the equal protection and equal opportunity standard—and the job-specific qualifications that grew out of the affirmative action programs—short white men in Mississippi could become state troopers if they could perform the tasks of a state trooper.

Thus, an unintended consequence of ending discrimination against minorities, and providing an equal opportunity and job-specific criteria on a level playing field for all, was to end discrimination against white women and men.

Growing out of experience, three basic forms of affirmative action programs evolved: a voluntary commitment to make the extra effort to include people who had previously been excluded; a legally mandated affirmative action plan that used flexible goals and timetables; and—after a finding of discrimination and the absence of any genuine effort to end or correct it—rigid court-imposed quotas that remained in place until the goal was achieved.

A basis for affirmative action can even be found in the Bible. Luke 15:4–6 tells the story of the one lost sheep. The responsible, sensitive, and wise shepherd left the ninety-nine sheep already in the fold—those who were already working or in school, those who already had a promotion or a contract—to affirmatively search out and bring the one lost (or rejected or excluded) sheep back into the fold. The Bible doesn't tell us whether it was a black, brown, yellow, red, white, female, disabled, or aged sheep, only that one sheep was lost and the shepherd sought it out. The shepherd was determined to leave not one sheep behind. Certainly, there are many lost, rejected, or excluded "sheep" in the American flock. We, therefore, must work as individuals, as corporations, and as a government to make sure that all of the American sheep are brought into the fold, and none is left behind.

Unfortunately, there are many demagogic code words and myths that opponents of affirmative action perpetuate in order to undermine equal opportunity. My father often says, "If someone else defines you, they can confine you." Proponents of affirmative action have allowed themselves to be boxed into a defensive posture because they have not taken the time to appropriately and accurately define the issue (as equal opportunity), or to teach it to others on a broad enough scale.

Opponents usually deliberately open their anti-affirmative-action arguments at the end of the process rather than at the beginning, using anti-equal-opportunity and negative buzz words. They commence by railing against quotas—"I'm against quotas and affirmative action"—when in reality quotas are the last resort of a protracted judicial process. Or, "I'm against reverse discrimination and affirmative action," when, as we have seen, reverse discrimination is illegal. Too many current conclusions are based on a lack of actual facts, ignorance of the law, little understanding of the process, and erroneous concepts that, not surprisingly, lead to false understandings and conclusions.

Some people are just not knowledgeable about affirmative action. For uninformed but sincere and concerned people, education is the answer. There are others, however, who understand the concept, but choose to be deceptive on the subject for personal or political gain. Using emotionally charged code words, they deliberately cloud and confuse the discussion rather than enlightening the American people on the subject of race and gender remedies. I am suspicious of the motives of all those who link affirmative action with the concepts of quotas, preferences, or reverse discrimination without a substantial discussion of what they mean in the full context of affirmative action.

But just as it is important to first define what affirmative action is, it is equally important to clarify what affirmative action is not. Affirmative action is not: quotas; reverse discrimination; preferential treatment; group rights over individual rights; against merit; a lowering of standards; a catering to unqualified people; a benefit only to the middle class and the elite; a program that hurts its beneficiaries; a program that is based on race and gender over economic need (class); or reparations.

Affirmative action is not quotas! That was the outcome of the 1978 *Bakke* decision—rigid quotas are illegal, flexible goals and timetables are acceptable, and race may be "a" factor, alongside other factors, for admission.

Measurement, however, is important in affirmative action plans. Measurement is not just "bean counting" as President Clinton once complained about NOW President Patricia Ireland's criticism of his administration's appointments. Numbers take us beyond goodwill and good intentions. While both goals and timetables, and quotas, deal with numbers, they are not the same. We should distinguish between and not confuse goals and timetables, which are legally required and flexible, with quotas, which are court imposed and rigid. Numbers allow us to measure progress toward our goal.

Affirmative action laws with only goals and timetables, but without the threat of effective enforcement, would be meaningless. Without quotas—an enforceable court remedy against corporations and schools that do not take the law seriously—affirmative action's teeth would be weak. It would mean that these entities could claim "good intentions," say they had put forth great effort to reach their goals, whether they had or not, and suffer no legal consequences for continuing either personal or institutional discrimination. The issue then is: Is there a penalty for failure when a good faith effort has not been made? When persevering on civil rights and equal opportunity laws, the courts have insisted, as a last resort, on the punishment of fines and quotas to remedy the wrong.

Others argue that although there is a difference between flexible goals and rigid quotas, some corporations and schools use a quota system as a defensive legal posture while insisting to the public that they are simply trying to achieve goals and timetables. The simple answer to this argument is they shouldn't be operating this way. They have no legal obligation to do so and, in fact, if it could be proven that they were actually operating a quota system it would be declared illegal.

The discussion, however, does raise another interesting point. How can we tell the difference between a successful affirmative action program with goals and timetables, and quotas? Externally we can't tell the difference, because in both instances the exact same ends are achieved. Only by analyzing the actual process of the means to the end could we distinguish between them.

Finally, there is the issue of how different people see quotas because of their historic experience with them. Some Jewish Americans, reflecting on their experiences in Eastern Europe, where quotas were used as a ceiling, and some Asian Americans, see quotas as a number beyond which they cannot grow. To my knowledge no institution in America, including the courts, has used affirmative action this way—to impose a limit to opportunity. The law is not currently used in this way, and I oppose any intentional use of affirmative action in such a manner. Asian Americans in the California higher educational system may be experiencing something like this, because they have become disproportionately high academic achievers. But if that is an unintended consequence, the only solution is to make sure that every student who has the aptitude and the interest be given an equal opportunity to pursue a quality public or private university education, and that neither the lack of money, nor the lack of good schools, nor affirmative action will deny them that privilege. Of course, there is no system currently in place (nor can one be created) that allows everyone their first choice every time!

On the other hand, the experience of exclusion by African Americans, other minorities, women, the aged, and the disabled is quite different. The problem for these groups has not been discrimination based on a ceiling, but discrimination based on the denial of an equal opportunity to get in on the ground floor. This difference between the two varied definitions of quotas constitutes a fundamental divergence.

Affirmative action is not reverse discrimination! But the late *Chicago Sun-Times* columnist Carl Rowan may have given some insight into how many whites may think about affirmative action when he wrote in early January 1995: "Social and political predators know that ordinary white Americans have been indoctrinated up to their gullets by propaganda that blacks are inferior to Caucasians. So it becomes natural in every work or study session for the dumbest white person to assume that any black person landing a spot above him or her is inferior, and just the beneficiary of reverse discrimination." If affirmative action is equal opportunity, then it cannot be reverse discrimination. Reverse discrimination would be the opposite of equal opportunity.

The charge of reverse discrimination is the allegation that white males are being excluded from jobs, promotions, schools, and contracts, while minorities and white females are being chosen instead. And it's true that if *only* those previously excluded were included in the pool for consideration or were eligible to be chosen, that would be reverse discrimination. But affirmative action is not that. If everyone is in the pool and has an equal chance to be chosen, and a member of a previously excluded group is selected while white males are not, that does not amount to reverse discrimination. It is simply equal opportunity at work. To reiterate, the only thing affirmative action does is get people into the pool for equal consideration. It does not mean any particular person will be chosen or not chosen, whether of a previously discriminated against group or not. Equal consideration does not amount to reverse discrimination.

And in fact, the vast majority of white males don't feel they are being discriminated against because of affirmative action. In an April 9, 2000, *Newsday* report, relatively few white men (10 percent) blamed affirmative action for their being denied a job or passed over for promotion. Even more objectively, the same article reported that the Equal Employment Opportunity Commission showed that job bias against white men is minuscule compared with that affecting blacks. The article said, "Since 1992, the federal agency has received on average 1,400 discrimination complaints per year from white men, or about 2 percent of all claims received nationwide from whites and blacks. And of the complaints filed by white men, no more than 168 were found to have merit in any year."

Affirmative action is not preferential treatment either, but this charge does have a small amount of limited truth attached to it. What do I mean?

The *Bakke* decision said that race could be "a" factor, alongside other factors, in a school's admissions policy. It also said that if two people are equally qualified, the scale of justice may be tilted toward the side of race (and gender)—to compensate for historical discrimination. In this very limited sense, I acknowledge some degree of "preferential treatment." However, this is not the dominant pattern in affirmative action programs.

The charge that affirmative action places group rights over individual rights is also invalid. Next to quotas, this charge is the most repugnant to the public. In refuting that claim, I remind every American that being a member of a previously excluded group does get a person into the general pool, but once inside the pool, each *individual* must make it on his or her own hard work and abilities. I repeat, it is illegal to admit to the pool an unqualified or unqualifiable person merely because he or she is a member of a historically excluded group. Thus, affirmative action is not against merit.

There are those who charge that affirmative action has lowered standards. In fact, almost the exact opposite has taken place. One of affirmative action's biggest contributions has been not to lower standards, but to normalize them. In some instances, it may have actually raised them. As previously mentioned, before affirmative action job standards were often subjective or unrelated to actual job performance. Affirmative action has helped objectify the standards.

By making the rules objective and putting all qualified people in the pool, the free enterprise system creates a level playing field, increases competitiveness, and raises the level of everyone's performance, not lowers it. On the other hand, monopolies, or limited pools of competitors, decrease competition and lower the level of individual performance.

Robert Woodson, a black conservative and founder of the National Center for Neighborhood Enterprise, has consistently opposed affirmative action. He charges that "it only benefits the upper echelon and middle classes in the African American community, not the poor masses."

That is not true on either count, but there is another point. Opponents of affirmative action can't have it both ways. They can't demand that individuals be qualified and then, when they become the best and most qualified, complain because these same individuals get the job, promotion, admission, or contract. Indeed, one by-product of affirmative action is that it reinforces and enhances America's social and family values of preparedness, hard work, and discipline. It does not destroy or undermine them.

But the "talented tenth" have not been the only beneficiaries of affirmative action. Mr. Woodson can only claim such a result if he ignores the facts. According to a comprehensive Labor Department study of race and gender discrimination, the Glass Ceiling Commission's *Good for Business: Making Full Use of the Nation's Human Capital*, the best and brightest have only gradually benefited under affirmative action, but they have not been the primary beneficiaries.

According to the *Good for Business* study, affirmative action has *mostly* benefited the lower levels of the African American community. Blue-collar positions in police and fire departments and on construction sites have been opened to blacks mainly because of affirmative action. In fact, it is affirmative action that has helped create the new black middle class.

Woodson further argues "that affirmative action has been of more benefit to white women than to African Americans," which is true. The *Good for Business* study points out that white women hold close to 40 percent of the jobs in middle management, but black women hold only 5 percent and black men even less. This means, not surprisingly, that white men adjust more easily to white women in the workplace than to people of color, especially African Americans. It may also suggest that racism is deeper and more resistant to change than sexism in our society.

However, on the basis of the data in the rest of the Glass Ceiling study, sexism continues to exist in the workplace. I favor renewed efforts at ending both sexism and racism, but with a special new emphasis on ending the apparently deeper and more protracted problem of racism. I would not suggest abandoning affirmative action for all because it is working better for some.

Still other critics say they are opposed to affirmative action because it is based on race and gender, not on economic need. This is an interesting argument, coming as it does from conservative opponents of affirmative action. The inference is that if affirmative action were applied to economic "class" rather than to ethnic and gender "caste," they would be more inclined to support it. Yet I know of no evidence that conservatives will enthusiastically embrace affirmative action if it is based on class instead of caste, because it is already based on both.

In fact, affirmative action proponents anticipated this argument and built its resolution into the legislation. The actual language of affirmative action legislation, regulation, and executive orders states that affirmative action is designed to assist and benefit the "economically and socially disadvantaged."

Thus, those who want affirmative action to help the "economically disadvantaged" already have the language to do so. The white poor in Tennessee, Kentucky, Alabama, Maine, and South Dakota are already being admitted into colleges and universities on the basis of affirmative action. Any worthwhile affirmative action program factors in economic plight as well as gender, race, or disability, and makes an overall judgment about the particular individuals involved. Thus, the argument about whether an affirmative action program would favor a rich African American doctor's son from Beverly Hills over a poor white farmer's son from West Virginia is moot at best, and a little silly at worst.

The truth is that essentially the conservative members of Congress and the media who lead the economic fights against workers' rights, oppose raising the minimum wage, and advocate overturning the *Davis-Bacon* law (which pays workers on federal construction projects the prevailing wage) are the same people who lead the social fights in opposition to civil rights, women's rights, and voting rights.

In short, most opponents of affirmative action support the status quo of privilege on the basis of class, gender, and race. They generally do not support any change that results in greater racial justice, gender equity, or economic equality.

In these arguments over affirmative action, it should also be made clear that affirmative action is not reparations. Reparations are repair for past damage done. Reparations involve morally justified positive actions to *compensate* for past immoral and negative actions that have resulted in serious damage. While minorities, women, and the handicapped may (morally) deserve reparations on the basis of the damage that racism, sexism, and discrimination have done, affirmative action is not reparations. It is a more conservative approach. It merely provides for equal opportunity in the current circumstances.

The United States provided reparations to Western Europe and Japan with the Marshall and McArthur Plans after World War II to help them recover from the destruction of the war. The United States did this for both moral and economic reasons—the same basis that we could use for reparations here at home.

U.S. Ambassador Ralph Bunche, a black man, worked through the United Nations to help establish the state of Israel in 1948—for which he received the Nobel Peace Prize. The reparations were compensation for damage done to Jews by Hitler's Germany during World War II. In essence, the United States said, "If Jews are discriminated against, made scapegoats, or massacred, never again should they be left with no place to go. They should be able to go home, to their own state, Israel." It was morally and economically justified. We should do the same thing for the Palestinians for the same reasons.

Another example of reparations occurred after Iraq immorally and illegally invaded Kuwait. In January 1991, a United States–led U.N. force drove Iraqi forces back across their own border. Following that victory, our government demanded that Iraq provide reparations to Kuwait—repair for damages done—prior to our reestablishing normal diplomatic relations with it. Even now, we are engaged in providing reparations to Eastern Europe (through the Polish American Economic Development Plan, for instance) and Russia.

Thus it appears that America has been more committed to helping former enemies (Germany and Japan in the case of World War II, Russia and Eastern Europe in the case of the Cold War) and foreign allies (Western Europe and Kuwait) than it has been to helping our own people.

These reparations I believe are justified, but they were and are not simply morally benevolent efforts to help other people and countries. They were and are also calculated economic attempts to develop other markets for the export of our own products, so that we may in turn become an even wealthier society. After all, Russians and Poles cannot buy what our industries produce if they are too poor or broke to do so. And if these countries become destabilized, we will have to spend more on our military. So developing them will aid in our own economic development. The same argument also applies to the home front. It is in the moral and economic self-interest of everyone—business, labor, white males, minorities, women, and the handicapped—for individuals, the private sector, and the government to turn tax consumers into revenue generators. Affirmative action is a conservative program that helps achieve this goal.

But affirmative action is not a jobs program! Though it aids in the fair distribution of jobs and openings that already exist, it does not in and of itself create new jobs. Without a national commitment to actual full employment, affirmative action raises the broader social and political problem of too many people chasing too few jobs. In that context people look for scapegoats—especially immigrants, minorities, and women, but also homosexuals, the aged, and the disabled.

For nearly four decades jobs in the private sector have been growing slowly by historical standards, or declining in some industries due to downsizing. Multinational corporations are moving plants and jobs to foreign countries to take advantage of cheap labor markets. The North American Free Trade Agreement (NAFTA) and the World Trade Organization (WTO) agreements have stimulated some jobs for the highly educated and technically trained, but these agreements also meant the loss of jobs for those with less education and training. This population is where much of the "angry white male" message is coming from.

Jobs in the armed forces have been reduced from 2.2 million to 1.6 million men and women because of a reduction in defense expenditures. After his first term, President Clinton brandished more than 100,000 jobs eliminated from the federal government as a downsizing accomplishment to run on for reelection in 1996, while reaching his ultimate goal of eliminating more than 250,000 jobs by the end of his second. Conservatives have forced a greater focus on job *reductions* in government, deficit reduction, balancing the budget, and retiring the debt than on job creation, economic stimulus, and investment for the nation's future.

Thus, while jobs are growing, jobs are also going—especially those requiring little education or technical training. Have these lesser-skilled jobs gone to minorities, women, the aged, and the handicapped through affirmative action, or to cheap labor markets abroad? I think primarily the latter. In fact, we are bringing highly trained foreign workers into the country rather than training our own workers.

There would not be the same negative reaction to affirmative action in a truly full-employment economy. However, when not enough well-trained people or well-paying jobs and openings exist, as in the current context, it makes being generous more difficult for those who are shakily holding on to the jobs they have.

Finally, affirmative action is not psychologically damaging to recipients. One of the favorite arguments of conservative African American and other intellectuals is that affirmative action damages the psyche of its beneficiaries. The underlying implication in this conservative charge is that the job, promotion, or admission to school was "given" to the minority because of affirmative action rather than "earned" because of work and merit, thereby attaching a stigma. One of the favorite lines used by conservatives is, "How would you like to be operated on by a 'quota doctor'?" This implies such a doctor would be unqualified.

But do such attacks work? Is such language and labeling effective? When Lani Guinier was nominated by President Clinton to head the Civil Rights Division of the Justice Department, the *Wall Street Journal* labeled her a "quota queen." This roughshod, indecent, and politically motivated attack was effective enough to intimidate the most powerful man in the world, the president of the United States, into withdrawing the nomination of his former classmate and personal friend.

Another important component of equal opportunity is voting rights. If democracy is government "of, by and for the people," then in a representative democracy there is nothing more fundamental than the right to vote. The logical democratic extension of the right to vote is the right to have your vote counted equally with others, and for all candidates running for office to have an equal opportunity to be elected.

Maximum voter participation optimizes political representation, strengthens democracy, and increases government legitimization. Minimum voter participation ensures assailable representation, weakens democracy, and makes any government less accountable. The decision by our nation's founders to limit the right to vote to white male property owners excluded too many people, and over time others fought to expand the Constitution and laws to include more.

In 1870 the Fifteenth Amendment prohibited states from voter discrimination on account of "race, color, or previous condition of servitude." The Nineteenth Amendment in 1920 broadened the right to nondiscrimination to women. The Twenty-fourth Amendment of 1964 banned poll taxes, but only in federal elections. The Twenty-sixth Amendment passed in 1971 allowed eighteen-year-olds to vote. The equal protection and due process clauses of the Fourteenth Amendment and the Voting Rights Act were finally interpreted by the courts in the 1960s and 1970s to mean that states could not write laws or construct barriers of discrimination to voting on the basis of race.

Even though the post–Civil War Fifteenth Amendment appears unambiguous in its meaning, as a practical political matter, because of racial discrimination, most southern blacks still could not vote ninety-five years after it was added to the Constitution. A combination of obstacles—poll taxes, literacy tests, grandfather clauses, white primaries, psychological and physical intimidation, violence and murder—kept most southern blacks away from the polls. During the late nineteenth and early and mid–twentieth centuries, these blatant tactics were replaced by more covert devices to disfranchise black voters: at-large elections, racial gerrymandering, second primaries, the purging of voter rolls, inconvenient and unannounced hours and places to register and vote, "show-cause notices"—notices sent to registered voters telling them unless they reported to the board of elections within a short time and "showed cause" why they should not be removed from the voter list, their names would automatically be taken off—abolishing elective offices and making them appointive, increasing the qualifying requirements of candidates running for public office, and more. And while state and local legislatures draw political district lines, local districts control the political apparatus: voter registration, keeping the voter lists, purchasing and operating voting machines, counting and interpreting the ballots, and more, as we saw in Florida during the presidential election of 2000.

A series of Supreme Court decisions gradually attacked and brought an end to many of these practices. In *Terry v. Adams* (1953), the Court dealt a final blow to the practice of all-white Democratic Party primaries in the South. Beginning in 1889 the Jaybird Democratic Association, also known as the Jaybird Party, was in reality an exclusive, self-governing, voluntary, all-white association of Democrats in Fort Bend County, Texas, that selected candidates for county offices in an unofficial primary election. These preselected white candidates then entered the Democratic Party primary, where they were unfailingly nominated and usually elected uncontested in the general election. This all-white club was purposefully organized to exclude and disfranchise black voters by circumventing the Fifteenth Amendment. *Terry* outlawed such practices.

In *Baker v. Carr* (1962), the Supreme Court embraced the principle of "equal representation," which meant that every ten years, after the census had been taken, electoral district lines had to be redrawn so that elected officials represented an equal number of people. Before this decision, rural interests protected and gave themselves disproportionate power to the exclusion of urban interests. It may have been an exaggeration, but Chief Justice Earl Warren, author of the 1954 *Brown* decision, considered *Baker* "the most vital decision" during his service on the Court. It did bring about a revolution in redistributing political power among rural, urban, and suburban districts.

In *Gray v. Sanders* (1963), the equal opportunity principle of "one person, one vote" first appeared, which was later confirmed in *Wesberry v. Sanders* (1964) and *Reynolds v. Sims* (1964) with regard to congressional and legislative districts.

On August 6, (following passage of the 1964 Civil Rights Act, which desegregated public accommodations, and the Selma-to-Montgomery voting rights march of March 21–25) President Lyndon B. Johnson signed into law the 1965 Voting Rights Act, effective for five years. The law originally applied to Alaska and seven southern states—Alabama, Georgia, Louisiana, Mississippi, part of North Carolina, South Carolina, Virginia—and sections of three other former Confederate states, Arkansas, Texas, and Florida. Other areas were later added.

In the meantime, in *Harper v. Virginia State Board of Elections* in 1966, the Court's application of the equal opportunity principle ruled against the imposition of a poll tax in state elections because it unconstitutionally singled out the poor.

If the Republican Party of 1865 was known as the Black Republican Party, the 1965 Voting Rights Act is the single largest reason the Republican Party of 2001 is known as the White Republican Party. Enfranchised in 1965, African Americans in the South and North voted overwhelmingly Democratic (they had mainly voted Republican until FDR's second election in 1936). Republicans concluded there was only one way back, only one card could be played that would restore them to national political power. It was the same card Democrats in the South played after the Civil War in 1865 to reclaim their lost power from Republicans. Thus, since 1965, the race card has been primarily played by Republicans to get back their lost power from Democrats.

The Voting Rights Act represented a shift from a case-by-case litigation strategy to a federal legislative, executive, and judicial interventionist strategy brought about as a result of the civil rights movement of the 1950s and 1960s. It also shifted the burden of proof from the victims to the victimizers, and from proving intent to proving effect.

The two most important sections in this legislation were Section Two, which outlawed "all forms" of voter discrimination, and Section Five, which required the "preclearance" of any voting process changes in these states and counties by either the federal district court in the District of Columbia or the U.S. Justice Department.

At the time, the preclearance provision was considered a catchall safety net in case new schemes were invented to deny southern blacks access to the polls. "In 1969, however, in *Allen v. Board of Elections*, the Supreme Court enlarged the meaning of a 'voting' change to include new electoral district lines, the institution of at-large elections or of multi-member districts, the relocation of a polling place, and even urban annexations of adjacent suburban or rural areas."[2]

The law was renewed in 1970 for five years. In 1975 it was extended until 1982 and broadened to cover other racial minorities such as Latino, Asian, and Native Americans. It also expanded the definition of "disfranchising devices" to include the use of English-only ballots, which helped Eastern Europeans and others. When it came up for renewal in 1982, the Reagan administration and its conservative cohorts in the Congress went after and attempted to weaken Sections Two and Five. They failed in their task, and the Voting Rights Act was extended for another twenty-five years, until 2007.

Between 1971 and 1982, the Supreme Court struggled with the question of "group rights" and how to ensure the inclusion of individuals from a previously excluded group (such as African Americans) in the political process by providing them with an equal opportunity—the Fourteenth Amendment standard—to be elected to office. In *Whitcomb v. Chavis* (1971), the Court noted that criteria other than race could be the basis of their loss—for instance, running as a Democrat in a predominantly Republican district. In *White v. Regester* (1973), the Court held for the plaintiffs, but laid out no coherent criteria of electoral exclusion. In *Mobile v. Bolden* (1980), the Court made proving racial intent, not just racial effect, the test of electoral exclusion. Just two years later, however, in *Rogers v. Lodge* (1982), the Court reversed itself and established that a plaintiff need only meet the evidentiary test of finding a discriminatory effect, not intent, to prove a case.

Prior to *Rogers*, when President Reagan came to office in 1981, he and his administration, led by Brad Reynolds, head of the Civil Rights Division at the Justice Department, attempted to shift the criteria of proof—in judging whether a voting rights violation had taken place or not—from "effect" to "intent." The Reagan people did not want a positive finding of voting rights violations unless it could be shown in court that there was an "intention" to discriminate. It is similar to asking an NBA referee to blow the whistle only when there are intentional fouls. Such a legal test is much harder to prove, takes longer, and is very costly. The Reagan administration and its Republican friends and colleagues were practicing the same old pattern of southern racist resistance. But Congress defeated these attempts to weaken the Voting Rights Act.

Still, resistance to equal opportunity in voting continues. Our current conservative states' rights Supreme Court, in *Reno v. Bossier Parish School Board* (2000), ruled that the Justice Department had no authority to object to a voting plan submitted to the department for review under Section Five of the Voting Rights Act unless the plan was "retrogressive"—that is, unless the voting changes made matters worse for minorities. In effect, the Court ruled that if injustice is in place, it's all right to keep it that way; it just can't get any worse. In the 106th Congress, Representative Mel Watt (D-NC) introduced the Voting Rights Clarification Act of 2000 to restore the authority of the U.S. Department of Justice to object, under Section Five of the Voting Rights Act, to intentional discriminatory voting practices.

The 1980 case *Mobile v. Bolden* was Brad Reynolds's and Dixiecrat Reaganites' impetus to attempt to gut the Voting Rights Act. Though no black had ever served on the five-member city commission in Mobile, Alabama, since its inception in 1911, the Supreme Court in *Bolden* had rejected a discriminatory "effects" test in favor of a discriminatory "intent" test. Justice Thurgood Marshall wrote a lengthy and angry dissent, labeling the Court an accomplice to perpetuating racial discrimination. He rejected the "intent" test, arguing forcefully for a test proving discriminatory "effects." In 1982 Congress agreed with Justice Marshall and amended the Voting Rights Act to establish the criteria of effect and not intent, frontally disagreeing with the Court and the Reagan administration with regard to *Bolden*. In 1986 the Court specifically upheld the constitutionality of the 1982 amendments in *Thornburg v. Gingles*. It was against this background that state legislatures thereafter determined that the Constitution required that majority-minority districts be drawn to avoid violating the law and to assure those of color of an equal opportunity of being elected.

Historically, the struggle over equal voting rights had long been entangled with the relative power of rural and urban interests. Predominantly a rural country in its beginning, the United States, through industrialization, evolved into an increasingly urban society, even though its politics was still dominated by rural white legislators and their agrarian interests. The South, of course, was overwhelmingly a rural society. Thus, another dimension of the North–South divide was the growing white urban European immigrant power in northern cities against a declining white rural power in the South, which was also being threatened by an emerging new black vote and the growing restlessness among women suffragettes.

Before the late nineteenth century, there was no voter registration in this country. The idea came about as the result of a combination of forces. Following the Civil War, former slaves were voting in large numbers. That threatened southern white rural interests. Freeing the slaves and the addition of the Fifteenth Amendment to the Constitution had inspired women to demand the right to vote, and the women's suffrage movement was gaining strength. That too was a threat to southern white male rural interests. As industrialization lured large numbers of European immigrants and a few blacks to the North, activists organized them politically. This combination of growing political power—blacks in the South, women everywhere, and white urban European ethnics in the North—was primarily a challenge to rural southern Democratic interests. But organized labor was politicizing these European ethnic workers, and their strong urban Democratic Party identification was also becoming a threat to the various industrial and Republican Party interests in the North. Thus, voter registration was gradually introduced by conservative forces both North and South, not to facilitate voting, but to inhibit, control, and limit our democracy for the purpose of preserving (especially southern) elite rural political power, but also to protect elite industrial and Republican Party interests in the North.

Until the early 1990s, Voting Rights Act interpretations by the Supreme Court had not clearly defined two important legal concepts on the question of equal opportunity in voting. The Court had used, and I believe the legislation had clearly intended, that its decisions and actions should bring about "full and effective participation" and an "equally effective voice" among all voters. Neither legislation nor Court decisions had succeeded on those two fronts because Jim Crow, Esq., had devised new schemes and ways of politically disfranchising black voters, as noted earlier.

On June 26, 1993, in a five-to-four *Shaw v. Reno* Supreme Court decision, the "intent" question was resurrected by turning the Voting Rights Act on its head. Illogically, *Shaw* recognized the right of *white* plaintiffs to challenge majority-minority districts, even though the intent of previous Court decisions and the original legislation was to overcome historical racial discrimination against blacks by securing greater minority representation. *Shaw*, like another case involving economic set-asides—*City of Richmond v. Croson*—denied or ignored the historical facts of racial discrimination in order to give white plaintiffs standing to challenge districts that were purposefully designed to overcome centuries of prior discrimination in political representation. In short, because majority-minority districts were intentionally drawn to give minorities an equal opportunity of being elected, the Court held that its intent was to discriminate against whites and, therefore, districts drawn in such a manner were illegal.

In another case, the court was asked to decide whether there was a compelling state interest in allowing "race" to be used as one of the criteria in designing congressional districts that provided minorities with an equal opportunity of winning. Political district architects used party affiliation, income, urban and rural composition, and other demographic criteria, but could race be used? The southern-based Fifth Circuit ruled in *Hays v. Louisiana* that the Louisiana plan—with specific reference to Representative Cleo Field's Fourth Congressional District seat in Louisiana—was not narrowly tailored to further a compelling state interest, which the Rehnquist Supreme Court upheld.

Hays was troubling for a number of reasons. First, in order to recognize the standing of white citizens to attack majority-minority districts, the court cited *Bakke* (1978)—which had ruled that race could be "a" factor, alongside other factors, in a university admissions program—in addition to *Shaw* and *Croson*. Thus, the alleged "fact" of a "color-blind" Constitution and country had been elevated and used by *Hays* to strike down the Louisiana plan.

The *Hays* decision also relied on a 1964 decision, *Wright v. Rockefeller*—decided before the Voting Rights Act of 1965—to define a racially gerrymandered districting plan as one that "intentionally" draws one or more districts along racial lines or otherwise segregates citizens into voting districts based on their race. The court also cited *Bolden* in support of this point. The decision in *Hays* seemed to ignore the fact that the 1982 amendments were specifically added to overturn *Bolden*. The only claim the court made from the 1982 amendments was to assert that Section Two expressly declared that "proportional representation" was not required. Additionally, because white voter registration and turnout was greater than black registration and turnout, the Court had previously determined that a majority-minority black district should be at least 65 percent black in order for an African American candidate to have an equal opportunity—not a guarantee—of winning the seat.

The Fifth Circuit was actually deciding these cases on political grounds, but using a legal rationale to do it. The political goal was to attack, undermine, and negate majority-minority districts. This was happening during the all-out attack on Lani Guinier by conservatives who called her a "quota queen." Frightened, President Clinton and Democratic senators quickly abandoned her.

What was even more troubling was that African American voters did not seem to understand what was at stake in these assaults on majority-minority districts, or the consequences of not voting in important local elections. Black voter turnout was significantly down in the Los Angeles mayor's race, which occurred only six weeks after the worst urban uprising in this country. It was also down in Chicago's and New York's mayoral races, and in the New Jersey governor's race, all of which occurred in this same time frame. Many African American voters interviewed by the media in Mel Watt's Twelfth Congressional District in North Carolina were not particularly upset by the attack on Congressman Watt's district because they seemed to agree it was a "funny-shaped" district. There was little appreciation of the historical context of the reapportionment decisions.

There seemed to be a growing feeling—perpetuated by the media and right-wing politicians and ideologues, both black and white—that if a Doug Wilder, a David Dinkins, or a Carol Moseley Braun could get elected, "we don't really need a Voting Rights Act anymore." However, those holding such a view failed to realize that those elections were won by less than 1 percent of the vote or under very unusual political circumstances. Senator Carol Moseley Braun was the first and only African American woman or African American Democrat ever elected to the U.S. Senate. Indeed, there have been only four African Americans in the Senate in the nation's entire history.

With reapportionment again coming before state legislatures in 2001, the African American and other communities of color, and the general American public, need a massive public education campaign on redistricting that puts it in its proper historical context and perspective. We have been through this before. During the First Reconstruction, twenty-two African Americans were elected to Congress between 1870 and 1901 after the federal government had registered more than seven hundred thousand black citizens in the South. However, after the Tilden-Hayes Compromise of 1877 in which federal troops were pulled out of the South (the way the law is being pulled out today); after the Supreme Court rendered its infamous *Plessy v. Ferguson* decision in 1896; and after the narrow interpretation of the Thirteenth, Fourteenth, and Fifteenth Amendments commenced, the black representatives were out of office by 1901. It was not until 1992 that a similar number of southern black representatives was sent to Congress, and now virtually every one of these new districts is under attack by Republicrats and Dixiecrats.

If those who are opposed to giving African American and other people of color an equal opportunity of voting, of having our vote count equally, and of being elected to office are allowed to dictate the terms of the debate on the basis of "bizarre shapes" and "quota representatives," then the remembrance of 1901 in 2001 should become more apparent. It is time to change the context and content of the debate!

Finally, if politics is the distribution system for the economy (and I believe it is), and if all economics takes place in a political context (and I believe it does), then there should be no higher priority in the African American or other communities of color, among the poor and working people than an increase in political education, complete voter registration, and full political participation. There should also be candidates with a social justice vision of a more perfect Union running for office at every level and strongly advocating for the real long-term economic interests of their constituents. I cannot say it too strongly. *While many other avenues of change are valid and important, fully registering, voting to the maximum, and running for office should be the top priority of progressives!*

Equal opportunity in education is another important issue. Discussion of this issue usually centers on three concepts—segregation, desegregation, and integration—which then also inform other broader issues of equal opportunity, such as housing.

During and since the modern civil rights movement of the 1950s and 1960s, most Americans would say that the goal is to build an integrated society. I agree with this goal, but the terms of the debate must be made much clearer and the use of language must be much more precise. There are at least five terms and options that we need clarify—segregation, accommodation, assimilation, desegregation, and integration—and they all have to do with choices.

"Segregation" is a legal term that has two dimensions, de jure (by law) and de facto (by custom), but the end result is the same: no choice. Prior to the 1964 Civil Rights Act, laws prohibited African Americans from staying at the hotel or motel of their choice, eating at certain restaurants, or using the public drinking fountain or rest room of their choice. In some states there were many other things African Americans could do by law, but not by custom, such as going to the church or dating the person of their choice.

Faced with such overwhelming legal and social obstacles, most people chose to adjust to an unjust arrangement. That is what I call accommodation. The consequences of not accommodating were often quite high—loss of a job, destruction of a family, violence, or even loss of life. My father tells the story of how, when he was a child, his mother would try to protect him from the harshness of southern segregation with rationalizations. When he would ask why he could not sit in the front of the bus near the bus driver, his mother would say, "Don't worry about that, Jesse. The back of the bus will get there at the same time as the front of the bus. Besides, if the bus hits something, it's safer to be in the back of the bus." Accommodation to a bad situation.

Another option is assimilation. If your position within an unjust arrangement is, relatively speaking, better than that of your friends or colleagues, or if you have more access and perks, you may decide to identify yourself with that arrangement. My father often tells me stories about how some of the old black preachers in Chicago would assimilate into Mayor Richard J. Daley's Chicago Democratic machine. One black minister used to end his prayers with, "Give us this day our Daley bread." That was complete assimilation.

The marches and struggles of the civil rights movement primarily achieved desegregation. The movement was fighting to desegregate America. The purpose was to get the "legal structures" of the society to provide equal opportunity for all, and not to discriminate against anybody. The movement was fighting to change the "no choice" option of segregation, and the limited choices of accommodation and assimilation, into unlimited and equal opportunity choices for all in every area of American life.

African Americans (and other Americans) may or may not choose to eat, drink, work, live, party, go to church, date, or marry any particular person of any particular race, but the civil rights movement wanted all Americans to have the equal right to choose among those options, with no legal or social barriers inhibiting them. The goal of the civil rights movement was built on America's ideals—freedom and equality of opportunity—which, of course, had been denied to African Americans.

Where, then, does integration take place? Integration, I believe, is spiritual choice. Integration is a possible by-product of desegregation that we should strive for as individuals and as a society on religious, moral, and humane grounds. It is the most human and God-like thing we can do. Desegregation automatically makes some degree of social interaction between the races inevitable. It also gives us a greater opportunity to get to know and understand those of another race or culture. Then perhaps the spiritual option of integration will manifest itself.

Finally, it seems to me that we must also distinguish between working to better the worst features of discrimination in a system, improving a situation, establishing a floor or minimum standard of decency below which no one should fall—and working toward the goal of true and full equal opportunity for everyone. Obviously, all the goals of amelioration are worth achieving and represent progress. But if we are to build a more perfect Union, we must have our eye on a higher goal, and strive and fight for genuine and complete equal opportunity in the fullest sense of that term—yes, including an equality of results—in every social, economic, legal, political, and spiritual dimension of our society and personal lives.

To build a more perfect Union with genuine equal opportunity for all, we must be highly motivated, disciplined, and committed to a long-term struggle to achieve our goals. At the same time, we must insist that an actual level playing field of equality of opportunity be present in employment, education, health care, housing—every aspect of American life. Equal opportunity must become concrete and authentic in every dimension of our lives and nation.

A MORE PERFECT UNION—
HUMAN RIGHTS

I am not an advocate for frequent changes in laws and constitutions. But laws and institutions must go hand in hand with the progress of the human mind. As that becomes more developed, more enlightened, as new discoveries are made, new truths discovered and manners and opinions change, with the change of circumstances, institutions must advance also to keep pace with the times. We might as well require a man to wear still the coat which fitted him when a boy as civilized society to remain ever under the regimen of their barbarous ancestors.

—Thomas Jefferson

True compassion is more than flinging a coin to a beggar: it understands that a society which produces beggars needs restructuring.

—The Reverend Dr. Martin Luther King, Jr.

What have "rights" been historically in the United States if not an evolving societal sense of justice and entitlement, won, always, in political struggle (frequently undergirded by various intellectual efforts)? The right of slaves . . . of women . . . workers . . . the Civil Rights movement of the 1960s . . . in all of these instances, the appeal was to a higher sense of justice, to fundamental principles of a democracy, and to foundational documents embodied in the creation of our country.

—Chester Hartman, Poverty and Race Research Action Council

Ideas, whether conscious or unconscious, underlie all action. Both the North and the South in the American Civil War were motivated, in part, by abstract ideas—republican democracy, liberty, interpretations of the Constitution, flags, Union, states' rights, the right of secession. No one should underestimate the power of ideas.

Human rights is that kind of powerful idea—and it is still emerging. In this sense human rights are like Maslow's hierarchy of needs—they start with a base and develop upward. Thus, the human species has moved from the "Divine Right of Kings" to the "democratic rights of the people." Governments have gone from a monarchy—"God's representative on earth"—to the democratic notion of self-government. Even some religions have adjusted from a strictly structured priestly hierarchy to a more divine democracy of the "priesthood of all believers."

In American democracy, we have the idea that certain "inalienable rights" are given by God and not bestowed by governments. Natural rights are "the idea that people by their nature have certain basic rights that precede the establishment of any government."[1] But even a representative democratic government "of, by and for the people" still codifies the will of the people in law.

The actual legal meaning of these God-given inalienable rights of the people is vague in the Constitution. What does the document's "right to life, liberty and the pursuit of happiness" and to "promote the general welfare" mean in a democratic society? Antichoice people use this "right to life" phrase in the Constitution as the basis for their opposition to abortion. But could not the "right to life, liberty and the pursuit of happiness" also mean the right to a fuller and higher quality of life: the right to such things as gainful employment, comprehensive health care, safe and affordable housing, a high-quality public education, genuine equal opportunity, and a clean environment?

In the real world in which we live there is one simple fact about rights: *All human rights are politically determined. Ultimately, human rights in a representative democracy are whatever the people say they are!*

This means we must struggle and organize politically to protect old freedoms as well as to secure new rights. Labor unions had to struggle to win workers' rights. The right to directly elect senators, and the right to nondiscrimination in voting for former slaves, women, and eighteen-year-olds also came through a political struggle to codify those legal advances in the Constitution, in legislation, or in constitutional interpretation by the Supreme Court.

Dr. Martin Luther King, Jr., seemed always to clearly understand that codifying human rights in the law was the central goal of his various campaigns. He wrote about it and preached about it. At one point he said that the law may not make you change your heart or attitude toward a man, and it cannot make you love him, but it can keep you from lynching him. He understood that the law could dictate a change in behavior that could foster a new social climate in which understanding between people is more possible.

He understood the significance of the 1954 *Brown* decision—which established the legal principle and provided the legal foundation of "equal protection under the law." He cited *Brown* in his very first struggle, the Montgomery bus boycott, as the legal basis for expanding African American rights. Dr. King always used nonviolence to bring about enough creative tension in the society to change the law. The Montgomery bus boycott culminated nine years later in ending legal segregation with the passage of the Civil Rights Act. Dr. King went to Selma to fight to codify the right to vote. He went to Chicago to lead open-housing marches to change the laws that were creating segregated neighborhoods and communities and, upon his death, as a tribute to his life, the 1968 Open Housing Act was passed.

At the time of his death Dr. King was organizing a Poor People's Campaign, trying to secure through the political process and the law an expansion of human rights that would end hunger. That, of course, can best be achieved through the creation of jobs paying livable wages and by providing other basic human rights. Words of racial tolerance and diversity ring hollow without genuine equal economic and political opportunity for all, and the creation of an economic system that leaves no American behind. Whatever else he may have contributed, Dr. King's struggle and campaigns were always, at bottom, about expanding human rights by changing the law.

My father's two presidential campaigns were the logical extension of Dr. King's work. The difference was that his quest for the presidency was done directly through the electoral process rather than through a protest movement. His campaigns, in essence, said that it was time for the human rights movement to go beyond influencing politics through protest and move directly to making policy through the law.

The shortcoming of his two presidential campaigns was the failure to build a sustained grassroots political organization that specifically helped find, train, and elect genuinely progressive candidates; something highly politically organized within the Democratic Party just short of a third party. Had he created a lasting progressive wing of Democrats, conservative Democratic presidential candidates—and conservative Democrats generally—could not say to progressives that they needed to get on board because "they have no place else to go." Under such circumstances, progressives just might be able to go someplace else.

Am I suggesting that that means progressives should, at some point, consider bolting the Democratic Party en masse for a third party? Not necessarily. Perhaps we should try something never tried before, seriously organizing political progressives within the party so we will be respected for what we bring to the table and treated as full participants in the existing Democratic Party. Conservative Democrats have much more of a destructive history of leaving the party (and the Union) than progressives. Ralph Nader is the rare modern-day exception.

The independent Democratic experience in Chicago is that when progressive Democrats won fair and square, conservative Democrats abandoned the party. When Harold Washington won the primary for mayor of Chicago, the current Mayor Richard M. Daley and other Democratic conservatives organized a third and fourth party rather than support the Democratic nominee. And most of the Democratic leaders who came back did so only after a white regained the mayor's office. Progressive Democrats, but especially the African American community, have invested much more in local Democratic parties, Congress, and the president than they have received from the current Democratic Party. Yet they have remained more loyal than the conservative, southern, Blue Dog, and DLC-type New Democrats who have the inside track and have received the most lucrative returns on their investment.

Progressives didn't abandon President Clinton during his impeachment proceedings. We weren't particularly strong supporters of his politics or his policies; we thought the Monica Lewinsky affair was reprehensible and undermined his moral authority as president; but we didn't think his actions met the "high crimes" constitutional standard for impeachment. It was his conservative and southern Democratic supporters—the people he had worked most closely with to push their mutual conservative agenda through Congress, those who took credit for electing a mainstream "New Democrat" on a platform of opportunity, community, and personal responsibility—who were the first to dump the president and jump overboard. Currently, Democrats haven't won in the white South since the civil rights movement. White men abandoned a conservative Democratic Party that stopped fighting aggressively for *economically universal* programs.

All politics may be local, and I agree that politics should emerge and build from the bottom up, but only the Congress of the United States can bestow new human rights in this country because it is the only body that writes national laws. New constitutional amendments must first pass by two-thirds in both houses of Congress, then in three-quarters of the state legislatures. We have federal district and appellate courts, but only the U.S. Supreme Court renders decisions for the entire nation. Thus, the ultimate political aim of any grassroots and human rights movement must be to codify these new rights in new constitutional amendments and laws, and secure new constitutional interpretations to protect these rights.

In the next several chapters I spell out what I think these new fundamental human rights are that Americans must struggle to codify. Obviously, these rights will cost, but not having them will cost even more—in lost production, slower growth, a weaker GNP, inefficiencies, waste, crime, and much more.

I believe that God created all of us just a little lower than the angels and that these eight democratic fundamental human rights—voting, employment, health care, housing, education, equal opportunity, a clean environment, and fair taxes—should now become a part of the God-given inalienable rights provided in our Constitution. But they too, like all past human rights, must be struggled for politically. Some progress may be achieved through new laws and new constitutional interpretations by these or a new set of progressive justices, and such progress should be pursued. But I believe these fundamental rights must ultimately be anchored in new constitutional amendments. New amendments should not be added thoughtlessly, precipitously, or carelessly, but neither should they be frivolously denied. Constitutional amendments are the most effective way that "we the people" can democratically secure these new rights.

These new American rights are also what I understand the Constitution to mean when it mandates us to build "a more perfect Union, establish justice, insure domestic tranquility, provide for the common defense, promote the general welfare and secure the blessing of liberty to ourselves and our posterity."

We must never take our current rights for granted. We should also have an understanding of the evolutionary nature and history of law, as well as an appreciation of the long and sacrificial struggle for human rights.

2350 B.C.: Urukagina's Code is the oldest known set of "laws."[2] While not actually discovered, they are referenced in other documents as a consolidation of "ordinances" of Mesopotamian kings confirming that the "king was appointed by the gods," and affirming the right of citizens to know why certain actions were being punished.

2050 B.C.: Ur-Nammu's Code is the earliest known written law. Only five articles can be deciphered, but archaeological evidence shows it was supported by an advanced legal system that included specialized judges, testimony under oath, a proper form for judicial decisions, and a judge's ability to order damages be paid to a victim by the guilty party.

1850 B.C.: The earliest known legal decision involved the murder of a temple employee by three men in this year. Recorded on a clay tablet, the murder became public, and the three men and the murdered man's wife were indicted. She was indicted because she knew of the murder but remained silent. Nine witnesses testified against them, and the death penalty was sought for all four. The wife had two witnesses who testified of spousal abuse, but added that she was not part of the murder plot and that things were worse after her husband's murder. The three men were found guilty and put to death in front of the victim's house.

1700 B.C.: Hammurabi's Code, carved in columns on a large rock in 1700 B.C., was developed for this Babylonian king who had come to power fifty years before. "An eye for an eye" was the guiding judicial principle underlying his code. Its 282 clauses regulated an array of obligations, professions, and rights, including commerce, slavery, marriage, theft, and debts. Punishment by modern standards was barbaric, including cutting off a finger or a hand for theft; cutting out the tongue for defamation; putting to death the builder of a house (and his son) if the house collapsed and killed the owner (and his son).

1300 B.C.: The Ten Commandments, according to the Jewish Hebrew Bible and the Christian Old Testament, were received directly from God and written on a tablet of stone by Moses. Many of these commandments underlie our modern laws against murder, adultery, and stealing. The commandments are found in the book of Exodus, which also contains other rules largely based on the "eye for an eye, tooth for a tooth" legal philosophy.

1280 B.C.: About this same time in India, known rules passed down orally through generations were formally written in the Laws of Manu. They were the basis of India's caste system, which established people's social standing and regulated most facets of Indian society. Punishment was used sparingly and only as a last resort. Interestingly, members of the higher castes were punished more severely than those in the lower castes.

621 B.C.: Draco's Law was written for Athens. A Greek citizen chosen to write their first code of laws, Draco's punishments—often death—were so harsh that we derive our word "draconian" from his name. However, Draco's Law also introduced the idea that the state, rather than private parties or vigilantes, had the "exclusive role" in trying and punishing a person accused of a crime. Draco was wildly loved by the Athenian people. One day at a reception honoring him, they showered him with such affection—in the traditional Greek way of throwing their hats and cloaks over him—that by the time they dug him out he had smothered to death.

600 B.C.: In a military state in southern Greece, the world was given the oral Law of Lycurgus (he never wrote them down) by this renowned king of Sparta. Lycurgus's Law held that women had a duty to have children, but if the children were born deformed, they were killed. Those who lived became wards of Sparta at the age of seven, when they began their preparation for military duty. Lycurgus's Law covered virtually every aspect of life; given the military orientation of Sparta, the greatest crime was considered to be retreat in battle.

550 B.C.: Solon, an Athenian statesman and lawmaker, refined Draco's Law by "democratizing" or making it more accessible to the citizens of Athens.

536 B.C.: China created the Book of Punishments, a legal book limiting the ways in which someone could be punished after conviction for a serious crime. Still, the punishment could include tattooing, mutilation, castration, amputation of the feet, and death.

450 B.C.: The Twelve Tables were originally ten laws written by ten Roman men to govern the conduct of Roman citizens. Subsequently, two more were added. The Twelve Tables form the basis of all modern law, both public and private. Under these laws a system of public justice was developed whereby injured parties could seek compensation from guilty defendants; the lower classes (plebes) were given greater protection from legal abuses by the ruling classes (patricians), especially with regard to debts. The Twelve Tables also prohibited marriage between differing classes; severely punished theft; and gave fathers the right of life or death over their sons. The Tables survived for nearly a thousand years, until the wood and bronze tablets were destroyed by invading Gauls in A.D. 390.

350 B.C.: The first Chinese imperial code of laws, the Code of Li k'vei, dealt with the issues of theft, robbery, prison, arrest, and other general subjects. It served as a model for the Chinese T'ang Code, which came about a thousand years later.

339 B.C.: The trial of Socrates played a role in the development of law. Socrates was not a religious man, but an Athenian philosopher who taught logic. When Athens lost the Peloponnesian Wars, conservative Athenians looked for a scapegoat. Three citizens accused the popular seventy-year-old of corrupting the minds of the youth with his logic and of not believing in the gods. They tried him before a jury of 501 citizens, who found him guilty by a vote of 281 to 220. He was asked to speak to the jurors with regard to his sentencing. Instead, in his speech, he chose to mock the jurors—who swiftly sentenced him to death by a vote of 361 to 140. His trial, however, advanced the role of "conscience" in legal proceedings.

33: While not part of a normal "legal" history, the following is important to my own understanding of the law. Christians saw Jesus the Christ as introducing a new dimension to Moses' Law. Under Jesus' "law," pure motives, a mature love and grace (unmerited love), as well as nominal justice, good behavior, and honorable ends became important. Jesus was not replacing Moses' Law, but was seen as fulfilling and perfecting it. In the New Testament, Matthew 5:17–18, Jesus is quoted as saying, "Think not that I have come to abolish the law and the prophets; I have come not to abolish them but to fulfill them. For truly, I say to you, till heaven and earth pass away, not an iota, not a dot, will pass from the law until all is accomplished." In Galatians 5:14 Paul writes, "For the whole law [of Moses] is fulfilled in one word, 'You shall love your neighbor as yourself.'" And in Romans 13:10 he writes, "love is the fulfilling of the law." Thus, this Judeo-Christian understanding of the law as both a commitment to justice and the application of a knowledgeable understanding of love is important to the spiritual framework that underlies and undergirds much of my and the nation's philosophy toward the law, as well as the purpose and function of law in a society. This understanding is important where Christianity is the predominant religion, but particularly in Western civilization.

529: Justinian's Code organized Roman law into a series of books called *Corpus Juris Civilis*. This legal collection was guided by Greek logic and English common law, the two main influences on contemporary Western society. Many legal maxims in use today, indeed the very spelling of the modern word "justice," all emanate from Justinian, the emperor of Byzantine.

604: Written by a Japanese prince for a country that had just begun to develop and become literate, the seventeen-article Constitution of Japan shaped its morality and law. Paternalistic in orientation, it espoused such legalisms as: "peace and harmony should be respected because they are very important for intergroup relations"; "There are very few evil men. If we teach them [the Buddha beliefs], they may become obedient"; "equality, speediness and integrity should be maintained in court procedures"; and "the basic philosophy in all matters should be 'against privacy' and 'toward public benefit.'" One distinction that characterizes two different legal traditions is that Oriental law seeks to prevent disputes, whereas Western law seeks to resolve disputes.

653: What is known today as China was originally several kingdoms occupied for thousands of years by various feuding kings. In A.D. 221 the king of Ch'in finally defeated the other six kingdoms and unified China. Some four hundred years later, the empire developed a code of law called the T'ang Code. The code revised earlier existing Chinese laws and standardized procedures—including the 350 B.C. Code of Li k'vei—and listed crimes and their punishments in 501 articles. One article allowed only two forms of capital punishment for a convicted criminal: beheading or hanging.

700: China invented the use of fingerprinting as a means of identifying people.

1100: The first law school came into existence in medieval Italy, when students hired a teacher to teach them Roman law, especially *Corpus Juris Civilis,* Justinian's Code. One of these teachers, Irnerius, became especially popular; students from all over Europe flocked to Bologna to learn from him. The number of students became so large that he had to hire other teachers and, thus, formed the world's first law school. By 1150, Irnerius's law school had more than ten thousand students. Such numbers and enthusiasm contributed to the revival of Roman law and helped spread it throughout Europe.

1215: The basis of English common law is the Magna Carta, signed into law at Runneymede, England, on June 15, 1215, by King John. It forced the king, for the first time, to concede a number of legal rights to his barons and the citizens of England. In financing foreign wars, King John had heavily taxed the people, and many of his barons threatened rebellion. With this threat hanging over the king's head, the barons were able to extract a number of rudimentary concessions from him, such as freedom of the church, fair taxation, controls over imprisonment *(habeas corpus),* and the right of all merchants to freely come and go except in time of war. The Magna Carta was comprised of sixty-one clauses, the most important of which was number thirty-nine. It said that "No freeman shall be captured or imprisoned . . . except by lawful judgement of his peers or by the law of the land." For the first time, even the king was restrained by the law from merely exercising his personal will against another citizen.

1689: The English Bill of Rights was enacted. It became a precursor to the American Bill of Rights. It set out strict limits on the royal family's legal prerogatives, such as a prohibition against the arbitrary suspension of Parliament's laws. More importantly, it limited to Parliament the right to raise money through taxation.

1692: The Salem Witch Trials took place in Salem, Massachusetts. A group of young women accused several other women of practicing witchcraft or worship of the devil. The accusations turned the atmosphere surrounding the judicial proceedings into a frenzy, creating a delirium where more than three hundred people were accused of witchcraft, of whom twenty were eventually executed, including a priest. Eventually people of New England rose up against any more prosecutions of witchcraft.

1740: The infamous South Carolina Slave Code, which regulated the use of slaves, became the model for slavery in other states. It said that "all Negroes, Indians . . . and all their offspring . . . shall be and are hereby declared to be and remain forever hereafter slaves; and shall be deemed . . . to be chattels personal in the hands of their owners."

1765: Law became more accessible to the common man when a British barrister named Blackstone wrote down the entire English law in an easy-to-read, four-volume *Blackstone's Commentaries on the Laws of England.* It also became a standard reference work for all lawyers and law students. The many reprintings of *Blackstone's Commentaries* made the transport of English law into the American colonies easy, an important legal development in the New

World. Many legal scholars contend that *Blackstone's Commentaries* were the law for the first hundred years in the independent American colonies.

1776: On July 4 the American Declaration of Independence from Great Britain announced that "all political connection between [the united colonies] and the State of Great Britain is and ought to be dissolved" and that "we the people" of these new United States rebuke the medieval legal theory that certain people possess, by divine or royal right, the power to rule others. It affirmed that "all men are created equal" and have "certain inalienable rights, that among these are life, liberty and the pursuit of happiness. That to secure these rights, governments are instituted among men, deriving their powers from the consent of the governed."

1787: The Constitution of the United States of America was signed in Philadelphia on September 17, 1787, and ratified by the required nine states on June 21, 1788. The U.S. Constitution formed the legal basis for the first republican government in the history of the world. It defined the institutions of government and the powers of each institution, carefully carving out the duties of the executive, legislative, and judicial branches. Its shortcomings with respect to compromises involving slavery, along with the power struggle between the federal government and the states, have been documented elsewhere in this book. Nevertheless, the U.S. Constitution has served as a model for many other nations attaining independence or becoming democracies.

1788: Sydney became the site of the first British settlement in Australia. It was to serve as the prime location of a British penal colony. For fifty years, Britain sent its worst men there. They were quickly assigned to chain gangs and put to work building roads and bridges. By 1821, there were thirty thousand British settlers in this British commonwealth, of which 75 percent were convicts. Thus, through the operation of penal law, a country was formed.

1791: The American Bill of Rights, the first ten amendments to the U.S. Constitution, was approved and ratified. These ten amendments, in the Jeffersonian tradition, declared rights in the areas of free speech, freedom of press and religion, the right to a jury trial by one's peers, and protection against "cruel and unusual punishment" or "unreasonable searches or seizures," among many other things. The Bill of Rights has influenced many modern charters and bills of rights around the world.

1803: In *Marbury v. Madison*, the Supreme Court upheld the supremacy of the Constitution and stated unequivocally that it had the power to strike down actions taken by American federal and state legislative bodies that, in its opinion, offended the Constitution. This has come to be know as the power of "judicial review." This case is considered by many in the legal profession to be the most important milestone in American law since the Constitution was ratified.

1804: In the Napoleonic Code, France adopted a comprehensive code of law that canonized many of the victories attained during the Revolution, such as individual liberty, equality before the law, and the "consent of the governed" character of the state. It also incorporated most parts of Roman law. Additionally, with respect to its influence beyond France, it served as a model for civil law systems in Quebec, Canada (1865), Germany (1900), Switzerland (1907), and California and Louisiana in the western territories of the United States. It was written in nontechnical language, which made it more available to the common people.

1864: The Geneva Convention set forth minimal human rights standards during times of war. It included such things as protection of military medical personnel and provided for the humane treatment of the wounded. It was later supplemented by a Prisoner of War Convention. While frequently ignored or violated during actual military operations, the Geneva Convention remains an important legal document.

1865: After the Civil War, the U.S. Congress passed and the states ratified on December 18, 1865, the Thirteenth Amendment to the Constitution, officially ending legal slavery.

1945–1946: The Nuremberg War Crimes Tribunal (Trial) brought together eight judges from the United States, Great Britain, France, and the Soviet Union in a special panel to try Nazi military officers for crimes committed against humanity (war crimes) during World War II. Twenty-four Nazis were put on trial and convicted. Half of them received the death penalty for their crimes, though one of them, Hermann Göring, committed suicide hours before his execution. The trial was important in establishing a legal principle that, even in times of war, basic moral standards apply. "The true test," wrote the tribunal, "is not the existence of the [superior] order but whether moral choice [in executing it] was in fact possible." The Nazi crimes included torture, deportation, persecution, and mass extermination. Nuremberg was a small town in Germany.

1948: The General Agreement on Tariffs and Trade (GATT) was originally written. Modified and updated several times since, GATT was developed by the United Nations and served as a catalyst for the lifting of legal barriers against the free movement of goods, services, and people. Now, under the auspices of the World Trade Organization (WTO), the implementation of GATT by almost all countries is causing commercial interplay among differing legal systems and, in most cases, is providing the impetus for those legal systems to move toward similarity and compatibility. GATT is also reflecting a new emphasis in the development of international law: from legal agreements providing military and basic human rights, to trade and economic rights. The problem is that the old politically conservative "Golden Rule" is too often being applied, rather than the new spiritually progressive Golden Rule of "do unto others as you would have them do unto you." That is, under the old "law," too often nations with the most "gold" (economic power) make the "rules" in their favor, to the disadvantage of weaker and developing economies, while often ignoring or placing on a lower legal level of priority basic and fundamental human, labor, and environmental rights.

1948: The General Assembly of the United Nations adopted the Universal Declaration of Human Rights, which puts forth a legal code of internationally recognized human rights. It served as a basic guide to the fundamental rights I will discuss in the coming chapters. Following this historic act of statesmanship, the assembly called upon all member countries to publicize the text of the declaration and "to cause it to be disseminated, displaced, read and expounded principally in schools and other educational institutions, without distinction based on the political status of countries or territories." (See appendix 3.) The United States is a signatory to this document, but our government and educational system have done virtually nothing to give exposure to or educate the American people on the contents of this extremely important document.

The U.N.'s Universal Declaration of Human Rights, in addition to raising consciousness of the rights to which all people are entitled, gives these same people a tool with which to fight for their human rights: The Supreme Court has ruled that all international treaties and legal principles to which the United States are signatories are considered legally binding on all citizens and the government of the United States.

Thus human law and political rights have evolved through history to ever-higher forms and the granting of more rights. This has also meant that responsibilities and obligations have moved away from external sources of appointed governmental power (divinely appointed leaders, successive royal bloodlines), to the voice and majority vote of democratically elected representatives of the people. The word "democracy" is comprised of two Greek words, *demos* (people) and *kratos* (strength or power)—people power. It means "we the people" have the strength and the power, in the end, to elect people to make our laws and rules. We the people have the right to declare what "rights" we have and don't have, what rules we will live and play by, and under which laws we will be governed. A representative democratic government is a political structure and arrangement whereby the supreme governmental authority is accepted, and the rules are made, with the consent of a majority of the common people.

Thus, the contrast between the organic, evolutionary, and political nature of the law, versus the static, strict constuctionist, and natural view of the law, should be clear in terms of the creation and preservation of political rights in human development. The approach of conservatives to play down or advocate an antipolitical, antilegislative, and anti-federal-government philosophy of social change is therefore certainly not a strategy designed to advance the public interest or real economic interests of a majority of the American people. These conservatives are acting on behalf of the special interests of the few who do not want mass democratic participation and action. This antigovernment and undemocratic conservative approach is a strategy to undermine progressive economic change intended to benefit the public good.

In a living democracy we must continually criticize and reform politics, government, and policies to keep them relevant, effective, efficient, accessible, accountable, and responsive to the people's real needs. This is very different, however, from criticizing politics and government per se as irrelevant and ineffective as instruments of change, of protecting old rights or advancing new ones.

It is quite clear that the strict constructionist constitutional approach of conservatives like Dan Quayle, Patrick Buchanan, Pat Robertson, Ed Meese, Robert Bork, and George W. Bush is a frozen-in-time, backward-looking, and fearful philosophical view of government, history, and the Constitution.

Strict constructionism runs contrary to the whole legal development of rights in human history. Strict constructionists look back to the founders' original document only—before the Thirteenth, Fourteenth, Fifteenth, and other progressive amendments to the Constitution were added; before nonlandowners could vote; and before Lincoln's Gettysburg Address. Strict constructionists, as former Supreme Court Justice Thurgood Marshall said at an event celebrating the two hundredth anniversary of the writing of the Constitution, "believe that the meaning of the Constitution was 'fixed' at the Philadelphia Convention."[3] That would require us to know their original intent and rigidly preserve the Founding Fathers' philosophy, even though they were all men, most were slaveholders, and they allowed slavery in the Constitution. A strict constructionist interpretation of the Constitution also means a re-affirmation of states' rights as the preeminent guiding legal principle.

A broader interpretation, on the other hand, sees the Constitution as a forward-looking, living, positive, and hopeful document. We respect the past and the positive contributions that the founders made, seek to understand their intent in the full context in which the Constitution was written, and seek to understand to the fullest its original meaning. But we also know that it has been changed and improved along the way in order to be more inclusive of all the American people. Therefore, we also know that we have an obligation today to improve it even further.

The more people are made aware of the rights to which they are entitled, that have already been written in national and international law; the more politically educated and conscious people become of these rights; the more politically active and organized the common people become in the struggle to achieve these rights; and the more accessible and responsive our democratic institutions of politics and government become to the democratic will of the people, the faster and more nonviolently we will be able to achieve a new and higher set of human rights.

A MORE PERFECT UNION—
FULL EMPLOYMENT

When men are employed they are best contented.

—Benjamin Franklin, *Autobiography*, published 1868

Working men and women aspire to more humane conditions, to greater security, to a fairer participation in the fruits of their common labor regarding wages, social security, and opportunities for cultural and spiritual growth. They want to be treated as free and responsible men and women, able to participate in the decisions which affect their lives and future. It is a fundamental right of workers to freely establish organizations to defend and promote their interests and to contribute in a responsible manner to the common good.

—Pope John Paul II, *Laborem Exercens*—On Human Work

All of the policies of the Federal Government must be geared to the objective of sustained full production and full employment—to raise consumer purchasing power and to encourage business investment.

—President Harry S. Truman, State of the Union Address, 1946

PROPOSED FULL-EMPLOYMENT AMENDMENT
TO THE U.S. CONSTITUTION

Section 1. Every citizen has the right to work, to free choice of employment, to just and favorable conditions of work, and to protection against unemployment.

Section 2. Every citizen, without any discrimination, has the right to equal pay for equal work.

Section 3. Every citizen who works has the right to just and favorable remuneration ensuring for themselves and their family an existence worthy of human dignity, and supplemented, if necessary, by other means of social protection.

Section 4. Every citizen who works has the right to form and join trade unions for the protection of their interests.

Section 5. The Congress shall have power to implement this article by legislation.

(Based on Article Twenty-three, United Nations Universal Declaration of Human Rights, to which the United States is a signatory)

Our nation has a peculiar work ethic. It insists that people work for a living, which is a valid expectation, but it does not insist that the private and public sectors provide enough jobs at livable wages for everyone who wants to work.

Our society's rhetoric values and rewards those willing to work the hardest or take the greatest financial risks, but, in reality, it sometimes rewards company executives and financial investors who work the least and assume the fewest risks.

We reward our professional athletic heroes and their owners with billions, because the market can afford it, but often pay our teachers a barely livable wage.

The country historically criticized the work ethic and sometimes humiliated the individuals on welfare, yet seldom questions the work habits or resulting product or service of the largest beneficiaries of the government's largesse—corporate welfare.

I believe gainful employment is a human right. And if we truly value work and believe in the work ethic, we should provide every American with the constitutional right to work, the right to organize, and the right to make a livable wage.

I recognize this is probably the most controversial amendment I shall propose. In many ways, it is also the most important. A full-employment constitutional amendment, if realized, would generate unprecedented balanced economic growth, spawn astronomical sums of taxes at every level of government to pay for education, health care, housing, and a clean and sustainable environment, and provide these huge sums in a more balanced and natural way.

There are a variety of ways to rhetorically raise the full-employment challenge. Is our nation actually willing to practice what it preaches with regard to the work ethic? Will we put our money where our mouth is? In biblical terms, are we really willing to make the word of work become the flesh of work? If the answer to all of those questions is yes, then America will be moving in the most progressive, humane, and just direction ever in the history of the world.

In 2000, as the stock market climbed to more than eleven thousand points during the height of the Clinton administration's robust economy and with the official unemployment rate at around 4 percent, there were still more than fifteen million Americans who were either unemployed or underemployed. The unemployed included people who had given up looking for work, and the underemployed included those who were overqualified, under-challenged, or paid less than at a previous job, as well as people who were working part time when they wanted to work full time.

I presented these facts in a question to Federal Reserve Chairman Alan Greenspan once when he was testifying before a House Banking and Financial Services Subcommittee, and he never challenged them. These facts are not the conventional economic wisdom, but neither are they unknown to those who study the economy or are concerned about such things.

This more realistic economic profile, which includes the unemployed and underemployed, I contend, is an economic crisis, a human disaster, and a political failure. Some economists and politicians argue that nothing can or should be done about it. It should be left to natural economic or market forces to work itself out. I argue it is ultimately the responsibility of the federal government to democratically plan and coordinate a national and international economic policy in such a way as to ensure the employment of every American willing and able to work.

The Preamble to the Constitution vests in the Union—the federal government, not the states—the power and responsibility to "promote the general welfare." Without full employment there can be no general welfare; or, to put it another way, the general welfare can only be promoted to the degree that we achieve full employment.

My number one political goal in Congress is full employment. This goal underlies everything else I fight to achieve. Poor people should be coaxed away from idleness, off welfare and part-time work through financial incentives that allow them to "learn and earn" their way into gainful employment. Full employment is my core economic belief, and there is nothing more central to my political philosophy and agenda.

Americans need economic security, and full employment is the means to give it to them. Full employment will do more to provide a climate where equal opportunity is socially acceptable and politically possible. Full employment is the foundation upon which we can best enhance the possibility of enriching the aesthetic and spiritual dimensions of our lives.

Exceptions and exceptional individuals sometimes use tragedy and hardship to climb to unknown human heights and explore new spiritual depths, but as a society we need a secure economic context to best explore the deeper dimensions of meaning in our personal lives, as well as give greater depth and meaning to the collective and political life of the nation. Full employment provides the best opportunity to do all of this.

Employment for all is the best economic and political cornerstone upon which to build a nation that has universal and comprehensive health care, affordable housing, a quality public education system, a clean and healthy environment, and fairer taxes for all Americans.

If the private sector can provide full employment, I welcome it. I have no ideological opposition to this. The private sector, however, hasn't provided full employment, and I doubt it can achieve this on its own. In fact, left to its own machinations, and without the coordination and assistance that a democratically responsive government brings, it gave us a stock market collapse and a Great Depression, with 25 percent unemployment. It took more than a decade and a half and the economic stimulus of a world war to pull us out of that catastrophe.

I want to make it clear that while World War II in the 1940s did provide a huge economic stimulus toward our recovery after the Great Depression of the 1930s, it was not the only way the recovery could have occurred. If we had given our economy the same kind of economic investment, but directed toward a peacetime domestic economy, we could have achieved a recovery similar to the war stimulus. Indeed, planned rationally, instead of created in the heat of the moment because of war needs, we may have created an even faster and stronger recovery and a better society more efficiently.

The central economic point I'm making is we didn't need a war to stimulate the economy. We can accomplish the same or better economic results through rational democratic planned investment if we will but create the political will. That didn't happen in the 1930s because politicians didn't have the economic vision and, to a lesser extent, didn't have the knowledge to do it. But even more central than the vision or the knowledge, the political will was lacking to adequately invest in the domestic economy. The political will was hampered because leaders were wedded to an underlying economic ideology of a free-labor market economy that saw government as only a helpmate, not a direct vehicle of primary assistance to the American people.

I believe capitalism is the most powerful economic engine in the world, but it must have a democratic political body to monitor and guide it. An engine this powerful, running wide open without a democratic governing body to contain it, resting on solid shocks, wheels, and tires to absorb the business cycle bumps in the road (monetary and fiscal policy directed toward full employment), and guided by a steering wheel to direct it properly (rational democratic planning), will go nowhere or everywhere very fast. It is also subject to crash or explode and hurt everybody in its path.

Capitalism is the most dynamic, responsive, and productive economic system ever devised. But a political context must be created to sustain and democratically reform it in order to bring about and maintain a more reasonable balance of power between capital and labor. Currently, capital dominates labor. Ultimately, a balance can only happen by creating a common market both within and among countries. Then the competitive dimension of capitalism would tend to function very well to improve the quality of products and services and reduce prices for consumers. We are a long way, however, from creating either a balance of power between capital and labor or of creating a common international market. Left on its own, then, capitalism will not create a more perfect Union or world.

I am neither a purist nor an ideologue. I'm a practical politician, but I think it is likely that achieving full employment will require a democratically directed and accountable public–private partnership. My only point here is there should be no acceptable excuse, no ideological or self-interested reason, why full employment is not the material goal that we as a society are striving to achieve.

We are supposed to be a democratic and representative government of, by, and for the people. Therefore, in the final analysis, the people's government should guarantee every able-bodied person who wants to work a socially useful and meaningful job at a livable wage. That must be our nation's number one economic and political priority.

To achieve the goal of full employment will require a national—indeed, an international—effort. Therefore, we cannot leave it to the private sector alone. The private sector has a self-interested motive not to achieve full employment. Its goal is minimum employment, wages, and benefits, with maximum production and profits—a surefire formula for overproduction and underconsumption that will guarantee high unemployment.

The private sector also has an ideological bias against a democratically directed and accountable public–private partnership. Such an approach, from its point of view, is unnatural. It believes in the utilitarian operation of "natural blind market forces," which are being directed by a ghostlike "invisible hand." I know, of course, that the religiously mature can be educated, rational, and spirit filled, but the irrational, antirational, and so-called spirit-filled wing of Christianity has nothing on these economic true believers.

The unfettered market approach rationalizes every dimension of the productive process to make it most efficient, but leaves the overall purpose of the productive process to be determined by the natural and invisible (irrational or beyond rational) blind market forces of capital.

Analyzing the theory of this market-driven point of view, we can guide the productive process with pinpoint precision, but the "ends" of this rational process are beyond anyone's control. In other words, such a system has rational means but fatalistic and deterministic ends. Such an economic system has "choice" relative to means, but "no choice" relative to ends. In the end, however, a democratic and representative government of, by, and for the people must make rational judgments and choices, about both the means and the ends of the overall productive process, so that it will lead to an economy that has full employment as our nation's highest economic policy goal.

That Americans are an optimistic and a forward-looking people is well known. And we tend to prefer the new to the old. We were founded on new ideas, conquered new frontiers, and built an agricultural and industrial economy on new inventions. What is not so well known or understood is the material basis for our optimism or the economic context that inclined us to look toward and build for the future.

The nation's idea of almost inevitable progress did not emerge from the abstract; it grew out of individual Americans actually experiencing a material gain and betterment in their daily lives. Economist Ben Friedman argues, "As Americans' standard of living doubled roughly once every thirty years—not as a one-time phenomenon but as an ongoing process that compounded itself from one generation to the next"[1]—citizens began to assume that a better life for their children was a basic element of the American experience, whether native-born or immigrants from elsewhere. "The idea that each generation of Americans would enjoy a noticeably greater level of material well-being was a fact, not just a hope."[2] Thus, the idea of American optimism and hope for the future had an economic and a material foundation. It was based on a concrete economic experience in America, not just related to other Americans as some abstract thought or theory.

Friedman continues, "A rising standard of living is worth having not only on its own account but even more so because it provides the material basis for a free and democratic society. The nature of the choices any society has to make is different when its citizens' incomes are regularly doubling every generation than when incomes stagnate. The openness, the social mobility, the breadth of individual opportunity, and the tolerance of diversity that have given American society its unique flavor are inseparable from a continually rising overall living standard. . . . Economic policy, not individual behavior, has made the difference."[3] Economic security for all is the key. And full employment is the key to economic security. To the degree that we achieve genuine full employment, such a society can continue to exist.

While the Clinton administration focused on the positive and upbeat characteristics of the economy, its propaganda did not always match the facts. Because the Clinton-Gore economic policies *structurally* paralleled the Reagan-Bush and Bush-Quayle corporate-oriented policies—they were only less extreme and slightly more benevolent—the more basic negative economic trends continued down the same path. We should not confuse the latest upside of a relatively long-term business cycle with the more important and revealing longer-term trends of the overall economy.

Yes, the extreme budget deficits of the Reagan and Bush years were reversed and turned into surpluses, but George Bush began that process by breaking his "no new taxes" pledge, which may have cost him the election. And the public investment ratio—investment in infrastructure, research and development, and education and training, the important ways in which the government stimulates economic growth and private sector productivity—was actually lower under Clinton than under Reagan. "In fiscal year 1997, such spending was estimated to reach $136 billion. The President's original budget proposed a reduction in public investment to $133 billion in FY-98, or to 1.6% of gross domestic product. In contrast, such spending was as much as 1.9% of GDP in the Bush Administration and 2.5% when Ronald Reagan was President. Merely returning to the Reagan-era level would [have] required more than an additional $60 billion annually."[4]

Bill Clinton ran and was elected on an "it's the economy, stupid" platform, and as the investment candidate. As president—choosing to switch rather than fight—he became the deficit reduction president. As a result, while many middle-class Americans said they felt better economically under Clinton, objectively, most working Americans—about 80 percent—didn't really begin to benefit from the so-called economic good times until the very end of his administration, and that boom seems likely to be short lived. Real wages and the real standard of living had only begun to inch back up as we neared the end of the Clinton administration, but they were still far behind America's economic path and pace historically.

President Clinton's preoccupation with deficit reduction and the Fed's preoccupation with inflation control have continued the trend or pattern of imbalanced and slow growth and stagnant wages for workers begun in 1973 during the economically conservative Nixon administration. The pattern was the same under an economically conservative Ford administration, whose **WHIP INFLATION NOW** buttons revealed its priority and contributed to high unemployment. The same direction was apparent under an economically conservative Carter administration, whose reliance on fiscal restraint and monetary policy created something wholly new in American economic history, stagflation. American economists had in the past used one to fight the other, but for the first time they had high unemployment, high inflation, and slow growth together. The economy, stagflation, not Americans held hostage in Iran, was the underlying cause of Carter's defeat in 1980.

An even more economically conservative Reagan administration had campaigned on reducing deficits and promising a balanced budget by 1984. In reality, it actually quadrupled the debt with record-setting deficits. From George Washington through Jimmy Carter in 1980, the nearly two-hundred-year cumulative national debt was $908 billion. In just the next twelve years, 1980 to 1992, during the conservative administrations of Ronald Reagan and George Bush, and with the support of conservative Democrats, the debt reached more than $3.5 trillion. Thus, the unprecedented and extreme deficits, debt, and resulting slow growth were the consequences of the policies of so-called economic conservatives in both parties and the go-along-to-get-along economic liberals who supported or weakly opposed these conservative Reagan-Bush policies.

Why did the debt grow so rapidly? How did this happen? The Reagan-proposed budget passed in 1981 (fiscal 1982 budget) escalated military spending by $750 billion and gave essentially the rich a $750-billion tax break (reduced in 1983 to $600 billion because the original so blatantly favored the wealthy and large corporations). It doesn't take a brain surgeon to conclude that if you have $750 billion more going out and $750 (or $600) billion less coming in—a gap of $1.5 trillion—the result will be huge, huge deficits and rapidly growing debt.

With tax hikes in 1993 and continual budget cuts since, the Clinton administration reversed the extreme budget deficits of the Reagan-Bush years, even eliminated them, and started back on the growth path, but the Robin-Hood-in-reverse (rob the poor to give to the rich) trends in terms of income and wealth continued unabated. Our underfunded public schools continue to crumble; we still have housing and health care crises; and taxes are still grossly unfair for the average American.

The self-interested politicians, economists, stockholders, and communications giants continued to tout the "robust" economy and demonstrate through all kinds of graphs, charts, and tests how vibrant and strong our economy was, how more than twenty-two million new jobs had been created, and how many people were working. But in my district, the Second Congressional District of Illinois—and I'm sure there are many others just like it—the economy failed the toughest test of all, the "eyeball test." All I had to do to judge the economy in my district was open my eyes and look, and my eyes told me that the economy was not doing very well in my district.

And if the economy is so good throughout the rest of the country, why is there so much economic anxiety in the land? Why are Patrick Buchanan and David Duke even known in American politics at any level? Why are the forces of reaction, racism, sexism, classism, homophobia, and xenophobia—and some bordering on fascism—so rampant in the country? Why is there so much mean-spirited legislation being proposed and passed in the Congress? These are hardly characteristics of economic good times.

I confronted such meanness of spirit in the debate over the proposed housing legislation of H.R. 2 in 1997. Republicans and many conservative Democrats wanted to single out the poor and force them to work for free—otherwise known as slavery—for their federal benefits (nineteen billion dollars); these same legislators felt the middle class and the rich were entitled to their much more generous federal tax deduction for their home mortgages (eighty-six billion dollars). I thought the poor should be treated like other people and given equal protection and equal treatment under the law.

More than 20 percent of all children—and half of all African American children—are now born into poverty in the richest nation ever known. That's according to government statistics, which are conservative and undercount poverty. Thus, children, one of the most vulnerable groups in our society, are being devastated.

Or look at the poor generally. While the percentage of poverty has declined, there are actually more poor people today than when the War on Poverty began in the 1960s, and the trend is not being reversed. However, since the New Deal, for sixty years, our country—for both moral and economic reasons—had put a safety net beneath the poor. That is no more! Most current Republicans have been against such a safety net all along—for economic and moral reasons. But only the combination of Republicans and conservative Democrats in the Congress, and conservative Democratic President Clinton—"I will end welfare as we know it"—in the name of reform, ended up in a legislative social retreat, ending it instead of mending it.

The same trends are seen in the debates over Social Security, Medicaid, and Medicare. They are all in some degree of trouble because virtually everyone is operating with the same conservative economic assumptions—giving priority to balanced budgets, reduced debts, and curbing inflation, rather than investing for more balanced and greater economic growth through full employment.

The commission that oversees the viability of the Social Security system bases its projections on conservative assumptions, as it should. The alleged Social Security crisis, however, is based on one central and very conservative economic assumption: that the economy will grow at an annual rate of 1.8 percent. According to the Twentieth Century Fund's *Social Security Reform: A Twentieth Century Fund Guide to the Issues*, if the economy grows so that it averages just 1 additional percentage point, to about a 2.8 percent average annual rate of growth over the next seventy-five years—well under modern historic rates of growth, and which a full-employment economy would easily reach and likely surpass—the Social Security crisis would be over. We may need to make a few simple adjustments as we have done in the past, but the so-called *crisis* would completely disappear. Indeed, even with the imbalanced growth toward the end of the Clinton administration, in March 1999, it was reported that both Social Security and Medicare would not be in crisis as soon as expected. The Social Security timeline was extended two years, to 2034, and the Medicare timeline was extended by seven years, to 2015, because of the increased level of economic growth, which clearly was not the result of a truly full-employment economy.

When President Clinton held his Social Security dialogue in New Mexico in the summer of 1998, I don't know or understand why this point was never raised or discussed, but it wasn't. Neither was changing the regressive nature of Social Security taxes to make them more fair discussed. The solution of full employment, leading to at least a 1 percent increase in economic growth and making Social Security taxes more progressive, was not even on the table as a possible solution to the current problem.

These economic circumstances and trends are very different from the twenty-eight-year period of unparalleled and more balanced economic growth between 1945 and 1973, known as the Golden Age of American economic growth and development. During this period, economic policy—monetary and fiscal—was directed at achieving and maintaining a greater degree of full employment. "The average unemployment rate since 1974 has been almost 50 percent higher than it was in the earlier Golden Age."[5]

During the Golden Age, 80 percent of the American people saw their relative share of income increase. The exact reverse is true today. The relative share of Americans' income and wealth is more unequal today than it was in 1947. In fact, in this regard, during President Clinton's first term we became the most unequal industrialized democracy in the world. The actual buying power of the American worker—known as real wages—has actually declined since 1973. The percentage of all families earning between $25,000 and $74,999 shrank between 1973 and 1990 from 59.7 percent to 54.5 percent.

Rather than looking at the facts and the reality of the very rich (especially the top 10 percent) rising at the expense of everyone else below them, the squeezed middle class is becoming even angrier at the poor and average workers for allegedly pulling them down. The bottom 80 percent of our nation—the poor, the working poor, the middle class, and the upper middle class—should be working together for the benefit of everyone (even the top 20 percent) through greater economic growth in a more balanced economy with a fairer tax system. Too often, however, the vast majority of us who ought to be turning to each other and working together are, instead, turning on each other with suspicion, fear, and hostility. Unless more of us become conscious of and educated about the actual underlying and systemic causes of our economic and social woes, they will continue to grow and go untreated. And untreated problems give politicians too much leeway to peddle their snake oil of scapegoating. If we come to know better, however, we don't have to indulge them.

As we watched the 2000 presidential campaign unfold, all of the candidates were of course looking for the right message to attract enough of a following to catapult them into the White House, or influence the process. The Republicans were trying to fit right-wing extremists, angry white males, and moderate Republican women under one tent. Pat Buchanan was looking for a platform to project his racist, sexist, homophobic, xenophobic, openly Confederate, and quasi-fascist beliefs on an American constituency vulnerable to his appeal to their worst fears, lack of jobs, and accompanying economic insecurity. He is living his life, as the late Reverend Dr. Samuel DeWitt Proctor proclaimed, in the "anti"—anti–affirmative action, anti-immigrant, anti–public education, anti-women, anti–gay and lesbian.

Al Gore, following his mentor Bill Clinton, looked for the will or courage to stand for something other than a poll. Gore had trouble connecting with average Americans or communicating a message that related to them. Even Republican Herbert Hoover in 1928 found a message that the common man on the street related to—a chicken in every pot. The only recent "presidential candidate" who had a message that reached the average American was Ken Griffey, Jr. In a 1996 commercial, this star baseball player wanted to put a shoe on every foot.

Why did no substantive economic message emerge in the 2000 campaign? Because we are living in an era in which politicians have the courage of Pontius Pilate: Let the crowd decide; follow the polls; which way is the wind blowing. People whose real wages have declined over the past quarter century are voting their fears and not their hopes—if they're voting at all, and not just seething below the surface, waiting to explode. The pollsters know this, and the political consultants exploit it through negative television and radio attack ads. And politicians, without courage, wear signs on their backs that read FOR SALE. Without meaningful campaign reform, this trend will continue.

The Bible says, "Where your treasure is, there will your heart be also." It does not say, as conservatives in both parties imply, that "where your heart is, there will your treasure be also." The Republicans and conservative Democrats profess pure motives, tender hearts, and good religion, but they are mostly unwilling to back it up with the nation's treasury. They're unwilling to spend enough money to put all Americans to work rebuilding our nation's infrastructure.

When we leave people unemployed and underemployed there are costs for our society, such as lost productivity and taxes. But it also burdens our society in other ways, including supporting a massive and rapidly growing prison-industrial complex. In 1978 we had fewer than four hundred thousand men and women in prison. Today, because of systemic changes such as mandatory minimums and a massive increase in jailing nonviolent drug offenders, we have over two million behind bars. According to an ABC-TV *Nightline Special* on "Crime & Punishment," the federal government went from spending twenty-two billion dollars annually on prisons in 1993 to twenty-seven billion dollars in 1998. Today black men are imprisoned in the United States at a higher rate than in South Africa under apartheid. Our military budget continues at 90 percent of what it was during the Cold War, while national violence prevention programs and investing in people, infrastructure, and the environment are sacrificed on the altar of tax cuts for the rich and the unnecessary goal of eliminating the national debt.

After World War II, our political leaders didn't focus on investing enough money to implement a progressive economic program of full employment, comprehensive and universal health care, affordable housing, and quality public education. Instead they spent our treasury on the Cold War. When the Cold War ended, our political leaders still didn't invest in the American people's material needs, prioritizing reducing and eliminating budget deficits instead. Now that the budget is balanced and in surplus, they tell us we can't invest in the American people because of the debt, yet in 2001 leaders in both parties supported a tax cut of between $800 billion and $2.3 trillion. I have come to the not-too-insightful conclusion that neither party wants to invest in the real material needs of the American people because both have other priorities. The nation lacks the political will, and our leaders lack the political courage to create the will among the American people to demand that the basic material needs of all of us be met.

Those who have actually conducted class warfare protest when you merely describe the state of America today. A few years ago a not-exactly-liberal magazine, *Business Week*, pointed out that "the combination of high productivity and tepid wage increases is pushing corporate profits through the roof." And indeed, profits have gone through the roof. Even after adjusting for inflation, they have been 50 percent higher than levels of ten years ago.

In 1997 Representative David Obey gave a speech before the Center for National Policy. In that speech he pointed out that the total value of U.S. stocks had jumped by $4.2 trillion during the previous ten-year period—$2 trillion in just the previous three years.

"To give some perspective on how much $4.2 trillion is," he said, "if you distributed that amount on a per capita basis, it would amount to about $65,000 for each family of four in the U.S. That would more than triple the financial assets now held by a typical middle-class American family."

Corporate managers have benefited as well. In fact, the combination of merging corporations and purging thousands of workers from the payrolls—politely called restructuring or downsizing—often drove up the price of their stock, and they were financially rewarded.

Representative Obey pointed out, however, that corporate CEOs have not really been the greatest winners in the explosion of the stock market. Federal Reserve data show that in 1983, two-thirds of all the individual wealth in this country was held by the richest 10 percent. If you exclude nonfinancial assets, such as housing and cars, the richest 10 percent held four-fifths of the financial assets of the country, leaving 20 percent to be shared with the bottom 90 percent of the population.

And the wealth of that top 10 percent was incredibly concentrated in the hands of the richest 1 percent. Over half of the financial assets of the richest 10 percent are owned by the richest 1 percent. And nearly 80 percent of the assets of the top 1 percent are owned by the richest 0.5 percent, about five hundred thousand families.

By 1989 the richest 0.5 percent increased their share of the nation's wealth from 24 percent in 1983 to 29 percent. And that is before the doubling of stock market values since 1989, which would take it to a considerably higher percentage today.

The holdings of those five hundred thousand families were worth $2.5 trillion in 1983. By 1989 this figure had risen to $5 trillion. To put that into perspective, the holdings of those families grew by almost three times as much as the national debt grew during that same period. If you want to talk about reducing the deficits and debt, those five hundred thousand families could have paid off the entire national debt, not just its growth, and still have owned 10 percent more wealth than they did in 1983. And remember, this does not include the increase in their wealth due to the doubling of the stock market since then! So however the up-and-down variations in the stock market may affect their portfolio, the average American need not worry about the top 0.5 percent or compare themselves to them. They are in a league of their own.

During this same period, 61 percent of the growth in financial assets, such as cash, stocks, bonds, and insurance policies, went to the wealthiest 0.5 percent. Some 28 percent went to the next richest 9.5 percent. The remaining 90 percent of the population got 11 percent of that increase—table scraps. So much for the poor, minorities, and workers putting the squeeze on the middle class!

To divert attention from this massive inequality—the greatest disparity in wealth of any industrialized nation in the world—and away from the historic slow economic growth rates, demagogues tell the middle classes in America that their problem is the poor, the people of color, the immigrants, and—especially—affirmative action.

Republicans, especially, spend millions of dollars and thousands of hours diverting the attention of the American people from the very real hard-core economic issues of the working class, instead focusing on the hot-button social issues of the religious and political right.

It's the old Sugar Ray Leonard boxing trick: Divert the attention of your opponent by circling and wildly swinging your left hand in the air, then, when his attention is on the left hand, hit him with a hard right! That's the role that the socially conservative political right plays. I don't believe I have ever heard a Republican or a conservative Democrat say that the number one item on their political agenda is full employment. I am certain I have never seen them fight for it.

These are not the economically liberal Golden Years of 1945 to 1973. They are the economically conservative years of Nixon, Ford, Carter, Reagan, Bush, Clinton, and another Bush. Most Americans are pretty clear that the modern-day Republican Party is no longer the "Black Republican Party" of the 1860s, but are instead more like the old antebellum southern Democratic Party of the white, the rich, and big business. Then, of course, the white, the rich, and big business were the owners of slaves. Today, they just own finance and industry—and exploit all workers.

One of the negative by-products and Democratic Party political travesties of the Carter and Clinton presidencies—two former-Confederate-state conservative Democratic governors—is that the American people have come to believe and feel that our economic problems are so complex and so out of control that it makes no difference whether a Democrat or a Republican is in the White House or in control of Congress. Too many Americans have concluded, erroneously, that our material problems just can't be fixed by either party and, therefore, they have given up on politics.

Economically speaking, because of this long and unbroken line of conservatives in the White House, in terms of real wages, fair taxes, economic growth, and full employment, it *hasn't* mattered much who was in charge. Recently a great many Americans have concluded, not irrationally or incorrectly, that neither party has made a discernable difference in their lives. Unfortunately, both political parties have made the American people feel that everyone is helpless; that no one can do much to significantly change the course of our economy so that it benefits all Americans. It appears that too many Americans have concluded that it makes no difference whether Republicans or Democrats control Congress, because neither is in charge of the economy. That attitude is reflected in increasingly lower voter turnouts. In fact, the American people seem to be saying that politicians and politics generally are irrelevant—a conclusion that works in favor of the monied interests and against average Americans. We should conclude the exact opposite if we want to change the present economic direction of the nation.

To change directions, we need more citizen involvement, not less. We need greater voter participation. We need more hope and action, and less cynicism and pessimism, because it is not true that we can do nothing. I still believe that "we the people" can make a difference. We *can* build a more perfect Union.

The Chinese symbols that comprise the word "crisis" are a combination of "danger" and "opportunity." That is what we are confronted with today—danger and opportunity. If we keep our heads, our wits, and our democracy about us, we can again create another Golden Economic era, with full employment as the primary policy goal.

If we massively increase democratic participation in every election; if we reform our labor laws to strengthen organized labor, allowing it to grow into a strong social and political force again; if we increase informed grassroots activism in the interim between elections; if we defeat the fatalistic economic ideology that is dominant today; if we begin again to reinvest in public infrastructures that will allow our economy to growth more vigorously; if we rekindle the spirit of a capitalist-energized, but democratically planned and directed public–private economic partnership; and, most important of all, if we develop the political will to fight for full employment, then, to paraphrase my father, "We will have kept hope alive."

I believe there are underlying causes of our failure to create a full-employment economy and I offer some alternative economic solutions that would help create such an economy. My arguments revolve around five key concepts: philosophy, politics, policy, practice, and product.

All economies are shaped by an economic philosophy and society's politics. Whether we are aware of it or not, what we produce and what we often think of as practical economic actions are really based on an economic policy and philosophy.

With regard to modern economics, theory precedes action. John Maynard Keynes said, "The ideas of economists and political philosophers, both when they are right and when they are wrong, are more powerful than is commonly understood. Indeed the world is ruled by little else. Practical men, who believe themselves to be quite exempt from any intellectual influences, are usually the slave of some defunct economist."[6]

Understanding the importance of underlying principles, presuppositions, and assumptions is basic. Let me illustrate. William is your best friend, and both of you have joined the army. After boot camp and specialized training, both of you are given special assignments to serve behind enemy lines. The army tells you—and you accept as true—that William is a loyal American, but that his assignment is to work as a counteragent within an enemy country. You are told that many of the things that you will hear about your friend, and may actually see him do, will *appear* to be unpatriotic and un-American. But just know that he is acting as a counteragent and is still a loyal American.

If you accept the army's basic premise—that William is a loyal American who is working for America as a counteragent—there is literally nothing that William can do to persuade you that he is anything other than a loyal American. If you accept the army's premise, then William can blow up American bridges and meet with known American enemies and spies. You would still conclude that he is a loyal American.

The acceptance of an underlying economic premise is no less powerful. If you assume that your economic philosophy or theory is correct, then you will interpret or fit all objective economic factors—employment, unemployment, the role of government with regard to fiscal and monetary policy, national and international finance, trade—into your philosophy.

What are the philosophical assumptions underlying the American economy? The most fundamental assumption is that the economy works "naturally." There are economic forces that, when released to compete against each other, work in a *natural* way to bring about the most good for society and for each individual in that society. Nature works so that the effort and competition of every individual and every individual business mysteriously—an "invisible hand" in nature, "blind market forces" in the economy—somehow work it all out for the common good of all.

Since this process is natural, nature and market forces work out all of the complicated and interdependent factors that go into producing an economy. What emerges from this economic nature mixer is a natural rate of employment and unemployment, a natural rate of interest, and a natural rate of economic growth. So for the human hand or mind—not to mention the political order—to touch this process or try to alter this economic nature mixer would be *unnatural*. Furthermore, to interfere in such a manner would not only be destructive to the economic process, it would also be destructive to society.

The logical conclusion of accepting assumptions based on such a natural economic philosophy, of course, is that there is nothing collective—that is, political—that we can or should do about it. Don't mess with nature! It is akin to the theological construct of Calvinism's predestination. In the final analysis, you don't really have a choice in the matter. God is in charge of the universe and history, and natural forces are in charge of the economy.

If nature is *a priori*, then politics and government are quite secondary. But if politics is the democratic choice of a representative means whereby the people choose an end—a democratic and representative government—then there is an inherent conflict between the political order and the economic order. One, the political order, involves the ability of the people to choose. The other, the economic order, involves a process where there is penultimate, but no ultimate or overall choice.

In fact, assuming a pure natural economic philosophy, politics and government are more than that. Politics and government are intruders and interferers in a natural process.

If the economic naturalists really believed what they say, or, even more to the point, if their economic philosophy were really true, no political and governmental action or inaction would be necessary—or even possible. Nature would simply run its course. But since there *is* politics and government, nature does not just run its course. Thus, it's not a matter of all or nothing, but a matter of degree. For economic naturalists, that's how we arrive at the liberal and conservative political divide.

In the American context, to be an economic naturalist is to be on the political right, with all its gradations of radical, conservative, and moderate. To challenge the philosophy of economic naturalism is to be on the left, with its varieties of radical, liberal, and moderate.

Economic conservatives say they want as little political and governmental interference in the economy as possible. That's not really true, and that's not the way they behave, but it is what they say. Conservatives in reality structurally interfere with the "natural" workings of the economy on behalf of the interests of capital (money) over labor (workers); they then use the rhetoric and ideology of naturalism to prevent the participation of others in the process or in the economic benefits.

Economic liberals, on the other hand, say they are not opposed to some democratic governmental direction or intervention in the economy, but most are so enthralled with the raw power of the economic engine of capitalism that they are either intimidated or bought off. Liberals too, then, fail to put this supercharged engine into a well-designed aerodynamic body, put sturdy shocks, solid wheels, and tires on it, and install a steering wheel that will allow it to be driven safely to its proper destination: full employment and economic security for all Americans.

The social conservative's philosophy, of course, is different from the economic conservative's. While economic conservatives want minimal governmental interference, social conservatives have no problem with government interference. They don't mind using the government to impose their private religious and moral beliefs onto everyone else. They attempt to insert politics and government into areas of private, personal, and religious choice such as abortion, prayer in public schools, sexual lifestyle, creationism, and more.

While there is often tension between the two, the social conservatives do work hand-in-glove with the economic conservatives. The social conservative's job is to keep the American people's focus on the social issues—individual moral and spiritual renewal, creationism in school curricula, a cutoff in funding for the National Endowment for the Arts, affirmative action, abortion and its related issues, affixing the Ten Commandments to courtroom walls, prayer in school, vouchers for private schools—and away from our real economic concerns over jobs, health care, affordable housing, investing in public education, fair taxes, and a clean environment.

The Reverend Jerry Falwell's Moral Majority once played this conservative political role; currently, it's the part that the Reverend Pat Robertson and his Christian Coalition organization attempts to play. It was the function that Coach Bill McCartney's Promise Keepers represented, as well as the role the Reverend James Dobson's Focus on the Family and Gary Bauer's related Family Research Council plays.

The underlying philosophy of social liberals, on the other hand, values individual civil liberties provided in the first ten amendments to the Constitution and respects the rights and beliefs of other individuals as long as they do not interfere with the rights and liberties of others. Social liberals were the authors of the Bill of Rights.

Lastly, as radical individualists, libertarians are economic conservatives but social liberals. Overall, however, given their economic self-interest, they are much more comfortable in the Republican Party.

I believe there are only two material powers in the world, economic and political, and by definition poor people, working people, and middle-class people don't have economic power. Thus, the only power left to us is political power. But political power has to be organized. The most organized and institutional form of political power in America is organized labor.

Capital and labor struggle over economic power in the form of profits and wages. The relative power of capital and labor determines whether what they produce together gets distributed fairly between the two and—depending on how progressive organized labor is—to the society generally. A major role of a democratic government is to structure laws and rules that help balance the power between labor and capital.

Currently, capital has the upper hand. Republicans and conservative Democrats, primarily representing capital and industry, work to weaken the role of labor in this equation. "Big Labor," "Corrupt Labor"—here I am referring to a largely Republican-created image—is the enemy of a Republican-and-conservative-Democrat-led Congress.

Interestingly enough, the question that most steamed Governor Bill Clinton at the National Rainbow Coalition's Presidential Forum in January 1992 was not a question about the death penalty—he had put Ricky Ray Rector, a lobotomized black man, to death the night before—but a labor question about ending right-to-work laws. He was asked, "Right-to-work laws make organizing and collective bargaining more difficult. Management can refuse to bargain in good faith, threaten and intimidate their workers. Would you support legislation, including repeal of Section Fourteen-B of the National Labor Relations Act, to reform and strengthen our nation's basic labor law?" Clinton's face turned beet red in anger as he lectured the Rainbow against even raising such a question because, he said, it could be used by the Republicans in a campaign commercial against Democrats.

In practice, "right-to-work laws" mean almost the exact opposite of the common understanding of the words. My amendment, by contrast, means that workers have a real right to work and to protect their work and other economic interests by organizing into strong labor unions. Right-to-work laws are specifically designed to undercut workers' ability to organize into strong labor unions to collectively protect their interests. In the twenty-one right-

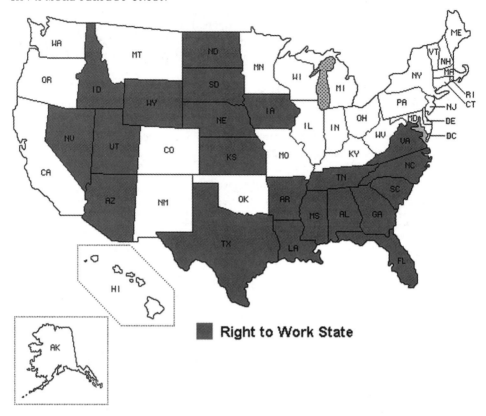

Right to Work State

to-work-law states, workers cannot be required to join or pay dues or fees to a union. Federal laws also permit workers to join and then resign as union members, but when a worker resigns, he or she is still fully covered by any collective bargaining agreement negotiated between a union and an employer, and the union is still obligated to represent that person. Thus, any benefits that are due a union member by an employer as a result of a collective bargaining agreement (wages, seniority, vacations, pension, health insurance) will still accrue to a worker even after resigning from the union. Obviously, if workers can work and benefit, whether they are union members and pay dues or not, it weakens labor's ability to organize workers into solid labor unions.

Unions have historically argued that those who benefit from their collective work ought to be obligated to join the union and pay union dues. Workers should not be "freeloading" off other people's labor, sweat, sacrifice, and money. In labor language this was referred to as having a closed shop (barred by the Taft-Hartley Act of 1947), and labor argued, rightfully, that nonunion workers should not be allowed to work in closed shops. But the individualistic anti-union and pro-corporate forces argue that a worker has a "right to work" in nonunion businesses even if he doesn't join the union or pay union dues. These right-to-work laws are concentrated in the former Confederate states, including Clinton's former home state of Arkansas and the West. (See the map.) They inhibit labor's ability to organize workers into strong unions, which affect their ability to become a political force in the South. That, in turn, perpetuates an economic elite, who perpetuate a political elite through the promotion of economic naturalism and states' rights. Right-to-work laws have their roots in the South's repressive labor laws of the late nineteenth century and were designed primarily to suppress black workers' rights during and after Reconstruction.

Clinton was afraid that if the Democratic Party took a position against right-to-work laws, the Republicans would run a television commercial that would offend his Democratic and Confederate-legacy southern friends. That, he thought, would undercut his ability to carry the South and win the presidency should he win the nomination.

These southern conservative politics are reinforced with a culture of individualistic and personalistic religion, which diverts the people's attention away from what is most needed materially, collectively, and politically in the poorest region of the country—an economic agenda of jobs, health care, affordable housing, and a quality public education—onto conservative and diversionary social issues. And these conservative politics play themselves out mainly through the two major political parties.

The economic philosophy of laissez-faire naturalism and its accompanying conservative politics of states' rights and local control protect the interests of capital. Out of an economic philosophy and politics comes an economic policy or, more accurately, economic policies. What economic policies has economic naturalism brought us? The first and most important policy is the policy of "antigovernment." Economic naturalism is against government even trying to achieve full employment, trying to democratically and rationally determine interest rates, or trying to stimulate or maintain a particular rate of growth. Economic naturalism is against government trying to regulate worker or consumer health and safety, setting a minimum wage, enforcing civil rights, regulating environmental safety, providing a social safety net for workers, the unemployed, or the poor, overseeing trade, or supervising international finance. And if such things do exist, the role of the economic naturalist is to "get the government off our backs"—to weaken, deregulate, devolve, or eliminate these unnatural governmental interferences.

Economic naturalists are not interested in a policy that, periodically, genuinely reforms the laws and regulations so as to allow the economy to function better and more efficiently for everyone and the society. Instead, they use the rhetoric of reform to eliminate all the government involvement they can—all, that is, that is not in the economic self-interest of capital and industry.

Economic naturalism dominates our current economic thought, our politics, and our economic policies. But what is the practical result? How does this trilogy work itself out in practice? In law? Especially in law, since law is what affects the structure of the economy and the society.

This trilogy, in practice, has manifested itself by increasingly removing government from regulating labor markets, by so-called welfare reform (knocking out the safety net), by refusing to raise and index the minimum wage, by reducing the number of people and length of time that people are eligible for unemployment insurance, by focusing on the budget deficit and debt instead of full employment and infrastructure investment, by deregulating international capital, and by an increase in the mobility of industry.

A major practical goal of the economic naturalists is to take the government out of the labor market to the greatest degree possible. Since, left to its own natural workings, capital will dominate labor, the only real chance workers have to compete on a relatively equal footing with capital is, hopefully, for their democratically elected and representative government to intervene on their behalf through the law, and enforcement of the law, to even the playing field. In this regard, the Congress and a long line of presidents have largely failed the American worker.

Apparently, unlike today's economic naturalists, Henry Ford understood that it made economic sense to pay his workers a more reasonable wage so they could buy the cars that he and they made. What good would it do for Ford to produce a huge supply of cars if workers' wages were so low that there would be no consumer demand to buy them? He understood that if the Ford Motor Company was to be economically profitable and stable there would have to be adequate consumer demand for his cars. Thus, even apart from the moral and humane arguments, there is an economic "demand" reason to establish a floor below which no American falls. In purely economic terms, such a floor always guarantees producers a certain minimum demand for their goods and services, which enhances their and the society's economic stability. Full employment at livable wages is the best guarantee of generating enough demand to keep the economy strong and society stable.

Thus, providing an economic floor underneath workers and the poor—a minimum wage, unemployment compensation, food stamps, welfare, or other forms of economic security— helps stimulate economic demand for the producers of goods and services, and gives at least a minimum of economic stability to the entire society. Again, however, creating a full-employment economy at livable wages would minimize the need for such a social safety net and increase demand even more.

But the economic naturalists want to undermine the wage floor. In practice, one form of undermining the wage floor was "ending welfare as we know it," which ended a humane and an economically enlightened sixty-year-old social policy. The poor—whether we have full employment or not, whether we are on the high or low side of a business cycle, whether there is a depression—can now stay on welfare for only two years continuously, and a total of five years in a lifetime. That is their guarantee in law. They have no similar legal guarantee of a job.

Why must the *federal* government "promote the general welfare"? Why don't we let the states do it? The shortest answer is also found in the Preamble to the Constitution—in order to "establish justice." There can be no just standard if it is left to the states' rights movement! "A 1996 report by the House Ways and Means Committee showed that states have not increased benefits nearly enough to keep up with inflation. As of January 1996, the maximum cash assistance within the 48 contiguous states for a family of three ranged from $120 a month in Mississippi to $703 in Suffolk County, New York."[7]

A second manifestation of this attempt to undermine the wage floor has been the refusal of conservatives in Congress and conservative presidents, including Democrats Carter and Clinton, to fight hard for a significant increase in the minimum wage. The increases granted have not kept pace with living standards. The minimum wage was originated in 1938 and attached to official poverty statistics. The minimum wage was set at 46 percent of the official poverty level for a family of three. It reached its peak in 1968 when the minimum wage was 118 percent of the official poverty level for a family of three, but has since fallen continuously as a percentage of poverty. In 1995 the minimum wage represented only 72 percent of the official poverty level. "Professor Ed Wolff of New York University has calculated that, if the minimum wage had kept pace with inflation since 1965, then the current wages of 30 percent of American workers would fall below the minimum wage. In effect, nearly one of three American workers is currently working for a wage that would have been illegal 30 years ago."[8]

The federal minimum wage was signed into law by President Franklin Delano Roosevelt on June 25, 1938. In the 104th Congress (1995–1997), the Democrats' proposal increased the minimum wage from $4.25 to $5.15 over two years during 1996 and 1997 through two 45-cent increases. The last increase, passed by an overwhelming bipartisan vote in 1989 and implemented in 1990 and 1991, was also a 90-cent increase in two 45-cent stages. In 1996 full-time minimum wage workers earned $8,500 a year, and a 90-cent increase over two years raised their yearly income by $1,800—as much as the average family spends on groceries in seven months—to $10,712. In 1996 the purchasing power of those earning the minimum wage was at a forty-year low.

Minimum wage workers are not primarily high school and teenage workers! In 1996–1997, nationally, about twelve million people benefited from the ninety-cent-per-hour increase in the minimum wage. Two-thirds were adults over age twenty who bring home half of the family's earnings; and the majority of minimum wage workers are women. For example, in Michigan in 1996 there were about 324,000 workers, representing 11.9 percent of all hourly workers in the state, who benefited from a raise in the minimum wage.

The Republicans and Democrats opposed to a raise in the minimum wage were acting against their own conservative economic interests. A 90-cent-per-hour raise for twelve million people added $10.8 million an hour to the purchasing power of workers. It contributed $432 million a week in consumer power to the economy. It boosted annual demand by an additional $22.5 billion. Yet the rich business and financial friends of the Republicans and conservative Democrats who voted against a raise in the minimum wage didn't even want the money of poor working people. How economically shortsighted can they be?

We need to raise the minimum wage to a livable wage and index it to inflation so that there is a floor below which a working person, and below which the national economy, will not fall. Such a policy would be good for workers, for the economy, and for our society.

One economic effect of establishing an economic floor—be it welfare, unemployment insurance, or a minimum wage—is that it tends to increase wages for everyone. With no economic floor, there will be a rush to the bottom. There will always be a desperate four-dollar worker waiting to take a five-dollar worker's job. And an illegitimate economy of drugs, gambling, prostitution, and the accompanying crime will always be established when a legitimate economy cannot be found. With an economic floor, the wind shifts in favor of the worker. Employers, if they are to remain competitive, are forced to pay a little more in wages in exchange for competency, efficiency, and productivity—which in the long term raises everyone's wages.

Without an economic floor, the rush to the bottom that such a policy creates also has the effect of pitting desperate or economically insecure workers against one another and, because of the resulting slow economic growth, forces them to compete for a limited number of jobs. It should come as no surprise, then, that there are growing tensions and hostilities between and among workers. Add to this the dimensions of gender, immigration, and race, and the situation is a political tinderbox ready to explode—or be exploited by demagogue politicians.

Unemployment insurance is another area where the wage floor is being chipped away from under workers' feet. Unemployment insurance (UI) has steadily paid workers roughly

40 percent of their wages, called the wage-replacement rate, and maintained a fairly constant duration of twenty-four weeks. But the percentage of unemployed workers receiving UI has changed rather dramatically. In 1975 the UI recipient rate was 75 percent of total unemployed; but by 1995 it had fallen by more than half, to just 36 percent. "In effect, changing the rules regarding qualification for UI has excluded more and more unemployed persons. Qualifying for UI has become increasingly dependent on a history of high-wage stable employment, whereas the economy has been producing more low-wage and contingent jobs."[9]

These antigovernment attacks have also taken the form of focusing on the budget deficit and national debt. Many economists, politicians, and journalists believe that the Reagan and Bush administrations deliberately ran up huge budget deficits and dramatically increased the national debt as a strategy for reducing federal spending. Others disagree and argue that the Reagan-Bush deficits and debt were unexpected. But a second Bush administration seems much more conscious of the effect on spending that pursuing such a policy will have. Whether deliberate or not, the net effect is the same. They know that with large deficits and debt Congress's first response will be to cut social spending, weaken government regulation, and underfund enforcement of our civil rights, workers' rights and environmental protection laws. Most conservative politicians want to "get the government off the back" of business, finance, and industry, and they're willing to use deficits and debt to do it.

These Reaganites and Bushites succeeded in weakening or eliminating laws and regulations that the American people had long struggled to put in place to improve the quality of their lives. In some instances, Clinton desired and was able to institute a temporary stay on such unraveling and resist the 1995 plan of Gingrich and the Republicans to devolve government. But his triangulation politics led him to assign Gore to "reinvent government," which played into the hands of conservatives. Now the second Bush administration has designs on finishing what the original Reaganites and Bushites started. Under such attacks, legislation related to nondiscrimination, voting rights enforcement, clean air and water, worker health and safety, and the regulation of business will all be sorely tested, if not diminished.

While conservatives like to focus on the debt, by historical standards the debt-to-GDP (gross domestic product) ratio is still very low. The biggest problem is not so much the debt itself, but the nature of the debt—what created it. If you invest fifty thousand dollars in a business, a house, or an education, there are future returns on your investment. If you "invest" that same fifty thousand dollars in a gun collection and ammunition, what are the future returns? Both investments result in a fifty-thousand-dollar debt, but will not render the same future return. Social investments should create a good rate of balanced social economic growth over the course of a lifetime—not unlike personal investments.

If the nation had invested, over a five-year period, $1.5 trillion of expenditures and tax breaks in roads, bridges, airports, railroads, mass transit, schools, housing, health care, cleaning up the environment, rebuilding our cities, and supporting family farmers, we might have the same debt (or even larger), but the future long-term returns would have been worth the investment.

Reagan's tax breaks for the rich and corporations, and military Keynesianism, brought about the short-term stimulus of consumer spending (much of this pleasure was borrowed, too), but it also ran up record government deficits and debt. Reagan's tax breaks for the rich came at the expense of investing in our nation's need for future long-term balanced economic growth. The Reagan administration neglected and cut back in real terms on our nation's infrastructure needs in the areas of education, health care, housing, job training, transportation, energy conservation and renewal, and more.

The inclination of most conservatives in both parties and the current President Bush (and Clinton before him) is to cut the debt by cutting programs for the most vulnerable among us—the poor, the children, the elderly, and the minorities. The two parties' only real disagreement is over the size of the cuts. This approach, however, is absolutely and totally the wrong direction to go. It is still not too late to go in the direction of full employment by investing in the American people and in our economic future.

A balanced budget amendment (BBA) is the mechanism conservatives have chosen to permanently "get the government off the back" of finance and industry. The BBA argument is as follows: Like families, businesses, and states, the federal government should balance its budget. But since it does not, we need a constitutional amendment to guarantee that it do so. That is the essence of the argument for the amendment. The amendment may sound good on its face, but it falls flat on its face when examined more critically.

According to the Center on Budget and Policy Priorities, Citizens for Tax Justice, and others, a federal balanced budget amendment would: damage our economy by making recessions deeper and more frequent; heighten the risk of default and jeopardize the full faith and credit of the U.S. government; weaken the principle of majority rule; lead to reductions in needed investments for the future; favor wealthy Americans over middle- and low-income Americans by making it harder to raise revenues and easier to cut programs; affect the financing of Social Security; not be the same as state balanced budget mandates; and not be necessary because we are making progress on reducing the debt without it. Therefore, passing the BBA is not a prudent path for the nation to follow.

The rigid fiscal policy prescription of the BBA proposed by both the House and the Senate would require the budget to be balanced (or in surplus) every year, regardless of whether economic growth is strong or weak. A sluggish economy, with fewer incoming revenues and more outgoing expenditures, would create a deficit that needs economic stimulation to reverse the cycle. Under a BBA, more deficit reduction would be required in periods of slow growth than in times of rapid growth—precisely the opposite of what is needed. Thus, a constitutional amendment risks making recessions more frequent and deeper.

Under the BBA, the government could no longer borrow funds unless there was a three-fifths vote in both houses of Congress to raise the debt limit. Under that scenario, a budget crisis, where a default is threatened, is more likely, and it would heighten the risk that such a default would actually occur. A default of only a few days could have long-term implications. It would erode confidence in the binding nature of U.S. financial obligations. The government pays relatively low interest rates on its loans because it pays its debts back in full and on time. A default would shake that confidence and, therefore, raise interest rates and government costs paid by taxpayers.

The requirement that the budget must be balanced at all times unless three-fifths of the members of Congress agree to raise the debt ceiling also weakens the current principle of majority rule. It would empower a minority (40 percent, plus one) willing to threaten economic turmoil and disruption unless they get their way with the ability to extort concessions or exercise unprecedented leverage over our national economic and fiscal policy.

Public investment that improves long-term productivity growth—such as investments in education, infrastructure, research and development—encourages increased private sector investment that results from lower deficits. A BBA, requiring a balanced budget every year, would result in less public investment and damage future growth.

Businesses that did not borrow to modernize could not remain competitive. Most families, if they could not borrow, could not purchase homes or finance college educations. State and local governments borrow judiciously to finance road construction, to build new schools, and to make other capital improvements, thus assuring their future economic development.

The BBA, while formally flexible in approach to deficit reduction, ultimately favors wealthy Americans over middle- and lower-income Americans because, under current law, legislation can pass by a majority of those *present and voting* by a recorded (roll call) or voice vote. The BBA, however, requires that legislation raising taxes be approved on a roll call vote by a majority of the *full membership* of both houses. Thus, the BBA would make it harder to cut the deficit by curbing the special-interest tax breaks of the oil and gas industries, and easier to reduce such programs as Medicare, veterans' benefits, education, environmental programs, and assistance for poor children. Wealthy individuals and corporations receive most of their government benefits in the form of tax entitlements (more than four hundred billion dollars in 1995), while low- and middle-income Americans receive most of their government benefits through programs.

When the baby boom generation retires, the ratio of workers to retirees will fall to low levels. This poses difficulties for Social Security, since Social Security has been based on a pure "pay-as-you-go" system, with the payroll taxes of current workers paying for the benefits of current retirees. This worked as long as today's workers could pay for today's retirees. But in the future, when there are fewer workers than retirees, the system will be out of balance. In 1977 and 1983 the Social Security Administration took important and prudent steps toward addressing this issue. It allowed the accumulation of reserves that will be used later when needed. These changes were akin to what families do by saving for retirement during their working years, and then drawing down on their savings after they reach retirement.

Senator Orrin Hatch's BBA and a similar House bill insists that total government expenditures in any year, including those for Social Security benefits, not exceed total revenues collected *in that same year,* including revenues from Social Security payroll taxes. Thus, the benefits of the baby boomers would have to be financed *in full* by the taxes of those working and paying into the system then, which undercuts the central reforms of 1983. Drawing down on any part of accumulated reserves, required under present law, under a BBA would mean the trust funds were spending more in benefits in those years than they were receiving in taxes. Under the BBA, that would be impermissible deficit spending. Theoretically, such drawdowns could be offset by cuts in the rest of the budget. But again, if such cuts could be made at all, politically they would likely be made on the most vulnerable among us.

Other BBA proponents argue that since states have to balance their budgets, so should the federal government. Indeed, many states are required to balance their *operating* budgets, but not their *total* budgets. No such distinction is made by the BBA. "Rainy-day" or reserve funds, which states can draw on to balance their budgets, are prohibited by the BBA. Many states require the governor to submit a balanced budget, but do not require actual achievement of it. Some states allow governors to act unilaterally to cut spending in the middle of a fiscal year. The BBA does not and, if it did, would upset the federal Constitution's separation of powers. The majority of states require the same number of votes to raise revenues as to cut programs, but the BBA does not.

These are some, but not all, of the arguments against the BBA. The truth is, the BBA is quite unlike the fiscal practices of businesses, families, and states and, contrary to popular myth, except in times of war and recessions, the country has a conservative record of keeping deficits in line. The only exception to this was the early Reagan years, which three administrations and both parties have since worked to correct. The ratio of debt to gross domestic product has declined from 5.1 percent in fiscal 1986 to 1.4 percent in 1996, a 70 percent decline over a decade.

Responsible fiscal policies by Congress and the president and responsive monetary policies geared toward full employment by the Federal Reserve System, not a constitutional amendment, are what is needed to keep our economy strong and growing, and our deficit and debt in line.

Today we don't live and work in a national economy; we are interdependent with a global economy. Thus we cannot achieve full employment in isolation. Therefore, another of the practical effects of the policy of economic naturalism has been the international deregulation of finance capital, or what William Greider defines as "the trading of stocks, bonds, currencies and other exotic forms of financial paper."[10] The key concepts in this debate are *fixed versus flexible exchange rates* and *capital mobility versus capital controls.*

In 1944, at a world financial conference in Bretton Woods, New Hampshire, a new system of international finance was designed to spur worldwide economic growth and employment. Its structure took the form of fixed exchange rates and capital controls.

A quarter century ago, however, that system faltered for a variety of reasons: three OPEC oil disruptions in the 1970s; countries addressing their trade deficits by borrowing; capital's increasing ability to evade existing international legal controls; the triumph of the philosophy of economic naturalism, which, Thomas I. Palley argues, meant "replacing fixed exchange rates with flexible exchange rates and eliminating capital controls";[11] and the need to discipline governments.

The result of replacing fixed exchange rates with flexible exchange rates was international financial speculation. International financial speculation, in turn, caused exchange rates sometimes to swing wildly or at times created a protracted shift, but both negatively impacted trade and employment. The system of exchange rates created at Bretton Woods that functioned relatively well between 1945 and the late 1970s was focused primarily on the question of employment and the problem of balancing exports and imports.

Beginning around 1975, however, the traditional financial cart was effectively turned upside down. Instead of finance being the *means* of supplying the needs of industry through international investment, trade, and the resulting employment, now the needs of finance became an *end*, an asset market unto itself.

Once finance was no longer a means but an end—it no longer played the secondary role of supplying the financial needs of industry—maximum profits became its driving force. Thus the lion's share of foreign exchange is used now not to supply the longer-term needs of industry and trade, but to satisfy the shorter-term needs of capital speculation.

Fixed exchange rates protected countries from capital flight. Flexible exchange rates naturally led to capital mobility. In a natural way, then, mobile or speculative capital goes to where it can receive the highest return. The word "arbitrage" means that when there is a difference in the price of something on two different markets, the arbitrageur simultaneously buys at the lower price and sells at the higher price. Thus, without controls, capital will arbitrage interest-rate gaps by leaving low-interest-rate countries to go to high-interest-rate countries, which impacts low-interest-rate countries negatively by driving up rates. "This ability to arbitrage and move between financial centers is the foundation of financial capital's economic power."[12]

We already understand what happens under this economic scenario when we look at our own economy. When the Fed raises interest rates the bond market is happy, because its investors will now reap a higher return, but the bottom line for the economy is that there is less demand. With less demand, the economy contracts because fewer people can borrow and fewer businesses need to borrow, which brings about slower growth, fewer jobs, more unemployment, bankruptcies, and business failures, and less business investment. Slower growth also means fewer taxes coming into the government, contributing to budget deficits and increasing the national debt, at the same time that the American people have greater needs—through no fault of their own—because of a deliberate choice and policy of the Fed to slow down the economy by raising interest rates. When that same pattern demonstrates itself in international financial markets, it has the same impact on the international economy, and its negative impact hurts the underdeveloped and smaller developing countries the most.

Because of increasing deficits and debt, both at home and abroad, pressure is now put on the politicians to cut spending in order to reduce the size of the budget deficits. But domestically, there are now Republicans and conservative Democrats who rail against the "big federal government" and "tax-and-spend liberals," pushing for economic austerity and cuts in government spending. Naturally, as a result of these conservative economic policies—not the decisions or actions of individual Americans—we seem to be trapped in a Catch-22 situation.

But in America, who gets cut and why? Congress cuts those who are the least organized, vote the least, and, therefore, have the least political power. That is, they cut the most vulnerable—the young who can't vote, and the poor, minorities, and least educated, who don't vote.

However, with a slow-growing economy and rising unemployment and in order to meet the increased needs of the American people, no matter how inadequately, the government begins to create deficits and increase the national debt because it has to borrow money from the economic naturalists to meet its obligations. But since the Fed raised interest rates to slow the economy, the government now has to borrow at a higher rate, which again makes the bondholders and the bankers happy.

Again, this is not unlike what happens internationally. International capital flows to the highest bidder. In order to remain competitive in the international trade and financial ball game, countries must keep their interest rates high to attract the huge sums of mobile capital that are now flowing around the world. William Greider reported in his 1997 book, *One World, Ready or Not*, that "the entire global volume of publicly traded financial assets (about $24 trillion) turns over every twenty-four days. . . . The entire traded volume of U.S. Treasury debt ($2.6 trillion) turns over every eight days."[13] Today, of course, the volume of capital speculation is even larger—and, because of technology, the speed is greater and the consequences more volatile and unpredictable.

High international exchange rates do internationally exactly what such interest rates do nationally—slow economic demand and growth. A United Nations report by the International Labor Organization a few years ago noted that over a billion people in the world were unemployed. Where there is unemployment there can be no demand. Where there is no demand there can be no growth, and all of the other negative mutually reinforcing results come into play internationally as they do nationally.

This "antigovernment" policy of economic naturalism has also made industry more mobile, both domestically and internationally, and helped strengthen the hand of finance capital and business, which enables it to divide and manipulate labor to further its own narrow economic interests.

Labor economist Thomas I. Palley argues that the economy actually works around four axiomatic principles: The levels of employment and output (GDP) depend on the level or demand for goods and services; the level of demand depends significantly on the distribution of income between wages and profits; the distribution of income between wages and profits depends on the relative bargaining power between workers and business; and firms are driven by the search for profits and will therefore shift their production to new sites if they can earn higher profits by doing so. This last principle applies to both manufacturing and financial firms.[14]

The bottom line is that business, naturally, is going where costs are cheapest. But this has not happened in a merely natural way. Governments have made choices, rendered decisions, and instituted policies that have reduced the costs to business of moving goods internationally. Whatever the stated intentions of business, finance, and conservative politicians, this has been the net effect of NAFTA and the WTO. The power of capital has been increased at the expense of labor.

A decline in the strength and numbers of trade unions has led to a weakened bargaining position for labor nationally and internationally in labor–management negotiations, which has led to firms like Manpower, Inc., hiring out more part-time workers, as well as shifting power, laws, and economic benefits away from workers and toward business.

Workers have been hurt, but so has government. Workers now, relative to capital, have proportionately less money to pay to the government in taxes, while capital has more but is paying less. As a result, there is less social investment and less return on the people's money. Fewer taxes are invested in infrastructure such as mass transit, commercial railroads, high-speed rail, airports, highways, seaways, research and development, education, health care, housing, and more. If taxes between capital and labor were fair and our nation made such social investments, the American people would be more supportive of government because workers and the middle class would be getting a social return on their collective economic investment.

Government shifts in tax laws to favor business and finance—through, among other things, cuts in the capital gains tax rate, which has reduced costs to business—have shifted the tax burden onto workers and the middle class, whose share of the tax burden has dramatically increased. The tax burden has been legally shifted "from people who can most afford to pay to those less able to pay; from corporations to individuals; from foreign corporations to domestic corporations; from foreign investors to American workers; from multinational companies to medium-sized and small businesses; and from the Federal government to state and local governments, whose taxes already fall most heavily on those in the middle and at the bottom."[15]

Again, Palley points out that taxes on growing corporate profits have been cut in half. In 1959 they represented one-quarter of government tax income, but by 1995 they constituted only one-eighth (12.5 percent) of government revenues.

The United States is the biggest financial player in the capital game and has the largest influence in setting the rules of international financial agencies. Thus, it is the combination of U.S. government and international financial organization economic laws and rules tilted toward business and capital that have created a world of high unemployment—and relatively low but unnecessary unemployment in the United States. The fifty states here and other nation-states compete for businesses and jobs. The states and the countries offering the best tax breaks and the most financial incentives land the businesses and the jobs. But this is a race to the bottom.

Advanced new production technologies and more efficient business organization, along with financial capital mobility, have changed the international economy's structure. This technologically and legally changed structure has made business, and the goods and services that business produces, much more mobile and less accountable to the democratic control of government at all levels.

Finally, trade is also affected by this antigovernment policy of economic naturalism. Is a more liberalized trading policy in our national interest? It depends on whether or not we are trading with economic equals. Trade with equals tends to contribute to balanced economic growth and to be good for the long-term interests of both trading partners. On the other hand, trade with unequal trading partners contributes to unequal economic growth and is bad for the long-term interests of both.

While economic naturalists theoretically assume that all trade takes place on an even playing field, again labor economist Palley points out that there are two forms of international trade: trade based on "market competition" between the products and services of two developed high-wage and high-employment economies; and trade based on "systems competition" between the disparate wages in a developed economy and those in an underdeveloped low-wage and surplus-labor economy.

In the United States slave labor in the agrarian South versus free labor in the industrial North created a similar uneven playing field. The recent movement of higher-wage and higher-cost union jobs from the "Rust Belt" of the North and Northeast to the lower-wage, lower-cost, right-to-work, nonunion states of the Sun Belt of the South, Southwest, and near West is still playing itself out in today's American economy. Politically, in 2001, virtually all of the former states were won by Gore and virtually all the latter states were won by Bush.

Trade based on market competition takes place between economic equals and leads to improved products and services as a result of competition over a product or service. Early-nineteenth-century British economist David Ricardo advanced this idea in his *Theory of Comparative Advantage* when he argued that such competition leads to improved quality, increased efficiency, and greater productivity, which leads to higher wages for workers and lower prices for consumers—a race to the top.

Competition based on systems competition between a developed and an underdeveloped low-wage and surplus-labor economy centers on cost competition. Systems competition does lead to lower prices for consumers and higher profits for business, but this kind of imbalanced economic growth also leads to employment insecurity, lower wages for workers, and weaker laws with respect to worker health and safety and the preservation of the environment—a race to the bottom. High-wage workers with higher overall standards of production and costs in the developed economies are undercut by low-wage and surplus workers with lower overall production standards and costs in the underdeveloped economies. Therefore, it is only natural for finance and industry to be attracted to the countries where the government and the laws are least likely to "be on their back."

Industry and finance are attracted to states and countries with the most antigovernment attitudes, politics, policies, laws, and regulations, and the most lax enforcement mechanisms. In the United States that's the South, the Southwest, and the near West. In the world it's the underdeveloped and developing nations. Business and finance rationalize their actions by saying that to stay competitive in such an international market there must be this race to the bottom. In other words, the antigovernment stance of economic naturalism naturally leads to a conservative race to the bottom.

Republicans and conservative Democrats in Congress—the Democratic Leadership Council, and Blue Dog and New Democrats—who primarily advocate for financial and business interests, and in turn are financed by them with campaign contributions and other favors, also reflect this anti-big-liberal-federal-government attitude. They prefer to be aligned ideologically with a more conservative states' rights form of government, because they too wish to get the "Big Federal Government" off the back of business and finance. But only a dynamic and representative democratic U.S. government is even potentially powerful enough to restructure U.S. and international laws in order to create a more even playing field between capital and labor. It is also the only power equal to the task of creating the economic structures, laws, and policies capable of fashioning a full-employment domestic economy that could put all Americans to work rebuilding America. And American workers deserve to fully benefit from the most powerful and economically productive system the world has ever known. After all, it wouldn't have been created without them. The goal of the economic naturalists and their states' rights advocates, of course, is to undercut, weaken, and stop this from happening.

While this powerful economic engine has provided portions of our nation and the world with unprecedented products, services, income, and wealth, there is another side. There have also been many negative consequences and by-products of this system. As early as four decades ago, Michael Harrington in *The Other America* documented the millions of broken, maimed, and unfulfilled lives that give testimony to this. And I still see the ongoing carnage playing itself out in the daily lives of many of my constituents in the Second Congressional District of Illinois.

While many feel that America is the greatest nation on earth, and I agree, ultimately we must judge our society not merely by our current achievements, but by our potential, by how great we can become. The ultimate measurement must be based on what is spiritually, materially, and politically possible; what we can and should become as a society if we fulfill our potential. To whom much is given, much is required. Our nation and its leaders must not have minimalist expectations. A glass half full is also a glass half empty. This book is about building a more perfect Union for all Americans, leaving no American behind.

Keeping the half-empty glass in mind, the single most important negative economic consequence of economic naturalism is the lack of market demand. And the only solution to reversing this lack of market demand begins and ends with a national commitment to full employment.

Mass prosperity requires "demand management" through representative and democratic government control and direction of economic policy, both monetary policy (interest rates and money supply) and fiscal policy (budget expenditures and taxes).

The first step toward achieving a domestic economy with a strong and steady market demand through full employment is overcoming the passive and superstitious philosophy of economic naturalism—that nothing can or should be done through the political process to achieve a full-employment economy. The underlying absurdity of an intelligent, informed, responsible, and democratic people relying on superstition and irrationality—turning the competing economic forces of capital and labor into quasi-religious beliefs about blind market forces and an invisible hand—must be ridiculed, defeated, overcome, and done away with. The idea that there is a "natural" rate of unemployment, a "natural" rate of interest, or a "natural" rate of growth must be seen as fatalistic and fatally flawed in a democratic society of choice. An economic philosophy that relies on "let nature run its course" must be replaced with an economic philosophy that understands and respects democratic planning.

Just as the economics departments in the universities, the graduate schools of business, and the mass media have "educated" students and the American people about economic naturalism, in a similar manner they can provide them with a basic alternative economic vision and framework. These same forces can provide the American people with the conceptual tools to understand the economic process well enough to make informed, intelligent, and basic economic judgments and democratic choices. Economics is not rocket science. With a concerted and sustained effort, the American people can be taught the basic options and consequences of their choices, and they can hold their elected representatives accountable for the democratic and economic choices they make.

Again, politics is economic naturalism's distribution system. Its rules and policies determine who gets what, when, where, and how much. They also determine our word choice—whether we call the distribution welfare, a tax break, or an entitlement. This distribution is the consequence of a larger political struggle between capital and labor. The broad mechanism through which the distribution is determined is monetary and fiscal policy. How income is distributed will be determined by the forces involved in the political fights over income distribution—battles over setting interest rates at the Federal Reserve, and executive and congressional fights involving taxes and spending. In the context of this chapter, whether we have full employment or not will be determined by political forces.

Full employment is a political choice, not a natural selection of the economic order. Whether we have an economy that is democratically directed toward full employment, demand management, and balanced growth, or whether we accept a fatalistic economic naturalism will be determined by political struggle and political choices based on the relative power of capital and labor.

In politics, an organized, informed, and participating minority will inevitably defeat an unorganized, uninformed, and uninvolved majority. Maximum voter registration, political education, and participation, therefore, are essential starting points. Becoming informed, being actively involved in issues between elections, and organizing to protect and expand our economic interests are essential to achieving our goals in politics.

The key political consideration or institutional strategy to be employed in changing our national politics is to strengthen the hand of organized labor through labor market reforms. Just as the laws and economic playing field over the last quarter century have been tilted in favor of business and finance, so too must the law be reformed to reflect a greater balance and a more even distribution of power between capital and labor.

No single policy shift can restore a high-wage, balanced-growth, full-employment domestic economy. Instead, any successful program will have a multitude of policies, including labor market reform, monetary policy, fiscal policy, international trade policy, international money markets, and international economic policy coordination.

The Wagner Act of 1935—guaranteeing the right to form unions, bargain collectively, and strike—helped create the economic Golden Age of 1945 to 1973. This twenty-eight-year economic span benefited more people, was more balanced, and was more affluent than any other period in the nation's history. Real wages and living standards rose significantly. The trends in the wealth and income gaps narrowed. There was greater social investment and fairer taxes. Virtually all of these trends have been reversed since 1973.

In *National Labor Relations Board v. McKay Radio and Telegraph Company* (1938), however, the Supreme Court weakened Wagner's right to strike by giving employers the right to permanently replace striking workers. In 1947 the Taft-Hartley Act prevented secondary or sympathy strikes and barred closed shops, further weakening labor's hand.

Even so, the Wagner Act resulted in 35.7 percent of the American workforce being organized into unions at their height in the mid-1950s. Labor's organized power also resulted in an increase in real wages. Labor now had greater input regarding working conditions, and there was also an income shift toward workers. This directly benefited organized workers, of course, but it also benefited the entire American economy and society, including business and finance.

In 1996 organized labor had fallen to just 14.5 percent of the total workforce, and by 1999, while the number of union members in the United States rose from 16.21 million to 16.48 million, the percentage of U.S workers belonging to unions was a mere 13.9 percent. Additionally, nearly half (42 percent) of unionized workers were employed in the public sector in 1996, with the private sector increasingly free of unionization with a rate of only 10.1 percent of its workforce organized. That means business and economic interests will continue to dominate labor for the foreseeable future.

A New Deal policy, backed up by economic, labor, and social legislation, of putting strict controls on international capital flight and creating a minimum wage and unemployment insurance allowed the country to make a policy commitment to full employment more than fifty years ago. We need new more progressive legislation and policies like this today, including international economic policies, to make a concrete commitment to actually achieving full employment at home and reducing unemployment in the world.

During the Golden Age, federal monetary and fiscal policy were directed in favor of full employment. Beginning in the early 1970s, however, these same federal policies began shifting away from full employment and social investments, and toward fighting inflation and a preoccupation with deficits and debt consistent with the philosophy and politics of economic naturalism. This did not just occur naturally; it was a deliberate political and policy choice by those whose economic interests it served. For example, the bond market currently implicitly dictates monetary policy by insisting on zero inflation as a policy goal; bondholders don't want their loans paid back in inflated dollars. But those whose interests are served by full employment, social investments, and fair taxes—the vast majority of the American people—must insist on no less. We must fight, through our politics, for policies that serve the material needs of all Americans. Monetary policy should not be ideological, but pragmatic and experimental, as it seeks to balance the concerns of employment, wages, and inflation.

Economically speaking, the federal government is currently talking out of both sides of its mouth. It doesn't want people on welfare, yet it won't create enough jobs to put everyone to work who wants to work. It demands welfare reform, but welfare reform has an unstated but underlying premise of full employment. The Federal Reserve's stated policy of full employment and price stability is on a collision course with welfare reform, because the Fed is dominated by those who protect financial interests first. Thus, fighting inflation reigns victorious over full employment as Wall Street pummels Main Street!

In fact, if the economy really begins to grow and official unemployment statistics approach a low percentage, say 3 or 4 percent, Federal Reserve Chairman Alan Greenspan and the Federal Open Market Committee threaten or actually raise interest rates for the purpose of cooling the economy. But slowing the economy reduces job creation, consumer demand, business investment, and economic growth. So just as the jobs begin to flow down, providing employment opportunities for former welfare recipients, Mr. Greenspan and the Fed turn off the spigot. Thus, the course is set for a clash between the stated goals of federal welfare reform or "welfare-to-work" and the Fed.

In the past, when the national economy slowed, unemployment rose, and hard times set in, the less fortunate could at least turn to welfare as a last resort. Under the new federal welfare reform policy, however, there is no such last resort. And there is no federal guarantee that when someone is forced off welfare, a job will be available through the private or public sectors. Thus, today's welfare recipients are left only with the mandate of a 1950s song, "Get a Job!" It's easier for politicians to get tough on poor people who don't vote than it is to get serious about full employment.

Underlying welfare reform is the moral principle that every person who can work, should work. This is morally sound, but it has no economic support. Government leaders should not impose the cultural standard of "the Protestant work ethic" on welfare recipients and the unemployed on the one hand unless they have an actual program of full employment on the other.

Logically, because of welfare reform, the government must now become the employer not of last resort, but of first resort. The first priority of the government's fiscal and monetary policies must be to actually achieve full employment and balanced economic growth. If full employment cannot be achieved in the private sector alone, then the government should guarantee every person who wants to work a meaningful job making a livable wage or an income. Until there are actually enough jobs to gainfully employ everyone, critics and political leaders don't have the moral authority to speak disparagingly about those who are unemployed or legitimately in need.

Currently, there is only an abstract policy contained in the 1978 (Humphrey-Hawkins) Full Employment and Balanced Growth Act, but no actual government programs to achieve full employment. Holly Sklar wrote in *Chaos or Community* (1995) that since 1932 the nation's leaders have had a lot to say about the work ethic, but the government's policies have been more committed to establishing entitlements to welfare or income transfer programs than to creating a full-employment peacetime economy.

In 1997 conservatives in Congress expressed great concern over the accuracy of the Consumer Price Index (CPI). And of course, the CPI should be accurate. But the politics of the CPI debate appeared to be a bipartisan exchange more about budget politics than about fiscal accuracy. In reality, the 1997 CPI debate sought to find a balance between the concerns of conservative Democrats over reducing the budget deficit by cutting programs for the poor, and the Republicans' desire to cut taxes for the rich on the road to reaching a balanced budget agreement. What struck me about the CPI debate, however, was that there is no similar debate about the accuracy of the unemployment statistics. While the official unemployment rate on February 2, 2001, was 4.2 percent (reflecting more than six million people who receive unemployment compensation but do not have a job), the actual number of unemployed and underemployed people is closer to fifteen or twenty million Americans.

Fiscal policy is also a key to full employment. The federal government and the American people must move away from the obsession with balanced budgets and reasonable debt, and focus instead on manageable deficits created by wise social investments in our nation's infrastructure that will result in future balanced economic growth and full employment for all Americans. Palley argues, "Saving does not cause investment; rather, investment causes saving. Increasing investment in turn calls for easier monetary policy and lower interest rates. Public investment is important for both growth and the quality of life; it should be funded for both reasons. A more progressive system of taxation, combined with the elimination of corporate welfare, can help restore income equality as well as fund increased public investment."[16]

There has also been an unproductive public debate going on for some time over trade policy. The argument is usually framed in the overly simplified terms of "protectionists" versus "free traders." It may have reached its zenith in the public's mind in the debate over NAFTA between Vice President Al Gore and Ross Perot on CNN's *Larry King Live* in late 1993.

Gore and Perot were both right and wrong. Vice President Gore was arguing that NAFTA would create jobs, while Perot was arguing that it would cost jobs. It actually did both, but for different groups of people. It created new jobs for already well-to-do, educated, entrepreneurial, and technically trained people. It cost old jobs for industrial workers who are less educated and less technically trained. But both free trade and protectionism are the wrong approach to international trade. Instead, trade needs a "common markets" approach in which countries agree to common environmental standards, workers' rights, and bans of forced labor, child labor, and discrimination in the workplace. Such requirements are usually referred to as core labor standards. Countries should also formulate basic workplace standards that regulate work conditions, such as hours of work, minimum wages, and pension and health benefits. It is interesting to note that while the rights of intellectual property are guaranteed under NAFTA and WTO, these core labor and work standards pertaining to fundamental human rights are not. And as previously noted, policymakers must be aware of and design policies that take into account the distinction between liberal free trade with developed versus underdeveloped countries.

In international money markets, the antigovernment policies of economic naturalism have freed capital to roam the world in search of the highest rate of return at the expense of trade, development, and jobs. The tail is now wagging the dog. This process must be reversed through changes in national and international law that allow governments to regain some control over runaway capital. "International money markets . . . need to be regulated through the imposition of appropriately designed capital controls, trading taxes, and trading requirements. This would reduce speculative distortions of the exchange rate and prevent financial capital from exercising a veto over domestic economic policy."[17]

The business and financial communities tout daily the reality of a new international and globally integrated economic system. I argued earlier that politics precede economics. By that I meant two things: that all economies function within the context of some politically created legal framework; and that politics, through democratically elected and representative governments, should determine basic economic direction and priorities—for instance, the priority of full employment over inflation. Therefore, in the tradition of Bretton Woods, the international political and financial regulatory community must again assert itself and take control over the economic direction of this new global economic reality. If it does not, the current dominance of business and financial interests over labor and democratic governmental direction will become even more entrenched and difficult to reverse. Such economic policy coordination is a necessary precondition for achieving full employment and sustained balanced economic growth and prosperity in a new globalized economy.

New progressive labor laws would help rectify the imbalance of power between labor and capital by strengthening the wage floor and consumer demand through higher minimum wages and improved unemployment benefits and coverage. In addition, labor laws should be amended to level the labor market playing field regarding workers' ability to form and join unions including, in the United States, repeal of Section Fourteen-B of the National Labor Relations Act. A full-scale intellectual and political attack against the "right-to-work" laws that proliferate in the South should be launched. The rules and regulations governing labor organizing must be enforced where now in place, and changed or reformed where not in place to make the playing field of labor and business more equal. More stringent laws should be passed by Congress to prevent the use of "replacement workers" by businesses when their workers go on strike. And the legislation governing the National Labor Relations Board (NLRB) must be strengthened and streamlined for more effective enforcement and more efficient processing of labor cases. The business practice of using delaying tactics with regard to NLRB cases must be stopped. We must put an end to the lack of aggressive enforcement of labor laws and impose stiff penalties for unlawful conduct by businesses in labor–management disputes. And we must put an end to undue influence by business at the NLRB.

There is a way out and up. With the political will we can create a more just society through a full-employment balanced growth peacetime domestic economy. Sheila D. Collins, Helen Lachs Ginsburg, and Gertrude Schaffner Goldberg and the "Jobs for All" coalition have offered a commonsense, practical, and progressive framework for a progressive economic program that I am pleased to support. It includes:

1. **JOBS FOR ALL.** Paid employment and phased reduction of work time—in other words, shorter hours. Certain forms of family care (such as of the very young and the infirm) should be recognized as productive work and should be compensated through paid family leave.

2. **ADEQUATE INCOME FOR ALL.** Individual and family income sufficient for the full realization of human potential, to be acquired from paid employment, income support, or a combination of the two.

3. **RIGHTS OF WORKERS.** To adequate compensation and benefits, to organize for their collective rights and interests, to job security during labor disputes (passage of striker replacement legislation), to training adequate to adapt to economic changes, to safe and healthy workplaces, to participation in decisions affecting their working life and security, to protection of wage and benefit standards for part-time and temporary workers, and to protection of workers' money (security of retirement plans).

4. **COMMUNITY INVESTMENT, PRESERVATION, AND SUPPORT.** To ensure that enterprises are accountable to the communities where they operate for all decisions that affect the level of employment and the economic and ecological well-being of the community.

5. **MILITARY CONVERSION.** Substantial and continuing reductions in military spending, with assurance that the "peace dividend" is committed to meeting the nation's large backlog of unmet social, physical, educational, and infrastructure needs, and that those at risk of job loss be fully protected and actively helped in the transition from the military economy to useful civilian work.

6. **ENVIRONMENTAL PRESERVATION AND SUSTAINABILITY.** Sustainable growth as the central principle in the restructuring of economic activity—as both a necessity for survival and beneficial to the economy and the people who work in it.

7. **FAIR TRADE AND ECONOMICALLY VIABLE LOCAL PRODUCTION FOR LOCAL CONSUMPTION.** Government commitment to develop international standards ensuring that globalized production preserves and enhances, rather than undermines or destroys, hard-won living standards, and that local autonomy and productive ability are protected.

8. **DEMOCRATIC PLANNING AND INDUSTRIAL POLICY.** Democratic planning at all levels of government to ensure balance between private and public investment, and between private needs met through market mechanisms and public needs financed through equitable taxation.

9. **REBUILDING THE NATION'S CITIES.** We must reverse the deterioration of urban America, reduce urban-based poverty and homelessness, and restore our neglected cities to their rightful place as the jewels of our civilization and engines of economic renewal.

10. **SOUND GOVERNMENT FINANCE.** We must move from our obsession with debt and deficits to creative use of fiscal and monetary policies to promote economic stabilization and renewal, through a more progressive tax structure, a level of taxation adequate to meet national needs, fiscal balance at a real full-employment level, and large-scale public investment to reduce our social, environmental, human capital, and other accumulated, damaging deficits.

11. **LIFELONG LEARNING.** Access to free education and training opportunities and support for workers displaced from declining industries, from industries undergoing changes in occupational structure, and for people reentering the labor market following family care, to enable people to realize their potential, and to assure adaptation of the workforce to rapid changes in the operations of the national and global economies.

To begin this century, Theodore Roosevelt offered the American people a "Square Deal"; after the Great Depression, Franklin Delano Roosevelt created a "New Deal"; following World War II, Harry Truman provided us with a "Fair Deal"; in 1960, the enthusiasm and vigor of a young forty-three-year-old John F. Kennedy challenged the nation to reach out for a "New Frontier"; and a poor Texas farm boy, knowing his segregationist past but remembering his economic roots—and seizing a new opportunity created by the civil rights movement—called the nation to a higher spiritual, moral, social, economic, and political plane with an appeal to create a "Great Society."

While he neither started nor finished it, in 1980, Ronald Reagan dramatically and effectively popularized conservative economic thought and rekindled the political cause of states' rights. In doing so, he radically escalated their dual economic and political effects on the American people by offering the few a "Royal Deal" and the rest of America a "Raw Deal."

The last three decades of the twentieth century were basically a steady march of the economic naturalists and the political states' righters walking hand in hand to undo the work of the previous four decades. For most it was a mission, but for a few it was a crusade. Only an organized mass democratic political movement to discredit the economic philosophy of economic naturalism and the political legacy of the Confederacy—states' rights' and local control—can reverse this direction and create a more perfect Union. That more perfect Union will provide the American people with a "Better Deal," a deal of balanced economic growth and full employment, comprehensive and universal health care, affordable housing, a quality public education system, equal opportunity, a clean environment, fair taxes, and voting rights for all Americans, not as a politician's campaign promise or a panacea of government programs, but as empowering *human rights* amendments for every American codified in the Constitution.

Such a mass democratic movement and organization must be respectful of and inclusive of the type of loosely organized and spiritually led moral crusade that characterized the civil rights movement of the 1950s, 1960s, and 1970s. But it must not be dominated by that style. Such a movement must have great appreciation for and never denigrate in any way the effective social movements of the past. But times and circumstances have changed. To democratically build a more perfect Union for all of the American people, and to change the current political direction of the country, will require whole new forms of communication and new styles of leadership and organization. These new forms will require much higher forms of organization and a much greater ability to communicate, independently, a democratic message with and to the American people.

This is the agenda I came to Congress to fight for. I invite all who share in that vision for social and economic justice to join in the political struggle and pilgrimage to achieve a full-employment peacetime economy.

12

A MORE PERFECT UNION—UNIVERSAL AND COMPREHENSIVE HEALTH CARE

[A 2000 report by the World Health Organization (WHO) analyzed health care systems in 191 countries. Africa's Sierra Leone ranked last. Other countries in sub-Saharan Africa also fared poorly, partly because they are some of the world's poorest nations, and are often plagued by disease and conflict. How well did the world's wealthiest nation do? Not so well; it ranked only thirty-seventh! While the United States spends more money on health care, thirty-seven hundred dollars per person a year, WHO said it got less bang for its health care buck than any other nation.]

In evaluating overall performances, WHO used healthy life expectancies, inequalities in health, responsiveness of the system, including diagnosis and treatment, inequalities in responsiveness, and how fairly systems are financed. . . . WHO says whether privately or publicly funded, a government's role is crucial. . . . WHO says a health care system is more than doctors, nurses, hospitals, and clinics. It is all the efforts society makes to improve health. And how well it performs is a matter of life and death to the people who depend on it.

—Margaret Lowrey, CNN correspondent
CNN-TV transcript, June 20, 2000

Lack of insurance is the seventh leading and most preventable cause of death in America. Lack of wealth must no longer condemn any citizen to a life cut short by inadequate health care.

—Senator Edward Kennedy (D-MA)
Speech before the Center for National Policy, January 19, 2000

**PROPOSED HEALTH CARE AMENDMENT
TO THE U.S. CONSTITUTION**

Section 1. **All citizens of the United States shall enjoy the right to health care of equal high quality.**

Section 2. **The Congress shall have power to implement this article by appropriate legislation.**

U NCLE SAM WANTS YOU! As part of the enticement to join the military during World War II, recruiters promised young men free lifetime medical care for themselves and their families if they spent twenty years serving their country in the military. The commitment made to these men—now part of an older generation of 1.8 million military retirees who are dying at a rate of 3,700 a month—is simply referred to as "the Promise" and was never a written law. Until recently the government had essentially fulfilled its commitment, but now it is wriggling and bordering on reneging on this promise. Thus, in the spring of 2000, veterans' organizations were protesting to Congress and filing friend of the court briefs before the Supreme Court in an effort to get the nation to live up to its word. It would be a difficult case to win before any court, not simply because it was only a promise to veterans, but because the Constitution contains no "right" to health care. Individual Americans, then, are left with only the option of appealing to and depending on the political will of Congress and state legislatures, presidents, and governors. Without a constitutional amendment, Americans have no direct individual right or power in their hands.

The cost of various proposed solutions to the veterans' plight ranged from $650 million to $9 billion. The response of Congress was timid. Big-spending and strong defense-minded southerners like Senate Majority Leader Trent Lott (R-MS)—who has fought long and hard to build a $375 million LHD-1 amphibious assault ship in his district that even the Pentagon said it did not need or want—and Armed Services Committee Chairman John W. Warner (R-VA) proposed minimalist solutions. They were joined in a bipartisan fashion by Senate Minority Leader Thomas A. Daschle (D-SD). Southern men, who are usually "military hawks" when they fight to secure the best weapons and spare no dime to protect the nation and defend its honor around the world, suddenly became penny-pinching "health care doves" with regard to dealing with the health needs of veterans—men who had risked their lives for the nation.

While veterans' groups were told by Trent Lott and House Speaker Dennis Hastert (R-IL) that the issue was money and they should lower their expectations, some members responded more sympathetically. House Appropriations Committee Chairman C. W. Bill Young (R-FL), a prominent defense hawk, told one reporter, "I think Congress has the moral obligation to provide the medical care that was promised when military personnel were recruited. I don't know if it's a major political issue, but it's a moral obligation."[1]

The nation has a moral obligation to fulfill its promise to these veterans. It also has a moral obligation—and the economic ability—to provide every American with universal and comprehensive health care of equal high quality. In a manner befitting the marine code on the battlefield, when it comes to health care, "we should leave no American behind." The only thing lacking in achieving that goal is the political will of the American people.

These veterans relied on a mere promise instead of the law, but even the law is not enough. Laws are written and passed in a political context. As the politics change in the country, so too the legislative process changes in Congress and the White House. What Democrats or Republicans provide the American people in the law today can be changed, reduced, or repealed altogether tomorrow. It all depends on the politics of the moment.

Currently, with regard to health care, there is no minimal "chin-bar"—not to mention a high and equal gauge—that Congress must continuously meet. Only a constitutional amendment, such as the one proposed at the start of this chapter, provides an eternal high touchstone for Congress to meet. Nothing in politics or the law is guaranteed, but a constitutional amendment is the best way to permanently codify the goal of high-quality health care. Having the right (an entitlement) is the only way all Americans are empowered to legally redress their health care grievances if the legislative and executive branches of government fail to provide such a system.

How the nation achieves this promise and goal—what the program looks like, how it is organized and funded—is a political issue that must be debated by Democrats and Republicans in the Congress. Many Republicans favor a system of portable individual medical savings accounts (MSAs) that each person funds, owns, and controls, out of which are paid routine health care costs. If unused, like an Individual Retirement Account (IRA), the MSA grows and can be applied later to health care expenses or used in retirement. Many Democrats prefer a single-payer national plan of comprehensive and universal health care equally available to all. It allows all individuals to choose their own private doctor, but sets the fees for services and controls prices. But both Republicans who support MSAs and Democrats who favor a single-payer health care system ought to be able to support a constitutional amendment that legally affirms as a right the goal of universal and comprehensive health care.

Over time, however, whatever health care system Congress creates today will need to be adjusted to meet additional demands, different needs, and future technologies in medicine. One example is the health care implications of completing the mapping of the entire human genome. This phenomenal new development will unlock health secrets with new insights into the causes of disease and potential new cures for cancer, AIDS, Alzheimer's disease, and more. Only a constitutional amendment continually forces Congress to meet the highest standard of care available at any given time. Such an amendment represents an unchanging standard within constantly changing circumstances.

Over the centuries every incremental advancement in the law and human rights has come as a result of a protracted political struggle. The journey of health care in America has been no different. In the United States it formally began with the Massachusetts Health Insurance Company issuing the first "sickness insurance" in 1847, an early form of health insurance. In that same year Nathan Davis founded the American Medical Association at the Academy of Natural Sciences in Philadelphia, where the AMA appointed a committee on medical education establishing standards for preliminary medical education and for the degree of M.D. A progressive French mutual aid society, La Société de Bienfaisance Mutuelle, established a prepaid hospital care plan in San Francisco in 1853, a plan resembling our current health maintenance organizations (HMOs).

The Civil War helped advance U.S. medicine. At the beginning, medical care was crude: The army featured only ninety-eight doctors and assistants, called surgeons. Limited hospital facilities were soon expanded, however, especially in Washington, D.C. The Washington Infirmary was a teaching and general hospital, the Washington Asylum (now DC General) housed indigent patients, and the Government Hospital for the Insane of the Army and Navy became today's Saint Elizabeth's Hospital. The Civil War forced the capital city to become a hospital city when a population of seventy-five thousand was obligated to care for fifty thousand patients. The military used the Capitol, the Patent Office Building, churches, large houses, and other buildings to care for wounded soldiers. Twenty-five military hospitals were established in Washington and surrounding townships, while at the peak of the Civil War the area may have boasted upward of eighty-five such facilities.

During the Civil War, amputation was the most common surgery. The pain and suffering of amputation was often followed by use of the leading painkilling drug morphine, sometimes administered as opium pills, but mostly just rubbed or dusted into a wound. Death occurred in only 25 percent of amputations conducted within twenty-four hours of a serious wound as medical techniques improved as the war progressed. The Civil War also turned embalming into a science: So many families wanted their dead relatives' remains returned that a whole new profession was created. Surgeons' work during the Civil War also advanced a new idea, that medical personnel were neutrals in war and should not be shot, taken prisoner, or captured alongside fighting soldiers. In Washington, "shortly after the Civil War, the government established Columbia Hospital for Women to provide health care for women coming into the city to look for missing and wounded relatives. . . . The Naval Hospital in downtown Washington was the forerunner of the Bethesda Naval Hospital. The Walter Reed Hospital also dates from the early 20th century."[2]

In the 1870s American industrial workers in the North became increasingly dissatisfied and militant in their labor demands. As a way of appeasing these workers, some railroad, mining, and other industries began to provide company doctors, funded by deductions from workers' wages—thus began employer-related health care. Montgomery Ward entered into one of the earliest group insurance contracts in 1910. The National Convention of Insurance Commissioners developed the first model around which states could regulate the new health insurance industry in 1912, and the International Ladies Garment Workers Union began the first union medical services in 1913.

A campaign between 1915 and 1920 to establish compulsory health insurance programs in sixteen states failed. A few years later a group of schoolteachers arranged to provide room, board, and specified services for a predetermined monthly cost at Baylor Hospital in Dallas, Texas—a forerunner to the Blue Cross plans of today. On August 14 President Franklin Delano Roosevelt signed the Social Security Act of 1935. In the middle of the Great Depression, progressive forces challenged FDR and called on the nation to take the next step and enact a national health insurance system, which both failed to do. But the Revenue Act of 1939 did provide an employee tax exemption for compensation, accident, or health insurance.

When World War II broke out the War Labor Board froze wages, so employers turned to health care and other benefits to lure workers to their plants. In Congress the McCarran-Ferguson Act of 1948 gave states broad power to regulate the health insurance industry. The Disability Insurance program was added to Social Security in 1956, broadening the nation's social insurance safety net. In 1962 President John F. Kennedy gave a speech at Madison Square Garden advocating Medicare for the elderly. By 1965, with only half of Americans age sixty-five or older having health insurance—contributing to very high rates of poverty among the elderly—Congress passed Medicare and Medicaid and President Lyndon Johnson signed them into law as amendments to the Social Security program. President Nixon appeared close to proposing a national health insurance plan in the early 1970s, but it was scuttled because of the Watergate scandal.

Alongside these legislative efforts over the years a Blue Cross Commission established in 1937 created a nationwide doctors' network, as the American Medical Association implored county medical societies to share in the burden of caring for poor patients. The AMA also became openly political as early as 1943 by establishing a congressional lobbying office in the nation's capital. Assuming ever-greater responsibility for the public's health, the AMA recommended a national vaccination program using the Sabin oral vaccine against polio in 1960 and adopted a report in 1964 on the hazards of cigarette smoking. It also launched a war against smoking, urging the government to reduce and control the use of tobacco products in 1972, and in 1983 called on the nation to create a smoke-free society by 2000. In 1978 it developed a national policy endorsing hospice care to enable the terminally ill to die in a more homelike environment.

The Health Maintenance Organization Act of 1973 established benefit, administrative, financial, and contractual requirements for entities seeking designation as federally qualified HMOs. The Employee Retirement Income Security Act of 1974 (ERISA) established uniform standards for all employee benefit plans, which had to be followed if they were to obtain and maintain their tax-favored status.

The postdepression Democratic Party Platform had always included a commitment to national health insurance until 1984, even though my father had campaigned on a commitment to a universal and comprehensive single-payer health care system as a centerpiece of his first campaign. With an employment-based health care system, dramatically rising health care costs, less skilled unionized industrial jobs moving overseas, part-time and independent contract and consultant work rising, and without full employment, there has been a significant decline in health care coverage in the United States. Private insurance through full-time employment is the way most citizens secure health care. But a quarter of all working Americans get their paychecks from part-time or temporary jobs, which are far less likely to offer health insurance or retirement benefits. Medicaid insures only about 10 percent of the low-income nonelderly population. Eighty percent of those without health insurance are workers or dependents of workers, with three-quarters living in families with at least one full-time year-round worker—in other words, not poor by official federal poverty standards. Children and people of color are particularly vulnerable, but they are only part of a much larger picture of those in the United States without health insurance. In the last twelve years the number of uninsured Americans has grown by thirteen million—seven million during the eight years of the Clinton administration—and at the start of the new millennium there are approximately forty-five million nonelderly Americans without health insurance (those over age sixty-five are covered by Medicare). Additionally, there are approximately forty-five million Americans with inadequate health insurance. If FDR could speak to the nation in 2001, he would have to tell us that one-third of America is still ill cared for in terms of health.

In 1990–1991 President Bush proposed expanding health insurance through tax breaks. His plan didn't pass, and health care has remained a major issue in subsequent presidential and other campaigns. A liberal Democrat from Pennsylvania, Harris Wofford, was elected to the U.S. Senate campaigning on a national health insurance platform as recently as 1991. In 1992 candidate Bill Clinton campaigned on health care, and early in his administration he sent to Congress the Health Security Act of 1993. Attacked by pharmaceutical companies, the smaller private health insurers, small businesses, and a series of politically effective "Harry and Louise" commercials, this poorly designed and unsatisfactory national health care plan was defeated. Even with its faults, however, if it had passed it would have represented an incremental step forward by giving some form of coverage to all Americans for the first time in the nation's history. He appointed First Lady Hillary Rodham Clinton as his point person in this failed attempt. In the 2000 campaign George Bush supported MSAs, Vice President Al Gore proposed an expansion of the CHIP program, the state-administered Children's Health Insurance Program to cover the eleven million uninsured children—the largest number ever reported by the Census Bureau—as a first step toward universal coverage, and former Senator Bill Bradley outlined a plan to cover 95 percent of the American people when signed into law.

In October 1996 Congress passed the Health Insurance Portability and Accountability Act with bipartisan support, which made it easier for workers to carry their health insurance from job to job. The next year Congress enacted the aforementioned state-administered CHIP in order to expand Medicaid coverage to the children whose families earn too much to qualify for Medicaid. The current debate in the 107th Congress is over strengthening Medicare by providing a prescription drug benefit for seniors and passing a patients' bill of rights.

Children, born innocently and into circumstances not of their own choosing, hold a special place in our hearts when their health care needs go unmet. Marian Wright Edelman, head of the Children's Defense Fund, speaks eloquently and powerfully on behalf of America's children when she describes the particular health problems confronting them. Every day, she says: 3 young people under age twenty-five die from HIV infection; 77 babies die; 151 babies are born at very low birth weight (less than three pounds, four ounces) and 798 at a low birth weight (less than five pounds, eight ounces); 399 children are arrested for drug abuse; 406 babies are born to mothers who had late or no prenatal care; 1,352 babies are born to teen mothers; 1,540 babies are born without health insurance; 2,140 babies are born into poverty; 3,445 babies are born to unmarried mothers; and 8,470 children are reported abused or neglected. Whatever reasoning we apply to the external demographics or social circumstances of parents, innocent children's health care needs should not be neglected or go unmet. Edelman says uninsured children are more than four times as likely to have an unmet medical need; three times as likely to have an unmet dental need; more than three times as likely to go without prescription medication; and almost twice as likely to have an unmet need for vision care. How can we expect children do well in school if they don't feel well, don't see well, and can't hear well?

The reality is more than 90 percent of uninsured children have one or more parents who work. Three in five live in two-parent families. Two-thirds have family incomes above the poverty level, but 70 percent have incomes below $26,580 a year for a family of three. In 1996, 70 percent of all Americans added to the ranks of the uninsured were children. Uninsured children are at risk for preventable illnesses. The majority of uninsured children with asthma, and one in three uninsured children with recurring ear infections, never see a doctor during the year. As a result of the U.S. infant mortality rate, 8.0 babies died for every 1,000 live births in 1994, and black babies died at almost twice that rate, 15.8 deaths per 1,000 live births.

I believe it is no accident—indeed, it is part of the legacy of slavery—that five of the seven states that ranked worst in terms of the following categories—children without health coverage; babies born to mothers receiving early prenatal care; low-birth-weight babies; infant mortality; two-year-olds fully immunized; children living in poverty; child support collected; and per-pupil education spending—are the former Confederate states of Mississippi, which appeared on the ten worst list in all eight categories, Arkansas (5), Louisiana (5), Alabama (4), and Tennessee (4). The other two were Oklahoma (5), a conservative state, and Washington, D.C. (5), which is without political power in Congress.[3]

Again, according to the Children's Defense Fund, while the United States is first in the industrialized world in GDP, millionaires and billionaires, military technology and exports, defense spending, and health technology, it ranks tenth and twenty-first respectively relative to eighth-grade science and math scores, fourteenth in the proportion of children in poverty, and twenty-second in infant mortality. If our infant death rate had equaled Japan's, fifteen thousand additional U.S. babies would survive their first year annually.[4]

In the late 1990s many poor workers lost their Medicaid coverage despite being eligible. Robert Pear of the *New York Times* reported in April 1999 that one unintended consequence of ending welfare in 1996 as we had known it was that hundreds of thousands of low-income people lost their health insurance. He reported that while the law was strong on advocating work, and workers were supposed to be able to keep their Medicaid coverage, in fact many lost it. In New York just two and a half years after Clinton had signed the welfare bill into law, roughly 265,348 (9 percent) people had been dropped by Medicaid. In New Jersey the number was 54,261 (8 percent); in Connecticut, despite a major effort to find eligible people, Medicaid rolls rose by only 3,258 (1 percent). Oregon was minus 43,000 (11 percent), and Texas dropped by 306,890 (15 percent) even though the state had expanded Medicaid eligibility. The number of people on Medicaid dropped by 213,614 (13 percent) in Pennsylvania, by 453,640 (8 percent) in California, and by 58,899 (4 percent) in Florida.[5]

For those states' righters who believe that states do a better job of administering programs than the federal government, Pear reported that Congress appropriated five hundred million dollars to help states carry out the Medicaid provisions of the 1996 law. For example, the states were allowed to use the money to hire workers to determine who was eligible for Medicaid and to help them enroll. The federal government reported that the states had used less than 10 percent of the money.[6] The result was this rather dramatic increase in the number of eligible poor workers who lost their Medicaid coverage.

The state-administered CHIP program, the states'-rights-oriented children's health program that Gore wanted to expand, has worked no better. While reflecting good intentions, CHIP has been a mess from the beginning because it was put together by Congress and the White House as part of the 1997 balance-the-budget deal. While the federal government provided states with additional money to insure poor children, it also requires state matching funds—and southern and conservative states have a documented history of not showing much concern for their children. CHIP also has complex eligibility requirements, and many states shied away because they didn't want to get stuck with additional outlays during the next recession. Thus, there are more kids without health coverage today than there were four years ago, because many former welfare families have lost their Medicaid coverage.[7]

There is not only a deficiency of health care for children, but also a disproportionate lack of health care for minorities. The disparities in health care leave too many minority communities with a health system that is separate and unequal. The Commonwealth Fund released a February 1999 study that showed, even after taking into account workforce and sociodemographic characteristics, blacks and Hispanics were 21 percent less likely than whites to have employer-sponsored health insurance. The report, "Employer-Sponsored Health Insurance: Implications for Minority Workers," found that minority groups tend to have lower rates of health care coverage because they are more likely to work in industries that do not provide coverage, have lower incomes, and hold part-time jobs.

HIV-AIDS in Africa has received considerable focus as a crisis worse than any war, famine, or other disease in Africa's history—2.4 million Africans died in 2000 alone, and 12 million children are now orphaned—but too often today's HIV-AIDS epidemic in the African American community is swept under the rug. HIV-AIDS in the black community was discussed recently at a 1998 Harvard conference of one hundred African American leaders. One participant, Mark Schoofs, argued that, apart from slavery, nothing in our history may have killed as many black people in such a short period of time as HIV-AIDS. The conference reported that HIV-AIDS kills more black Americans in the prime of their life, age twenty-four through forty-four, than any other cause. It also noted that one out of five deaths among black women in this age group is caused by AIDS; one out of three among black men. While blacks comprise just 12 percent of America's population, we claim 40 percent of all AIDS cases, more than half the female cases, and more than 60 percent of children with AIDS. Blacks are also six times more likely than whites to be infected with HIV, and twice as likely as Hispanics. Finally, it was reported that today it is likely that three hundred thousand to five hundred thousand African Americans are infected with HIV.

Dr. Beny Primm, executive director of Addiction Research and Treatment Corporation, described the current state of the crisis of HIV-AIDS in minority communities, particularly the African American community, in a similar way. He said that racial and ethnic minorities account for more than 54 percent of the total AIDS cases reported since the beginning of the epidemic. And according to the Centers for Disease Control and Prevention, three of seven people who contract HIV in this country every day are African Americans.

While federal enforcement pressure and the general strength of the economy have helped reduce barriers and bring many African Americans into the nation's economic mainstream, in the area of health care there has been little progress—and even growing disparities. Recent reports indicate that health gaps between blacks and whites with regard to higher death rates from nearly all major causes—life expectancy, asthma, diabetes, major infectious diseases, and cancer—continue to exist and, in most cases, are getting wider. Peter Kilborn reported in the *New York Times* that "the federal Centers for Disease Control and Prevention reports that from 1980 to 1994 the number of diabetes cases rose 33 percent among blacks, three times the increase among whites. The gap in cases of infectious diseases has grown by the same magnitude. With breast cancer, the CDC reports that from 1990 to 1995 the death rate for all women fell 10 percent, from 23.1 per 100,000 to 21. But black women's higher rate did not budge from 27.5 per 100,000."[8]

Poverty and bad health habits are clearly contributors to poor health, but, sociologically speaking, merely being an African American seems to be a major factor as well. Kilborn notes in the same article that Dr. Donald M. Berwick, a pediatrician in Boston who was a member of President Clinton's commission on health care quality, said, "Tell me someone's race"—not implying that poor health is genetically related. "Tell me their income. And tell me whether they smoke. The answers to those three questions will tell me more about their longevity and health status than any other questions I could possibly ask. There's no genetic blood test that would have anything like that for predictive value."[9]

It was reported in a newsletter published by HHS, *Closing the Gap*, that of "Toward the Year 2000 Health Goals" established by the administration, "many conditions . . . disproportionately touch blacks, including asthma, obesity, homicide, maternal mortality, diabetes and fetal alcohol syndrome . . . the incidences [are] not only falling short of the goals but also slipping in relation to the conditions in the late '80s and early '90s, on which the goals were based."

The report continued, "Other minority groups suffer from some diseases more than blacks. American Indians have higher levels of diabetes. Hispanic-Americans tend to suffer more fatal and disabling strokes. Puerto Rican children have the highest incidence of asthma. The CDC reports that in 1996, tuberculosis among Asian-Americans was nearly 15 times higher than among whites and nearly twice the level for blacks. But as the largest minority group and the one with the highest death rates from most diseases, blacks arouse the most concern among experts. 'There is a minority group that is very disadvantaged with respect to health, and that's African-Americans,' said Samuel H. Preston, a demographer and dean of the School of Arts and Sciences at the University of Pennsylvania. 'It's not a minority problem. It's a black problem.'"

Kilborn also reported on a study in the October 1997 issue of the *New England Journal of Medicine* that suggested there was "something peculiarly American to being black and unhealthy beyond genes." Two Chicago neonatologists, Drs. James Collins and Richard David, studied the birth weights of all children born in Illinois from 1980 to 1995. Isolating the lowest-risk group of mothers—those between the ages of 20 and 39 who were college educated, married to college-educated men, had prenatal care in their first trimesters, and had no prior miscarriages or stillbirths—they found 2.4 percent of 12,361 American-born white mothers delivered underweight babies compared to 3.6 percent of 608 mothers living in Illinois and born in sub-Saharan Africa. For African American mothers, however, the rate was 7.4 percent. Therefore, the doctors concluded at the annual American Public Health Association, the study's "findings discredit the genetic theory of race as it applies to birth weight. ... To understand this thing called race, we must turn our attention to the institutions and attitudes which perpetuate and justify unequal treatment of people on the basis of their physical appearance, language or culture." In the same article Dr. Berwick concluded, "It isn't enough to say we're going to close the gap by equalizing services. I don't think that's the heart of the problem. It's not equality of access. It's equality of result that we should seek."[10]

I have contended throughout that politics in Washington reflects more the economic divide between North and South than the traditional political demarcations of Democrats/Republicans, or the ideological labels of liberal/conservative and left/right. The accompanying chart listing the percentage of Americans without health insurance on a state-by-state basis illustrates the point.

STATE	PERCENT UNINSURED	UNINSURED
United States	18.1	43,056,000
Arizona	27.8	1,163,000
Texas	26.8	4,769,000
New Mexico	25.7	420,000
Arkansas	25.0	558,000
California	23.5	6,927,000
Florida	22.6	2,678,000
Louisiana	22.3	838,000
Mississippi	22.1	540,000
Oklahoma	21.7	618,000
Nevada	20.9	321,000
Montana	20.8	167,000
West Virginia	19.8	286,000
New York	19.6	3,128,000
Georgia	19.5	1,327,000
Idaho	19.5	214,000

Alaska	18.8	112,000
New Jersey	18.5	1,301,000
South Carolina	18.3	618,000
District of Columbia	18.1	81,000
North Carolina	17.7	1,131,000
Wyoming	17.7	76,000
Alabama	17.5	640,000
Colorado	17.0	603,000
Kentucky	16.9	576,000
Oregon	16.1	468,000
Delaware	15.7	103,000
North Dakota	15.7	86,000
Tennessee	15.6	769,000
Maryland	15.6	689,000
Maine	15.2	162,000
Virginia	14.8	854,000
Illinois	14.4	1,546,000
Utah	14.4	270,000
South Dakota	14.2	86,000
Missouri	14.0	644,000
Indiana	13.7	698,000
Washington	13.6	702,000
Connecticut	13.6	388,000
Massachusetts	13.4	711,000
Kansas	13.1	288,000
Michigan	12.8	1,100,000
Ohio	12.7	1,243,000
Iowa	12.5	311,000
New Hampshire	12.3	130,000
Rhode Island	12.0	95,000
Nebraska	11.8	173,000
Pennsylvania	11.6	1,191,000
Vermont	11.4	59,000
Minnesota	10.7	458,000
Wisconsin	10.6	483,000
Hawaii	10.2	102,000

[SOURCE: THE UNINSURED IN AMERICA, NEWS HOUR WITH JIM LEHRER/HENRY J. KAISER FAMILY FOUNDATION PARTNERSHIP, APRIL, 2000.]

Progressive economist Robert Kuttner says what's really wrong with our health system is that it relies too heavily on employers when Americans no longer have lifetime jobs—and portability is not the answer. He also argues that the health care system relies too much on the managed care industry's profit motive: HMOs make money in proportion to whom they can enroll, who doesn't get sick, and whom they can deny care. With more people without health insurance and increased fragmentation in the health care industry, if you change or lose your job you have to change doctors—that is, if you can get or afford insurance at all.[11]

Believing that every American has a right to health care does not commit us to supporting any particular health care approach, plan, or solution. But we ought to know what the broad range of approaches are.

What is the difference between a national health care system, national health insurance (private or government run), and national health service? The United States is the only industrialized nation in the world that does not have a national health care system (prior to ending apartheid, even South Africa had one for its white citizens). If President Clinton's 1993 health proposal had succeeded—after failed attempts by Presidents Roosevelt, Truman, Johnson, and Nixon—we would have had a national system for the first time in our history. But these various plans would not all have been the same. Roosevelt's, Truman's, and Johnson's plans were very different, with much better results for the American people, than Nixon's and Clinton's.

Differing underlying ideas and principles quite naturally lead to different health care proposals. National health insurance, run by the private insurance companies, is a national health care system designed to benefit the insurance and health industries, where economic competition and profit are the driving forces. It treats health care like peanuts, soybeans, beer, and cars—as just another commercial commodity to be produced, distributed, and sold efficiently and privately for profit. It is government regulated, in the same way that the Federal Trade Commission regulates other forms of commerce, but it is private-profit driven. President Clinton's "Managed Competition" proposal generally followed this model. I fully supported Clinton's goal of national coverage, but I was less supportive of his specific plan.

Paul Starr and Walter Zelman, who were part of a corporate-sponsored group of Democratic Leadership Council–type health theorists known as the Jackson Hole group, were the major architects of Clinton's plan. They argued for a plan designed to encourage the integration of health insurance and health care provisions into the same organization. The more integrated the plans, the better able the insurance companies would be to control costs. In other words, they wanted a unified rational national health care system, but they wanted it controlled by the big insurance companies and run for profit.

At the start, the first lady announced, "We are tired of insurance companies running our health care system"—and she initially received strong public support. But as she fought to sell "managed competition," it became increasingly clear that what the Clintons were in truth doing was putting the large insurance companies in charge of our health care system. The real beneficiaries would have been Aetna, Prudential, Cigna, Metropolitan Life, Travelers, and Blue Cross—all of whom supported Clinton's plan. It is also why the Health Insurance Association of America (HIAA), the representative of the smaller insurance companies—which Clinton attacked as a "special-interest" group—so strongly opposed it. When the American people found out that it was the highly profitable health insurance industry, with its skyrocketing health care costs—the same industry that was cutting back on coverage, providing fewer services, and charging ever-higher prices for drugs and services, while raising copayments—that would be running it, they turned their backs on the Clintons and checked out on the plan. When the Clintons introduced their plan in 1993 there were fifteen hundred private health insurance companies with different plans, benefits, and costs. Fifteen hundred private insurance companies cannot provide all Americans with an equal high quality of health care. If they could, they already would have done so, for profit.

In short, the Clinton plan would not have provided everyone with high-quality care at an affordable price (it was based on a hierarchy of costs and services, with the more expensive plans receiving more services and better care); consumers did not have real choices (for example, you could not choose your own private doctors); insurance companies, not consumers and caregivers, would have called the shots (based on the bottom line); the plan didn't control costs; it allowed large employers of five thousand—plus nationally to run their own health care plans (a disadvantage to individual and smaller businesses); and benefits were not guaranteed soon enough. In all of the proposals in the 1990s—except the single-payer plan—insurance-controlled plans would have reduced services to optimize profits.

We see this two-tiered multiquality approach from conservatives often. But these double-standard, blind-market-force-driven economic conservatives want to privatize Social Security with risky stock market schemes, privatize health care with medical savings accounts, privatize public education with educational savings accounts and vouchers (sometimes referred to as "personal empowerment" programs), and privatize publicly assisted housing. All of these privatizing schemes and their variations create a two-tiered system of services in these basic areas of human need—a better one for those on top, a lesser one for those in the middle and on the bottom. The Clinton plan fit this mold.

I believe that as societies, economies, and civilizations evolve to a higher plane, certain basics of material life—specifically employment, health care, housing, and education—should not be turned over completely to market forces (the "survival of the fittest" philosophy). In such a system, the few always wind up on top with the best and most of everything, while the many end up on the bottom with the least and worst of everything—in this case, health care.

A second approach to health care, a national health insurance program organized by the government (in other words, single payer), would provide comprehensive and universal health insurance for all Americans on an equal basis; would establish the fees of health care providers, with the states' help; would control price increases; and would allow the health care system to stay entirely in private hands, with unrestricted choice of private doctors. It sees health care as a human right. The single-payer approach is the one that I support.

A single-payer program would be federally administered, but not federally run. Local counties would likely oversee and be the primary operators of such a system. I support such a plan not out of any ideological bias or party loyalty, but for practical reasons. Fifty states and 3,067 U.S. counties, each running different cost and benefit programs, cannot provide all of the American people with an equal high quality of health care. This states' rights approach is illogical and will not work. There must be a high minimum national standard that every state and county must meet. My amendment does that by establishing an equal high standard and quality of health care for every American.

Logically and practically, fifty states, 3,067 counties, or fifteen hundred private health insurance companies with different cost and benefit plans cannot meet my constitutional standard on their own. Clinton's "Managed Competition" proposal did recognize the irrationality and bureaucratic nightmare that the current system has become, which is why the administration proposed to rationalize it on a national basis. The core problem, however, was that it tried to rationalize the system for the private gain of the big insurance companies rather than for the public health and good of the American people. The goal of universal and comprehensive health care was laudable. The actual plan was misdirected. The only entity large enough to plan, fund, and administer in a democratic manner a health care program that has the possibility of providing an equal high quality of care to all Americans—and that can be held accountable by the American people—is the federal government. But only if my amendment is in the Constitution are the Congress and the White House obligated to meet the highest standard of health care.

A third option, national health service, is a government-run not-for-profit system designed to benefit health consumers comprehensively by promoting a healthy lifestyle, health education, research, prevention, treatment, care, and cure. Such a system would not eliminate completely market competition—competition within the framework of a national health service system would help keep prices down, quality up, and improve efficiency. Market forces would influence the system, but not drive it. Like the single-payer approach, a national health service views health care as a human right and would be driven by social need, not by private greed.

Such a national health service approach to health care is often criticized as being "socialized medicine." I am a professional politician, practical, eclectic, democratic, and aware of various political ideologies. I am not, however, an ideologue, neither liberal nor conservative, left nor right, capitalist nor socialist. I assume it is understood that I am not a communist. I advocate for human rights and seek practical workable solutions that meet these human needs. However, the conservative charge of socialized medicine—or the general conservative charge of socialized anything—is interesting and should be answered.

Conservatives charge that any national or universal health care system will require a "big government bureaucracy." However, the reality is, it is the current system that requires the big bureaucracy—hundreds of private health insurance companies selling hundreds of separately priced and unequally beneficial health care plans in the 50 separate and unequal states. It is this private, state-centered health care bureaucracy that spends nearly one-fourth of the over $1.2 trillion of American's total health care costs on advertising and administration rather than on health care.

Any national health care system that—to paraphrase the U.S. Marines—"leaves no American behind" and provides health care of an equal high quality for all will be labeled by conservatives as "socialized medicine." The flip side of the conservative argument—of calling high quality and equality of health care for everyone "socialized medicine"—is actually more germane and revealing.

What is actually revealed in this socialist label is that conservatives are almost always arguing for programs that reflect narrow private economic interests and agendas, usually have dual and private (versus public) standards, and are elitist in outcome because their programs overwhelmingly benefit those at the top while leaving those in the middle and at the bottom not just somewhat, but usually far, behind—like the ninety million Americans who have no or inadequate health insurance. The proper question to put to conservatives who call any comprehensive and universal program socialistic is: If you don't want to cover everyone equally, who do you want to leave behind or with unequal coverage? Quite candidly, it must also be said that benevolent moderates and liberals sometimes operate off these same principles, except they are usually less extreme in application. Again, Clinton's Health Security Plan was such an example. Progressives, however, must support programs that are universal, have one equal public standard, benefit everyone and the public good, which will help to build a more perfect Union.

It seems the major fear that middle-class Americans have over adopting one standard is that it will be lower than their current standard. Struggling daily to maintain their standard of living and quality of life, they feel that raising the health care standard and quality of life of others will automatically lower their own. Many Americans would like to believe, or abstractly believe, that every American has the right to universal and comprehensive health care, but they just don't think such a program is practical, financially sound, or politically possible. I take issue with all of these arguments.

I believe such a program is practical and that the American economy has the financial resources and technological skills to provide such health care. We lack only the political will to do so.

Politically, conservatives argue that no candidate supporting such a national health program could ever get elected. But that contradicts most of the last seventy years of the Democratic Party's history. From the mid-1930s until 1984, Democrats supported national health insurance, and Roosevelt, Truman, Kennedy, Johnson, and Carter were all elected with it in the platform. Even Clinton's idea of universal health care was very popular until the American people learned its flawed details. It is since Democrats dropped national health insurance from their platform and stopped campaigning on it that they have had the most trouble winning elections.

And substantively, those who argue that the United States can't efficiently organize or afford a national health care system can't have it both ways. They can't argue that we have the greatest government with the most efficient financial and industrial sectors in the world, that have built our nation's economy into the most powerful and productive in the world— our nearly ten-trillion-dollar GDP dwarfs every other economy in the world—then turn around and argue that we don't have the organizational ability and cannot afford to provide for our citizens what every other industrialized democracy has provided for its people. We have just not organized the political forces to realize our goal.

Conservatives usually argue that our health care system is the envy of the world; that we have the best doctors, researchers, equipment, hospitals, and clinics in the world—and we do. They argue that when world leaders and others need the best care they can find they come to the United States—and again, they do. We do have the best health care system in the world—for the wealthy at the top who can afford it. But that same quality of care is not available to all of the American people.

Not only do we have the largest and strongest economy in the world, but the United States spends more money on health care than any other industrialized democracy in the world. We currently spend more than $1.2 trillion a year, 15 percent of our GDP, on health care, and this is growing. Canada, with a single-payer system that ranks second in health care spending, spends only 9 percent of a much smaller GNP on health care. All the other countries spend about 6 or 7 percent, yet they provide health care for all their citizens. If we continued to spend 15 percent in a full-employment economy that was growing in a balanced fashion at a rate of around 4 to 5 percent, it would make the surpluses being generated today look meek by comparison. If that was combined with significant, but reasonable, cuts in unnecessary military expenditures, the combination of full employment, balanced economic growth, and new national priorities would generate enough money to sustain a national single-payer health care system—at an even higher quality of care for all Americans than we have today—and we could sustain it into the indefinite future. Spending this amount of money would create the high quality of health care that Americans want and would eliminate the kind of complaints that sometimes characterize Canada's health care system. Even with their waiting lists, the vast majority of Canadians would not exchange their health care system for ours.

To date, the state-by-state (states' rights) market approach to providing health care has not adequately met the American people's health care needs. It bears repeating that the federal government is the only entity that can accumulate the financial resources and coordinate a national health care system. Such a system can be run and controlled locally, but the minimum high standards, the overall coordination and administration, and the national financial planning for such a system must be administered and made democratically accountable at the federal level. While health care is clearly a more complex undertaking, if we can do it for Social Security—the most popular social program in America's history—we can also do it for health care.

Moderates accept the political status quo and try the incremental, piecemeal approach—a patients' bill of rights, small increases in the number of children covered, Medicare coverage for prescription drugs. The states'-rights-oriented CHIP effort at the end of 1998 reported that in the forty-three states in which it operates, only about 982,000 additional children received health insurance under the program. It has done a little better since then, reducing the number of children without health insurance from 11.3 to 10.8 million. I support all of these improvements, but it's a long way from what the American people deserve, what the American economy can afford, and what political leaders ought to be fighting for. We should continue to fight for all these advances, but my health care constitutional amendment is the logical conclusion to all of these bit-by-bit struggles and proposals.

I am not arguing that health care as a human right from womb to tomb is without complications, or that difficult personal decisions, economic considerations, and political choices will not still have to be made. The fact is, we are making such decisions today, but leaving ninety million Americans in the lurch. Given the new developments in science to sustain life in some form, clearly we need to have an enlightened and enlightening national dialogue over many issues. If individuals express their will, orally or in writing, about the conditions under which they are willing to have their life sustained, that must be factored in as well. Since most health care costs come in the final months of life, tough personal, family, medical, and politically considered judgments will still have to be made.

But instead of moving in this direction, conservative Republicans and Democrats have consistently tried to cut coverage or benefits or increase the costs of Medicare and Medicaid. Often today's differences between Democrats and Republicans are only in terms of the severity of the cuts, where and how they should be made, and how much and when the premium increases should come. Neither party appears to believe that all Americans have a *right* to health care. The regressive proposals of conservative Senator John Breaux (D-LA), Representative John Dingell (D-MI) charged, would have converted "Medicare from a universal guarantee to a government voucher for private insurance."[12]

The American people deserve better, and we can afford and achieve better. A constitutional amendment guaranteeing the right to high-quality health care can be achieved. The American people can and ought to make the personal and political choices that will create a more perfect Union.

A MORE PERFECT UNION—
AFFORDABLE HOUSING

The general welfare and security of the Nation and the health and living standards of its people require housing production and related community development sufficient to remedy the serious housing shortage, the elimination of substandard and other inadequate housing through the clearance of slums and blighted areas, and the realization as soon as feasible of the goal of a decent home and suitable living environment for every American family.

—Housing Act of 1949

Everyone has the right to a standard of living adequate for . . . housing.

—Article Twenty-five, Section One,
Universal Declaration of Human Rights

PROPOSED HOUSING AMENDMENT TO THE U.S. CONSTITUTION

Section 1. All citizens of the United States shall enjoy the right to decent, safe, sanitary, and affordable housing without discrimination.

Section 2. The Congress shall have power to implement this article by appropriate legislation.

After two terms and eight years in office of trying to lead the country back to prosperity from a collapsed economy, in his third inaugural address on January 20, 1941, President Roosevelt declared, "A nation, like a person, has a body—a body that must be fed and clothed and housed, invigorated and rested, in a manner that measures up to the objectives of our time." And in his State of the Union Address of 1945, FDR motivated the nation with this call: "The provision of a decent home for every family is a national necessity, if this country is to be worthy of its greatness—and that task will itself create great employment opportunities. Most of our cities need extensive rebuilding. Much of our farm plant is in a state of disrepair. To make a frontal attack on the problems of housing and reconstruction will require thorough-going cooperation between industry and labor, and the Federal, State and local governments."[1] It is as if FDR's speeches were written yesterday—and they remain relevant enough to deliver tomorrow.

As I document in this chapter, great strides have been made since the depression-era housing crisis, which prompted the nation, under President Roosevelt's bold leadership, to start down the path of federal involvement in the housing sector. Today record numbers of

American families own their own homes; the overall quality of housing stock and the diversity of housing choices available to Americans have both improved markedly. Federal policies have been instrumental in eliminating financial risk to homeowners and lenders through such vehicles as mortgage insurance and favorable tax treatment for homeowners, developers, and investors. Direct subsidies allowing for below-market interest rates and down-payment assistance have created a whole new class of homeowners. A secondary market for mortgages made possible through the creation of government-sponsored enterprises like Fannie Mae, Freddie Mac, and Ginny Mae, a HUD agency, provide liquidity and economic security to lenders, enabling extensions of credit to American families not possible before federal intervention. Though the political rhetoric often implies that only the poor have benefited from federal housing programs, it is clear that national housing policies have bolstered the housing conditions of American families at all income levels.

Despite the persistence of insidious discriminatory practices against people of color, the Community Reinvestment Act has replaced red lines with green lines, compelling banks to invest in cities and neighborhoods they once considered too risky. In effect, federal persistence in this critical arena has empowered lenders to discover a whole new market for their products that they had historically ignored. It is a win–win scenario. Banks now have new customers and markets, and urban and rural communities have been revitalized. Billions of dollars in investment have enabled individual consumers to establish equity and accumulate wealth, and nonprofit community-based organizations have leveraged these resources to improve the quality of life for their constituents. The resulting levels of economic and community development serve as testament to the wisdom of this national policy.

Likewise, federal production programs, when adequately supported, have yielded similarly successful results. During the New Deal era, labor unions and other private nonprofits sponsored mixed-income, government-subsidized co-ops, and provided housing and homeownership opportunities for their members and constituents. With the establishment of the public housing program, a safety net for America's neediest families was created.

The military's response to housing shortages exemplifies the potential for federal housing production programs, given successful advances in providing affordable housing opportunities for military families. All enlisted soldiers and career military personnel are entitled to some form of housing subsidy. As I document later in this chapter, wartime administrations created millions of housing units over relatively short periods of time to address the needs of returning veterans. Today the military owns and leases affordable units to military families both on and off base while providing housing subsidies or vouchers to others, who are then able to find affordable housing in the private market. Yet despite the demonstrated success of both the supply-side and demand-side direct subsidies, federal housing programs have been plagued by historically insufficient levels of funding and retrenchment. Yet we know that these programs can work to meet the magnitude of the national need.

Nearly sixty years after FDR's call to the nation, and despite unprecedented levels of productivity and financial prosperity, far too many Americans suffer from severe housing needs. Nearly fourteen million Americans—one in every seven families—are unable to live in both healthy and affordable conditions.[2] The provision of affordable housing affects not only the housing-burdened, but also, on a macro level, the nation's future economic health.

It is well documented that the state of the housing industry has always been closely linked to the nation's economic growth. This economic engine, once stalled, will undoubtedly reverse the advances in economic development enjoyed in recent years in communities across the nation. Additionally, when housing starts fail to keep pace with job creation in high-growth areas, shortages cause prices to spiral out of control. Sale prices for existing housing stock are driven up, out of the reach of low-income families, and increasingly of moderate-income families as well. Higher construction costs cause builders to cater to higher-end buyers, leaving behind workers who are essential to the community's continued viability. It is not only lower-wage public sector and service industry employees who are affected by these market circumstances. Faced with housing shortages and longer commutes, professional employees are turning down otherwise appealing job offers, posing serious recruiting problems for employers.[3] Without an appropriate federal response to this pervasive market failure at all income levels, this pattern will only worsen.

Perhaps no better example of this stark reality exists than in Silicon Valley, California—home of the high-tech industry that has arguably fueled this new information age. In San Francisco and San Jose, more than 20 percent of working families suffer from severe affordability crises—spending more than half of their income on housing[4] at the expense of other critical family needs, such as food, clothing, and health care. In order for minimum-wage-earning families in San Francisco to live affordably according to the federal guidelines,[5] they would have to work 174 hours per week.[6] Incredibly, 1999 figures indicate that 34 percent of Santa Clara County's homeless people have full-time jobs, up from 25 percent just four years earlier. As noted in a startling new report, Silicon Valley's teachers, police officers, firefighters, and salespeople working on commission, earning more than fifty thousand dollars annually (and solidly middle class by most national standards), are now seeking refuge in area homeless shelters. This does not bode well for the country; nationally, waiting lists for rental assistance are increasing dramatically. It is telling that in no major metropolitan area can full-time workers earning the minimum wage afford the fair market rents.[7]

Housing production not only provides the necessary housing stock to stem the disastrous effects of shortages, but it also creates jobs. Job creation, in turn, results in more disposable income, which workers then spend on more goods and services, in turn creating more jobs and increasing national levels of productivity. Economists call this the multiplier effect, because, in essence, the benefits to the economy keep multiplying. More jobs, more income, a larger tax base, and, ultimately, a healthier nation.

Symbolically, we have always believed that adequate housing is synonymous with "the American Dream." Unfortunately, it is no longer a foregone conclusion that hardworking Americans, even families with two adults working full time, can provide for their children and own their own homes, as was once possible in this great country. These days, home-ownership on its own is no panacea. While a majority of working-class families own their own homes, these families, struggling to make high mortgage payments relative to their incomes, cannot avail themselves of the primary federal housing subsidy—the mortgage interest deduction. Without sufficient income to itemize deductions on their income tax returns, 1.6 million low- and moderate-income working families struggle without any form of available federal assistance to meet their housing needs.[8] Only a comprehensive federal housing policy that meets the needs of all Americans—at all income levels—can guarantee the future strength of our nation and our economy.

After a job or an income that provides adequate economic security for all people and all families for life—and right next to universal and comprehensive health care of equal high quality—decent, safe, sanitary, and affordable housing stands as one of the greatest material needs of the American people.

I believe that adequate, safe, and affordable housing is a human right. As civilizations and economies develop, certain material basics (like food, shelter, health care, and education) should not be turned over completely to market forces, to a "survival of the fittest" philosophy and program. We know that in such a system, the few always wind up on top with the best and most of everything, while the many end up on the bottom with the least and worst. Such is the case with housing in America.

Adequate and fair housing for all of the American people should not be treated like peanuts, soybeans, beer, and cars—a commodity to be produced, distributed, and sold privately in the marketplace for profit. Let us be clear and disabuse ourselves of the notion that a "free market" for housing actually exists. The playing field for housing in inextricably linked to government policy—from local zoning laws to federal highway appropriations and tax benefits for homeownership. We know that housing is more costly in areas with good public schools, good roads, and public transit systems. Thus, the government essentially subsidizes housing markets through its disparate investments in public services and infrastructure among communities. History has demonstrated that this approach does not serve the housing needs or interest of all Americans, particularly poor and low-income—and increasingly middle-income—people. Clearly the market hasn't, it doesn't, and it won't or it already would have. Thus, as representatives of all of the American people—not just those who can survive in a private, "survival of the fittest," housing market—Congress and the executive branch of the federal government must assume its responsibility.

The federal government has a role and an obligation to accomplish this public goal. A federal government of, by, and for the people must ensure that every American is suitably housed. If the federal government reclaims this role, it will also reclaim the support of the American people.

A constitutional amendment unequivocally establishing an inalienable right to adequate housing lifts the federal housing goal, codified many times over, to its proper place as a critical national priority. If all the American people know and believe that they are entitled to housing, they will have a material reason to vote and will once again actively participate in this democracy. Policymakers and the judiciary always factor in the electorate's tolerance level as expressed through activism. If elected officials fail to do so, an engaged electorate will hold them accountable and vote them out of office.

As with the other rights advanced in this book—employment, health care, education—advocating for an entitlement to housing cuts against the grain of current political and budget priorities. The federal role in housing is declining, and direct subsidies are shrinking relative to historic levels of investment. In fact, a recent study reports that "In 1997, the number of new federal low-income housing subsidies, including subsidies to owners and developers of low-cost housing as well as subsidies to low-income renters, was only one-seventh the number of new federal subsidies provided 20 years earlier in 1977."[9] While political debate about housing policy always centers on incremental changes in HUD's budget, the reality is that HUD's budget is only *one-fifth* of all federal housing subsidies,[10] with tax expenditures comprising three-quarters of government housing assistance. In 1978 the federal government spent 3.7 times more on direct subsidies than on tax breaks. Today the ratio is reversed. By 1997 tax expenditures exceeded direct investment by 3.3 to 1. Relatively few low-income

Americans receive housing assistance (four million out of the nearly twelve million who are eligible), yet three-quarters of affluent Americans avail themselves of the system.[11] As noted above, the working poor—those well off enough not to qualify for public or assisted housing, yet too poor to receive favorable tax treatment—are left out of the equation altogether.

Conservatives in Congress don't want to reform HUD. They want to do away with it altogether. In fact, the 1996 Republican Platform called for the abolition of the entire agency.[12] During my tenure on the House Banking and Financial Services Committee, it became increasingly clear to me that conservatives not only want to dismantle public housing, but also aim to target government assistance to subsidize only the private housing market. This strategy, on its own, has proven time and again to be inherently flawed.

The reduction or elimination of other "safety net" programs—"five years on welfare and you're off for life despite the nation's economic or your personal circumstances"—is part of mainstream political thought today, and perfectly suits the politics of those who govern at the behest of polls. Such thinking may be in the current political mainstream, but it is not in the moral mainstream, nor is it in the long-term interest of the American people. The mean-spirited and shortsighted "politics of cutbacks and cutouts," by both conservative Republicans and Democrats, come at a time of increasing poverty, a widening income gap between rich and poor, and other growing social tensions.

Just because it isn't currently politically popular to call for the right to safe and affordable housing for all Americans doesn't mean that we should not demand it. I join Chester Hartman of the Poverty and Race Research Action Council, who aptly stated, "I proceed from a normative, philosophical stance that asserts the wisdom and justice of such a right, as well as our society's clear ability to achieve it."[13]

Providing decent, safe, and affordable housing is also cost beneficial and, addressed on the front end, reduces public costs that result from a lack of adequate housing. Massive Medicaid bills due to health problems associated with substandard and overcrowded housing conditions—lead poisoning, rat bites, communicable diseases, asthma—could be preempted. On the back end, taxpayers also fund emergency fire and police protection, not to mention the completely avoidable problem of homelessness.

Reducing overcrowding does more than increase space. It decreases stress, family tensions, and disease. Affordable housing allows families to spend more of their income on food, education, health care, and recreation—all vital elements of a wholesome and fulfilling life. Discrimination on the basis of race, ethnicity, and class further isolates families from the economic mainstream, depriving impoverished families of employment opportunities, public facilities, and quality goods and services (which ironically cost even more than the same products in higher-income areas). These costs and those resulting from lost productivity and educational deficits related to poor housing and neighborhood conditions are never properly taken into account by policymakers charged with crafting "solutions."[14]

It is important to reiterate that building a more perfect Union will admittedly cost, but not building it will cost even more. The American taxpayer will pay one way or another. I advocate allocating taxpayer dollars in the most efficient, effective, and productive way—an approach not reflected in current policy. We have decreased direct public funds for building affordable housing for all of the American people, for example, while dramatically increasing taxpayer funds for building prisons. America now incarcerates more than two million inmates, more than any other country in the world. Our prisons are state-of-the-art, costing taxpayers $80,000 to $150,000 per cell to build, and another $18,000 to $35,000 per year to maintain. This, too, is a choice we Americans are making. Shifting national priorities so that we invest in people on the front end—through adequate housing, health care, education, and job training—rather than on the back end (in what my father, the Reverend Jesse L. Jackson, Sr., has appropriately termed "the prison-industrial complex")—will improve our nation and our world.

Fighting for the right to housing places us on solid moral and religious grounds. A 1975 statement from the U.S. Catholic Bishops asserts, "We begin with the recognition that decent housing is a right" and quotes the Second Vatican Council: "There must be made available to all men everything necessary to live a life truly human, such as food, clothing and shelter." A 1985 document from the U.S. Catholic Bishops says, "The right . . . to shelter . . . [is] absolutely basic to the protection of human dignity. . . . These economic rights are as essential to human dignity as are the political and civil freedoms granted pride of place in the Bill of Rights of the U.S. Constitution."[15] Similar statements have been made by the General Board of the American Baptist Churches: "'We proclaim that each person being created in the image and likeness of God possesses an inherent dignity from which stems a basic human right to shelter.' And Pope John Paul II, in his 1997 Lenten message, asserted, 'The family, as the basic cell of society, has a full right to housing adequate to its needs, so that it can develop a genuine domestic communion. The Church recognizes this fundamental right and is aware of her obligation to work together with others in order to ensure that it is recognized in practice.'"[16]

Unfortunately, the United States shamed the American people at the June 1996 U.N. Conference on Human Settlements (Habitat II) in Istanbul. The State Department first gave strict instructions that it "must be made clear for the record that the U.S. does not recognize the international human right to housing." This is most revealing. While no government has completely lived up to the declaration's mandate—and unlike the United States, many governments are economically, technologically, and organizationally incapable of doing so—every other government in the world, at the very least, acknowledges that a human right to housing exists.

It is also surprising that the United States would take such a position in light of the Supreme Court ruling that signed international treaties and statements of principles have the force of law in this country. The United States is a signatory to the U.N. Declaration of Human Rights, which identifies housing as a human right. Perhaps it was for this reason that the State Department finally issued "the weak assertion that the U.S. recognizes the 'full and progressive (as opposed to prompt) realization of that right in the context of other international documents.'"[17] Given this context, however disturbing, it is not surprising to learn that proportionately among all Western democracies, the United States provides the least amount of federal housing assistance to its citizens most in need.[18]

Government involvement in providing affordable housing for the American people has always been slow in coming; when it did arrive, the forces of "localism" prevailed. When the government ultimately took action aimed at assisting the housing needs of the poor, historically such efforts mainly originated at the county level. Orphanages for children, shelter for the poor (deemed "poor farms"), and housing for military personnel occasionally were supported at the state level, but mostly such housing was financed, owned, and operated purely by county governments.

Federal action first came in response to a growing national housing reform movement born in the 1840s, out of religious and moral concerns for the pervasive unsanitary conditions suffered by the inhabitants of urban slums.[19] When the federal government finally accepted responsibility for providing housing, initial forays were limited to research and studies about housing and community development. The first congressional action came fifty years later, in 1890, when Congress allocated two hundred thousand dollars "for the documentation and investigation of conditions in slums in the core of four U.S. cities with populations more than 200,000."[20]

In 1908 President Teddy Roosevelt created the President's Housing Commission, a blue-ribbon panel charged with documenting slum problems in America's urban centers. For the first time in history, the committee's report advocated direct federal involvement in housing in the country's major cities, recommending an aggressive program of slum clearance and rehabilitation. Specifically, the committee called for the rebuilding of entire communities through the direct purchase of slum properties and direct loans to finance new construction. Its policy sought to enable the poor to buy or rent decent housing at low interest rates or rents.

These recommendations, however, proved to be far ahead of their time: They were largely ignored until after World War I. In 1918 Congress passed a program of loans authorizing real estate companies incorporated by shipbuilders to construct housing for their employees. Over a period of years, it stimulated construction of about nine thousand single-family homes, eleven hundred apartments, eight hotels, and nineteen dormitories in twenty-four different cities—a start, but hardly a program to meet the nation's growing housing needs. This same Congress created the U.S. Housing Corporation and authorized one hundred million dollars (of which only fifty-two million dollars was actually spent) to build, organize, or manage twenty-five community projects for war workers living near defense installations. This program provided thousands of additional units. Within a few years, however, all dwellings created through this program were either sold to private owners or demolished due to a measure included in the enabling legislation by Republicans for the benefit of the private real estate industry.[21]

When the stock market crash of 1929 occurred, the collapse of the housing market soon followed. President Herbert Hoover convened a Home Building and Home Ownership Conference in Washington, D.C., in December 1931, setting the stage for a long series of federal responses to the nation's housing crisis. The research and documentation at this conference laid the cornerstone upon which later reforms (1932–1937) were built.

FDR, elected in 1932 following the financial collapse, with Congress set the country on a new activist course of federal involvement in domestic issues—including, by standards of that day, a large-scale involvement in housing on behalf of the American people. The foundations of the financial and construction systems still in place today were born out of the experience of the private financial-market-created Great Depression. At the time, half of the nation's single-family homeowners found themselves in default; mortgage foreclosures occurred at the stunning rate of one thousand per day. In those days, a five-year loan (and often one- or two-year terms) was the accepted standard. Large down payments of 50 percent of the principal and high interest rates, in comparison to other types of loans, were the convention in the real estate industry. In response to this unprecedented crisis, Congress and the president, over the course of three years (1931–1933), created the Federal Home Loan Bank System, the Federal Savings and Loan Insurance Corporation, and the Federal Housing Administration (FHA), introducing the previously untried mechanism of long-term self-amortizing government-insured mortgages, along with low-rent public housing.

The Emergency Relief and Construction Act of 1932 provided direct federal funding for low-income housing and slum clearance by creating the Reconstruction Finance Corporation, which extended credit to local entities for the purpose of building housing for the poor. New York's Knickerbocker Village was one of the initial beneficiaries of eight million dollars in slum clearance and reconstruction loans. Additionally, Congress created the Federal Home Loan Bank System, which, in effect, reorganized the housing and thrift credit system through the establishment of twelve regional banks, supervised by the Federal Home Loan Bank Board, to provide short-term credit to various financial institutions. Among its members were savings-and-loan and building-and-loan associations, and cooperative banks.

Congress created the Home Owners' Loan Corporation (HOLC) in 1933, an agency charged with refinancing defaulted residential mortgages in areas of economic distress. Qualifying loans were restructured, giving borrowers more time to pay down their debt. One of the more successful New Deal programs, the HOLC refinanced more than a million loans and helped stabilize the private residential mortgage system during its most vulnerable hour. For the first time in our nation's history, home loans were available over a fifteen-year period, at a 5 percent maximum interest rate, through monthly principal and interest payments. The act authorized two billion dollars in funding and was financed through the issuance of tax-exempt bonds. Another lasting legacy of the legislation was the federally chartered savings-and-loan association known to us today. Originally local mutual thrift institutions regulated by the Federal Home Loan Bank Board, these associations were given a mandate to lend funds on the security of their deposits or mortgages located within fifty miles of their home office.

Congress also passed the National Industrial Recovery Act (NIRA) in June 1933 to combat record levels of unemployment—indeed the greatest crisis facing the country, with 25 percent of the workforce unemployed. Congress viewed the construction of housing as part of a job-generating program. The law authorized the use of federal taxpayer funds to finance slum clearance and low-rent housing. Under the rubric of the Public Works Administration, the NIRA eventually produced 21,600 units of low-rent housing and 15,000 units in "Greenbelt" new towns and other resettlement areas. In 1935 the low-rent program was halted by a federal court decision that declared the use of eminent domain to acquire private property for public housing construction unconstitutional.[22] The decision set the stage for a new approach to housing the poor, which would be enacted in 1937.

The National Housing Act of 1934, in the meantime, emerged as one of the most important pieces of housing legislation ever passed by Congress. By creating the Federal Housing Administration (FHA), it addressed some of the structural and institutional inadequacies of "the market" as applied to housing. The FHA was created to provide government insurance to private lenders for residential mortgages. By protecting private lenders against loss— essentially by providing economic security and largely eliminating financial risk to private lenders—the government in effect applied "socialist" principles that bolstered the private housing financial sector. Government action thus advanced the private housing market.

The FHA continued to pioneer and greatly expand the modern long-term mortgage, with relatively low down payments, interest rates, and monthly payments fully paying off the full principal amount over the life of the loan. The FHA originated a series of mortgage insurance programs to expand various types of housing, to include Section 203 for one- to four-family properties and Section 207 for low-income multifamily housing owned by specially designed government housing corporations or private limited-dividend corporations.

In 1938 the low-income restriction was lifted and ownership of such housing was expanded to include all types of public and private entities. The act also provided support for the savings-and-loan industry by insuring savings accounts through the Federal Savings and Loan Insurance Corporation. Originally, deposit insurance covered savings up to five thousand dollars, with the ceiling raised to one hundred thousand dollars in 1980.

Significantly, the 1934 act authorized the creation of national mortgage associations to provide a secondary market for FHA-insured mortgages, and the Federal National Mortgage Association (known today as Fannie Mae) was chartered in 1938. It could raise funds by issuing notes, bonds, and debentures. Today Fannie Mae, a private organization since 1968, in conjunction with Freddie Mac (created in 1970) provides a secondary market for mortgage loans by standing ready to purchase loans from financial institutions and convert them into mortgage-backed securities, thereby providing liquidity to expand homeownership.

Even after four years of hard work and effort to meet the country's needs, President Roosevelt stood before the American people on January 20, 1937, and in his second inaugural address declared, "I see one-third of a nation *ill-housed*, ill-clad and ill-nourished." He called for and delivered the Housing Act of 1937, which created the United States Housing Authority (subsequently renamed the Federal Public Housing Administration in 1942, and the Public Housing Administration in 1947). This subsidized the construction of low-rent public housing by local authorities. It was the second most significant housing law passed during the recovery from the Great Depression.

Originally established within the Interior Department, the agency issued loans, capital grants, and annual contributions to local public housing agencies to assist in the development, acquisition, or administration of low-income housing and slum clearance projects. Terms for loans and annual contributions contracts could run as long as sixty years, and tenant income limits were included in the contracts. The first public housing units in the nation built under the 1937 Housing Act were Atlanta's Techwood Housing Project, dedicated by FDR, and Santa Rita Courts in Austin, Texas.

Even though the nation was now primarily urban, the housing challenges faced by rural communities persisted. The first significant piece of federal rural housing legislation was the Bankhead-Jones Farm Tenant Act of 1937, which authorized the Agriculture Department to make forty-year loans at 3 percent interest to farm tenants, laborers, and sharecroppers who sought to purchase farms or repair their housing. Smaller, shorter-term loans were available for minor repairs and refinancing existing debt.

World War II, like World War I and the Great Depression, greatly impacted American life in all respects. Housing was no exception. As with much of America's progress, federal experimentation and involvement in housing began by providing housing assistance to servicemen and defense workers—even prior to the invasion of Pearl Harbor. In 1940 the Defense Homes Corporation was established and the U.S. Housing Act of 1937 was amended, so that affordable housing could first be provided to military personnel and defense workers. A flurry of congressional activity resulted in mortgage relief for servicemen and more than 945,000 new housing units for military personnel.[23] One year later FHA mortgage insurance was extended to defense housing, netting 350,000 new units in just the three years between 1941 and 1944.

During this period, however, funding for low-income Americans fell prey to conservative political forces. The election of anti–New Deal politicians to Congress from 1938 to 1942 resulted in wholesale cuts in funds for public housing. It wasn't until the Housing Act of 1949 that federal spending on public housing was again authorized. During World War II Congress funded only housing for the military and rejected all programs serving nondefense low-income families.[24]

Following the bombing of Pearl Harbor and America's entry into World War II, Congress enacted price controls in 1942, which, among other things, authorized federal rent controls. Through an executive order, President Roosevelt established the National Housing Agency, which oversaw virtually all non-farm- and non-military-base-related federal housing programs in the country.

In his 1944 State of the Union Address, FDR unveiled his "Economic Bill of Rights," casting adequate housing as a national priority.[25] Subsequently, the G.I. Bill of Rights[26] established the Veterans Administration housing program, including guaranteed home mortgages for returning veterans. The measure was the most significant and lasting piece of housing legislation to emerge from the war. To date, millions of veterans continue to finance the purchase of their homes through these VA-guaranteed loans. It is significant to note that the notion of affordable housing as a right received widespread acclaim at the time, and continues to receive such support vis-à-vis the military.

The Senate Committee on Postwar Economic Policy and Planning, in an August 1945 report, called for the construction of 1.2 million new housing units per year for ten years—not unlike the Kaiser Commission Report of 1969 (which called for 2.6 million new housing starts per year for ten years). Unfortunately, the Senate committee, despite the nomenclature (a committee whose stated mandate included "planning"), left the primary responsibility for generating these twelve million new units in the hands of non-long-range general planners. The nation's housing goal was subsequently placed in the hands of blind market forces, with the government playing a secondary and supplemental role. It was thus left, once again, to the private sector to accomplish this public goal.

While each private entity plans, of course, plans are crafted internally to achieve the self-interested goal of an individual firm's bottom line. By definition corporate strategic planning is not aimed at achieving the overall public goal of providing affordable housing for all Americans. Thus, if market forces fail to meet the needs of the nation, needs are necessarily left unmet. Only a democratically elected federal government, accountable to the people, is in a position to fully accomplish public aims. The private sector is not against planning; it just cannot plan on its own for the overall public good. Such an approach is therefore no substitute for democratic governmental planning.

Upon FDR's death, President Harry S. Truman pledged to continue the struggle for FDR's Economic Bill of Rights. In his first State of the Union Address in 1946, Truman delivered words that resonate today: "Our basic objective—toward which all others lead—is to improve the welfare of the American people. Every family should have a decent home. The new economic bill of rights to which I have referred on previous occasions is a charter of economic freedom which seeks to assure that all who will may work toward their own security and the general advancement; that we become a well-housed people, a well-nourished people, an educated people, a people socially and economically secure, an alert and responsible people."

In 1946 the Veterans' Emergency Housing Act and President Truman's creation of the Office of the Housing Expediter strengthened plans and programs aimed at providing veterans' housing at moderate prices and rents, and allocated materials and facilities for such housing production. Subsequently, a peacetime government gradually shifted most housing provision responsibilities once again to the private sector. The Housing Expediter Agency was terminated in 1951, while rent controls—partially because of the Korean War—lasted until 1953. Congress created the Farmers Home Administration in 1946 to make loans and grants for construction and repair of farm homes and assist rural self-help housing groups.

As World War II was winding up, Congress, through its committees, focused increased attention on the American people's postwar housing needs. Congressional committees, particularly House and Senate Special Committees on Postwar Economic Policy and Planning, recommended the liberalization of FHA mortgage insurance programs, the expansion of public housing, and federal assistance in the technical development of housing materials and construction methods, as part of a longer-range public works and construction program. Congress also recommended the establishment of a National Housing Agency to effectively meet the housing needs of all Americans—a recommendation that did not come to fruition until eighteen years later, with the creation of the Department of Housing and Urban Development in 1965.

Several urban redevelopment bills were also introduced in Congress, yet languished, due to the inherent tensions between government planners and the private real estate industry. Public housing was not specifically addressed in either legislative approach. Advocates articulated the need for the continued provision of public housing so as not to displace current residents and, thereby, create new slums. To forge a workable compromise and salvage public housing (which had since 1938 been completely unfunded), housing reformers endorsed the notion of federal aid to the private real estate industry.

With the support of this "strange-bedfellow" coalition for the cause of urban redevelopment, and Congress's failure to act upon the legislation before it over the course of three years, Truman seized the opportunity to make housing a political issue, ran against the "Do-nothing Eightieth Congress," and emerged victorious in his surprising and extremely close reelection bid over Thomas Dewey in 1948.[27]

After overcoming caustic ideological debate over the concept of public housing (a cause célèbre of Senator Joseph McCarthy), as well as a nondiscrimination amendment posed by arch-conservatives to effectively act as a "poison pill" in the hope that southern Democratic segregationists would then vote against the bill,[28] the Housing Act of 1949 passed by a 227–204 vote.[29] The act created the Urban Redevelopment Agency and gave it the authority to subsidize three-quarters of the cost of local slum clearance and urban renewal. Under the act, "primarily residential" and "blighted" urban areas could be condemned, cleared of buildings, and sold for private redevelopment. As the opening quote indicates, in its call for "a decent home and suitable living environment for every American family," it established a firm rhetorical federal commitment to affordable housing for all the American people, and created the most far-reaching program, urban renewal, under Title I.

Initially, the notion of slum clearance had divided public housing advocates (who called themselves "housers")—a coalition comprised of social workers and "public housers." The former considered slum clearance necessary to improve the lives of those suffering under the substandard conditions of urban slums. The latter group, proponents of regional planning and modernist architecture, sought to replace urban blight with "vibrant, human-scale communities that combined the best physical and social features of town and country living."[30] They disliked slums, yet contended that wholesale slum clearance would exacerbate the existing shortage in housing stock. Rather, they supported the relocation of the poor to new public housing developments on the outskirts of town.[31] In an effort to create a national public housing program, the two factions reached a strategic compromise, adopting an antislum position closer to the public houser's stance—support for slum clearance based upon the practical reality that inner-city land would be too costly for redevelopment.[32] As noted above, the coalition was successful in achieving passage of the 1937 act, which created public housing. Its limitation to very-low- and low-income families—an attempt to protect private sector interests by conservative lawmakers—however, stunted a public sector housing production program aimed at meeting the needs of all Americans. This limitation had long-standing consequences. Increasingly today, moderate-income families are joining the ranks of the severely housing-burdened, with no form of available federal assistance to meet their needs.

During this time, support for urban redevelopment and slum clearance was steadily growing at the municipal level and in the private real estate and downtown business sectors as well. The migration of wealthier white urban residents to the suburbs during the 1920s, and the continued proliferation of slum conditions in urban centers, increasingly drew focus to the implications of urban blight and flight for cities' tax bases. These forces began to mobilize to preserve the economic health of American cities.[33] The National Association of Real Estate Boards (NAREB) in the mid-1930s led the charge to develop a national urban redevelopment strategy to combat blight and flight in an effort to maintain urban real estate values. Its approach, however, significantly omitted public housing from the plan.[34] In fact, NAREB lobbied extensively against the 1937 act's creation of the public housing program, which it viewed as the "opening wedge in an eventual takeover of the private housing industry by the government, and undermined the initiative and independence of American cities."[35]

Undoubtedly as a function of the broad yet inherently conflicted coalition, the controversial urban renewal program, born out of compromise, had both successes and failures. The program changed the face of many American cities for better and worse through its initial authorization of one billion dollars in loans and five hundred million dollars in capital grants over more than five years. This law also provided for the expansion of public housing, with authorization for 810,000 new units, but Congress never fully appropriated the funding. Title V addressed rural needs through the Farmers Home Administration, which even today provides housing for low- and moderate-income rural and small-town families. Acknowledging that rural areas were confronted with a scarcity of private credit for housing, Congress directly engaged the federal government through the extension of rural loans.

During the Korean War, Truman, himself a supporter of public housing, cut back on production at the outset, just after the bill became law, in order to conserve materials for the war effort. A strategic error, this gave anti-public-housing conservatives the momentum to significantly cut back on production. In 1950 anti-public-housing members seized on this opportunity, and Congress funded only 5,000 out of the possible 350,000 units called for by the law.[36] This false start set the tone for a history of insufficient housing production and subsequently inadequate design (including the lack of appropriate community facilities) to accomplish the bold aims of creating new viable communities. Despite the controversy surrounding the act, the law's lasting legacy is the legitimacy of the federal government's role in matters of local housing and community development programs.[37]

Truman's successor, President Dwight D. Eisenhower, created an Advisory Committee on Government Housing Policies and Programs to address criticisms of federal housing programs and a series of FHA scandals in the early 1950s. The committee's December report called for more of the same: aid to end city slums, the reconstruction of older urban communities, mortgages to help low-income and minority families with housing, a continuation of public housing, and the creation of a private secondary market mechanism.

The committee's recommendations resulted in the passage of the Housing Act of 1954 to meet the basic postwar housing needs of the American people. Modifying urban redevelopment by replacing it with the term "urban renewal," the act required communities engaged in such activities to adopt code enforcement, relocation, and other measures that would prevent the spread of urban blight. In so doing, the law further empowered local agencies and private developers to increase nonresidential development, while new FHA mortgage insurance programs increased capital for private construction in targeted areas.[38]

From 1949 through 1968, Congress approved 1,946 urban renewal projects in 912 communities.[39] The liberalization of development guidelines in the urban renewal program resulted in a net loss of residences in targeted areas, with often conspicuously profitable commercial buildings constructed where residential neighborhoods once stood (whether blighted or not). Widespread displacement of African American communities engendered criticism of the program's "Negro removal" policy. The inequitable distribution of resources caused the displacement of ethnic communities and historic neighborhoods in urban centers across the nation for the benefit of downtown commercial interests. More housing was demolished than built, contributing to the program's legacy of social inequity. Communities were uprooted to make way for office buildings, convention centers, and, often, vacant undeveloped lots.[40]

Additionally, under this law, FNMA ("Fannie Mae") was reorganized so that private money would gradually replace federal money in its capitalization and operation—which it did completely in 1968. In 1959 Eisenhower additionally expanded federal housing programs to include the special housing needs and interests of colleges and two new programs for the elderly.[41]

Just two weeks after he was inaugurated, President John F. Kennedy sent a special message to Congress on housing, urging action to expand credit, more aggressively pursue urban renewal, and meet the housing needs of the poor and people of color. In his first State of the Union Address in 1961, Kennedy declared, "Our national household is cluttered with unfinished and neglected tasks. Our cities are being engulfed in squalor. Twelve long years after Congress declared our goal to be 'a decent home and a suitable environment for every American family,' we still have 25 million Americans living in substandard homes."

Just a month later he sent a second housing message to Congress, setting forth the national objectives of providing decent housing for all Americans, a commitment to rebuild our cities, and a determination to maintain a robust housing industry as part of an overall sound economy. In response, the Housing Act of 1961 increased the federal share of spending on housing in smaller cities and broadened the FHA insurance programs to cover all low- and moderate-income condominiums.[42]

In short, Kennedy expanded the nation's and the government's commitment to housing and development by enlarging middle-class housing programs, adding programs to repair existing housing, and providing federal dollars to acquire land for parks, recreation, and future development. In his second message he also recommended the establishment of a new Department of Housing and Urban Development. Congress was, at the time, dominated by southern segregationist Democratic committee chairs and thus refused to act on such a proposal. In January 1962 the House Rules Committee blocked legislation creating a Department of Urban Affairs and Housing from reaching the floor for consideration. The president then offered a government reorganization plan, which was also rejected by the House. Not until after Kennedy was assassinated and President Lyndon Baines Johnson won a landslide election in 1964 was HUD created, in 1965.

During the early Johnson years, the Housing Act of 1964 liberalized FHA procedures to speed up the processing of FHA-insured mortgages, set up a low-interest housing rehabilitation loan program,[43] and expanded rural housing programs. The Housing and Urban Development Act of 1965 created a new rent supplement program to assist lower-income tenants, adding a new Section Twenty-three (the precurser to the current Section Eight program) to the U.S. Housing Act of 1937 authorizing the use of leased private housing in the public housing program. The act further established the cabinet-level Department of Housing and Urban Development (HUD), consolidating the Federal Housing Administration, Federal National Mortgage Association, Public Housing Administration, Urban Renewal Administration, and Community Facilities Administration under its roof. A related bill[44] established the Economic Development Administration in the Department of Commerce to provide support for job-creating programs in economically distressed areas.

The Demonstration Cities and Metropolitan Development Act of 1966 created the Model Cities Program, authorizing grants to plan and coordinate the physical and social development of entire neighborhoods. It used both public and private resources in comprehensive health, education, welfare, housing, and employment programs designed to revitalize whole communities within selected urban areas. It also provided financial incentives for coordinated metropolitan-area planning for open spaces, water supply, sewage disposal, and mass transit, and established a loan guarantee program to encourage the development of "new communities."

The Housing and Urban Development Act of 1968 proved to be the decade's most significant piece of housing legislation. Creating the Government National Mortgage Association (GNMA, or "Ginny Mae"), Congress transferred certain FHA mortgage functions from Fannie Mae (which has since provided more than one hundred billion dollars in mortgage-backed securities). The law also established new housing subsidy programs that reduced the cost of loans, liberalized FHA loan programs, extended guarantees and grants to developers, liberalized grants for public housing and for housing rehabilitation, and created a Section 236 rent subsidy program and a Section 235 subsidy program for homeownership. While the FHA programs contributed greatly to both increases in housing starts and improved housing quality (all FHA-insured homes met "quality assurance" standards), the FHA's underwriting practices in effect contributed to discriminatory housing trends, because they encouraged white flight to the suburbs and divestment from urban centers. Even more blatant was the FHA's endorsement of racially restrictive covenants through its official underwriting standards.[45]

In 1966 Dr. Martin Luther King, Jr., led open-housing marches in segregated Chicago. The Fair Housing Act, enacted as Title VIII of the Civil Rights Act of 1968, prohibited housing discrimination based upon race, color, religion, sex, or national origin.[46] The 1968 act was passed in the aftermath of Dr. King's assassination on April 4. As a tribute to him, it included the strongest provision to date for an open, fair, and nondiscriminatory national housing policy. Following Dr. King's assassination, urban rioting occurred in many American cities. The act came to be known as the "Rap Brown Act," due to the inclusion of an amendment sponsored by southern Democrats and conservative Republicans. This measure provided that any individual who crossed state lines to deliver a speech could be apprehended for inciting a riot if a riot subsequently ensued. Two young militant African American leaders, known then as H. Rap Brown and Stokely Carmichael, were the symbols and main targets of the bill.

In June 1967 President Lyndon B. Johnson appointed the President's Committee on Urban Housing, chaired by Edgar F. Kaiser, which issued a comprehensive report on national housing needs in 1969. The Kaiser Report's most notable recommendation called for the construction of twenty-six million new and rehabilitated homes over a ten-year period. In support of this recommendation the committee reported, "Attainment of this goal should eliminate the blight of substandard housing from the face of the nation's cities and should provide every American family with an affordable, decent home."[47]

Even in advance of the official recommendation, LBJ, in his 1968 State of the Union Address, challenged Congress and the country to raise their vision and reach for this new twenty-six-million-unit housing goal, including six million new homes for low- and moderate-income people, over ten years. Demonstrating true leadership by articulating this challenge, LBJ highlighted the fact that Congress had funded only three hundred thousand units for 1968 (three times the inadequate one hundred thousand units appropriated in 1967). He underscored the unfortunate reality that a mere 530,000 units of housing for low- and moderate-income people had been cumulatively developed over the previous decade. It was a huge challenge, but one that he courageously embraced.

After decades of enacting and implementing housing legislation, Congress passed the Housing and Urban Development Act of 1968, which set as a goal the Kaiser Commission's twenty-six million new and rehabilitated dwellings over ten years, of which six million were to be federally subsidized. Yet over the course of the intermittent thirty-one years, not once have we, as a nation, reached the 2.6-million mark, and only four times did housing starts exceed 2 million annually. (See the timeline on page 324.)

In 1970 Congress authorized the Home Loan Bank System to reduce interest rates on home mortgages by means of a federal subsidy. It also established mechanisms for a secondary market in conventional mortgages and created a special-interest subsidy program for low- and moderate-income housing.[48] The Housing and Urban Development Act of 1970 authorized greater outlays for housing subsidy programs and rent supplements to moderate-income households and created a Community Development Corporation to encourage the formation of "new towns" by guaranteeing bonds used to finance land acquisition and development.

Housing production peaked during the years of 1968 to 1972, thus making President Richard Nixon's 1973 moratorium on all federally subsidized housing programs all the more shocking. Nixon's abrupt freeze was implemented even over the objections of his own "production-minded" secretary of Housing and Urban Development, Michigan Governor George Romney.[49] In August of that year, Nixon shifted a majority of the federal government's subsidized housing funding to Section Twenty-three, subsidizing private landlords who rent to public housing tenants. Under the program, tenants paid 25 percent of their income for rent (currently, 30 percent and allowable up to 40 percent under certain circumstances), and the government subsidized the difference through a housing allowance. In the aftermath of Nixon's moratorium, subsequent administrations, both Republican and Democrat, have pursued the path of demand-side (in lieu of production supply-side) policies, effectively setting the stage for the affordable housing shortage today, as well as the devolution of responsibility for affordable housing production from the federal government to the state and local levels.[50]

As a case in point, the Housing and Community Development Act of 1974 essentially rewrote the 1937 Housing Act, converting the Section Twenty-three leased-housing program into Section Eight, which became the major national housing program in the 1970s and remains so today. Tenants now pay 30 percent of their income for rent, instead of 25 percent, with HUD paying the difference in the fair market value but with fair rent ceilings established to control costs. The Ford and Carter administrations nominally increased housing production under Section Eight's "New Construction and Rehabilitation" components until President Ronald Reagan's election in 1980. In 1983 Reagan repealed all production programs, leaving tenant-based rental assistance (in the forms of Section Eight certificates and vouchers) as the primary form of housing assistance[51]—action that essentially set the course for the present-day affordability crisis plaguing the nation.

Indeed, inadequate increases (relative to the overall need) in the numbers of Section Eight vouchers were the only housing appropriation "victories" won by a Clinton administration embattled by a Republican-led Congress following the 1994 midterm elections. The first budget to emerge from the current Bush administration, while cutting public housing capital funds to modernize and rehabilitate housing stock, authorizes increases in the numbers of Section Eight vouchers by thirty-four thousand at this writing. As noted above, if the market does not provide sufficient housing stock to absorb new vouchers, however, such authorizations do little to address the critical housing needs faced by low-income Americans. It is clear that this national housing policy revolves around economic incentives for the private owners of rental housing—the market—and the federal government's concern with fiscal austerity, rather than focusing primarily on providing decent, safe, sanitary, and affordable housing for all the American people.

In keeping with the states' rights emphasis of both Republican and Democratic conservatives, the 1974 act also converted former federal categorical housing programs into community development block grants to states, with broad goals as directives but local control of programs. In 1977 a new component, the Urban Development Action Grant (UDAG), was added to the community development block grants, and the Community Reinvestment Act (CRA) of 1977 was passed. UDAG, which has since been repealed, provided funding for specific projects in communities that met minimum standards of economic hardship or distress.

The CRA is a federal law requiring banks to use affirmative action in lending to "help meet the credit needs of their entire community, including low- and moderate-income neighborhoods." Banks that fail to do so can be denied permission by federal regulators to buy other banks, engage in interstate banking, and open or close branches. CRA does not direct banks to make specific loans. Instead, it gives them a broad, affirmative obligation to serve the needs of their community. It is the bank's prerogative to determine how to best do this. While discrimination in mortgage lending persists, the CRA has made great inroads in reversing historical discriminatory lending practices resulting from banks' redlining of entire communities based on their racial or ethnic compositions. The Financial Services Modernization Act,[52] passed in 1999, retained the CRA's mandate yet weakened its purview.

With national housing starts slowing to below one million and a dearth of multifamily development (319,000 units nationally) in 1981, Congress essentially created a tax shelter for development—which ultimately led to reckless private development, the savings and loan crisis, and the federal bailout required later that decade.[53] In the Tax Act of 1986

Congress passed and President Reagan signed into law the Low Income Housing Tax Credit (LIHTC), essentially a "tax block grant" to states, once again distancing the federal government from housing production for the poor. The program provides private investors with a lucrative subsidy to cover the costs of development (via a dollar-for-dollar credit against other tax liabilities—thus creating a market for syndication of tax credits and equity investments by large corporate interests)—a subsidy now administered by state housing agencies. The LIHTC is allocated to states on a per capita basis (initially $1.25 per person, increased to $1.50 in 2001 and authorized to increase to $1.75 by 2002). The LIHTC—a program that, in effect, rewards corporate interests with "windfall" profit margins (thus rendering it inefficient according to conservative market-oriented analysis)—is now the primary housing production program in the nation, having financed more than one million units from 1987 to 1998.[54]

To qualify for tax credit awards, developers have the choice of developing either 20 percent of the units to house the "very low income" (below 50 percent of area median income) or 40 percent to meet the needs of relatively better-off low-income families (below 60 percent of area median income). Most developers select the latter, resulting in almost all developments being occupied by families at or below 60 percent. As a result, the LIHTC has failed as a program to meet the critical housing needs of families at the lowest income levels. In order to meet the housing needs of the working poor, LIHTC equity must be one source of funding among many others—a task often relegated to nonprofit community development corporations (CDCs), which are committed through their missions to serving low-income Americans.[55]

States are required to set aside at least 10 percent of tax credit allocations for nonprofit developers. CDCs (themselves usually strapped for cash and operating income) have been successful with the assistance of complicated (euphemistically called "creative") financing strategies. CDCs find it necessary to layer HUD's CDBG and HOME funds with foundation grants and other mechanisms for "gap financing," including loans or grants from foundations, financial intermediaries, or Community Development Financial Institutions (CDFIs), to meet their development costs. CDFIs' and CDCs' proven capacities to successfully finance and develop housing at levels untouched by private sector bottom-line financial analysis presents a moral and practical imperative to increase both the capacity of nonprofit organizations and the federal resources available to them and others to perform this public function that market forces will not.

During the first two years of President Bill Clinton's administration, a Democratic controlled yet increasingly conservative and centrist Congress defeated Clinton's major public investment programs. The 1994 midterm elections yielded a staunchly conservative Congress, with the House of Representatives led by Speaker Newt Gingrich of Georgia—a congressional majority convinced (however incorrectly) of its mandate to reverse thirty years of civil rights gains and the general legitimacy of the federal role in meeting the nation's needs. Reflecting this shift in the political winds, Clinton, in his 1996 State of the Union Address, declared that the "era of big government is over."[56]

Significantly, President Clinton never mentioned the genuine housing needs of the American people in either of his two inaugural addresses or any of his State of the Union speeches. In contrast to Democratic Presidents Roosevelt, Truman, Kennedy, and Johnson, Clinton's only references to housing centered on fair housing, his effort to "reinvent" the government, which he said would cut sixty public housing programs down to three, and praise for the work of Habitat for Humanity, a voluntary housing program. While Habitat is a worthy endeavor and everyone, conservatives, moderates, and liberals alike, can support such voluntary efforts, it can only aid—never meet—the nation's substantial housing needs. Only a comprehensive federal strategy matching the magnitude of the problem can accomplish this public goal.

Of Clinton's major presidential addresses, only one, his 1999 State of the Union Address, addressed housing in any significant manner. This centrist message from a Democratic president marked a true shift in national priorities vis-à-vis housing and community development:

> We must do more to bring the spark of private enterprise to every corner of America —to build a bridge from Wall Street to Appalachia to the Mississippi Delta, to our Native American communities—with more support for community development banks, for empowerment zones, for 100,000 more vouchers for affordable housing. And I ask Congress to support our bold new plan to help businesses raise up to $15 billion in private sector capital to bring jobs and opportunities to our inner cities and rural areas—with tax credits, loan guarantees, including the new American Private Investment Company, modeled on the Overseas Private Investment Company.

On its own, this strategy for growth represented a DLC, Blue Dog, New Democrat, corporate-based, private–public partnership, "we the market" approach, rather than a progressive, citizen-oriented, democratic-based, public–private partnership, "we the people" approach. History tells us that such a market-driven plan cannot operate in a vacuum. Without direct and adequate levels of investment in the real causes of the affordable housing gap and lagging economic development in impacted areas, this hit-or-miss private sector strategy, on its own, cannot be expected to meet the needs of all Americans.

It was in this political context that HUD Secretary Henry Cisneros, in an effort to prevent the conservative Congress from eliminating HUD altogether, reported his "Reinvention Blueprint" to Congress in 1995—a plan that proposed to downsize the agency, end project-based Section Eight housing in favor of portable vouchers, and continue the practice of flexible block grants to states and localities.[57] With the assistance of fifty million dollars in HOPE VI demolition and redevelopment grants, the administration charged local housing authorities with demolishing one hundred thousand of the "worst public housing developments." The plan called for the demolition of severely distressed housing developments and their replacement with smaller scattered site structures, as well as for an income mix among residents. While most housing authorities had, over the years, been well managed and maintained, a small but very visible minority of public housing projects had spiraled downward into what Cisneros and the nation identified as "islands of despair and poverty."[58] This circumstance was due, in large part, to congressional sabotage at the outset of the program's design and decades of federal underfunding, which necessarily resulted in deferred maintenance. Indeed, by the early limitations on public housing—it could serve only the very low income (over the protests of the "houser" reform movement)—Congress guaranteed that tenant income would never be sufficient to support the operating needs of large urban developments. Furthermore, by placing control over siting decisions with local governments (particularly suburban officials), and providing funding that could cover only rudimentary boxlike construction, Congress guaranteed that these public housing developments became racially segregated and stigmatized as "housing of last resort."[59]

The 1994 Republican Congress made further attempts to weaken the federal obligation for subsidized housing. For instance, former conservative Representative Bill McCollum (R-FL), in an effort to devolve powers to states and localities, introduced legislation that affirmed the right of states to set reasonable occupancy standards for assisted units.[60] To make matters worse, McCollum also attempted to strip the Justice Department of its ability to pursue cases of lending discrimination through the established tool of proving that an offender engaged in a "pattern and practice" of discrimination. Rather, McCollum sought to raise the standard of proof in court to require that injured parties prove affirmative discriminatory "intent" (and of course it is very difficult to prove what is in someone's mind), rather than a discriminatory "effect" (proof that is based in fact). This attempt to eliminate the use of the "disparate impact" theory of civil rights law (that a lender's actions disparately impact members of a protected class) would have increased both the level of difficulty in and cost of successfully prosecuting such illegal action. In practice, this measure would have made enforcement of housing discrimination laws much less effective.

The devolution of housing programs to the local level is detrimental on two fronts. First and foremost, of course, is the reality that only a large-scale and comprehensive federal solution can accomplish the goal of adequately housing all Americans. Additionally, however, we know that local governments often work against providing housing for all of their citizens, rather than working toward this end. Counties and local municipalities often permit exclusionary zoning practices that prevent inexpensive multifamily housing units from being built. The forces of NIMBYism (as in, "not-in-my-backyard") fill local political coffers with campaign contributions, thus exerting political influence against which low- and moderate-income people cannot compete. Local governments sometimes initiate strict building-code enforcement campaigns that prevent homeless shelters, single-room occupancy (SRO) structures, and affordable multifamily developments from locating in urban centers.

As such, those with the greatest need are isolated from the employment and supportive service facilities that could enable them to improve their quality of life. Occasionally, costly rent inspections, subjective interpretations of requirements, and impossibly expensive rehabilitation requirements preclude the efficient preservation of century-old housing. Antivagrancy laws often remove the homeless from view by pushing them out of lucrative sites where out-of-town visitors spend money. Yet cities have failed to provide those displaced with opportunities for decent permanent shelter.

In 1998 a Republican Congress–crafted public housing reform bill compounded the housing problems confronted by low-income Americans by changing so-called targeting requirements for public housing residents in favor of creating mixed-income communities. While a laudable goal in principle, and consistent with the original aims of early-twentieth-century reformers, the legislative changes did not address, in reality, the great numbers of very-low-income people who suffer in the law's hands. The so-called solution of vouchering out residents displaced by demolished units (or expiring project-based Section Eight apartment complexes) means nothing in high-rent markets (like my hometown, Chicago) where Section Eight voucher holders find safe, sanitary, and affordable housing nearly impossible to secure. In a condescending swipe, the 105th Congress instituted a provision that I likened to "involuntary servitude" during the floor debate on the bill. The law essentially required public housing authorities to require residents, as a condition of their lease, to engage in community service activities (a personal commitment ordinarily associated with volunteerism—by definition a free choice). Given the legislative practices over the course of the program's history, it should come as no surprise that no additional funding was associated with this program—the imposition of an "unfunded mandate" on public housing authorities by a party whose "Contract with America" demonized such federal actions.

While the Republican Congress was all too willing to impose the oxymoron of forced volunteerism on poor people who receive housing subsidies, the vast majority of housing subsidy recipients continue to exercise their free will in such personal matters. Relative to the numbers of Americans who receive housing subsidies, the poor comprise a small minority. In point of fact, the mortgage interest and real estate tax deductions cost the federal government $58 billion—twice the amount that the government spends on all of HUD's direct housing subsidies.[61] Roughly half the mortgage interest subsidy benefits the top 5.6 percent of all taxpayers (or those earning more than one hundred thousand dollars annually).[62] The larger the home, the larger the mortgage, the greater the tax deduction. This is a regressive tax benefit that lower- and moderate-income homeowners cannot access, because they rarely itemize their deductions (which are generally lower than the standard deduction).[63] Despite the political rhetoric to the contrary, the Treasury Department—not HUD—is the largest government housing subsidy agency.

Thirty-two years after the Kaiser Commission Report the U.S. population, in this new millennium, has grown significantly, and our existing housing stock is older and in dire need of repair. The reality is that our nation's housing needs are even greater today than they were in 1968. The affordable housing gap in rental units exemplifies the magnitude of our challenge. In 1970, 6.5 million low-cost units exceeded the 6.2 million low-income renters, a temporary surplus of 300,000 units. Decades of failure to implement an adequate federal production program have resulted in an enormous shortfall. Just eight years after Nixon's moratorium, in 1978, 7.4 million renters competed for 5.7 million units—a 1.7-million-unit shortage. By 1995 the gap had widened to 4.4 million, with 10.5 million low-income renters and 6.1 million affordable units.[64] According to a 1999 HUD report,[65] at least 4.9 million households still pay more than half of their incomes for rent and/or live in severely substandard homes—conditions HUD deems "worst case housing needs." This reverses an upward spiral over the previous ten years.

Even as the nation's housing crisis has grown exponentially, federal housing funds have not kept pace with the magnitude of the burgeoning need. In the name of deficit and debt reduction, programs for poor and working-class Americans have been woefully underfunded, while the vast majority of housing subsidies instead inure to the benefit of middle and primarily upper-income families in the form of tax deductions. On the tenth anniversary of the Stewart B. McKinney Homeless Assistance Act, a coalition of six national homelessness advocacy groups pointed out that, in 1992, candidate Bill Clinton pledged to convene a White House conference on homelessness as part of an overall plan to combat the growing problem of American homelessness.[66] To their dismay, however, this forum was never held. Homelessness is usually temporary and seldom a permanent status. Yet, as the advocates noted, "on any given night, at least 775,000 Americans have nowhere to call home." The groups cited two simultaneous trends as the overarching culprits—the growing shortage in affordable rental units and a concomitant increase in poverty.[67]

Poverty and homelessness are inextricably linked. Between 1985 and 1990, 5.7 million Americans found themselves without a home, reduced to finding shelter in bus stations, parks, emergency homeless shelters, and vacant buildings. At one time or another in their lives, 13.5 million Americans have reported being in this predicament.[68] The National Coalition for the Homeless (NCH) reports that the number of poor people in the United States increased by almost 26 percent (from 25.4 million to 31.9 million) during the years of 1970 and 1988.[69] By 1996, 36.5 million Americans lived in poverty, with the numbers living in extreme poverty proliferating. In fact, by 1996, 14.4 million people—essentially two-fifths of all poor people—had incomes less than half the poverty level, an increase of 500,000 in just one year, from 1995. Forty percent of those below the poverty line are children, with 1996 data casting the children's poverty rate at twice that of any other age group. Despite these desperate circumstances, 1996 was the year that the Clinton administration and a Republican Congress pulled the sixty-year-old floor out from under America's neediest families, with the repeal of Aid to Families with Dependent Children and a five-year lifetime limit on its economic safety net.

In response to the claims of virulent anti-federal-government crusaders and rigid free traders, the NCH underscores the dire consequences of policies driven by blind market forces:

> Two factors help account for increasing poverty: eroding labor market opportunities for large segments of the workforce, and the declining value and availability of . . . public assistance. . . . Until its repeal in August 1996, the largest cash assistance program for poor families with children was AFDC. . . . Between 1970 and 1994, the typical state's AFDC benefits for a family of three fell 47%, after adjusting for inflation. The Personal Responsibility and Work Opportunity Reconciliation Act of 1996 repealed the AFDC program and replaced it with a state block grant program called Temporary Assistance to Needy Families (TANF). Current TANF benefits are below the poverty level in every state, and in most states they are below 75% of the poverty level.[70]

Contrary to popular opinion, when the federal government is not committed to satisfactorily providing jobs, health care, housing, and education for all Americans, welfare does not provide relief from poverty either. If we are to resolve these issues, bold federal action is essential.

Since Nixon's moratorium in 1973, all subsequent administrations, have, in one form or another, replaced federal housing production programs with market-driven "solutions." Their differences spanned the spectrum, from rhetorical harshness and mean-spiritedness to political accommodation, with the end result being our current crisis state. During the last decade, and mostly during the Clinton years (in a political tug-of-war with a hostile Republican Congress), funding for HUD—the main source of funds for alleviating the housing crisis—was cut by 61 percent, more than any other domestic budget in the same period. The 2000 HUD budget of $28.5 billion met the needs of only one-third of the twelve million low-income families eligible to receive federal housing subsidies. Thus, two out of every three poor renters receive no housing assistance, with roughly two million low-income households serving desperate time on overcrowded waiting lists. As predicted by the Center for Budget and Policy Priorities, Congress has made it even more difficult for poor families to access the limited supply of public or assisted housing.[71] New Section Eight housing vouchers were increased by a mere 50,000 in 1999, 60,000 in 2000, 120,000 in the 2001 budget, and are scheduled to go back down to 34,000 in Bush's fiscal year 2002 budget, with record numbers of private landlords abandoning federal subsidy programs in search of higher market rents.

Preservation of existing affordable housing stock currently poses a significant challenge, in light of the fact that two-thirds of all project-based Section Eight units—fourteen thousand properties and one million apartments—are set to expire in the next few years. Forty-four states thus stand to lose more than half the affordable units subsidized through Section Eight. While the government promises that "portable" rental vouchers (which travel with the tenant) will mitigate this loss, these vouchers may, in certain circumstances, force tenants to pay up to 40 percent of their income in rent. To make matters worse, the housing markets in many of these communities are either so tight that renters are priced out, and/or highly saturated with Section Eight renters, creating new concentrations of poverty. Such are the challenges faced not only in urban centers, but also in older "inner-ring" suburbs, like the south suburban Chicago neighborhoods in my district. With once healthy industrial employment opportunities and supportive tax bases long gone, voucher holders have begun to overwhelm these financially strapped communities, far from access to jobs, which cannot provide the kind of services necessary to support such lower-income families.

In the past six years alone, homeownership has grown by roughly seven million, to around 66.8 percent, the highest in history. While hailed as an accomplishment, this figure does not truly reflect the fact that, relative to the 1980s, homeownership has actually decreased for families under fifty-five years of age. Young families, and particularly those in higher-cost urban centers, find it nearly impossible to accumulate enough equity to make a down payment on their first home. The disparity in homeownership rates between whites and people of color remains wide, yet is narrowing due to CRA enforcement and affirmative outreach efforts by Fannie Mae and Freddie Mac.

These record numbers, however, mask the fact that among homeowners, far too many are relegating far too much of their income to mortgage payments. Household debt, particularly among families earning less than fifty thousand dollars, has reached unprecedented levels.[72] Racial segregation has hardly changed in the thirty years. Poor African Americans and Latinos are more likely to live in high-poverty census tracts than are poor whites, and middle-income African Americans are more likely to live in segregated neighborhoods than are middle-income whites.[73]

While people of color are generally more likely to be housing-burdened, the challenges faced by Native Americans are rarely noted. Native Americans are nearly twice as likely as the population at large to suffer substandard housing conditions. In fact, 28 percent of Native Americans residing on tribal lands live without complete kitchen or plumbing facilities, or in overcrowded dwellings.[74]

A large majority of the new homeowners bolstering the national record live outside city limits—a noteworthy point, because it underscores the highbrow DLC, Blue Dog, suburban, and top-down political constituency of these groups. Their point of reference starts with the greediest and moves to the neediest, rather than looking from the bottom up. In other words, our current crisis is due to a lack of focus on how to convert America's real housing needs into a bold new comprehensive federal policy, with a plan to achieve and programs to meet the material needs of *all Americans*.

Centrists and conservatives demonized what they call the welfare state for poor Americans, hailing the termination or privatization of public benefits, for the good of the poor, as a panacea. But we have yet to hear the resounding call to terminate the panoply of middle- and upper-class "welfare state" programs such as homeownership tax deductions, VA- and FHA-insured loans, Social Security, Medicare, federal funds for highways, airports, and clean air and water. These programs are properly viewed as supporting basic needs of the American people—and federal investment in these necessities of a civilized society forms the basis of our social contract. If conservatives really want to significantly cut federal spending and be fiscally responsible, cuts in corporate welfare benefits are where they can achieve big savings. We know that this won't happen, of course, because the special interests that actively vote, lobby, and invest in campaign contributions are well represented by elected officials who are accountable to their interests.

The overarching challenge facing policymakers in the housing arena today is how to meet the affordability gap that threatens the viability of our future economic health as a nation. Only the federal government has the resources and ability to match the magnitude of this crisis. The stakes are simply too high to replicate the flawed incremental strategies of the past employed for the sake of political convenience and comfort. It is incumbent upon our national leaders to once and for all seize the reins of the power invested in them by their constituents, and achieve the vision so eloquently articulated by FDR more than half a century ago. Rather than quibbling over the minutiae of an anemic HUD budget, it's time to implement and invest in a bold and comprehensive federal policy that targets the real housing needs of all Americans. We have the resources and the technical capacity to do so. For the good of the nation and future generations, we must now make the commitment.

In essence, it is the gap between household incomes and housing expenses that must be closed. Rather than relying solely on private sector mechanisms to meet our public goal, the federal government must craft an approach that recognizes the necessity of bolstering a public–private partnership, matching new and increased levels of direct public investment with the operations of a primarily private (for-profit and nonprofit) housing industry. Housing is, admittedly, a complicated area, yet we know which approaches work and which don't, based on decades of empirical evidence.

First and foremost, the acknowledgment of housing as a constitutional right, and not a privilege, compels us to create a universal allowance for housing, whereby each eligible family is entitled to assistance. Rather than public or assisted housing continuing as a "lottery for the lucky few,"[75] rental assistance must be made available for all families that meet the federal guidelines. Furthermore, working families should not be made to suffer the indignities of forgoing food, medicine, and clothing for their children to cover excessive rent or mortgage payments. Housing assistance must be targeted as well to the growing numbers of low- and moderate-income working families that find themselves in the unfortunate circumstance of being too well off to avail themselves of assisted housing, and yet too income-poor to take advantage of tax benefits. Down-payment assistance, homeownership vouchers, and deeper-reaching tax benefits must be enacted so that the working poor can live affordably, without paying too much of their income for housing at the expense of material necessities.

We know, however, that providing vouchers in oversaturated high-cost markets does as much good as doing nothing at all. Thus, a truly effective federal approach would target such subsidies to those markets where the housing stock exists yet is out of reach to low- and moderate-income people. Communities facing shortages can only be served by direct federal investment and tax incentives, which are aimed at increasing the production of housing affordable at below-market levels. Nonprofit CDCs and for-profit developers, labor union collectives, and employer-assisted housing all require deeper subsidies to meet the growing need. The AFL-CIO's Housing Investment Trust (HIT) has, since 1981, invested three billion dollars in pension funds to create rental and homeownership units. In 1995 alone, HIT invested close to five hundred million dollars to build forty-five hundred units.[77] However, with six million working-class families paying more than 50 percent of their income for housing, deeper federal subsidies are necessary to match the magnitude of the problem.

Tax incentives should be targeted toward those who, absent government intervention, cannot make ends meet. The Earned Income Tax Credit should be increased at the federal and state levels to assist families in markets where housing prices have outpaced growth in wages.[78] Additionally, so long as preferential tax treatment remains an "entitlement" for middle- and upper-income Americans, equity demands that lower- and moderate-income Americans also be able to access favorable tax treatment. A new progressive refundable tax credit for first-time home purchases would enable these families to build equity and accumulate wealth.[79] Fannie Mae, Freddie Mac, and the FHA can help build a whole new class of homeowners through less rigid underwriting standards and supporting limited-equity cooperatives, among other mechanisms.[80]

The federal government also has the ability to deter localities from preventing affordable housing development with "snob-zoning" ordinances by rewarding inclusionary zoning plans with increased federal subsidies. The same incentives should apply to restrictive building codes and other local regulatory barriers to affordable housing development.

All housing markets are different, characterized by vastly disparate forms of housing stock and unique market needs. It is an often cited refrain that only localities, not a distant federal bureaucracy, are familiar with the unique characteristics and needs of their own communities. While this is, of course, true when it comes to knowing the particulars of a given housing market, it does not justify devolving the obligation and commitment for meeting the nation's challenge to states and local governments (a dynamic generally accompanied by decreasing levels of subsidy). Rather, it is the differential in local housing needs that justifies the adoption of a comprehensive federal plan (and adequate level of federal investment), which is targeted to meet those needs.

Clearly, housing programs are not one-size-fits-all. Rather, a program where federal investments truly meet the specific needs of qualified communities is a much more efficient approach. As noted above, high-cost markets that cannot absorb housing vouchers would be better served by increased production-oriented subsidies. Older communities confronting dilapidated and substandard housing stock would benefit from increased dollars for preservation and rehabilitation. A comprehensive federal plan to address the magnitude of America's housing crisis must be flexible enough to serve the specific needs of communities, while at the same time targeted enough to fully fund the variety of issues facing individual communities. The elevation of affordable housing to its proper place on the list of national priorities would necessarily benefit all participants in the housing sector and Americans at all income levels. And a "right to affordable housing" constitutional amendment would help, in Dr. King's words, "speed up the day."

The American people intuitively know that the private sector and state governments, as separate and uncoordinated entities, are not equipped to guarantee their economic security and basic material needs of employment, health care, housing, and education. Thus, when federal elected officials devolve responsibility for virtually everything that is materially important to private sector entities, the states, and volunteers, it is inevitable that the people will lose faith in the abilities of the federal government. If the leaders of the federal government don't want or expect the federal government to forge solutions to the American people's very real problems, how can we expect our participatory democracy to flourish?

The federal government's failure to address the concrete needs of the American people is contributing to low voter turnout. The loss of faith in the federal government's role—or as Ronald Reagan often stated, seeing the government as "the enemy of the people, the problem and not the solution"—represents a philosophy that is deeply rooted in the nation's racial history and culture, indeed, the politics of states' rights. Armed with this insight, it is much easier to understand how and why conservative politicians can play the race card in the economic class game. It is precisely because it engenders division and distrust among the people with regard to their federal government. In this fashion, they successfully maintain the economic and racial status quo that ultimately serves the special interests of an economic elite.

Americans remain loyal to the highest ideals expressed in our founding legal documents and democratic institutions, and thus have not lost hope. The American people believe that they do indeed deserve better leadership and service from their federal government. We can achieve this, but we must first respect ourselves enough to demand it. We must then be committed enough to organize politically, and with vigilance and steady focus, work toward our goals. In so doing, we will keep the democratic spirit alive and create a truly representative federal government that is responsive and accountable to all of its citizens. If we do, we can, among other things, achieve decent, safe, sanitary, and affordable housing for all Americans.

NEW HOUSING STARTS

More than three decades after the 1969 Kaiser Commission's call for 2.6 million housing starts per year, the country has reached a mere 2 million new housing starts in only four of the intervening thirty-one years—1971, 2.052; 1972, 2.357; 1973, 2.045; 1978, 2.020. Never have we even come close to reaching the 2.6-million-unit goal. At the time of this writing, we are averaging less than 1.7 million new housing starts per year—at a time when they say the economy is booming. The timeline below traces (in thousands) America's economic history and tracks the implications of major events and federal housing.[81]

Benjamin Harrison (R)

1889	342
1890	328
1891	298
1892	381

Grover Cleveland (D)

1893	267
1894	265
1895	309
1896	257

William McKinley (R)

1897	292
1898	262
1899	282
1900	189
1901	275
1902	240
1903	253
1904	315

Theodore Roosevelt (R)

1905	507
1906	487
1907	432
1908	416

William Howard Taft (R)

1909	492
1910	387
1911	395
1912	426

Woodrow Wilson (D)

1913	421	
1914	421	World War I
1915	433	World War I
1916	437	World War I
1917	240	World War I
1918	118	World War I
1919	315	
1920	247	

Warren G. Harding (R)

1921	449	"Roaring Twenties"
1922	716	
1923	871	
1924	893	

Calvin Coolidge (R)

1925	937
1926	849
1927	810
1928	753

Herbert Hoover (R)

1929	509	stock market collapse
1930	330	
1931	254	
1932	134	

Franklin D. Roosevelt (D)

1933	93	
1934	126	
1935	221	
1936	319	
1937	336	
1938	406	
1939	515	
1940	603	
1941	706	World War II begins
1942	356	World War II
1943	191	World War II
1944	142	World War II
1945	326	World War II ends; 1945 Housing Act sets 12-million-unit (1.2 million per year) 10-year housing goal

Harry S. Truman (D)

1946	1.023	
1947	1.268	
1948	1.362	
1949	1.466	
1950	1.952	
1951	1.491	Korean War
1952	1.504	Korean War

Dwight D. Eisenhower (R)

1953	1.438	Korean War
1954	1.551	
1955	1.646	
1956	1.349	
1957	1.224	
1958	1.382	
1959	1.531	
1959	1.554*	

John F. Kennedy (D)

1960	1.274	
1960	1.296*	

1961	1.337
1961	1.365*
1962	1.469
1962	1.492*
1963	1.635*

Lyndon B. Johnson (D)

1964	1.561*	
1965	1.510*	Vietnam War
1966	1.196*	Vietnam War
1967	1.322*	Vietnam War
1968	1.545*	Vietnam War; Kaiser Commission sets 26-million-unit (2.6 million per year) 10-year housing goal

Richard M. Nixon (R)

1969	1.500*	Vietnam War
1970	1.434	Vietnam War
1970	1.469*	
1971	2.052	Vietnam War; rising unemployment; Nixon jawbones Fed for lower interest rates; in August he imposes wage and price controls
1972	2.357	Vietnam War
1973	2.045	Vietnam War ends; Nixon imposes a federal housing moratorium
1974	1.338	

Gerald R. Ford (R)

1975	1.160
1976	1.538

James "Jimmy" E. Carter (D)

1977	1.987
1978	2.020
1979	1.745
1980	1.292

Ronald W. Reagan (R)

1981	1.084
1982	1.062
1983	1.703
1984	1.750
1985	1.742
1986	1.805
1987	1.620
1988	1.488

George H. W. Bush (R)

1989	1.378
1990	1.193
1991	1.014
1992	1.200

William "Bill" J. Clinton (D)

1993	1.288
1994	1.457
1995	1.354
1996	1.477
1997	1.474
1998	1.617
1999	1.666

*Includes farm housing.

A MORE PERFECT UNION—
A QUALITY PUBLIC EDUCATION

It is an axiom in political science that unless a people are educated and enlightened it is idle to expect the continuance of civil liberty or the capacity for self-government.

—Texas Declaration of Independence, March 2, 1836

Let the children of the rich and poor take their seats together and know of no distinction save that of industry, good conduct, and intellect.

—Townsend Harris, New York City Board of Education, 1840s

The right to an education is not guaranteed, either explicitly or implicitly, by the Constitution, and therefore could not constitute a fundamental right.

—U.S. District Judge Michael P. McCuskey
Decatur Illinois School Board Ruling, January 11, 2000

Reading is a new civil right.

—Governor George W. Bush, Republican presidential nominee
Philadelphia, Pennsylvania, August 3, 2000

1. Everyone has the right to education. Education shall be free, at least in the elementary and fundamental stages. Elementary education shall be compulsory. Technical and professional education shall be made generally available and higher education shall be equally accessible to all on the basis of merit.
2. Education shall be directed to the full development of the human personality and to the strengthening of respect for human rights and fundamental freedoms. It shall promote understanding, tolerance and friendship among all nations, racial or religious groups, and shall further the activities of the United Nations for the maintenance of peace.
3. Parents have a prior right to choose the kind of education that shall be given to their children.

—United Nations Universal Declaration of Human Rights
Article Twenty-six

PROPOSED EDUCATION AMENDMENT
TO THE U.S. CONSTITUTION

Section 1. All citizens of the United States shall enjoy the right to a public education of equal high quality.

Section 2. The Congress shall have power to implement this article by appropriate legislation.

Rightly or wrongly, many Americans believe they have a *constitutional* right to protect their family with a gun. But Illinois U.S. District Judge Michael P. McCuskey said it as plainly as it can be said. In the United States, American citizens have no constitutional right to protect their family with an education. Can there be any greater irony of misunderstood, misplaced, or missing priorities in the Constitution?

If the American people were polled and asked: "Which one of the following do you think would provide your family with greater security and protection—an education, or a gun?" I think it would be nearly unanimous that the American people would reply, "An education." If that is the priority of the American people—and I believe it is—then we should have the wisdom and political will to codify it in the form of a constitutional amendment that guarantees every American citizen the legal right to a public education of equal high quality.

What the 2000 presidential election revealed, if it revealed nothing else, is that the candidates offered the people from Virginia to Texas, and in other rural and small communities throughout the United States, no constitutional amendment to provide a high-quality public education for their children that could occupy a greater place in their hearts and minds than their perceived Second Amendment right to a gun. The right to a gun claimed a higher political allegiance than fixing their children's broken public school system.

I believe Americans should still have the right to pursue a private education of whatever quality or orientation they desire or is available in the "education market"—and pay for it with their own private funds, even as their fair share of taxes continue to support a public education system. But since more than 90 percent of Americans get their elementary and secondary education in public schools—and if they were of a higher quality, the percentage would be even higher—that is where public policy and a constitutional amendment should be focused. Public education is what my constitutional amendment addresses.

If we created a public school system of equal high quality, we would turn the conservatives' "competition" argument on its head. Yes, competition would improve all education in the United States. But with this amendment the real competition would be among the public schools to reach, maintain, and even improve on the standard of "equal high quality." Then it would be the private and parochial schools that would have to vastly improve in order to attract students away from the public schools—and get parents to spend additional private money to pay for it.

Why would that be the case? Because of the standard proposed in the new constitutional amendment. It's not a low, minimalist, mediocre, or "rush to the bottom" standard. It's a high maximum constitutional standard—of equal high quality. The competition would always be upward! The amendment would challenge and pull America toward achieving the highest standard of educational excellence that we are capable of producing at any given time. It's a standard and a reach for educational excellence that we don't presently have in our public schools—and can't have without this new constitutional amendment.

For a great nation, when it comes to excellence in public education, we sometimes have a beggar's mentality. On Friday, June 16, 2000, President Clinton and entertainer Billy Joel were guests of Matt Lauer on NBC-TV's *Today Show*. The setting was P.S. 96 in East Harlem. All week the show had been leading a campaign to acquire voluntarily donated musical instruments from the public. The show assumed responsibility for having them placed in the public schools. Over the week they had received about five hundred instruments.

The music video television network VH-1 had meantime initiated a national effort by donating five million dollars, including one million dollars to the New York public school system, of which P.S. 96 received twenty-five thousand dollars. All of those involved had every right to be proud of their efforts. But is this any way to systematically educate America's children for the challenges before them in the twenty-first century—plugging holes through public appeals and voluntary sporadic contributions?

The *Today Show's* news "hook" of voluntary donations of instruments was also a way for the show to focus on the importance and need for music education in the public schools. Over the last two decades, music education had been taken out of the curriculum of an increasing number of public schools. Only about 25 percent of the public schools in America now offer music education as a basic course. Music has joined art, physical education, and extracurricular activities on the fiscal chopping block of American education.

When public schools cut music, art, physical education, and extracurricular activities, or have an inferior system or poor physical facilities, where can these students or their parents seek relief? They can't appeal to a constitutional amendment that tells them they have the right to an equal high-quality public education. The only avenue currently open to them is legislative or executive action, but increasingly the American people are losing faith and turning away from these political avenues. And current law provides them with a hard road in the courts with little hope of improvement during the educational life of a student.

In some cases when there are enormous differences in educational expenditures and the quality of education between counties and school districts within a state, lawyers have gone to court—in Kentucky, Texas, New Jersey, Illinois, New York, and elsewhere—and argued circuitously for "equal educational protection" under a state constitution. In some instances victories in the courts led to improvements. In others, like Illinois, they didn't. Even though such a court case was won in Illinois, and the state constitution says, "A fundamental goal of the People of the State is the educational development of all persons to the limits of their capacities. . . . The State has the primary responsibility for financing the system of public education," the court refused to enforce the court's finding of discrimination by making the state legislature come up with an equitable funding formula. Mostly, inequality and mediocrity in our public schools continue, and will continue. These court decisions have not spoken (and cannot speak) to a common national standard of equal high quality among counties and districts, and among the states, because their is no federal constitutional basis for doing so.

Illinois Federal District Judge McCuskey, in the Decatur Illinois School Board case cited at the beginning of this chapter, was unambiguous and unequivocal in his ruling. The U.S. Constitution contains no fundamental right to a public education, and therefore America's parents and children cannot legally appeal to a national educational standard, that is, "a right to a public education of equal high quality." Substantial legal relief is not possible. And given the current conservative political orientation of both parties and the conservative political climate in the country, positive change coming from the federal legislative or executive branches will be extremely difficult to achieve. With few legal court levers, and unresponsive legislative and executive branches, there appears to be little chance of significant change or relief in sight. Admittedly, while the current Supreme Court is also very conservative and could potentially interpret my amendment narrowly—all Supreme Court interpretations reflect the Court's current legal orientation and politics—the Court's reasoning would still have to come to grips with each of those concepts, "a right" "to an equal" "high-quality" "public education." Just as a conservative Court rendered a narrow interpretation of the Fourteenth Amendment in *Plessy v. Ferguson* in 1896, fifty-eight years later the Court in *Brown* brought forth a broader interpretation. The more liberal interpretation of *Brown*, however, would not have been possible without the Fourteenth Amendment. So just as a conservative Supreme Court might render a conservative interpretation of my amendment today, a liberal Court could later interpret it more broadly. The central point is that every parent and child in the future would have greater federal legal protection and, therefore, a better chance for a good education with my amendment than without it.

According to the American Society of Civil Engineers, "One-third of all schools need extensive repair or replacement. Nearly 60 percent of schools have at least one major building problem, and more than half have inadequate environmental conditions. Forty-six percent lack basic wiring to support computer systems. It will cost about $112 billion to repair, renovate and modernize our schools. Another $60 billion in new construction is needed to accommodate the 3 million new students expected in the next decade."[1]

The U.S. Department of Education said recently that just to bring the physical infrastructure of the nation's public schools to a reasonable level, the nation should spend $127 billion more than it intends to spend over the next ten years. That does not include costs for smaller class sizes, increased teachers' pay, or improving the curriculum, including putting art, music, physical education, and extracurricular activities back into our public schools. That amount is needed just to build new schools and repair old ones. The National Educational Association (NEA) put the cost of these same basic physical infrastructure needs at $322 billion. In 1998, a Republican-led Congress refused to pass Senator Carol Moseley Braun's mere five-billion-dollar bill for this purpose. That's about the level of legislative remedy we can currently expect from conservatives, whether Republicans or Democrats. And without a constitutional amendment, even if we did get a progressive Congress or president or both, the next conservative Congress and president could reverse the course.

Of course, laying waste to the elements necessary to create a successful public educational system is always done in the name of the highest motives and rhetoric. Thus, conservative Presidents Nixon, Carter, Reagan, Bush, and Clinton—Reagan and Clinton were known as "Great Communicators"—always spoke of progress and wore smiles as they made their cuts or failed to make significant improvements. For example, Ronald Reagan's last budget proposed eliminating Section Four of the National School Lunch Act, which granted schools fourteen cents for each lunch served. Reagan argued that the lunch program was an unnecessary subsidy to the parents of children who could afford to pay full price for school meals. But schools subsidized their entire nutrition program with this money, and many would have dropped out of the federal lunch program if the subsidy had been eliminated. Still, who could fault this affable and bewitching president? After all, he was only trying to save the taxpayers a little money.

Clinton's education record improved incrementally over eight years. After mostly remaining silent on the issue in his first year, Clinton initially proposed an education budget in fiscal 1994 that was short on discretionary spending, attempted to eliminate several programs, and focused most of its expenditure increases on Clinton's new initiatives. Barmak Nassirian, the assistant director for federal relations for the American Association of State Colleges and Universities, said at the time, "We were disappointed that this Democratic Administration really didn't differ that much from the previous Republican administrations when it came to putting your money where your mouth is with education."[2]

Both conservative Republicans and Democrats use noble motives and responsible language to articulate their destructive priorities. The catchphrases include "being fiscally responsible," "exercising fiscal and monetary restraint," and "practicing necessary economic austerity." The program implementation is called "balancing the budget," "eliminating the debt," and "slowing down growth to fight inflation." But since the Civil War, these conservative economic priorities have applied only to domestic programs of economic and social reconstruction.

Economic stinginess, fiscal responsibility, austerity, tight money, and necessary cuts do not apply to national defense or security expenditures, which are always conceived and defined in narrow military terms alone. In fact, American education has sometimes been the accidental beneficiary of this obsession with defense, along with our spontaneous and unplanned approach to public education. The increased spending on teaching science in our public schools in the late 1950s and 1960s was not the result of supporting science to improve the quality of life in America. The 1959 National Defense Education Act (NDEA) was passed because the Soviet Union's launch of Sputnik left the country feeling vulnerable.

Instead of mostly reacting defensively out of fear, what we should do is go on the offensive and democratically plan and pay for the finest public school system the world has ever known. We have the money, the organizational skill, the technology, and the knowledge to create such a system—and the amendment would help to frame the issue and set the standard. Again, the only missing element is the political will.

Our budget surpluses are projected to reach over five trillion dollars over the next ten years, even as our public schools continue to crumble and overall the system failed to meet the modest Clinton "Education Goals 2000" agenda, which established a federal role in developing a voluntary national system of academic standards and assessments and provided grants to fund state and local reforms. In 2000 a conservative Clinton administration's priority was not on creating the world's greatest public education system, but on starting a new arms race by breaking with the 1972 Antiballistic Missile Treaty and spending a minimum of sixty billion dollars on an unproven "Star Wars" defense shield. This strategy was undertaken not for proven reasons of national defense, but for partisan political reasons—to make sure that Al Gore didn't look weak against George W. Bush on national defense and military spending in the 2000 election campaign.

The goal of the more extreme Republican conservatives—those who are for eliminating all or most of the federal government, or for "privatizing" as much as is politically possible, or tolerable, of public education, government jobs, the U.S. Post Office, Social Security, health care in the form of Medicare and Medicaid, public and federally assisted housing programs, and federal services generally—is to discredit any federal role in public education. The purpose of these *economic* and *political* conservatives appealing to *social* conservatives by using their diversionary tactics of posting the Ten Commandments in public schools and insisting on violating the Constitution's prohibition of an "unconstitutional act of prayer" in the public schools is to undermine a federal role in public education. Diverting the American people's attention from the real economic issues in public education by using the vouchers tactic has the same goal. Conservatives are using the legitimate frustration of parents over failed public schools to illegitimately entice them with money and spirituality —a voucher, the Ten Commandments, and a prayer—to enroll in their private school scheme. Privatization is the only way conservatives can fulfill their dual ideological fantasy of a "market-driven" world without the "enemy" of private progress—big government.

The bottom line, however, remains that children in America have no federal constitutional right to a quality public education. Apart from the legislation created by local, state, and federal officials—legislation that is usually created in the political climate of "the least taxes the market will bear"—parents have few alternatives and little hope. They can't redress their grievances by going the judicial route, because there is little in state or federal laws that protects their children's right to a good education either. It has gotten so bad that real estate agents now sell homes and school systems together. In other words, legally, parents are in the same boat as the World War II veterans in regard to health care. They have no real or effective place to turn.

When I was a little boy my mother taught me, "If you fail to plan, you plan to fail." It is a miracle that America's public school system is a good as it is considering the lack of national democratic planning that has gone into it. It has been pieced together. It has never really been approached—in terms of policy, program, and practicality—from a rational national perspective.

Why is that? Because the politics of states' rights has been carried to the next level down—localism! Education is seen primarily as a state and local responsibility in the United States. In the truest sense, then, we really don't have an American educational system or a national commitment to education. We have stratified layers of different educational systems in America, with huge discrepancies in the quantity of money spent and the quality of public education available. Bona fide equal opportunity, under the current stratified structure, is impossible and will always be a hoax.

I believe local communities should continue to administer and operate local public schools, but they should do so within the framework of a high minimum standard that a constitutional amendment would provide. The amendment, however, should be accompanied with a new federal commitment to provide a public education to every American child of equal high quality.

We don't currently have such a system. In the fifty states and 3,067 counties in the United States, there are fifty-three million students in fifteen thousand school districts and eighty-five thousand public schools, with the expectation that we will have sixty-two million students in public school in the relatively near future. These students come from widely divergent economic, social, cultural, and religious backgrounds. Various city, county, and rural systems exist amid differences in funding and educational priorities. Many students attend schools that are currently de facto segregated or have a history of systemic racial segregation. Others are enrolled in multitiered systems that reflect disparate or inadequate funding. Some school systems are well funded with federal and state monies, along with local property taxes, while others remain underfunded with that same combination, even with the addition of lottery and gambling money. Some school systems have the private sector significantly involved, while others can't even entice parents to meet their child's teacher. Thus, fifty-three million children come to school from a wide variety of personal and community income strata, different family situations, and a multitude of religious, ethnic, and cultural backgrounds.

Additionally, standards vary among teachers' unions from state to state, while many students are taught by nonunion teachers where the standards vary even more, especially in southern and small rural western states and on Indian reservations. Teachers' pay and benefits differ from state to state, and within states. Some students are required to learn one or more foreign languages, while others struggle to learn our own. Many schools have art, music, gymnasiums, radio and television studios, libraries, swimming pools, debate, chess, and bowling clubs, as well as a wide variety of extracurricular activities, while other students are seldom exposed to these choices. Some state legislatures adequately fund education; others do not. Unless there is one high federal legal standard in the Constitution, it is a hopeless task to "leave no child behind."

Reflecting the context and diversity of public education in America, the National Center for Education Statistics recently reported that of the approximately four million babies currently born annually in the United States, one in eight is born to a teenage mother. The center indicated that parental education, income, and family expectations also tend to parallel student achievement. Today one out of every four babies is born to a mother with less than a high school education, one in four is born to an unwed mother, and one in three is born into poverty. In the end, these children make up the bulk of those who have learning disabilities, experience learning difficulties, repeat grades, require more expensive special education services, are the most socially maladjusted, are suspended more, and end up dropping out. Rather than emerging as educated and productive citizens, they end up on the streets, hooked on or selling drugs, committing crimes, in jail, killing someone else, or dying prematurely themselves.

Racial and ethnic minority and low-income students are at a greater risk of performing poorly in school at the same time that they are becoming an increasing proportion of the total student population. The National Center for Education Statistics concluded recently that "the social context of education has changed over the past few decades. The structure of families is shifting away from the two biological parent families. The percentage of children from minority backgrounds is increasing, as is the percentage of children who have difficulty speaking English. . . . Black and Hispanic children remain much more likely than white children to be living in poverty, a factor associated with poor school outcomes."

The national center also reported, "Minority students are more likely to attend schools with a high level of poverty. This is significant since in many ways the climate in high poverty schools appears to be less conducive to learning than that in low poverty schools. Similarly, high poverty schools are, on average, worse off than low poverty schools with regard to human and financial resources. . . . The social context in which schools operate can influence their effectiveness. Changes in social context present challenges that schools must address to enhance their effectiveness and ensure that education progress can occur."[3]

While schools must address the social context to enhance their effectiveness, they cannot fundamentally change the social context. Only political action can do that. The basic rights being raised and advocated in this book as needing constitutional protection—equal opportunity in employment, health care, housing, education, equality for women, a clean environment, progressive taxation, and voting rights—must be seen as interconnected and part of a whole. It would be difficult, if not impossible, to provide a first-class public educational system in an economy with high unemployment, or millions of Americans without health care, living in substandard housing or in poverty.

While much of urban education, especially as it pertains to many African American students, is a particular problem, the media's stereotypical negative image of an urban black student is wrong and must not blind us to the fact that *America* needs a new public educational policy and system. Former Congressman William H. Gray III, currently president of the United Negro College Fund (UNCF), commissioned a recent study that found that "contrary to the widespread belief that black students are a dominant presence in urban public schools, less than one-third of black public school students attend schools in large cities. Young black children participate in preschool programs at a higher rate, or 53 percent, than white students, who represent 44 percent. Black preschoolers display abilities comparable with those of white students in verbal memory, social behavior and physical development, but fall behind in vocabulary skills."[4]

With real estate taxes providing the bulk of local school funds, the richest communities actually pay the lowest percentage of their income for school taxes. But that amounts to more money per student than in the poorest communities, which pay the highest percentage of their income in taxes. (See *San Antonio Independent School District v. Rodriguez*, 1973.) That sometimes results in rich suburban schools that look like well-endowed private universities, while some inner-city schools resemble systems in poor developing nations.

The answer to this education amalgam is clearly not private and religious school vouchers. Nor is it teaching the Ten Commandments and praying in public schools; turning schools into an extension of the church; or teaching religion-based creationism, as if true religious belief cannot exist alongside science-based evolution.

This social, economic, and political context of education sets the stage for public education. If left to current politics alone, or politics narrowly conceived—given the nature of race and class relations, racism, race manipulation, and states' rights localism—it is difficult for the nation to support policies and fund education at a level that will actually provide every student with a public education of equal high quality. A constitutional education amendment provides not a guarantee, but, in a legal and political sense, the best insurance policy that such an educational system can and will be achieved in this country. No educational outcomes can be guaranteed, but such an amendment would guarantee that the judicial, legislative, and executive branches of government could be directly appealed to in order to improve education. That would significantly improve the chances of impacting public education for the better.

In the final analysis, in a democracy, the only real guarantee that an educational system of equal high quality can be established and sustained will come from an informed, active, and continually politically engaged majority. And this kind of involvement is more likely to come from a well-educated electorate than a poorly educated one—which, of course, makes our current political task and challenge all the more difficult. That's why the downturn in voting and civil activism should concern us all, not just political activists.

A constitutional amendment also encourages and challenges federal, state, and local legislatures, executive branches, and school boards to organize, fund, and operate from the start an educational system that meets this high constitutional standard. Otherwise, they'll know they can be sued and taken to court by individual students and parents.

Trying to provide an equal educational opportunity to all of America's fifty-three million elementary and secondary schoolchildren on a state-by-state basis, in fifteen thousand local school districts, is nearly impossible. To reach the proposed constitutional amendment standard, we must have a shared national standard and commitment.

What is the nation's and the federal government's commitment today? With an economy in 2000 that generated a gross domestic product (GDP) of more than nine trillion dollars, the nation merely spent six hundred billion dollars on education at all levels—with 91 percent of the funds coming from state and local governments and private sources. The federal commitment is only 9 percent, and that includes 3 percent spent on education programs administered through a variety of federal agencies, including the Departments of Defense, Agriculture, Health and Human Services, and Labor. Minus those dollars, the federal share is only 6 percent. Thus, out of a federal budget of approximately $1.8 trillion in fiscal 2000, the Education Department spent only $38 billion or 2 percent of the overall budget. But federal budgets represent more than just levels of spending. They represent values and priorities. And a 2 percent federal budget appropriation doesn't reflect a nation that highly values education or is making it a high national priority.

Again, as my mother often reminds me, "You get what you pay for." Why then should we be surprised that we have world-class bombs and first-class jails, but a second-class public school system, especially for our economic and minority underclasses?

When did a national role in education begin in America? And how did this hodgepodge of locally oriented educational systems evolve into a federal network? For the most part, accidentally. It was a kind of "put your finger in the dike" response to an emergency such as Sputnik, or a "fill in the blank, do whatever's not being done" approach of volunteerism and federal afterthought.

The federal Education Department's stated mission is "to ensure equal access to education and to promote educational excellence throughout the Nation." But what really controls public education in America is "localism." The small federal budget, the legal limitations, and the historical lack of political will by Republicans and Democrats in the White House, in Congress, and on the Supreme Court to actually achieve excellence and enforce desegregation laws for all of America's children all tell us that public education is a political game played by highly skilled politicians. Without a constitutional amendment that sets a national standard of equal high quality, this offensive and ineffective game will continue with our children.

In regard to desegregating our schools, the federal government has chosen the path of a political roller coaster. The *Brown* decision in 1954 ruled that a segregated education was and would always be an inherently unequal education. It overturned the "separate but equal" legal principle of *Plessy v. Ferguson* and replaced it with "equal protection under the law." The Court required schools to desegregate "with all deliberate speed." In 1955 the modern civil rights movement and Dr. Martin Luther King, Jr., picked up the Court's new legal principle, applied it more broadly to public accommodations generally, built a movement to desegregate a de jure segregated South, legally brought down the cotton curtain that separated blacks and whites, and moved to end de facto segregation in the North.

By 1970, in just sixteen short years, totally de jure segregated schools in 1954 were more desegregated than de facto segregated northern schools, because there had been stricter federal enforcement in the South than in the North. In seventeen southern and border states, desegregation had risen to 43.5 percent by 1988, and these states comprised more than one-third of our country. However, by 1996, Harvard's Gary A. Orfield, one of the most learned desegregation specialists in the country, documented that the percentage of desegregation in these same seventeen states had shrunk to 34.7 percent.

What brought about this reversal? It was a slow process of political resistance that gradually built up steam, beginning with the "states' rights" campaign of Goldwater in 1964, the "law and order" and "antibusing" presidential campaigns of Wallace and Nixon in 1968 and 1972, that changed the politics around school desegregation. With a brief reprieve in the political climate (but not much change in substance) under President Carter—he acciden-tally won over Ford in 1976 because of Nixon's criminal conduct—the elections of Reagan in 1980 and 1984 and Bush in 1988 brought it to a head. Their elections put in place the political climate—and financial and legal mechanisms—for a retreat on enforcing all civil rights laws. This was accompanied with a weakened resolve and ruling reversals by the Supreme Court. And under Clinton-Gore there was no serious funding or revving up of civil rights legal enforcement. Clinton's record only looked good in comparison to the anti-civil-rights records of Reagan and Bush pertaining to education, employment, and housing. This political process resulted in our public schools being more segregated going into the new millennium than they were in 1970.

Whether because of demographics, policy, or lack of enforcement, school resegregation has slowly been taking place—especially in the southern and border states. Mr. Orfield, in a series of Harvard studies in the 1990s, has shown that this resegregation trend is contin-uing and escalating. And a report issued by a New York panel in the early 1990s said that its state had two public school systems—"one urban, minority, poor and failing, and the other suburban, white, affluent and successful."

With the national legal and political will becoming weaker, our schools resegregating in the South, and northern schools never having been desegregated in the first place, many parents, educators, and politicians have now lost both the vision and the will to fight for desegregation and are just focusing on improving the quality of public education in whatever situation—segregated or not—they find themselves. Or they feel compelled to abandon a fail-ing public school system with the false hope that private schools are the answer to America's educational dilemma. The real tragedy, however, is that the arguments are usually framed in an either/or and not in a both/and context. Politically, if not yet legally, we seem to have returned to a kind of de facto (if not de jure) social acceptance of the "separate but equal" prin-ciple—a position that Justice Clarence Thomas clearly articulated in 1995 in *Jenkins*.

Local control, small federal budgets, and few national legal levers pretty much leave the top federal education official as what he or she has always been, a kind of preacher or cheer-leader for education, touting its virtues and sharing ideas with the states and local school boards—with little money, political power, or legal leverage. It's definitely not the way to create the best and most equally accessible national school system in the history of the human race. It's not structured to do that. And I say that it is deliberately so because of a deeply embedded and underlying conservative political philosophy called states' rights, and its grandchild, localism.

Given this Jeffersonian states' rights and "government closest to the people is the best government" orientation, the federal government was an afterthought, and its role was to voluntarily fill in the gaps left by state and local governments and the private sector. Any re-view of the history of federal legislation and key educational Supreme Court "equal oppor-tunity" decisions affecting the nation's schools will confirm the basic arguments I have been making about the federal government's and the Court's inconsistency.

Surprisingly, a national role did begin early, even before the formal founding of the United States. The Northwest Ordinance of 1787 authorized land grants for the establish-ment of educational institutions. Early on in the nation's history, too, President Thomas Jef-ferson launched the U.S. Military Academy in 1802 in upstate West Point, New York. The U.S. Naval Academy, located in Annapolis, Maryland, was established in 1845 by the sec-retary of the navy under President James Polk.

Representative Justin Morrill (R-VT), in the first Morrill Act of 1862, authorized public land grants to states for the establishment and maintenance of agricultural and mechanical colleges. (Conservative and racially insensitive Republicans, who want to do away with the IRS and other Reconstruction programs, need to be reminded that it was also Republican Morrill who drafted the first Internal Revenue Act in 1861 to pay for the Union's war against slavery and the wayward southern states of the Confederacy.)

Congress passed the Department of Education Act of 1867 authorizing the establishment of the U.S. Department of Education. It was later identified as the Office of Education, and its purpose was to do research and collect information to be passed along to the states for the improvement of their educational systems—a practice that continues even today. One hundred thirteen years later, in 1980, under President Jimmy Carter, it became a cabinet-level department. During Reconstruction after the Civil War, with 4 million former slaves (plus 250,000 free blacks, Native Americans, poor whites, and others) needing an education and training in order to be brought into the Union's economic mainstream, a lot of emphasis was put on black education. For example, during the last session of the Thirty-ninth Congress (1865–1867), Howard University was formally incorporated when Congress granted its charter on March 2, 1867. North Carolina A&T, where I went to school, is a public land grant university that was founded in 1891. There are currently 118 historically or predominantly black public and private colleges and universities around the country and in the Virgin Islands. In 1969 the National Association for Equal Opportunity in Higher Education (NAFEO) was formed to advocate for their interests, and for the interests of equal opportunity in higher education generally. According to NAFEO, these 118 institutions enroll upward of 370,000 students and graduate approximately one-third of all black students annually with undergraduate, graduate, and professional degrees. Since 1966, these institutions have awarded approximately half a million undergraduate, graduate, and professional degrees.

In 1876 the Republican National Platform contained the following statement: "The public school system of the several states is the bulwark of the American republic." It called for a constitutional amendment to forbid the use of public funds for any private, religious, or sectarian school.[5] In that same year the Department of the Treasury established the U.S. Coast Guard Academy. A second Morrill Act in 1890 provided federal grants for administrative support of instruction in the agricultural and mechanical colleges.

In 1896, of course, the infamous *Plessy v. Ferguson* case upheld an 1890 Louisiana law requiring railroads to provide "equal but separate accommodations for the white and colored races."[6] The Court ruled that if segregation is seen as "a badge of inferiority," it is only because "the colored race chooses to put that construction upon it." *Plessy* was the de jure underpinning for state-sanctioned racially segregated schools in the South. This decision created what is referred to as Jim Crow segregation throughout the South, and the "separate but equal" interpretation of the Constitution lasted fifty-eight years, until the 1954 *Brown* decision.

In the *Cumming v. Richmond County Board of Education* case of 1899, the Court rejected a bid by blacks to force the Augusta, Georgia, schools to end secondary education for whites until the district restored it for blacks. The ruling, the first school segregation case to reach the high court, allowed for wide disparities in the quality of education afforded blacks and whites in the South. In another case in 1908, *Berea College v. Kentucky*, brought by a private college with a tradition of mixed-race education, the Court upheld a state law that prohibited integrated classes for blacks and whites. In *Gong Lum v. Rice* (1927), the Court affirmed a Mississippi district's right to require a Chinese American girl to attend a segregated black school, rejecting her bid to attend the school for whites.

The Smith-Hughes Act of 1917 was a major boost in federal aid to schools, providing grants to states for vocational education, and the Vocational Rehabilitation Act of 1918 provided grants to rehabilitate World War I veterans through training. A law to provide additional educational facilities in 1919 authorized the federal government to sell surplus machine tools to educational institutions at 15 percent of cost.

The Bankhead-Jones Act of 1935 authorized grants to states for agricultural experimental stations. The Agricultural Adjustment Act in that same year authorized 30 percent of the annual customs receipts to be used to encourage the exportation and domestic consumption of agricultural commodities. Commodities purchased under this law began to be used in school lunch programs in 1936.

In 1938 *Gaines v. Canada* was the first challenge to racial discrimination in graduate programs to reach the Supreme Court. It ruled in *Gaines* that Missouri's failure to provide an equal law school for blacks was unconstitutional and established that the legitimacy of legally segregated institutions "rests wholly upon the equality" they offer the separated groups.

The beginning of World War II in 1941 led to a significant expansion of federal support for education. The Lanham Act, and later the Impact Aid Laws of 1950, authorized federal aid for the construction, maintenance, and operation of schools in federally impacted areas, and made payments to local school districts to ease the financial burden on communities affected by the presence of military and other federal installations.

In 1944, reflecting on education as an afterthought, the Surplus Property Act authorized the transfer of surplus property to educational institutions.

The Servicemen's Readjustment Act, known as the G.I. Bill, also became law in 1944 and provided postsecondary educational assistance that ultimately sent nearly eight million World War II veterans to college. It provided one free year of higher education for each ninety days of service, plus one additional month of paid education for each month of service up to forty-eight months. In the late 1930s about 160,000 Americans graduated annually from college, but by 1950 that number had increased to 500,000. In 1947, 49 percent of U.S. college enrollments were veterans. The cost of this World War II education program was $14.5 billion. In 1985 Congress passed a new G.I. Bill for members of the Selected Reserve, including the National Guard.

The Court in *Sipuel v. Board of Regents of the University of Oklahoma* (1948), citing *Gaines*, directed Oklahoma to provide a legal education to a black student denied entry to its all-white law school. Oklahoma slapped together a school for blacks, an action the high court refused to overturn. Again demonstrating the kind of afterthought and piecemeal approach to American education, the Federal Property and Administrative Services Act of 1949 provided for the donation of surplus property to educational institutions.

The *Sweatt v. Painter* case in 1950 found that a hastily invented law school for blacks in Texas was unconstitutionally inferior, and ordered the white law school to admit the black plaintiff. A decision issued the same day in *McLaurin v. Board of Regents of the University of Oklahoma* struck down an elaborate set of rules physically segregating a black student from whites in a graduate education program. The Court cited harm caused by intangible as well as physical inequalities. The rulings foreshadowed the demise of state-sanctioned segregation in *Brown*. Congress's Housing Act of 1950 authorized loans for construction of college housing facilities.

In the 1954 *Brown v. Board of Education of Topeka, Kansas* case, the Court unanimously declared that segregating elementary and secondary students by race violated black children's constitutional right to equal protection of the law—but not that they had a constitutional right to an education of equal high quality. Even so, many see *Brown* as the Court's most far-reaching ruling ever. The May 17 opinion arose from cases in four states (Delaware, Kansas, South Carolina, and Virginia). The same day, the Court invalidated school segregation in the District of Columbia on the grounds that it violated black students' constitutional rights to due process—but again, it did not rule that they had the right to an education of equal high quality. The Court deferred judgment on implementing its ruling. In 1954 Congress passed legislation establishing the U.S. Air Force Academy in Colorado Springs, Colorado; authorized cooperative arrangements with universities, colleges, and state educational agencies for educational research; and provided funds to purchase milk for school lunch programs.

The Court finally ordered the districts in the original *Brown* cases to make a "prompt and reasonable start toward full compliance" in 1955. Known as *Brown II*, the ruling obligated local school authorities to overcome obstacles to desegregation "with all deliberate speed" and directed federal district judges to oversee the process. The Court also stressed that constitutional principles cannot be sacrificed "simply because of disagreement with them." In 1957 President Eisenhower had to send federal troops into Little Rock, Arkansas, to uphold the *Brown* decision by protecting nine black students enrolling in classes at Central High School, including my good friend Ernie Green. In 1958, in *Cooper v. Aaron*, the Court rejected a bid by the Little Rock, Arkansas, school district to delay desegregation because of the upheaval surrounding the opening of Central High School the year before. "Law and order are not here to be preserved by depriving the Negro children of their constitutional rights," the justices unanimously ruled. It was a major shock to southern resistance to desegregation. It was also the beginning of the private and religious school movement in the South by the states' rights advocates.

Thus, the same political forces that represent the legacy of slavery; of the Confederacy; of resistance to Reconstruction; of Jim Crow segregation; of the 1948 Dixiecrats, the Goldwaterites of 1964, the Wallace-ites of 1968, the Nixon southern strategists of 1972, the Reagan Democrats of 1980, and the Bush (Willie) Hortonizers of 1988; and some of the forces that in 1992 Clinton and Gore sought to bring back into the Democratic Party as New Democrats—who in 2000 returned to become George W. Bush "compassionate conservatives"—these are the same conservative political leaders and operatives who are the primary movers and shakers behind Charlton Heston and the NRA, and the Ten Commandments, Prayer in School, and voucher movements, because their private school race habits have become too expensive for their followers' poor, working-class, and middle-class pocketbooks. And generally, Democrats don't know how to handle them because they don't want—or don't know how—to deal with the race question either.

The Cold War stimulated the first national experiment at comprehensive education legislation when Congress passed the National Defense Education Act (NDEA) in 1959 in response to the Soviets' launching of Sputnik. To help ensure that highly trained individuals would be available to help America compete with the Soviet Union in scientific and technical fields, the NDEA provided assistance to state and local school systems to strengthen instruction in science, mathematics, and modern foreign languages. Congress also wrote laws for training teachers of the handicapped and established a loan service of captioned films for the deaf.

The antipoverty and civil rights laws of the 1960s and 1970s brought about dramatic changes in the areas of equal access to education and training, including training or re-training people in redevelopment areas. In 1962 Congress passed laws to provide new and improved skill training for the unemployed and underemployed, as well as loans, advances, and grants for the education and training of refugees. In 1963 federal laws provided funds for expanding teaching facilities, student loans in the health professions, increased support for vocational education, and supply grants and loans to public community colleges.

School segregation continued as a problem in the South. Prince Edward County, Vir-ginia, understood that the Court had ordered public schools to desegregate, but it said that the Court did not state that a county had to have public schools. So rather than integrate, in 1959 it closed its public schools and opened private ones. But in *Griffin v. Board of Edu-cation* (1964), the Court ruled that Prince Edward County, one of the districts involved in *Brown*, could no longer avoid integration by keeping its public schools closed. Voucher sup-porters should take note that on the same day as *Griffin*, the Court affirmed a decision block-ing tax breaks and tuition grants used to subsidize private schools for whites.

Congress passed Title VI of the Civil Rights Act of 1964 to assist educators in dealing with desegregation problems, and the Economic Opportunity Act supplied grants for col-lege work-study programs for students from low-income families. Congress also established a Job Corps and gave support to community action programs, including Head Start, Fol-low Through, and Upward Bound, and established Volunteers in Service to America (VISTA).

The Elementary and Secondary Education Act of 1965 launched a comprehensive set of programs, including Title I, a program of federal aid to disadvantaged children that ad-dressed problems in poor urban and rural communities. The Higher Education Act assisted in postsecondary education with financial aid programs for needy college students, insured student loans, established a National Teacher Corps, and provided for graduate teacher-training fellowships. Other laws provided grants and loans for projects in the creative and performing arts, set up scholarships to aid needy students in the health professions, estab-lished a residential school for postsecondary education of the deaf, and offered assistance for recovery from a major disaster. In 1966 Congress established Gallaudet College as a model secondary school for the deaf.

In *Green v. New Kent County School Board* (1968), the Court declared in a case from Virginia that districts that formerly operated "dual systems" for blacks and whites had an affirmative duty to eliminate racial discrimination "root and branch." It told districts that they must promptly dismantle segregation not just in student assignment, but also in faculty, staff, transportation, extracurricular activities and facilities. These six areas became the "Green factors" later used by courts to gauge whether a district had met its obligation to desegre-gate. Congress also passed laws to assist with the education of handicapped, deaf-blind, and rural children, supported school dropout prevention projects, and supported bilingual edu-cation programs.

In 1969 *Alexander v. Board of Education* overturned an appeals court ruling that gave thirty-three Mississippi districts more time—fifteen years after *Brown*—to come up with plans to desegregate. The unanimous ruling said districts must end their dual systems for blacks and whites "at once, and to operate now and hereafter only unitary schools." *United States v. Montgomery County Board of Education* upheld the use of numerical quotas for the racial balancing of school faculty in a case arising in Alabama.

In another important desegregation case in 1971, *Swann v. Charlotte-Mecklenburg Board of Education*, the Court authorized mandatory busing, redrawn attendance zones, and the limited use of racial balance quotas as desegregation tools. It held that individual schools need not reflect the districtwide racial balance, but that districts bear the burden of proving that any one-race schools do not result from discrimination. In one of three related rulings issued on the same day, the justices struck down a North Carolina antibusing law that prohibited assignment of students on the basis of race.

Congress wrote Title IX of the Education Act and Section 504 of the Rehabilitation Act in 1972, which prohibited discrimination based on race, sex, and disability, respectively. In separate rulings issued on the same day, *Wright v. Emporia City Council* and *United States v. Scotland Neck Board of Education*, the Court in 1972 rejected bids to carve out new school districts in Virginia and North Carolina. In both cases, the districts would have had enrollments with a greater ratio of white students than in the desegregating districts they were leaving. The Court also, for the first time, in *Keyes v. Denver School District No. 1* (1973), held a district liable for intentional segregation, even though it had never required separate schools by law—a decision that extended the "affirmative duty" to desegregate districts beyond the southern and border states. A majority on the Court also found that official discriminatory acts affecting some schools or neighborhoods created a legal presumption that the whole district should desegregate. And the justices held that Hispanics should be counted with blacks in determining whether a school is segregated. In *San Antonio Independent School District v. Rodriguez* (1973), which was a case on behalf of poor schoolchildren challenging the Texas system of financing public schools based on local property taxes, the Court ruled that the system did not violate the Fourteenth Amendment's equal protection clause because education is not a fundamental right and property is no reason to hold otherwise. This is the cornerstone case establishing that the Constitution contains no right to a public education. In 1973 Congress passed education programs for older Americans as well as the Comprehensive Employment and Training Act (CETA), which provided opportunities for employment and training to unemployed and underemployed people.

In a close five-to-four ruling in *Milliken v. Bradley* in 1974—following two antibusing presidential campaigns, Wallace and Nixon in 1972—and in the first major curb on the expansion of desegregation, the Court struck down a plan to merge the Detroit schools with fifty-three largely white suburban districts. It cited a lack of evidence that those districts were guilty of intentional segregation and ordered a new desegregation plan confined to the city, where student enrollment was more than two-thirds black. The decision made it much harder for courts to order city–suburban desegregation plans to counteract the concentration of minorities in the cities.

In 1976, in *Pasadena City Board of Education v. Spangler*, the Court reversed a ruling requiring this California district to adjust attendance zones annually to preserve court-ordered racial ratios. A lower court had ordered that no school have a majority of any minority group, a directive with which the district fell out of compliance after only one year. In a six-to-two vote, the justices concluded that the enrollment shifts stemmed from demographic changes and not deliberate "segregative acts." In *Milliken v. Bradley*, the Court in 1977 authorized lower courts to require remedial education programs as an antidote to past segregation, a decision known as *Milliken II*. It upheld a ruling directing the city of Detroit and the state of Michigan to split the cost of programs in four areas: reading, in-service teacher training, student testing, and counseling. It opened the door to broader use of remedial programs and extra funding for racially isolated schools across the country.

The *University of California Regents v. Bakke* (1978) case was about a young premed student twice denied admission to medical school. He sued the University of California's affirmative action program for giving a "preference" to a black student whom he said was a less qualified applicant. In a carefully defined five-to-four ruling, the Court agreed that Bakke's right to equal protection had been denied, that he should have been admitted, and that affirmative action "quotas"—sixteen slots out of a hundred had been set aside for minorities—should be discarded. At the same time, the Court acknowledged race as "a" factor in admissions and hiring decisions, and permitted the establishment of flexible "goals and timetables." Thus, affirmative action could continue as long as rigid quotas did not constitute, in effect, "reverse discrimination."

Two cases in 1979, *Columbus Board of Education v. Penick* and *Dayton Board of Education v. Brinkman*, upheld mandatory busing in two districts in Ohio, ruling that school officials had perpetuated segregation, to varying degrees, by their actions and inaction since the *Brown* decision. In dissent, future Chief Justice William H. Rehnquist said the rulings so blurred the line between de jure and de facto segregation that the only way urban districts could avoid court-ordered busing, given residential segregation, was to get rid of neighborhood schools. This was Justice Rehnquist playing his political race card—defending local neighborhood schools while remaining silent on getting rid of residential segregation.

In 1980, under President Carter, Congress established the U.S. Department of Education and passed legislation to inspect schools for the detection, removal, and replacement of hazardous asbestos materials. A year later, also under Carter and in keeping with the history of southern states' rights and local control of education, Congress consolidated forty-two programs into seven to be funded under state elementary and secondary education block grants.

Still struggling with school desegregation, in *Washington v. Seattle School District No. 1*, the Court in 1982 struck down a state antibusing initiative passed by voters after Seattle voluntarily adopted a desegregation plan involving extensive crosstown busing. The Court concluded that the antibusing initiative was racially motivated. *Crawford v. Board of Education* upheld an amendment to California's constitution that prohibited state judges from ordering busing for integration in the absence of a violation of the U.S. Constitution. The amendment followed a state supreme court order requiring Los Angeles to desegregate on the grounds that it was obligated under the state constitution to attack de facto segregation.

In 1983 and 1984, despite Reagan's attempt to get rid of the Education Department and his lack of commitment to public education, Congress was still able to make public education more inclusive by adding an architectural barrier amendment; clarifying the participation of handicapped children in private schools; adding new science and mathematics programs for elementary, secondary, and postsecondary education, including magnet schools, excellence in education, and equal access; providing aid to the states to make vocational education programs accessible to all people, including the handicapped and disadvantaged, single parents and homemakers, and the incarcerated; and establishing a National Talented Teachers Fellowship program, a Federal Merit Scholarships program, and a Leadership in Educational Administration program.

Signaling that the Court was weakening in its commitment to desegregated educational opportunities, it ruled in *Board of Education of Oklahoma City v. Dowell* (1991) that court orders to desegregate were designed to be temporary. The ruling said federal judges should lift such decrees if districts have complied with them in good faith and remedied past discrimination "as far as practicable"; by a five-to-three vote the Court allowed the district to return to neighborhood schools. In 1991, in response to a series of strict constructionist interpretations of civil rights laws by the Supreme Court, Congress amended the Civil Rights Act of 1964, the Age Discrimination in Employment Act of 1967, and the Americans with Disabilities Act of 1990 with regard to employment discrimination. Weakening the commitment to desegregation even more, in 1992 in *Freeman v. Pitts*, courts were authorized to relinquish supervision over some aspects of a district's desegregation-related obligations, such as extracurricular activities, while retaining it in others. The decision also granted judges leeway to consider issues beyond the "Green factors," such as educational quality, in assessing whether districts should be declared unitary.

In 1994 Congress passed Clinton's Goals 2000 Educate America Act, which established a new voluntary partnership through a system of grants to states and local communities to reform the nation's education system. It also established School-to-Work programs, charter schools, and grants to local educational agencies with serious crime to implement violence prevention activities. Also, under the Clinton administration, Congress passed legislation in 1997 establishing Hope Scholarships and a Life-Long Learning Tax Credit.

In a major desegregation case, *Missouri v. Jenkins*, the Court said in 1995 that an ambitious magnet school plan in Kansas City aimed at luring suburban whites amounted to judicial overreaching. The five-to-four ruling said neither the goal of attracting whites nor the persistence of substandard test scores in the city justified the plan, which the state subsidized and wanted ended. Justice Clarence Thomas, the court's only African American, said in concurrence that the plan reflected an assumption "that anything that is predominantly black must be inferior." It is clear that Judge Thomas's understanding of American history and the law is limited. As a strict constructionist and color-blind judge, he apparently just doesn't understand.

This, then, is the basic federal legislative history with regard to education, integrated alongside a brief history of key Supreme Court decisions affecting the desegregation of America's schools.

Imagine comparing this history of how our schools have evolved and operate to the way America's trains and railroad tracks function. Suppose you wanted to travel from Maine to California by train, but every state had a different gauge of railroad track. In such a circumstance, as you crossed each state's border, you would have to disembark one train and board another. Also, some states would put a higher priority on trains than others, and their tracks would be in better condition. But imagine how unequal, inconvenient, and inefficient such a system would be. It was important that the federal government establish one standard gauge of track so that the railroads, country, and economy could grow and flourish in all of the states and territories.

This is analogous to the state of education in America today—except instead of dealing with fifty different state standards, we are dealing with a wide range of different standards in fifteen thousand school districts and eighty-five thousand public schools. The educational quality within and between Illinois and Minnesota is different from that of Mississippi and Alabama. We need one standard that can be applied to all our schools, and the only way to establish that high minimum standard is to ratify the right to a public education of equal high quality in the Constitution of the United States.

As I considered this history and these decisions, it became clear to me that the educational system in America has been put together piecemeal basically around two political principles with respect to federal involvement: First, volunteerism—states and localities voluntarily relate to, cooperate with, or receive educational help from the federal government; and second, localism—the primary educational power source. Politically, I've concluded that if local communities disagree with Supreme Court rulings or the federal government on equal racial access or economic equality in education, their task is to get their political leaders "to get the federal government off our backs." Both principles, volunteerism and localism, derive primarily from a Democratic Party states' rights history and political philosophy baptized in racism. That's why today southern Democrats vote heritage in local elections and vote for Republicans in national elections.

But volunteerism and localism have largely failed to provide a public education of equal high quality to all of America's children—and have for most of our history legally locked large numbers of our children out of public schools or assigned them to inferior schools. Periodically, but inconsistently, the Supreme Court and the federal government have stepped in to try to do something about it—with varying degrees of understanding or commitment by justices, presidents, and legislators as to educational excellence, equality, and inclusion. This history tells us that the federal government and the courts have had to force uncooperative states and local school districts to "do the right thing" if they were unwilling to do so voluntarily.

It is also clear to me from this history that this patchwork federal system has had its priorities. Education for young military men (and later women) who risked their lives or served their country in the military benefited first from a federal presence in education. Second, the federal role in education—legislatively and in legal decisions—has been about opening up and giving greater access (the "Green factors" and more) to those who have been locked out historically or otherwise disadvantaged, including African Americans, Hispanics, Asians, Native Americans, women, adults and older Americans, aliens and immigrants, bilingual and the language impaired, the blind, deaf, disabled, rural, homeless, school dropouts, poor, low-income, and, more recently, financially strapped middle-income students. Third, I saw in this history a few weak attempts to address questions of educational context (breakfast, lunch, antiviolence, and asbestos programs) and quality of education issues.

Nearly all Americans say they see education as the main route to upward mobility in our society. Education is seen as the path to employment; education and employment are seen as the course to health care and housing; economic security in the form of a job, education, health care, and housing are seen as the tracks to less discrimination and greater equal opportunity; education is seen as the way to guide Americans toward a cleaner, safer, and more sustainable environment; and education and economic security are the keys to generating enough fair taxes to make all these areas better and sustainable.

So what is the result of this long train of federal educational activities and legislation, and Supreme Court decisions affecting school segregation? In keeping with my central idea that politics in America is mostly North and South, I suggest one of the best ways of evaluating our educational efforts to bring about greater economic security for all Americans is to look at a chart that documents the most economically needy region in our country, the South, and specifically the eleven southern states of the former Confederacy—Alabama, Arkansas, Florida, Georgia, Louisiana, Mississippi, North and South Carolina, Tennessee, Texas, and

Virginia. Is there an economic legacy of slavery, states' rights, volunteerism, localism, and the Confederacy? If so, how has it manifested itself? And can it be documented?

In the following table our fifty states are ranked in twelve categories. A state receiving a "1" rank is at the top (the highest) in that category; a "50" puts that state at the bottom (the lowest).

1. Employment: Employment/population ratio (1997)
2. Economic: State governments—general revenue per capita (1997)
3. Economic: Average annual pay (1997)
4. Economic: Personal income per person in constant (1992) dollars (1998)
5. Economic: Household income in constant (1992) dollars (1998)
6. Economic: People below poverty level (1998)
7. Education: Public elementary and secondary teachers' average salaries (1998)
8. Education: Full-time college enrollment (1996)
9. Health: Doctors per 100,000 population (1997)
10. Health: Infant mortality rate (1996)
11. Health: Births to teenage mothers (1997, preliminary)
12. Crime: Violent crimes per 100,000 population (1997)

STATE	(1)	(2)	(3)	(4)	(5)	(6)	(7)	(8)	(9)	(10)	(11)	(12)
AL	38	39	31	40	33	13	39	9	39	2	5	20
AR	44	29	46	46	49	12	45	11	42	3	2	22
FL	46	50	30	19	39	20	29	46	17	22	19	1
GA	19	40	19	23	26	17	20	11	33	4+	12	15
LA	49	23	32	41	44	2	47	5	14	6	3	4
MS	48	28	47	50	48	4	48	3	49	1	1	25
NC	21	26	29	31	35	15	37	17	22	4+	14	15
SC	34	32	37	42	42	16	35	19	35	13	7	2
TN	39	47	28	33	40	19	27	15	13	10	8	9
TX	24	49	15	25	36	10	34	38	38	36	10	17
VA	29	37	16	13	10	46	24	33	16	17	32	34

+Georgia and North Carolina are tied.

SOURCE: U.S. CENSUS BUREAU.

As you can see from the chart above, these former Confederate states rank near the bottom of almost everything positive and near the top of most things negative. The chart shows, statistically, the material legacy of slavery, states' rights, and the Confederacy. The question then becomes: With the majority of black and white southerners having so many material needs and problems, why would genuine representatives of the people—religious, educational, and political leaders, Republicans or Democrats from these former Confederate states—ever have been economically conservative, not to mention their remaining economically conservative today? What are they conserving? The economic legacy of slavery documented above? And who are they conserving it for? A few "inheritors" of this former privileged economic system?

We need this constitutional education amendment to overcome the legacy of slavery, states' rights, and the economic elitism of the Confederacy—and the current vehicle, delivery system, and form of it, economic conservatism as delivered to us by conservative Democrats and Republicans. We must have such an amendment to assure every American the educational path to economic security.

The economic motives and political judgments of conservatives may be debated, and different conclusions reached. But the facts have been corroborated throughout this book. Since the Civil War, the legacy of slavery, states' rights, and a top-down elitist economic arrangement, the economic tracks to Reconstruction—employment, health care, housing, and education—have basically been missing, delayed, or, when present, bent, torn up, blown up, sabotaged, subverted, unfunded, underfunded, and more. But the job of economic Reconstruction is still ongoing and unfinished—and education is still the main rail. That is why today America must have this constitutional education amendment—to provide a public quality educational system for every American.

Can you imagine America without the right to free speech? Without the right to a free press? Without the right to peaceably assemble and to petition the government for a redress of grievances? An America without the freedom of choice of religion, or to choose no religion at all? I can't imagine that! Yet making available those legal rights to common citizens, to every individual American, in a Constitution, was wholly new thinking in the history of humankind just over two hundred years ago.

It is equally astounding to me that we have not included in our Constitution a right so basic, so fundamental to our social progress, our well-being, and a higher quality of life for our country and every individual American, as the right to a good public education! Therefore, it is time to insert another missing link in our constitutional chain of guaranteed rights—a constitutional amendment that provides every individual American with the right to a public education of equal high quality.

Constitutional amendments set minimum floors below which no law or American can fall. Laws can be written to improve on constitutional rights, but none can fall below them. My constitutional amendment sets a high minimum floor that incorporates ever-upward competition. All fifty states can improve upon my amendment, but none can fall below it. If a state constitution already speaks to the issue of education but does not meet the new constitutional standard, that state must change its constitution to satisfy the new higher standard.

Because my amendment is an individual right, it empowers every parent and child in America's public schools with the legal right to go to court and show that the legislative and executive branches have failed to meet the constitutional standard and demand relief—a remedy that meets the constitutional standard. The implication of this remedy is that no longer will some kids go to school hungry or have potato chips, candy, and pop for breakfast—which leads to hyperactivity, overall poor health, and dysfunctionality—while others have a wholesome and healthy breakfast. No longer will some children have their eyes tested while others don't, or will some get vaccinations while others don't, even though by law they're all required to. Parents will no longer have to tolerate some schools offering a full-service health facility while other kids never see a doctor, dentist, or nurse.

With my amendment, state and local school boards will no longer be able to hide behind the Tenth Amendment and will be obligated to address the inequities that exist in our schools. And because the standard is high, and it's an individual right, no parent who has a child in a public school will be left behind. It only requires one parent to make the school better. Because of the Tenth Amendment, states have reserved the right not to comply with federal standards or to accept federal funds with strings attached if it involves racial desegregation, or educating the handicapped or anyone else they choose not to include. The choice of block grants and the present system of varying standards is a by-product of the Tenth Amendment.

For every American, not just a few, we must overcome Tenth Amendment prohibitions and limitations that keep us from raising the educational standard for every single child with an explicit constitutional right to a public education of equal high quality. There must be no confusion about constitutional interpretation. Any proposal by Republicans or Democrats that uses a state-centered federalist approach of local control and volunteerism with regard to education will always doom a majority of America's children to a low-quality and inadequate education that leaves some children behind. The Tenth Amendment, since slavery, has perpetuated the status quo.

My amendment is also a living amendment. It allows the broadest discussion by both current and future jurists about what, at any given time, constitutes the "equal high quality" standard. It's an objective standard that still allows education to be lifted ever upward. Today's values and information may be different from tomorrow's. For example, the First Amendment didn't originally apply to women or people of color. It meant something different in 1787 than it meant after January 1, 1863. The founders could not have imagined the Internet. Equal high quality is broad enough and high enough so that every American in the future can also appeal to it to make their schools better. The strict constructionists want to consider only rights that strengthen the Tenth Amendment, but my constitutional right is not designed necessarily to strengthen the federal government either. What it actually does is return power to each parent. Right now parents have no power to direct the destiny of the education of their children except through volunteering, home schooling, buying some language tapes, or sitting their kids down in front of *Sesame Street*.

As I anticipate where attacks against this constitutional amendment might come, I think one will surely be about "unanticipated consequences." Why? Because it's a question and a line of attack that can't be fully answered. No one can anticipate all of the consequences of any proposed amendment, because we don't know the future consequences of the amendments we already have. So maybe the more important question to ask is: Do you think you (and the country) would be better off with this amendment? I think the answer is clearly yes. An education amendment is absolutely vital and necessary to building a more perfect Union.

A MORE PERFECT UNION—
EQUALITY FOR WOMEN

In the new Code of Laws . . . put it out of the power of the vicious and lawless to use us with cruelty and indignity with impunity.

—Abigail Adams to John Adams, March 31, 1776

As to your extraordinary Code of Laws, I cannot but laugh. . . . Depend upon it, We know better than to repeal our Masculine systems.

—John Adams to Abigail Adams, April 14, 1776

We hold these truths to be self-evident; that all men and women are created equal.

—Elizabeth Cady Stanton, Declaration of Sentiments
First Woman's Rights Convention
Seneca Falls, New York, July 19, 1848

Use any excuse you want . . . all we [men] are trying to do in our own little way is to maintain the right to declare a difference.

—Representative Stewart McKinney,
ERA debate, U.S. Congress, Oct. 12, 1971

PROPOSED EQUAL RIGHTS AMENDMENT
TO THE U.S. CONSTITUTION

Section 1. Equality of rights under the law shall not be denied or abridged by the United States or by any State on account of sex.
Section 2. The Congress shall have power to enforce, by appropriate legislation, the provisions of this article.
Section 3. This amendment shall take effect two years after the date of ratification.

The millennium ended appropriately enough for women—with a protest. The U.S. Women's Soccer Team had a dispute with the U.S. Soccer Federation over equal pay for its players. Led by one of its stars, Michelle Akers, in January 2000, twenty members of the team refused to play in an Australian tournament because, as a result of a 1996 agreement with the federation, the most experienced players were being paid only $3,150 per month and $250 per game, while the federation was paying the U.S. Men's Soccer Team $5,000 per month with an additional $2,000 for the eighteen players who were going to Australia. Many of the women had to work at outside jobs to adequately support themselves.

In the end, facing embarrassing and unfavorable publicity, the federation granted women a new five-year contract guaranteeing ongoing pay parity with the men's team. Even though this example is elitist, in that it had an effect only on the top echelon of women, the women's soccer team pay controversy is still illustrative of why we need an equal rights amendment (ERA). An ERA would help women at the "top," but it would be most beneficial to the masses of average women. After more than two hundred years under the present Constitution, and despite the progress that has been made as a result of federal laws, women are still not treated as first-class citizens. They still don't have equal protection under the law. Women should be granted that protection not just under federal law, but under the highest law in our land—the Constitution of the United States.

The lack of a clear constitutional guarantee of equality for women leaves America's democratic promise unfulfilled for half the population. It is a shameful truth that 225 years after this nation was established, equality between the sexes remains more hope than reality. The disadvantaged status of women is so pervasive and so supported by cultural mandates that many people—women and men—see these conditions as "normal" and accept them. But in fact our entire society suffers greatly from the subjugation of women, maintained and perpetuated by the threat or reality of men's violence against women. That injustice is widespread and institutionalized does not make it less abusive.

A national dialogue leading to adoption of an amendment that would prohibit discrimination based on sex will have the most profound impact yet in reshaping the legal and economic landscapes. For if women—who constitute the majority of the population—were to have their basic human right to equal treatment under the law, every aspect of their current disadvantaged status would be forever changed.

Women's fundamental human rights, including the right to bodily integrity, personal safety, equality of opportunity, and equal protection of the law continue to be sacrificed to men's freedom to privilege themselves at women's expense. In economic terms, depriving women of legal equality translates into a difference of many billions of dollars. Barriers to education, employment, and freedom of movement, as well as systematic deprivation of access to contraception and assistance with child care, impose severe constraints on women's freedom to compete for achievement and rewards in professions, corporations, and paid workplaces at all economic levels.

Unimpeded by the U.S. Constitution, men have at various times barred women's admittance to sex-segregated public schools, to law and medical schools, and to the practice of these professions. They have prohibited women from serving on juries, voting and running for office, owning or inheriting property, establishing personal credit, and obtaining loans that would allow them to finance their own businesses. Using the draft exemption as a pretext, they have excluded women from the basic claim to full rights of citizenship that vulnerability to the draft confers on men, as well as access to the training, educational opportunities, and veterans' benefits that military service affords. They have denied women custody of their own children in the event of separation or divorce and have made it illegal for a woman to protect herself against assault by her husband. For women of color, the constraints have been even more severe. Thanks to feminism and the progressive movement, some of these restrictions have been removed during the last century, but sex discrimination and unequal treatment still prevail.

Held back by educational, employment, and other social barriers, women then provide little competition for corporate and political control. At base, it is this opposition by the male system to sharing the mantle of power that has impeded women's progress throughout our history.

The exclusion of women from the U.S. Constitution is not accidental. From the founding of this country more than two centuries ago to the present day, men have repeatedly refused constitutional recognition to women's legal and civil rights. There were three key occasions when this was done:

> In 1776 Founding Father John Adams denied his wife, Abigail's, demand that the constitution of the new nation "put it out of the power of the vicious and lawless to use [women] with cruelty and indignity with impunity," as English law allowed. To her clear demand for a guarantee of equal protection of the law, John Adams responded with cutting ridicule. "As to your extraordinary Code of Laws, I cannot but laugh," he wrote. "We have been told that our Struggle has loosened the bands of Government every where. That children and apprentices were disobedient— that schools and Colleges were grown turbulent—that Indians slighted their Guardians and Negroes grew insolent to their Masters. But your Letter was the first intimation that another Tribe more numerous and powerful than all the rest were grown discontented. Depend upon it," he assured her, "We know better than to repeal our Masculine systems."

> In 1868, after the Civil War, Congress adopted the Fourteenth Amendment, which guaranteed to all "persons" the right to equal protection of the law. However, in the second section, which determined the number of congressional representatives that each state would be due, use of the words "male citizens" for the first time marked the explicit, intentional exclusion of women from the Constitution. Further affirming this exclusion, the Fifteenth Amendment, ratified in 1870, granted to all men—but not women—nondiscrimination in voting. A minority of women thus were granted protection on the basis of race but, along with white women, denied it on the basis of sex. Splitting the Fourteenth Amendment on this invidious basis made it vulnerable to further restriction of its power to protect human and civil rights. The fifty-year campaign to secure a guarantee of nondiscrimination in voting for women resulted in passage of the Nineteenth Amendment in 1920. This completed the Fifteenth Amendment, but left the Fourteenth Amendment with no counterpart for women. To enable women to use their vote to remedy this discrimination, suffragist leader Alice Paul drafted the Equal Rights Amendment and began the campaign for ratification in 1923.

> In 1982, after a final ten-year campaign, ratification of the Equal Rights Amendment was denied by legislatures in fifteen states. Sex discrimination remains constitutionally permissible.

Why fight to secure a constitutional amendment rather than work to pass more incremental and easily achieved federal laws? Because laws—federal and state—must be made and interpreted on a foundation of constitutional principle to be reliably enforceable. Until the Constitution is amended to explicitly prohibit discrimination on the basis of sex, sex discrimination can be legally treated as justified or unimportant and laws can continue to privilege men overtly or by disparate impact.

Hard-won laws against sex discrimination can be weakened by amendment, reinterpreted, underfunded, enforced inconsistently, repealed outright, or simply ignored. Sex discriminatory laws, such as barriers to abortion, can be enacted without challenge to their invidious effect on women as individuals and as members of a class. Court challenges to sex discriminatory law are not subjected to the "strict scrutiny" standard of review that must be applied to cases involving discrimination against classes such as race where a constitutional right to equal protection is established. Without the vigorous public dialogue from the grassroots up that must precede passage of a constitutional amendment, there is neither an informed consensus as to the need for laws against sex discrimination nor a political mandate to honor and enforce them.

If the public is generally unaware of women's lesser constitutional status, the Supreme Court is not. During arguments before the Court in 1983 in the *Bob Jones University v. United States* case, involving a private college's ban on interracial dating, Justice Powell asked Justice Department attorney William Coleman, Jr., if his arguments against racial discrimination applied to sex discrimination as well. "No," Coleman replied, "we didn't fight a Civil War over sex discrimination and we didn't pass a constitutional amendment against it." The Court did not disagree.

The fact that women are allowed to vote creates an illusion of equality. But the power of the vote can be devastatingly undercut by the power of the press to minimize, trivialize, or demonize women political leaders and initiatives that constructively address women's needs. For example, shortly after the Nineteenth Amendment was passed in 1920, and fearing the new power of the women's vote, Congress passed the Sheppard-Towner Act (1921) supplying the first federal health care funds for women and infants. But after two decades in which no strong "women's voting block" was seen to materialize, Congress let the law expire. Meanwhile, legislatures freely allowed discrimination on the basis of sex, both on the face of the law and in the form of disparate impact on women. Even laws against sex discrimination can be applied in a sex discriminatory way.

It took just one Supreme Court decision invoking the Fourteenth Amendment in *Fitzpatrick v. Bitzer* (1976) to prohibit sex discrimination against men employed by the state of Connecticut who took early retirement and to award compensatory pension back pay, retroactive not just to passage of Title VII of the Civil Rights Act of 1964 prohibiting sex discrimination in employment, but back to the start of the pension fund itself. As to where the money would come from, Justice Stevens opined that the state would simply have to put more money into the fund.

That precedent was nowhere to be seen in *City of Los Angeles Department of Water and Power v. Manhart* (1978) and yet again in *Arizona v. Norris* (1983), dealing with sex discrimination in women's pensions. Here the Supreme Court ruled against lower pension payments for retired women but required only prospective relief. In clear defiance of the civil rights legal principle of making the victim whole, they disallowed the back pay award in the Manhart case, openly sympathizing with the burden on employers of having to pay equal pensions to men and women and emphasizing that this decision did not apply to privately funded pensions.

What difference would an ERA have made in these cases? A constitutional amendment affirming equal rights for women would shift the burden of proof from those fighting discrimination onto those who discriminate. An ERA shifts the argument from women protesting ongoing discrimination and discriminators justifying it, to requiring the courts to apply strict scrutiny to cases of apparent inequality.

In the year 2000, Equal Pay Day was observed on May 11. The date was chosen to highlight the fact that a woman would have to work an extra 137 days—until May 11—to make up for the 1998 average difference between a woman's salary of $25,862 and an average man's salary of $35,345, a difference of $9,483 or 37 percent. Moreover, federal laws do not cover the issue of equal pay for work of comparable worth or jobs that are different but should be compensated at a corresponding value.

Putting it another way, women's pay averages around 75 percent of what men are paid, according to Bureau of Labor Statistics information. Women still tend to be hired into traditional "women's jobs" at the low end of the pay scale. Whether a registered nurse, an elementary school teacher, a computer operator, or a retail cashier, women's salaries are still lower than men's, even though both have the same education and perform the same tasks. The National Committee on Pay Equity (NCPE) reported that "the pay gap exists, in part, because women and people of color are still segregated into a few low-paying jobs. Studies show that the more an occupation is confined to women or people of color, the less it pays."[1] Yet people of color must pay the same as whites and women must pay the same as men for groceries and education, and—given race and sex profiling—maybe more than white men for a home or a car. Using census data, NCPE contrasts a dollar of white men's pay with the seventy-two cents paid white women, sixty-five cents paid black women, and fifty-two cents paid Hispanic women.

According to a 1995 Federal Glass Ceiling Commission report, "97 percent of the senior managers of Fortune 1000 industrial and Fortune 500 companies are white, and 95 to 97 percent are male; in the Fortune 2000 industrial and service companies, only 5 percent of senior managers are women and almost all of them are white."[2] The commission documented ongoing discrimination against women, African Americans, Hispanics, Asians, Pacific Islander Americans, and American Indians in the business community. This discrimination persists despite the fact that in our society, two-thirds of the population—and 57 percent of paid workers—are women, minorities, or both.

Further, racial discrimination is evident within sex classes. The average twenty-nine-year-old white woman with a bachelor's degree will lose about $990,000 in pay during her lifetime, while the average woman of color will lose even more. Women saw their inflation-adjusted median annual earnings increase by 2.4 percent from 1995 to 1996, but 1996 earnings were still lower than in 1989. And while 48 percent of men earned less than twenty-five thousand dollars in 1996, 70 percent of employed women did. Fifty-eight percent of workers who gained from the last increase in the minimum wage were women. And the Institute for Women's Policy Research estimates that the average working family annually loses four thousand dollars in income because of inequitable pay.

The loss of wages also has a lifetime impact. Social Security was formed in the employment context of FDR's New Deal. But in 1940, only 14 percent of women worked outside the home; most were wives and homemakers. Today 70 percent of women with school-age children are employed in the paid workforce, and the number of single women is growing substantially. With the divorce rate nearing 40 percent and an extended life expectancy—especially for women, many of whom now live into their mideighties—the demographics of society have shifted dramatically, but the benefit formula of Social Security has not. Married men receive 100 percent lifetime benefits, while wives, widows, and divorced women receive significantly less, even though many elderly women are either mostly or totally dependent on these meager benefits. Since Social Security is based on lifetime earnings, when women are paid less during their working years they receive less in retirement—on average, about half of what a man receives.

This system of social insurance fails to adequately recognize women's important contributions to the family unit and to society in general and is in serious need of updating. Under Social Security, women are penalized for raising the next generation; their years out of the paid workforce count against them. Credits for caregiving should be established and other improvements made that would increase retirement benefits for caregivers. Accordingly, the payroll tax upon which revenues are generated to the Social Security Trust Fund falls most heavily on lower-income earners—most of whom are women and people of color—because it is not a progressive rate. High-income earners do not have to pay tax on any amounts earned above eighty thousand dollars annually. And, as I argue in another chapter, regressive taxation is an unfair burden on low- and middle-income working families.

Insurance and pensions are also significantly impacted by discrimination against women. Of the four million elderly, some three-quarters are women. Women have only about half the income of elderly men, and elderly women of color have significantly less income than their white counterparts. Thus, women of color are subjected to discrimination in the form of sex, income class, and caste.

Because employment history and pensions are tied together, women are only half as likely to receive a private pension as men (22 percent of women versus 49 percent of men). And when women do receive a pension, on average it amounts to only half that of men ($5,432 per year for women, $10,031 for men). An ERA could help women receive compensatory relief to make up for this loss of pension income based on demographic and historic circumstances, which are allowed to have a disparate impact on women as a class.

Under state insurance codes, insurance regulators allow different rates of premiums and payouts for women and men in five different types of insurance: auto, disability income, medical expenses, life, and retirement income insurance. Despite this obvious state involvement, ERA opponents argued that "lack of state action" would prevent the amendment from disallowing such costly discrimination and threatened that women would lose benefits if sex discrimination were eliminated. The claim that male-dominated state legislatures are advantaging women, an underrepresented group, defies the basic principle of representative government. Research by the National Organization for Women (NOW) has conclusively demonstrated that sex-divided insurance of all types discriminates against women.

While in the previously cited case of *City of Los Angeles Department of Water and Power v. Manhart*, the Supreme Court ruled that Title VII of the 1964 Civil Rights Act outlawed discrimination in employer-paid insurance policies, it did not outlaw such discrimination in privately purchased insurance policies with private insurance companies. The *City of Los Angeles* decision was further weakened by a New York federal district court that exempted some employer plans from Title VII coverage.

In the case of *Bartholomew v. Foster* (1988), the Pennsylvania Supreme Court found sex-divided auto insurance rates discriminatory against young men under the state ERA but spurned a remedy using cents-per-mile rates that would not have resulted in raising young women's rates—an outcome falsely used to argue that equality would harm women. Moreover, the finding of discrimination against men in the auto insurance case has never been applied to end sex-divided rates that openly discriminate against women in medical expense, disability income, and life insurance, along with annuities. NOW estimates that if there were sex equality in insurance prices, coverage, and benefits, women would annually gain $2.5 billion.

Adding an ERA to the Constitution would help prevent such disparities by subjecting patterns of discrimination against women to the highest standard of judicial scrutiny. It would provide a solid basis for equalizing employment opportunities, wages, income, Social Security, insurance, pensions, education, and more. It would respect women's right to self-ownership. But an equal rights amendment can only provide strong constitutional protection for women's human and civil rights if a strong definition of what equality would mean when it includes women is developed. That definition must be built into the ERA throughout the political process of gaining ratification.

Some of the economic results of pregnancy discrimination would be positively affected by an ERA. The Fourteenth Amendment guarantees men's—but not women's—right to bodily integrity, leaving government free to enact laws and regulations targeting pregnancy for punitive treatment. Congress has done so in denying the right of poor women to choose a legal abortion by prohibiting the use of federal funds for such a purpose. But if abortion is legal for anyone—and it is legal for everyone—then it should also be accessible to everyone. Anything less is a denial of equal protection under the law. Also, in 1995, Congress passed a law denying pregnant federal workers and women in the military serving abroad access to safe abortions. An attempt in 1998 by Representative Nita Lowey (D-NY) to repeal provisions of existing law that prohibit women serving in the military overseas from using their personal funds to obtain abortions in U.S. military hospitals failed by a vote of 190 to 232.

A recent congressional assault on women's reproductive rights has been directed against a rarely used medical procedure known as dilation and extraction (D&X). It is used when a medical decision has been made that the life or health of the mother is at stake, or a decision by a physician and a pregnant woman that the fetus is severely deformed. Congress has passed legislation (which was later vetoed) prohibiting this critically needed medical procedure, and thirty-one states have done so, even though a Supreme Court decision has ruled such a ban unconstitutional (*Stenberg v. Carhart*, 2000). State legislatures continue to debate and enact an endless parade of bills whose only discernible purpose is to harass pregnant women and girls. The National Organization for Women argues that "the real issue for women is the right to bodily integrity, and without this basic right women can have no true freedom."

In the twenty-eight years since the *Roe v. Wade* (1973) decision, a backlash has intensified against women's enhanced ability to control their reproductive lives and their bid to gain full legal and economic equality. Right-wing politicians and Christian fundamentalist activists have exploited a predictable public unease about profound social change to expand their political base—not only in the conservative South, but in the Midwest and mountain states as well. The "family values" theme—a code term for patriarchal control—combined with other well-tested but deceptive political messages has enabled them to assume control of a majority of state legislatures, Congress, and a substantial number of governorships. Antifeminist leadership by conservative politicians, combined with the ambivalence of most male politicians to sharing political power with women, has meant a serious retrenchment for women's rights generally, and specifically for women's reproductive rights.

Since 1995, when conservative anti-choice Republicans took control of Congress, more than one hundred federal laws limiting a woman's right to obtain an abortion or utilize contraceptives have been passed. At the state level, 262 anti-reproductive-rights measures have been enacted over the last six years, making these rights more restricted now than they were in 1973 when *Roe v. Wade* was decided. The restrictions take several forms: bans on abortion procedures, "informed" consent laws, limits on counseling, so-called conscience-based exemptions, and limitations on insurance coverage—to name just a few. There are repeated threats to repeal *Roe v. Wade* and to pass a constitutional amendment prohibiting abortion and a real fear by women's reproductive rights advocates that an even more conservative Supreme Court will overturn *Roe*.

The conservative backlash has encouraged a violent fringe element to see it as their "religious" duty to bomb clinics and murder physicians. Since the 1980s, hundreds of bombings, acts of arson, vandalism, anthrax hoaxes, and butyric acid attacks have been made against women's health clinics. Worse, thirty-one physicians and clinic personnel have been cold-bloodedly murdered or injured by these extremists. For years, local law enforcement authorities made only halfhearted gestures to prosecute these crimes; it took a federal law with the force of the Department of Justice and the FBI before such crimes began to be vigorously investigated and prosecuted. But the Ninth Circuit Court *(Planned Parenthood of the Columbia/Willamette v. American Coalition of Life Activists)* recently found that the First Amendment protected a Web site posting the names of women's health clinic staff in a "Wanted"-style format with names crossed out for those doctors and personnel who had been murdered.

When First Amendment guarantees of freedom of speech can be invoked to sanction harassment of women and tolerate Internet hate-mongering against abortion providers, women are being sent a dire message that the Constitution is not obliged to recognize and protect their human rights. Even though we focus much attention on acts of violence, the following question must be asked: If it is only extremists who want to punish women for trying to remedy a condition that men create, where are the moderates? Women cannot consistently count on the support of friendly male politicians to effectively advocate for their rights. A constitutional amendment is the best and most reliable means to safeguard basic rights.

Women's well-founded concern about personal safety circumscribes their daily lives; the ever-present fear of assault means that women must be cautious in unlit parking lots at night or on running paths; they do not venture into certain areas alone. The number of rapes, as estimated by the National Crime Victimization Survey with 1994 data, places them at 432,100 annually (age twelve and over); more than half of rapes in another survey found to have been committed on girls age seventeen and younger. Severe stalking—once thought to be rare—happens to one out of every twelve women, as estimated by the Violence Against Women Survey in 1998. The problem is especially serious for young women in college, where 13 percent of respondents indicated that they had been stalked since the beginning of the school year, as reported by the National Institute of Justice and the Bureau of Justice Statistics in January 2001.

Approximately 1.9 million women are assaulted each year, according to a National Institute of Justice and Centers for Disease Control survey (1998). More than half the women interviewed indicated that they had experienced a physical assault (anything from slapping or hitting to using a gun) at some point in their lives. Violence against women is primarily due to partners. The Bureau of Justice Statistics in 2000 estimated 876,340 violent victimizations of women by intimate partners, down from 1.1 million in 1993. Women are five times more likely than men to be a victim of partner violence. Women are more likely to be injured as a result of rapes and physical assaults, with one in three requiring medical attention. Women of color were as likely to be attacked as their white counterparts; however, levels of violence increased among respondents with incomes less than ten thousand dollars per year in the 1998 survey.

The Federal Bureau of Investigation reports that about 11 percent of all murders in 1998 (1,830 homicides) were the result of intimate partner violence—down from 3,000 intimate partner homicides in 1976. However, the proportion of women murdered in intimate partner homicides has grown from 50 percent in 1976 to 72 percent in 1998. The most common cause of death among pregnant women is murder, according to researchers at the Maryland Department of Health and Mental Hygiene reporting in the *Journal of the American Medical Association* (March 2001). Sexual assault of women in prison is now recognized to be a pervasive problem that remains unaddressed in most states; Amnesty International has documented more than one thousand cases of sexual abuse over a three-year period in U.S. prisons. Sex profiling of women by police has recently been described by an Eastern Kentucky University professor, who has documented hundreds of cases in which women have been sexually assaulted by police officers during traffic stops.

Domestic violence—once an accepted cultural practice—is no longer overlooked, but it remains prevalent at every income level and for all races. So prevalent that a Web site by a Dallas, Texas, company features men's tank T-shirts emblazoned with the words WIFE-BEATER and offers even an infant-sized shirt that says LI'L WIFE-BEATER.

Such grim statistics and stories remind us that women continue to be the targets of male violence and that violence is effectively used to intimidate women into accepting their second-class status. As African Americans and other people of color are harassed, threatened, and brutalized to perpetuate discriminatory treatment, so women continue to be treated.

The organized women's movement can be traced directly to the abolitionist movement, the Civil War itself, and the disappointment and anger of women after the Civil War when they were told that they would have to wait indefinitely for recognition of their rights as citizens.

In 1840 Elizabeth Cady Stanton and Lucretia Mott attended an antislavery conference in London, England. While the U.S. delegation sent both men and women, the conference denied women official delegate status and relegated them to the gallery as spectators. Thus, at an antislavery conference in Europe, these two women were forced to recognize the social, legal, and political status of women. It was there that they vowed to come back home and fight to change women's circumstances.

Following up on their 1840 commitment in London, they convened the first women's rights convention in Seneca Falls, New York, at the Methodist chapel in July 1848. After writing a Declaration of Principles modeled after the Declaration of Independence, the women drafted several resolutions. The idea of women voting was so radical at the time that even at a women's rights convention the only resolution that did not pass unanimously was the ninth—"Resolved that it is the duty of the women of this country to secure their sacred right to the elective franchise." Only when Frederick Douglass added his eloquent affirmation to Elizabeth Cady Stanton's did the resolution pass. Resistance to women's vote was so prolonged that only one of the sixty-eight women who signed the Declaration at Seneca Falls, Charlotte Woodard, lived to vote in the 1920 election—at age ninety-three. And by the time she did, twenty-six other nations had already granted the right of their women citizens to vote.

The Seneca Falls ideas resonated strongly with many women's experiences and were widely explored in the numerous meetings and conventions held in the following years and reported on by an anxious press. Women actively gathered petitions and lobbied state legislatures on practical issues such as the Married Women's Property Act, which would protect a woman's property and earnings from being owned by her husband as English common law allowed. Their work soon had to be set aside, however, under pressure to devote all efforts to supporting the abolitionist cause.

Harriet Beecher Stowe's novel *Uncle Tom's Cabin* was enormously influential in building northern opposition to slavery, and also provoking a negative reaction in the South in defense of it. Susan B. Anthony's neighbors and countless other women opened their homes to hide slaves using the Underground Railroad to escape slavery and the Fugitive Slave Act. Abolitionist activism also allowed women the opportunity to hone their skills as organizers, writers, and public speakers—all skills they later used as advocates for women's suffrage.

During the Civil War, many women served as nurses, binding up the wounds of young men and soldiers injured on the battlefields. Out of such Civil War activity Clara Barton emerged as a strong voice and forceful leader—and founder of the American Red Cross. Today the American Red Cross is physically located just a couple of blocks from the White House, and carved in stone atop its headquarters are the words: IN MEMORY OF THE HEROIC WOMEN OF THE CIVIL WAR. Some women's nursing service, essential as it was, was not invoked the way some black soldiers' military service was to justify awarding them the vote.

After the war white women went South to teach in newly formed schools for black children, often founded by churches. White women also helped establish and run colleges and universities for young black men and women. They also formed organizations to lobby Congress to create pensions for widows and orphans who were the survivors of soldiers killed in the Civil War, and worked to provide charity for the impoverished.

In the North and South women worked for free public schools, temperance, and especially in organized labor to outlaw child labor and to improve the working conditions of women in the textile and other industries; and in social welfare and other "social uplift" movements, as they were called. In Illinois the ongoing presence of Jane Adams's Hull House and the Women's Christian Temperance Union, which started out with a focus on individual workers' drinking habits but advanced to fighting against the underlying economic and structural causes of poverty and unjust working conditions, are reminders of this work and activity.

While women were moving in ever-larger numbers from the "private sphere" of the home into the "public sphere" of paid employment and public service, their right to be treated as adult citizens and members of society, as symbolized by voting, was still denied. The work that northern—and even some southern—abolitionist women had done to free the slaves was disregarded. Men's political commitment to end slavery and bring about Reconstruction that culminated in the Thirteenth, Fourteenth, and Fifteenth Amendments for African Americans after the Civil War was not combined with an equal commitment to ending the social oppression, economic inequality, and political impotence of women—including African American women.

For African American women, discrimination has been doubly oppressive. The situation was stated clearly in 1890 by Mary Church Terrell, suffragist leader and founder of the National Association of Colored Women: "A white woman has only one handicap to overcome—a great one, true, her sex; a colored woman faces two—her sex and her race. A colored man has only one—that of race."[3] The inherent conflict this creates is enshrined in post–Civil War amendments to the Constitution.

Elizabeth Cady Stanton and Susan B. Anthony were the best-known leaders in the fight for equal rights for women in the postwar period, but they were joined by large numbers of women in their own generation and the next. Cady Stanton's daughter, Harriott Stanton Blatch, who was born in 1856 in Seneca Falls, New York, grew up to become the chief strategist of the women's rights movement in the largest and most important state, New York. As a key participant in the radical Woman's Party founded by Alice Paul, she was a senior stateswoman in the campaign that produced the Nineteenth Amendment to the U.S. Constitution. The perspective she had gained from long residence and political activism in England informed her democratic viewpoint and determination to build the American women's movement as a working-class political movement.

I am fascinated by her story because, at least in some respects, it parallels my own. Blatch's mother, Elizabeth Cady Stanton, was a militant and strongly focused feminist leader, not unlike my father with regard to civil rights. She joined Susan B. Anthony in courageously opposing the Fourteenth and Fifteenth Amendments to the Constitution after all efforts had failed to persuade male political leaders to stand up for equal rights for all—women included. Throughout her long career as a writer and public speaker, she braved men's wrath by attacking patriarchal oppression wherever she found it—in marriage and in the Bible, as well as in the Constitution.

Blatch had been raised not only to pursue the goal of women's suffrage, but to regard it as a crucial part of a larger mission of social democracy, economic equality, and political justice. Even though she was just seven years old at the time, she remembered the New York City draft riots of mid-July 1863, and her thinking was greatly influenced by the Civil War and its aftermath. Sojourner Truth had been a guest in her home.

Blatch was one of the modern era's first great women politicians. She insisted that "the vote" for women would not be gained by education, moral improvement, civic uplift, or any of the other women's traditional methods of social action—including direct action and civil disobedience. While all of these may be necessary and play a part, she insisted that political equality must be won politically, and to secure it, women would have to learn how to wield legislative, partisan, and electoral tools. Carrie Chapman Catt, her counterpart in the National American Women's Suffrage Association, applied the same understanding to a broadly pragmatic legislative strategy.

While not claiming to be a great politician, I have come to the same conclusion as Blatch and have the same orientation with regard to social democracy, economic equality, political justice, and progress for African Americans. African Americans can achieve justice and equality only to the degree that all Americans achieve social, economic, and political justice and equality, and all of it must be achieved through politics and political action. There will be no black or female justice apart from white, yellow, red, brown, and male justice. What affects one of us directly affects all of us indirectly. We must fight politically for the principle of equal protection of the law for all Americans. As a fundamental guarantee of the human and civil rights of half of the population, an equal rights amendment in the Constitution for women is an essential way to advance the cause of justice and equality for all.

Even though conservatives are the political constituency and elected leaders most opposed to equal rights for women and, therefore, an equal rights amendment to the Constitution, they are certainly not shy about proposing constitutional amendments of their own. In the 106th Congress (1999–2001), clearly understanding the greater power and force contained in a constitutional amendment than in mere federal legislation, conservatives proposed a large number of constitutional amendments: a balanced budget amendment; term limits; right to life; prohibition against flag desecration; voluntary school prayer; line-item veto; English as official language; provision of a procedure by which the states may propose constitutional amendments; limiting the public debt; tax limitations; abolition of the federal income tax; prohibiting courts from levying or increasing taxes; protecting the rights of crime victims; religious freedom; spending limitations; and abolition of personal income, estate, and gift taxes.

These proposals are very narrow, not very popular, and outside the purview of basic American values. More important, they do not work to benefit all Americans, and especially not average Americans. And according to polls, a large majority of the American people oppose them. Certainly the vast majority of the members of Congress oppose them. They do not consider these proposals to be in the best interests of the American people. In fact, they are generally seen by members as frivolous.

If we are to build a more perfect Union, we must think beyond the next election and legislative session. Progressives, especially, need to combine short-term strategies and tactics, regular election choices, and incremental legislative changes with a longer-term strategy and goals.

You may legitimately disagree with my proposed amendments philosophically and politically—that all Americans should have a constitutional right to vote, employment, health care, education, housing, a clean environment, and fair taxes—but no one can say such issues are frivolous or unimportant to the vast majority of the American people; or that they would not eventually make a significant positive difference in all Americans' lives and their lifetime opportunities; or that they go against the basic values and goals shared by virtually every individual in every American family.

But since it is clear that conservatives aren't opposed to new constitutional amendments, why do they object to a constitutional amendment that would provide equal legal protection for women under the Constitution? And do the politics surrounding and growing out of the Civil War have anything to say about the denial of equal rights for women today?

Most Americans just see the Constitution as a legal document. I don't see it quite that simply. When I put on the lens of race to view American history through the eyes of the African American experience, it forces me to look at the original Constitution not merely as a plan of government drafted by and for white men only, but as an "economic deal." I see it as an economic deal designed to protect the financial interests of white men who were landowners through the highest legal structure available to them, a Constitution of the United States. Why would slavery be structured into it five times if not to protect the economic interests of slaveholders?

Thus, the Founding Fathers were framing not just a plan of government, but also an economic deal for white male landowners. After all, it was essentially the same Founding Fathers who resisted and led a revolution over "taxation without representation" who also wrote the Constitution. White men who were not landowners, as well as women and people of color (none of whom paid taxes), were written out of the bargain. Much of our history since then has been a struggle to broaden this original economic arrangement to include more of the American people, and many of these struggles culminated and were crowned with the inclusion of new rights in the form of constitutional amendments. All of my proposed new amendments are in that lineage of greater inclusion and of broadening participation in the original economic deal.

After studying most of the previously cited amendments proposed by conservatives I came to two conclusions, one economic and one social. The effect of the economically oriented amendments would be to perpetuate the original economic dominance of the wealthiest white men. The balanced budget amendment, term limits, line-item veto, restrictions on annual spending, deficits, and the overall debt, and all of the antitax and tax limitation proposals would result in the status quo (or worse) of white men's economic dominance. Second, the political effect of the socially oriented amendments diverts attention from the basic issues of economic fairness, material inclusion, and freedom from crushing authority. Flag desecration, voluntary prayer in schools, English only, crime victims' rights, and religious freedom amendments all serve this diversionary purpose.

Further, the original deal of selective white male inclusion and economic domination also translated into social control and racial manipulation—to protect their economic hegemony. Thus, the conservative "right to life" amendment is an attempt to continue men's social and physical domination of women and is a direct challenge to the full equality of women. It implicitly denies women's status as human beings and their right to control their own bodies, make their own decisions, and determine their own direction and destiny.

It is a predictable effect of oppression that institutional sexism can be supported and advanced by women, just as institutional racism can be supported and advanced by African Americans—as in the case of some of the decisions and rationale given or supported by Supreme Court Justice Clarence Thomas. Cases involving states' powers *(Board of Trustees of the University of Alabama v. Garrett)*, voting rights *(Shaw v. Reno* and *Miller v. Johnson)*, and school desegregation *(Jenkins)* come quickly to mind.

Likewise during slavery, as self-designated protectors of cherished but subordinate white women, white men used the racial/sexual social scare tactic as a diversion to protect and preserve the dominance they held over their women, their slaves, and their patriarchal and slave systems. These tactics became part of the post–Civil War strategy to control the black population by terrorism, because endemic violence and the threat of violence serve at all times to enforce the ownership of women's bodies by male relatives and strangers alike.

Support for slavery and the strongest resistance to black civil rights came, and still comes, from these same conservative forces in the South, and it should be no surprise that southern conservatives have also consistently opposed women's rights. Looking at American history through the lens of race heightens awareness of this aspect of anti-women politics.

For example, in a roll call vote that required a two-thirds majority for the ERA to pass in the first session of the Ninety-eighth Congress (1983–1985), it was defeated by a vote of 278 to 147. The Republicans voted 53 to 109 against and the Democrats 225 to 38 in favor. But of the 38 negative votes by Democrats, 25 (66 percent) were cast by southern Democrats from the eleven former Confederate states, with 31 out of 36 southern Republican votes (from their total of 109 against) coming from those same eleven states voting "no." Southern Democrats and Republicans (as well as many northerners) today, of course, are in the lineage of the slaveholding, Jim Crow, racially and sexually discriminatory, and patriarchal Democrats of a century and a half ago. Thus, of the 129 total congressional districts in thirteen southern states (the total survey included Oklahoma and Kentucky), nearly half of all southern representatives, Democrats and Republicans, voted against the ERA. In other words, the bill was essentially killed in the South.

As the history of the Fourteenth Amendment demonstrates, however, it would be incorrect to lay blame for the defeat of the Equal Rights Amendment exclusively on southern conservatives. They may simply have served as the front-line defense for men throughout the country who, in the words of John Stuart Mill, "cannot yet tolerate the idea of living with an equal."[4] It was, after all, northern liberal men who drafted the sex discriminatory Fourteenth and Fifteenth Amendments and engineered the "Negroes' Hour" strategy, to which Frederick Douglass assented, in the vain hope of winning the 1872 election by enfranchising black men and excluding women. Their early strategy to destroy any possible political alliance between former slaves and abolitionist women meshed only too well with white southerners' exploitation of the black rapist myth in promoting mutual resentment and distrust.

With both economic and social conservatism still strong in the South, my guess is that, politically, if the same vote were taken today the "no" vote would be similar, or possibly even stronger, in those 129 southern congressional districts. Again, looking at American history through the lens of race—and seeing the social, economic, and political consequences of the legacy of slavery's ideology, institutions, and structures—even allows us to see the underlying pattern of a vote on women's rights more clearly.

The law in our early history allowed women few rights. Colonists brought with them the common law of England, which gave single women only limited rights. Once married, the husband possessed and exercised any rights that did exist, including the right to vote.

Women sought to vote as early as 1647. Margaret Brent appealed to the Maryland Council. She was the rare wealthy owner of a plantation and an agent and representative of Lord Baltimore, the proprietor of the Maryland colony, and the executor of another estate. Possessing the self-worth, identity, and ego that property often bestows, she demanded not just one vote, but two—one vote for each of the properties. The Maryland Council denied her request.

In some rare instances, women voted until they were outlawed from it—as was the case in New Jersey until 1807. A few states (the first, Kentucky, in 1838) enfranchised women to vote in rural local school board elections. Following the "Go West, Young Man" trend, however, men found few white women out west. In order to attract more women to the frontier, Wyoming became the first state to grant full voting rights to women. Other western states followed Wyoming's lead and, in a rare exception to most other important events, the women's suffrage movement moved from west to east.

Women's suffrage had many opponents beyond men's general desire to cling to privileges that helped give them authority over women. Male-run businesses and male-dominated big-city Democratic machines were opposed. As new voters, if the women were honest, graft was at risk, and if they were corrupt, the cost of buying elections could rise. Railroad interests and industrialists employing child labor saw any bloc of new voters as a threat to their control over politicians.

The brewing and distilling industry saw women in the temperance movement as a threat to their economic interests and charged per-keg assessments to fund campaigns against the suffrage amendment. Ratification of the Eighteenth Amendment in 1919 signaled the demise of their powerful lobby and helped clear the way for ratification of the Nineteenth Amendment in 1920.

Intense opposition to women's right to vote came from southern political leaders. They resented the role that northern women had played in both the abolitionist movement, the Civil War itself, and now in Reconstruction—among other things, helping educate the former slaves in the South. Women were also a threat to the patriarchal and hierarchal social, economic, religious, and political structures of the South. The Roman Catholic Church, but especially the fundamentalist and conservative Protestant churches of the South—the large number of white southern Baptists in particular—all strongly opposed women's suffrage:

> The question of woman suffrage, if put into effect, is simply a key that's going to unlock the gates of hell and turn the demons loose upon the human family. . . . [T]hey are trying to bring women into public life. There she is distinctly out of place. She was made for man's glory—to mother man. . . . When you hand her the ballot, you simply give her a club to knock her brains out.

Southern fear-mongering frequently linked woman suffrage with the threat of black political dominance:

> MEN OF THE SOUTH: Remember that woman suffrage means a reopening of the entire Negro suffrage question, loss of State rights, and another period of reconstruction horrors, which will introduce a set of female carpetbaggers as bad as their male prototypes of the 'sixties.

But nonsoutherners had their say as well:

> In half a century the political equality of men and women will change the whole basis of social organization. . . . The smothered brutality of both sexes will be fanned into a blaze and the results easily imagined."

Even though the parties' commitment was weak in 1916, both Democrats and Republicans finally included a plank in their platforms in support of women's suffrage. President Woodrow Wilson endorsed the Nineteenth Amendment and the House passed it in 1918, but the Senate defeated it. Both houses of Congress passed it in 1919, and it was ratified in 1920 when Tennessee, on August 18, became the thirty-sixth state to ratify.

The United States was the *twenty-seventh* nation to provide women the ability to vote. U.S. women had to wait fifty years after the Fifteenth Amendment affirmed the same ability for African American men in 1870. In practical terms, however, after a short-lived period during Reconstruction, no African Americans, male or female, were permitted to register or vote in any significant numbers in the South until the 1965 Voting Rights Act.

Thirteen of the fifteen states that had granted women's right to vote in all elections by 1918 were in the West. It was understandable then why Jeannette Rankin of Montana, a Republican, was the first woman to be elected to the U.S. House of Representatives on November 9, 1916, even though the Nineteenth Amendment was not made part of the Constitution until 1920. She was an ardent suffragist and pacifist who, during her only two terms in Congress, the Sixty-fifth (1917–1919) and the Seventy-seventh (1941–1943), opposed U.S. involvement in both World Wars I and II.

Ironically, despite its support in 1916 for the Nineteenth Amendment, the Republican Party's 1980 platform took no position on the ERA, reversing a forty-year Republican tradition of support for the amendment in its platform begun in 1940. Its candidate, Ronald Reagan, publicly opposed the ERA. Conservative Republican leadership since then has continued to oppose an equal rights amendment to the Constitution. Democrats have reintroduced ERA legislation in Congress each session, but otherwise have done little to move it forward in recent years. Both Democrats and Republicans joined in the effort in 1971 to handicap ERA's ratification by placing a nearly unprecedented time limitation on the ratification process.

> Join the union, girls, and together say, "Equal Pay for Equal Work!"
>
> —Susan B. Anthony, *The Revolution*, March 18, 1869

Clearly, women have made progress and contributed much to America, as well as enduring many setbacks. Margaret Abbot won a gold medal in 1900, the first Olympics in which women were allowed to compete. Madam C. J. Walker, by creating a hair care and grooming system to meet the needs of African American women and providing employment and business opportunities for hundreds of African American women, became the first African American millionaire in 1905. She actively used her wealth and influence to promote black civil rights. Journalist Ida Wells Barnett boldly used the power of her newspaper and her international lecture tours to publicize and demand an end to lynching. As organizer of the first black women's suffrage club in Illinois and a delegate to the National American Woman Suffrage Association's 1913 March in Washington, D.C., she disregarded the officials' insistence that she march with black delegates at the rear of the procession and integrated the march by quietly stepping out of the crowd and joining her Illinois colleagues.

In a 1909 "Uprising of the 20,000" in New York, women struck for better wages and working conditions and forced three hundred shops to sign union contracts. In New York in 1912, twenty thousand women marched for the right to vote before a crowd of half a million. They were attacked, and forty were wounded and hospitalized. Suffragist Alice Paul and Woman's Party members in Washington, D.C., were repeatedly arrested for peacefully picketing the White House and sent to Occoquan Work House, where they were brutally treated and force-fed when they went on a hunger strike. History textbooks rarely mention these violent events in their brief accounts of how women were "given" the vote.

Taking advantage of a labor shortage during World War I, women began working in previously all-male industries and service sectors—heavy industry, manufacturing, automobile and railway plants; running streetcars, conducting trains, directing traffic, and delivering mail. After the war, however, women were pressured to surrender those jobs to male war veterans and go back to unpaid domestic work or lower-paid "women's jobs." The same pattern was repeated during and after World War II.

In 1930, 77 percent of school districts would not hire married women as teachers, and 63 percent fired women who got married. In 1932 the National Recovery Act prohibited more than one family member from holding a government job, resulting in many women losing their jobs. The protective labor laws for which women fought improved conditions for all workers but were later used as a pretext for "protecting" women out of more remunerative jobs. At the same time, political professionals like Eleanor Roosevelt and Esther Peterson succumbed to the pressure to agree with the argument used against the ERA in the 1930s and 1940s that women could not have both "special protection" and equality. Tactics like these held back progress on the ERA until women's participation in the civil rights movement, combined with their anger at their repressive and domestically subservient role after World War II, led to the renewal of the women's movement and new interest in the ERA.

The idea that political rights create and protect all other rights is as true for women as it is for men. Women will make progress, and America will make progress, to the degree that women achieve political parity with men at every level of government. More than eighty years after women's right to nondiscrimination in voting was recognized, the presence of women in elective and appointive office is not representative of their numbers in the general population. Significant barriers to running for office discourage women from making the effort, including the high cost of campaigning, lack of a support base akin to an "old boys' network," and public stereotypes about women's responsibilities to home and family. The numbers show that there is still a long way to go to equal representation.

There are approximately five hundred thousand publicly elected or appointed officials in the United States, with an estimated 20 percent being women, even though women constitute a majority of the population. It should be noted that the vast majority of these are local nonpaid positions and do not have offices or staffs. No accurate number is available for women in all of these positions, but in February 2001, according to the Center for American Women and Politics (CAWP) at the Eagleton Institute of Politics at Rutgers University, 89 women held statewide elective executive offices, which was 27.6 percent of the available 323 positions, and included 45 Democrats, 41 Republicans, 1 Independent and 2 who were elected in nonpartisan races. Five of the total (5.6 percent) are women of color.

At the state legislative level, of the 7,424 positions available, women hold 1,663 (22.4 percent)—a number that has increased fivefold since 1969, when only 301 (4 percent) of all state legislators were women—and 264 (15.9 percent) are women of color. Again according to the CAWP, women hold 394 (19.9 percent) of the 1,984 state Senate seats, and 1,269 (23.3 percent) of the 5,440 state House seats—which includes 71 senators and 193 representatives who are women of color, all but 8 of whom are Democrats. Women of color constitute 3.6 percent of the total of 7,424 state legislators.

The top ten states with the highest percentage of women as state legislators are: Washington (38.8 percent), Colorado (35.0 percent), Nevada (34.9 percent), Arizona (34.4 percent), Kansas (33.3 percent), Oregon (33.3 percent), New Mexico (31.3 percent), Maine (30.1 percent), New Hampshire (29.5 percent), and Connecticut (29.4 percent). Is it pure coincidence that six of these ten are western states, and not one southern state has ever been in the top ten? I surmise that it is because western states were the first to grant women the right to vote, and southern states have a history of keeping women powerless. Thus, established positive and negative traditions continue to play themselves out even today.

According to David Bositis at the Joint Center for Political and Economic Studies, at the end of 2000 there are a total of 8,936 African American elected and appointed officials, of whom 2,997 (33.5 percent) are women, a much higher percent than for white women.

In the entire history of Congress, as of this writing, there have been only 208 women elected or appointed to the body out of 11,639 (not including delegates) total members— 9,775 individuals in the House and 1,232 in the Senate, with 630 people having served in both. Of the 208 women in Congress, 178 served only in the House and 24 served only in the Senate, with 7 having served in both houses. One hundred thirty-four have been Democrats and 74 Republicans. A record 74 women (13.7 percent) are serving in the 107th Congress (2001–2003); 61 from 29 states and territories serve in the House and 13 from 10 states serve in the Senate (California, Washington, and Maine all have two women senators), including 43 Democrats and 18 Republicans in the House, and 10 Democrats and 3 Republicans in the Senate. This total includes Washington, D.C., and the Virgin Islands, which are represented by women delegates to the House.

A total of twenty-one African American women have served in Congress, including Democrat Carol Moseley Braun from Illinois, the only African American woman senator, from 1993 to 1999. Patsy Mink, a Democrat from Hawaii, was the first Asian American, and Ileana Ros-Lehtinen, a Republican of Florida, was the first Hispanic American women to serve in Congress. Twelve women have chaired congressional committees.

Until the October 23, 1991, oath of office put Clarence Thomas on the Supreme Court, after the controversy arising out of Anita Hill's testimony during the Senate confirmation hearings, there had never been more than three women at one time in the Senate. To some extent because of Clarence Thomas, in 1993 there were seven. In each of the three congresses thereafter there were nine, and now there are thirteen.[5]

The low percentage of women in Congress will begin to climb significantly when effective campaign finance reforms are adopted and when more women are able to gain political experience at state and local levels, enabling them to move up the political ladder. Recognizing that constraints to women holding office are often unfair, some nations have adopted policies that mandate that political parties allot a specific quota of their candidate slots to women. A few countries, such as India, have adopted a constitutional amendment reserving at least a third of local elective positions for women. In France, local election lists must have as many women as men, and in Argentina women must make up 30 percent of political parties' parliamentary representatives. Shouldn't we be asking why our exemplary democracy has not applied such affirmative methods to defeat systemic inequality?

Recognizing that women are grossly underrepresented in the higher echelons of decision making in government, the private sector, the judiciary, and in academic institutions, 189 nations at the fourth World Conference on Women, in 1995, committed themselves to take specific steps to ensure women's equal access. Since then, the United States has done little to reach a balance by sex in governmental bodies and to encourage women's full participation in public life. Could it be that conservative political leaders fear what may be the likely consequences of the more socially conscious women politicians? The presence of women in higher numbers in decision-making bodies means changes in the political agenda;

studies of the 103rd and 104th Congress show that women representatives are more likely to sponsor bills that speak to women's and children's health concerns, education, and child care. Further examination of the direction of legislative bodies in the U.S. western states will determine whether women politicians gaining critical mass will reshape dynamics of those institutions.

P rogressives, however, must not be satisfied to fight just for passage of a strong and meaningful equal rights amendment in the United States. We must join in the global movement toward equality for men and women by demanding of our national leadership an active commitment to eradicate discrimination based on sex. For nearly twenty years the U.S. Senate has refused to adopt a resolution recommending ratification of the United Nations Convention on the Elimination of All Forms of Discrimination Against Women that would require signatories to adopt laws to eliminate discrimination in education, employment and compensation, health care, family policies, financial credit, and all other spheres of political and public life. This failure in our nation's leadership is inexcusable; the United States must advocate strongly for women's human rights at home and abroad.

We must fight for greater social, economic, and political justice for women everywhere around the world. Despite what many may consider almost insurmountable obstacles of violence and social subordination maintained against women, especially poor women of color in the underdeveloped world, many activists still have a vision and see new possibilities. The World Conference on Human Rights in Vienna in 1993 stressed the theme that "women's rights are human rights." The International Conference on Population and Development in Cairo in 1994 placed "women's rights, empowerment and health—including reproductive health—at the center of population and sustainable development policies and programs." The Beijing Conference in 1995 reached general agreement on a Platform of Action that "seeks to promote and protect the full enjoyment of all human rights and the fundamental freedoms of all women throughout their life cycle."[6]

At a gathering of nearly all the world's leaders—the largest such meeting ever held—the three-day United Nation's Millennium Summit ended on September 8, 2000, by issuing a statement of agreed-upon goals and common values. Among the common goals and values were freedom—"men and women have the right to live their lives and raise their children in dignity, free from hunger and from the fear of violence, oppression or injustice. Democratic and participatory governance based on the will of the people best assures these rights"—and equality—"No individual and no nation must be denied the opportunity to benefit from development. The equal rights and opportunities of women and men must be assured."

The U.N. statement also said that the world has shared responsibilities—such as that, by the year 2015, "children everywhere, boys and girls alike, will be able to complete a full course of primary schooling; and that girls and boys will have equal access to all levels of education. By the same date, to have reduced maternal mortality by three-quarters, and under-5 mortality by two-thirds, of their current rates." The final document said, "We also resolve: to promote gender equality and the empowerment of women, as effective ways to combat poverty, hunger and disease and to stimulate development that is truly sustainable."

Passing the ERA will bring to fruition the idea and ideal of legal equality for women in this country at the highest level—the Constitution. It is our democratic principles that best serve our long-term national interests: They will be emulated and promoted by others around the world. The ideals contained in an ERA inspire women—and all justice-loving people—to want to import them into their own legal structures and forms of government. People of the world want us to export such ideas, and it appears that some are moving faster than the United States is to implement them. Advocates know that if equality to a human standard can be achieved and work in our multicultural and multireligious society, it has the possibility of working elsewhere as well.

Passing the ERA will legally empower women in America, but it will also embolden and, therefore, contribute to empowering women everywhere. Women are not alone in the fight for recognition of their human and civil rights. The endeavor to achieve an ERA in our Constitution has worldwide social, economic, and political ramifications and implications. Therefore, passing and ratifying the ERA will contribute not only to building a more perfect Union, but to constructing a more perfect international community as well.

A MORE PERFECT UNION—
THE ENVIRONMENT

The earth is the Lord's and the fullness thereof, the world and those
who dwell therein; for he has founded it upon the seas, and established it upon the rivers.

—Psalms 24:1–2

All creation is the Lord's, and we are responsible for the ways in
which we use and abuse it. Water, air, soil, minerals, energy resources, plants, animal life, and space are to be valued and conserved
because they are God's creation and not solely because they are useful to human beings. Therefore, we repent of our devastation of the
physical and nonhuman world. Further, we recognize the responsibility of the Church toward lifestyle and systemic changes in society that will promote a more ecologically just world and a better
quality of life for all creation.

—United Methodist Church, Social Principles, The Natural World

Humanity stands at a defining moment in history. We are confronted with a perpetuation of disparities between and within nations, a worsening of poverty, hunger, ill health and illiteracy, and
the continuing deterioration of the ecosystems on which we depend
for our well-being. However, integration of environment and development concerns and greater attention to them will lead to the
fulfillment of basic needs, improved living standards for all, better
protected and managed ecosystems and a safer, more prosperous future. No nation can achieve this on its own; but together we can—
in a global partnership for sustainable development.

—U.N. Agenda 21, Preface 1.1, 1999

The common underlying factor of conflicts today is the issue of insecurity prompted by the prospect of exclusion or the perceived
threat of starvation for both people and communities. The circumstances of this feeling of insecurity are often brought about by
degradation of the environment. An Earth Charter will make every
one of us conscious of this and help develop a culture of peace, care
and solidarity.

—Ambassador Mohamed Sahnoun,
Earth Charter commissioner, Algeria

Not one cent for scenery.

—"Old Foul Mouth" Joseph G. Cannon,
Speaker of the House, 1903–1911, rejecting
a request for a conservation appropriation[1]

PROPOSED ENVIRONMENTAL AMENDMENT TO THE U.S. CONSTITUTION

Section 1. All citizens of the United States shall enjoy the right to a clean, safe, and sustainable environment.
Section 2. The Congress shall have power to implement this article by appropriate legislation.

Conservatives argued for years that industrial and economic expansion were incompatible with a clean environment. Modern technology, of course, disproves that theory. Today we can have both—if we want both.

I am acutely aware of environmental hazards, and environmental racism, because my congressional district in some ways is ground zero for both.

The Second Congressional District of Illinois is the longtime home of Chicago's industrial corridor. The landscape is dotted with steel mills, car and train manufacturers, refineries, and other smokestack industries. While many factories' heyday is long since past, the old plants that remain are saddled with outdated technology and safeguards that leave the public at risk.

Adding insult to injury, the Second District is greater Chicago's historic dumping ground. For more than one hundred years, the area housed some of the nation's largest garbage dumps—legal and illegal—hazardous waste reservoirs, and sewage treatment plants.

In fact, one of the most forsaken one-half square miles in North America might well be located in my district. It is the Chicago Housing Authority's Altgeld Gardens housing project. Altgeld, as it is known, has a huge garbage dump immediately to the south and east, a mammoth sewage- and sludge-treatment facility, plus several foul-smelling paint and petrochemical factories immediately to the north, and the hulking Acme Steel Company mill immediately to the west. As if that weren't enough, Altgeld is built on top of what many believe was the city of Chicago's first (albeit undocumented) garbage dump, now a century old.

Altgeld's problems are well documented. Local pollutants, including PCBs, lead, hydrocarbons, various carcinogens, and a witch's brew of toxic air, ground, and water contaminants have been recorded by the federal and state EPAs. Recent state health studies found heightened incidences of asthma and numerous other health ailments. In 1998 the Chicago Housing Authority's own study recommended a massive relocation of residents. Ignoring its own study, however, the Chicago Housing Authority recently proposed a Band-Aid rehabilitation of the nearly two thousand units.

But you need not be a scientist to detect Altgeld's problems. A casual observer couldn't help but notice that Altgeld Gardens has no gardens; that noise from the mills and factories is nonstop; and that the pungent odors from the nearby sewage, sludge, garbage, and factories, particularly on muggy summer days, requires motorists on a nearby highway to literally hold their breath while they speed by.

Nevertheless, amid all this, there sits Altgeld Gardens—an isolated patch of land, detached from the rest of the city of Chicago, surrounded by contaminated air, ground, and water—where five thousand people live in one of the most dilapidated public housing projects in America. Even so, out of the midst of this poverty and environmental disaster came one of the most famous basketball players and finest human beings Chicago has ever produced, Terry Cummings. While raised in the nearby Roseland community, he became a star at Altgeld's Carver High School and DePaul University in Chicago; he was the second overall pick in the 1982 NBA draft by the San Diego Clippers, where he was voted the 1982–1983 Rookie of the Year. I got to know him as a willing volunteer participant in an annual fund-raising game in Chicago sponsored by Operation PUSH called the PUSH-EXCEL Pro-Basketball Classic. Cummings, superbly conditioned at six feet, nine inches and 235 pounds in his prime, nevertheless takes medicine for a heart condition. I have often wondered if there was a relationship between his ailment and the unsafe environment in which he grew up—and how many others from Altgeld are suffering similarly, or even worse, as a result.

Altgeld residents, of course, deserve much better. For decades they have fought to up-grade their quality of life. Local activist Hazel Johnson has visited with many presidents and is often featured in newspapers, magazines, and books. But despite the efforts of Ms. Johnson and her organization, People for Community Recovery, living conditions in Altgeld have not notably improved since the low-rise structures were built sixty years ago. The conditions in Altgeld would not be politically tolerated in any but a poor or people of color community. The politicians would have bulldozed it many years ago.

While Altgeld may sound like a perfect example of environmental racism in the Second Congressional District, tragically there are two better examples. They are the south suburban villages of Ford Heights and Robbins.

Ford Heights has been the poorest suburb in America for thirty years running, according to Roosevelt University urbanologist Pierre deVise, whose findings are based on U.S. Census reports. Robbins, meanwhile, has been in the bottom ten nationally and is currently the second poorest suburb in the state of Illinois, behind Ford Heights. Their recent tales of environmental racism are remarkably similar, and scandalous.

Back in the late 1980s, America was facing a perceived landfill crisis. You may recall the infamous garbage barge, which for weeks floated up and down the East Coast looking for a harbor to dump its load of municipal waste. With the image of that garbage barge fresh in their minds and seeking to capitalize on a potential crisis, the Illinois General Assembly approved lucrative incentives for any incinerators relocating to Illinois. Practically overnight, Illinois was inundated with applications from incinerator companies worldwide seeking to cash in on the state's generosity.

At one point fifteen incinerator plans surfaced, virtually all looking to locate in impoverished neighborhoods in South Chicago or some nearby impoverished southern suburb. The incinerator developers targeted small poor and mostly black communities where they knew local officials craved development of any kind.

Predictably, heated public debates ensued. Most pitted working- and middle-class whites in neighboring communities who opposed the incinerators against poor blacks from these two economically depressed villages who, in desperation, welcomed them. It was a classic case of corporate interests investing heavily in a PR campaign to take advantage of a community in desperate straits. After months of bitter, often racially tinged, feuding, the corporations prevailed.

Thus, two giant waste incinerators were built in Illinois's two poorest communities—a garbage burner in Robbins, and a tire and rubber burner in Ford Heights. The Robbins facility was said to be the largest trash burner in North America.

Those incinerators were built before I took office, but I warned other communities that such projects were not development but "de-development," meaning they would preclude future development. After all, what grocery store, strip mall, tool shop, car dealership, or fast-food restaurant wants to locate next to a huge garbage incinerator? Beyond that, I warned that the tension created between the white opponents and black proponents would create unnecessary racial divisions between otherwise diverse but generally friendly neighboring communities.

Then, just as the Robbins and Ford Heights burners were nearing completion, the story took a cruel twist.

Waste management officials unveiled a new study that concluded that, thanks to increased local "reduce and recycle" efforts, local landfills had extended their useful life by at least ten years. Whoosh, the perceived landfill crisis evaporated overnight.

Illinois lawmakers, realizing that their incentive package was no longer necessary and fearing it could prove quite costly, took the nearly unprecedented step of repealing the incentives.

The repeal was devastating to Ford Heights and Robbins. Without the state subsidies, both incinerators suddenly found themselves unneeded, teetering on bankruptcy, and operating at bare minimum levels. To this day, neither facility has generated the business, jobs, tax base, or local benefits that were promised. Instead, the villages are left with hulking plants that stand as symbols of economic failure in Illinois's poorest communities.

The fact that no incinerator was proposed, much less approved, in more affluent communities begs the question of whether color, poverty, and the environment came together around something called environmental racism.

However, regardless of the color or economic condition of a community, because there are no clear-cut legal protections for individual residents, there is little legal recourse. Without change, it is inevitable that corporations will continue to exploit poor and desperate communities, government watchdog agencies will continue to bow to corporate pressure, and stories like those in Altgeld Gardens, Ford Heights, and Robbins will continue unabated.

The environment is so important to life that when Sandi gave birth to our daughter Jessica, the doctors' first concern was an environmental one—making sure the path to Jessica's lungs was clear so she could get air. When we brought her home, as first-time parents, there was nothing over which we lost more sleep than making certain our daughter could breathe and did not suffocate. Our daughter's birth and early months drove home to us a most simple environmental point—nothing is more fundamental to life than air. In fact, however, virtually all of life is that way if we only take the time to think about it. It's just that we've taken the environment for granted. We shouldn't, and we can't do it any longer.

Among the American people, a clean and safe environment may be our most understandable and least fear-laden national and international quest. The environment is an area where almost all people—young and old, rich and poor, conservatives, moderates, and progressives—can understand the need for greater national and international resources, cooperation, and coordination. We know that protecting our air, water, earth, and atmosphere is essential to our very existence.

Most people understand that pollution will destroy the ozone layer and, unless they protect themselves, the more direct exposure to the sun's ultraviolet rays will increase their risk of skin cancer. The resulting warming of the sea will also increase turbulent weather all over the world, while the wind spreads industrial pollution everywhere. More people have come to understand that an oil spill at sea can damage or destroy an ecosystem, which can eventually, if not immediately, negatively effect the earth and the whole human family.

Our world is so vast and extensively interconnected that environmental damage and catastrophes affect all of us. For example, fallout from a nuclear explosion—underground, on earth, at sea, or in space—poses the risk of potentially serious alterations to our environment and even annihilation of life on earth as we know it. While Dr. Martin Luther King, Jr., may not have been fully aware or referring directly to the environmental impact of a nuclear explosion, his words are still applicable and appropriate because he understood that our choice for the survival of the human race now is "between non-violence and non-existence"—and I'm sure he would have understood and connected his concepts of violence and nonviolence to the environment. He also understood that whatever affects each of us directly and individually affects all of us indirectly and collectively.

The world is so vast and interconnected that environmental damage, problems, and issues that affect all of us cannot be solved by individual nation-states. We must have a much broader perspective, and more cooperation and coordination if we are to sustain the earth with a high quality of life. While the modern-day environmental movement was born in the 1940s, it is in this broader context and more mature understanding of our universe that a worldwide environmental movement is growing. We need a national and international approach. That is why a strong environmental amendment to the U.S. Constitution would be a good first step.

While our global village shares the common goal of a clean, safe, and sustainable environment, our efforts to achieve that goal are sometimes diverted by economically self-interested businesses, often by approaches that are disjointed and uncoordinated, and occasionally by effective, but limited, grassroots activism. Most important of all, however, is the lack of a set of legal standards contained in a superlaw, our Constitution. My amendment would address this.

The fact that the political right, center, and left seem to share the same environmental goals makes it reasonable to propose codifying them in the form of a constitutional amendment. The discussion needs to move beyond the realm of good intentions, well-meaning speeches, lofty resolutions, volunteerism, economic incentives, and mere legislation—which is sometimes drafted by interests opposed to the public interest—to the level of our highest law.

Unfortunately, it won't be easy. While the reality is that international business and finance have created our new globally connected world, conservatives, with their rhetorical and ideological emphasis on individuality and localism, express great fear that such an amendment would just be another step down the road toward a "New World Order" or "World Government." Ultimately, they fear the loss of some individual freedoms or our sovereignty as a nation. Their reasons are often vague and lack accurate, sufficient, or important information. Nevertheless, such fear is real and must be taken into account if we are to build a more perfect Union and world. More democracy, greater citizen participation, and more education—not less—in the United States and around the world are important keys to alleviating such fear.

In politics this fear manifests itself in many ways, such as opposition to world trade agreements, refusal by the United States to pay its fair share of money to sustain the United Nations, and threats to pull out of the U.N. altogether. Those fears also, sometimes unwittingly, impact environmental issues.

I am a strong supporter of staying in the U.N. and of paying our fair share of the U.N. budget for peacekeeping and other purposes. However, I did oppose NAFTA, the WTO, the fast-tracking of GATT, the African Growth and Opportunity Act (AGOA), and permanent normal trade relations (PNTR) with China, but for very different reasons than conservatives like Pat Buchanan and Ross Perot. I opposed them not because I'm a conservative or a liberal, against "free trade" or for "protectionism," but for progressive reasons. These corporate-oriented trade agreements and organizations lack transparency (openness) in their deliberations and public accountability in their legal protection of human and workers' rights and the environment.

I'm against protectionism and an enthusiastic supporter of international trade, if it protects human and workers' rights and the environment and benefits middle-class entrepreneurs and working people in the trading countries, not just the international financial speculators and multinational corporations.

Therefore, I support establishing a set of guiding principles for an international environmental policy through the United Nations. International cooperation and coordination are absolute necessities, even as each individual and nation does its part as well. That's why we in the United States need a constitutional amendment—to give the environment the status it deserves and the legal protection it needs at the highest level of our law.

An amendment, of course, does not spell out the legislative or other specifics with regard to the kind of environmental policies or programs Congress, states, businesses, and individuals should put in place. But it does provide an environmental framework accompanied by the force of law. A constitutional amendment is the best way to show whether we are serious about protecting and sustaining the environment.

Conservatives like to argue that their goal is to "empower the individual." An environmental constitutional amendment empowers every American with a right and a legal remedy, as an individual or as part of a class action, which would guarantee each individual's right to a clean, safe, and sustainable environment. A constitutional amendment would also encourage industry to produce and distribute products with greater sustainability and minimal environmental damage.

If we are to effectively fight to secure a new right in our Constitution to protect the environment, it is important to understand what has transpired before us. After several decades of insecurity and major wars at the beginning of the twentieth century, the United Nations was established in 1945 to try to bring about greater security in the world. It focused principally on the issues of peace, human rights, and equitable socioeconomic development as the keys to that security. At the time, the environment was not seen as one of the critical links to security.

This is changing, however, as our environmental consciousness evolves. Our modern-day environmental laws took root in the 1940s and 1950s. For example, Congress passed the initial Clean Water Act and Clean Air Act in 1948 and 1955 respectively.

Many consider a book written by Rachel Carson in 1962, *Silent Spring*, to be the springboard for first understanding the interconnectedness of the environment, the economy, and human well-being. Professionally a marine biologist, Carson worked for the U.S. Fish and Wildlife Service and authored *The Sea Around Us* and *The Edge of the Sea*. *Silent Spring* investigated DDT and the pesticide industry and how it was polluting our environment. Rachel Carson made environmentalism respectable. Before her book, most Americans saw science in simple terms, as a force for good. She exposed its darker side as well. She showed how DDT and other chemicals used to enhance agricultural productivity were also poisoning our lakes, rivers, oceans, and people. Carson made Americans look anew at the market's criteria of progress—tons of wheat produced and insects killed—and helped us redefine progress as economic growth that benefited the human family as well as sustained the environment.

In a most moving and graphic way the environment was brought to earth when an *Apollo 8* crew traveled to the moon in 1968. On the way, astronauts focused a television camera on a distant object, and the American people saw for the first time the earth looking like a big blue marble suspended in space. In that one moment, people of the world felt spiritually connected. It gave us a new perspective on our environment.

In 1969 Congress passed the National Environmental Policy Act, which established a basic legal framework and set policy and goals.

Determined to raise the consciousness of Americans about the environment, in 1970 Senator Gaylord Nelson, a Democrat from Wisconsin, created the first Earth Day. National Coordinator Denis Hayes, on April 22, organized more than twenty million Americans to participate in peaceful environmental demonstrations and teach-ins. Until then, many different environmental organizations had been fighting against oil spills, polluting factories and power plants, raw sewage and toxic waste dumps, pesticides, the loss of wilderness, and more. Earth Day helped them realize that they shared many common values and goals. Earth Day activities—and ongoing environmental agitation and political organizing—eventually led to the creation of the U.S. Environmental Protection Agency (EPA) and passage of the Clean Air Act in 1970, the Endangered Species Act in 1973, and the Clean Water Act in 1977. Senator Nelson was awarded the Presidential Medal of Freedom, the highest honor given to civilians in the United States, for his role as founder of Earth Day.

In 1970 the Savannah River nuclear power plant near Aiken, South Carolina, experienced a meltdown of its fuel rods, even though the incident was not officially acknowledged for eighteen years. That same year the Occupational Safety and Health Act was passed to ensure worker and workplace safety. The goal was to make sure employers did not expose workers to toxic chemicals, excessive noise levels, mechanical dangers, heat or cold stress, or unsanitary conditions. In that same year, Congress also passed the Resource Recovery Act, intended to encourage recycling. In 1971 Congress passed a law to prevent lead-based paint poisoning, and in 1972 it passed the Federal Water Pollution Control Act, which set the basic legislative framework for regulating discharges of pollutants into U.S. waters.

Internationally, however, it wasn't until the Stockholm Conference on the Human Environment in 1972 that the environment emerged as a fourth major area of focus for the United Nations, alongside peace, human rights, and equitable socioeconomic development. Since Stockholm, many governments, international bodies, coalitions, and countless individuals have sought to establish a common environmental framework of shared values and mutual principles that balance development, conservation, and a sustainable way of life.

The aforementioned Endangered Species Act of 1973 provided a program for the conservation of threatened and endangered plants and animals and their habitats. The U.S. Fish and Wildlife Service at the Department of the Interior maintains a list of 632 endangered and 190 threatened species of animals and plants. Also in 1973, the OPEC oil crisis created a debate over sustainable development. And in response to deforestation and environmental degradation, the Chipko Movement was founded in 1973 in India, with women and foresters emerging as important environmental players. Chipko, which has influenced natural resource policy in India, was a spontaneous movement, mainly village-level women, protesting logging abuses in Uttar Pradesh in the Himalayas. The name of the movement comes from a word meaning "embrace." Following in the footsteps of Dr. Martin Luther King, Jr., the women practiced satyagraha—nonviolent resistance—by putting their bodies between the trees and the contractors' axes, thus becoming the environmental movement's first tree huggers.

Congress passed the Safe Drinking Water Act in 1974 to protect the quality of our drinking water and the Resource Conservation and Recovery Act (RCRA, pronounced "rick-rah") in 1976, which gave the EPA authority to control hazardous waste from cradle to grave. The law addressed the generation, transportation, treatment, storage, and disposal of hazardous waste. RCRA also set forth a framework for the management of nonhazardous wastes. In that same year, Congress passed the Toxic Substances Control Act (TSCA), giving the EPA authority to track seventy-five thousand industrial chemicals produced or imported into the United States, to continually screen, test, and report chemicals that pose an environmental or health hazard, and to track the thousands of new chemicals that industry develops each year. The EPA also had the power to ban the manufacture or importing of dangerous chemicals.

In 1977, focusing primarily on toxic pollutants, Congress amended the Clean Water Act of 1972. Congress also passed the Surface Mining Control and Reclamation Act in 1977, even as the Greenbelt movement began in Kenya, Africa—an indigenous, grassroots environmental campaign that used tree planting as the focal point around which other environmental and economic issues were brought to the attention of the public and decision makers. The Amoco *Cadiz* oil spill took place off the coast of Brittany in 1978, and in 1979 the Three Mile Island nuclear accident occurred in Pennsylvania.

In 1978 a state of emergency was declared at Love Canal, New York, as a major gap was revealed in our environmental laws—harm from wastes buried long ago. So Congress passed what is officially known as the Comprehensive Environmental Response, Compensation and Liability Act (CERCLA). Unofficially, it is known as the Superfund. It was signed into law on December 11, 1980, by President Jimmy Carter. This law created a tax on the chemical and petroleum industries and provided broad federal authority to respond directly to releases or threatened releases of hazardous substances that may endanger public health or the environment. Taxes collected went into a trust fund for cleaning up abandoned or uncontrolled hazardous waste sites.

According to a variety of environmental organizations and reports, as of its twentieth anniversary, the EPA's Superfund had made significant progress by taking more than sixty-four hundred actions to immediately reduce threats to public health and the environment; had completed cleanup at 757 Superfund sites; had done at least some work at 70 percent of the sites on the EPA's list of national priorities; and reached settlements valued at over eighteen billion dollars with private parties. By the same token, however, according to many respected environmental organizations and experts, the Superfund has still fallen far short of its goals and potential to protect the environment and the public's health. It has been far more responsive to the private corporate interests of polluters than to the public interest of protecting the environment and public health under both Democratic and Republicans administrations—differences have been a matter of degree, varying with the different presidents in office.

Congress passed the Nuclear Waste Policy Act and the U.N. adopted the World Charter for Nature in 1982. The latter was a very forward-looking document that set forth a first set of ethical and environmental principles designed to help guide nation-states toward a cleaner environment. Similar to the United Methodist Church's environmental principles, it emphasized the *intrinsic* value of all life-forms and took a principled position respectful of nature itself—not just an anthropocentric or utilitarian position. Most documents since the World Charter for Nature have not reached its balance or progressiveness.

In August 1982 an international debt crisis occurred when Mexico, a large debtor, suspended payments, an act that threatened to disrupt the world's financial system. It was caused by a widespread economic slowdown, largely the result of sharp increases in international interest rates. The crisis was arguably the most serious event to affect the world economy since the financial crisis of 1981. As a result, the 1980s became "the lost decade" for much of Latin America. Debt dominated discussions on international economic issues, and the world financial system came under intense scrutiny. But by not properly balancing human and humane concerns in resolving the debt crisis, the resulting fiscally austere policies of the world's economic managers wreaked havoc on the environmental concerns of poor and developing nations. My father raised the debt issue, and a more humane way of dealing with it, to a very high level during his 1984 presidential campaign when he visited Mexico and several Central American countries, but to little avail.

In 1984 a toxic chemical leak killed 10,000 and left 300,000 injured in Bhopal, India, and a drought starved to death somewhere between 250,000 and 1 million Ethiopians. An ozone hole was discovered over the Antarctic by American and British scientists in 1985, and the Chernobyl nuclear accident occurred in the Soviet Union in 1986, turning an entire region into an eerie ghost town. Also in 1986, Congress passed the Emergency Planning and Community Right-to-Know Act, designed to help local communities protect the public and the environment from chemical hazards.

During the reauthorization of the Clean Water Act in 1987, the Reagan-Bush administration delegated many of the previous federal EPA functions, such as issuing permits, administration, and enforcement, to state governments. This states' rights approach weakened environmental enforcement. A fifty-state enforcement structure helps protect the economic elite and big industry. It is far easier for greedy national and multinational corporations to manipulate and pit fifty needy state governments against each other than to deal with one reasonable public interest standard—a constitutional amendment—established by the federal government. This state-centered plan, as many others, is a direct descendant of the southern slaveholding class, which used states' rights to protect the industry of slavery.

Internationally, work growing out of the World Commission on Environment and Development (WCED) in 1987—the Brundtland Commission's report, "Our Common Future"—called for a new charter "to consolidate and extend relevant legal principles to guide State behavior in the transition to sustainable development." The Brundtland Commission was named for Gro Brundtland, the prime minister of Norway, its head. From 1983 to 1987 the commission conducted worldwide public hearings to critically appraise the concept of sustainability, then drafted "a legal framework for existing and future international and national environmental and sustainable development law and policy." The commissioners also unanimously concluded that our common future depends on sustainable development. Their report defined sustainable development as that which "meets the needs of the present without compromising the ability of future generations to meet their own needs" and concluded, "to be sustainable, development must improve economic efficiency, protect and restore ecological systems, and enhance the well-being of all peoples."

In 1988 the growing worldwide environmental movement was spotlighted when a South American rubber tree tapper named Chico Mendes was assassinated for resisting the destruction of a Brazilian rain forest, even as scientists used satellite photos to document what Amazon fires were doing to damage and destroy it. In that same year, in response to a growing environmental push, Congress passed the Indoor Radon Abatement Act, the Lead Contamination Control Act, the Medical Waste Tracking Act, the Ocean Dumping Ban Act, and the Shore Protection Act. Yet the oil tanker *Exxon Valdez* ran aground in 1989, dumping eleven million gallons of oil into Alaska's Prince William Sound, causing astronomic environmental damage.

In 1990 a group of environmental leaders asked Denis Hayes, national coordinator of the first Earth Day in 1970, to organize a second big environmental campaign to commemorate twenty years of work, further heighten environmental awareness, and sharpen focus for a future course of action. This time Hayes took Earth Day global, mobilizing two hundred million people in 141 countries to participate. This action increased the environment's status and helped to put it more firmly on the world stage. Following Earth Day 1990, Gaylord Nelson and Bruce Anderson—a solar-energy architect, author, and New Hampshire Earth Day organizer—cofounded Earth Day USA. Their goal was to make Earth Day a highly visible annual event.

Congress began the 1990s by passing the Oil Pollution Act (OPA), which streamlined and strengthened the EPA's ability to prevent and respond to catastrophic oil spills, and the Pollution Prevention Act, which focused on reducing pollution at its source and on conservation. This approach, reducing pollution through prevention and conservation, was fundamentally different and more desirable than the previous approaches of either waste management or pollution control. The law encouraged practices such as recycling, source reduction, and sustainable agriculture. Congress also passed the National Environmental Education Act.

The environment was damaged in 1991 when hundreds of oil-field fires burned uncontrollably for months in Kuwait following the Persian Gulf War. Meantime the Canadian east coast cod-fishing industry collapsed when only 2,700 tons of spawning biomass remained after a harvest of 190,000 tons.

Internationally, an Earth Summit was held in Rio de Janeiro in 1992, where a Declaration on Environment and Development was adopted. The Rio document also called for the development of an Earth Charter, a document that the U.N. and others might follow as an ethical foundation and set of principles for the world community's shared environmental values and goals. There is a continuing international effort to compose and reach agreement on a Peoples' Earth Charter.

Two organizations, the Earth Council and Green Cross International, supported by the Dutch government, convened a meeting in the Hague in 1993 to continue the effort to develop a People's Earth Charter, relying on people's participation and commitment. This coalition of more than sixty representatives proposed a broad-based international consultative process that they hoped would eventually lead to a universally accepted People's Earth Charter.

In 1995 the two groups' collaboration led to the "Principles of Environmental Conservation and Sustainable Development: Summary and Survey," which provided an overview of principles of environmental conservation and sustainable development. The U.N.'s World Commission on Environment and Development (WCED) likewise recommended that a final People's Earth Charter "be subsequently expanded into a Convention [an agreement or understanding], setting out the sovereign rights and reciprocal responsibilities of all states on environmental protection and sustainable development."

Also in 1995, the execution of environmental activist Ken Saro-Wiwa in Nigeria brought international attention to the linkages among human rights, environmental justice, security, and economic growth. In Congress in 1996, the important Food Quality Protection Act (FQPA) amended the Federal Insecticide, Fungicide and Rodenticide Act (FIFRA) and the Federal Food, Drug and Cosmetic Act (FFDCA). These amendments rewrote pesticide regulation, requiring a new safety standard of "reasonable certainty of no harm" to be applied to all pesticides used on foods.

In 1966 the Earth Council, along with various other environmental groups, initiated the People's Earth Charter Consultation in preparation for the Rio+5 Forum. The Rio+5 Forum (five years after the Earth Summit in Rio de Janeiro in 1992) brought together twenty-three distinguished individuals from every continent to form a People's Earth Charter Commission to oversee the drafting and consultation process. In March 1997 this commission proposed a "Benchmark Draft" of a People's Earth Charter, which reflected the penultimate conclusions of all efforts between 1972 and 1997 to create such a document.

Also in 1997, an Asian economic and ecological crisis occurred in Indonesia (and Southeast Asia) when land-clearing fires were intensified by the El Niño–induced drought. As a result, large regions in the area were covered with haze, which caused more than $1.4 billion in short-term health costs and fire-related damages. I was briefed on and witnessed some of this on a congressional trip I took at the invitation of Chairman Jim Leach while I was serving on the House Banking and Financial Services Committee.

In 1998 environmental groups and other activists successfully lobbied against the Multilateral Agreement on Investment (MAI) because of its potential harm to the environment. Also, controversy erupted in Europe and in some developing countries over genetically modified food and, in particular, concerns about "terminator technology"—seeds developed via biotechnology that do not germinate if saved and planted a second time. Finally during the turbulent environmental year of 1998, unusually severe weather left China with its worst floods in decades; two-thirds of Bangladesh was underwater for several months following torrential monsoons; Hurricane Mitch destroyed parts of Central America; fifty-four countries were hit by floods and forty-five by drought; and the earth reached the highest global temperature ever recorded.

In March 2000 the Earth Charter Commission meeting in Paris released its final document to the public to further educate and build public support for the People's Earth Charter. While it is still open for comment and revision, it is hoped that the U.N. will consider and endorse it in 2002. (The March 2000 People's Earth Charter can be found in appendix 4 of this book.)

The environment needs a universal code of conduct to guide people, organizations, and nations toward sustainable development that reflects a multiracial, multicultural, and multireligious democratic quest for an integrated ethical vision for our common future. The People's Earth Charter Campaign is an umbrella group helping bring that vision to fruition.

The People's Earth Charter affirms within four broad categories the following general interdependent principles "for a sustainable way of life and as a common standard by which the conduct of all individuals, organizations, businesses, governments and transnational institutions may be guided and assessed":

1. **RESPECT AND CARE FOR THE COMMUNITY OF LIFE.** Respect Earth and life in all its diversity; care for the community of life with understanding, compassion, and love; build democratic societies that are just, participatory, sustainable, and peaceful; secure Earth's bounty and beauty for present and future generations.

2. **ECOLOGICAL INTEGRITY.** Protect and restore the integrity of Earth's ecological systems, with special concern for biological diversity and the natural processes that sustain life; prevent harm as the best method of environmental protection and, when knowledge is limited, apply a precautionary approach; adopt patterns of production, consumption, and reproduction that safeguard Earth's regenerative capacities, human rights, and community well-being; advance the study of ecological sustainability and promote the open exchange and wide application of the knowledge acquired.

3. **SOCIAL AND ECONOMIC JUSTICE.** Eradicate poverty as an ethical, social, and environmental imperative; ensure that economic activities and institutions at all levels promote human development in an equitable and sustainable manner; affirm gender equality and equity as prerequisites to sustainable development and ensure universal access to education, health care, and economic opportunity; uphold the right of all, without discrimination, to a natural and social environment supportive of human dignity, bodily health, and spiritual well-being, with special attention to the rights of indigenous peoples and minorities.

4. **DEMOCRACY, NONVIOLENCE, AND PEACE.** Strengthen democratic institutions at all levels, and provide transparency and accountability in governance, inclusive participation in decision making, and access to justice; integrate into formal education and lifelong learning the knowledge, values, and skills needed for a sustainable way of life; treat all living beings with respect and consideration; promote a culture of tolerance, nonviolence, and peace.

The People's Earth Charter, which has reviewed the environmental statements and concerns in existing United Nations and international documents, argues that our increasingly interdependent and fragile world now stands at a critical moment in the history of the earth. The choices that we make on the environment must encompass our diverse cultures and perspectives even as we develop a unified sustainable global society founded on respect for nature, universal human rights, economic justice, and a culture of peace. The earth is our home and we must protect its "vitality, diversity and beauty as a sacred trust."[2]

One objective of the International People's Earth Charter Campaign is to promote a worldwide dialogue around shared values and global ethics as they pertain to the environment. Its inclusion as an appendix to this book is an effort to contribute to that process. By circulating the charter throughout the world as a people's treaty, environmental awareness is promoted, as well as commitment to the implementation of its values. It is hoped that the Earth Charter's principles will find expression in individual lifestyles, in educational curricula, religious teachings, the work ethic of professionals and organizations, as well as in public policy and government practices. Eventually it is hoped that the Earth Charter will share a revered place alongside the U.N.'s Universal Declaration of Human Rights and other legal documents that help guide human and international conduct.

In the United States the charter should serve as a guide for federal, state, and local legislation, and for everyday business and individual conduct. Indeed, it could and should be used by the Supreme Court for any interpretation of an environmental constitutional amendment.

O ur current patterns of production and consumption are causing environmental devastation, depleting our resources, and extinguishing species. The unjust distribution of resources between rich and poor nations and the general global overpopulation are widening this gap and resulting in increased poverty, ignorance, and violent conflict in the world. The very foundations of global security are being threatened.

But we still have choices. We can act in a way that protects and enhances our common humanity and the earth on which we live, or we can continue down our current path, which appears to be leading to greater destruction. The People's Earth Charter reminds us that "fundamental changes are needed in our values, institutions and ways of living"; that once we meet our basic needs, human development and the purpose of life should be "primarily about being more, not having more."

We know better. We know how to create a cleaner, safer, more democratic, humane, and sustainable world. The question is: Will we choose to do and be better? The People's Earth Charter tells us that "our environmental, economic, political, social and spiritual challenges are interconnected, but together we can forge inclusive solutions." What is lacking, and what we must teach and develop, is a sense of universal responsibility. We must maintain a healthy sense of pride in our country, but at the same time do away with any unhealthy nationalism. Again, the charter reminds us that "the spirit of human solidarity and kinship with all life is strengthened when we live with reverence for the mystery of being, gratitude for the gift of life, and humility regarding the human place in nature."

We have an opportunity, as never before in history, to seek a new beginning for a common destiny, but it will require us to change hearts and minds, including our own. It will demand the recognition of a new sense of universal responsibility and global interdependence. And even in the midst of our diversity of cultures and heritage, all of us must imaginatively develop our own distinctive ways of realizing the vision of a sustainable way of life locally, nationally, regionally, and globally.

Life and the environment sometimes force us to make difficult choices between competing values, yet we must accept the responsibility of finding harmony and unity amid diversity. For example, even as we value and fight to protect our personal freedom, the environment forces a paradox on us: It shows us that the only way to maintain our individual freedom is by pursuing the common good. For if the common good cannot be preserved with respect to the environment, then neither can our individual democratic freedoms. The environment also forces us to recognize and accept short-term objectives, even as we harmonize them with our long-term goals. And because every little bit helps, every individual, family, organization, and community must affirm and assume its vital role in preserving a sustainable environment. Additionally, art, science, religion, education, the media, business, nongovernmental organizations, and official governments must all assume a role and offer creative leadership. A government, civil, and business partnership is essential to achieving these shared environmental goals.

The People's Earth Charter reminds us to "let ours be a time remembered for the awakening of a new reverence for life, the firm resolve to achieve sustainability, the quickening of the struggle for justice and peace, and the joyful celebration of life."

The people of the United States should do our part by recognizing the world's environmental interdependence and assuming our proper responsibility, beginning with the addition of an environmental amendment to the Constitution. Such an amendment would go a long way toward guaranteeing that our generation, and all future generations, will continue to exist and to enjoy the full blessings of the earth. A clean, safe, and sustainable environment is absolutely critical to building a more perfect Union and world.

A MORE PERFECT UNION—
FAIR TAXES

Taxation without representation is tyranny.

—James Otis, 1761

The subjects of every state ought to contribute toward the support of the government, as nearly as possible, in proportion to their respective abilities; that is, in proportion to the revenue which they respectively enjoy under the protection of the state. . . . As Henry Home (Lord Kames) has written, a goal of taxation should be to "remedy inequality of riches as much as possible, by relieving the poor and burdening the rich."

—Adam Smith, *Wealth of Nations* (1776)

I am in favor of an income tax. When I find a man who is not willing to bear his share of the burdens of the government which protects him, I find a man who is unworthy to enjoy the blessings of a government like ours.

—William Jennings Bryan
Democratic National Convention, July 8, 1896

Taxes, after all, are the dues that we pay for the privileges of membership in an organized society.

—Franklin D. Roosevelt
Worcester, Massachusetts, October 21, 1936

In a sense we have come to our nation's Capital to cash a check. When the architects of our republic wrote the magnificent words of the Constitution and the Declaration of Independence, they were signing a promissory note to which every American was to fall heir. This note was a promise that all men would be guaranteed the inalienable rights of life, liberty, and the pursuit of happiness.

It is obvious today that America has defaulted on this promissory note insofar as her citizens of color are concerned. Instead of honoring this sacred obligation, America has given the Negro people a bad check which has come back marked "insufficient funds." But we refuse to believe that the bank of justice is bankrupt. We refuse to believe that there are insufficient funds in the great vaults of opportunity of this nation. So we have come to cash this check—a check that will give us upon demand the riches of freedom and the security of justice.

—Dr. Martin Luther King, Jr.
March on Washington, August 28, 1963

PROPOSED FAIR TAXES AMENDMENT TO THE U.S. CONSTITUTION

Section 1. **The Congress of the United States shall tax all persons progressively in proportion to the income which they respectively enjoy under the protection of the United States.**

Section 2. **The Congress shall have power to enforce this article by appropriate legislation.**

On August 28, 1963—a hundred years after President Abraham Lincoln issued the Emancipation Proclamation—Dr. Martin Luther King, Jr., said, "I have a dream." The "dream" of which he spoke was the poetic conclusion to a speech about racism and economics. The substantive theme of the march that drew 250,000 people to the nation's capital was "Jobs & Justice"—economics and racism. It was not an abstract dream.

When Dr. King uttered these words in 1963, he was looking toward the Capitol from the Lincoln Memorial, speaking to the Congress, referring to the denial of rights to African Americans, and calling on the U.S. Congress and the country—its national budget and the total public and private economic resources of our nation—to fix the long-standing problems of caste and class, that is, of race and poverty.

Today the media and conservatives come close to projecting Dr. King as an unrealistic dreamer—a sort of impractical utopian. The constant focus on the "I Have a Dream" portion of his speech, to the exclusion of the parts addressing racism and economics, does a disservice to Dr. King and his legacy. In fact, Dr. King was a morally, economically, and politically grounded activist with a realistic economic dream for America, the richest, most organized, and most technologically advanced country the world has ever known.

Five years later Dr. King was even clearer and more realistic about his dream. Congress, in large part in response to the march in 1963, passed a Civil Rights Act in 1964 desegregating public accommodations. In response to the march in Selma, Congress passed a Voting Rights Act in 1965 knocking down barriers to black voter registration and political participation. Some progress had been made in at least highlighting the issue of northern segregated housing patterns as a result of his 1966 open-housing marches in Chicago. In 1967 he spoke out against a war conducted against people of color in Vietnam (racism) and said that we were using our national treasure (economy) to destroy and kill abroad instead of using it to build and heal at home.

When King was assassinated in 1968 he was not organizing primarily on the basis of race, but on the basis of economics—the need for jobs, health care, housing, and education. He was organizing a "Poor People's Campaign" that would bring to Washington masses of people to dramatize the plight of the poor regardless of color or ethnicity. He was prepared to disrupt the national government and fill up the jails to make his economic point about poor and working people generally. He had gradually shifted his focus from fighting for civil rights historically denied to people of color to pursuing economic rights for all. After all, what good is it to have the civil right to stay in any hotel or motel you wish, eat in the restaurant of your choice, and matriculate at any school, but then not have the economic resources to pay for it?

Dr. King did have a dream, but it was a dream about both racial reconciliation and economic justice. He was not naive, though. He also understood that the nation must pay for its dreams if it was to approximate its stated ideals and achieve its highest potential. He knew that social, economic, and political justice would cost—including significant public tax dollars. He also knew that continued injustice would cost even more.

We can go down only four avenues to achieve our social, economic, and political justice goals: the public economy; the private economy; foundations and other charitable organizations and institutions; and volunteerism.

I believe Dr. King would have supported efforts down all four paths of the social, economic, and political order to bring about the social justice, fairness, and humane change he sought, but I also believe he understood and knew the political priority of the order listed above.

I recognize that the private sector of the economy is and will remain the largest piece of the total economic pie—and is currently the most powerful—but even so, it still operates within the context of the political order and its rules. Currently, private sector priorities dominate public sector rules, both practically and ideologically, because it supplies the goods and services for the American people and in international trade. The private sector has used its economic power to co-opt, corrupt, and pervert the political rules to serve its narrow special economic interests—yes, through financial contributions to candidates, but even more so through an ideological and legal bent that puts private interests first and the public interest second.

The private sector currently reigns over the political order. More important, it also dominates the ideological debate underpinning of this arrangement. In truth, a fully conscious and participating democratic political order ought be steering and directing, through the law, policy, and regulation, the private sector's important contribution toward the public good. The political order should be making rules designed to protect the public interest and to build a more perfect Union.

Most people complain that taxes are just killing them. This is more than simply the normal human trait of not liking to pay taxes. Objectively, albeit in varying degrees, the majority of the American people are hurting economically, and taxes are contributing to their pain and anguish. They look at their paycheck and see more and more of it going to taxes, and they're mainly thinking of federal taxes—paying for that big federal government. Republicans and conservative Democrats rail against "tax and spend" liberal Democrats as they propose or support federal "tax cut" and "rate cut" policies in the name of tax reform, and support legislation designed to disproportionately benefit the very rich and the largest corporations. But what are the tax facts?

The gross domestic product (GDP) is the total value of goods and services produced in this country. In the year 2000 our nation's GDP approximated nine trillion dollars. The U.S.

economy currently dwarfs every other economy in the world. For a simplistic understanding of how large it is, dividing a $9-trillion GDP equally among 275 million Americans gives a (mean) average GDP value of $32,727 per American. For a family of four, that's an annual income of $130,908, which would rank comfortably in the top 5 percent nationally in terms of current family income. The annual income in a two-earner family would be $65,454, again ranking that family in the top 60 to 80 percent of income in America.

The point of the illustration is not to redistribute the nine trillion dollars equally, but to indicate that if income in the American economy were not so maldistributed—and wealth is even more so—all Americans could live in a "practical utopia"—that is, minus hunger and poverty, with a decent job, affordable health care and housing, and a public education that prepared students for today's and tomorrow's world of work. If the economic fruits of the labor of the American people were not so grossly maldistributed to its roots—the workers— we could achieve the "riches of freedom and the security of justice" that Dr. King talked about in 1963.

It is the role of the political order to distribute the goods and services that the economy produces. Specifically, the two houses of Congress—the Ways and Means Committees on taxes and the Appropriations Committees on spending in both—take in and distribute, through their laws, rules, and regulations, the taxes that the American people produce.

When measured in terms of tax receipts as a percentage of GDP, the United States is one of the least taxed major industrialized nations in the world. Japan and the United States have the lowest tax rates as a percentage of GDP, while France, Italy, Germany, Canada, and Great Britain all have significantly higher rates. Taxes in France approach 50 percent of GDP.

Prior to World War II, the federal budget (taxes) comprised about 7 percent of GDP. During World War II, the federal budget increased to 20.9 percent of GDP in 1944. However, from World War II to the present, federal taxes as a percent of the GDP have remained relatively constant, averaging 18.5 percent. Also, because of the growth of the economy, we've seen the recent irony that federal tax rates have actually fallen within every income group even as total revenues have increased. Put another way, the rich and superrich are making so much money that they are actually contributing more aggregate tax dollars to the federal budget than ever before, even though their tax rates, along with those of everyone else, have been lowered.

The share of adjusted gross income (AGI) accruing to high-income taxpayers grew dramatically between 1980 and 1998. According to the IRS, in 1980, 932,388 taxpayers with an AGI of $80,580 made it into the top 1 percent income bracket. By 1998, 1,237,758 had to earn $269,496 to get there. The average tax rate nationally in 1980 was 15.38 percent, but it shrank to 14.42 percent in 1998. The tax rate for the top 1 percent dropped from 35.06 percent in 1980 to 27.12 percent in 1998, but their increase in income was even more dramatic. The top 1 percent claimed 8.46 percent of adjusted gross income in 1980 but 18.47 percent in 1998—almost a 120 percent increase in just eighteen years. As high-income taxpayers' share of total AGI dramatically increased, so did their share of total federal taxes. This has been the mechanism that has fueled the increase in federal tax revenues. A much larger percentage of total income is now earned by taxpayers at the top of income distribution where marginal income tax rates are the highest, which has in turn significantly increased federal revenues. The share of total income tax for the top 1 percent went from

19.29 percent in 1980 to 34.75 percent in 1998, an increase of only 80 percent. Thus, while the top 1 percent's share of income increased by nearly 120 percent, their share of taxes increased only 80 percent, yielding them a net gain of 40 percent in the highest tax bracket. The rich are still making out like bandits.

As a result, our current tax code is still grossly unfair, and our unfair tax policies have resulted in the United States being the most unjust industrialized democracy in the world today in terms of wealth and income. The gap between those at the very top and the vast majority of Americans has increased dramatically over the last two decades, especially since President Ronald Reagan's Economic Recovery Act of 1981. The top 1 percent's share of AGI was 15.2 percent in 1988 but 18.5 percent in 1998, while the bottom 50 percent's share went from 14.9 percent in 1988 to 13.7 percent in 1998.

This is a point that bears repeating: It is to divert attention from this massive inequality—the greatest disparity in income and wealth of any industrialized nation in the world—that conservatives define our economic problem as federal taxes and spending on the poor, people of color, immigrants, and affirmative action.

Let's examine in even greater detail why most Americans are experiencing a tax squeeze. The average American is feeling pinched because the burden of federal taxes has shifted from corporations to individuals.

It was reported in early 2000 that individuals were paying a much higher percentage of federal taxes while corporations were paying significantly less. According to a February 13, 2000, *New York Times* report by David Cay Johnston, in 1990 individual Americans paid 13 percent of earned income in taxes, but by 1997 that had risen to 15 percent. In contrast, corporate taxes paid on profits fell from 26 percent in 1990 to 20 percent in 1997. In 1999 corporate income taxes paid fell 2.5 percent from 1998, while individual income taxes paid surged by 6.2 percent. Individual incomes had risen 131 percent between 1990 and 1997, but taxes were 164 percent higher. Again, in contrast, corporations, with a tax rate of 35 percent, reported a gain of 252 percent in profits between 1990 and 1997, but a tax increase of only 191 percent. Johnston reported that "because of these trends, in 1997 alone, companies paid $60 billion less in income taxes than they would have if they had paid taxes at the same rate as in 1990. But individuals paid $80 billion more."[1]

In 1941 individual income taxes comprised 1.2 percent of GDP, corporate taxes 1.9 percent, Social Security taxes 1.7 percent, excise taxes 2.2 percent, and other taxes 0.7 percent, for a total of 7.6 percent of GDP. In 1946 individual income taxes comprised 7.2 percent of GDP, corporate taxes 5.3 percent, Social Security taxes 1.4 percent, excise taxes 3.1 percent, and others 0.5 percent, for a total of 17.6 percent. In 1998 individual income taxes comprised 9.9 percent of GDP, corporate taxes 2.2 percent, Social Security taxes 6.8 percent, excise taxes 0.7 percent, and others 0.9 percent, for a total of 20.5 percent—the highest level since World War II, but only slightly higher than the 18.5 percent average for the last fifty years.

Over the past fifty years federal corporate taxes have dramatically been reduced, while federal individual and Social Security taxes have skyrocketed for workers and the middle class. (See table 1.) The individual American has assumed a greater share of the aggregate burden of federal taxes, while the corporation is assuming a far lesser share of the aggregate federal tax burden. How much more in taxes would corporations have paid each year during the 1980s had their 1970s average tax rate not been cut but merely stayed the same? One hundred thirty billion dollars!

Table 1. FEDERAL RECEIPTS AS A PERCENT OF GDP, FISCAL YEARS 1941–1998

Fiscal Year Taxes	Individual Income Taxes	Corporate Income Taxes	Social Security	Excise Taxes	Other Receipts	Total
1941	1.2	1.9	1.7	2.2	0.7	7.6
1942	2.3	3.3	1.7	2.4	0.6	10.1
1943	3.6	5.3	1.7	2.3	0.4	13.3
1944	9.4	7.1	1.7	2.3	0.5	20.9
1945	8.5	7.2	1.6	2.8	0.5	20.4
1946	7.2	5.3	1.4	3.1	0.5	17.6
1947	7.6	3.7	1.5	3.1	0.6	16.4
1948	7.5	3.8	1.5	2.9	0.6	16.2
1949	5.7	4.1	1.4	2.8	0.5	14.5
1950	5.8	3.8	1.6	2.8	0.5	14.4
1951	6.7	4.4	1.8	2.7	0.5	16.1
1952	8.0	6.1	1.8	2.5	0.5	19.0
1953	8.0	5.7	1.8	2.6	0.5	18.7
1954	7.8	5.6	1.9	2.6	0.5	18.4
1955	7.3	4.5	2.0	2.3	0.5	16.6
1956	7.5	4.9	2.2	2.3	0.5	17.4
1957	7.9	4.7	2.2	2.3	0.6	17.8
1958	7.5	4.4	2.4	2.3	0.6	17.3
1959	7.5	3.5	2.4	2.2	0.6	16.1
1960	7.9	4.1	2.8	2.3	0.8	17.8
1961	7.8	3.9	3.1	2.2	0.7	17.8
1962	8.0	3.6	3.0	2.2	0.7	17.6
1963	8.0	3.6	3.3	2.2	0.7	17.8
1964	7.6	3.7	3.4	2.1	0.7	17.6
1965	7.1	3.7	3.2	2.1	0.8	17.0
1966	7.4	4.0	3.4	1.7	0.9	17.4
1967	7.6	4.2	4.0	1.7	0.9	18.3
1968	7.9	3.3	3.9	1.6	0.9	17.6
1969	9.2	3.9	4.1	1.6	0.9	19.7
1970	9.0	3.3	4.4	1.6	0.9	19.1
1971	8.0	2.5	4.4	1.5	0.9	17.4
1972	8.0	2.7	4.5	1.3	1.0	17.6
1973	7.9	2.8	4.8	1.2	0.9	17.7
1974	8.3	2.7	5.2	1.2	1.0	18.3
1975	7.9	2.6	5.4	1.1	1.0	18.0
1976	7.6	2.4	5.2	1.0	1.0	17.2
TQ*	8.5	1.9	5.5	1.0	0.9	17.9
1977	8.0	2.8	5.4	0.9	1.0	18.0
1978	8.2	2.7	5.5	0.8	0.9	18.1

*Transition Quarter, referring to the year in which the start of the fiscal year was changed from July 1 to October 1.

1979	8.7	2.6	5.6	0.8	0.9	18.6
1980	9.0	2.4	5.8	0.9	1.0	19.0
1981	9.4	2.0	6.0	1.3	0.9	19.7
1982	9.3	1.5	6.3	1.1	1.0	19.2
1983	8.4	1.1	6.1	1.0	0.9	17.6
1984	7.8	1.5	6.3	1.0	0.9	17.5
1985	8.2	1.5	6.5	0.9	0.9	17.9
1986	8.0	1.4	6.5	0.8	0.9	17.6
1987	8.5	1.8	6.6	0.7	0.9	18.6
1988	8.1	1.9	6.7	0.7	0.9	18.4
1989	8.3	1.9	6.7	0.6	0.9	18.5
1990	8.2	1.6	6.7	0.6	1.0	18.2
1991	8.0	1.7	6.8	0.7	0.9	18.0
1992	7.7	1.6	6.7	0.7	0.9	17.8
1993	7.9	1.8	6.6	0.7	0.8	17.8
1994	7.9	2.1	6.7	0.8	0.9	18.4
1995	8.2	2.2	6.7	0.8	0.9	18.8
1996	8.7	2.3	6.7	0.7	0.8	19.2
1997	9.2	2.3	6.7	0.7	0.8	19.7
1998	9.9	2.2	6.8	0.7	0.9	20.5

SOURCE: OFFICE OF MANAGEMENT AND BUDGET, BUDGET OF THE UNITED STATES GOVERNMENT, FY 1998, HISTORICAL TABLES.

Additionally, while the federal aggregate tax burden relative to GDP has remained relatively constant for half a century—conservatives, states' righters, and localism advocates take note—the broad combination of state and local taxes has *doubled!* As a result, total taxes (federal, state, and local taxes combined) have increased by 9.5 percent—or more than 33 percent from the 1947 level.

"Progressive" taxes are based on the biblical concept of "to whom more is given, more is expected." The term means the more you earn, the more you should pay. "Regressive," on the other hand, means the more you earn, the less you pay. While most citizens focus their anger on the IRS and federal income taxes, it should be noted that federal income taxes are more progressive than Social Security and state taxes—both of which are regressive—and local taxes, which are the most regressive of all. The basic progressive federal tax rates currently (2000) are 15, 28, 31, 36 and 39.6 percent, depending on income. The rates range from 15 percent on incomes of $26,250 to $63,550, to 39.6 percent for incomes over $288,350. The more you earn, the higher your tax bracket.

The bottom line is this: The tax squeeze is coming essentially from two sources. First, at the federal level, it is coming from a shift in the burden of taxes off corporations and onto individuals; and second, the squeeze is coming from dramatic increases in state and local taxes—mainly sales and excise taxes, property taxes, and state income taxes. According to a June 26, 1996, study by Citizens for Tax Justice titled "Who Pays?" the richest families pay about 7.9 percent of their incomes in state and local taxes, families in the middle pay about 9.8 percent, while the poorest families pay a whooping 12.5 percent of their meager incomes in state and local taxes. The middle class, workers, and the poor are taxed the most because they spend a higher percentage of their income on the necessities of life. For example, the poor spend a higher percentage of their income on consumptive items such as food, clothing, and medicines that are subject to sales and excise taxes, which are the most regressive.

The central problem of unfair taxes then is not the "national liberal Democrats" who are charged by conservatives with advocating federal "tax and spend" policies for "big government programs for the poor"—it will be shown later that the biggest federal benefits in fact go to the rich and middle class, not the poor. Instead, it is the conservative Republicans and Democrats who advocate tax rate cuts for corporations and the rich who are shifting the tax burden to middle income families. It turns out that those states' rights conservatives who want to shift government power to the state and local levels are the biggest taxers of all. Given the tax facts, it is understandable why the American taxpayer is peeved—but also deceived.

While the media has focused attention on the big central government in Washington—raising expectations of what we should expect in return for our taxes—it has not consistently reported these shifts in the structure of taxation and in related tax burdens, or interpreted properly the inevitable political consequences.

The political consequences are that the media's consistent emphasis on the big federal government with its trillions of dollars in spending ($1.83 trillion in 2001, an amount that staggers lawmakers as well as the average American) fails to put this in context—the context of our $9-trillion GDP and relatively unchanged federal spending pattern (18.5 percent of GDP) over the past fifty years. It does not constantly reiterate the changes in taxes the way it does the rise in aggregate spending. Neither does it regularly educate us on the unfair taxes we pay, which should be the source of our anger. Also, a dispersed fifty-state and local media does not have the same expectations of state and local governments, and cannot hold these governments to the same standards to which the national media holds the one federal government. By definition, such reporting is simply too diffuse. Given all this, how could the American people be anything but angry at the "Big Federal Government"! I'm angry too, but mainly at the politicians and the media who will not tell the American people the truth and educate them about taxes.

The American people do need a tax cut, but not the one the conservative Republicans want to give them that disproportionately benefits the very rich and the large corporations. But neither do the American people need the one that the DLC Rockefeller Republican-Democrats like President Clinton and Vice President Gore wanted to give. While it's true that moderate Democratic proposals are clearly better than the conservative Republican ones, the Democrats are still just tinkering around the edges of tax reform. What the American people really need most is fair taxes, which would mean a significant tax cut for 80 percent of the population.

My proposed constitutional amendment, with its progressive language, would come closest to giving it to them on a constant, ongoing, and institutional basis. Such an amendment would also likely press Social Security taxes into a more progressive mode, and force state and local governments to construct more progressive tax schemes. Progressive or fair taxes would reduce the burden on 80 percent of the American people and on small businesses. Then, in the famous words of conservative Republicans, average American workers and middle-class businesspeople could keep more of their own hard-earned money, and they could save it, invest it, or spend more of it as they please.

The federal government is actually providing more service to the American people with proportionately the same amount of money that it had fifty years ago. On the other hand, state and local taxes have doubled, rising from 5.3 percent of GDP in 1947 to 10.7 percent in 1998. The so-called liberal federal government has been fiscally conservative, while it is the so-called conservative state and local governments that have been the "spendthrifts" and offered rather dramatically rising "tax and spend" policies over the past half century.

If it's bureaucracy that troubles the public, clearly another political consequence of decentralized taxing and spending policies is that fifty separate state entities—plus thousands of local governments—add bureaucracy, rather than reducing it. Jeffersonian conservative local control, or atomization, contributes to society being more, not less, bureaucratic. The more we can nationalize standards, collect and spend general revenues at the federal and state levels, and provide national programs for education, health care, and housing, similar to what we do with Social Security, the more perfect a Union we will have. There is a localism, within broad national standards, that I can and do support. More rational national government policies and programs does not mean that there cannot be genuine and even more meaningful local control.

There is yet another, even bigger, consequence of so-called local control of government. If political power can be decentralized while economic power is becoming ever more centralized, it is simply one more way that private special economic interests can keep their dominance over the public interest. Local political power cannot compete with and will be overwhelmed by centralized economic power. Local political power will not have genuine choice if economic power dominates, as demonstrated by the communities of Robbins and Ford Heights in my congressional district when the large incinerator companies descended on them. Deregulated economic power will force local governments—as we see today with U.S. state governments, and with poor governments in the international arena—to compete with each other to see who will offer them the best tax deal and incentives package. Economic power will obviously go where costs are cheapest and profits are greatest. This "rush to the bottom" is in the short-term special interests of private economic power but not in the long-term public interest.

Finally, there has been a steady but dramatic growth in the Social Security tax. As a result of the 1937 Federal Insurance Contributions Act (FICA) and the Self-Employment Contributions Act (SECA), more than 150 million employees and employers (each pays half) contribute a portion of their wages (or a portion of net income for the self-employed) to pay for the Old Age, Survivors and Disability Insurance, and Hospital Insurance portions of Medicare. But Social Security taxes are regressive. In 1937 the FICA tax was first set at 1 percent on earnings up to $3,000 a year. In 2001 the rate is 7.65 percent and is levied on earnings up to $80,400 (the level rises annually at the same rate as average earnings in the economy).

So in addition to the primary weight of federal income taxes falling on individual taxpayers, a disproportionate amount of Social Security taxes also falls on the poorest workers and the middle class. It's regressive because the less you make, the more you pay: A higher percentage of your overall gross income goes to paying Social Security taxes. It's a regressive flat tax on everyone earning less than $80,400. Both the employee and the employer stop paying Social Security taxes once the employee's annual gross income reaches $80,400. It makes no difference if an individual earns an additional $1 million or a corporation earns an additional $100 billion; both stop paying Social Security taxes when the employee reaches $80,400. And Social Security taxes have become an ever-larger share of each person's overall federal tax burden.

The Citizens for Tax Justice study that I cited earlier documented how state sales and excise taxes, property taxes, and state income taxes fall more heavily on middle- and low-income families than on the wealthy. But the study also showed tremendous differences of regressiveness or unfairness among the states, with some taxing their poorest citizens up to four times the rates paid by the rich. The "Terrible Ten," as the study referred to them, are shown in table 2.

Table 2. THE TEN MOST REGRESSIVE STATE TAX SYSTEMS: TAXES AS SHARES OF INCOME BY FAMILY INCOME GROUP

TAXES AS A % OF INCOME ON:				RATIO OF TAXES PAID BY:	
Income Group	Poorest 20%	Middle 60%	Top 1%	Poor/Top 1%	Middle/Top 1%
Washington	17.1%	10.5%	3.9%	435%	267%
Florida	14.0%	7.7%	3.6%	390%	216%
Texas	13.8%	8.5%	4.4%	314%	194%
South Dakota	11.7%	7.7%	2.9%	408%	269%
Tennessee	12.3%	7.5%	3.6%	340%	208%
Louisiana	13.4%	9.9%	6.0%	224%	167%
Pennsylvania	13.3%	10.2%	6.1%	220%	168%
Illinois	13.6%	9.8%	6.1%	223%	160%
Alabama	11.6%	9.0%	4.8%	242%	187%
Michigan	13.3%	10.6%	6.9%	193%	154%

Note that half of the ten most regressive state tax systems cited are in the South. While I am not alleging that this is the only cause, it would be wise to recall that 75 percent of the state lawmakers in the eleven former Confederate States were slave owners, and they set a pattern of paying few taxes on their private property of land and slaves. The result of this permissive southern tax legacy is a top-down private economic arrangement protected by an elite group of conservative Democrats and Republicans who preserve this historic unjust economic pattern with their conservative politics.

It is interesting that the states of Washington, Florida, and Texas brag that they are "no-income-tax" states, but that claim is deceptive. They are definitely not "no-tax" states for the poor. The "Who Pays" study reports that in Washington, "when all state and local sales, excise and property taxes are tallied up, poor families in the State of Washington pay 17.1 percent of their total income in taxes. . . . Florida and Texas . . . tax their poor families at rates of 14 percent and 13.8 percent, respectively (fifth and sixth highest in the country). . . . Many so-called 'low-tax' states are, in fact, high-tax states for the poor. Most of them do not offer a good deal to middle-income families either. The wealthy in such states, however, pay relatively little."

The study sites certain common characteristics of states with particularly regressive tax systems. In the ten most regressive tax states, several items particularly stand out:

> Five of the ten states lack a broad-based personal income tax.
> Of the five very regressive tax states that do have broad-based personal income taxes, three have flat rate taxes and two (Alabama and Louisiana) allow a deduction for federal taxes paid.

> Seven of the ten states—Washington, Florida, Texas, South Dakota, Tennessee, Louisiana, and Alabama—rely very heavily on sales and excise taxes. In these seven states, about half to three-quarters of the total state and local taxes imposed on the families in the study came from these consumption taxes (compared to the national median of 35 percent for all states).

In contrast, those states with the fairest tax systems have the most progressive personal income taxes and rely the least on consumption taxes to fund state services. Thus, it is not merely taxes, but the kind of taxes that citizens pay that creates the huge differences in who pays. A state with progressive income taxes, where the more you earn the more you pay, is fairer and less reliant on consumption sales and excise taxes for money. Consumption taxes are very regressive and force poor families, on average, to pay more than six times more in taxes as a percentage of their income than wealthy families pay. And the study also revealed that even middle-income families paid four times more than wealthy families in state taxes.

Currently, several "tax reform" ideas, including reducing or eliminating capital gains taxes, capital depreciation, the flat tax, the valued-added tax, the marriage penalty tax, and estate taxes, are the magnificent obsession of conservative Republicans, with some conservative Democrats tagging along.

The two primary vehicles through which the shift in the tax burden from corporations to individuals has taken place are a reduction in capital gains taxes and corporate depreciation write-offs—which go primarily to large corporations and rich individuals.

Capital gains are profits from an increase in the value of stocks, bonds, investment real estate, or other capital assets. Income earned on capital investments is taxed much more favorably—especially for the rich—than income earned with the sweat of one's brow. Approximately two-thirds of total capital gains reported on individual tax returns went to those earning more than two hundred thousand dollars. In comparison, 75 percent of the American people with reported incomes of fifty thousand dollars or less reaped a mere 7.6 percent of capital gains benefits. More than any other type of income, capital gains benefit the people at the very top of the income ladder.

When the income tax laws were first written, capital gains were taxed at the same rates as other income. That soon changed, and there has been a variety of other rate changes over the last three-quarters of a century. The rationalization for the favorable treatment of capital gains, supposedly, has been to stimulate savings, foster investment, create jobs, and generate economic growth. However, the results intended by their conservative proponents have not been achieved. In fact, the effect of capital gains tax cuts has been almost the opposite.

For example, prior to a drop in capital gains tax rates from 39 to 28 percent in the 1978 Revenue Act, the GDP grew at 5.8 percent. For the two years following, GDP growth was 0.3 percent. A similar pattern preceded and followed the 1981 capital gains cut from 28 to 20 percent. Unemployment also rose following both the 1978 and 1981 capital gains tax cuts. On the other hand, increases in capital gains taxes have resulted in increased economic growth, largely because investments were made in real economic growth rather than to take advantage of capital gains tax shelters.

President Clinton expressed concern that on his watch inequality in the United States had reached new heights. Thus, in mid-1999 he touted a "New Markets" strategy to focus attention on those who had been left behind during the relative good economic times of his administration. But Bob McIntyre of the Citizens for Tax Justice (CTJ) testified on January 25, 1995, before the House Ways and Means Committee that "in the 1993 budget bill . . . capital gains preference(s) was greatly expanded to provide what amounts to a 30 percent capital gains exclusion for top-bracket taxpayers (the difference between the new 39.6 percent top regular tax rate and the continuing 28 percent maximum capital gains rate). The 1993 act provided an additional 50 percent capital gains exclusion for profits from certain 'risky' investments that are considered likely to fail. A staggering 96 percent of the tax savings from the current 28 percent maximum capital gains tax rate for individuals goes to the best-off 1 percent of all taxpayers." Could it be that this 1993 capital gains bonanza contributed significantly to the growing inequality?

Created during the corrupt Nixon administration by executive fiat and later incorporated into Nixon's 1971 Revenue Act, the accelerated depreciation allowance is the other large corporate tax loophole. The Nixon administration called it the Asset Depreciation Range (ADR). The ADR front-loaded deductions in the early years that equipment was used and shorted the overall depreciation write-off periods by 20 percent across the board.

Bob McIntyre also pointed out in his testimony that things got worse in 1979 when a business-oriented Republican and two southern Democrats—Senators Lloyd Bentsen (D-TX), Barber Conable (R-NY), and James Jones (D-OK)—pushed through a big corporate tax cut bill. "They proposed to shorten depreciation periods and accelerate write-offs much more radically even than ADR," McIntyre said, and part of it was later written into Reagan's extreme and radical supply-side 1981 tax cut package, the biggest gift to corporations and the rich since the Hoover administration.

It was also McIntyre who told the Ways and Means Committee that by 1983 half of the biggest and most profitable businesses in America paid no federal income taxes in at least one of the years the depreciation changes were in effect. He also found that more than a quarter of 250 companies surveyed paid zero in federal income taxes over the entire three-year period, despite making fifty billion dollars in pretax U.S. profits. One example, General Electric, got a $283 million tax rebate on $6.5 billion in pretax profits. Another, Boeing, received a rebate of $267 million on $1.5 billion in before-tax profits. DuPont received a mere $132 million rebate on pretax profits of $2.6 billion.

The supply-side economic results were so woeful, the public was so outraged, and the tax breaks were so unjust that President Reagan himself joined with then Senator Bill Bradley and lobbied to close many of the loopholes through the Tax Reform Act of 1986. "The changes greatly scaled back corporate tax avoidance opportunities and made taxpayers out of most of the former corporate freeloaders," McIntyre concluded.

Despite this dismal record of capital gains tax reductions, conservative Republicans, supported by some conservative Democrats, continue to press their case for reducing capital gains taxes for their rich and big corporate friends. According to the CTJ, in 1999 the Republican leadership proposed capital gains tax cuts that would have the following effects:

> Three-quarters of all tax cuts would go to taxpayers with more than one hundred thousand dollars in reported capital gains. (This group represents only 2.6 percent of all capital gains recipients.)
> Nearly half the total tax cuts would go to seventy-three thousand taxpayers with more than five hundred thousand dollars in capital gains. (People in this group constitute less than 0.5 percent of all taxpayers with capital gains.) Their average tax cut would exceed $102,000 a year.

> Almost a quarter of the total tax cuts would go to 3,061 taxpayers with capital gains exceeding ten million dollars. Their average tax cut under the plan would be $1,236,400.

In addition to capital gains tax cuts and depreciation, conservatives also favor a "flat tax." It is based on a book written in 1983 by two Stanford University economists, Robert Hall and Alvin Rabushka, titled *Low Tax, Simple Tax, Flat Tax*. Two southerners, Representative Richard Armey (R-TX) and former Dixiecrat Senator Richard Shelby (R-AL), are the chief supporters of the flat tax legislation. Additionally, former congressman and vice presidential candidate Jack Kemp, two-time presidential candidate Steve Forbes, and Senator Phil Gramm (R-TX) have their own, but similar, versions of the flat tax.

The basic idea is to replace the current progressive federal personal and corporate income tax structure with a flat tax, one designed to tax all income only once and at the same rate. The very poor and the very rich would pay few if any income taxes. The plans would replace corporate taxes with consumption taxes—taxes that fall heaviest on the middle class and the poor. All of the plans would result in a bonanza for the rich and large corporations, significantly higher taxes for the middle class, estimates of massive budget deficits ranging from nearly two hundred billion dollars to more than three hundred billion dollars annually, a massive increase in the national debt, an increase in interest rates, and slower but even more unbalanced economic growth.

Lars-Erik Nelson wrote in New York's *Newsday*, July 9, 1995, that states' righter and House Majority Leader Dick Armey "seeks to undo virtually every governmental accomplishment for working people, Democrat and Republican, of the past 60 years. Armey is a shiny-eyed ideologue who wants freer immigration plus an end to minimum-wage laws, abolition of the earned-income tax credit for the working poor, no taxes on dividends or capital gains, abolition of environmental regulations and an end to both the current Medicare system and employer-paid health insurance. Armey is another of these latter-day Ronald Reagans who have neither Reagan's charm nor Reagan's intellect."

Again, Robert McIntyre of the CTJ has pointed out that the conservative apostles of Hall and Rabushka in Congress are not nearly as candid as their teachers. The authors admitted that their flat tax "will be a tremendous boon to the economic elite." They honestly delivered what they admitted was "some bad news": "it is an obvious mathematical law that lower taxes on the successful will have to be made up by higher taxes on average people. . . . They calculated that their flat tax would raise taxes by $1,400 to $2,400 a year (in today's dollars) on families earning between $25,000 and $75,000." But "the truly successful get a better and better deal," they pointed out. "Families with incomes around [$295,000] receive tax breaks of about 7 percent of income, those with incomes of [$1.5 million] get 10 percent, and the handful with incomes approaching [$4 million] get 13 percent."

The real meaning of the flat tax is that it would knock flat out virtually everyone who was not earning more than $130,000, or the top 20 percent of today's income earners!

Another favorite conservative approach to taxes is the value-added or national sales tax. The conservative Americans for Fair Taxation, based in Houston, Texas, advocates for a FairTax Plan that amounts to a "national retail sales tax on new goods and services at the final point of sale for personal consumption above the poverty level." It would not tax used items. The organization argues that its plan would eliminate the complexity and injustice of our current system by repealing all federal individual and corporate income taxes, payroll taxes (such as Social Security), and estate taxes. These taxes would be replaced with a simple 23 percent federal retail sales tax on new goods and services. But as I have shown, such consumption taxes are the most regressive and unfair. Such an approach was supported by another southerner, former Representative Bill Archer (R-TX), chairman of the House Ways and Means Committee, the tax-writing body in Congress.

It is simply a reality of life that, for a variety of reasons, some people making the same amount of money pay different taxes. It may be that someone is living on Social Security and tax-deferred income that is taxed at a different rate than wages on earned income. Or it could be that two people are taxed differently because one is married and the other is not. According to Robert S. McIntyre: "It's one of life's little annoyances, at least for the majority of adults who are married."

The "marriage penalty" was written into our tax code in 1969 because the law effectively treated everyone as a single taxpayer. That meant a single person earning the same income as a married couple paid additional taxes because, with fewer deductions, he or she moved more rapidly into the higher tax brackets. So the new rate table in 1969 was adopted to offset protests that the system was discriminating against singles.

Now alleging discrimination against married couples, on February 10, 2000, the House passed a Republican-sponsored bill to end the marriage penalty. It slightly boosted the Earned Income Tax Credit for the poor and doubled the standard deduction of a married couple over a single person. Most important, however, the legislation increased the point at which the 28 percent tax bracket began for couples, to twice the level for singles. As a result, two-thirds of the ten-year $182-billion cost of the bill went to couples earning over $75,000. Couples earning more than $75,000 received an annual $994 tax break, while couples making less than $50,000 a year got a $149 average tax cut. So, it turns out, the Republican marriage penalty is essentially another conservative tax scheme to reduce taxes on wealthier Americans.

Many tax policies supported by conservative Republicans and Democrats, including President Bill Clinton, added to increased disparities between taxpayers with similar incomes because of their more favorable treatment of investment income than income from wages. It is therefore demagoguery to have expressed such concern over one tax difference, the marriage penalty—which conservatives often overstate.

Additionally, the marriage penalty for lower-income earners (up to about sixty thousand dollars in combined income for a couple in 1998) applied mainly to those couples who took the standard deduction on their tax return. Most high-income earners, however, itemize their deductions and are not affected by the standard deduction. Higher-income earners are faced with rate schedules that are different for singles and marrieds. If two partners earn forty thousand dollars each, a decision to get married could, on its face, cost them more than a thousand dollars.

To completely eliminate the marriage penalty would result in billions in lost revenue, but conservative Republicans provided no offset. Such lost revenue, then, would have to be made up in other ways: either by increasing taxes on the same married taxpayers who already pay three-quarters of all income taxes; enacting an overwhelming tax hike on a much smaller group of single taxpayers, which is politically unfeasible; or cutting government services. Thus, for the states' righters, doing away with the marriage penalty would accomplish another of their purposes, cutting the size and role of the federal government in Americans' lives.

It should also be noted that the biggest disparity in the marriage penalty is found in its application to married and unmarried couples receiving the Earned Income Tax Credit (EITC). EITC is a tax rebate program for lower-income working families. The CTJ points out that "two cohabiting single parents each making $15,000 can get as much as $2,870 apiece in tax rebates. But if they marry, their tax rebates are eliminated. As a result, in the worst cases, two-earner couples with four children and a joint income of $20–25,000 can face marriage penalties exceeding $5,000." While conservative Republicans are willing to spend huge sums on higher-income married couples, they apparently are unwilling to target marriage penalty relief to EITC couples. According to this Republican marriage penalty tax correction, marriage and family values should only be applied to the most well-off.

The marriage penalty advocates also use accounting gimmickry. They compare what married couples pay now with what they would pay if overall taxes were a lot lower. Again, as Robert S. McIntyre has said, "Saying that taxes would be lower if taxes were lower is true, but not edifying. The correct comparison is with a revised tax system that raises as much as current law."

When tax rates are fiddled with, you can always find some perceived "penalty" on somebody. The marriage penalty, however, is not one of the great tax injustices in our system. It is not even in the same ballpark as the disparities created by the tax mechanisms of reduced capital gains and accelerated corporate depreciation allowances.

Estate or so-called death penalty taxes are another favorite whipping boy of conservatives. Bard College President Leon Botstein reminded us in a *New York Times* op-ed piece on Sunday, July 23, 2000, that "James Madison, in his defense of the Constitution, admitted that the over-riding purpose of government was to protect the unequal acquisition of property. Inequality in wealth resulted from the manner in which the natural inequalities among human beings played themselves out." Traditionally, Americans have said it is one thing to labor and earn personal wealth, but it is quite different to have another's labor passed on from one generation to the next. It was this latter form of aristocratic inheritance to which Madison objected.

The inheritance tax was the democratic response. Botstein described it as a sort of "self-renewing equality of opportunity." The inheritance tax helped keep the idea of upward mobility credible and keep equality of opportunity believable (over actual material equality), encouraged the rich to give money they could not pass on to their children to charitable causes in which they believed, and served as an incentive to establish major foundations, such as Rockefeller, Pew, and Ford. It also helped keep class conflict at a minimum. Thus, Horatio Alger's "rags to riches" story could remain alive.

One of the first proposals of President George W. Bush in 2001 was repeal of the inheritance or estate tax. He and his Republican friends preferred to call it the "death penalty" tax as they focused public attention on small farmers and small businesses, even though they would not be the biggest winners under the Bush plan. Under current law, until 2006, anyone can inherit up to $675,000 without paying any estate taxes. In 2006 this amount will be raised to one million dollars. Small farmers and small businesses can already pass along even larger amounts. The Bush proposal, to repeal the estate tax altogether, would apply to everyone. A universal tax elimination program that is applied to every single American sounds equal and fair, but it is a far cry from both.

Currently, only 2 percent of Americans are wealthy enough when they die to pass along estates of more than $675,000 on which their heirs will have to pay estate taxes. Few people inherit such a large amount, including the small farmers and businesses Bush and Republicans talked so much about, which totaled a mere 3 percent of the 2 percent with more than $675,000. The Center on Budget and Policy Priorities, a progressive group in the nation's capital that studied Bush's plan, concluded that when fully implemented in 2010 the forty-five hundred largest estates in the country would receive fully half of the fifty-five billion dollars in tax breaks, while 142 million Americans in eighty-one million families with the lowest incomes would receive the other half, about twenty-eight billion dollars. Again, according to the center's study, "IRS data show that in 1998, the most recent year for which such data are available, the 2,900 largest estates paid half of all estate taxes." The Bush plan was a bonanza only for the super-superrich.

For Bill Gates, worth more than eighty billion dollars, it would have meant tens of billions of dollars. For the Forbes 400 richest Americans, it would have meant two hundred to three hundred billion dollars. For 98 percent of Americans, it would have meant paying even higher personal taxes to make up for the $28.2 billion missing in estate taxes from the federal budget over the first five years, $104.5 billion over ten years, with most of it kicking in after the first ten years—a twenty-year estimate in the neighborhood of $386 billion taken out of the federal budget.

As my father often says, the kind of alleged "equality" represented by Bush's across-the-board elimination of estate taxes for everyone represents chicken and egg justice. As the story goes, two men enter a restaurant and tell the waiter they'll have bacon and eggs for breakfast. From their human standpoint, that sounds good, fair, and just—bacon and eggs. The animals, however, have a different take on that breakfast. The chicken didn't mind, because all it had to do was give up a couple of eggs and go on about its business. But the hog had to give up his life! The chicken and the hog didn't view the sacrifice each of them would have to make for this common breakfast as equal. The elimination of the "death penalty for everyone" is essentially just as unfair.

The counterproductive nature of some tax cuts is also revealed when we take a closer look at Republicans' attempts to cut federal taxes by attacking the arts and humanities, and specifically the National Endowment for the Arts (NEA)—which benefits many of their white middle-class constituents. Additionally, most of the money in federal entitlement programs and tax breaks (Social Security, Medicare, tax write-offs, deductions, credits, and more) goes to the middle class, not to the poor. As shown in an earlier discussion on affordable housing, the homeownership deduction on two houses of up to a million dollars is one glaring example.

Tax expenditures on both tax breaks and programs equal revenue losses. But middle-class and wealthier Americans receive their benefits largely through the tax code, which is generally enacted as permanent legislation, and can be taken advantage of privately by any qualified taxpayer. What did these mostly silent, hidden, or little-recognized tax expenditures to the rich and middle class cost? They equaled $582.8 billion in the 1999 budget, which was still $1.7 trillion, and these same expenditures under Clinton were estimated to cost $670.8 billion in 2003 when the federal budget was projected to be slightly over $2 trillion! Under the Bush tax plan, they would be significantly higher, and concentrated at the very top. Workers and the poor, on the other hand, benefit mostly from public programs. The public perceives tax breaks received in private as closer to entitlements, while viewing public programs as taxpayer "giveaways" to undeserving Americans who engage in "waste, fraud, and abuse."

Many tax breaks are corporate and do not affect average taxpayers directly. Most analyses of capital income suggests that capital gains taxes are likely to be borne by the rich. According to a recent Congressional Budget Office (CBO) report, the top 1 percent of the population receives 40 percent of capital income. Sixty percent goes to the top 5 percent, 67 percent to the top 10 percent, and 76 percent to the top 20 percent. Those in the bottom four quintiles receive 1, 6, 7, and 10 percent, respectively. Thus, higher-income individuals are the prime beneficiaries of corporate tax expenditures. Is anyone surprised then when the rich want to reduce, even further, capital gains taxes?

Conservatives like to tout charity and volunteerism as a means to social justice. The private economy clearly provides the biggest slice of the national economic pie in terms of jobs and contribution to the GDP. The distributional laws and policies of the national political order ought to be designed to ensure that every American has access to life, liberty, and the pursuit of happiness—and that no American is left behind. The government should, and often does, help those who, through no fault of their own, were born or have become disabled, or can only make a limited contribution to society—the mentally retarded and the permanently disabled.

Failing that, however, if some are still left temporarily behind, charitable organizations such as the YMCA, the United Way, the Urban League, churches, synagogues, mosques, and foundations have always been willing and able to contribute to helping people who have fallen on hard times or between the cracks of society. Even when money is not available, many Americans have always been generous with their time and volunteered to help the less fortunate and the society generally in countless ways.

In light of the massive tax giveaways provided to the corporations and the wealthy, you might think they would be among the most charitable givers. But a 1997 study by Yale University's Program on Non-Profit Organizations found that "most high income Americans are modest to stingy givers and only because a tiny minority are exceptionally charitable do the wealthy have a reputation for generosity."

Former Labor Secretary Robert Reich once noted that "most voluntary contributions of wealthy Americans go to the places and institutions that entertain, inspire, cure or educate wealthy Americans—art museums, opera houses, theaters, orchestras, ballet companies, private hospitals and elite universities."

Thus, over the past couple of decades of Reaganomics—"I got mine, you get yours," survival of the fittest economics—while the rich were getting much more wealthy, they remained stingy.

After all of these examples and analysis of unfair taxes, I am obligated to ask: What constitutes fair taxes? What criteria should be used to determine whether taxes are fair or not? government documents suggest five interrelated and sometimes integrated principles.

The first principle is source. Fair income taxes should be equitable in terms of the source of gross income. There are two types of source equity: vertical equity, which shares the tax burden equitably between individuals or groups with different gross incomes; and horizontal equity, which shares the tax burden equally between individuals or groups with the same gross income. Fair taxes should reflect a system that divides the tax burden fairly both vertically and horizontally between individual and corporate gross income (that is, equitably between big corporations and small businesses or rich and poor individuals, and equally between corporations or individuals with the same gross income).

Vertically, for example, if collectively corporations generate 50 percent and individuals 50 percent of the nation's gross income, then the tax burden (contribution to the nation's budget) should reflect taxes of 50 percent from corporations and 50 percent from individuals. Horizontally, the burden of taxes of differing gross income groups within corporations and individuals (large and small; rich and poor) should reflect the same taxes as everyone else in their gross income range.

The second principle is that the fairest taxes are progressive. The principle of progressivity expands on the first principle of vertical equity by citing the morally sound biblical mandate of "to whom more is given, more is required." That means the greater your gross income, the greater the share of the tax burden that falls on you, whether a corporation or an individual. By contrast, a proportionate tax system—sometimes referred to as a flat tax—taxes everyone at all income levels at the same rate. A proportionate tax is equal but not equitable because a greater share of the overall tax burden falls on low-income people than falls on high-income. A regressive tax is a tax where those with a higher income pays a smaller proportion of taxes than those with lower incomes.

The third principle is that fair taxes should go into a general fund as much as possible, and the programs these taxes support should be universal in application. This is why, like Social Security, a single-payer comprehensive and universal health care system would be popular among Americans. With universal programs and systems (politically) everyone has a stake in preserving and improving them.

Social Security provides both a sound and a contradictory example of this third principle. Social Security is sound and popular because of the universality of its application—at a certain age, everyone qualifies and is entitled to it. Therefore, the first step of conservative opponents of Social Security—whether Republicans, Democrats, or independents—is to weaken its political support by eliminating its *universal* nature and attaching a means test to it, usually on the basis of income. But a means test severs its universal nature, which is the basis for its strong political support. Conservatives who advocate means testing often use an appealing "fairness" argument—that the rich don't really need it. In reality, however, this is a tactic designed to begin to weaken Social Security's political support so conservatives can bring forth their various schemes of privatizing—which will better benefit a few, but will be a greater threat to the economic security of the many. Conservative privatizers want to take both the "social" and the "security" out of Social Security!

The contradictory part of Social Security is that the universal spending part of the program is so popular that it masks the regressive nature of Social Security taxes. Social Security insurance was designed as one leg of a tripod—the other two legs being private pensions and personal savings. However, Social Security, in combination with Medicare health insurance, has actually been the government's best antipoverty program, as it has dramatically reduced poverty among the aged in America.

In 1959 more than 35 percent of elderly Americans were poor. By 1994 poverty among senior citizens was only 11.7 percent. An important segment of the elderly need Social Security merely to survive: 26 percent of elderly recipients rely on Social Security for 90 percent of their total income. For 14 percent of recipients, Social Security is their only source of income—and 40 percent of the elderly rely on Social Security for 90 to 100 percent of their total income. Although women generally receive smaller monthly checks from Social Security than do men, they typically have a greater need for the money. Only 13 percent of women age sixty-five and older receive a private pension, compared to 33 percent of men. The mean private pension income for older women in 1995 was $3,940 annually, compared to $7,468 for men.

Progressive Social Security taxes could potentially generate even more money for the trust fund, allow us to increase Social Security payments, reduce poverty even more, and increase aggregate consumer spending—and thus make a contribution to building a more perfect Union.

The fourth principle is that taxes should be as simple as possible. This is often easier said than done. The principles of fairness and simplicity sometimes work against each other. Changes to make taxes fairer often also make them more complex. That does not mean that tremendous improvement in simplifying the tax system is beyond our reach. If our best minds seriously tried and applied these four principles, massive improvements in both simplicity and fairness in our tax code would be the result.

The fifth principle is greater efficiency. Economic efficiency is a measure of how effectively an economy satisfies the basic material needs and desires of its participants. Generally, taxes are most fair and cause the economy to function most efficiently when they treat different activities, investments, and types of income the same. Thus, for example, conservatives are both unfair and economically inefficient when they tax investment income less stringently than they tax income from wages.

A mericans pledge allegiance to the flag and to the republic for which it stands. We accept the five broad goals that are outlined in the Preamble to the U.S. Constitution. We affirm the idealism that Thomas Jefferson wrote in the Declaration of Independence that "all men (and women) are created equal" and that President Abraham Lincoln set forth and made even clearer in his Gettysburg Address. And we are also inspired by the dream of Dr. Martin Luther King, Jr. While in many ways we have improved and progressed as a nation, in other ways we have not always—if ever—lived up to those ideals.

One legitimate reason for this failure is that, while we always could have done better, through much of our history we have not been financially, organizationally, or technologically capable of fulfilling or making gigantic leaps of progress toward social and economic justice. But that is no longer true! We now have the ability to pay for our dreams. But how?

We can pay for our dreams through fair taxes, taxes shared equitably and invested in the development of all of the American people. We can also choose new priorities, with more money invested in education, health care, and housing, and less money wasted in the military and on unnecessary and imagined, but unrealistic, threats to our national security.

Another way is through balanced economic growth, not just aggregate growth. Planning for full employment is the best way to assure balanced economic growth. Full employment will generate more money to invest in health, housing, and education. And investing in these things will allow us to have even greater balanced economic growth, resulting in higher living standards and even more tax revenue.

Finally, we need to invest the American taxpayer's money—and the government needs to provide economic incentives for the private sector to spend its money—on these same human and humane priorities in the international community. If we do those four things, we will no longer just have uplifting utopian dreams, we will also be able to pay for a whole series of practical material dreams.

A U.S. constitutional amendment guaranteeing the right of every individual American to be taxed fairly and progressively would, in the words of Dr. King, "speed up the day" when we could actually build a practical utopia. Such an amendment would have a positive revolutionary impact on our society. It would require not only that federal taxes be fair, but that state and local taxes meet the minimum federal standard as well. Therefore, the most regressive taxing systems of all—state taxes, local taxes, and consumption taxes—would all have to be revised or reversed, in varying degrees, in order to comply with the new federal standard established by a progressive and fair tax amendment.

A fair tax amendment would actually do what President Bush and other conservatives say they want to do—put more of the people's hard-earned money in their own hands to spend as they see fit. But it would do many other things as well. By putting more money into the hands of a broader consumer base, fair taxes contribute to balanced economic growth as well as aggregate growth. Fair taxes would limit the negative effects of the boom and bust of the business cycle and the rise and fall of the stock market by adding stability to our economy, which is beneficial to the stock market, business, workers, and consumers. Another result of fair taxes and balanced growth would be even more taxes with which to develop the American people and the economy by providing them with ever-better education, health care, housing, and more. Such human development would make every American even more productive. Operating in the global economy with a fairer tax structure would have a similar effect on the justness and stability of the world economy as well. In short, fair taxes would help build both a more perfect Union and a fairer world—which would allow us to cut back on wasteful and unnecessary military spending.

I have consistently shown that the United States now has the means—the economic strength, money, organization, technology, communications, transportation, gross income, and GDP—to pay for our practical utopian dreams of full employment, comprehensive and universal health care, affordable housing, high-quality public education, a clean environment, and an end to abject poverty. What is currently missing is the moral and political will!

A MORE PERFECT UNION—
FOREIGN POLICY

Over the past two years, as I have moved to break the betrayal of my own silences and to speak from the burnings of my own heart, as I have called for radical departures from the destruction in Vietnam, many persons have questioned me about the wisdom of my path. At the heart of their concerns, this query has often loomed large and loud: "Why are you speaking about the war Dr. King?" . . . it grows out of my experience in the ghettos of the North over the last three years, especially the last three summers. As I have walked among the desperate, rejected and angry young men, I have told them that Molotov cocktails and rifles would not solve their problems. I have tried to offer them my deepest compassion while maintaining my conviction that social change comes most meaningfully through nonviolent action. But they asked, and rightly so, "What about Vietnam?" They asked if our own nation wasn't using massive doses of violence to solve its problems, to bring about the changes it wanted. Their questions hit home, and I knew that I could never again raise my voice against the violence of the oppressed in the ghettos without having first spoken clearly to the greatest purveyor of violence in the world today: my own government. For the sake of those boys, for the sake of this government, for the sake of the hundreds of thousands trembling under our violence, I cannot be silent.

For those who ask the question, "Aren't you a civil rights leader?" and thereby mean to exclude me from the movement for peace, I have this further answer. In 1957, when a group of us formed the Southern Christian Leadership Conference, we chose as our motto, "To save the soul of America." We were convinced that we could not limit our vision to certain rights for black people, but instead affirmed the conviction that America would never be free or saved from itself until the descendants of its slaves were loosed completely from the shackles they still wear. In a way we were agreeing with Langston Hughes, that black bard of Harlem, who had written earlier:

"O, yes, I say it plain.
America never was America to me,
And yet I swear this oath—
America will be!"

—Dr. Martin Luther King, Jr.
"Beyond Vietnam" speech, New York City, April 4, 1967

Be the change you want to see in the world.

—Ghandi

If you want to make the world a better place, take a look at yourself and make that change.

—Michael Jackson, "Man in the Mirror"

During the presidential campaigns and debates of 1984 and 1988, when the press would challenge my father's foreign policy credentials, he would often say, "I know foreign policy. I've studied history. We came to America on a foreign policy."

That is true but, even more important, it was his way of saying that foreign policy is an extension of domestic policy. Building an early southern domestic economy based on slavery led to its logical foreign policy extension—a growing slave trade in the United States until 1808. Slavery also influenced how we related to Cuba and Nicaragua, as southerners tried to expand U.S. political slave power into the Caribbean and Central America. Cuba was coveted by some southern leaders periodically throughout the early and mid-1800s; in 1848 Mississippi Senator Jefferson Davis argued for exercising the Monroe Doctrine by claiming it for the expansion of slavery. During the mid-1850s, William Walker led a gang of filibusters (pirates) to conquer Nicaragua, with the financial support of Cornelius Vanderbilt. Walker was embraced by the South because on September 22, 1856, he ended Nicaragua's emancipation edict of 1824 and again legalized slavery.

There is another major way in which U.S. domestic policy has influenced and continues to influence foreign countries. Many new democracies, South Africa being the latest, have modeled all or significant parts of their constitutions on ours. Therefore, what is in our Constitution, such as freedom of speech, press, and religion, and what is not in, like the right to an education and health care of equal high quality, gets exported. In these instances, by helping to shape another country's constitution through ideas that are often copied from us, the U.S. Constitution extends both our domestic and foreign policies. In this way, my eight proposed constitutional amendments would affect other countries as well, thus having a positive influence on our domestic as well as our foreign and trade policies.

The original molders of our Constitution were fundamentally drafting an economic deal in the form of a legal document to protect, expand, and benefit primarily the special interests of well-to-do white male property owners, rather than the common economic interests of all citizens. Fundamentally, it is still this original economic arrangement we are exporting—admittedly amended to include more people. However, if the proposed human rights amendments were added to the U.S. Constitution, it would have the potential to influence new democracies around the world with a broadened set of rights. Such amendments are particularly important in poor developing countries, because poor and working people need a democratic government on their side. A democratic government, with the law under a constitution on the side of meeting the basic needs of common people, is the only protection the poor and workers have against the ravages of an unregulated market-driven globalized economy. Currently, the concerns for total human and humane development are not present in the U.S. Constitution. Therefore, if other countries are looking to us as the model, these new democracies will feel less of a need to consider them either.

New American human rights, codified in the Constitution, could completely change the face of international trade agreements such at the North American Free Trade Agreement (NAFTA), the permanent normal trade relations (PNTR) agreement with China, and organizations like the World Trade Organization (WTO), the World Bank (WB), and the International Monetary Fund (IMF). Current trade agreements ignore or scale down concerns for such rights. Business and financial interests are uppermost and prevail over human rights, in part because such rights are not in the trading countries' constitutions or laws. Thus, current international trade agreements largely reflect the original U.S. Constitution's priority of protecting the special interests of the few, favoring business and finance over common economic interests.

Foreign policy is the relationship one nation has with another. It is not limited to defense, although defending the nation and its people is any government's first responsibility and must always be taken seriously. But national defense and security are sometimes misused and manipulated for political purposes. Nationalism, religion, and fear—all strong human emotions and motivators, almost instinctual drives—used in the name of defending a nation's people can also be manipulated by gifted political leaders who choose to push these emotional buttons for domestic or foreign policy purposes. Checking and balancing our leaders in this regard is another reason for making sure that we keep our democracy alive, vibrant, resilient, and well.

While thoughtful and good people with integrity may have differing viewpoints about what constitutes an adequate or effective national defense, most people are clear that real national defense and national security involve more than military might and economic hegemony. People working at good jobs, well educated, healthy, properly housed, living in a clean environment, enjoying equal protection under the law, and paying fair taxes should also be seen as part of any holistic strategic plan for building a strong national defense. Thus, amending our Constitution with these eight new American rights would contribute mightily to our nation's defense and security. And promoting democracy and raising the living standards of people in the developing world as part of an enlightened foreign policy would also advance our own national security.

Obviously, the world is not always a safe place, and there are people and organizations that exist to do harm. There are thugs, criminals, and murderers at home who represent a danger, and there are revolutionaries and counterrevolutionaries abroad who wish to hurt America. However, that is not our fundamental problem, either at home or abroad. Individuals and small-group leaders, apart from an unjust economic and political context, generally are not serious threats to our interests. Therefore, a foreign policy that works to eliminate underlying unjust economic and political circumstances, and works toward greater democracy and justice, is the best way to prevent a leader, a movement, or a society from emerging that threatens our national security interests.

Some argue that we must deal with the real world in *realpolitik* terms and, unfortunately, sometimes I am forced to agree. But we also need to remember that there are several kinds of *realpolitik* in the world. In the real world of democracies, where the rule of law prevails and people have genuine freedom and a relative degree of economic security and prosperity, they don't fight each other. So the best way to protect America's real national interests and security needs is to identify with those legitimate leaders, movements, and nations that are fighting for democracy, a humane agenda, and justice under the law, and support them morally, politically, and financially, using means that are respectful of other human beings.

The root material cause of virtually all international conflicts is social, economic, and political injustice. However, the United States and the other leading economic powers usually ignore and do not take seriously real preventive measures that would help stem conflicts and prevent wars: the demographics of population, international job security, health, housing, and education needs, democracy and human rights, balanced and sustainable economic growth. When we do move in this direction, it is usually too little or too late to prevent a firestorm. Even when confronted with a terrible conflagration, we mostly give lip service to the people's legitimate needs and real concerns. As a result, grievances fester as the common people are left poor, frustrated, and behind. Cuba, Vietnam, Chile, Grenada, Haiti, Nicaragua, El Salvador, Bosnia, Iran, the Philippines, Panama, and most conflicts in Africa, including Liberia, Sierra Leone, Rwanda, and Congo, are all recent examples of failing to deal with underlying long-standing patterns of injustice.

Frustrated people sometimes turn to militant leaders and more violent means, which threatens the status quo. Then our leaders rally the American people by claiming revolutionaries are threatening our national interests. In reality, it's mostly business and financial interests that the American government is protecting. It reminds me of when the South wanted the federal government out of its life, until the slaves escaped. Then Congress passed a Fugitive Slave Law and the South wanted strong federal enforcement. In a similar way, the minimally regulated business and financial communities, which always want the government to "let them alone" and "get off their back"—businesses are usually in developing countries in the first place to escape stricter business, worker, and environmental regulation by government—now want their economic interests protected or rescued by the government. It is another instance of the tail wagging the dog.

We experienced a similar pattern of behavior in the United States when FBI Director J. Edgar Hoover saw and treated Dr. Martin Luther King, Jr., as a national security risk. Hoover saw Dr. King, as well as the Black Panthers, the NAACP, and almost all other relevant black organizations and their sympathizers, as a threat to our internal security. Mr. Hoover and our political leaders did not look inward to see and address centuries-old injustices and grievances. They looked outward to find a scapegoat—communism.

The Kerner Commission documented the grievances of African Americans in 1968. But our society's response was not to nonviolently and legislatively deal with the underlying grievances of unemployment and lack of good educational opportunities, health care, housing, an end to media stereotypes, discrimination, and police brutality. Instead, the primary societal and political reaction was to support the forceful and violent suppression of those who were raising the issues, articulating the problems, and organizing to address them. Eliminating underlying causes is still not our highest priority today.

Again, my mother's simple wisdom comes to mind. She taught me an old value, that an ounce of prevention is better than a pound of cure. Unfortunately, prevention is still not America's fundamental orientation, either at home or abroad. Rather than seriously analyzing problems and finding preventive solutions, lazy minds would rather rely on the government's solution of spending 30 to 100,000 taxpayer dollars per inmate building first-class jails, and another twenty thousand dollars annually to keep each inmate incarcerated and dependent on the state. As a result, we have caught and surpassed Russia as the world's largest jailer of its citizens, with more than two million locked up. This at a time when we can educate students in the best universities for fifteen to twenty-five thousand dollars a year and make them independent, taxpaying, and productive citizens in the private economy. We need a revolution in values and priorities to apply both in the states and abroad—and new human rights amendments to the Constitution would help us get there.

While I happily and thankfully acknowledge that much progress has been made in our society, much more remains to be done. But if our response to social, economic, and political problems at home remains shortsighted and police oriented, I'm afraid that the principle of exporting such domestic policies through our foreign policy will continue as well. If our national priorities remain on an expensive incarceration over a valuable education, internationally we can expect to spend additional billions of dollars squelching rebellions or invading other countries to rescue our financial and business interests—which have often been propped up and protected by a brutal dictator who has exploited his citizens and the American people for personal economic and political gain—rather than fighting on the side of economic justice and political democracy. Such patterns and expenditures in the past are well documented: Batista in Cuba; Diem in Vietnam; Pinochet in Chile; Samoza in Nicaragua; to a lesser extent, Duarte in El Salvador; the Shah of Iran; and Ferdinand Marcos in the Philippines, just to name a few.

During this century, with some exceptions in Europe, we mostly sided with the unjust and antidemocratic forces in South and Central America and the Caribbean. In most cases we did not support legitimate freedom fighters and anticolonial movements in the struggles for independence in Africa. We belatedly supported Nelson Mandela, the African National Congress, and other democratic forces in South Africa. In the Middle East, we didn't have a balanced policy and couldn't even talk to one side (Yasir Arafat and the Palestine Liberation Organization, the PLO) until relatively recently. Under President Clinton we finally began to use our power to pull the two sides together in an attempt to mediate the conflict and facilitate a negotiated just and lasting peace. After a long association with the tyrant and self-proclaimed "President for Life" Francois Duvalier (Papa Doc) and his son Jean Claude (Baby Doc), we begrudgingly supported democratic forces in Haiti. But we have not engaged in the kind of continuing military, economic, and political commitment that will be necessary to bring Haiti into the twenty-first century. Our policy in Cuba has always been hypocritical and still makes no sense. We had normal relations with the Soviet Union and China when they were communists, and—no longer a satellite of the Soviets—Cuba is not a threat to U.S. interests. And while the situation is more complex, by approving the PNTR with China we have basically chosen business rights over human rights.

President Clinton toured Africa in 1998. On the trip he acknowledged our nation's foreign policy participation in the sin of slavery and human and economic exploitation, stopping just short of an official apology for our past conduct. He proposed a new relationship based on respect and mutual benefit. President Clinton said one purpose of his trip was "to put a new face on Africa for Americans." It could equally be said that he was trying to put a new face on America for Africans.

This historic antidemocratic and unjust foreign policy is why Peter Vaky, the second-ranking diplomat at the U.S. embassy in Guatemala in the late 1960s, wrote a memo on March 29, 1968—it only became public on March 10, 1999—condemning America's tolerance for state-sponsored terrorism that targeted innocent civilians and undermined stated American principles during Guatemala's thirty-six-year civil war. The *Washington Post*, on March 12, 1999, reported that, "Taken as a whole, the documents show that Washington not only was aware of the Guatemalan military's excesses against civilians but continued to support it—sometimes openly, sometimes not—throughout the bloodiest days of the conflict, which killed 200,000 people."

In a visit to Guatemala in early 1999, President Clinton said that U.S. support for military forces that "engaged in violent and widespread repression was wrong." In the same March 12 article, the *Washington Post* reported that Vaky stated in his memo why such an apology was necessary: "We HAVE condoned counter-terror; we may even in effect have encouraged and blessed it. . . . We have been so obsessed with the fear of insurgency that we have rationalized away our qualms and uneasiness. . . . Murder, torture and mutilation are alright if our side is doing it and the victims are Communists."

President Clinton could have gone to Chile, El Salvador, Panama, Nicaragua, Zaire, Uganda, South Africa, Angola, Iran, the Philippines, and elsewhere and made essentially the same speech. In each of these countries we did not side with the common people, economic justice, and democracy, but with various levels of antidemocratic forces and tyrannical leaders who were often economically exploiting the poor and enriching themselves with America's help.

By ignoring leaders who advocate longer-term, nonviolent, and democratic preventive economic policies, we make more peaceful ways of resolving disputes, such as economic incentives, leverage, and diplomacy, next to impossible. Angry, ideologically driven, or religiously motivated zealots who are supported by the people's resentment from long-standing grievances do not listen or respond to such reasonable appeals and overtures. The *realpolitik* result, then, is that we also make the faster, violent, military, reactive measures more likely. Dr. King once said, "Those who make non-violent evolutionary change impossible, make violent revolutionary change inevitable." Thus, for both economic and humane reasons, we ought not choose the shortsighted Catch-22 scenario that inevitably leads to military attempts to solve human problems; that, in turn, becomes the measure of the nation's strength, defense, and security. Military action is neither the best protection of our security interests nor our most effective option for solving problems.

The United States needs a strong defense comprised of military might, economic strength, diplomatic skill, moral authority, and the political will to act in just and preventive ways to protect our national security and long-term interests.

In a long series of presidential campaigns, both Democratic and Republican politicians have exploited our national defense fears with so-called bomber, missile, nuclear, technological, and other military "gaps" for narrow political advantage and economic military-industrial gain. Our military-industrial-based economy solidifies itself politically by distributing its goods, services, and jobs domestically in enough states and congressional districts to be assured that Congress will continue its federal "welfare" benefits by funding what they make or buying what they sell. This, of course, assures sustained and hefty amounts of unnecessary military spending. Under such a scenario, however, a holistic and realistic national defense strategy is guaranteed to remain a distant secondary concern. In the 2000 presidential race the national security question became whether we needed a "Star Wars" defense shield; if so, what size, how sophisticated, and how much money should we spend? Bush supported it because he wanted to appear strong on defense, and Gore supported it because he didn't want to appear weak. The American people were caught in the middle, basically without an alternative view.

One of the best examples of the domestic politics of defense spending—pursued in the name of a foreign policy based on protecting our national security—was former Congressman

Newt Gingrich (R-GA). He rose to become Speaker of the House by being strong on defense, castigating the federal government and urban programs, while preaching the virtues of the individual, family, and an entrepreneurial suburban lifestyle. Yet from a 1993 Common Cause study, we learn that Cobb County—the heart of his former Fifth Congressional District—received $3.4 billion in federal funds in 1992, ranking it third among suburban counties nationally. Cobb County's "hungry hog at the federal trough" was 41 percent higher than the national average for the more than three thousand counties in the United States. Mr. Gingrich often criticized big cities like New York for being dependent on taxpayer dollars and living off the public dole, which he claimed was creating a "culture of waste and dependency." Yet Cobb County residents received $9,878 in federal aid per capita, about $4,000 more than New York City residents. Thus, it turns out that the economic health and wealth of Cobb County was inextricably tied to federal spending, particularly defense spending. Defense contractors in his district, Lockheed and Dobbins, claimed $2.7 billion in 1994, or more than three-quarters (79 percent) of the federal dollars flowing into Cobb County.[1]

In economic terms, that's military Keynesianism, or the liberal economics of using the federal government's money to prime the pump of the private sector, yet Cobb County is called conservative and strong on defense. Are they really politically and economically conservative and strong on defense or are they just strong on economic prosperity and job security? Would their conservative politics and political ideology change and become more liberal or progressive if they could enjoy the same degree of wealth and job security, and maintain the same high quality of life and lifestyle, in a domestic-based and peace-oriented civilian economy? I think so!

The 2001 federal budget totaled $1.8 trillion, of which $284 billion (15.5%) went for national defense. NATO's defense of Western Europe took $80 billion, which, among other things, sustains 135,000 American troops there. The Asian Pacific region got $30 billion for defense, including $3 billion for maintaining 37,000 American troops in South Korea. Approximately $20 billion keeps U.S. troops in the Persian Gulf region.

However, in fiscal 1995, $802 million in aid for seven hundred million sub-Saharan Africans—that's slightly over $1 per person for the poorest people in the world—was removed as a line item in the budget by a Republican-led Congress because, it was argued, we couldn't afford it. We had to balance the budget—and it was supported by a Democratic president. Would such aid have given sub-Saharan Africa special treatment, something that no other region in the world would have? No. In fact, with its removal, Africa became the only region in the world that did not have a line item in the U.S. budget!

Foreign aid seems always to be the target of conservatives, yet in the 2001 budget it totaled only $14.9 billion, a mere 0.8% of the overall federal budget. That places the United States last among twenty-one industrialized nations in terms of the percentage of our GNP allocated to foreign aid. And it is hardly a giveaway! By law, nearly all U.S. foreign aid must be spent on American-produced goods and services. In fiscal year 1997, 87 percent of all foreign military assistance was used to buy U.S. military equipment and training—another federal subsidy to the U.S. military-industrial complex. More than 90 percent of food aid dollars was spent in the United States, another federal subsidy to the agricultural sector, and more than 75 percent of the agricultural products were shipped on U.S. ships. According to the U.S. Department of Commerce, all U.S. exports—of which only part is due to foreign aid—support twelve million American jobs. Thus, it turns out, foreign aid is really federal aid to American businesses, farmers, and workers, which may also happen to benefit the countries to which it is given.

During the second half of the twentieth century, American foreign policy was dominated by a policy of virulent communist containment. With the breakaway of the Soviet bloc nations, the breakup of the Warsaw Pact, and the breakdown of the Soviet Union, the Cold War is over. While there has been some strategic rethinking, many of the assumptions, institutions, policies, and practices generated by the Cold War are still in place and can be seen in any annual federal budget appropriation.

In the last century more than a hundred nations gained their independence, but are struggling with grinding poverty, illiteracy, disease, tribalism, nationalism, religious fervor, debt, and financial austerity. Yet our nation's and the world's basic response has been a sort of economic determinist, market-oriented, one-approach-fits-all solution that, again, serves primarily the economic interests of multinational corporations and financial institutions rather than the multiple needs of the common people in these developing countries.

I consider and take into account political philosophy and economic ideology as I go about my job in Congress. Indeed, we need to have such a general orientation and commitment; otherwise, as the saying goes, we will fall for anything. But we must not be rigidly married to any particular philosophy or orientation, and we must get beyond all of them if we are to meet common people's real needs. That's another advantage in fighting for human rights and not exclusively for any particular program, party or ideology.

My politics are guided by putting people first. People don't exist to serve the needs of or validate any particular party, economic ideology, political philosophy, or social system, regardless of its form, whether state controlled or market driven. Whether national or global, economic systems exist to serve the real interests and basic needs of all the people. All of them are means to an end. And while I have a political orientation, I consider many factors and try to listen to the various arguments before making a final public policy decision. In the end, however, I have two underlying questions in mind with regard to domestic, foreign policy, and national security questions: What are the underlying moral dimensions of this problem? And what will be the actual long-term human impact of this decision or policy?

In early 1998, at the invitation of the House Banking and Financial Services Committee chairman, Jim Leach, a Republican from Iowa—for whom I have enormous respect and great admiration, even though I differ with him on many economic and political points— I had the privilege to journey with a congressional delegation to East Asia on an eleven-day fact-finding mission with regard to the international financial crisis then gripping that region. It was recognized that, given the nature of an increasingly global financial market and economic system, the effects of a crisis in Asia would not be limited to Asia. It would negatively impact the entire world if it was not dealt with appropriately. While the U.S. eventually bailed Asia out at a cost of $17.8 billion, I doubt that the economic "structural adjustments" Congress required of them will make for a more just solution in the long term. Ongoing turmoil in the global economy will periodically demonstrate the limitations of the World Bank's and IMF's model of trade and capital liberalization.

Just prior to my visit to Asia, in late 1997, my staff provided me with a document written in May 1997 titled, "Moral Imperatives for Addressing Structural Adjustment and Economic Reform Measures" by the Religious Working Group on the World Bank and IMF. It helped immensely in crystallizing my thinking prior to and during the trip, and continues to give me tremendous guidance as I study foreign policy and national security issues. Written from a Judeo-Christian religious point of view—but recognizing that virtually all credible religions acknowledge the same general principles and values—it gave a religious framework for applying moral values to my institutional responsibilities as a member of Congress.

Its religious orientation makes it clear that economic decisions, whether by individuals, institutions, or governments, involve moral choices and have human consequences. There are no "economic laws" that place policy decisions beyond moral scrutiny. Policymakers and implementors are morally accountable for their choices and their effects—intended or otherwise. Only economic determinists feign moral and human neutrality and blame the consequences on "blind market forces" or "the forces of history." Human beings make choices and choices have human consequences, for which we are all individually and collectively responsible and should be held accountable.

Foreign policy, like domestic politics, is fundamentally about economic distribution. Therefore, economic justice should always be the end toward which our foreign policy works. Only economic justice can truly guarantee our national interests and security. My friend the Reverend Al Sharpton's words are as true internationally as they are domestically: "No justice—no peace!" I would only add, in a foreign policy context, "No security either!" And in foreign policy, we should strive to make our foreign policy means as consistent as possible with our stated foreign policy ends. It is difficult, if not impossible, to achieve a just and lasting peace and security using unjust means.

The Religious Working Group (RWG) set forth a set of moral imperatives relative to a sound foreign policy, beginning with, "All of life exists within the sphere of God's care and judgment." This means that all of us, whether acting individually or collectively through institutions, businesses, governments, or economics, are morally accountable. And since "the earth is the Lord's and the fullness thereof," we must use the earth's resources in a sustainable manner to benefit everyone, not just a select or privileged few. In practice, the recent economic "structural adjustment" policies imposed by the World Bank and the International Monetary Fund on poor and developing countries, with strong U.S. backing, violate this principle. Structural adjustment policies have forced cutbacks in public expenditures on education and health care, caused environmental destruction, and resulted in a significant increase in pain and suffering among the poor.

"Human beings are created in the image of God," was another of the RWG's imperatives. Since God loves everyone and considers each person of equal worth, every person deserves the same fundamental human rights and responsibilities. Each of us should be able to democratically and meaningfully participate in the basic decisions of our society, reap an equitable share of the fruits of our labor, and not be subject to denial on the basis of any human criteria. "Therefore," the group argued, "our social, economic and political decisions and policies must respect and enhance human dignity and gender equity. Economic and political policies must be flexibly designed and implemented with the consent of the people, as expressed through authentic and genuinely participatory democratic processes. In both the domestic and international spheres, 'reforms' must be held accountable to international human rights standards and treaties. There must be public debate and civil society participation."

"Human beings are persons-in-community, intended to live in relationships of human solidarity according to the norms of love and justice," also reflected RWG thinking. In essence, this is the Golden Rule of loving our neighbor as we love ourselves. Thus, lines of ethnicity, gender, generations, class, or nation-state are ultimately arbitrary human creations. Justice, which is love distributed, also means that everyone should have access to enough "resources to live in dignity, meet their family's needs and fully participate in the shared life of their community." Maldistributed income and wealth should be avoided, and when it exists corrected.

In the international economic community, however, the North is getting richer and the South is becoming poorer. Gaps in per capita income, share of world GDP and wealth, unemployment, a devastating debt, negative growth, infant mortality, disparities in access to safe drinking water, and suffering due to diseases, famine, and war are just some of the indications and reasons for this growing rich–poor gap. Domestically, during the Clinton-Gore administration, the United States became the world's most unjust industrialized democracy in terms of wealth and income, while within the United States the rich–poor gap grew as well. In fact, many of Clinton's policies actually increased these inequities. I always found it curious that Clinton and his DLC friends, who often speak of family values, equal opportunity, mutual responsibility, and community, seldom discussed their mutual responsibility for this accelerating domestic and international economic inequality. Such unjust economic arrangements, however, are the major contributing factors in weakening families, lessening genuine equal opportunity, and destroying communities.

"God is redeemer and liberator, calling us to a special concern for people living in poverty and oppression," was another RWG guide. God's truest work involves empowering people, but especially the poor, to liberate themselves "from every kind of oppression—personal, social, economic and political." Our focus, then, must be on "the least of these," but not merely in a call for personal, community, or voluntary help to solve our social problems. That approach often provides some immediate relief and, as such, is valid. But our primary task is to eliminate the underlying causes of poverty and injustice. Thus, public policies, laws, and economic relationships must "become instruments of emancipation by giving preference to the dignity of those who labor, to human rights, to gender equity and to sustaining the earth," yes, even above the interests of capital. The goal is not the easing of poverty (or conscience), but the objective eradication of poverty and the establishment of economic justice in our society and around the world.

The RWG also argued that "creation is an expression of the goodness of the Creator and is endowed with dignity and value." The creation of the human race and world is good, must be respected, and should sustain life with all it beauty, diversity, and richness.

The religious group also stated that "sin is social and institutional, as well as personal." What is social sin? Among other things, social sin is evident where there are growing economic disparities, increasing concentrations of economic power, a lack or lessening of genuine full political participation, and accelerating environmental abuse.

Only God is worthy of ultimate worship. Thus it is a form of idolatry when any economic model or political system is viewed as complete, fully adequate, and not needing reform. Therefore, economic justice cannot and "must not be based on any one economic model." Guided by principles (many articulated here, but also found in the eight proposed constitutional amendments), all economic systems must flexibly adapt to specific social, economic, and environmental contexts, be open to innovative designs, and be responsive to popular and democratic needs and initiatives.

"All humanity is called to forgiveness and reconciliation," was the RWG's last moral imperative. Dr. King once said that if God were merely just—an eye for an eye and a tooth for a tooth—and not also merciful, we would all be blind and toothless. Jesus' most famous prayer contained the words, "forgive us our debts as we forgive our debtors." When applied to our foreign policy, one practical application of his prayer of mercy and justice would be to forgive the crushing international debt burden imposed on millions of poor people living in impoverished countries, a debt we can afford to forgive, and one that is not of the people's making. I proposed such total debt forgiveness in my HOPE for Africa bill in 1999. While Republicans refused to even hold hearings on the bill, it did stimulate broader discussion of the issue both nationally and internationally, and caused the Clinton administration to make some token gestures in that direction.

Such moral imperatives are to be kept in mind and pursued. Yet I am not naive. In public life and policy we may not always be able to follow them. But we ought to be aware and grapple with them. Too often, we take an easier path. We put on the easy blinders of economic and political self-interest, or *realpolitik*, and remain oblivious to the tougher and deeper dimensions of questions, and we shouldn't. Our moral, mental, economic, and political lives will be better in the long term if we contend with these more difficult, profound, and troubling questions. We need to struggle with them before we are confronted with a critical situation—so these values can become a more natural part of us—as well as, if we have time, when we are actually confronted with a crisis.

The work of the RWG reminded me of Peter Vaky's observation that the morality of U.S. support for the military in Guatemala was never discussed at the embassy. "We never debated it as an ethical question. The issues were never really posed that way," Vaky said.[2] Yet underlying every social, economic, and foreign policy issue are the moral and ethical dimensions. Clearly, our political and governmental leaders' understanding of these critical religious-moral-spiritual-ethical issues and their modus operandi should be more comprehensively informed and inclusive of such factors.

If the first level of foreign policy discernment is seeking to understand the underlying moral dimensions of any given policy issue (which are usually not obvious), a second level, which is sometimes stated, is political principles. When carved out in a systematic way, they are often referred to as "doctrine." Thus, the Monroe Doctrine, as it came to be known— a new American foreign policy spelled out by President James Monroe in 1823 as part of a message to Congress—basically announced that France and Spain were no longer welcome in the American hemisphere. Because the United States had acquired the industrial and military might, it enforced the policy.

While anticommunism among both Republicans and Democrats in Congress and the White House was the key element in America's foreign policy following World War II— Vietnam destroyed Lyndon Johnson's administration—the Reagan administration epitomized this point of view most clearly, especially when it came to the Soviet Union and the so-called Third World. From President Reagan's point of view, "The Soviet Union was an evil empire and it lay behind all the trouble spots in the world." Therefore, the world was a chess board where moves and countermoves with the Soviet Union in Africa, South and Central America, the Caribbean, and elsewhere constituted foreign policy.

The Jesse Jackson presidential campaign in 1988 argued that "from this perspective came the Reagan Doctrine, the commitment to intervene against any government or frustrate any movement which did not meet American approval. Inevitably, the Reagan Doctrine entailed open contempt for international law, illustrated in our withdrawal from the World Court after mining the harbors of Nicaragua. It entailed unilateral action, spurning the opinions and objections of our allies. It finally entailed secrecy and deception to avoid the protests of our people and the constraints of Congress."[3] The doctrine was based on a fundamental error. Poor countries, struggling to survive and fighting poverty, illiteracy, and disease, were drawn not to communism, but to help from wherever they could get it.

During the campaign, in an Iowa debate, my father put forth a set of five foreign policy principles upon which I have built my own foreign policy perspective. While Reverend Jackson never achieved the presidency and put them into practice, he referred to them as the Jackson Doctrine.

Respect and strengthen international law and international institutions was the Jackson Doctrine's first foreign policy principle. It is important for the most powerful nation in the world, now its only superpower, to strengthen international law and institutions because, in a lawless or unstable international order, the United States has the most to lose. Unless our presence in the world is seen as legitimate and contributing to the common good, no amount of economic or military power can protect or sustain our interests.

We must build a more perfect international community for the same reasons that we must build a more perfect Union. Some problems are so large, extended, or in need of financial resources or centralized coordination that there is no other way to solve them. AIDS doesn't stop at the water's edge. Acid rain knows no national boundaries. Economic collapse in one area now affects us all to one degree or another. In terms of international peace, Dr. King used to say that "the choice now is not between violence and non-violence, but between non-violence and non-existence." The human mind has now harnessed the power that could bring about the total annihilation of the human species.

Strengthening and supporting international law and international institutions does not mean support for the international status quo. Many of the RWG's moral imperatives are being violated by the "structural adjustment" and "reform" policies and programs that the United States is pursuing through the International Monetary Fund and the World Bank. For example, poor countries are being forced to export food and other products in order to pay their debts, but sometimes just the interest on the debt is greater than their exports. As a result, many poor countries are falling farther behind on their debt and are unable to feed their own people. That is all the more reason why moral imperatives must undergird the political principles of any political doctrine.

At one point during the 1990s, the United States owed $1.6 billion in back dues to the United Nations, despite needed reforms having largely been implemented. This irresponsible act by Congress—led by southern Senator Jesse Helms of North Carolina and perpetrated mainly by the Republican Party—was clearly contemptuous of respecting and strengthening international law. And in the end, the negotiated lower U.S. payment was an insult to the international community. We are a founding charter member of the United Nations and the largest among the host countries in which U.N. governing units are located. Its presence in our country contributes to the U.S. economy.

Respect for the right of self-determination was the second principle of the Jackson Doctrine. Virtually every nation-state lives in its own context and out of its people's experiences. Not everyone will model their economic or political system on that in the United States— and we should respect those choices. Within this context, and keeping in mind the moral imperatives, it does mean that we will help or cooperate more with those who support democratic processes and work toward achieving economic justice than with those who don't. But before we or the international community interferes with another country's right to self-determination, or uses military might against them, we ought to make sure that we are on strong moral and legal ground, and that we have a decent respect for the opinion of humankind. Short-term military expediency usually leads to longer-term political and foreign policy problems.

The third principle of the Jackson Doctrine was respect for human rights. Our foreign policy ought to strive to respect, protect, and export our most cherished values. Gross and repeated offenders of human rights should not be given U.S. aid or trade preferences. America's influence in the world, even more than its economic and military might, is in its ideas and ideals. Even more than our scientific and technological prowess, it's our high degree of respect for human rights; freedom of speech, religion, the press, and assembly; due process; equal protection under the law; and tolerance of differences that most appeal to the world. Adding the right to vote and the right to work, the right to an education, health care, housing, equal rights for women, a clean environment, and progressive taxation to our Constitution will only increase America's influence in the world in that regard. The common workers and people of the world welcome and are voluntarily importing many of our ideas and ideals, sometimes long before they accept the exporting of our goods and services, which are sometimes resented. If we export the former, rest assured, at the appropriate time, the latter will also be welcomed.

Jackson's fourth principle was to seek to lift the living standards of the common people in the developing world, not to lower the living standards of working people in America. Again the campaign argued that "development in the Third Word is a security need of the United States. Without development, there will be no peace; without peace, there can be no growth. Without growth in the Third World, our own prosperity will be threatened. We will not succeed as an island of affluence in a sea of misery, and we will pay a heavy price for trying."[4]

Raising the living standards in the developing world helps secure our own living standard and quality of life. If we exploit the lower living standards of those in the developing world through cheaper wages, fewer workers' rights and protections, and environmental degradation, U.S. corporations will relocate American jobs to cheaper labor markets. This is the recent and continuing pattern even in the United States. Businesses first moved higher-paying organized workers' jobs in the North to lower-paying unorganized workers in right-to-work states, primarily in the South, but in the Southwest and Far West as well. Then the companies moved the jobs to an even cheaper labor market across the Mexican border. Now business has the ability to move its productive capacity and jobs to wherever the cheapest labor and the weakest government standards in the world are located. My father often says in his speeches that if a four-dollar-an-hour worker is willing to take a six-dollar-an-hour worker's job, somewhere in the world there is a two-dollar-an-hour worker waiting to take away that four-dollar job. That is a "rush to the bottom" policy, and we will all lose.

Such a downward spiral of jobs, income, and worker and environmental protections does not enhance our security, but threatens it. It threatens the stability of countries where the mass of common workers are being exploited for the benefit of a few, and it contributes to the anxiety of U.S. workers who feel vulnerable. It contributes to worldwide economic instability because low-priced workers cannot buy what high-wage workers make—only better-paid workers can purchase what well-paid workers make. Thus, it is in our own and the world's economic and political interest to raise the living standards and quality of life of the poorest nations. Our country and the world cannot be any stronger or more secure than its weakest link.

The final political principle in the Jackson Doctrine is perhaps the most challenging: applying the other four principles as consistently as possible everywhere in the world. It is hard to be constant in our family relationships, so to be dependable in the application of political principles in very complex international situations where two or more valid principles may be in conflict is a major test of political skill and wisdom. Such political ability may even involve the apparent paradox of applying essentially inconsistent principles in a flexible way. This does not mean, however, we should not try for consistency, at least to the degree that is humanly and situationally possible.

The issues of war and peace must be a part of any consideration of a sound foreign policy. Like the previous moral imperatives and political principles above, my purpose here is not to deal with any particular concrete situation. In the end there is no moral imperative, political principle, or other guiding light that can substitute for sound human judgment when faced with an actual situation. But it is important to weigh various criteria when considering the use of military force. In the final analysis we must ask: When is it right to go to war or use military force?

I'm not a purist or a pacifist. In the real world of nation-states, where violent forces and men and women determined to do great harm to our nation and the world operate, military might and violence are sometimes necessary—when confronted with limited choices—to protect lives and our real national security interests. It is a serious and grave undertaking, however, when a democratic leader makes the judgment to use force or violence.

If considered necessary, the use of force and violence in war should never be seen as a positive good. War is the result of moral, economic, political, and human failure. In war, lives are lost and maimed, mental and physical suffering abound, homes and families are destroyed and disrupted, the means of making a living are often crippled, and, ever more in modern warfare, serious or even permanent damage can be done to the environment, which threatens the very existence of us all.

But even nonviolent approaches can also have relative degrees of violence associated with them. For example, an international embargo conducted against a nation may be effective in making that country behave in a certain way, but it may also hurt the most vulnerable, such as children, by causing the loss of basic necessities like food and medicine—which is violent. Thus, politically, even a nonviolent approach may not be absent some violence. It may simply be the least violent means of achieving legitimate or just ends.

Democratic leaders must consider moral, rational, and practical questions before using force and violence. They must also recognize and acknowledge that people of goodwill, using the same criteria and answering the same questions, may come to different conclusions and make different judgments, and this must be respected. Again, in the end, no principle or guidelines can substitute for a leader's sound judgment.

In a democratic society, when a leader is confronted with the issues of war and peace or the use of violence, it is important to consider motive. The motive must be to advance the cause of a just peace, which is the only basis for building a lasting peace or permanent stability in a region or in the world.

Military force should be used only to achieve morally sound and legitimate goals. The goals should be stated as clearly as possible, and subjected to public scrutiny, questioning, and debate prior to any action taken, if possible, so the American people and the world community can make a reasoned and sound judgment. Force should not be used to go beyond the stated goal—for example, merely to punish. During the series of Iraqi conflicts in the 1990s, some members of Congress hinted that we should go beyond the goal of driving Iraq out of Kuwait and later of ensuring inspections and eliminating dangerous weapons. They argued or hinted that we should eliminate President Saddam Hussein by attempting to assassinate him. President George H.W. Bush was right in resisting such advice.

Before using military force or engaging in war, leaders must exhaust all alternatives and do everything humanly possible to solve a problem or resolve a dispute through less violent means. That may include, but not be limited to, moral and rational persuasion, political leverage and diplomacy, and economic incentives or disincentives.

A rational and justifiable response must also be commensurate with the transgression. Just as this principle has traditionally guided and directed our legal system, so must it be applied in the context of international diplomacy and foreign relations. In other words, the means used must be proportionate to the desired end. The Vietnam War rationale of "destroying villages in order to save them" was not proportionate and should not have been acceptable.

Political leaders in a democratic society, especially under the pressure of war or when using violence, must maintain a high degree of humility and be aware that unknown consequences will likely occur as a result of their actions. Inherent in using military might or declaring war is arrogance—we are right, you are wrong, and we are going use violence to make you do right or stop you from doing wrong. Such arrogance often takes the form of dehumanizing the enemy in the heat of war by describing their people or soldiers as less than human. For example, the North Vietnamese people were often referred to as "Red Communists" and their soldiers were called "Vietcong" and "gooks." The consequence was to rationalize and justify the violence and inhumanity directed against them. It's an attempt to put a kind of salve, anesthesia, analgesic, or medical ointment on our conscience. Democratic leaders, however, should always maintain a high degree of humility, because our motives and goals, means and ends, and roles in causing or in not preventing such conflicts often aren't as pure and righteous as we would like to believe. Additionally, there are consequences of the use of violence and war that cannot be known in advance of a conflict—consequences that we may regret in the future or wish we could have avoided. Having the humility to recognize all people's common humanity and understand the limitations of our own humanity, judgments, and mortality is difficult in a time of war when violence is all around. But it is necessary for our leaders to behave in such a manner if we are to survive as a human species and community.

It is important to take into account world opinion and to build public support domestically for any violent action deemed necessary. When I was a child and a teenager growing up I would sometimes defy my parents' and friends' best judgments and advice. It sometimes worked out, but more often it didn't and I suffered the consequences. By the same token, those democratic leaders who choose to use military force or violence to solve conflicts must have a decent respect for the opinion of mankind. If possible, they must take the time to build domestic and international consensus in advance of any violent action. Leaders should seek and secure United Nations resolutions in support of the application of such military force. There should be joint congressional resolutions at home to ensure support by the American people and their elected representatives for any contemplated dangerous or prolonged military action. To do so is both morally and politically wise. President Bush's actions at home and internationally relative to driving Iraq out of Kuwait in 1991 are an example of such leadership.

While I have emphasized many factors and dimensions of our foreign policy, in the final analysis I hope that two factors have shown through above the rest: that U.S. foreign policy should be directed toward support of democracy, and of social, economic, and political justice around the world, and less about defending injustice; and that the United States should have as its priority prevention over cure.

As a member of Congress I strive not to be isolationist, imperialist, colonialist, or neo-colonialist, or to support oppressive policies anywhere in the world. I also strive not to have a Messiah complex. To borrow from biblical language, I am not trying to be my brothers' and sisters' "keeper" or their savior. I simply want to be their brother and for them to be my sister. And in my role as congressman, my goal is to provide and fight for public and foreign policies that support democracy, human rights, and social and economic justice around the world. Such policies should result in providing the maximum opportunity possible for all individuals to achieve their highest degree of personal development, and every nation to improve and eventually thrive.

The elimination of injustice is the surest way of preventing war, and working toward justice is the unavoidable way of achieving a permanent and lasting peace. Such a peace can only be advanced by fostering the development of democratic freedoms, balanced economic growth, and economic justice throughout the world, which should be the primary focus of U.S. foreign policy. If we stand and fight for this "preventive doctrine," the vast majority of the human family will not only admire us and what we have achieved, but will be on our side. And "we the people," democratically organized, fighting for balanced growth and economic justice, built on sound moral imperatives and political principles, standing up for our national and international democratic political institutions, can build not only a more perfect Union but also a more perfect world.

Obviously, it is easier to outline moral imperatives, formulate political principles, and draw up checkoff lists than it is to apply them to concrete situations. That has certainly proven true in my political life. As a congressman it is one thing to have what you think is a good idea. It is a completely different task and more difficult matter to translate that good idea into concrete legislation and have it become law.

Most laws are passed as a result of compromise and are not built on a consistent set of pure principles. Passing a bill in Congress must take into account many and divergent interests, and that's not necessarily a bad thing. In fact, it's generally a good thing, since no one side and neither party has all the wisdom. Thus, with virtually all congressional proposals, relative not pure judgments must be made.

I have this legislative experience almost daily, but it took on a more personal note during the 1998 and 1999 debates over the African Growth and Opportunity Act (AGOA). AGOA was intended to authorize a new trade and investment policy for sub-Saharan Africa and expand trade benefits to the countries in the Caribbean Basin. The Clinton administration, my longtime and good friend Representative Charles Rangel (D-NY), and my own father, as the president's special envoy to Africa, all supported the AGOA on the eve of the president's historic visit to Africa. It was clear that the president was going to tout it throughout his Africa trip. Even though Nelson Mandela initially rejected it in the presence of President Clinton, most African leaders accepted it or remained silent. African ambassadors to the United States and members of the Congressional Black Caucus mostly went along with it.

Although the countries of sub-Saharan Africa have vast natural and cultural wealth, and enormous economic potential, the standard of living for most of Africa's seven hundred million people has been falling. The region's per capita income is less than $500 annually, down from $613 in 1988 (in constant 1980 U.S. dollars)—versus $752 in 1980 when the IMF first began to work its will and its neoliberal market-driven development model on African economic policy.

Many sub-Saharan African countries have made notable progress toward democratization in recent years. Despite this enormous potential, Africa has the largest number of the poorest countries in the world. Thirty-three of the forty-one highly indebted poor countries (HIPC) are located in sub-Saharan Africa. Indeed, 50 percent of Africans live below the poverty line, and 40 percent live on less than one dollar per day. In addition, 40 percent of Africans suffer from malnutrition and hunger, while one in five children in Africa die before the age of five.

Africa is the only continent where economic production per person has declined throughout the last two decades. According to the World Bank, in sub-Saharan Africa wages have not grown since 1970; in the last decade alone family incomes have fallen by a third and the number of African families unable to meet their basic needs has doubled. In 1996 twenty sub-Saharan African countries were still below their per capita incomes of twenty years before. African women, the region's chief food producers, are often excluded from the benefits of current trade and investment regimes. Africa's wealth in natural resources, oil, and minerals is immense. However, current development and economic models have denied the majority of African people any benefits from this vast wealth.

Certain fundamental preexisting hindrances to African development and trade must be addressed. Sub-Saharan Africa's people, especially the poorest, are inordinately burdened by tens of billions of dollars of debt, and servicing these debts now take more than 20 percent of the export earnings of the sub-Saharan African region, excluding South Africa. The debt burdens of sub-Saharan Africa constitute a serious impediment to private sector development, stable democratic political structures, broad-based economic growth, poverty eradication, the expansion of small and women-owned businesses, food security, agricultural development aimed at feeding the continent's people, environmental sustainability, and regional integration.

Any policy for development in Africa that is intended to benefit Africa must be premised on unconditional debt cancellation. The history of U.S. cancellation of debt includes reversal of our demand that Germany pay 10 percent of its post–World War II export earnings to recover debts owed prior to the war. Germany successfully negotiated for a rate that resulted in annual payments of less than 3.5 percent of export earnings. Currently, Mozambique, one of the world's poorest countries, pays more than 20 percent of its export earnings to cover its debt.

The International Monetary Fund, the World Bank, and other international financial institutions and aid agencies have required African nations to adhere to "structural adjustment programs" that have imposed enormous preventable suffering on African people. These adjustment programs orient economies toward export production, placing downward pressure on wages, encourage unsustainable resource exploitation, and undermine food security, or the ability of societies to feed their people. These IMF and World Bank programs have led to major reductions in government spending, including in the crucial areas of education, health care, and environmental protection, and they particularly harm women, who are most severely hurt by the elimination of the social safety net and the policy's neglect of small and domestically oriented farmers.

Such programs impose a deregulatory and trade liberalization agenda that removes crucial government protections for society and leaves local business vulnerable to foreign multinational corporations. They also encourage wage cuts, including reductions in the minimum wage, weakening of labor laws and labor rights, and government and private sector reductions in employment. Structural adjustment programs force recessionary policies that most seriously victimize the poor, and these programs tend to exacerbate income and wealth inequalities and undermine basic well-being, as measured by access to food, shelter, medical services, and a sustainable livelihood, even when traditional economic indicators show economic growth.

Many economic and development policies imposed on sub-Saharan Africa under International Monetary Fund programs and other international loan programs are focused on generating hard currency through exports to service foreign debt rather than on production for domestic African food and other needs. Net transfer of resources from sub-Saharan Africa to developed countries has increased substantially for almost every sub-Saharan African nation. Two prominent examples are Zambia, whose debt service ratio was 25.3 in 1980 and 174.44 in 1995—a 600 percent increase—and Sierra Leone, whose debt service nearly tripled from 1980 to 1995.

Certain industrial agricultural practices imposed on sub-Saharan Africa under International Monetary Fund programs and other international loan programs, including substitution of export crops for staple food production, and use of chemical fertilizers, hybrid seeds, and other products, have resulted in damage to local farmers and agriculture and loss of food security. Current large-scale development projects have not been designed in a manner that produces benefits for most Africans.

Most sub-Saharan African countries are also suffering from an epidemic, indeed a pandemic, of HIV-AIDS as well as tuberculosis, malaria, and other diseases, many of which are treatable or preventable with existing pharmaceutical and medical treatments. Yet the AGOA legislation did nothing about the debt crisis or the HIV-AIDs pandemic, and its structural adjustment provisions forced these governments to cut back on domestic spending on education and health care while leaving the environment more vulnerable. Separately, Congress did pass some African debt relief legislation in 1999, virtually over conservative Republicans' dead bodies, but it was of little real assistance.

Fair trade and mutually beneficial investment can be important tools for broad-based economic development. A plan for sustainable, equitable development for, and trade with, Africa must recognize the asymmetries of power and different levels of development that exist between countries. Global production utilizing free trade between developed countries that have a common economic and social system often carries significant benefits—an expansion of demand, employment, and productivity, and a general increase in living standards.

However, trade between developed and underdeveloped countries with significantly different standards produces unjust results. Usually, there is a general reduction of wages and demand resulting from overproduction and underconsumption. That is accompanied by a reduction in workers' rights and safety, and fewer environmental protections and social welfare mandates. It results in a transfer of income and wealth from underdeveloped countries to the wealthy in developed countries, thus increasing income and wealth disparities both within developed countries and between developed and underdeveloped countries. Finally, there is the general lowering of living standards in the developed countries, or a rush to the bottom.

Therefore, mutually beneficial trade arrangements between countries with significantly different levels of development will require a more comprehensive approach that combines trade opportunities with other necessary policies that raise living standards rather than lower them.

It was in this context that I had immense problems with the AGOA because it didn't contain the kind of economic justice and humane policies that I thought developing countries in Africa needed and deserved. It contained nothing on the HIV-AIDS or debt crises that were pummeling Africa. Its multinational and corporate orientation didn't protect human rights, workers' rights, or the environment, and its austerity policies forced countries to cut back on public funds for education and health care to pay for the interest on their debt. But I had no alternative piece of legislation to offer. My dad even told me I was "against Africa" for opposing and voting against AGOA. It was a hard pill to swallow and swallow it I did, but not without first putting up a fight. I asked tough and critical questions of Representative Rangel and Representative Phil Crane, a conservative Republican from Illinois, its original sponsor. I spoke on the House floor and elsewhere against it. And I voted against the bill. It still passed in the House and was sent to the Senate.

When the bill failed in the Senate, I told my staff and several of my advisers outside Congress—Lori Wallach of Ralph Nader's Public Citizen Trade Watch among them—that in the next Congress I wanted to offer an alternative bill for Africa. I added, however, that I didn't want it designed merely with Africa in mind. I wanted it built on principles and laid out in terms that set new precedents for how the United States should engage in all trade agreements generally in the future. I said it should be seen as a challenge and as an alternative to NAFTA, the WTO, MFN status for China, and the general terms of trade that were currently being espoused by the IMF and the World Bank. I wanted it to reflect the moral imperatives and the political principles described above.

The president was using the right rhetoric, but he was advocating the wrong policies. In his 1999 State of the Union Address, President Clinton said: "Trade has divided us, and divided Americans outside this chamber, for too long. Somehow we have to find a common ground on which business and workers and environmentalists and farmers and government can stand together. . . . We must ensure that ordinary citizens in all countries actually benefit from trade—a trade that promotes the dignity of work, and the rights of workers, and protects the environment. . . . We have got to put a human face on the global economy."

I agreed completely. However, the only piece of legislation mentioned in the president's address, and the first trade bill he pushed in the 106th Congress, was the same mostly Republican-sponsored AGOA—which was a continuation of the old face of trade. How would this old approach address the total picture that we found in sub-Saharan Africa? I was even clearer that we needed more than a new face. We needed a new approach and a new substance.

With this knowledge, and to overcome a nearly four-hundred-year legacy of unregulated business, investment, and trade that had given us slavery, colonialism, and widespread human and economic exploitation, on February 23, 1999, I introduced H.R. 772, the HOPE for Africa bill of 1999. HOPE stood for human rights, opportunity, partnership, and empowerment, the basis for a new respectful and mutually beneficial trading relationship with Africa as well as other developing nations.

The key dimensions of the bill were in harmony with my core beliefs and were modeled after the Lagos Plan, a set of developmental principles outlined by African finance ministers from the sub-Saharan African countries, in coordination with the Organization for African Unity, nearly twenty-five years earlier. The Lagos Plan emphasized the freedom for each African country to self-determine what economic policies suit the needs of its people. Among the priority goals were food self-sufficiency and sustainability, broad access to potable water, shelter, primary health care, education, and affordable transportation—many of the same basic human needs my new human rights amendments address.

Most of my colleagues initially only saw it as an alternative to the AGOA bill. A few, especially among the Democratic leadership and those with significant labor support, saw in it my original intention, which was to set a precedent for all future U.S. trade and development agreements.

The HOPE for Africa bill was a new and different approach to development in sub-Saharan Africa. It was a comprehensive policy, a Marshall Plan for Africa. I saw no reason why our approach to Africa should be any different from our approach to the rebuilding of Europe and Japan after World War II—except that Africa had many more problems and many more needs and, therefore, it would be a more difficult and protracted task.

Thus, the HOPE bill was designed to promote sustainable, equitable development in Africa, and fair and mutually beneficial trade between our two regions. Specifically, HOPE represented the new approach to international commercial policy that the president said he was seeking: access for African countries to U.S. markets; broad benefits to ordinary Africans; corporate adherence to labor, human rights, and environmental standards; employment of African workers; promotion of African capital accumulation and investment partnerships; emphasis on establishing small and medium-sized businesses in Africa; and partnerships between Africans and Americans.

HOPE provided for mutually beneficial trade by taking a holistic approach to interlocking the trade, investment, business facilitation, debt relief, and aid elements that are vital to any successful economic relationship between sub-Saharan Africa and the United States.

Moreover, HOPE included the purchase, at a significantly discounted market rate, and cancellation of African debt, which had a face value of $230 billion and an annual debt service that devoured more than 20 percent of all African export earnings. Cancellation of an uncollectible debt would provide a clean slate for African countries facing the challenges of the global economy. HOPE also targeted U.S. foreign aid toward uses with broad public benefits, such as the prevention and treatment of the HIV-AIDS epidemic ravaging Africa. The original AGOA did not even mention debt relief or HIV-AIDS, and the final version that became law contained only "sense of Congress" resolutions, which express good intentions but do nothing.

I argued that the HOPE bill provided trade remedies that could be embraced by both working Americans and working Africans because it raised the living standards of both. It would not raise some African living standards at the expense of lowering some American living standards. It was also good for long-term business development and economic investment because average workers on both continents would be able to buy the goods and services that they produced and, in the process, build a fairer and more perfect economic world.

While I agreed with President Clinton that we needed to put a new and human face on trade, I also believed that this new face must be built on a new foundation. I argued against the current policies that Congress has set regarding Africa, which will negatively affect the economic future of the continent for decades to come. With such high stakes, it was vital that we get the initial policy right, but we didn't.

HOPE had the broad-based support of African and U.S. development, trade, and economic experts, and civil society organizations in Africa and the United States, representing the interests of the majority of the people who would be affected.

But the HOPE for Africa bill did not pass in Congress. In fact, House Republicans would not even give it a hearing. Still, it can be used to educate Americans about a new way to look at and conduct trade. And if we continue to educate and agitate, it could pass in some future Congress if we elect more progressives to the body. I took solace in the fact that a new standard of expectations was set in terms of relating to Africa, a lot of good progressive education and organizing took place, a model for future trade agreements was cast, and many Democrats joined in supporting it.

I still believe it is the future direction of trade agreements. It is a path leading to greater economic justice, which should be the primary goal of U.S. foreign policy. And increasing economic justice and political democracy at home and abroad is the best way to assure that our national security interests will be protected both now and into the future. Indeed, moving in this direction will create both a more perfect Union and a more perfect world.

POLITICS

Our flag is red, white and blue, but our nation is a rainbow—red, yellow, brown, black and white—and all are precious in God's sight. America is not like a blanket, one piece of unbroken cloth—the same color, the same texture, the same size. It is more like a quilt— many patches, many pieces, many colors, many sizes, all woven and held together by a common thread. The white, the Hispanic, the black, the Arab, the Jew, the woman, the Native American, the small farmer, the businessperson, the environmentalist, the peace activist, the young, the old, the lesbian, the gay and the disabled make up the American quilt. Even in our fractured state, all of us count and fit in somewhere. We have proven that we can survive without each other. But we have not proven that we can win or make progress without each other. We must come together.

—Reverend Jesse L. Jackson
Democratic National Convention, July 17, 1984

PROPOSED VOTING RIGHTS AMENDMENT
TO THE U.S. CONSTITUTION

Section 1. All citizens of the United States, who are eighteen years of age or older, shall have the right to vote in any public election held in the jurisdiction in which the citizen resides. The right to vote shall not be denied or abridged by the United States, any State or any other public or private person or entity, except that the United States or any State may establish regulations narrowly tailored to produce efficient and honest elections.

Section 2. Each State shall administer public elections in the State in accordance with election performance standards established by the Congress. The Congress shall reconsider such election performance standards at least once every four years to determine if higher standards should be established to reflect improvements in methods and practices regarding the administration of elections.

Section 3. Each State shall provide any eligible voter the opportunity to register and vote on the day of any public election.

Section 4. Each State and District constituting the seat of Government of the United States shall establish and abide by rules for assigning, on the day designated by the Congress for holding an election for President and Vice President, electors of President and Vice President for the candidate for each office who receives a majority of the popular vote in the State or District.

Section 5. Congress shall have power to enforce this article by appropriate legislation.

The 2000 presidential election revealed several things: Candidates seemingly have the ability only to look out for their most narrow and selfish political interests (the people and the democratic process were completely secondary concerns); the voting infrastructure and system by which we choose U.S. presidents (and others) is broken, not only in Florida, but virtually everywhere, and needs to be repaired; and, perhaps most important, we have no explicit fundamental right to vote in our Constitution.

Gore first wanted to count only the votes in the four counties where he thought he would win, not in all sixty-seven Florida counties. Bush reasonably responded by arguing, "Why not recount the votes in the whole state?"—but he then engaged in obstructionist legal tactics to make sure that such a recount never took place. Bush initially didn't want to count ballots where there were technical errors, until such irregularities had an impact on mail-in votes cast by military personnel and two counties where he ran well. After a statewide vote count looked like it might help him, Gore changed his mind and wanted "to count every vote." Bush didn't want a true statewide count—that is, making the best effort to count every vote in an imperfect system—because he feared it would cost him the election. Winning and politics was the only game for both candidates and both parties, not a concern for the voters or democracy. The 2000 campaign reminded us that we can't trust politicians to play fair in elections if left on their own.

In the 2000 election Americans also discovered another problem, that the voting *infrastructure* in our country is broken. Because of the pivotal role of Florida in the election, it received the lion's share of coverage, but virtually every state's election system would have revealed similar fault lines if given thorough scrutiny. The pattern across the country reveals that some ballots have confusing designs. The best machines with the lowest error rates are generally located in the wealthier and whiter counties, while the cheapest machines with the most mistakes are disproportionately located in counties with the poorest people and the highest number of people of color, especially African Americans. Additionally, county election administrators use inconsistent methods of counting votes. Electronic scanners reject ballots marked with pencils instead of pens. They also discard ballots marked for two different candidates, or properly punched ballots that also have a candidate's name written on it. The scanner sees both ballots as erroneous double votes and rejects them, even though, in many instances the voter's true preference is clearly indicated. In Florida, while many voters' choices were easily discernible on ballots rejected by optical scanners, some election officials never bothered to look at the actual ballot if the machine rejected it. Following the election, the *Orlando Sentinel* reported in late January that an initial examination of the fifteen Florida counties with the highest rate of discarded votes revealed that a voter's choice for president could be easily determined on more than 1,700 of the 15,596 rejected ballots.

Most Americans believe that the right to vote is cardinal among all human rights. This right, when seen in its entirety as a right to have your vote counted and weighed equally throughout the political process, is the key to all other rights. Therefore, this chapter on politics, a by-product of voting, in many ways is the most important in the book.

Even though the right to vote is the supreme right in a democracy, the Supreme Court in *Bush v. Gore* told Americans there is no explicit fundamental right to suffrage in the Constitution. Chief Justice William Rehnquist and Associate Justice Antonin Scalia besieged Gore's lawyer with inquiries premised on the assumption there is no constitutional right of suffrage in the election of a president, and state legislatures have the legal power to choose presidential electors without recourse to a popular vote. My voting rights amendment fixes these flaws.

George W. Bush was elected the forty-third president of the United States by one vote— a five-to-four Supreme Court decision. Most Americans thought the Constitution called for Supreme Court justices to be selected by the president. In 2000, however, with no fundamental right to vote in the Constitution, Supreme Court justices selected the president. Thus we witnessed a Supreme Court used as an extension of the Republican Party and a willing tool of the Bush campaign. Even more important than partisan politics, however, the votes should have been fully counted in the name of democracy in order to give the maximum amount of credibility and legitimacy to the eventual winner.

As a member of Congress, I swore to uphold the Constitution and the laws of the United States. When Bush was elected I reaffirmed that oath and affirmed that we are a nation of laws and not just of men and women. Even as I recognized and abided by the Supreme Court's decision, I strongly disagreed with it. In Third World countries, when democratically cast votes are not counted, or the person who most likely lost wins in a highly questionable manner, we usually refer to that as a coup d'état—the overthrow of a government, usually by a small group of people. Not all legally cast votes in Florida (as elsewhere) were counted. If they had been, according to the consortium of credible newspapers that conducted the post-election investigation, it appears Vice President Gore received the most votes in Florida, as he did in the country.

After the Soviet Union collapsed, many of its satellites fell. In the case of the Czech Republic, Václav Havel became the new president on the basis of a broad-based legitimate people's uprising, and a democratic "Velvet Revolution" was the result. In contrast, in the United States, in an illegitimate and narrow use of judicial power, the U.S. Supreme Court in 2000 overruled the will of more than one hundred million voters and orchestrated a highly questionable velvet legal coup.

Most Americans thought the legal right to vote in our democracy was explicit (not just implicit) in our Constitution and laws. However, our Constitution only provides for *nondiscrimination* in voting on the basis of race, sex, or age in the Fifteenth, Nineteenth, and Twenty-sixth Amendments, respectively. Therefore, the *Bush v. Gore* decision and the 2000 presidential election are among the many reasons why Americans should amend our Constitution to make the fundamental right to vote explicit. We should no longer leave that right to the whim or in the hands of election commissioners in over three thousand counties, or of nine Supreme Court justices, without the protection of a high constitutional standard. Our equal right to vote should be secured by explicitly putting a voting rights amendment in the Constitution that guarantees the people elect our highest leaders.

Beyond the right to vote, however, if political progressives' agenda is jobs, health care, housing, education, peace, and justice, what is the path, the means, for moving toward and achieving these goals? Is it better private religion and good personal moral behavior? A better or higher quality of education? Financial investment, corporate economic development, or an entrepreneurial spirit?

It is obvious there is no simple single answer. Societies do tend to thrive and be more wholesome if they practice good religion and pursue high ethical conduct. An educated country does progress better and faster than one with less emphasis on education. A "can-do" attitude toward finance and economic development and an aptitude for business and technological acumen that is open to change, efficiency, and increased productivity will be more competitive in the world economy. The latter, however, if left unchecked, or not made democratically accountable and regulated, will dominate all else—religion, ethics, education, culture, and politics. That is one of the lessons of slavery and states' rights.

While there is no single answer, for progressives there is one priority and one context in which all the other areas, in fact, do operate, and that is politics. For progressives, however, that precedence must not be just any kind of politics, it must be democratic politics! Both words—"democratic" and "politics"—are important for achieving the goals of jobs, peace, and justice and for building a more perfect Union. Unless our politics are genuinely democratic and participatory in the broadest possible sense, inevitably they will increasingly become elitist, undemocratic, unrepresentative, two-tiered, and dominated by an ideology conducive to corporate interests and business-first economics. And the latter can ultimately become authoritarian.

I understand that singling out politics, not as the answer but as the priority, along with increasing democratic participation, is not a popular answer in an age of corporate-dominated economic priorities and an antigovernment and antipolitics ideology. But increased and informed democratic political participation is the only path and the only chance that the poor, working, and middle classes of America—more than 80 percent of the American people— have of improving their material lives and of building a more perfect Union.

Actually, in the grand scheme of society, politics are inevitable and unavoidable. Politics affect you whether you're actively involved in them or not. No one is above their direct impact. The only question is whether they take place with or without our knowledge, participation, or consent. Our only option is what kind of politics we will have—democratic or undemocratic, informed or uninformed.

American "democracy" was founded to preserve and protect an elite economic system that allowed in only white male landowners as the initial participants and cut out all other nonlandowning white males, women, and all people of color. Landowners, large commercial enterprises, and other sectors of the economic elite of today, as a small minority with special private economic interests to protect, usually want lower taxes and less government, except for a military big enough to protect their economic interests anywhere in the world. They do not see the broader public–private partnership necessary for building a more perfect Union as being in their economic interests. It is my view that a more perfect Union is in the financial and business communities' long-term interests because it gives them greater economic, social, and political stability, and a broader and more dependable consumer base. But many businesses have trouble seeing it that way because their vision is narrow and short-sighted—they can see only maximizing short-term profits.

Landowners, the business and financial elite, and the very wealthy dislike and distrust genuine democracy and mass participation because building a more perfect Union and world for everyone interferes and leaves less protected their more short-term, narrow, private, and privileged economic interests. And in the final analysis, they are for protecting and advancing their own narrow economic interests, not for building a more perfect Union. That too is a lesson to be learned from the legacy of slavery and states' rights.

To some extent, after the first ten amendments to our Constitution, the struggle from America's beginning has been a quest to include more and more excluded Americans in our democracy. The Fifteenth Amendment to the Constitution in 1870, the Nineteenth in 1920, and the Twenty-sixth in 1971 were intended to politically enfranchise the former slaves, women, and young people, respectively. The Seventeenth Amendment in 1913 was enacted to ensure the people's direct election of U.S. senators. The Twenty-third Amendment in

1961 was adopted to see to it that the excluded people of the District of Columbia could at least cast electoral votes for president and vice president of the United States. The Twenty-fourth Amendment in 1964 prohibited poll taxes as the basis for voting—a Jim Crow tactic long employed by southern states primarily to exclude African Americans from voting.

In more than two hundred years, only seventeen amendments have been added to our Constitution since the Bill of Rights, and of those seventeen more than one-third (six) have been directly related to voting and increasing democratic participation. Additionally, several other amendments impact directly or indirectly on voting and our democracy, including the Twenty-second, which limits a president to two terms. I think the Twenty-second Amendment is undemocratic and should be repealed. Irrespective, my point here is that there must be some extremely important reason why people amend constitutions, fight, and die over the vote.

Despite long struggles to expand voting, there are some who try to play down the importance of voting and participating in politics. The conservative columnist and commentator George Will considers most practical efforts to increase voter registration and voter participation as misguided and ill founded. He usually argues that people have a right not to participate and should be left alone. "Apparently, they are fairly content with the way things are," he often says.

Of course people have a right not to participate. But this is a disingenuous argument designed to support a climate of minimum democratic political participation disguised as informed wisdom. The fewer people who are politically active and voting, and making sure that they get their fair share of the economic pie, the better off it is for those who already have an unfair amount and are voting to protect and expand their economic interests.

Limited voting and low political participation benefit the status quo, especially of conservative Republicans, but also of conservative and incumbent Democrats. This is why neither party devotes much serious time, effort, or money to increasing voter registration and participation unless it is clearly in their most narrow political interests to do so.

It's also why conservative Republicans in particular devote so much time, money, energy, and, in some instances, illegal activity to discouraging African American political participation. My father has told me about Nixon's Republicans funding Jeff Fort, a leader of the Black Stone Rangers and Disciples gangs in Chicago, to conduct a "Don't Vote" wall graffiti campaign in the black community in 1968 to discourage voting. Nixon won, and Jeff Fort was at his inauguration. In Louisiana and Alabama, Republicans have sent out intimidating notices to voters in targeted black neighborhoods warning that they could be put in jail for voter fraud. In New Jersey and other states, Republicans have created "ballot security teams" to be present at the polls, also designed as an intimidation tactic to discourage black voters from voting. Former conservative Republican "B-1" Bob Dornan tried similar demoralizing tactics against the current Democratic representative, Linda Sanchez, in his former congressional district in Orange County, California, among Latino voters. These modern-day Republican tactics are but a shadow of similar, but much more vicious, tactics perfected by the historical Democratic Party. David A. Bositis, senior researcher associate at the Joint Center for Political and Economic Studies, contends that political consultants probably put more resources into driving down votes for opponents than increasing their own.

Conservative Republicans don't want increased political participation among currently disenfranchised black voters, because they know they'll vote Democratic. But conservative and many moderate Democrats don't aggressively encourage increased black political registration and participation either, because they fear these new voters will vote for black or more progressive white Democrats. The voting records of conservative Democrats and Republicans on the Voting Rights Act of 1965 and its extensions in 1970, 1975, and 1982, on statehood for the District of Columbia, and on the motor voter bill—and the lack of aggressive implementation by governors in many states after passage—shows how much real opposition there is among the political elite to bringing every citizen fully into the political process.

The National Voter Registration Act (motor voter) passed the Senate on May 20, 1992, by a vote of 62 to 38. Of the 38 who voted "no" on the bill, 37 were conservative Republicans and the other, Ernest Hollings, was a conservative Democrat from South Carolina. The same measure was passed in the House on June 16 by a vote of 268 to 153. Of the 153 voting against the bill, 135 were Republicans and of the 18 Democrats who voted "no," 11 were from the South, 2 were from the border states of Missouri and Maryland, and 5 were from northern states.

An even clearer pattern emerged on a House vote that failed on statehood for the District of Columbia on November 21, 1993, a vote that, if it had been successful, would likely have seen three additional Democrats elected, including two blacks in the Senate and one in the House. The vote, in a majority Democratic House, was 153 "for" and 277 "against." The vote breakdown was 151 Democrats and one Independent, Bernard Sanders of Vermont, voting for statehood, with all Republicans voting against it except Wayne Gilchrest of Maryland. What was even more revealing about Democrats, however, was how the conservative legacy of slavery impacted the vote. Of the 105 Democrats who voted against statehood (and likely black representation), 59 (56 percent) came from southern congressional districts, even though more than 50 percent of blacks still live in the South. Four were from the border states of Missouri (3) and Maryland. Another 11 votes came from small, farming or western states and included Arizona (2), Colorado, Iowa, Idaho, Montana, Nebraska, North Dakota, South Dakota, and Utah (2).

With voter participation around 50 percent of eligible voters in recent presidential elections, including 1996 and 2000, and with politicians of both parties seemingly uninterested in attracting new voters to the rolls and polls, it is inevitable that both parties' preoccupation will be with the better-educated and more well-to-do suburban voters who are already registered and voting. Therefore, any emphasis on increasing voter registration and democratic participation will likely have to come from political activists and the disenfranchised voters themselves. It is they who must gain the knowledge and have the will to act in their own economic and political self-interest by making voter registration and voter participation a top priority in everything they do. If the disenfranchised and their allies act and organize, the politicians will adjust and adapt.

The 1965 Voting Rights Act, equal opportunity minority political districts, motor voter registration, and statehood for the District of Columbia should be seen as part of the unfinished business of the American Civil War, indeed, of American democracy itself. The problem of politically enfranchising the former slaves, poor whites, people of color, or the disenfranchised generally has yet to be solved. Indeed, politically enfranchising all Americans has never been a top priority of America's political, economic, business, and governmental leaders. A constitutional amendment guaranteeing equal voting rights for every American is not the total answer, but it would help immensely.

While African Americans may not always understand the meaning of the constantly evolving racial code words and political games, most blacks are aware that white politicians may not always have their best interests in mind. That's why many African Americans were concerned when they heard about a 1998 inflammatory e-mail, passed on through talk radio, that blacks' "right to vote" would be up for consideration in 2007 and could be taken away. Again, all Americans, not just African Americans, need to know that there is no explicit right to suffrage in the Constitution. The Constitution contains only the right to nondiscrimination in voting on the basis of race, sex, and age. Thus, the only voting rights protections we have are in federal laws. This e-mail rumor is still widely known and sometimes accepted in the black community. I and other African American members of Congress are asked about "losing our right to vote" a lot on black talk radio and elsewhere. Such belief correctly interprets the motive and goal of weakening black political power by those who do not have our best interests at heart, but most of the facts in the e-mail were wrong. Even so, the spirit of caution inherent in the rumor—to remain eternally vigilant with regard to our voting rights—was correct.

Congressman John Lewis (D-GA) provided members of Congress with information to help clarify voting rights issues raised by this e-mail. The Voting Rights Act (VRA) was enacted in 1965 to end Jim Crow laws and practices that prevented blacks from voting mainly in southern states. Most sections of the act were permanent, but Section Four was set to expire in 1970. Section Four defines which political subdivisions are subject to restrictions outlined under Section Five. Without Section Four, Section Five has no effect.

Specifically, Section Four declares that a state or other political subdivision is subject to Section Five if: "(a) it maintained a test or device as a condition for voter registration on November 1 of 1964, 1968, or 1972; and (b) either less than 50 percent of those citizens of legal voting age were registered to vote or less than 50 percent of such citizens voted in the presidential election held in the year in which it used a test or device." "Test or device" includes such instruments as literacy, educational achievement, and good moral quality tests. Section Four also provides that states can be exempted from Section Five if they can meet a strict standard of nondiscrimination in voting practices during the previous ten years. Sections Four and Five are the only temporary sections in the act.

Section Five applies only to those states with a history of using discriminatory voting procedures as defined in Section Four. Under Section Five, covered jurisdictions must submit any proposed voting procedure or election law changes to the Federal District Court for the District of Columbia, or the U.S. attorney general, for what is commonly called "preclearance." The covered jurisdiction must prove that the proposed change does not have the intent or effect of discriminating against any minorities. If the jurisdiction does not meet this burden, the proposed voting procedure or election law change cannot take effect. The expiration of Section Four would end Section Five federal preclearance for covered states that seek to change their election procedures.

Originally only applied to southern states, in 1970 Congress extended Sections Four and Five for five years and expanded coverage to all states. In 1975 Congress extended these sections for another seven years, while expanding coverage to protect the voting rights of ethnic groups whose language is other than English. In 1982 Congress again extended Sections Four and Five, this time for twenty-five years—through 2007. The 1982 extension also expanded federal oversight of state voting procedures.

The heart of the VRA is Sections Two, Four, and Five. Section Two outlaws all forms of voter discrimination and allows states and individual citizens to challenge discriminatory voting procedures enacted by states (like Jim Crow laws). To challenge a voting practice, a plaintiff need only show that the voting practice has a discriminatory result, not that a discriminatory intent existed when the policy was implemented. Section Two applies to all states and citizens. Section Two also served as the impetus for the creation of equal opportunity minority political districts. However, some of those districts have subsequently been interpreted as unconstitutional by a strict constructionist and conservative Supreme Court using narrow interpretations.

Writing for the majority in *City of Mobile v. Bolden* (1980), Justice Potter Stewart argued that "racially discriminatory motivation is a necessary ingredient of a Fifteenth Amendment violation." So when the VRA came up for renewal in 1982, the Reagan administration did not so much try to *end* our protections of nondiscrimination in voting as it tried to *weaken* the enforcement provisions in Sections Four and Five by ending the preclearance provision. Ending that enforcement mechanism would have made the VRA much less effective. Consistent with *Bolden*, Reagan also tried to weaken Section Two by changing the criteria for court-determined voter discrimination by altering the standard of proof from "effect" to "intent." Proving intent is obviously more difficult, time consuming, and costly than proving effect. But in renewing and extending the VRA in 1982 for twenty-five years, Congress preserved the preclearance provision and insisted that the standard in voter discrimination cases was proof of a "discriminatory effect," not a "discriminatory intent." Such attempts at weakening the VRA must be resisted now and into the future.

Because Section Two is permanent, any election procedure with a discriminatory effect would continue to be illegal and could be challenged by an individual citizen or the federal government. In conjunction with the Fifteenth Amendment to the Constitution outlawing voter discrimination on the basis of race, color, or previous condition of servitude, Section Two ensures that African Americans will not be denied the federal legal right to vote, even if Sections Four and Five expire in 2007. However, without Sections Four and Five the burden falls to the aggrieved *individual* to remedy any voting discrimination, rather than the states having an affirmative duty not to discriminate as currently enforced through the preclearance provision.

No provision of the VRA is scheduled to expire before 2007. As the August 6 expiration date nears, Congress will examine the VRA's history and effectiveness and decide whether changes should be made and expiring provisions extended. In each of the last three instances in which Congress considered the VRA, it has strengthened and reauthorized it for an increasingly longer period of time (five years in 1970, seven years in 1975, and twenty-five years in 1982). However, if Republicans are in control of the House, the Senate, or the White House in 2007, and are joined by some conservative or southern Democrats, an effective 1965 Voting Rights Act could definitely be endangered through weakening its Sections Two, Four, and Five provisions. However, the greater immediate danger, before 2007, is a narrow interpretation of an equal opportunity minority political redistricting case by a strict constructionist and conservative Supreme Court, which could undermine the effectiveness of the Voting Rights Act.

I do understand the concern of many African Americans that there could be a threat to our voting rights. After all, it was only a little more than thirty-five years ago that southern states used Jim Crow laws and violence to deny blacks the ability to exercise their vote. A majority of African Americans alive today lived in a period where segregation and the denial of constitutional rights to blacks were not uncommon. Until we affirm the right to vote in the Constitution, the only real protection or "guarantee" of protecting our right to vote is to be politically informed with accurate information, and to maximize voter registration and political participation among all Americans. That is the one thing conservatives fear the most!

Jobs and employment, health care, housing, education, equal opportunity, the environment, and fair taxes are all aspects of the content of politics, but democracy is politics' dynamic. Equal voting rights, maximum registration and participation, political education and activism, dissent, agitation, and more will make the political order more dynamic and the economic order more accountable to the public good. The capitalist economic order operating in our country and around the world is inherently dynamic—as it must be. This vibrancy for change, efficiency, and productivity, however, must be matched with the political energy of democracy in action, or the economic enterprise will overrun and dominate our politics to the detriment of us all.

It is impossible to have politics without ideology, even though it is usually unstated. That's why I was fascinated by the underlying ideology at the new "Third Way: Progressive Governance for the 21st Century" meeting of world and local leaders in Washington immediately after NATO's fifty-year celebration on April 25, 1999. Convened by Al From, president of the conservative and southern-based Democratic Leadership Council, it included President Bill Clinton, a former chairman of the group; Tony Blair, prime minister of Great Britain; Wim Kok, prime minister of the Netherlands; Gerhard Schroeder, chancellor of Germany; Massimo D'Alema, president of Italy; Lieutenant Governor Kathleen Kennedy Townsend of Maryland; former Colorado Governor and Democratic Party Chairman Roy Romer; Mayor Wellington Webb of Denver; and Commissioner Michael Thurman of Georgia.

At the start of the conference From articulated the ideological form of the DLC's public philosophy as follows: "Its first principle and enduring purpose is equal opportunity for all, special privilege for none. Its public ethic is mutual responsibility. Its core value is community. Its outlook is global and its modern means are fostering private-sector economic growth, today's prerequisite for opportunity for all, and promoting an empowering government that equips citizens with the tools they need to get ahead." Candidate Clinton in 1992 said he "put people first," but conceptually Al From was saying the DLC puts private sector economic growth first and an empowering government second; only third does it equip citizens to then complete and participate in this private sector growth. From's ideological priority is clearly the private sector's special interests and aggregate economic growth. He claims this is progressive because he is willing to use public tax dollars to provide education, training, and research to citizens, who in turn then aid and abet his real priority, private economic interests.

Thus, according to From and the DLC, the private sector's aggregate economic growth has ideological priority because its blind market forces can best lead us toward achieving the public good. Putting people first for the DLC means using government to advance private sector economic growth, which is done, of course, to benefit the people. Talk about economic elitism! The DLC formula is simply designed for the narrow elite economic tail to wag the broad democratic political dog.

It should also be understood that these so-called blind market forces are not all that blind when it comes to their own private economic interests. Indeed, within their dynamism and creative destruction, these market forces are the most rational, efficient, measured, and planned economic forces in the world. It is this ideology of public assistance to these rational (for their own) private interests that, the DLC believes, will achieve the public good and build the more perfect Union. This is neither a new nor a very progressive political philosophy. In fact, it is an old, illogical, and regressive political philosophy that puts the elite private economic interests of the few over or ahead of the public interest, the democratic public will, and the public good.

While progressives believe, along with the DLC, in the dynamism, growth, productivity, power, innovation, and creativity that private market forces generate, it is precisely because these forces are blind and private that they must be given public democratic direction to achieve the public good. It is the only way to truly put the American people first. For progressives, then, while we need a partnership between the public and private sectors, the order of that partnership must be public–private, not the DLC's private–public. From the start, to achieve the public good, the democratic will of the American people must have first claim on the nation's priorities and resources, assisted by the private sector. If the democratic will of the people, as expressed through their elected representatives in Congress, the White House, and polling, concluded that the public good is best served by providing all Americans with an equal high-quality health care system, then today we should not have forty-five million Americans without health insurance. And politically, if that will were expressed in a health care constitutional amendment, it would speed the day when no American was without high quality health care.

It is worth noting that Al From correctly identified the DLC as an "idea action center, dedicated to developing a Third Way philosophy and a Third Way governing agenda." That is important to understand because the DLC has no mass-based constituency or following. It is, not surprisingly, largely funded by corporate interests and collects elected leaders at small conferences to project its top-down corporate-led point of view through the media to influence public opinion. It sells its ideas through slick public relations, salesmanship, and "imaging." One of its best salesmen, of course, has been former President Bill Clinton.

It was also interesting to note that at this DLC conference—an organization that has been the most ideological of all Democratic organizations—it took pains to de-emphasize ideology, even as it discussed it endlessly. An example was British Prime Minister Blair's remarks:

Now, the way that I define the Third Way is this . . . what I would call . . . if I could use British or European terms . . . the old left would have almost tried to resist change, would just have said, we don't like this change. And we became associated with high taxes, producer interests, big government. In terms of crime, for example, we were often perceived as simply soft on crime, indifferent to it, more worried about the rights of those committing crimes than those people that were victims of it—and, basically, didn't appear to have answers to these problems of the future. That was the old left.

The new right that was produced in a sense as a sort of counter-revolution to that, in the '80s, thought the solution to everything was just get rid of government, just get it out—as little of it as possible, get rid of it all, economics of *laissez faire* and socially, often I think indifferent to what was actually breaking apart the bonds of society.

Now, I think that our whole process, really, for the center and center-left is a voyage of rediscovery. What is it that we're really, really about? And I believe what we're really, really about is the politics of community, summed up as Al From put it—community, opportunity, responsibility. . . . It's an agenda of values and principles that ends up with practical policies that make a difference to the people whose lives we're looking after and trying to help.

I was amazed that at the highest levels of government, these straw men and light arguments passed for serious economic thought and political ideology. Or was such lightness and lack of serious intellectual thought part of the blurring or attempted cover-up of their actual conservative ideology?

The DLC is obviously not naive about ideology. The organization was formed in reaction to and to offset the progressive impact of Jesse Jackson's 1984 and 1988 campaigns on the Democratic Party—which they claimed had ideologically pulled the party too far to the "left." Apparently the DLC does not distinguish between the legacy of slavery and racism and liberal economic and political thought. The Jackson campaign had emphasized enforcement of the 1965 VRA and an end to second primaries in 1984 as a way of enfranchising the masses of unregistered African American voters in the South, which, if embraced, would have benefited the Democratic Party. Instead, it upset one of the conservative parties in the South, the one with the legacy of slavery, From's own Democratic Party, the one that has dominated southern politics since the country's founding with the exception of the brief period of Radical Republican Reconstruction following the Civil War—and conservative Republicans recently.

In 1988 Jackson campaigned on putting America back to work by rebuilding America and on a national comprehensive and universal single-payer health care system for all Americans. The DLC interpreted the Jackson candidacy and defined these issues as "liberal" and "left." I guess, for the DLC, for all Americans to have a job and health care is somehow considered liberal or left. But I know that similar labeling and name calling is also how supporters of American apartheid and Jim Crowism and opponents of civil rights defined being able to eat in the public cafeteria of your choice or use the nearest rest room or stay in any hotel or motel of your choice in the 1960s. The demand by African Americans to have access to the same facilities as whites was interpreted by conservative segregationists, Republicans and Democrats alike, as liberal, left, and even communist. It seems the demand that all Americans have the right to vote, a decent job, health care, housing, and an education will also be called liberal, left, and even communist by conservatives. But why is meeting the basic human needs of all Americans—needs that the majority virtually take for granted—always defined by conservative opponents as liberal and left? I believe this is an obvious political strategy used by conservatives to scare the public and protect an unjust economic and political status quo.

Jackson's candidacy, following the gains of the civil rights movement, the divisiveness of the Vietnam War, the rise of the women's, environmental, and student movements, and the northern urban unrest of the 1960s, emboldened the Republican Party to abandon the philosophy of the "Party of Lincoln" and adopt the racist and states' rights legacy of the historic southern Democrats. This positioned Republicans to try to make some political inroads among historically conservative white Democrats. These generally better-off traditional southern conservative Democrats became the Reagan Democrats, joined by many northern suburban and western white conservatives.

The Reagan Democrats are the people the DLC, Clinton, and conservative Democrats generally targeted in 1992 and 1996, and Gore and Bush valued in 2000. Democrats campaigned and projected a barely acceptable message to their so-called "special-interest" constituencies, a voter base of workers, women, young people, academics, and people of color. The political calculation was that these constituencies had few other places to go. This was evident by the low turnouts in recent elections since the 1970s. It backfired in 2000, when the liberal votes that Ralph Nader and the Green Party received cost Democrats the White House. Decreasing turnout among the Democratic base, in a shrinking pool of active voters, is not how traditional modern Democrats win elections or change things progressively! But when a party cannot come to grips and deal with the history and legacy of slavery, Jim Crow, and discrimination, it becomes ever more economically and politically conservative in order to appeal to an even smaller pool of white, educated, and affluent voters as the only door left to walk through.

But this base constituency was neither the chief target nor intended to be the chief economic beneficiary of a "New Democrat" victory. Given their corporate private sector, top-down-oriented political philosophy, it is the only political constituency New Democrats can go after. They did not want maximum political participation because that would bring millions of new voters into the process whose justified expectations of improving their material lives would have to be met. But the DLC orientation and political ideology cannot satisfy such demands. Therefore, these Democratic conservatives simply want to divide up the smaller number of voters who are already in the process. Their approach is not bottom-up—worker and public good oriented—but corporate, private good, and top-down oriented.

One foreign policy consequence of this DLC approach was support by the Clinton-Gore administration of conservative Illinois Republican Congressman Philip Crane's African Growth and Opportunity Act. This legislative approach to African economic development was corporate oriented and top-down rather than people oriented and bottom-up.

But how do we revitalize democracy and increase political participation so as to be able to put people first? Several steps need to be taken to increase the mass participation of the American people and to improve the dynamics of American politics. There are several practical steps that can and should be taken in the form of legislation.

There was nearly 100 percent voter participation in the very first South African democratic election, while the United States—a country with the longest history of voting and the so-called cradle of democracy—ranks near the bottom in voter participation among the industrialized democracies in the world. The South African turnout was more than just the initial infatuation with voting. It included many South Africans with little formal education, no history or tradition of voting, and high rates of illiteracy. Part of its overwhelming success was political will, but much of it was in the very structure of the South African voting system.

Slightly more than a century ago there was no such thing as voter registration in the United States. Admittedly, voting was limited then, but people who were eligible to vote by age, citizenship, residency, gender, and race were simply allowed to vote on election day. What undemocratic politics changed this democratic policy?

Just over a century ago the United States was primarily Protestant and rural. The emerging industrial revolution, however, was changing that dramatically. Urbanized industry was attracting large numbers of formerly rural, but also European ethnic Catholic immigrants, to industrial jobs in the cities. Such growing mass migration to the cities was a direct threat to rural Protestant economic and political power that dominated both the U.S. Congress and state legislatures. At the same time, the women's suffrage movement was growing—finally coming to fruition with a constitutional amendment in 1920—and the recently freed slaves were trying to emerge as a political force.

Rural Protestant power dictated that something be done to stymie the potential political power of urban European ethnic immigrant Catholic industrial workers, women, and African Americans. Fundamentally, then, conservative white rural males in state legislatures began to introduce voter registration as a barrier to voting and an obstacle to mass democratic participation!

Along with voter registration, especially in the South, came additional structural and legislative barriers—early cutoff dates for registration, voting on a workday, roll purges, gerrymandered political lines, poll taxes, literacy tests, grandfather clauses, at-large elections, second primaries, and, of course, violence, including murder. Thus, it was neither an accident nor apathy that led Americans not to develop the habit of voting. The majority were structurally, legally, and politically hampered from voting. Vested economic and political interests at the top have worked long and hard, and in sophisticated ways, to keep those at the bottom from voting. This is less true today, but not completely untrue. When it comes to voting, old habits are often hard to break, new traditions are hard to establish, and candidates and their platforms must appeal to mass interests if we want mass participation.

Today we have a high degree of admiration for South Africa. While not without serious and ongoing problems, politically South Africa is one nonracial democratic country. Apartheid, which in Afrikaner means "separate, apart," is dead. The ten "black homelands" and the legal absurdities of apartheid are no more. South Africa, twice the size of Texas, had a population of 39 million at the time of its first election: 29.2 million (73 percent) black; 7.2 million (18 percent) white; 1.2 million (3 percent) colored (mixed race); and 1.2 million (3 percent) Asian. Its people are mainly Christian, with Hindu and Moslem minorities.

There were systemic differences that nurtured the high turnout of voters in the South African election compared to the low turnout in U.S. elections. The first difference between South African and U.S. voting is that in South Africa the new government *intended* for the masses of the people to participate in the democratic process. In the United States our government shows little interest or intention of having the masses of the American people participate by voting. How do I know that? Because good intentions are translated into good and effective government policies, legislation, and procedures. The South African government spent $70 million ($35 million from the United States) on voter education and voting procedures for 39 million people and 23 million eligible voters. A similar program for 280 million Americans and nearly 200 million voters would cost more than $500 million. In South Africa on the day prior to official voting, the government took the polls to the infirm in hospitals, to the incarcerated in jail, and to soldiers in the military. In the United States registering and voting is left mostly to individual initiative.

In South Africa the election was conducted over two days, which were national holidays, and everyone was off from work. They even extended it into a third day in the middle of the election to accommodate everyone who wanted to vote. All U.S. national elections (and most local ones) are held on Tuesday, a workday, usually between 6 AM and 7 PM. Our elections are thus conducted when most Americans are expected to be at work.

For most of the people who could vote at the turn of the nineteenth century—white male plantation owners, small businessmen, and small independent farmers (which most Americans still were at that time)—daytime Tuesday voting was not a problem. They had the flexibility to vote during the allotted time. Plus there was no need to accommodate women, who couldn't vote; or blacks and common farmworkers, who did not have the same flexibility during the week. This group of elite voters didn't want the masses of common people voting anyway. If they had really wanted them to vote, then Saturday, often a day for workers and their families to shop in small towns, and Sunday, a church day and day of rest, would have been better choices. The very process of voting midday on a weekday was designed to discourage most people from participating. Thus, this old white aristocratic and rural notion, carried over from another era, has the effect of disproportionately disenfranchising workers, minorities, and the poor, who face some of the same obstacles even today.

To simplify voting for the less educated, South African voters simply placed an "X" next to the picture, not just the name, on the ballot for the candidate of their choice—technically, in South Africa's proportional representative system, they were actually voting for the party.

South Africa also had same-day, on-site, universal voting. For three days citizens could vote anywhere in the country by just showing up at an election poll on the days of the election. Fraud was prevented by dipping a voter's thumb in invisible ink that would not wash off for a week. Ultraviolet light revealed whether a prospective voter had voted before or not. In the United States the problem of voter fraud is overwhelmingly related to those who run and control the voting system, not individuals who cheat. In the four American states that do have same-day, on-site, universal voter registration—South and North Dakota, Maine, and Minnesota—voter participation is about 15 percent higher than the national average.

Despite the fact that voter interest rises as the election nears, with interest being highest on election day, in the United States voter registration is cut off in different states between ten and forty-five days before an election. Yet if the police stop you on the highway in any state, they can tell within ten minutes on a computer whether you are driving a stolen vehicle and if there is a warrant out for your arrest. But the overseers of elections need up to forty-five days to prepare for you to vote. The difference is that the government actually *wants* to find stolen vehicles and people with outstanding warrants of arrest. The government has much less concern about whether you vote or not.

Finally, in South Africa, all minorities received protection—the white minority, as well as political minorities within the major racial groupings. Any party that got 5 percent or more of the vote was included in the government in proportion to its vote total. Winning seats only took one four-hundredth of the vote (0.25 percent). Winning 5 percent meant gaining a cabinet position, although this provision has since been dropped from the law. Thus, almost everyone had an interest in voting. Dr. Mangosuthu Gatsha Buthelezi's Inkatha Freedom Party won approximately 10 percent of the vote; former President DeKlerk got 20 percent. They were included in the cabinet and as vice president respectively, even though Nelson Mandela got 63 percent of the vote. In the United States the winner takes all. Clinton got 43 percent and he won it all with no (political) obligation to the 57 percent majority who voted for someone else. Our elections are not a shared-power win–win system for everyone, but a winner-take-all electoral system where the *majority* is often the loser. The U.S. election system is structured with a disincentive to vote as a way to discourage mass political participation.

We need not switch to a parliamentary system of government to implement significant changes that would dramatically increase the participation rate in America's democratic elections. Same-day on-site universal voter registration, changing our one election day to two weekend days, and eventually simple consumer-friendly electronic or Internet voting could dramatically increase voter participation and turnout.

The U.S. election system is based on individual candidates running in single-member winner-take-all districts. Proportional representation would be one good reform. There are a number of ways that proportional voting systems work, but the essence is that candidates run in multimember districts that elect several members at once based on a proportion of the total votes. The basic principle underlying proportional representation is all voters and political groups deserve representation in legislatures in proportion to their strength in the electorate.

Robert Richie, executive director of the Center for Voting and Democracy, proposes an additional idea: instant runoff voting (IRV). In the general election, IRV would allow voters to rank candidates in their order of preference rather than simply voting for one candidate. The highest turnout in the world among nations without compulsory voting has been in Malta, where they use an IRV-type system of proportional representation, and turnout has been more than 95 percent in recent elections. Of countries with compulsory voting, Australia has had the highest turnout, also with IRV. Because many Americans are fed up with voting for the lesser of two evils, they are either not voting or looking for a third-party alternative. Richie suggests, as a first step, changing the rules of our political elections that usually keep voters from taking independent candidates seriously.

As used in Ireland, Australia, and London, IRV requires the winner of an election to earn a majority of votes—unlike Clinton in 1992 or Bush in 2000. Voters rank candidates, in case their favorite candidate is eliminated, in which case the votes of the candidate's supporters count for their second choice in an instant runoff that is accomplished through the voting equipment in an immediate second tally. This process continues until one candidate earns a majority of the votes.

For example, in 2000 progressive voters might have chosen Ralph Nader as their first choice and Gore second, with conservatives selecting Buchanan first and Bush second. Buchanan finished last, so he would be eliminated, but his voters' ballots would be assigned to those voters' runoff choices, most likely Bush. That would not have given Bush a majority, however, so Nader's voters' second choice would then be awarded, most likely to Gore. In 2000 Gore would have gained a majority and won. This simple change for greater voter choice would allow for a different method of tabulating results. The candidate with the most first-place votes would not automatically win as he or she does under the present plurality system. Instead, a candidate would need a 50-percent-plus-one majority to win. Such a winning democratic majority would also provide a mandate to govern.

The most recent IRV election in the United States occurred in Ann Arbor, Michigan. The Democratic and Human Rights Parties had been splitting votes, allowing Republicans to win. The Human Rights Party was the antiwar and more progressive party, and the people adopted IRV in a 1974 charter amendment. It was first used in the mayoral election of 1975. In that election the Republicans won 49 percent of first choices, the Democrat won about 40 percent, and the Human Rights Party candidate won the rest. The Democratic candidate eventually won because nearly all the backers of the Human Rights Party candidate ranked the Democrat as their runoff choice. As a result, Albert Wheeler became the first black mayor in the city's history. Conservative Republicans, of course, went ballistic, primarily blaming the new voting system for their loss, and they were able to repeal IRV in a 1976 special election. But IRV could just as easily work in the Republicans' favor in other circumstances. For example, if IRV had been in place nationally in 1992, Bush likely would have defeated Clinton. But without it, Perot probably cost Bush the election. In Ann Arbor the majority of voters won in 1975. In 1992, nationally, the majority of voters and democracy conceivably lost. And of course, the same thing happened in the presidential election of 2000, with Gore actually receiving the most votes.

IRV is the system used to elect the Australian parliament and the Irish president. It could be adopted by states and cities for all elections, from city council and school board elections to state legislative and federal congressional races. With IRV, our politics would take a strong step toward what democracy should be all about: majority rule, providing voters with real choices, encouraging debate on issues, and building coalitions among people.

If in 2004 or beyond a popular progressive Democrat ran for president on a third-party ticket in the general election, I believe that many currently frustrated progressive and liberal Democrats and other so-called disinterested voters would have a reason to vote and would. But almost all Democrats fear that such a candidacy would split the Democratic vote and allow a Republican to win—as was the case with Ralph Nader and the Green Party in 2000. IRV is the way to eliminate that fear.

With IRV, for example, a Ralph Nader candidacy would help beat the Republican candidates, not hurt Democrats. Nader would bring progressives out to vote, and they would likely list other Democrats as their second and third choices. Likewise, a Pat Buchanan candidacy would help to galvanize conservatives and neo-Confederates, and with their second and third choices would likely choose the most conservative Republicans on the ticket—which would help Republicans defeat Democrats, not hurt Republicans.

IRV would encourage a more diverse range of candidates to run and thereby help remedy a flaw in the current system: Many citizens feel left out by its limitations. This more inclusive process would give voters a greater reason to vote, with an increased chance of their vote counting toward a winner. By opening the field to more choices, which, according to polls, a majority of Americans would welcome, IRV could help lift voter turnout in the United States.

It would take a constitutional amendment to make IRV applicable when electing a U.S. president. However, IRV could be introduced nationwide by simple statute for electing members to Congress, legislation that I have introduced. It could also be implemented by state and municipal legislatures for state and local elections. Some states would need to find new ways to tabulate ballots, but such a one-time reform would be a small price to pay in exchange for providing democratic majority rule and engaging the electorate in what is the most important public choice they will make—who will represent their interests when it comes to dividing up the economic pie. Such technical infrastructure advances in our voting procedures would cost additional dollars, so I have also introduced federal legislation to pay for these additional costs.

With a wider choice of candidates, voters would not have to choose between the "lesser of two evils." There would be increased voter participation because no one need fear that his or her vote is going to elect someone with a dramatically different ideology or platform. The candidate preferred by a majority of the voters would win. And the winner would have a bigger mandate to govern.

Let me illustrate how instant runoff voting works using two examples of 100 voters:

> Assume that in 2004 Gore was the first choice of 43 voters, Bush the first choice of 37 voters, Ventura the first choice of 11 voters, and Nader the first choice of 9 voters. As the lowest vote getter, Nader would be eliminated, but 8 of his voters chose Gore and 1 chose Ventura as their second choice. Ventura would now have 12 votes, Bush would still have 43 votes, and Gore would now have 51 voters, a majority, and would be declared the winner.

> Assume that in 2004, as above, Gore got 43 votes, Bush 37, Nader was the first choice of 11 voters, and Ventura the first choice of 9 voters. As the lowest vote getter, Ventura would be eliminated, but 7 of his voters chose Bush and 2 chose Nader as their second choice. Bush would now have 44 votes, not a majority, but the lead over Gore, who would remain at 43 votes. Bush could still not be declared the majority winner, and Nader

would now have 13 votes. Nader now becomes the lowest vote getter and is eliminated, but all 11 of his first-choice voters chose Gore as their second choice; also, the 2 Ventura voters who chose Nader as their second choice, chose Bush as their third choice. Bush would now have 46 votes. Gore would be declared the winner by garnering a majority with 54 votes.

Table 1. INSTANT RUNOFF VOTING HYPOTHESIS FOR 2004

FIRST EXAMPLE "BALLOTS"   SECOND EXAMPLE "BALLOTS"

Candidates	First-Choice Totals	Second-Choice Totals	Candidates	First-Choice Totals	Second-Choice Totals	Third-Choice Total
Gore	43 (+8)	51	Gore	43 (+0)	43 (+11)	54
Bush	37 (+0)	37	Bush	37 (+7)	44 (+2)	46
Ventura	11 (+1)	12	Nader	11 (+2)	13 Out	
Nader	9 Out		Ventura	9 Out		

In addition to reforming our system by giving voters more choices and altering our method of counting votes, we need campaign finance reform, and more than just shutting down large contributions of soft money from individuals, corporations, and labor unions. We need public financing of federal campaigns. Whoever puts the gas in the tank determines where the car goes. If private sector corporations, highly financed special-interest political action committees (PACs), and wealthy individuals put the money in the political tank, they will determine the economic direction of the country. In 2000 both the Republican Convention in Philadelphia and the Democratic Convention in Los Angeles were corporate dominated. If the public genuinely wants their elected representatives to represent their real needs and economic interests, and the public good, only campaign finance reform that includes the public financing of federal elections will allow them to do so. This is especially true of the preselection process of the parties' "wealth primaries." It is these primaries, more than the final general election process—which is mostly decided by the basic partisan leanings of large political constituencies—where money is most important. No campaign financing system is foolproof or a panacea, and all systems will require periodic reform, but public financing of campaigns would be a strong step in the right direction.

Another legislative initiative that could help with public financing of campaigns would be to give a tax write-off or, even better, a tax credit to any individual or business that contributed to a Federal Election Commission (FEC) fund to publicly finance federal and/or local elections. Contributions would go into a fund similar to the one-dollar checkoff option currently available when we file our income taxes, but with the ability to make unlimited contributions. We would then see—by who contributed—who was genuinely civic minded and public spirited. Any excess moneys could be used to improve the system or to engage in strictly nonpartisan voter education (teaching students and others how to use voting equipment, for instance), buy voting machines, or eventually set up the Internet for purposes of voting. Any shortfall in the goal or allotment could be made up out of general revenues. Such voluntary contributions would have the added advantage, like a charitable contribution, of allowing taxpayers who wish to see their personal, collective or corporate money used in this public manner to contribute directly to such a fund.

Lastly, with regard to improving the political process and increasing political participation, we must come to grips with the growing issue of ex-convicts who have served their time in jail and paid their debt to society but in most states are still by law not permitted to register and vote for the rest of their lives. This is a gross injustice and is becoming a bigger problem every day, especially in the black and brown communities. It is worth noting that New Mexico recently became the first state in a long time to restore ex-convicts' right to vote, with a Republican governor signing the bill.

The Bureau of Justice Statistics recently released prison population figures that show the nation's prison and jail population at more than two million inmates—the most of any industrialized democracy in the world. In 1999 nearly 3.9 million Americans, including 13 percent of African American males (1.4 million), were politically disenfranchised because of a felony conviction; 4.6 million black men voted in 1996. Ironically, the same number, 3.9 million, was the entire population of the United States when George Washington was elected president in 1789.

Regardless of race or color, we must fight to re-enfranchise American citizens who have done their time and paid their dues. If people make mistakes, serve their time, and pay their debt to society, then their right to vote should automatically be restored to them as well. Most people are reluctant to raise the issue, because they are afraid they will be labeled "soft on crime." But I think democracy and fairness are worth standing up and fighting for. That is not being weak on crime. That is being strong on democracy.

It is also in society's self-interest to do so. Powerless people are more apt to commit future crimes. People with political power, who have been informed about its importance and how to use it, are less inclined to commit crimes—especially of a violent nature. If we leave ex-convicts, who have paid their societal dues, politically impotent, then we have taken away one of their most important and powerful tools to rehabilitate themselves.

This is an increasingly serious problem in the country, affecting approximately four million people, and it is especially serious in the black community among black men, as you can see by studying the accompanying table. I am sure that the vast majority of these black male felons are quite young, joined by young brown and poor white men in the same predicament.

Table 2. DISENFRANCHISED FELONS BY STATE

State	Total Felons	Rate for Total*	Black Felons	Rate for Black Men**
Alabama	241,100	7.5%	105,000	31.5%
Alaska	4,900	1.2%	500	6.3%
Arizona	74,600	2.3%	6,600	12.1%
Arkansas	27,400	1.5%	10,700	9.2%
California	241,400	1.0%	69,500	8.7%
Colorado	15,700	0.6%	3,500	6.1%
Connecticut	42,200	1.7%	13,700	14.8%
Delaware	20,500	3.7%	8,700	20.0%
District of Columbia	8,700	2.0%	8,100	7.2%
Florida	647,100	5.9%	204,600	31.2%
Georgia	134,800	2.5%	66,400	10.5%

Hawaii	3,000	0.3%	100	0.9%
Idaho	3,800	0.5%	100	2.7%
Illinois	38,900	0.4%	24,100	4.5%
Indiana	16,800	0.4%	6,800	4.6%
Iowa	42,300	2.0%	4,800	26.5%
Kansas	7,800	0.4%	2,800	5.6%
Kentucky	24,000	0.8%	7,000	7.7%
Louisiana	26,800	0.9%	19,600	4.8%
Maine***	0	0.0%	0	0.0%
Maryland	135,700	3.6%	67,900	15.4%
Massachusetts***	0	0.0%	0	0.0%
Michigan	42,300	0.6%	22,700	5.4%
Minnesota	56,000	1.6%	7,200	17.8%
Mississippi	145,600	7.4%	81,700	28.6%
Missouri	58,800	1.5%	20,100	11.3%
Montana	2,100	0.3%	0	2.9%
Nebraska	11,900	1.0%	2,100	10.2%
Nevada	16,800	1.4%	4,000	10.0%
New Hampshire	2,100	0.2%	100	3.8%
New Jersey	138,300	2.3%	65,200	17.7%
New Mexico	48,900	4.0%	3,700	24.1%
New York	126,800	0.9%	62,700	6.2%
North Carolina	96,700	1.8%	46,900	9.2%
North Dakota	700	0.1%	0	1.1%
Ohio	46,200	0.6%	23,800	6.2%
Oklahoma	37,200	1.5%	9,800	12.3%
Oregon	7,300	0.3%	900	4.5%
Pennsylvania	34,500	0.4%	18,900	5.2%
Rhode Island	13,900	1.8%	2,800	18.3%
South Carolina	48,300	1.7%	26,100	7.6%
South Dakota	2,100	0.4%	100	3.5%
Tennessee	97,800	2.4%	38,300	14.5%
Texas	610,000	4.5%	156,600	20.8%
Utah***	0	0.0%	0	0.0%
Vermont***	0	0.0%	0	0.0%
Virginia	269,800	5.3%	110,000	25.0%
Washington	151,500	3.7%	16,700	24.0%
West Virginia	6,700	0.5%	900	4.4%
Wisconsin	48,500	1.3%	14,900	18.2%
Wyoming	14,100	4.1%	400	27.7%
U. S. Total	3,892,400	2.0%	1,367,100	13.1%

*Percentage of adult population who are disenfranchised.
**Percentage of black men who are disenfranchised.
***Not reported.

SOURCE: THE SENTENCING PROJECT

There are many young trained professionals in the fields of law, business, medicine, and other important areas. I am a young professional trained in business, theology, and law. Why did I choose politics as a profession? Basically because I think it is the highest art form available to the human family for doing the most good for the most people. It is also an effective forum for conflict resolution, and politics affects everything we do in life. Finally, politics is the distribution system for our economic system. It determines who, gets what, when, where, how, how much, and what it is called—a tax write-off, a subsidy, a tax credit, or welfare.

Politics is sometimes a rough-and-tumble profession, but it's also a noble one, and citizen political involvement is a righteous cause. While I disagree with James Carville on some issues, we totally agree that the art and science of politics counts, and that it's a noble profession.

Politics is often referred to as a "game"—and yes, there are goals, joys, and challenges in both. But I prefer to think of politics as an artistic and scientific profession rather than a game. Like any art, science, or profession, there are rules, guidelines, principles, strategies, tactics, and other dimensions that you learn in order to win or succeed.

I see three fundamental strategies in politics: Unify your friends; divide your opposition; and maintain the moral high ground. At base, politics is about numbers—do you have the numbers (that is, the power) to get your agenda through?

In politics, friends and opponents are built around interests, usually economic interests. When people have essential interests in common, they usually establish a formal organization—such as a political party or an interest group. Sometimes in politics, on a particular issue, opponents may cross organizational lines and become allies temporarily, such as when southern Democrats join with northern Republicans to oppose economic justice and racial equality. Most of the time, however, politics proceeds along partisan and economic interest lines.

While politics is almost always influenced by feelings and emotions, it is driven by protecting and expanding our objective economic, legal, social, and political interests. Politically, race has blinded many Americans from seeing clearly their real economic, legal, and social interests—the issues I have argued comprise building a more perfect Union. For example, it makes no political or economic sense for most of the people of the South, the poorest region of the country, to be economically conservative. Conserve what? The lowest wages in the country? The highest poverty? The poorest schools? The worst health care? The most substandard and inadequate housing? The highest crime rate?

It may make sense for the political *leadership* of the South to be conservative. Most southern leaders, from the founding of our nation to the present, have always either been the conservative economic elite (as slave owners) or have worked out an arrangement with the economic elite (the corporate sector today). But such economic conservatism does not add up for the *majority* of southern people. Southern political opposition to organized labor and support for "right-to-work" laws and tax breaks for the rich make sense to political leaders who socialize with and are funded by wealthy and corporate interests. However, it's not in the real economic, legal and social interests of most people in the South to support a conservative economic and political agenda.

Southern individualism and moralistic religion have always been key elements in promoting and preserving conservative southern politics. While the South's political branches have reached out and influenced the whole country, the religious roots of conservative economics and politics are in the South.

The vast majority of the most highly visible personalizing and evangelizing religious leaders on television and radio today (or recently) are from the South: Jim and Tammy Bakker's
PTL (Praise the Lord) television show was based in the Carolinas in the 1980s; Reverend
Jimmy Swaggart Ministries, including his church, television ministry, and university, reside
in Baton Rouge, Louisiana; the Reverend Oral Robert's television healing ministry and
university are housed in Tulsa, Oklahoma. The Reverend D. James Kennedy's church and
television ministry are located in Coral Gables, Florida; the Reverend Jerry Falwell's former conservative political organization, the Moral Majority, his church, his *Old Fashion
Gospel Hour* television ministry, and Liberty University are set in Lynchburg, Virginia; the
Reverend Pat Robertson's *700 Club* television show, his Regent University, and his political
organization, the Christian Coalition (formerly headed by Ralph Reed from Georgia), are
located in Virginia Beach, Virginia. The Reverend Billy Graham hails from North Carolina
even though his Billy Graham Crusades are based in Minnesota; the Reverend Kenneth and
Gloria Copeland and the Reverend James Robison are grounded in Fort Worth, Texas. The
Reverend James Dobson's Colorado-based Focus on the Family and his D.C. associate
Gerald Bauer's related conservative Family Research Council; Coach Bill McCarthy and the
Promise Keepers of Colorado; and Dr. Robert Schuler's *Hour of Power* international televi-
sion ministry, based in Orange County, California, are the exceptions to the rule.

Virtually all of these conservative religious leaders' approaches—either consciously or unconsciously—spiritually and intellectually support and undergird conservative economics and
politics. CNN's *Both Sides* television show and the Rainbow/PUSH Coalition human rights
organization hosted and headed by my father, who also was born and raised in ultraconservative South Carolina, are the only variants to this national conservative religious phenomenon
of which I am aware. However, even some of the more conservative social positions my father
has taken (for example, he originally opposed the public policy of abortion) and conservative
economic projects he has run, like his current Wall Street Project, reflect this top-down
conservative southern religious, economic, and political upbringing as well.

One of the basic strategies in politics is to divide your opposition. This conservative
southern religion and the conservative Republican political opposition in Congress combine to strategize and use tactics that divide their Democratic opposition throughout the
country and in the Congress. Two recent examples of how they achieved this were the
Promise Keepers demonstration in Washington in 1996 and Clinton's impeachment and
trial in 1998 and 1999.

On October 5, 1996, former Colorado Head Football Coach Bill McCartney brought a
million men to the nation's capital for a Promise Keepers "Stand in the Gap" religious rally.
Joining together with other men, a Promise Keeper was to be committed to high spiritual,
moral, and ethical values and to building strong marriages and families through love, protection, and biblical values. However, because many of its religious leaders had a history of
conservative political activity, including Coach McCartney, there was a suspicion that this
demonstration was not just a religious and spiritual gathering, but that at least its leaders
secretly had a political agenda. This was consistently denied by everyone associated with the
Promise Keepers rally and, on the surface, it certainly appeared to be that way. Below the
surface, it was less clear.

To better understand the potential political implications of the Promise Keepers rally, it
is helpful to be familiar with the thinking of Ralph Reed. In his book *Politically Incorrect*—
subtitled *The Emerging Faith Factor in American Politics*—Ralph Reed, former Christian

Coalition executive director and student of Republican "take no prisoners" strategist Lee Atwater, said he was not just thinking about political tactics from election to election, but strategizing for where he wants the country to be twenty-five years in the future. Further, he outlined a specific strategy recommendation for increasing minority participation in the conservative political movement through the churches.

Reed suggests that the religion-based political right pursue two themes in order to break the color barrier:

> First, social issues are the key to unlocking support in the minority community. Republican candidates traditionally run on taxes and cutting government spending. The result is that they have won only a small percentage of the minority vote since 1936, when blacks left the party of Lincoln for the party of FDR. Moderates in the Republican Party who call for the inclusion of more minorities in the party want to beat a retreat from the social issues, a flawed strategy that would virtually lock the GOP out of the minority vote for the remainder of this century. Jesse Helms, for example, received a higher percentage of the black vote than Ronald Reagan in North Carolina in 1984 by campaigning in minority churches on issues like school prayer.
>
> The second theme is the need for religious conservatives to work more actively within the Democratic Party. Despite their essentially conservative views on the issues, blacks and Hispanics remain strongly Democrat in their loyalties, partly because of the legacy of civil rights. If the pro-family movement hopes to make realistic gains among these voters, it must become more aggressively bipartisan and resist the temptation to become a wholly-owned subsidiary of the Republican Party. The Traditional Values Coalition has understood the importance of this strategy, working the minority pastors in a bipartisan way to oppose legislation granting minority status based on sexual preference. *Religious values cross racial lines; all too often, party loyalty does not* [emphasis added].[1]

Thus, while the Promise Keepers organization had gone to great lengths to distance themselves from the Christian Coalition, they may have been taking a page from Reed's playbook. Political conservatives know that African Americans have economic needs and are, therefore, economically liberal. But they also know that the African American and Latino communities are, at the same time, deeply religious and socially conservative. So, Reed says, if the political right wants to attract people of color to its movement, focus on social issues and values and stay away from economic issues.

Reed's strategic advice to political conservatives is therefore to focus on social issues and values that the religious and socially conservative minority churches, both black and Latino, identify as moral issues and reflective of moral values—support for voluntary school prayer, the Ten Commandments in public schools, opposition to abortion generally and to "partial birth" abortions specifically, homosexuality, pornography, and support for school choice (code words for vouchers), because the poor and people of color are so disgusted with many of the disastrously failing inner-city public schools.

On the other hand, Reed preaches that religiously based political conservatives cannot win if they try to organize minorities around their economic and material needs; what they really need from politics—jobs, fair taxes, health care, housing, affirmative action, an end to job discrimination, and so on. Conservative Republicans, however, carefully avoid making the distinction between "social" and "economic" conservatism. They use the word "conservative" in conjunction with social values, these limited social issues, *and* economics, as if conservative social values and issues, and conservative economics, are one and the same.

Family is a conservative social value and issue that both I and Harriet Beecher Stowe of *Uncle Tom's Cabin* support. Slavery was conservative economics. In *Uncle Tom's Cabin* she used the conservative social value of the family to expose the contradiction between and hypocrisy of the conservative family values that the slave owners preached and the conservative economics of slavery that they practiced. Deliberately mixing, confusing, and blurring conservative "social" values and conservative "economics" to maintain an unjust economic and political status quo is pretty much what most conservative Republicans, and some conservative Democrats, do today. It's the only sensible explanation why the neediest and poorest economic region in the country, the South, would be the most conservative. To be an *economic* conservative in the South is almost a contradiction of human nature.

This political strategy, then, has the form of the classic Republican tactic: "wedge issue" campaigns that organize around social issues that unite political conservatives with minority religious and social conservatives, but which also divide them from economic and political progressives. If political conservatives try to organize around economic issues, it will unite even socially and religiously conservative minorities with economic and political progressives, and keep them away from economic and political conservatives.

A chapter in Reed's book titled "The Curse of Ham" illustrates his point by citing the Bishop Knox incident in Mississippi. Bishop (his first name, not a religious title) Knox is the African American principal who created a national controversy by allowing student-initiated prayer in an integrated public high school.

Reed writes, "The Bishop Knox incident . . . exemplified the unity among white and black Christians on social issues such as prayer in school. In a statement that could have been made by Pat Robertson or Jerry Falwell, Knox argued that anything that restored moral values in our young people, including prayer, could hardly be viewed as harmful."[2]

The practical political advantages of this approach should be obvious. The social issues will attract and unite a segment of the conservative black and Latino churches, which will allow their pastors and congregants to coalesce with the white economic and political right, which is overwhelmingly Republican. At the same time, they become divisive and confusing wedge issues in the minority community and for multiethnic economic liberals and progressives, who are overwhelmingly Democrats.

Why is attracting blacks to the Republican Party and decreasing Democratic Party turnout so important to Republicans? More than 50 percent of all African American people live in the eleven former Confederate states of the South, and focusing the attention of African Americans on economic issues is the key to changing the conservative politics of the South. Thus, Republicans can take the country in a conservative economic direction to the degree that they can convince America that they are not racists and intolerant, and pick off, bit by bit—through the use of these conservative social issues and moral values—an ever-larger slice of the African American and Latino vote. Republicans can do this only because Democrats, North and South, haven't come to grips with the legacy of racism either. Again, changing the Republican face of racism and intolerance was the purpose of the "imaging" going on at the party's 2000 convention in Philadelphia.

The impeachment and trial of President Bill Clinton was also part of this social issues strategy and a tactic used by Republican conservatives, mostly southern based, to further their narrow economic and political agenda.

Republicans maintained that the underlying issue in the impeachment proceedings was not sex, it was perjury and obstruction of justice. Democrats claimed the underlying issue was sex— a private consensual sexual relationship—and the president lied about it to the American people, possibly committing legal perjury in the grand jury process. But perjury had not been established in a courtroom, and since lying about sex to the American people was not an act that involved using his official position against the state, as Nixon did, Democrats argued that Clinton's sins did not reach the constitutional standard for impeachment.

This is the essence of the arguments we heard presented by members of the House Judiciary Committee and members on the floor of Congress who voted, mainly along partisan party lines, to impeach President Clinton. That is what Republicans and Democrats were saying during the impeachment, but history many render a different judgment.

Underlying the Clinton impeachment and trial was neither sex, nor lying, nor perjury, but conservative politics and American history itself. Essentially the same economic and political forces that drove the presidential impeachment process against Andrew Johnson in 1868 drove the impeachment process against Bill Clinton 130 years later. The roles were reversed—the Republicans of 1998 were the Democrats of 1868—but the underlying issue was essentially the same: Reconstruction. Our nation's first effort at economic and political reconstruction after the Civil War was at issue in 1868. Our nation's second effort at economic and political reconstruction—which began with *Brown* in 1954 and continued with the progressive legislation of civil and voting rights passed in the 1960s—was at issue in 1998.

Lincoln fought the Civil War to preserve the Union and to stop the spread of slavery westward, which he believed would eventually end slavery. He defeated the southern slave forces militarily at a national cost of more than 620,000 lives and, to some degree—to what degree, we will never know—was prepared to reconstruct the nation with a Republican program of economic inclusion and political enfranchisement. "Former" Democratic Confederates opposed and resisted such a big centralized Republican federal government and wanted "the government off their states' backs" so they could go back to a system of states' rights and local control that protected their economic interests. After 1865, however, that local economic system was not slavery, but the ability to control a system of labor—the former slaves' and white fieldhands' pay, working conditions, and ability (really inability) to organize. Again, southern "right-to-work" laws are an offshoot and manifestation of this phenomenon today.

It's important to briefly recall the context: A "Black" President Lincoln was in office, and a Republican Party identified as antislavery was commencing Reconstruction; blacks remained loyal to Republicans until 1936, when they were attracted to the economics of FDR's New Deal and a new more inclusive Democratic Party; Senator Andrew Johnson, a Tennessee Democrat, after refusing to join southern Democratic Confederates, was rewarded by Lincoln with a nomination for vice president in the 1864 campaign.

After Lincoln's assassination, a Democratic President Johnson focused on putting the Union back together, but lacked the Republican commitment to build a "more perfect Union" for all Americans. Unlike Lincoln and the Republicans, he was willing to preserve the Union by leaving some Americans behind. Johnson was willing to sacrifice the rights and interests of the former slaves. As a result, angry northern Radical Republicans investigated a vulnerable Johnson—who was not unlike Bill Clinton in terms of his personal foibles—to try to come up with an excuse to impeach him. It was a partisan Republican attack on a Democratic president in order to preserve the Republicans' First Reconstruction program.

The struggle between these radical progressive northern Republicans and these radical conservative southern Democrats continued following the Civil War. It finally came to a head in the 1876 presidential election and Tilden-Hayes Compromise of 1877, which ended Reconstruction politically. Rutherford B. Hayes, a Republican, was finally elected president by one vote in the House in exchange for pulling out federal troops protecting the newly freed slaves in the South, picking up some of the southern states' Civil War debts, and agreeing to appoint conservative Democrats to the Supreme Court. These southern Democrats, with the help of new Black Codes of discrimination, psychological intimidation, physical violence, and murder, were now on their way back to power in the South.

By 1896 the Supreme Court appointments resulted in *Plessy*, which ended Reconstruction legally and ushered in Jim Crow, and by 1901 the first Congressional Black Caucus was completely eliminated from Congress, not to return for three decades.

The southern Democratic Party, with the legacy of slavery, the Confederacy, and Jim Crow, generally found itself on the wrong side of history again in the 1960s. Governors George Wallace of Alabama, Lester Maddox of Georgia, and Orville Faubus of Arkansas were all Democrats from Dixie. Renowned segregationists like Senators Richard Russell and Herman Talmadge of Georgia, Russel Long of Louisiana, and Congressman Howard Smith from Virginia were Democrats. It is the same elitist southern political forces, and their continuing anti-federal-government ideology, that undid the First Reconstruction that now want to undo the nation's second effort at reconstruction. The difference is that over the last four decades the original Black Republican Party of Abraham Lincoln has transformed itself into the old White Democratic Party of Thomas Jefferson and Andrew Jackson. Today's Senators Strom Thurmond of South Carolina and Richard Shelby of Alabama, who were originally Dixiecrats, are today strong defense, anti-tax, fiscally conservative, reduce-the-deficit-and-debt, and "era-of-big-government-is-over" Republicans. Conservatives John Breaux of Louisiana, Ernest Hollings of South Carolina, and Zell Miller of Georgia are their closest parallel today still sitting on the Democratic side.

The Second Reconstruction, begun with *Brown*, attempted to desegregate all aspects of American life, from public facilities to private corporate behavior, and took the form of a 1964 Civil Rights Act, a 1965 Voting Rights Act, affirmative action, equal opportunity minority political districts, elementary and secondary education acts, Medicare, Medicaid, and more. Until 1992, most African American members of Congress came from somewhere other than the South, even though a majority of all African Americans live in the South. But black votes didn't count equally with white votes in southern states—and still don't. Given our electoral college system, even though most blacks live in the South and voted more than 90 percent for Gore in 2000, not a single black vote went to Gore because Bush won every one of those southern states' electors.

Also, lines were drawn in a particular way to protect white economic and political interests, which both white Democrats and Republicans had in common. The federal government, in the form of a 1965 VRA, imposed on white southerners—mainly Democrats, but also some Republicans—a new legal structure for African American inclusion at every level among elected officials. The Supreme Court insisted that political lines be drawn in such a way that African Americans and others have an equal opportunity of being elected. Because current Democrats have failed to come to grips with racism and economic justice for all, in 1991 Democrats were vulnerable to African Americans cutting a deal with Republicans to increase black representation in the South. African Americans chose self-determined self-representation over conservative southern Democratic representation, whether Yellow Dogs, Blue Dogs, Dixiecrats, or DLC New Democrats. Thus, after the 1991 redistricting and the 1992 election, the CBC went from twenty-seven members with five southern representatives in the 102nd Congress (1991–1993) to thirty-nine representatives with seventeen southern members in the 103rd Congress (1993–1995).

The target of today's conservative southern-based Republicans is the liberalism of Johnson's Great Society, ultimately encompassing many of the economic programs of Roosevelt's New Deal, including Social Security. Republican presidential candidate Steve Forbes advocated an end to Social Security in favor of privatized pensions. Candidate George W. Bush, when asked about privatizing Social Security, answered: "Maybe so, maybe not." Thus the real underlying dynamic and goal of the impeachment and trial proceedings was not the immediate removal of Bill Clinton, but continuing to put in place the politics that would lead to the gradual removal of the social and economic programs of the New Deal and the Second Reconstruction programs of the Great Society, a weakening of the big federal government generally, and the destruction of liberalism as a viable political ideology in particular.

Clinton's private behavior and poor judgment played perfectly into Dixie's religious fundamentalism, individualistic, and moralistic social politics. President Clinton's comportment contributed mightily to conservatives' ability to nationalize southern politics by electing Texan George W. Bush as president in 2000, retaining Republican and southern control of the House and Senate, as well as Republican control of state legislatures and governorships—and thus redistricting in 2001 and potential Supreme Court appointments over the next four years. It will be interesting to see if Senator James Jeffords's resignation from the Republican Party, turning control of the Senate over to the Democrats, makes any significant substantive difference. Progressives must clearly understand that conservatives' real goal now, as it always has been, is to undermine a century and a quarter of social, economic, and political progress. Racial politics were central to that progress, and will also be front and center in attempts at regress. Progressives must not underestimate or miscalculate this either. Politically, President Clinton risked all of that history of progress by lying about an issue of personal pleasure. He did not commit treason as defined by the Constitution as an impeachable offense. His real "treason" was against the underlying politics that sustained the New Deal, the Great Society, and the cause of building a more perfect Union.

There were a few pro-impeachment southern Democrats (such as my good friend Charlie Stenholm of Texas) thrown in for good measure, because they must factor in the Old Democratic political forces in the South, now dominated by Republicans. Over one hundred years ago, the diversion was the threat of interracial sex. In 2000 it appears the Republicans misled the American people again with a new sex diversion, Clinton and Monica Lewinsky. What America needs is a strong political leader who is able to focus Americans' attention on their real economic interests of full employment, comprehensive and universal health care, affordable housing, and a quality public education. Whether these conservative anti-federal-government Republicans are ultimately successful in turning back the clock or not will be determined by future elections and history.

Today the political epicenter, ideological base, and geographical roots of this anti-reconstruction and anti-more-perfect-Union effort are in the South, though its tentacles have spread beyond the South. With ten of the eighteen Republicans on the House Judiciary Committee from southern congressional districts, the Republican impeachment effort allowed us to look at the roots and current political dynamic of this post–Civil War conservative political movement. One hundred and thirty-five years after the "Great Quake," the impeachment of President Clinton was merely another aftershock in the ongoing struggle to reconstruct America.

To capture a new political base, Republicans abandoned the essence of Lincoln in deciding to go after Dixie, using moral and social issues as cover for their narrow conservative economic and political agenda. Mr. Conservative, Barry Goldwater, launched this modern anti-federal-government movement with his 1964 states' rights presidential campaign—at the height of the civil rights movement. Nixon's and Wallace's "law and order" and "antibusing" campaigns in 1968 and 1972 continued this racial thrust as cities burned and desegregation spread northward. Ronald Reagan picked up the theme, at the behest of then Representative Trent Lott, and sent the same race signal by launching his southern campaign from Philadelphia, Mississippi, in 1980, where two Jews and a black fighting for black voting rights were murdered in the name of states' rights. Willie Horton was front and center in the first Bush's campaign. George W. Bush's appearance at Bob Jones University and his "let South Carolina decide" what to do with the Confederate flag added up to the same race signal. The goal of Republicans following the 2000 election is to complete Mr. Gingrich's 1994 "Revolution of Devolution" by defeating and eliminating their twin forces of evil—liberalism and big government. The 2002 federal budget was the supreme expression of these conservative politics.

I suspect that Republicans knew ahead of time—based on the information they had gathered—that if the president was impeached in the House, he would not be convicted in the Senate. They didn't want him convicted and out of office, with President Al Gore given two years to solidify his hold on the White House. They wanted an impeached—but not convicted—immoral president twisting in the wind for two years leading up to the 2000 election. This was a continuation of Tom DeLay's and the Republican hardliners' November 3, 1998, strategy of motivating and building their conservative "family and social values" political base as a diversion from economic justice issues. The Republicans would not permit censure, because that would have allowed Democrats to say that they had taken some action against the president for his shameful actions, which would have taken away their "social, moral, family values" 1998 congressional and 2000 presidential campaign issue, tactic, and strategy. And the Republicans' strategy worked! The election of Bush, along with Republican retention of the House, state legislatures, and governorships in a redistricting year, could set the country back dramatically.

What the Republicans wanted out of the impeachment crisis was a "moral and family values" issue for the 2000 presidential campaign—to use Bush's rhetoric, in order "to restore dignity to the Oval Office." They are trying to say subliminally that Clinton's sexual misconduct was the inevitable result of the "decadent values" of the 1960s—and, subliminally, economic liberalism and the "welfare state" generally. In other words, the Lewinsky matter became a Republican "wedge issue" in the 1998 and 2000 campaigns. The fact that African Americans were so closely identified with both President Clinton and liberal "Big Government" programs fit perfectly with their consistent use of race to divide the electorate in presidential campaigns. Except in 1998 and 2000, Republicans could use race in the campaign without having to use "race" or its more obvious code words. Republicans didn't want to be accused of using race in the 2000 campaign; after all, former All-American football player Representative J. C. Watts of Oklahoma was one of their leaders and chief spokespeople.

Even though Bush's instincts wouldn't allow him to resist using Bob Jones and the Confederate flag in the heat of a battle with John McCain during the South Carolina primary campaign, thanks to the Lewinsky matter Bush didn't feel obligated to so openly "race-bait" during the general election. In fact, Bush could campaign as a "uniter not a divider." In light of the Lewinsky matter, Republicans could now more naturally send the subliminal race signal during the campaign with less fear that it would be detected or interpreted as such. Indeed, they could have a virtually all-black show on the opening night of their convention in Philadelphia and go on the offensive to show socially liberal—but economically conservative—white southern "Reagan Democrats" and suburban independents (their real political targets) that they were not intolerant or racists. They now could say, with a straight face, that they were only for restoring honor and dignity to the Oval Office, and programmatically they were simply for a strong defense and believed in a conservative political philosophy that called for lower taxes, smaller government, and being fiscally responsible. Who could be against that, call it racist, or be offended? And it projected Bush as a moderate, rather than as the extreme conservative he actually is.

The Republican goal in 2000 was to use this strategy to retain control of the House and Senate and to gain control of the White House—and it worked. Now they can interpret census data and redraw district boundaries to their advantage, and potentially can appoint hard-core right-wing conservatives to the Supreme Court and lower courts, all of which will affect the country for at least a decade or more. It's important to remember that Kenneth Starr's ambition, before being sullied by the Lewinsky affair, was to be appointed to the Supreme Court. That's why the defection and departure of Senator James Jeffords of Vermont from the Republican Party is potentially a huge monkey wrench in the plans of the hardcore conservative Republicans.

Republican and Democratic conservatives, with Dixie as their geopolitical and theological center, in control of the federal government, state legislatures, governorships, 2000 census data, redistricting, and Supreme Court appointments, can potentially turn back the clock to a twenty-first-century version of the states' rights days of the 1850s and the 1896 "separate but equal" days of *Plessy v. Ferguson*. It will not be a return to slavery or Jim Crow de jure segregation, but a return to the days when equal opportunity for all in jobs, admissions, and voting is *interpreted* by courts, legislators, and the executive branch in a way that is essentially unequal and restricts the economic and political growth of people of color and women.

If you think this is a preposterous statement, an African American Supreme Court justice is laying the legal and ideological basis for a return to *Plessy*. In *Jenkins*—a Kansas City, Missouri, school desegregation case—Justice Clarence Thomas wrote in 1995: "It never ceases to amaze me that the courts are so willing to assume that anything that is predominantly black must be inferior. [The theory that] segregation injures blacks because blacks, when left on their own, cannot achieve [is the result of] a jurisprudence based upon a theory of black inferiority. . . . The point of the Equal Protection Clause is not to enforce strict race mixing, but to insure that blacks and whites are treated equally by the state without regard to their skin color." In my view, that is a gross misunderstanding of the Fourteenth Amendment—it is most assuredly a conservative and strict constructionist interpretation—and a return to the underlying logic and rationale of *Plessy* and a legal case for "separate but unequal." It is unbelievable that such an historically blind and, therefore, illogical argument could be written by anyone, much less a black man, on the eve of the twenty-first century!

But after economically and socially conservative Presidents Nixon, Ford, Carter (an economic conservative, but more liberal socially), Reagan, and Bush had allowed the economy to deteriorate for nearly three decades, a moderate-to-conservative southern Democrat, President Clinton, finally helped to prepare an economic bridge that would allow us to again begin to work on the unfinished tasks of the Civil War. President Clinton grew teary-eyed toward the end of his speech at the Democratic Convention when he said, "I have waited, not as president, but as your fellow citizen for over thirty years to see my country once again in the position to build a future of our dreams for our children." Also recognizing this new economic opportunity of growth and surpluses, Bush, during his acceptance speech in Philadelphia, referred to it as an opportunity to have a "presidency with a purpose" and to "use these good times for great goals."

The underlying racial component in our politics is what the Clinton and Gore campaigns sometimes tried to address in the 1990s and 2000 campaigns. However, in these elections the political pundits most often focused on the gender gap between the parties, and Democrats' huge advantage with women voters in 1992 and 1996. The racial gap between the two parties was not given the same high-profile interpretation. The reality, however, is that since the 1960s civil rights days, white males have been leaving the Democratic Party for the Republican Party in droves over resentment of government programs they perceive as only benefiting minorities and, to a lesser extent, women—even though the facts show that women have been the prime beneficiaries. Democratic DLC and Blue Dog spinning of conservative social issues (such as school uniforms) will not bring them back. The only way to bring southern working-class white males back into the Democratic Party is to fight for universal and equal economic programs—like my human rights amendments. Only ideas and programs that will actually change the objective economic conditions of common people will bring the estranged and the disillusioned back to the Democratic Party.

Republicans' conservative and narrow economic proposals will not positively meet the broad objective economic needs of the vast majority of white males, especially southern working-class white males. And politically, they have always been exploited by the economic elite, first by Democrats and now by Republicans. The end result of the inevitable failure of conservative Democratic social spin and Republican wealth-oriented economic programs will either be an external revolutionary force poised for a violent political explosion (most likely aimed at African Americans), or a repressed counterrevolutionary implosion that orients people toward dropping out of politics. We know, however, that repression always manifests itself in unhealthy ways. Thus, neither external revolution nor internal repression is good for the country. Neither consequence will contribute to building a more perfect Union.

Ignoring liberals and progressives, and practicing ever-more-conservative politics, produces ever-smaller turnouts among eligible voters, automatically shifting politics to the right. As a result—and without the will, ability, or vision to come to grips with overcoming the history and legacy of African Americans in this country by using universal economic issues such as full employment, health care, education, housing, the environment, and taxes to combat it—President Clinton and Vice President Gore spent most of their time cultivating the conservative wing of the Democratic Party. They "ended welfare as we know it," "fought crime," declared "the era of big government over," cut "balance the budget" deals, set "eliminating the debt" goals, and "reinvented government" to curry favor with southern and conservative Democrats and independents.

Even after snubbing the liberal base of the Democratic Party for most of his administration, when impeachment hit, only the party's liberal and progressive base, especially African Americans, sustained Clinton in office. Those southerners and conservatives Clinton had cultivated and spent virtually all of his political capital with were the first to abandon him. In 2000, even after a primary and general election strategy of ignoring the party's base and cultivating conservative southern and suburban Democrats and independents, following the DNC Los Angeles convention southern Democrats were still not satisfied with Gore-Lieberman.

Democratic Senator John Breaux of Louisiana, still pouting over Clinton's rejection of his Medicare Commission's conservative privatization recommendations, complained during the campaign that Bush was closer to him on his Medicare position than Gore. Many southern senators and governors refused to campaign or appear with national Democrats. "The Democratic candidate for governor of North Carolina, state Attorney General Mike Easley, chose not to appear with Gore during a June visit to meet with flood victims. . . . When Gore and his running mate, Sen. Joseph Lieberman of Connecticut, held a rally in downtown Atlanta on Aug. 10, there was no sign of Georgia's newest statewide Democratic candidate, Sen. Zell Miller, the state's former governor. Miller was . . . appointed to replace the late Paul Coverdell, and [had] only a few weeks to campaign to keep the job in a special election in November. . . . Jim Hodges, the Democratic governor of South Carolina, left the convention rather conspicuously on Tuesday, before the acceptance speeches of Gore and Lieberman. . . . All three seem painfully aware that voters in the region continue to distinguish between national Democrats and Southern Democrats."[3]

Citing progress toward religious tolerance in the South, Jay Kaiman, Atlanta's Southeast regional director of the Anti-Defamation League of B'nai B'rith, said Lieberman's "biggest problem here won't be that he's Jewish. It's that he's a Northerner."[4] Yet southerner Gore and northerner Lieberman, two conservative candidates with a conservative platform and convention, could only be elected with a reasonably good turnout by their base constituencies whose issues they largely ignored and who would have benefited the least under a Gore-Lieberman administration.

For those Democratic leaders who are uncertain or nervous regarding the racial justice question, the Republicans will always have a law and order, antibusing, welfare queen, Willie Horton, liberal, or quota attack campaign—or a blackface minstrel show, as in Philadelphia. What the Republicans are not prepared to handle is a Democratic leader who will take on the economic justice questions as the foundation for tackling head-on the racial justice and gender equality issues.

If there is a Democratic Party economic common-ground progressive agenda, what are the *politics* that will allow the country to elect such a Democratic candidate? That is where a progressive African American on the Democratic ticket comes into play.

I agree that general elections are won in the center, but putting a progressive African American on the ticket automatically shifts the center significantly to the left by increasing voter registration, participation, and turnout. By insisting that an African American on the ticket be politically progressive and identified with progressive economic issues, not just progressive African American issues, many of the large majority of disenfranchised voters and potential voters—Naderites, average white workers, even some Buchananites who are fed up with the status quo and will vote for change, and the more than 50 percent who are not currently registered and voting in presidential elections—would be galvanized into registering and voting for Democrats in record numbers.

If economic common ground is the agenda that pulls all of the patches and pieces of the Democratic quilt together, then putting a progressive African American on the Democratic ticket as the vice presidential candidate is the politics. Such a move will energize the largest, most loyal, and most strategically located base in the Democratic Party. It is also the most expeditious way of putting an end to the southern-based conservative legacy of slavery, racism, "states' rights," and constructing the political supermajority in Congress that it will take to build a more perfect Union.

The Democratic Party's legacy of slavery and states' rights still affects the party's and the nation's politics. These politics must be changed if we are ever going to be able to build a more perfect Union. The key to changing the politics is the African American vote. Putting a progressive black on the ticket is the key to mobilizing this vote in a national election. Putting a black on the ticket is also the key to winning back Democratic control of both the House and the Senate by galvanizing the margin of victory in many congressional districts and states.

Throughout the entire 1992 Democratic presidential primary campaign, former California Governor Edmund G. "Jerry" Brown, Jr., had said that if he was the Democratic nominee, Jesse Jackson would be his choice for running mate. Whatever his motivation— sincere commitment or calculated political cultivation of the African American and progressive voting constituencies—having a progressive African American on the Democratic ticket was a sound idea.*

A progressive African American, more than any other Democrat, including a liberal Democrat, would bring massive numbers of voters into the Democratic column in strategic electoral states and help the party's nominee win an electoral college victory in a general election.

The ethnic, religious, or racial characteristic of any candidate helps mobilize others who identify with that feature. Thus, Kennedy's nomination in 1960 mobilized Catholics. Carter and Clinton had a greater appeal to southerners. Dukakis energized Greeks. Lieberman's nomination was a major breakthrough and helped marshal the Jewish community. A black on the ticket would do the same for African Americans. The difference, however, is that the black vote is the largest, most loyal, and most strategically located voting bloc within the Democratic Party. It has the most unregistered voters, so additionally Democrats would also gain the most. After the 2000 census, it now appears that blacks are basically tied with Hispanics in terms of sheer numbers. While I'm not opposed to a Latino or a woman on the ticket, a progressive Hispanic or a woman would not have the same political effect on the most needy area of the country, the former Confederate States of the South. Also, Hispanics don't vote as a bloc to the same degree as blacks for the Democratic Party.

Gore chose Lieberman to be on his ticket in 2000. I supported that courageous choice. Knocking down Jewish political barriers opens more doors for everyone. But the number of Jewish voters in the country is very small when compared to the African American vote (four million Jewish voters to twenty-four million black voters). And a very high percent-

---

*In the arguments ahead, while there will be many references to the Jesse Jackson presidential campaigns of 1984 and 1988, references to him or his campaigns are not designed to argue for him being on a Democratic ticket. I refer to his campaigns simply because his were the only serious national presidential campaigns that an African American has run. The general underlying factual and rational political arguments I will make should stand or fall on their own merit, apart from any particular political personalities.

age of Jews are already registered and voting. However, only about 14 million of the potential 24 million eligible black voters are registered and only about 10.5 million actually voted in 2000, with black women representing 60 percent and black men 40 percent. This means there is still a tremendous 50-percent-plus growth potential for voter registration and participation in the black community. Approximately one-third of the vote in New York City is Jewish (mostly registered and voting) and one-third is black, with nine hundred thousand blacks unregistered. While Gore easily won New York, a progressive black on the ticket would have helped him even more than Lieberman. Perhaps as important, it would have benefited Hillary Rodham Clinton even more than Gore.

A progressive African American on the ticket would also help the Democratic Party gain and retain control of Congress. Looking back to 2000, beyond New York, a progressive black, more than a conservative Lieberman, would have helped Democrats in senatorial, congressional, gubernatorial, state legislative, and other local races throughout the country, but especially in the South. That is only natural, with more than half of black voters residing in the South. For example, I believe Chuck Robb, who was running for reelection to the Senate from Virginia, would have fared better with a progressive black on the ticket than the conservative Lieberman. And even though Zell Miller won a senate seat from Georgia, I believe he too would have performed even better with a progressive black on the ticket. The same would have been true throughout the South, but also in other important electoral states like Pennsylvania, Ohio, and Indiana.

I advocate for a *progressive* African American candidate because Democrats should not deceive or confuse themselves. African American leaders are not fungible. Black voters know which black politicians represent their real economic interests and which do not. Governor Doug Wilder of Virginia, and the conservative DLC white Democrats who were prepared to fund and pull for him, found that out in a hurry in 1992 after Jesse Jackson's two historic campaigns in 1984 and 1988. Wilder did not even make it out of the starting blocks. He attracted neither black nor white voters in 1992, while Jackson attracted 4.5 million black votes and 2.5 million white votes in 1988—more white votes than any black man has received in the history of the world.

That was because Jackson's "economic common ground" and "keep hope alive" message had universal appeal. He was a winner and a motivator because he had something deeper than name recognition, he had service recognition. He carried in his body and soul the scars of an authentic suffering servant who has spent all of his adult life struggling for social and economic justice.

While the Democratic nominee in 2000 considered a great many fine men and women, and each would have brought certain positive attributes to the ticket, I suggest that no other Democrat would have brought as many votes into the Democratic column in both the presidential and congressional campaigns as a qualified progressive African American vice presidential candidate.

Bill Clinton designed a 1992 Democratic primary campaign to appeal to the Reagan Democrats, independents, suburbanites, and disillusioned and economically pinched Republicans in the general election. Perot came along and took many of those voters and some of that strategy away. Thus, politically, Clinton had to return to his dependable Democratic base—labor, women, and people of color. It was no accident that the moment he wrapped up the nomination on June 2—yet was playing third fiddle to Ross Perot and George Bush on the basis of polling—the first stop he made on June 3 was to appear on the *Arsenio Hall Show* in an appeal to black voters. It was not just to circumvent the major news media, it was also to appeal to a certain important political constituency that he needed to offset the Perot factor.

In a strange political paradox that is often the case in politics, by putting an African American on the ticket, Democrats would automatically increase and solidify the core constituencies at the base of the Democratic Party. And with a morally centered, traditional Democratic family values economic message—a message designed to meet all Americans' real economic needs—Democrats should feel comfortable taking that message to white suburban voters as well. In other words, the top of the ticket could remain consistent with its basic Democratic message and politically have the best of both worlds.

In 1992, for the first time in American history, suburbanites made up a plurality of the voters in the presidential election. Clinton won the White House in 1992 using a suburban voter strategy, but since then Democrats have lost almost everything else. In order for Democrats to be sure of winning back the White House and regaining control of the Senate, the House, governorships, and state legislatures—for redistricting purposes every ten years— they need someone on their ticket who will massively increase voter registration and turnout in the general election. Only a progressive African American will do that to the maximum degree possible. With a progressive African American at the top of the ticket, blacks will turn out in record numbers for the presidential election, but also increase the vote for all other Democratic candidates running for lesser offices. And that doesn't include reinvigorating the progressive wing of the Democratic Party that went for Nader in 2000.

Many will argue that there will be a backlash if a progressive African American is put on the ticket. They are correct. There will be a backlash in some quarters. But more important, for Democrats, there will be an even larger forward bounce—if the candidates keep the focus on universal and equal economic justice issues and programs for all Americans.

In Chicago we even know the objective increase in registration and turnout of the forward bounce. There was a voter backlash when Harold Washington ran for mayor of Chicago in 1983. It was a major recoil led by local Democratic Party leaders. But the jolt forward added 275,000 registered voters to the rolls in five months, and Washington won. The original Mayor Richard J. Daley, "King Richard," never got more than 600,000 votes in an election in his two decades in office—with 3.3 million people in Chicago. Harold Washington won his first primary election with 600,000 votes and the general election with 668,000 votes, even though Chicago had dropped to just 3 million in population.

Similar increases in registration and turnout took place in Philadelphia (Wilson Goode, 1983), in New York (David Dinkins, 1989), in Memphis (Willie Herenton, 1991), and virtually everywhere that African American, Hispanic, and progressive enlightened political self-interest were involved.

During his two presidential campaigns, Jackson always did better in the actual vote than he did in pre-election polls or pundit predictions because of the number of new voters he brought into the process. Never did he do worse! What is little known is that Jackson ran strong in every part of the country in 1988, finishing first or second in forty-six of fifty-four contests. He won thirteen and finished second in thirty-three races. To use an Olympic analogy, that was more gold and silver medals than the nominee Michael Dukakis won. Jackson's seven-plus-million votes and 1,218.5 delegates were the most that any second-place finisher in either party had ever received in the history of the country.

The black vote is also strategically located in key electoral states, but it is especially heavy in the South. With a progressive African American on the ticket, voter registration would increase dramatically in strategic states and regions of the country, and voter turnout would probably set a record. That bodes well for Democrats.

For Democrats, the biggest source of potential sure support can be found among the reluctant voters and the nonvoters who live in America's cities. In recent presidential elections they have voted with their feet—staying home on election day more than any other group. According to the Census Bureau, cities accounted for 55.3 million eligible voters in 1992, with a similar pattern in 1996 and 2000. But less than two-thirds (63.2 percent) were registered to vote, which is why Clinton, Gore, and Lieberman concentrated on suburban and Reagan Democratic voters—because they are registered and they vote! Among those in the city who are registered, 86 percent voted. However, in 1988 only about half (54.4 percent) of the eligible urban voters went to the polls.

When city residents register and vote, their loyalties are to the Democrats. In the fifty largest cities, with more than thirty million eligible voters, residents who went to the polls cast their ballots for the Democrats by dramatic margins: 73.5 percent in Baltimore, 66.6 percent in Philadelphia, 68.6 percent in San Francisco, 69.2 percent in Chicago, 85.6 percent in Detroit, 82.6 percent in Washington, D.C., 66.3 percent in Boston, and 79.7 percent in New York City.

For a Democratic victory, it is not only how city residents vote, but how *many* vote— particularly in key electoral college states. Why have urban residents stayed away? Because the Democrats have not spoken to their concerns—and the national party organization has made little effort and committed few resources to reaching them. They have not left the Democratic Party; the Democratic Party has left them in the lurch.

The first rule of politics is to consolidate your base. Few people realize that Dukakis won back the Reagan Democrats 52 to 48 percent in 1988—they liked Reagan's racial appeal, but couldn't afford his economics. Dukakis won the urban areas, too, but not by as much as Mondale won them in 1984. If he had won as many votes in urban areas in 1988 as Mondale won in 1984, he would have been elected president. The Dukakis campaign had a deliberate strategy to avoid minorities (and especially Jesse Jackson), and it cost Democrats the election. Jackson campaigned hard for the ticket in 1988. Campaigning hard, off the ticket, however, is obviously not enough for Democrats to win.

The year Clinton won, 1992, was the first anniversary of the class of 1986 that won back Democratic control of the Senate as a result of the 2.5 million new Democrats Jackson's candidacy put on the rolls through his 1984 campaign, many in the South. Democrats winning back the Senate in 1986, among other things, meant they were able to defeat the nomination of Robert Bork to the Supreme Court in 1987. Democrats owe many victories to Jesse Jackson, but they have never been able to acknowledge them.

With a progressive African American on the ticket, there would be record high registration and turnout, which helps Democrats. Without an African American on the ticket, and a weak economic message, there was a relatively low turnout in 2000, even though in Florida the black vote increased significantly. We know low black turnout hurts Democrats, as the votes of 1994, 1996, and 1998 show. In 1998 African American turnout, while low, was higher than white turnout and helped Democrats make a small gain during the Lewinsky impeachment proceedings in the House.

Turnout in the 1992 Democratic primaries should have been an omen of grave concern to the Democratic Party. In some southern states more Republicans voted than Democrats, which was unprecedented. In New York only 25 percent of registered Democrats bothered to vote at all. Of particular concern should have been the low African American turnout. During the primaries, Governor Clinton received from 51 to 86 percent of the African American vote—but it was a solid majority of a very low overall turnout.

Clinton won Georgia with 57 percent in 1992 and Jackson won Georgia with only 40 percent in 1988. But Jackson got 248,000 votes in 1988 while Clinton received 258,000 votes in 1992—a mere 10,000-vote difference. In Connecticut Jerry Brown won the state with 63,600 votes in 1992 while Jackson finished a distant second—28 percent to Dukakis's 58 percent in 1988. However, Jackson won more votes finishing second (68,300) than Brown did finishing first. The 1988 and 1992 New York results are similar. Bill Clinton won the state with 398,000 votes while Jackson finished a respectable second (37 percent) in 1988 with (only) 585,000 votes. Again, Jackson got 187,000 more votes than the 1992 winner.

According to independent political analyst and strategist Steve Cobble, 4.5 million voters disappeared between the 1988 and 1992 presidential primaries. The overall voter turnout rate declined in twenty-five of the thirty-one states where primaries were held in both election years. The total number of people casting primary ballots in those states was down by 13.3 percent in just four years. During the entire four-month primary season, there were 28.8 million ballots cast in thirty-one states for candidates running in both parties—down from 33.3 million in 1988. The primaries saw much more severe declines among Democratic voters than Republican, even though it became clear to Republicans much earlier who their nominee was going to be.

There were 17.5 million Democratic ballots cast in thirty states in 1992, nearly a 20 percent decline from the 21.8 million cast in 1988. Long before Texas billionaire H. Ross Perot became a potential independent candidate, voting in Texas's March 10 primary was off more than 25 percent. Democratic participation declined in Texas by 525,000 votes.[5]

The downturn in participation by Democrats in 1992 should not be seen as unrelated to the fact that Jackson was a candidate in 1988 and not a candidate in 1992. Both the potential of a progressive African American on the ticket for the presidential and the congressional races and the antithesis for the party if an African American is not on the ticket are contained in the above numbers.

Baltimore Sun syndicated columnist and television analyst Jack Germond acknowledged this specific point on a *McLaughlin Group* show in 1992 with regard to Carol Moseley Braun's candidacy in Illinois. He observed that Illinois is more likely to go Democratic in the presidential race now because of the increase in voter registration and turnout her candidacy would bring. In fact, that is exactly what did happen: She carried Clinton to victory in the state—Clinton did not carry her. However, Mr. Germond stopped short of projecting that keen observation more generally—of saying that a similar thing would happen to the top of the ticket, as well as in congressional races around the country, if a progressive African American was on the national Democratic ticket.

If Democrats think they can win without an African American on the ticket, then they can win even bigger with an African American on it. The difference is that, without mass support, even if Democrats win the presidential election they may not regain control of the Senate and House. Or Democrats may win the presidency but have no mandate to govern or to build a more perfect Union. Democrats can govern successfully only with a popular mandate to take the country in a new direction, or in the same direction faster, which is the only way the country can make progress in actually correcting the serious economic problems and trends that face the nation.

My personal choice for Gore's vice president in 2000 was Mel Watt (D-NC). He is from the South and progressive. He was elected in a majority-white congressional district, so I know he could have attracted white southern voters. He is a constitutional expert who serves on the House Judiciary Committee. In pure political terms, if Mel Watt, instead of Joseph Lieberman, had been put on Gore's ticket, it would have totally wiped out any gains made at the Republican National Convention and destroyed the Republicans' electoral strategy. Watt's candidacy also would have annihilated Ralph Nader's Green Party candidacy and energized the base of the Democratic Party. And Gore would not necessarily have had to change his mostly conservative message. Gore's problem would have been that he would have had to change his conservative policies and programs after the election to meet the needs of those who voted for him. But the resulting Democratic-controlled House and Senate would more than likely have pushed him to do that anyway. Democrats would likely have regained some governorships and state legislatures as well, which would have affected redistricting in 2001.

Stability and predictability are a campaign manager's dream. Putting a progressive African American on the ticket is a Republican campaign manager's nightmare. The conventional calculation in 2000 was that somewhere around one hundred million people would vote in 2000 and, given the present cynicism and disinterest of many voters, possibly less. A certain number of voters on each side would vote Republican and Democratic if one party had run Mickey Mouse and the other Donald Duck for president. The winning strategy is to design a message and campaign that win the biggest share of the middle.

As a result of increased interest, voter registration, and expected higher turnout, an African American on the ticket in the general election automatically shifts the political center leftward and forces the Republicans to retool their campaign strategy and message. Now the Republican conventional political wisdom, based on traditional expectations of overall turnout and strategic electoral college calculations, no longer applies. If they engage in race-baiting or pursue their conservative social agenda, moderate, independent, and young Republicans may abandon the party. If they merely liberalize their message to capture a broader share of the middle, they run the risk of alienating their socially conservative core vote on issues such as abortion or civil rights. The Pat Buchanan and Reverend Pat Robinson Republican voters become estranged.

An African American on the ticket enhances the chances of winning for a good candidate with sound economic ideas and solid economic issues. It also converts a conventional campaign into an enthusiastic crusade. Even with his bad economic ideas, this is how Ronald Reagan upset an incumbent Democrat in 1980. He ran a crusade, with a simple and clear economic message—and an underlying southern racist theme thrown in for good measure—and projected optimism and conviction about his vision for the country. The Democrats should do no less, minus the racism. Such a ticket is just what the Democrats need—a spark that would create the energy at the grassroots that would lead to a bottom-up campaign.

The structure of the electoral process—especially with regard to the South—strengthens the argument for a strategic vice presidential nomination of a progressive African American. The electoral college, not the popular vote, elects the president and vice president. As Frank Clemente and Frank Watkins point out in their book on the 1988 Jackson campaign, *Keep Hope Alive*, Dukakis won a total of 112 electoral votes from ten states and the District of Columbia. He lost twelve other states by small enough margins that a Jackson vice presidency would likely have made the difference for victory.

In raw numbers, those twelve states translated into 1,232,018 additional Democratic votes needed for victory; only 616,010 voters needed to be motivated to switch from the Bush to the Dukakis column for Dukakis to have won—a switch of a mere ten votes in each of the 64,780 precincts in those twelve states. Winning those twelve swing states would have added 168 Dukakis electoral votes, for a total of 280 electoral votes—eight more than he needed to win. The 1988 election was much closer than it has been portrayed.

Table 3

State	Electoral Votes	% of Votes Bush/ Dukakis	Margin of Dukakis Loss	Votes Needed to Switch	# of Pcts	Voters per Pct
IL	24	51/49	94,999	47,499	11,696	4
PA	25	51/48	105,143	52,572	9,459	6
MD	10	51/48	49,863	24,931	1,570	16
VT	3	51/48	8,556	4,278	300	15
CA	47	52/48	352,684	176,342	23,627	8
MO	11	52/48	83,534	41,767	4,695	9
NM	5	52/47	25,844	12,922	1,175	11
CT	8	52/48	73,657	36,829	743	50
MN	4	52/46	21,456	10,728	965	12
SD	3	53/47	19,456	9,928	1,153	9
CO	8	53/45	106,855	53,362	2,752	20
MI	20	54/46	289,703	144,852	6,645	22
Subtotal	168	1,232,018	616,010	64,780	10	
Dukakis	112					
TOTAL	**280**					

SOURCE: ABC NEWS ELECTION SYSTEMS[6]

There were at least twelve other states (six of which are the same as the states above) in which the number of unregistered and nonvoting African Americans alone exceeded the number of votes by which Dukakis lost. With nearly nine out of ten African American voters supporting Dukakis, if these states could have been added to the 112 electoral votes that Dukakis won, he would have had 308 electoral votes and victory, with a mandate to govern in a progressive direction.

Table 4

State	Electoral Votes	# of AA in VAP*	# of AA Who Voted in 1998	Bush's Margin of Victory in 1998	# of AA Who Didn't Vote in 1998
CA	47	1,576,000	736,391	347,373	839,609
IL	24	1,213,000	671,896	94,657	541,104
GA	12	1,138,000	343,836	366,539	794,162
NC	13	993,000	424,433	232,458	568,567

MI	20	896,000	473,581	289,703	422,419
LA	10	873,000	341,922	166,242	531,078
MD	10	833,000	244,221	40,263	588,779
PA	25	783,000	402,770	105,143	380,230
AL	9	697,000	275,695	266,070	421,305
SC	8	693,000	197,201	235,889	495,799
MS	7	587,000	209,907	193,969	377,096
MO	11	370,000	188,391	83,534	181,609
TOTAL	**198**				

*Voting-age population.

SOURCE: ABC NEWS ELECTION SYSTEMS; JOINT CENTER FOR POLITICAL STUDIES. NUMBER OF AFRICAN AMERICANS WHO VOTED IN THE 1988 ELECTIONS IS A ROUGH ESTIMATE BASED ON EXIT POLL DATA.[7]

Republicans and the political pundits in the media argue that census changes—the demographic shift to the South, Southwest, and West and the loss of congressional districts in northeastern and midwestern industrial states—have benefited Republicans. To some degree, they are right. But mere demographic population changes are no more important than the economics in regions. Gore-Lieberman had trouble in the Midwest Great Lakes and the lower Southeast regions of the country because in those regions the issue was still "the economy, stupid."

As table 5 shows, in the categories of per capita income, disposable personal income, and per capita disposable personal income, the Southeast and Great Lakes regions clearly ranked next to last or last, respectively. These regions needed a strong economic message from the Democratic team, but that message was not consistently delivered.

Table 5

Regions	Per Capita Income		Disposable Personal Income		Per Capita Disposable Personal Income	
New England	+.1996%	(1)	+.1868%	(4)	+.1737%	(2)
Mid-Atlantic	+.1792%	(5)	+.1597%	(7)	+.1536%	(5)
Great Lakes	+.1626%	(8)	+.1595%	(8)	+.1438%	(8)
Plains	+.1804%	(4)	+.1849%	(5)	+.1655%	(3)
Southeast	+.1637%	(7)	+.1843%	(6)	+.1448%	(7)
Southwest	+.1823%	(3)	+.2191%	(2)	+.1636%	(4)
Rocky Mountain	+.1984%	(2)	+.2335%	(1)	+.1800%	(1)
Far West	+.1774%	(6)	+.1947%	(3)	+.1491%	(6)

Regions	Per Capita Income		Disposable Personal Income		Per Capita Disposable Personal Income	
New England	**+.1996%**	**(1)**	+.1868%	(4)	+.1737%	(2)
Rocky Mountain	**+.1984%**	**(2)**	+.2335%	(1)	+.1800%	(1)
Southwest	**+.1823%**	**(3)**	+.2191%	(2)	+.1636%	(4)
Plains	**+.1804%**	**(4)**	+.1849%	(5)	+.1655%	(3)

Mid-Atlantic	**+.1792%**	**(5)**	+.1597%	(7)	+.1536%	(5)
Far West	**+.1774%**	**(6)**	+.1947%	(3)	+.1491%	(6)
Southeast	**+.1637%**	**(7)**	+.1843%	(6)	+.1448%	(7)
Great Lakes	**+.1626%**	**(8)**	+.1595%	(8)	+.1438%	(8)

Regions	Per Capita Income		Disposable Personal Income		Per Capita Disposable Personal Income	
Rocky Mountain	+.1984%	(2)	**+.2335%**	**(1)**	+.1800%	(1)
Southwest	+.1823%	(3)	**+.2191%**	**(2)**	+.1636%	(4)
Far West	+.1774%	(6)	**+.1947%**	**(3)**	+.1491%	(6)
New England	+.1996%	(1)	**+.1868%**	**(4)**	+.1737%	(2)
Plains	+.1804%	(4)	**+.1849%**	**(5)**	+.1655%	(3)
Southeast	+.1637%	(7)	**+.1843%**	**(6)**	+.1448%	(7)
Mid-Atlantic	+.1792%	(5)	**+.1597%**	**(7)**	+.1536%	(5)
Great Lakes	+.1626%	(8)	**+.1595%**	**(8)**	+.1438%	(8)

Regions	Per Capita Income		Disposable Personal Income		Per Capita Disposable Personal Income	
Rocky Mountain	+.1984%	(2)	+.2335%	(1)	**+.1800%**	**(1)**
New England	+.1996%	(1)	+.1868%	(4)	**+.1737%**	**(2)**
Plains	+.1804%	(4)	+.1849%	(5)	**+.1655%**	**(3)**
Southwest	+.1823%	(3)	+.2191%	(2)	**+.1636%**	**(4)**
Mid-Atlantic	+.1792%	(5)	+.1597%	(7)	**+.1536%**	**(5)**
Far West	+.1774%	(6)	+.1947%	(3)	**+.1491%**	**(6)**
Southeast	+.1637%	(7)	+.1843%	(6)	**+.1448%**	**(7)**
Great Lakes	+.1626%	(8)	+.1595%	(8)	**+.1438%**	**(8)**

Source: Bureau of Economic Analysis, U.S. Department of Commerce.[8]

The focus in 2001 will be on the census and redistricting. Demographic population changes may affect the U.S. House to the benefit of conservative Republicans, but this may be short lived and potentially could have the opposite effect in terms of presidential politics. Minorities did not leave midwestern and northeastern industrial states, at least not to the same degree as whites, and those blacks who did are returning to a South where blacks still have large numbers of voters. And it is the more educated, trained, and affluent white Republicans who are socially more liberal than the traditional Bible Belt believers and similarly situated conservative white suburban Reagan Democrats, who have moved back to the South. Thus, in the future minorities will potentially have even more power or electoral strength, not less, in those big midwestern and northeastern states with heavy electoral college weight. If the more affluent and conservative white population has left these states, leaving a poorer and more progressive population of people of color, then the poorer people of color potentially (if they had reason to register and vote in big numbers) have more power, not less, in that state than when the general population was greater. However, minority voters must have an incentive to participate if they are to be brought into the process in enough numbers to make the difference. A progressive African American as vice president is one dimension of such a motivating force. The other is a progressive economic platform and program—properly presented.

More affluent white conservatives from the Northeast and Midwest who have moved to small rural western and southwestern states are in states that were already voting Republican, so there is only a small electoral gain for them. And those who have moved to the conservative South are more socially liberal than traditional southerners. These new Republicans in the South have also moved to where most African Americans live, but are massively unregistered. Thus, there are enormous opportunities for Democratic gains in the South, and a progressive black on the Democratic ticket could help to bring about those gains.

The accompanying table shows the potential for black voter gains.

Table 6. 2000 ELECTION

State	Won By	Electoral College Votes	Total VAP	Black VAP	Black VAP % by State	Total Turnout % by State	Black Share Actual Vote %
AL	Bush	9	3,212,000	832,000	23.9	50.3	25
AR	Bush	6	1,835,000	318,000	14.3	47.8	11
CA	Gore	54	19,016,000	1,505,000	7.1	n/a	7
FL	Bush	25	10,033,000	1,178,000	13.4	50.7	15
GA	Bush	13	5,417,000	1,712,000	26.5	43.3	25
IL	Gore	22	8,009,000	1,161,000	13.9	52.5	14
LA	Bush	9	3,073,000	972,000	29.6	54.2	29
MD	Gore	10	3,555,000	876,000	26.7	49.1	22
MI	Gore	18	7,029,000	979,000	13.2	57.2	11
MO	Bush	11	3,879,000	335,000	10.1	57.5	12
NY	Gore	33	11,545,000	1,665,000	16.6	45.4	11
NC	Bush	14	5,392,000	1,273,000	20.5	49.4	19
OH	Bush	21	8,123,000	804,000	10.5	54.3	9
PA	Bush	23	8,694,000	755,000	8.8	53.3	7
SC	Bush	8	2,793,000	741,000	27.8	47.6	22
TN	Bush	11	4,050,000	635,000	15.0	49.1	18
TX	Bush	32	12,528,000	1,559,000	11.8	43.1	15
VA	Bush	13	4,786,000	1,010,000	19.0	51.8	16
Total		**332**	**122,969,000**	**22,074,000**			
Gore		**137**					
Bush		**195**					

In the eleven Deep South states, rarely has 50 percent of the voting-age population turned out to vote in a presidential election; in some, like South Carolina, 50 percent of the voting-age population has never voted. Georgia was at the bottom in 1988 with a 38 percent turnout. Ten other southern states were not far behind. In 1996 only one southern state, Louisiana, had a turnout of 50 percent. (See table 7.) Again, this is another part of the legacy of slavery and its related political consequences for both blacks and whites. If you were poor and a basic field worker, regardless of race, you were not encouraged to vote and did not develop the habit or tradition of voting, and you never saw that a vote made an economic difference in your life. In my mind, all these factors suggest that a Democratic ticket with a strong economic message and a progressive African American on it in the general election poses the greatest challenge to a Republican presidential candidate in the South.

Table 7. VOTER REGISTRATION AND TURNOUT, 1996

STATE	1996	1996 VAP*	Percent Registered VAP**	Turnout***	Percent Turnout
Alabama	3,220,000	2,470,766	76.73%	1,534,349	47.65%
Arkansas	1,873,000	1,369,459	73.12%	884,262	47.21%
Florida	11,043,000	8,077,877	73.15%	5,300,927	48.00%
Georgia	5,418,000	3,811,284	70.34%	2,298,899	42.43%
Louisiana	3,131,000	2,559,352	81.74%	1,783,959	56.98%
Mississippi	1,967,000	1,715,913	87.24%	893,857	45.44%
NC	5,519,000	4,318,008	78.24%	2,515,807	45.58%
Tennessee	4,035,000	2,849,910	70.63%	1,894,105	46.94%
Texas	13,597,000	10,540,678	77.52%	5,611,644	41.27%
SC	2,771,000	1,814,777	65.49%	1,151,689	41.56%
Virginia	5,083,000	3,322,135	65.36%	2,416,642	47.54%
Alaska	425,000	414,815	97.60%	241,620	56.85%
Arizona	3,145,000	2,244,672	71.37%	1,404,405	44.66%
California	22,826,000	15,662,075	8.62%	10,019,484	43.90%
Colorado	2,862,000	2,346,253	81.98%	1,510,704	52.78%
Connecticut	2,479,000	1,881,323	75.89%	1,392,614	56.18%
Delaware	548,000	421,710	76.95%	270,810	49.42%
DC	422,000	361,419	85.64%	185,726	44.01%
Hawaii	890,000	544,916	61.23%	360,120	40.46%
Idaho	858,000	700,430	81.64%	489,481	57.05%
Illinois	8,754,000	6,663,301	76.12%	4,311,391	49.25%
Indiana	4,374,000	3,488,088	79.75%	2,135,431	48.82%
Iowa	2,138,000	1,776,433	83.09%	1,234,075	57.72%
Kansas	1,897,000	1,436,418	75.72%	1,063,452	56.06%
Kentucky	2,928,000	2,396,086	81.83%	1,387,999	47.40%
Maine	945,000	1,001,292	105.96%	679,499	71.90%
Maryland	3,820,000	2,587,978	67.75%	1,780,870	46.62%
Massachusetts	4,649,000	3,459,193	74.41%	2,556,459	54.99%
Michigan	7,072,000	6,677,079	94.42%	3,848,844	54.42%
Minnesota	3,422,000	3,067,802	89.65%	2,192,640	64.07%
Missouri	3,995,000	3,342,849	83.68%	2,158,065	54.02%
Montana	656,000	590,751	90.05%	407,083	62.06%
Nebraska	1,211,000	1,015,056	83.82%	677,415	55.94%
Nevada	1,212,000	778,092	64.20%	464,279	38.31%
NH	871,000	754,771	86.66%	499,053	57.30%
New Jersey	6,034,000	4,320,866	71.61%	3,075,860	50.98%

New Mexico	1,224,000	851,479	69.57%	556,074	45.43%
New York	13,564,000	10,162,156	74.92%	6,439,129	47.47%
North Dakota	476,000	N/A****	N/A	266,411	55.97%
Ohio	8,347,000	6,879,687	82.42%	4,534,434	54.32%
Oklahoma	2,426,000	1,979,017	81.58%	1,206,713	49.74%
Oregon	2,411,000	1,962,155	81.38%	1,377,760	57.14%
Pennsylvania	9,197,000	6,805,612	74.00%	4,506,118	49.00%
Rhode Island	751,000	602,692	80.25%	390,247	51.96%
South Dakota	535,000	459,971	85.98%	323,826	60.53%
Utah	1,333,000	1,050,452	78.80%	665,629	49.93%
Vermont	445,000	385,328	86.59%	258,449	58.08%
Washington	4,115,000	3,078,128	74.80%	2,253,837	54.77%
West Virginia	1,417,000	970,745	68.51%	636,459	44.92%
Wisconsin	3,824,000	N/A	N/A	2,196,169	57.43%
Wyoming	356,000	240,711	67.62%	211,571	59.43%
United States	**196,511,000**	**146,211,960**	**74.40%**	**96,456,345**	**49.08%**

*VAP refers to the total voting-age population of the state as reported by the Census Bureau. Please note that the VAP includes all people over the age of 18—including a significant number of people not able to vote in U.S. elections.

**Registered VAP refers to the total number of registered voters as reported by the states.

**In this instance, turnout refers to the total vote cast for the highest office on the ballot in 1996 (president). These figures may be inconsistent with other reported turnout figures since research suggests that approximately 2% of voters fail to vote for the highest office on a fairly consistent basis.

****Not applicable. North Dakota has no voter registration and Wisconsin has election day registration at the polls.

SOURCE: REGISTRATION AND TURNOUT STATISTICS COURTESY OF STATE ELECTION OFFICES AND THE CONGRESSIONAL RESEARCH SERVICE (GOVERNMENT DIVISION), WITH DATA PROVIDED BY ELECTION DATA SERVICES, INC., WASHINGTON, D.C. THE TABLE WAS GENERATED BY THE INTERNET ASSISTANT WIZARD FOR MICROSOFT EXCEL. IT CAN BE FOUND AT HTTP:// WWW.MICROSOFT.COM/MSOFFICE/FREESTUF/ MSEXCEL/INDEX.HTM.

Former residents of New York, New Jersey, and other northeastern and midwestern industrial states moved to Florida (which ten years earlier gained four congressional seats and, thus, electoral votes), Arizona, and other western and southwestern states. But from an electoral college point of view, in 2000 we saw that it makes no difference if the Republicans win Florida by five hundred or five million votes; they still gained only four additional electoral votes. In 2000 Florida happened to make all the difference, but this unusual occurrence does not counteract my basic point.

If the nine hundred thousand African Americans, 700,000 Hispanic Americans, and thousands of other alienated voters in New York can be attracted to the Democratic ledger with a progressive African American on the ticket, who would not give up four additional electoral votes to Florida (and other small gains elsewhere) for a sure thirty-three electoral votes in New York, twenty-three in Pennsylvania, twenty-one in Ohio, and other gains elsewhere? Tables 5, 6, and 7 demonstrate that such an electoral potential exists in key states across the nation precisely where an African American vice presidential candidacy would bring massive numbers of new voters onto the rolls.

I would suggest that those who think an African American as vice president would mean sure defeat for the top of the ticket, and infer that it would cost Democrats in the Senate and House, are misguided. In fact, I believe the exact opposite is true. The resounding losses by Mondale in 1984 and Dukakis in 1988 in the presidential races were combined with Democratic gains in the House and Senate. In 1984, at the height of Reagan's popularity, Democrats actually unexpectedly defeated four Republicans and made a net gain of two seats in the Senate, clearly demonstrating that voters know how to split their ticket if that is the concern. Current voters in the various states and congressional districts voted simultaneously against the national Democratic candidate and for their local Democratic congressional candidates.

For much of the 1990s, there was a tremendous anti-incumbency mood among conservative Republican voters in the country. It was reflected in the number of resignations, along with primary and general election defeats, of members of Congress. This anti-incumbent mind-set, in turn, nurtured the term-limits movement. But there is no such dominant mind-set in the black community or the Democratic Party. Thus, the onrush of new straight-Democratic voters that an African American on the ticket would bring would also quite likely effectively eliminate any Republican term-limits appeal by electing a Democratic-majority Congress.

A black on the national ticket would be the Democrats' greatest asset at every level, including in the approximately one-quarter of all 435 congressional districts where African Americans—not including Hispanics and progressives—make up 20 percent or more of the voters. Such an increase would also be important in statewide senate and gubernatorial races in the southern, midwestern, and northern industrial states where Democratic senators are up for reelection every six years.

Earlier I showed how many southern Democrats ran from the Gore-Lieberman ticket. But with a majority of all African Americans living in the South and making up large percentages of the Democratic vote—for example, nearly 65 percent of Zell Miller's general election vote in Georgia came from African Americans—if blacks were registering and voting in even greater numbers because a black was on the ticket, these conservative southern Democrats could not have run from a Gore-Watt ticket and won themselves. There would be a completely new election and electoral college *dynamic* at work in the South and elsewhere in bigger states like Pennsylvania, Ohio, and Indiana that Democrats need to carry in order to win the presidency.

Reflect on the off-year elections of 1994, when Republicans gained control of both the U.S. House and Senate, and the voter turnout was near a historic low. Contrast this with the net gains of Democrats in 1984 in Congress, and then how Democrats won and regained control of the Senate in 1986 because of the millions of new voters added by the Jackson candidacy of 1984. Despite these and many other Jackson contributions, too often the Democratic Party leadership—and especially the DLC—has acted instead as if his two campaigns were an albatross around the Democratic Party's neck. In light of these facts, such irrationality can only be understood in the context of the southern history of slavery and racism within the Democratic Party previously described in this book. Democrats' obvious nervousness is gleefully exploited by the Republicans. Contrary to such irrational fears by Democrats, a progressive African American on the ticket would be the best and strongest political weapon the Democrats could have.

While I think I'm arguing a strong case for why a Democratic would win with a black on the national ticket, even assuming a Democratic defeat under these circumstances would still provide Democrats with the surest strategy for regaining and continuing to control and increase their numbers in Congress, governors' mansions, state legislatures, city councils, and school boards, and assure more Democratic victories in the future. There is no logical way that activating an additional four to eight million new solidly Democratic black voters would not massively aid the Democratic Party at every level of elections if the political program was targeted at equal economic programs for all Americans.

The Mondale and Dukakis losses suggest that congressional candidates would still get their basic core vote, plus an avalanche of new hard-core Democratic voters that a progressive African American vice presidential candidacy would bring into the mainstream.

If President George H. W. Bush and the Democrats haven't understood this, George W. Bush sure has. *Time* magazine reported in 1992 that he had warned his father of the potential impact of an H. Ross Perot candidacy on his chances for reelection. He pointed out that his father's victory in 1988 was much closer than most realized. Though Bush won 426 electoral votes in 1988, 120 of those came from states that he won with margins of less than 5 percent of the popular vote—Illinois, Pennsylvania, Maryland, Missouri, California, New Mexico, Michigan, Colorado, Louisiana, Texas, Oklahoma, and Tennessee—almost all states with significant numbers of potential black voters where having an African American on the Democratic ticket would likely have made a dramatic positive difference.

Republicans now take winning the South in presidential elections for granted. That's the base from which their political strategists begin to build their electoral victory. If Gore, a southerner, had chosen a progressive African American as his running mate, which would bring strength in both the South and the urban North, Northeast, and Midwest, the entire political dynamic would have changed. It would have forced the Republicans to campaign harder in the South, which takes time, money, and energy away from other critical states and regions that they needed to win.

With a moderate white Democrat at the top of the ticket to appeal to white moderate and conservative southern voters (Reagan Democrats and DLC types), and an African American on the second spot to appeal to African Americans (more than half of all of the twenty-four million African American voters live in the South, but nearly five million are unregistered), along with Hispanics, organized and unorganized workers, farmers, students, environmentalists, and other progressives, Republicans would have found themselves in a strategic dilemma.

Such a ticket would have been equally appealing in the industrial centers of the North. Take again, for example, New York. The *Village Voice* ran an article after the 1992 New York primary that showed that the "spin" by the mainstream media that Jackson had hurt Jerry Brown because of the Jewish vote was not an accurate assessment. Brown was damaged most by his regressive flat tax. He was not harmed by his close proximity to Jackson among those who voted, including Jewish voters, and he was helped by Jackson among African Americans. In New York, Brown and Jackson were projected by the media as being closely linked, and it paid off for Brown. It was the state where Clinton received his lowest percent of African American votes—51 percent.

Despite the media controversy about Jackson and Jews that followed him in New York in 1988, and with voters voting for him alone (not on the second spot on someone else's ticket), he still won New York City with a multiracial coalition that included 15 percent white, mainly Jewish, voters. There were also more than nine hundred thousand African Americans and seven hundred thousand Hispanics unregistered in New York—hundreds of thousands of whom would be brought onto the rolls with a progressive African American on the ticket.

The *Los Angeles Times* survey of voters leaving the polls after the June 2, 1992, California primary indicated that the largest number (17 percent) of those responding thought that a Clinton-Jackson ticket would do the most to inspire them to vote Democratic that fall.

Traditionally, campaigns that have put both wings of their party together on their tickets have won. Jackson himself said, "It takes two wings to fly." The DLC one-wing ticket of 1992 won—with a mere 43 percent of the popular vote—but it had no mandate to govern or to take the country in a significantly new direction. That is why Clinton, once elected, politically caved to the Perot forces, becoming the "deficit reduction" instead of the "investment" president he promised during the campaign. Candidate Clinton told us he would put the American people first, not the deficit. In 2000 Democrats again tried the DLC one-wing strategy and lost. But even if they had won, there would have been no significant mandate, only support for incremental programs like expanding the Children's Health Insurance Program (CHIP) to eleven million children without health insurance. That would have been a step in the right direction, but there are forty-five million Americans without health insurance who need it. Democrats need a platform that is ambitious enough to include them.

In 2000 the Republicans, too, fielded a one-wing ticket. Conservative George W. Bush picked ultraconservative Richard Cheney as his running mate, and they are initially governing as pretty extreme conservatives. That pleases the right wing that nominated them, but not the moderate wing that elected them. For example, lurching to the right on the environment, they pushed to drill in the Arctic wildlife preserve, reneged on a campaign promise to regulate the emissions of carbon dioxide, overturned arsenic limits in our water, and tried to open up sixty million acres of national forest to corporate development. Bush's appointment of Gale Norton as his interior secretary, a protégé of James Watt (who was quite possibly the worst secretary of the interior in the history of the country), and Norton's statements regarding her longing for the good ol' days of the southern Confederacy and states' rights will make their administration vulnerable in 2004. John Ashcroft's selection as attorney general sends the same signal. The Bush-Cheney campaign disguised this conservative and right-wing agenda during the campaign enough to win. But unless the Bush administration changes course and selects a running mate at the opposite political spectrum of his party in 2004, I predict that this Bush, too—like his father, but for very different reasons—will be a one-term president. As for the Democratic Party, it will be in serious trouble if Bush happens to replace Cheney with Colin Powell.

Such traditional winning combinations have been true whether it involved the Democratic Party or the Republican Party. Democrats, for example, won because both wings were represented on the ticket with Kennedy and Johnson in 1960; with Johnson and Humphrey in 1964; and with Carter and Mondale in 1976. They lost with two liberals on the ticket—McGovern and Eagleton-Shriver in 1972, and Mondale and Ferraro in 1984. Recent Republican victories featured Reagan and Bush in 1980, and Bush and Quayle in 1988—candidates from different wings of their party.

Obviously, other factors were involved in these wins and loses, but a contributing factor for victory in each of them was a "balanced" ticket. Such inclusion means the maximum number of people feel their interests are being represented by the ticket, and it is one motivation for them to participate and vote. It is one element in a formula for victory.

If confronted with the new political reality of a progressive African American on a national Democratic ticket, how does a Republican team alter its message and campaign strategy and tactics to gain more voters than it loses? A difficult matter to calculate in such a clearly unpredictable campaign. A progressive African American on the ticket becomes a major headache for Republican strategists.

Undertaken because of the weakness of the "Quayle factor" on the Bush-Quayle ticket, research and polling during and after the 1988 campaign showed that the American people vote for or against the top of the ticket, not against the second spot. They voted for George Bush and against Michael Dukakis, not against Dan Quayle or for Lloyd Bentsen. I don't accept as true today that the top of the ticket dominates—except if an African American is on the ticket. The American people vote for president, not for vice president.

In another way, however, an African American on the ticket is an exception, but a positive one for Democrats. Whoever is on the top of the ticket, and regardless of nonfundamental character issues or controversies, the new voters that an African American will bring to the Democratic column will not abandon the candidate or the Democratic Party in a crisis. The Lewinsky matter, which was very wrong but not an impeachable offense, made that clear and laid all doubt about it aside! In fact, if there are crises or attacks it may even stimulate black voters more. It did in the case of Harold Washington in Chicago. This cannot be said of anyone else Democrats may choose to put on their ticket in the vice presidential spot. No other candidate brings the same number of passionate, committed, loyal, and reliable voters to the ticket.

Let's not kid ourselves or be naive. All posturing or protestations aside about picking the "best-qualified" vice presidential candidate, the person on the second spot on the ticket is selected to bolster an electoral strategy. Obviously, Bush's selection of ultraconservative Dick Cheney was not about the three electoral votes from Wyoming. In fact, Cheney moved his voting address from Texas to Wyoming just so he could be nominated and not violate the Constitution's prohibition of two candidates from the same state. Cheney's nomination was about energizing a southern base of conservatism, and its electoral votes, with the hope and confidence that the affable manner and friendly face of Bush could still appeal to moderates and independents nationally.

When Gore won the nomination, hypothetically, if former Senator Bill Bradley had been a "former Democrat from Wyoming," a state with the smallest population in the country and three electoral votes—Rhodes scholar, college and NBA basketball hero, and all—he would have been much less appealing and likely to be on the ticket than former Senator Bill Bradley of New Jersey, a populous state in the center of other eastern industrial states with big populations, many voters, and large blocs of electoral votes. He would have been no less qualified—except in the electoral sense.

In 1988 Bush selected Quayle to hold conservatives in his column. He chose a conservative who was weak politically, however, for fear that a strong vice president with an active constituency would do within his administration what Pat Buchanan did to him in the primaries—make him toe the strict conservative line on policy and issues.

What does actually qualify a person to be president of the United States? Five U.S. presidents, 12 percent of those elected, never held elective public office before becoming president. Intelligence, judgment, negotiating skills, the ability to work and communicate with others, to build coalitions, inspire and motivate people, handle the press, set priorities, articulate a vision, and set a clear direction for the country are all closer to the real qualifications for the office of president of the United States—or vice president capable of being president—than merely having elected legislative or executive experience. In today's climate of political disaffection and economic pain at the bottom, and uneasiness in the middle, the ability to make people feel that the government cares about people like them may be the preeminent qualification for being president or vice president—a qualification that Clinton demonstrated in abundance. I understand that John F. Kennedy was not a particularly good administrator, but he inspired a whole nation and set it on a new and historic course.

The selection of other candidates, even liberals, to serve on a national ticket will have its advantages, but having a progressive African American on the Democratic ticket is the only way to defeat the legacy of slavery, racism, and states' rights that has its roots in Dixie. The other side of that coin, politically, is that it is also the most dependable way to build a more perfect Union of jobs, health care, housing, education, equal opportunity, a clean environment, and fair taxes for all Americans. African Americans are the least likely political constituency to abandon such a progressive agenda, or get diverted by Republicans on a conservative social and moral values agenda. For African Americans, jobs, health care, housing, and education are also moral and family value issues.

To set the country on a truly progressive course today will require a Democrat in the White House and a supermajority of Democrats in the House and Senate. That supermajority cannot be obtained anywhere but in the South. Only a progressive African American on a Democratic ticket that focuses on these bigger economic needs of all of the American people even has the potential of winning the White House and creating that supermajority of Democrats in Congress.

From a theological perspective, we could posit that in God's omniscient and omnipotent Providence, politically, God has placed African Americans in key and strategic electoral locations in the United States, locations that can help to build a more perfect Union, not only for themselves but also for all Americans—and make a significant contribution in helping to build a more perfect, stable, and secure world as well.

Table 8. NATIONAL VOTER TURNOUT IN FEDERAL ELECTIONS, 1960–1996

Year	Eligible Voters	Registration	Turnout	%T/O of VAP*
1996	196,511,000	146,211,960	96,456,345	49.08%
1994	193,650,000	130,292,822	75,105,860	38.78%
1992	189,529,000	133,821,178	104,405,155	55.09%
1990	185,812,000	121,105,630	67,859,189	36.52%
1988	182,778,000	126,379,628	91,594,693	50.11%
1986	178,566,000	118,399,984	64,991,128	36.40%
1984	174,466,000	124,150,614	92,652,680	53.11%
1982	169,938,000	110,671,225	67,615,576	39.79%
1980	164,597,000	113,043,734	86,515,221	52.56%
1978	158,373,000	103,291,265	58,917,938	37.21%
1976	152,309,190	105,037,986	81,555,789	53.55%
1974	146,336,000	96,199,020**	55,943,834	38.23%
1972	140,776,000	97,328,541	77,718,554	55.21%
1970	124,498,000	82,496,747	58,014,338	46.60%
1968	120,328,186	81,658,180	73,211,875	60.84%

1966	116,132,000	86,288,283	56,188,046	48.39%
1964	114,090,000	73,715,818	70,644,592	61.92%
1962	112,423,000	65,393,751***	53,141,227	47.27%
1960	109,159,000	64,833,096****	68,838,204	63.06%

*Percent turnout of voting-age population.
**Registrations from Iowa not included.
***Registrations from Alabama, Arkansas, Washington, D.C., Iowa, Kansas, Kentucky, Mississippi, Missouri, Nebraska, New Mexico, North Carolina, North Dakota, South Dakota, Tennessee, Wisconsin, and Wyoming not included.
****Registrations from Alabama, Alaska, Washington, D.C., Iowa, Kansas, Kentucky, Mississippi, Missouri, Nebraska, New Mexico, North Carolina, North Dakota, Oklahoma, South Dakota, Wisconsin, and Wyoming not included.

SOURCE: DATA DRAWN FROM CONGRESSIONAL RESEARCH SERVICE REPORTS, ELECTION DATA SERVICES, INC., AND STATE ELECTION OFFICES. THIS TABLE WAS GENERATED BY THE INTERNET ASSISTANT WIZARD FOR MICROSOFT EXCEL. YOU CAN FIND THIS ADD-IN ON HTTP://WWW.MICROSOFT.COM/MSOFFICE/ FREESTUF/MSEXCEL/INDEX.HTM.

Table 9. NATIONAL VOTER REGISTRATION AND TURNOUT IN PRESIDENTIAL ELECTIONS, 1960–1992

VAP*	Total REG**	Turnout***	% REG	%	Turnout
1960	109,159,000	64,833,096	68,838,204	59.40	63.06
1964	114,090,000	73,715,818	70,644,592	66.24	61.92
1968	120,328,186	81,658,180	73,211,875	69.54	60.84
1972	140,776,000	97,328,541	77,718,554	70.84	55.21
1976	152,309,190	105,037,986	81,555,789	68.97	53.55
1980	164,597,000	113,043,734	86,515,221	68.68	52.56
1984	174,466,000	124,150,614	92,652,680	71.16	53.11
1988	182,778,000	126,379,628	91,594,693	69.15	50.11
1992	189,529,000	133,821,178	104,405,155	70.61	55.09

*Total VAP refers to the total voting-age population of the state as reported by the Census Bureau. Please note that the VAP includes all people over the age of eighteen—including a significant number of people not able to vote in U.S. elections.
**Total REG refers to the total number of registered voters as reported by the states.
***Turnout in this instance refers to the total votes cast for the highest office on the ballot (president). These figures may be inconsistent with other reported turnout figures since research suggests that approximately 2 percent of voters fail to vote for the highest office on a fairly consistent basis.

SOURCE: REGISTRATION AND TURNOUT STATISTICS COURTESY OF STATE ELECTION OFFICES AND THE CONGRESSIONAL RESEARCH SERVICE (GOVERNMENT DIVISION), WITH DATA PROVIDED BY ELECTION DATA SERVICES, INC., WASHINGTON, D.C. THIS TABLE WAS GENERATED BY THE INTERNET ASSISTANT WIZARD FOR MICROSOFT EXCEL. YOU CAN FIND THIS ADD-IN ON HTTP://WWW.MICROSOFT.COM/MSOFFICE/ FREESTUF/MSEXCEL/INDEX.HTM.

GOD THROUGH US

When a religion is good, I conceive it will support itself; and when it does not support itself, and God does not take care to support it so that its professors are obligated to call for help of the civil power, 'tis a sign, I apprehend, of its being a bad one.

—Benjamin Franklin

Christianity has sufficient inner strength to survive and flourish on its own. It does not need state subsidies, nor state privileges, nor state prestige. The more it obtains state support the greater it curtails human freedom.

—Justice William O. Douglas

If men were angels there would be no need for government.

—James Madison

God is often described as omnipotent or all-powerful, omniscient or all-knowing, and omnipresent or ever present. There are also cosmological or an orderly universe, teleological or a purposeful universe, and ontological or first-cause arguments for God's existence. I certainly encourage serious people to study and wrestle with these various philosophical and theological concepts. While we can certainly have a vibrant and valid faith without reason and science, it is generally more desirable to have such a faith beyond them. A mature faith recognizes the potential benefit of intellectual curiosity and the scientific method's relentless inquiry, but it also clearly understands their limitations. At the center of my personal faith and relationship with God is the conviction that the God I worship and serve is someone who has been active and is still able to do great things in nature and history.

Philosophically, there are only two basic views we can hold of history. All philosophies of history are mere variations or adaptations of these two fundamental approaches. One view of history sees the world and life as cyclical, while the other sees it as linear. The cyclical view of history sees the universe and world as an unending series of repetitions and cycles, not unlike the seasons of the year, which have no beginning and no end. History is not "going anywhere" and thus has no ultimate purpose or design. A linear view of history says our universe and world has a beginning and will have an ending. Linear history may have many different views of what that beginning and ending are or may be, and various interpretations of its ultimate purpose. There may be a variety of numerators, but "beginning," "ending" and "ultimate purpose" are the common denominators of a linear view of history.

The Judeo-Christian faith holds a linear view of history. God, who is "Spirit," created the world *ex nihilo*, "out of nothing." It's logically true that *ex nihilo, nihilo fit*, that is "out of nothing, nothing comes," but God creating the world out of "nothing" means God created it out of nothing material. Thus, God created the world, not "out of nothing," but out of nothing material. God created the material world out of Spirit.

From the Judeo-Christian linear view of history, God is not merely an idea or ideal, a principle, or "First Cause." God is something more and God did something more. God is a personal God who cares about each of us and is and was involved with us throughout history. Through this linear view, God can be known in many ways, through using reason and the scientific method of observing and studying people, their social arrangements, nature, or the universe. But most important for Christians, God is truly known not in the abstract or impersonal realm of things or nature, but through men and women working throughout history, and uniquely so in Jesus the Christ. Thus, through him we learn most fully that our purpose in the world is to be co-creators with God in the universe, working toward better personal and social relations, and respecting the world that God the Creator has given us to take care of as good and responsible stewards.

While the theological particulars may differ, Jews, Christians, and Muslims all share a linear view of history and believe that a monotheistic God is revealed to us in history. God worked through a specific "chosen people" to send all people a universal message of God's concern and involvement in their human affairs. God revealed through Moses a set of universal laws for basic conduct as human beings in societies—the Ten Commandments. God spoke through the Prophets, who were primarily forthtellers of the present, not foretellers of the future, so we would know God's will and the demands of justice. For Christians, God spoke most dramatically through Jesus the Christ to let us know that faith, hope, and love, but especially a genuine and mature love of self and neighbor, who is every person, was the key to life and God's will for us.

As a Christian I affirm that there is only one way to God and the afterlife of Heaven, and that way is through Jesus the Christ. But I must immediately follow that statement with a question, "What was Jesus' one way?" My answer is that Jesus' way was the way of *agape* or selfless love for another and others. Thus, all those of any religious faith, or of no "religious" faith, who strive after and manifest the most mature love they are capable in their personal and collective relationships have found Jesus' one way to God. That is the Kingdom of God on earth as it is in Heaven.

As a U.S. congressman I use my Christian faith and my Judeo-Christian heritage, principles, and moral values to inform my legislative and political decisions, but I do not use my position to impose my religion, heritage, or moral values on others through the law. My role as a lawmaking member of Congress is to protect the constitutional rights and fight for equal protection under the law for all of the American people.

When I became a member of Congress, I put my hand on the Bible and swore to uphold the Constitution. I did not put my hand on the Constitution and swear to uphold the Bible, the Torah, or the Koran. The people of the Second Congressional District of Illinois did not elect me to be their pastor, priest, rabbi, or imam for the purpose of shepherding their souls. They elected me to be their political representative and the guardian of their constitutional rights.

To uphold my oath of office and the Constitution, I have to defend the rights of Christians of all denominations, Jews, Muslims, and people of other faiths in America, as well as unbelievers, even hostile unbelievers, agnostics, and atheists. The greatness of our country and our Constitution (as amended) is that it puts believers in the position of defending the rights of unbelievers, while unbelievers must defend the rights of believers.

Even this principle is derivative from the best of the Judeo-Christian faith and tradition, which respects everyone's inherent value and worth as well as the freedom of choice of every individual even when, within the law, we may disagree with their choice. I must defend the rights of all Americans even when I cannot defend the choices of some Americans. Therefore, as a matter of public policy, we must support public policies and laws that grant the maximum amount of individual freedom that is compatible with the demands of social justice and societal stability. One of the greatest contributions that any person or institution—but especially religious leaders and institutions—can make to society is to teach humility and tolerance. This is especially true of the Judeo-Christian faith in America, since it is the country's dominant religion.

Leaders should not teach a false humility that is actually a weak ego, or teach a tolerance that in reality is a lack of courage or principles. We should teach a genuine humility based on a mature understanding of both God and our human finitude. Sometimes a failure of leadership is sold as humility or tolerance. Appointing commissions to study issues thoroughly, with the intent of bringing back sound recommendations to better a situation, which I generally fully support, can sometimes be used as an excuse for inaction, then sold to the public as humility and tolerance. The lack of presidential and congressional leadership—after more than two hundred years of political disenfranchisement—on the question of statehood and full political enfranchisement for the nearly six hundred thousand people of the District of Columbia is one example that comes immediately to mind.

False humility and tolerance must not be allowed to serve as excuses for inaction or for not standing up for things that are morally, socially, economically, and politically sound. Our society should cultivate a hope and expectation that our leaders, even when it's difficult, will have a real commitment to equal protection under the law for all Americans, and strongly and aggressively enforce the rule of just laws. We should not concede to a more cynical view of society and leaders that they will always follow public opinion polls rather than mold public opinion. It is honest, courageous, and realistic for us to say that, at our best, Americans hope, expect, and urge our leaders to be the kind of people who have the courage not just of their convictions, but also of sound moral convictions, to lead us in such a manner and direction.

For example, the Supreme Court was correct when it overturned the 1896 ruling in *Plessy v. Ferguson* with the 1954 *Brown v. Board of Education* decision, which replaced the legal precedent of "separate but equal" with the legal doctrine of "equal protection under the law." But the Court also should have meant it when it said school segregation should end "with all deliberate speed." Nearly half a century later it is clear that the Court didn't really mean it. While affirming that in some school districts there has been significant progress, and affirming that the Court's decision may have been well intended, so far neither it, nor our leaders, nor our society as a whole has had any real sustained commitment to achieving the result of a desegregated and truly integrated high-quality public school system or society for all Americans.

Good religion deals with the "ought," while good politics deals with the "is." The religious "ought" should always be challenging the political "is" to get better; the political "is" should be forced to struggle with the religious "ought" as it concretely grapples to solve societal problems in ethical ways. Both, at their best, create a good and healthy tension in a morally alive and democratic society.

America is a multiracial, multicultural, multireligious, democratic, and secular society, not a religious theocracy. While our nation may have been founded by mostly Judeo-Christian leaders espousing Judeo-Christian values and principles as outlined above, we do not believe that our laws come directly from God or through a monarchical representative of God. Instead, we are a secular and representative democracy whose leaders and the laws are derived from the will of the people themselves. We have a republic and a democracy where, as the late Senator John Stennis (D-MS), quoting Benjamin Franklin, would often say, "In America, the people govern." That is what makes our Constitution and America great.

Having said that, we do need strong leaders with well-founded moral convictions and political beliefs who will lead us by appealing to the best and highest, not the lowest and worst, within us.

I see two critical problems confronting people who are both religiously and politically committed, but who live in a multicultural, secular society such as the United States. Religion tends to deal with the absolute and the eternal, while politics deals with the relative, the temporal, and the politically possible. How to mesh, balance, or integrate the two is the challenge.

Finite people cannot know absolute truth or eternal principles, except by faith. To take our faith absolutely seriously, but also to make the relative judgments that must be made as finite human beings, requires us to see ourselves as both purposeful but also limited human beings. Again, this requires us to be both genuinely humble and tolerant relative to the differing points of view of others. And in a democracy, we should be more than just tolerant or respectful of other people's points of view. Hopefully, we can be appreciative and celebrate our differences.

It was Reinhold Neibuhr in *Moral Man, Immoral Society* who taught that as individuals, one on one, we can sometimes approximate Jesus' standard of *agape* love for one another. But, he argued, as we move higher up the social structure or ladder to more complex relations such as family, friends, neighborhood, church, state, economic interest group, political party, and, finally, relations between nation-states, we are less able to approximate Jesus' individual love ideal because of sin—which he defined as an inevitable, but false, human pride. This innate "original sin," as manifest in human pride, is, as social relations become more complex, the inability to see from another's point of view.

Therefore, Neibuhr said, while we should maintain the ideal of love, and certainly strive to achieve it at the individual and family levels, at the more complex levels of social and political organization a "balance of power"—especially a balance of economic power—is necessary to achieve justice. Even the opportunity for the ideal of individual and family love becomes more available and possible within the context of social, economic, and political justice.

He argued that those seeking social justice should make moral and humanitarian appeals; they should try to persuade through reason; they should use education to achieve their socially just ends; and, through politics, they should fight to change the laws to better society. But, he said, unless there is also a balance of economic power, then the use of morality, reason, education, politics, and the law, in the end, will all tend to reinforce and serve the special interests of those with the most economic power.

This should not be read as a form of economic determinism, whether of the inevitable-progress or the inevitable-failure variety. I believe in neither. I believe that God has given every individual and society at all times genuine, if limited, human freedom. Obviously, some individuals and societies, because of their human, social, or political circumstances, have relatively more or less freedom than others. But God has given everyone and every society, in whatever circumstance they may find themselves, a degree of genuine freedom to make real choices that have consequences and for which they are accountable. The focus on economic interest is merely an underlying principle of reality and social organization that those engaged in the struggle for social change and social justice must keep in mind.

I believe that Neibuhr's view is a true analysis of our human and political situation. Therefore, I believe an active participatory democracy is necessary not only for secular and civic reasons, but for spiritual and religious ones as well. In a secular sense, an active democracy that maximizes the participation of all of the people is necessary to assure genuine representation. Morally and religiously, I believe democracy is required as the best antidote to the original sin of not being able to see from another's point of view. A balance of economic power is necessary to offset human pride and sinfulness. The phrase "power corrupts and absolute power corrupts absolutely" is true for both secular and religious reasons. The democratic and spiritual correction for this problem is not the absence of power, less participation, bigger contributions, and more reliance on an expert class or a political elite. A balance of power will only be achieved through greater democratic participation. Just two simple changes—the public funding of our elections and a 95 percent turnout of all eligible voters —would dramatically alter politics in the United States!

Our nation and our politics would be very much different if 95 percent or more of our people voted and remained politically active between elections instead of the current situation where only half of our eligible voters vote in presidential election years, with even fewer voting in off-year and local elections. The United States, the so-called leader of world democracy, has the lowest voter participation rate of any industrialized democracy in the world, therefore our democracy is not truly representative of all of the American people. All studies show that the whitest, brightest, oldest, and best off economically are voting. People of color, the less educated, the young, and the poorest among us are not voting, and their interests are not being protected. Thus, inevitably, in a democracy, only those with accountable elective power will be represented in politics and government.

If politics is the distribution system for the economic system, and the economic order finances the election of the political order, we should expect a sizable gap between the "haves" and the "have-nots" in terms of income and wealth—which is precisely what we have in the United States and in the world today. The top 1 percent of Americans own as much wealth as more than one hundred million Americans at the bottom, and one individual, Bill Gates, is worth more than most of the poorest countries in the world combined. And the wealth and income gaps between the North and the South in the global community continues to grow.

If tolerance and humility are the antidotes to intolerance and arrogance, and a balance of economic and political power is required to achieve justice, then we must analyze the nature of power. I do not discount moral and spiritual power, but there are only two forms of material power in the world, economic and political. By definition, poor people, workers, and the economic middle class have relatively little material power individually. That includes 80 percent or more of the American people—anyone making under about eighty thousand dollars per year.

At the height of Britain's class-based society, the top 1 percent owned 19 percent of its wealth. The latest studies show that in the so-called classless society of the United States, the top 1 percent owns nearly 40 percent of the wealth, and this disparity is growing and becoming more pronounced, not staying the same or receding. The United States is now the most unjust society, in terms of distribution of wealth and income, of any industrialized democracy in the world. In the global economy, more than twenty-four trillion dollars changes hands every twenty-four days, and this money is held and manipulated by a very small group of global economic elites.[1] Thus, there is only one material power that has the potential to offset this level of concentrated global economic power, and that is democratic political power. And the only way "we the people" can get political power in a democracy is to organize it.

My father taught me three principles of organizing: Need is the basis of organization; self-interest is the sustaining force; and work and service on behalf of this need and self-interest will give you power—because it obligates others and makes you or your institution necessary. And he taught me that the only protection against a range of things—from going out of business to genocide—is to remain necessary. Things, organizations, institutions, or people who become unnecessary tend to become irrelevant and disappear.

These principles can be applied to any local grassroots or national mobilizing effort, or to any effort at building an organization or sustaining institutional power, whether a church, a political organization, or a government. People organize around their needs, stay involved as long as their self-interest is being met, and gravitate to leaders and institutions that are working to meet their needs and self-interest.

The premise of this book is that, with a human openness of spirit to God's Spirit and guidance, the purpose of life on earth is to help create a society and a human and humane atmosphere or context where all people on earth are permitted to achieve their maximum individual human potential—spiritually, mentally, socially, economically, and politically—in a way that also allows all other human beings to achieve that same end.

Obviously, this is a stated goal and an ideal that we will never completely reach on earth. Having said that, however, I would quickly add that we do ourselves and our posterity a great disservice by not looking more closely at the man-made and freely chosen economic and political policies and structures that we put in place, which create the total individual, social, legal, economic, and political context in which we all live.

Without negating or denigrating any progress that has been made to date, if we look clearly and carefully at our current economic policies and political structures we may conclude that we cannot reach utopia on earth, but I think we will also realize that we can sure do a whole lot better. To whom much is given, much is required.

Speaking of the African American experience in America, Dr. Samuel DeWitt Proctor, the former pastor of the Abyssinian Baptist Church (succeeding the Reverend and Congressman Adam Clayton Powell, Jr.), said, "I believe that ultimately their experience may be a prophetic precursor to this new human paradigm in the world, one that underlines the absolute equality of all persons. This new paradigm is the fruit of high religion, and the concomitant of true democracy. It will foster the maximum cultivation of all human potential, and celebrate justice, fairness, and compassion. Evidence that such a model of responsible and decent humanity might come into being is shadowy, but the faith that piloted the emancipated slaves remains the substance of things hoped for, and the evidence of things not seen."[2]

Clearly, differing human and freely chosen economic policies and political structures contribute differently—more positively or negatively—to the stated goal and ideal of maximum human development for the maximum amount of people. In our American democracy we must always look carefully at these institutional and structural arrangements, and at these economic and political choices. They were freely chosen and, with leadership, new, more humane, and more just choices can always be made.

For example, religious and politically conservative leaders are fond of quoting Jesus' words about the poor—"The poor you will have with you always"—as a way of maintaining or solidifying their economically privileged place in society, or to justify doing nothing structural or political about the problem of poverty. It is one of the clearest examples of a text being taken out of context. While Jesus may have had the personal will to eradicate hunger and poverty, and even if he had been able to mobilize or organize the broader political will, he did not have the way, the means, to eliminate hunger in his day. That is, there was not the agricultural, scientific, communications, transportation, and other technological means of eliminating hunger and poverty, and sustaining plenty, in Jesus' day. That may have been tragic, but it was not sinful. Today, however, we know how and we have the way, the means, to eradicate hunger, but we lack the political will. That is more than tragic. It is a sin of both omission and commission.

Creating the political will to eradicate poverty will take a combination of spiritual clarity and human determination, along with scientific, skillful, and artful democratic political organizing and planning. Economic power left unregulated—or regulated around principles other than truly putting people and their human betterment first—will always dominate, and it will always dominate for the benefit of a privileged few.

Only people power, or politics—democratically elected representatives functioning in democratically responsive institutions and processes—can bring about economic justice. Only democratically organized people power can put in place the economic policies and political structures for us to best be able to approximate our loftiest goals and achieve our highest ideals.

God works through us in politics and history because God, as Spirit, is able to communicate with our spirit in a variety of ways. A spirit absent the body is a ghost. A body absent the spirit is a cadaver. God's Spirit connects to us through our spirit and "speaks" to us through human channels. Individually, then, God's Spirit communicates with our spirit through our body, psyche, and mind—through the vast physical universe of science, our deep and complex emotional makeup, and our utilized and underutilized intellectual potential. Collectively, God's Spirit communicates with our collective and communal need for justice (our spiritual, moral, and ethical center) through our social, legal, economic, and political institutions, as well as through aesthetics—literature, paintings, sculpture, architecture, music, movies, and other art forms.

At the center of every individual and collective dimension of our lives is the spiritual, moral, and ethical dimension. To the degree that the spiritual and moral dimension is sensitive and just, holistic growth can occur; to the degree that we are insensitive or unjust, our individual and collective growth will be stymied. A strong and good society needs sensitive, fair, and merciful individuals, as well as informed, just, and responsive social, economic, and political institutions.

Unfortunately, too often political conservatives begin (and end) with the individual and his or her personal soul. Equally unfortunate, frequently political liberals and progressives begin (and end) with the social, economic, and political structures, and show less regard for the inner life of the individual. We need both in proper balance.

Clearly, we are all individuals living in a collective context. Our ends can be achieved by a variety of means. Some people, as individuals, can think themselves into a way of acting, while others need the assistance of the collective to act themselves into a way of thinking. For me, strategically, it is the ends—holistic individual lives and economically and politically just democratic institutions—rather than the means of getting there that ought to preoccupy us. Tactically, we need to start where people are and take them to where they need to go.

Whenever the question of God's activity, or the activity of God's servants as actors in history, surfaces—that is, those who feel "led" to speak or act on God's behalf, whether clergy or laity—red flags go up. However, in a democratic society, there is nothing wrong with "religiously called" individuals or groups being active and involved in politics. It is only proper and fitting that they are. Indeed, it is both their religious and their civic duty to be involved! There are dangers, however, and a certain cautionary note is necessary.

While it is perfectly sound and legitimate for religiously motivated individuals or groups to feel "called" by God to achieve some purpose in society or history, when it comes to their input and participation in a multicultural democratic secular society of law, economics, and politics, they must play by the same rules and be held to the same standards, measures, and laws as everyone else. They get no special treatment because they are religious actors, as though others are lesser or merely civic participants.

Caution is also necessary because religion is socially powerful and there has been a history and a current misuse of religion—both in our society and in the world—often resulting in awful human consequences. The Crusades of the Middle Ages used violence to spread Christianity. European missionaries practiced colonialism. The white-minority Dutch Reformed Christian Church of South Africa imposed apartheid on a black majority. Southern Baptists (and other religious individuals and groups North and South) in America gave biblical and theological justification to slavery. The Ku Klux Klan calls itself a Christian organization.

Dr. Martin Luther King, Jr., sent a "Letter from a Birmingham Jail" to white Christian clergy who were not resisting southern racial apartheid, and were challenging his right to do so. Good Christian Founding Fathers declared African Americans to be three-fifths of a person as part of the "original intent" of the U.S. Constitution. Those same founders practiced genocide against Native Americans, stole the land of Mexicans, and denied women the right to vote.

In Congress today, many who call themselves devoutly religious and Christian vote against laws to provide food, health care, housing, jobs, education, and an equal opportunity to millions of Americans who desire these services or have these needs. There is an old Negro spiritual that goes, "Everybody talkin' 'bout Heaven ain't goin' there."

This history of religiously sanctioned, supported, and inspired violence, colonialism, racism, genocide, sexism, and discrimination is why we need to be aware of the issues involved when it comes to "mixing" religion and politics.

For me it comes back to the fact that the greatest religious and moral dilemma of our day is human arrogance and intolerance. That is why I believe that if religion has anything to offer politics beyond a vision of the sacredness of life, the human dignity of every individual, and a commitment to justice, it is to teach and practice humility and tolerance. The twin diseases of arrogance and intolerance have infected all religions.

Religiously trained or motivated people may have a unique or special understanding of human nature and God, but they must participate in a secular democratic society and politics using the same rules, laws, and constitutional standards as everyone else. They must not be thought of as having a unique or special social, economic, or political understanding or be allowed to play the political or economic game using a different or separate set of rules.

Religious people must be allowed to participate fully and on an equal basis with everyone else, but they must also make their case in the public square just like everyone else. That's where I differed with the pope and the Roman Catholic Church when they banned Father Robert J. Drinan S.J. (D-MA) and other Catholic clergy from serving in public office. I see no reason why anyone, officially religious or nonreligious, should be barred from public office as long as they uphold the Constitution, engage in the science and art of politics in a democratic manner, and obey and uphold the law of the land.

Jesus had a partial answer to the question of mixing religion and politics and church and state. He said: "Render unto Caesar the things that belong to Caesar and unto God the things that belong to God." That was a wonderful answer to a tricky and perplexing question, but it is only partially helpful because he did not tell us "which things belong to Caesar" and "which things belong to God." This, then, is where the public debate over religion and politics begins in a democracy.

The original Constitution was written in 1787 and ratified in 1788; the first ten amendments, the Bill of Rights, were added in 1791. The part of the Bill of Rights that is most important to the "separation of church and state" debate—the rendering unto Caesar and to God that which properly belongs to each—is the First Amendment, and in particular the two religion clauses of the First Amendment. These two clauses deal precisely with the issue of what government can and cannot do with respect to religion.

The establishment clause makes up the first ten words of the First Amendment, and reads: "Congress shall make no law respecting an establishment of religion. . . ." The free exercise clause makes up the next six words of the Amendment, which are: "or prohibiting the free exercise thereof."

Together, these clauses constitute two sides of the same coin and comprise the most specific statement in the Constitution about the powers of the federal government over religion. The framers of the Constitution gave us maximum freedom on this question—by neither permitting the establishment of an official religion nor prohibiting anyone from worshiping freely in a manner of their choosing—which allows us to advance the debate even farther. It is interesting to note that both clauses are phrased in the negative—that is, they describe what the federal government cannot do with respect to religion. It cannot establish or tilt the government to officially support any religion; and it cannot prohibit a people from worshiping as they understand or wish.

Broadly speaking, two schools of thought grew up around these "religion clauses." Conservative interpreters are generally known as accommodationists. Liberal interpreters are usually referred to as separationists.

The accommodationists believe that the Constitution gives government the power to regulate some aspects of religion. It just cannot establish an official religion or a national church. The separationists believe that the Constitution gives government no power to establish any religious belief or practice by law and that the First Amendment bans all types of interference with religion. I am philosophically aligned with the separationists.

Religious and political conservatives often argue that "God and the Bible have been expelled from the public classrooms of America." They claim that "secular humanism" is the "new religion" in our public schools. I have heard them preach and teach, "When God, the Bible, and the Ten Commandments were taken out of our public schools, guns, drugs, violence, sexual promiscuity, teen pregnancy, and AIDS went in." In an era of "soundbite" politics and simplistic analyses, such statements may sound plausible to an unsuspecting public. But there are also some hidden, not-so-hidden, and underlying politics here.

It was mainly southern conservatives who initially postulated this direct link between a Supreme Court decision in the early 1960s that upheld the constitutional principle of separation of church and state with regard to prayer in school, and the issue of crime and violence. It was the same Supreme Court that in 1954 ordered an end to racial segregation in our public schools in *Brown*, which initially mainly affected federal enforcement of de jure segregation in the South. These political conservatives deliberately linked, subliminally, prayer out of public schools with desegregation in public schools—throwing in crime, violence, drugs, sexual promiscuity, and teen pregnancy in our public schools for good measure. And the linkage of "prayer out and decadence in" is completed when the media constantly projects people of color, the victims of segregation, as the main perpetrators of such social decadence.

The South has a history of sexual fears relative to black males and white females coming closer together, especially a fear of what might happen if our children go to public school together. That is one of the psychological undercurrents in the political opposition to school desegregation. White politicians also sometimes use the rhetoric of crime and violence as subliminal code words for blacks, to gain votes. Southerners George Bush and Al Gore, since they both know the region's hot-button issues, from my point of view, were playing racial politics with the death penalty in the 2000 campaign. Governor Bush's death penalty killing spree in Texas, which made him a virtual state-sponsored serial killer, had the subliminal effect of a racial political appeal for the purpose of gaining votes, as Gore said nothing. And Gore's proposed victims' rights amendment, adding ten thousand new prosecutors and fifty thousand new police, and wanting to be the enforcement president was just a new form of the original Willie Horton appeal of 1988.

When the openly hostile and sometimes violent mass resistance to Brown in the South died down and went North (for example, to Boston), and the issue became politicized throughout the country, this religious nomenclature of resistance became national. We sometimes forget or overlook the time frame (and possible racial motive involved) when these religious issues and catchphrases were developed. These so-called religious concerns over public education were being raised mainly in the South, then spread to the North as the North too was affected by the *Brown* decision.

All of this may have been purely coincidental, but viewing American history through the eyes of the African American experience could lead us to conclude otherwise. It may be deliberately political. The timing and connection by religious and political conservatives of these two Supreme Court decisions—desegregation and separation of church and state—and politically linking them to social issues like school prayer, posting the Ten Commandments, crime, drugs, and violence seems more than coincidental. It appears to be part of a continuing, calculated, and deliberate conservative political strategy of resistance to school desegregation, societal integration, and the building of a more just and perfect Union. It is aided by a media-enforced white stereotype of blacks, crime, sex, and drugs. This approach to maintaining economic and political power is in keeping with conservative southern history and tradition. The history is of an elite economic, religious, and political leadership that uses conservative social issues—and the South's large conservative religious community as a political base—for preserving the status quo of southern economic injustice. It retains in power an elite group of politically conservative leaders who maintain, through the law, its economic privilege.

Religious and political conservatives (and sometimes liberals) may misuse religion and abuse politics, but there is a proper role and constitutionally protected relationship between religion, education, and our public schools. The law does permit certain forms of religious instruction that are both educationally sound and constitutionally legal.

The church–state question is not new in U.S. history. Prior to public education in America, organized education was religious education. Thus, prayer, Bible reading, memorizing the Ten Commandments, and early-morning devotions were seen as a normal and natural part of the school curriculum and a regular part of classroom activities. This pattern rather naturally continued with the creation of the public schools.

The relationship of religion and education was brought to a head, however, with the development of the public education system in the 1800s, which was almost exclusively established in the industrial North. Religion in the public schools was always a contentious issue, because it involved the place of religious values and convictions in a public institution that now welcomed children of all faiths or of no faith.

Questions involving different religious faiths and practices often led to severe conflicts. In Philadelphia, for example, full-scale riots and bloodshed erupted in the 1840s over which translation of the Bible should be used in classroom devotions. Cincinnati was sharply divided by the "Bible War" in the 1870s. Many Americans came to realize that interfaith harmony and community goodwill could best be realized by keeping public schools neutral on religious questions.

Immigration at the turn of the twentieth century added to the religious diversity of American society. The Protestant orientation of the religious instruction in public schools offended many of these newly arriving Roman Catholics. In the late 1940s, attacks on the First Amendment and calls for public aid to parochial education led to the founding of the organization Americans United for Separation of Church and State (now just Americans United). However, it was not until the year of their official founding, 1947, that the Supreme Court in *Everson v. Board of Education* applied the Constitution's establishment clause to the states—that "Congress shall make no law respecting an establishment of religion"—through the Fourteenth Amendment's due process clause.

The state of New York tried to circumvent this decision by creating a "nonsectarian" prayer. But in 1962 in *Engel v. Vitale*, the Supreme Court ruled that, "the state could not compose an official prayer and that aid to all religions was as impermissible as aid to any one religion. The voluntary nature of student observance was also found immaterial. Compulsion was not a necessary component of an Establishment Clause."[3]

In 1963, the Court in *Abington School District v. Schempp* (which also jointly decided the *Madalyn Murray v. Curlett* case) disallowed the common practice of beginning each day of school with a prayer or devotional Bible reading. The Court said that the weakness in *Engel* was not primarily the nature or author of the prayer, but that the prayer's primary purpose was to advance the cause of religion through a public institution—public education. To drive home the point about the timing of the connection between desegregation and prayer in public schools, Representative L. Mendell Rivers, the former arch-segregationist from Mississippi, accused the Court of "legislating—they never adjudicate—with one eye on the Kremlin and the other on the NAACP."[4] Thus, politically, Rivers was connecting a conservative religious appeal to "Godless communism" and white racism.

The argument that reciting the Lord's Prayer and Bible reading fulfilled the secular purposes of promoting moral values and diminishing materialism was also rejected by the Court. However, the Court emphasized that studying about religion and reading the Bible as part of a secular program of education was acceptable. In fact, in its 1963 Bible-reading decision, the justices maintained that a student's education is not complete without instruction on the influence of religion on history, culture, and literature. Also, for the first time, the Court spelled out an establishment clause "test," which said that legislation must have "a secular legislative purpose and a primary effect that neither advances nor inhibits religion."[5]

Justice Tom Clark, representing the court, wrote in *Schempp:* "Nothing that we have said here indicates that such study of the Bible or of religion, when presented objectively as part of a secular program of education, may not be effected consistent with the First Amendment." Justice Clark also argued that the government may not establish a "religion of secularism," in the sense of actively opposing or showing hostility toward religion.

This has consistently been the Court's ruling. The state of Kentucky posted the Ten Commandments in public classrooms, but in 1980 the Court ruled against it in *Stone v. Graham*. Alabama's "moment of silence" law was found unconstitutional in *Wallace v. Jaffree* in 1985. Note the southern origin of all of these religion cases.

Consistent with this legal path, the Court in *Widmar v. Vincent* (1981) held that if state university facilities were available to a wide variety of student groups, they must also be available to student organizations with a religious orientation. Shortly thereafter, in 1984, Congress passed the Equal Access Act, which applied *Widmar* to public high schools. This law said that any school receiving federal funds that allowed non-school-related student groups to meet on campus beyond regular school hours created what it called a "limited open forum." Therefore, the school could not deny other student groups equal access because of their religious, political, or philosophical views. The Court upheld Congress's equal access law in *Board of Education v. Mergens* (1990), which permitted student groups wishing to read and discuss the Bible, share Christian fellowship, or pray together to use school facilities. The Court interpreted the equal access principle as neither endorsing nor disapproving of religion. "Essentially, the court distinguished between 'government speech endorsing religion, which the establishment clause forbids, and private speech endorsing religion, which the Free Speech and Free Exercise clauses protect.'"[6]

The Supreme Court has consistently ruled that the home, family, and private religious institutions are the appropriate places to make religious decisions and give students personal religious guidance and instruction, not the government or institutions of government, like our public schools. Justice Clark concluded in *Schempp:* "The place of religion in our society is an exalted one, achieved through a long tradition of reliance on the home, the church and the inviolable citadel of the individual heart and mind. We have come to recognize through bitter experience that it is not within the power of government to invade that citadel, whether its purpose or effect be to aid or oppose, to advance or retard.

In the relationship between man and religion, the State is firmly committed to a position of neutrality." While there are some difficult church–state issues that remain to be solved, the Court has not been hostile to religion.

For example, according to Americans United, these court decisions mean that, in practice, students in our public schools may use the Bible or other religious books as resources in teaching about religion; schools may offer elective courses in the Bible as literature and history; they may offer objective instruction in comparative religion; students may study the history of religion and its role in the story of civilization; teachers may utilize historic documents such as the Declaration of Independence that contain references to God; students may voluntarily sing the national anthem and other patriotic songs that contain assertions of faith in God; instructors may refer to faith in God in connection with patriotic ceremonies if participation is voluntary; children may be released for religious instruction off school premises; reading the Bible or other religious literature during a student's free time at school is permitted; and students may pray voluntarily and silently anytime they wish. All of these do not violate the principle of separation of church and state.

Again, according to Americans United, the Court has prohibited schools and teachers from doing the following: using compulsory attendance laws to impose religious worship or instruction on children; providing compulsory reading from the Bible as part of a devotional activity or religious service; requiring or encouraging students to recite prayers; teaching a "religion of secularism" any more than they may teach a theistic religion; composing or sanctioning official prayers for recitation in school; offering sectarian instruction in school classrooms during school hours; promoting, organizing, or recording student attendance at sectarian instruction, even though it is offered off school premises; sponsoring or encouraging the distribution of religious literature on school premises; giving academic credit for off-campus religious instruction; erecting permanent religious symbols in classrooms or posting religious scriptures on classroom walls in a way that suggests advocacy of a particular religion.

Most religious denominations and organizations, with wide-ranging biblical and theological differences—Protestants, Roman Catholics, Jews, and Muslims—have supported Supreme Court separation of church and state decisions through formal votes in their denominational meetings and through statements issued by their ecclesiastical bodies. These general guidelines are perceived by most informed Americans as fair. They preserve the freedom of conscience of each individual student, parent, and public school employee.

Yet there is a conservative movement of religious and political leaders, both inside and outside Congress, who are out to destroy this delicate balance, a balance that has, thus far, been achieved with great sensitivity and careful legal thought.

The private and Christian school movement in the South is primarily sponsored by southern Protestant churches—and most were formed originally to avoid desegregation in the public schools. Private elementary and secondary schools are overwhelmingly religious and sectarian in nature, including 60 percent of all private schools that are Roman Catholic, mostly in the North. In recent years these northern Catholics have been joined by southern and northern evangelical Protestants, to some degree, both black and white.

Private religious schools certainly have every right to exist, are legal, and are making a rich contribution to the education of America's children. Private religious schools are exercising their legitimate right of free expression. I graduated from two of them. However, private religious schools do not have the right to double-tax the American people by forcing taxpayers to pay for public schools, where all children may attend, and then asking taxpayers to pay a second time for a voucher for private schools where only some people of a certain faith or similar beliefs may attend.

Virginia's Reverend Pat Robertson has regularly attacked the public schools and called on the public to give tax dollars to aid private religious schools, and has insisted in the past that "the Constitution says nothing about the separation of church and state." He's had second thoughts about the Black Muslims getting such money since Bush introduced his Faith-based Initiative program. Robertson, a Yale Law School graduate, is not ignorant of the law or the meaning of the Constitution. Despite the Pat Robertsons of the world, it is still clear that most Americans want to preserve a nonsectarian public school system. But given the number of ideologically conservative and states' rights justices currently on the Supreme Court—including the only African American, Justice Clarence Thomas—it would be wise for us to keep a sharp and watchful eye on the Court as future church–state issues come before it.

Beyond constitutional wording and interpretation, there are two critical concepts and propositions that need further clarification. Conservatives like to cloud the difference between "religion and politics" and "church and state." Religion and politics cannot be separated. The religious and ethical demands of justice will always and inevitably bring challenges to the political order. On the other hand, church and state should never be joined. For example, one of the biggest obstacles to ending southern slavery was its religious endorsement and the moral support it enjoyed among most of the religious communities in the South.

The Reverend Dr. Martin Luther King, Jr.'s, application of religion to politics (civil rights and the Vietnam War), and the Reverend Dr. William Sloane Coffin, Jr.'s, religious challenge to the war in Vietnam while chaplain at Yale University, and his later commitment to the SANE/Nuclear Freeze Campaign, are good examples of people who properly "mixed" religion and politics but did not cross the line of "intertwining" church and state.

Religion, which gives people spiritual security in God, and nationalism, a political concept that gives economic, social, and political security, are the two most powerful forces in the world to unleash on the human personality. That's why both religion and politics must be handled carefully and responsibly.

My father, the Reverend Jesse L. Jackson, is an ordained Baptist minister and clergyman who has been involved in religion and politics virtually all his adult life, even running for president of the United States on two different occasions. While he enjoys wide public support among many people, he has also been severely criticized by religious and political conservatives for "mixing religion and politics." However, he has consistently made this important distinction between "religion and politics" and "church and state."

For him the application of religion to politics has meant that the justice demands of his religion inevitably led him into the political arena in order to make our democracy a more just society. He is not a politician who is covertly using religion as a means of achieving his political ends. He has pointed out repeatedly that his religion has made him political—for instance, trying to feed hungry people inevitably led him to agricultural policy and the Agriculture Department—unlike some "family values" conservative politicians whose politics have made them "religious." He has never had any intention or desire to cross the constitutional line separating church and state.

Religion, morality, ethics, and politics should not, indeed cannot, be separated. At the center and core of every political policy debate are religious, spiritual, and moral dimensions of what is right, what is fair, what is equal, what is humane.

The only real issue of concern here is the need to protect the constitutional rights of all Americans to freely practice the religion of their choice, or to practice no religion at all. This obligates us to protect the legal doctrine of the separation of church and state. The essence of the Judeo-Christian religion and tradition, which is shared universality by all major religions of the world, is to love God and your neighbor, who is everyone and everywhere in the world; and to be good stewards and co-creators with God in leaving the world a better place in which to live than when we entered it. This religious mandate should be carried out in the world of democratic politics, properly executed, and within the bounds of the Constitution.

The religion and politics question also raises the issue of whether there can or should be a distinction made between our personal ethics and our public morality. There is no doubt that our personal ethics and our public morality should be as close together as is humanly possible. As a congressman, I am a public servant, not a perfect servant. Neither religionists nor politicians should be self-righteous or hypocritical. Having said that, however, we should not at all be confused about distinguishing between the two. In a secular democratic society, I am very clear that it is far better for us to be well governed by sinners than to be misgoverned by saints.

The interplay of religion and politics also demands that our "means and ends" should be as consistent as is humanly possible. I was disturbed by a statement made in Washington in 1997 in *The Hill* newspaper by Ralph Reed. The former executive director of Pat Robertson's Christian Coalition and founder of Centuries Strategies remarked regarding his style of politics: "I want to be invisible. I do guerrilla warfare. I paint my face and travel at night. You don't know it's over until you're in a body bag."

Advocating such a political style of secretive, clandestine means is not the way genuine religiously motivated and mature people should function and achieve their ends in a democratic society. I've studied some literature and I know about "Onward Christian Soldiers" hidden in Trojan horses. We should be aware and wary of letting any more Trojan horses enter Troy. Such secret and hidden soldiers need to be exposed and burned with the cleansing rays of sunlight.

One of the most troubling and explosive current religious and political issues involving both personal ethics and public policy is abortion. Probably no other issue so confuses the American people with regard to "religion and politics" and "church and state" as the issue of abortion. Make no mistake about it, abortion is a morally difficult and religiously troubling issue. Abortion is both a moral, spiritual, and religious issue, as well as a legal public policy and political issue.

It is perfectly legitimate and proper to mix religion and politics by teaching and preaching against abortion in the church, and speaking and marching about it in the public square. Religious leaders should feel free to argue that abortion is a sin and immoral. This is legitimate religious, personal, and public persuasion directed at the political order.

I exercise those same rights when I advocate against the death penalty, which I see as a moral and religious issue as well. I am morally and religiously opposed to the death penalty, but it's legal in America—the only industrial democracy in the world to have the death penalty—and the current public consensus is clearly against my position. I will need to continue to work within the current legal framework and political climate to try to persuade, over time, the public, Congress, and the Supreme Court to see it a different way—my way. The point is, we must always be careful to separate church and state by not imposing our personal, moral, and religious convictions on others through a public policy, a law, or a constitutional interpretation while there are legitimate religious, rational, and scientific differences on the issue—and, in a democracy, no public consensus.

From a religious or moral point of view, some Americans see abortion as immoral. However, the majority do not see it that way. Plus, in America, under constitutional guidelines, abortion is legal. That is why the choice should be left to an individual's personal conscience rather than having the government impose a collective choice on the individual—which is anti-choice. Humility and tolerance are necessary around such a highly charged and important issue.

We live under a Constitution and on January 22, 1973, the Supreme Court held in *Roe v. Wade* that abortion, under certain conditions, is legal. Even if I disagreed with that decision —which I don't—as a member of Congress I am sworn to uphold the Constitution, not my personal conscience or views.

Some taxpayers will argue that their religious convictions are being violated because they don't want their public tax dollars going to pay for poor people's abortions. However, living under a republican and democratic representative form of government doesn't give taxpayers this individual choice. John Q. Public may not want his tax dollars spent on a missile defense system, but if a majority of Congress votes for it and the president signs it into law, that missile defense system will go forward regardless of John Q. Public's religious convictions. In a representative democracy, we don't have a specific choice of how our individual tax dollars are to be spent collectively. Such spending is done within a legal framework by our elected political representatives. If we don't like their choices and priorities, we can try to vote them out of office, change choices, and get new priorities—as the public has done with respect to using federal dollars to pay for abortions.

While as a taxpayer, I disagree with not being able to use federal dollars to pay for abortions if poor or military women voluntarily make that choice, that's the current law and there is nothing this taxpayer can do about it except continue to fight, within the law, to change the law. I *know* the Supreme Court has said abortions are legal, therefore I *believe* if abortions are legal for everyone they should be available to anyone. No one should be denied equal protection under the law merely because they are poor or in the military.

Getting beyond the traditional and stereotypical language, I am both pro-choice and pro-life. The real question is whether we see women as whole and equal human beings who can be trusted with the freedom to make their own responsible choices. I believe that abortion is just one (the latest controversial example) of the many choices in life that women must be trusted and respected to make. My pro-choice and pro-life stance also supports legislation and programs that will contribute to the quantity and quality of a baby's, a child's, a young person's, a teenager's, an adult's, and an older person's entire life. To me, that's the real pro-choice and pro-life position!

Pro-choice is not a pro-abortion position. Being an advocate of choice is not the equivalent of urging women to have abortions. Choosing to have a child, advocating abstinence until marriage, choosing to appropriately educate boys and girls about sex, and teaching young people how to avoid getting pregnant in the first place are all pro-choice and pro-life positions.

The politically conservative position of opposition to legal abortions is anti-choice—and often anti-life. Not only do the conservative anti-choice people and their congressional representatives oppose the choice of abortion for women, but once a baby is born they're often against virtually everything that would actually give that person a decent quality of life: jobs, minimum and livable wages, workers' rights, equal opportunity, worker safety, comprehensive and universal health care, affordable housing, a high-quality public education, protection of the environment, Head Start, Women Infants and Children (WIC), school breakfast and lunch programs, sex education, due process, Social Security, Medicare, Medicaid. And after having ignored our youth for most of their early years, if they get in trouble as teenagers or young adults, these same conservatives are usually the strongest advocates of lock-'em-up-at-any-cost law and order and the death penalty. And all of these conservative positions are most pronounced in the religiously saturated politics of the eleven former Confederate States of the South!

The same conservatives who are most strongly for getting the government off their backs and defending individual economic rights want the government involved in the most intimate and personal rights of a woman's life. But that's the same politics southern conservatives played relative to states' rights and slavery. The South was for states' rights to protect the institution of slavery, but when the slaves escaped North they wanted the strong arm of the federal government to powerfully enforce the Fugitive Slave Law to get their slaves back. Using a political double standard is nothing new to southern Democratic and Republican conservatives.

From a Judeo-Christian perspective, abortion is a very sensitive issue. If you believe, as I do, that human life is sacred and that human life must be protected, abortion is a very troubling issue. It forces a moral confrontation and a political choice between two powerful and valid claims: a fetus or potential human being's right to life versus a women's right to choose. But it is a very tough and very sensitive issue for virtually all women as well. Most women are hardly casual about it. In the end, we must respect those who disagree morally, religiously, and scientifically and allow women to make responsible individual and personal choices. As a man I can't have a baby, so I don't know how I would feel as a woman or what decision I would make. That's why I have to see women as fully grown and equal adults who are responsible human beings capable of making good judgments about their own lives—and trust and respect a woman's choice.

Homosexuality is another hot-button issue in America today that involves "religion and politics" and "church and state" issues. Gay and lesbian rights is an area that confuses the American people when it comes to personal morality and public policy. Many Americans see the gay and lesbian lifestyle exclusively in religious and moral terms. They may or may not be right, but they certainly have the moral, religious, constitutional, and legal right to see it that way. This issue has one level of complexity if the lifestyle is a matter of personal choice. It becomes much more complicated if genetics plays a significant role in whether a person "chooses" a gay or lesbian lifestyle or not.

But there are also legal and constitutional issues at stake. I voted to uphold my oath of office to defend the Constitution and to support equal protection under the law for all Americans by voting "no" on the so-called Defense of Marriage Act in 1996. This was a law proposed by an ultraconservative southern Republican, Bob Barr (R-GA), that said, "no State, territory, or possession of the United States or Indian tribe shall be required to give effect to any marriage between persons of the same sex under the laws of any other such jurisdiction or to any right or claim arising from such relationship." It also established a federal definition of "marriage" as "only a legal union between one man and one woman as husband and wife"; and "spouse" as "only a person of the opposite sex who is a husband or wife."

I argued that public policy and the law should not be used to discriminate against people in the civic arena, including gays and lesbians, in the areas of banking, bankruptcy, civil service, consumer credit, copyright, education, federal lands and resources, housing, immigration, judiciary, labor, military, Social Security, taxation, veterans, and the Soldiers and Civil Relief Act, which were the areas of federal law to be affected by this bill.

In effect, this bill denied gay men and lesbian women hospital visitation rights, health coverage, and other forms of insurance, inheritance, and taxation rights; government benefits for spouses; immigration rights for spouses; and other rights. I thought that just as the states should not interfere in any way with religious ceremonies, religious groups should not govern who receives a civil marriage license.

The issue was not what anyone personally believes morally or religiously about whether marriage is sacred or not. I happen to believe that marriage is both a sacred religious act and a legal civil act. However, moral and religious views should remain with individuals and with religious institutions. But whether or not public policy and the civil law should be used to discriminate against people because of their sexual orientation and private conduct is a constitutional and legal question. I said that I did not believe the civil law should be used to discriminate in such matters.

I thought the so-called Defense of Marriage Act was a mean-spirited homophobic bill, politically motivated and designed by conservative Republicans as a "social wedge issue" to divide the American people by diverting their attention from real economic problems and solutions that would actually help defend the family, such as full employment, comprehensive and universal health care, affordable housing, and a high-quality public education.

I also voted "no" because Article IV, Clause One, of the Constitution, the full faith and credit clause, says that each state must fully recognize the acts and proceedings of other states—and never once has Congress implemented laws allowing states not to recognize certain "Acts, Records and Judicial Proceedings" of another state. In fact, Congress had heightened each state's recognized responsibilities under the clause by enacting several pieces of legislation: the Parental Kidnapping Prevention Act of 1990, which required states to enforce, not ignore, other states' child custody determinations; the Full Faith and Credit for Child Support Orders of 1994, requiring other states to enforce and not turn a blind eye to child support determinations of other states; and the Safe Homes for Women Act, which also required states to recognize the orders of other states to protect victims of domestic violence. Why then was Congress singling out Hawaii's laws relative to civil unions between gays and lesbians to treat constitutional law differently? I thought the answer was obvious. It was the usual perversion and misinformation campaign, followed by the political exploitation of an emotionally charged and religious hot button social issue spearheaded by southern economic conservatives.

Thus, the same conservative people who fight against increasing the minimum wage, which would help stabilize marriages financially; the same ones who are cutting domestic programs designed to help stabilize families; the same conservative congresspeople who say they support states' rights and local control; who almost always oppose the idea that "we here in Washington know better than the local people how they ought to behave"; these same conservatives were now supporting "outside interference by the Big Federal Government" or what they are always opposed to almost everywhere else. It was hypocritical, homophobic, wrong, discriminatory, and unconstitutional—and I voted against them.

The covert nature of religious and tax-exempt organizations, and their illegal use for political purposes, are two of the biggest problems perpetuated by many of the conservative organizations on the political right. That is what got the Christian Coalition in trouble with the IRS, and it is also what got former Speaker of the House Newt Gingrich in trouble with the law and the Congress—for which he had to pay thousands of dollars in fines.

The conservative religious right's representatives in Congress—consistent with the spirit of covertly using "religion" to achieve their political ends—often try to introduce deceptive patriotic- and religious-sounding stealth legislation that violates the Constitution's establishment clause of the separation of church and state. By "stealth legislation" I mean legislation that deliberately uses words and symbols that sound good, but are meant to deceive or hide the true intent or content of the legislation.

The following pieces of legislation, at various times, have been proposed in the U.S. Congress or elsewhere. The bills may sound great and appear innocent, until you look at the substance. Then you often discovers that they violate the Constitution's separation of church and state.

> **VOUCHERS.** Conservatives in the U.S. Congress frequently propose legislative measures that would divert millions of dollars from the federal treasury into religious, parochial, and sectarian schools. Also, in many state legislatures across the country, bills have been introduced to fund private sectarian educational institutions. Currently, the most popular form of such "parochiaid" is vouchers. Vouchers violate the constitutional principle of separation of church and state because they provide public funding for religious education.

> **CHARITABLE CHOICE.** Former Senator John Ashcroft (R-MO), now Bush's attorney general, created a new piece of legislation that he termed Charitable Choice. The only problem is that it violates the principle of separation of church and state by allowing "pervasively sectarian" institutions, including churches and other houses of worship, to receive direct federal funding to administer social services and public health benefits on behalf of the government. President Bush calls this program his Faith-based Initiative, which could open the door to federal regulation of religion.

> Unlike Catholic Charities, a separate secular legal entity organized by the Roman Catholic Church that receives federal funds to provide public social services on a nondiscriminatory basis, Bush's Faith-based Initiative does not require religious organizations to create separate organizations. It directly funds sectarian religious organizations. Bush's publicly financed plan also does not outlaw proselytizing while providing social services. And despite federal financing, his proposal permits religious groups to discriminate in hiring on religious grounds.

> Additionally, the Charitable Choice legislation would adversely affect the religious mission of houses of worship by funding social services that may already be performed with voluntary contributions. Many religious institutions have a religious mission to provide social services to their communities with the voluntary contributions of their membership. Such

contributions would likely diminish if the religious institution can receive public dollars to provide such services. This would make the religious institution dependent on the government for money.

> **THE AMERICAN COMMUNITY RENEWAL ACT.** Representative J. C. Watts, a conservative black Republican from Oklahoma, introduced the American Community Renewal Act on March 12, 1997. It proposed to amend the IRS Code to allow HUD to provide financial assistance for the renewal and economic development of poor urban and rural communities, but included both the Charitable Choice language and a voucher program. These two sections clearly violate the principle of separation of church and state. It also made sectarian religious organizations eligible to participate in the program on the same basis as any other nonprofit private organization.

> **THE RELIGIOUS FREEDOM CONSTITUTIONAL AMENDMENT.** On May 8, 1997, Representative Ernest Istook, also a Republican conservative from Oklahoma, introduced the so-called Religious Freedom Amendment. This "school prayer and public funding of religious institutions" amendment was introduced in the House with more than 130 cosponsors.

One of the top priorities of the conservative religious right is to amend the First Amendment of the U.S. Constitution in order to destroy the founding principle of separation of church and state. This proposed constitutional amendment would obliterate the separation of church and state and result in government-sanctioned worship, taxation to benefit religion, and majoritarian oppression. This amendment is an unnecessary and dangerous assault to the religious liberty enjoyed in this country. Changing the First Amendment is a radical step that has never been done in the more than two-hundred-year history of the Bill of Rights. Yet this resolution would have gutted the First Amendment's religious freedom protections.

> **PARENTAL RIGHTS LEGISLATION.** The conservative religious right has mounted a new stealth campaign they are calling parental rights, which will destroy public education and break down the wall between church and state. This misleading legislation has been introduced in Congress, as well as in myriad state legislatures. Under this broadly written and vague legislation, any parent of a public school student would be allowed to file a lawsuit against the local public school challenging almost every aspect of the school's curriculum. Parents could argue, and then sue, over every test, homework assignment, and school program. They could sue to have books, materials, or educational programs removed from the classroom.

For example, parents who disagree with the science of evolution could sue to have such materials altered or completely removed and have them replaced with religion-affiliated dogma. This would permit one parent's personal or religious views to supersede the education of the rest of the public school's students. The "parental rights" movement is a mask for the voucher movement.[7]

Religiously motivated American citizens should be involved with God as co-creators trying to build a more perfect Union for all Americans. But these are just some of the dangers associated with not clearly understanding the difference between mixing religion and politics and separating church and state.

Like Dr. Martin Luther King, Jr., I can say that at the center of my faith is the conviction that in the universe there is a God of power who is able to do abundant things in nature and in history. I too believe in a God who is able to beat back gigantic waves of opposition and to bring low prodigious mountains of evil. For many African Americans, and other Americans, this is a belief born of experience and a faith tested by time.

In the Bible the greatest sin was idolatry—putting something or someone, a false god, above the one true God. So there have always been attempts to substitute by man-centered, thing-centered, or nature-centered gods above the one true God. There is nothing new under the sun in the modern age about that. In the period of the Renaissance, and subsequently in the Age of Reason, the talented gifts of artistic expression and intellectual reasoning of humans were elevated to the stature of God. In the industrial age, the necessity of God was questioned. During the scientific revolution, a belief in the inevitability of progress became the God substitute.

In modern times, the conversion of the economic theories of Karl Marx and Adam Smith into undemocratic economic determinist intellectual and political movements of the left and the right do not suggest that "God is able," but that men and women through the "forces of history" or "market forces" are able. But "man is not able to save himself or the world. Unless he is guided by God's spirit, his new-found scientific power will become a devastating Frankenstein monster that will bring to ashes his earthly life."[8]

In his book *Strength to Love*, in a sermon titled "The Answer to a Perplexing Question," Dr. King says that "human life through the centuries has been characterized by man's persistent efforts to remove evil from the earth."[9] In effect, Dr. King is also posing the question of "religion and politics." He is asking: Is the answer to the human family's quest to build a more perfect Union and a more perfect world in "human effort" or in "letting God do it"? Is human ingenuity or divine goodwill the path to international peace, social and economic justice? It is a question that many religionists and nonreligionists wrestle with daily.

King suggests that sincere and dedicated human effort in the areas of reason, science, invention, agriculture, education, technology, industry, and all humanitarian efforts to eliminate the social evils in the world today must be respected, be encouraged, and continue. But he also warns that unless we recognize our mortal nature, our human limitations, and the presence of sin in the world, we are self-deluded and doomed to failure. Through my own observations of people involved in the civil rights movement, I understand that such human failure and frustration can turn to bitterness, disillusionment, and despair, and even manifest themselves in violence against ourselves, our families, neighbors, or society.

Dr. King wrote, "The second idea for removing evil from the world stipulates that if man waits submissively upon the Lord, in his own good time God alone will redeem the world."[10] Here he contrasts the overly optimistic Renaissance with the overly pessimistic Protestant Reformation with regard to human nature. The Renaissance saw our capacity for good and overlooked our capacity for evil. The Reformation saw our capacity for evil and overlooked our capacity for good, and turned both God and man into absolutes. God was absolutely sovereign with man having no freedom, and man was absolutely helpless and could make no difference in the world.

The overemphasis on human sin and evil led people to give up on this world and instead concentrate on a Christian religion that was otherworldly and that left the troubles of this world behind—concentrating almost exclusively on getting to Heaven after this life, or a "pie in the sky by and by" religion.

This kind of religion has no application of religion to politics. This pessimistic view of religion is otherworldly oriented or, in a modified form, concentrates only on meeting the physical or emotional needs of an affected individual. It seldom, if ever, comes to grips with working to eliminate the underlying systemic social, economic, legal, or political causes that created the individual human need in the first place.

Prayer, in this kind of religion, becomes a substitute for effort and makes a mockery of work. This limited-hope religion is concerned only with the issues of an afterlife, not with the issues of life. This false and heretical Christianity—Christian heretics were not people who did not tell the truth, but those who did not tell the whole truth—creates too rigid a wall of separation between the sacred and the secular, between the human and the divine, between the mortal and the immortal, and between the religious and the political. Dr. King put it this way:

> We must pray earnestly for peace, but we must also work vigorously for disarmament and the suspension of weapon testing. We must use our minds as rigorously to plan for peace as we have used them to plan for war. We must pray with unceasing passion for racial justice, but we must also use our minds to develop a program, organize ourselves into mass nonviolent action, and employ every resource of our bodies and souls to bring an end to racial injustice. We must pray unrelentingly for economic justice, but we must also work diligently to bring into being those social forces that make for a better distribution of wealth within our nation and in the underdeveloped countries of the world. . . . We must learn that to expect God to do everything while we do nothing is not faith, but superstition.[11]

How then do we reconcile the two—human effort and divine guidance? Dr. King says the answer is with two different kinds of faith in God working together—a rigorous intellectual faith that is tough minded (a faith that "believes that"), and a tender faith of the soul that engulfs and commits the whole person to God's will and service (a faith that "believes in"). "So by faith we are saved. Man filled with God and God operating through man bring unbelievable changes in our individual and social lives."[12]

We cannot build a more perfect Union by sheer human will and making New Year's resolutions. Neither can we build a more perfect world merely by calling on God through prayer to change our circumstances and to save us. God, through us, can build a more perfect Union. Through faith we must surrender ourselves to become instruments of God's love, justice, and peace.

"Now faith is the substance of things hoped for, the evidence of things not seen" (Hebrews 11:1). Those in America and around the world who will allow God to work through them in history have this kind of faith, and are held and sustained by this kind of faith.

The Reverend Dr. Samuel DeWitt Proctor argued that:

> Faith in God, faith in their own worth and dignity, and faith in the idea that America's 270 million diverse peoples can cohere in a true community that gives space to ethnic preference, but gives loyalty to the basic values of equality, compassion, freedom and justice. Through the long, winding trail of political fortunes, with a disci-

plined transcendence over movements and individuals who would impede their progress, they have survived every challenge and still press forward toward helping America fulfill a unique and unprecedented role in the history of humankind.

Like millions of other black Americans, I am heir to the faith that was born the day twenty frightened black captives were unloaded at Jamestown in 1619. Their slow, courageous journey from the Dutch slave boat to the present, in the face of unrelenting oppression, is the story of their faith; and therein I believe lies the clue to the answer to today's dilemma.

Faith put steel in their spines to endure physical bondage, and zeal in their souls to prevail against evil; it illumined their minds to keep the vision of a better day, and inspired their hearts to learn and embrace the great human conversation. Faith gave them a sense of eternity, a mystical transcendence that transposed their pain into song and their agony into a durable, resilient quest for complete humanity, the substance of things hoped for.[13]

I have a faith that gives me the courage to believe that the same Constitution that freed the slaves can improve upon our democracy by providing for our right to vote, create and sustain full employment, advance public education, extend health care and affordable housing, sustain the environment, provide equal rights for women, and render taxation fair for all Americans. It is with this faith that I press on, with God's help and guidance, to build a more perfect Union. We can all be instruments of God's love and peace and justice if we will but open and surrender ourselves, and let God work through us.

EPILOGUE

How do we as a nation go about fulfilling the Constitution's proclamation "to build a more perfect Union?" It can't be accomplished through fifty separate and unequal states. Nor through 3,067 separate and unequal counties; nor local control of thousands more separate and unequal cities. Building thousands of separate and unequal health care and educational systems won't work. Nor can a multilayered approach provide a clean, safe, and sustainable environment, or solve the affordable housing crisis. And if we rely on a similar approach to creating a tax structure that meets our basic material needs, many will be left behind—especially when one revenue stream comes from an agricultural-based economy, another from an industrial-based economy, a third from a service-based economy, and a final one from an information-based economy.

Common sense tells us it is impossible to build a more perfect Union using the *Plessy v. Ferguson* "separate but equal" model to meet all Americans' basic material needs. Yet it is exactly such a structure that is largely in place today. As a result, only a holistic structural adjustment will provide a high, mandatory, and equal set of standards that each state, county, and local entity must meet. Constitutional amendments are the only way to achieve this.

Why struggle for rights? And why fight for constitutional amendments that embody these rights? Because constitutional rights precede political party platforms and government policies and programs, and constitutional amendments are more enduring. Policies, programs, budgets, personnel, and ideologies ebb and flow according to the political climate of the times. Rights do too, in the sense that judicial interpretations of the law may be broader or narrower at any given time. But constitutional rights are more durable and constant and less subject to political whims.

A More Perfect Union offers a peaceful but revolutionary strategy for meeting the American people's basic civic and material needs by calling for new American rights in the form of eight constitutional amendments. The first ten amendments that comprise the original Bill of Rights are essentially "negative rights"—that is, they properly limit the role of government in order to protect certain individual rights. But I am proposing to balance these negative individual rights with mostly positive individual rights. My amendments affirm the government's role in appropriately satisfying certain material needs and fulfilling basic defined rights.

What I propose constitutes nothing less than a Second American Bill of Rights. Such a bill will establish a framework of positive rights and, in essence, instruct the government's legislative and executive branches to fulfill them. The judicial branch, over time, would interpret and more clearly define each of them.

Some will say that amending the Constitution once, not to mention eight times, takes too long, requires too much energy, and costs too much money—that it's an inefficient stewardship of time and resources.

The answer to the first argument is that the Constitution has been amended twenty-seven times, including seventeen times since the original Bill of Rights was passed. (The Bill of Rights itself required 811 days—from September 25, 1789, to December 15, 1791—for ratification.) Following the initial, usually lengthy struggle to get an amendment through two-thirds of the House and Senate, the time frame for ratifying amendments varies widely. Look at our latest two amendments: The Twenty-sixth Amendment (giving eighteen-year-olds the vote) required one hundred days, whereas the Twenty-seventh Amendment (regarding congressional salaries) took 202 years. The more common time frame ranges from 189 days (the Twelfth Amendment, dealing with the election of the president and vice president) to 1,439 days (the Twenty-second Amendment, presidential tenure).

Once an amendment is passed by two-thirds of the House and Senate, there is no time limit for ratifying it—that is, no seven-year limitation on ratifying amendments, as many people believe. This schedule was arbitrarily placed on the Equal Rights Amendment (and later extended to ten years) and the D.C. Statehood Amendment. Once a state legislature votes for an amendment, that affirmation remains in place, unless a later body reverses it.

How long it takes for my amendments to be passed by House and Senate, and ratified by three-quarters of the state legislatures, will be determined by a combination of political leadership and the will of the American people. If Americans have a strong desire for these rights—have a political fire burning in their bellies—such amendments can be shuttled through the House and Senate and ratified relatively quickly after a legitimate national debate on their substance and implications.

If the political leadership or political will is lacking, obviously, more time will be needed.

And what about the questions of attention and money? My answer is that I do not consider it poor stewardship to fight to establish fundamental rights that will make the lives of all Americans much better; contribute to greater justice; generate trillions of dollars through accelerated balanced economic growth; and save taxpayers trillions of dollars through preemptive preventive action.

There will be naysayers. Conservatives and libertarians may go on the political offensive against these new constitutional rights. And beyond the expected and necessary debates and discussions, reactionary forces will be highly funded to aggressively spread distortions about the amendments and the issues surrounding them. That too will be part of the political struggle.

Another favorite tactic of conservatives is to buy into an issue, agree to a goal, and support a constitutional amendment—then try to change the amendment's language in order to alter its meaning or weaken its impact. I am not married to the particular language of any of the amendments in this book. I wrote them with my best understanding of the issues involved in building a more perfect Union. I am open to improving the specific language of any of them as long as the clear intent and goal of all these amendments remain intact. And since it takes two-thirds of the House and Senate to pass any of them, I feel confident that there are enough members of the House and Senate who share similar values and goals that any attempt to pass them in a diluted form could be stopped.

There are other Americans interested in convening a constitutional convention to dramatically rewrite or overhaul the entire U.S. Constitution. Such a convention is unnecessary and unwarranted. We should add these new amendments to the existing Constitution the way military people earn stripes—one at a time. Our Constitution and its amendments have evolved over two hundred years and provide a good foundation on which to build. Focusing on one amendment at a time allows us to focus our debate on the issues it involves and the ramifications of adding it.

Still others, mostly liberals and progressives who generally support the goals of the amendments, will claim that these amendments are morally right and desirable, but politically utopian and impractical. Obviously, I agree that they are morally sound and politically worthy. I also believe, however, that if they are utopian, they represent a practical political utopia. These rights can be achieved politically, because they represent the American people's values and goals. Further, we have the ability to organize the structures, institutions, and programs necessary to fulfill these rights: We are developed and rich enough as a nation to afford it. Moreover, these amendments will allow us to become even wealthier as a nation into the indefinite future. To make them a reality, we need only rekindle our belief in democratic representative government.

There is also a fear among some progressives that the current Supreme Court and federal judiciary—not to mention the strict constructionists President George W. Bush will try to appoint—is so conservative that even good amendments could turn out bad with the wrong interpretation. The problem with this argument is that the Supreme Court can and sometimes does interpret our Constitution in bad ways; just look at *Dred Scott* and *Plessy*. On the other hand, the 1954 *Brown* decision would not have been possible without the Fourteenth Amendment, ratified in 1868. Constitutional amendments require such a long-term perspective and strategy.

Courts reflect the political climate of the times. Over the last three decades, conservatives have organized to change America's political climate—to some extent by organizing around constitutional amendments they consider fundamental: those that would provide a balanced budget, term limits, a right to life, protection of victims' rights, and voluntary school prayer, to mention just a few. By focusing on these issues and on a strict constructionist interpretation of the Constitution, they have created the current political climate, and the conservative judges elevated to the bench sustain it. Placing the Constitution at the heart of their fight has, in other words, worked for conservatives.

Progressives should organize in a similar way around rights. We must move forward with hope, not in fear. We must be for something positive, not just against the conservatives' negative. We must organize and change the political climate, and I can't think of any better way to do so than by fighting for constitutional amendments that provide fundamental human rights for the American people.

Substantively, adding these human rights amendments to the Constitution will "speed up the day" when the values and goals they represent can be accomplished. Politically, fighting for universal human rights—as opposed to arguing over various philosophies, policies, and programs—maximizes agreement among the American people, and minimizes division. For example, if we argue for a constitutional right to health care for all Americans, most white, African, Asian, Native, and Latino Americans will agree. If we argue over whether medical savings accounts or a single-payer health care plan is the best way to ensure health care for all Americans—then there would be much less unity. With the constitutional right in place, however, the means won't interfere or be confused with the end. Instead Republicans, Democrats, and Independents in Congress would be forced to come up with their best ideas, reconcile their differences, and develop legislation to meet the constitutional standard. And if they fell short, individual Americans would not be left out in the cold. They could go to federal court to have their right to health care enforced.

The fight to ratify these amendments would itself be valuable. Advocating for human rights can unite groups that are fighting for similar goals but use different strategies and tactics. For example, in the African American community, a rights movement and campaign could include the direct-action approach of a RainbowPUSH Coalition of the Reverend Jesse Jackson, the National Action Network of the Reverend Al Sharpton, and the Southern Christian Leadership Conference of Martin Luther King, III; the legal approach of Kweisi Mfume and the NAACP, and the NAACP Legal Defense Fund of attorney Elaine Jones; the research and job placement role played by the National Urban League of Hugh Price; and the educational and social service roles of National Council of Negro Women, the United Negro College Fund, and fraternities and sororities.

While we cannot fight for or achieve all of these rights at once, they should been seen comprehensively. Seeing them together will also allow us to build a political movement that includes diverse and broad-based coalitions both within and among various racially, ethnically, and culturally diverse groups. Political, religious, labor, business, civil rights, women's, health care, housing, education, environmental, voting rights, student, and other civil society groups can work together and cross-fertilize around these amendments in ways they never could around policies and programs, even good ones beneficial to each.

My eight constitutional amendments also set clear, objective, and measurable political and legislative goals. Fighting for specific rights in Congress will help the American people determine where their members of Congress, in the House or Senate, stand with regard to their human rights. It will help separate the political wheat from the chaff, the talkers from the doers, those merely willing to advocate for values and goals from those who are ready to vote for them in a real, concrete way.

Finally, since every human being is political and all human rights are politically determined, *A More Perfect Union* closes with one question that every American should ask her- or himself: Do you know in your mind, feel in your heart, and believe in your soul that you have more than a desire for, but indeed a *human right to* a secure job that pays a livable wage; to high-quality health care; to a high-quality public education; to safe, sanitary, and affordable housing; to equal opportunity; to a clean, safe, and sustainable environment; and to fair or progressive taxes?

We will attain a Second American Bill of Rights in the form of these new constitutional amendments when enough of us can answer "yes" to this question, translate it into political action, and leverage our votes among our political leaders.

Like Dr. Martin Luther King, Jr., I too have a dream. I dream of an America where every citizen votes to adequately fulfill the basic need and human right to employment, education, health care, housing, a clean environment, equal opportunity, and fair taxes. Indeed, I believe that my dream is consistent with, contributes to, and embodies the great American dream.

KEY DATES IN FORMING
THE U.S. CONSTITUTION

The First Continental Congress met in Philadelphia in September 1774 and adopted the Declaration and Resolves of the First Continental Congress, embodying rights and principles later to be incorporated into the Constitution of the United States.

The Declaration of Independence was issued on July 4, 1776.

The Second Continental Congress adopted the Articles of Confederation in November 1777, which the states approved in July 1778.

Upon recommendation of the Continental Congress, a convention of state representatives met in May 1787 to revise the Articles of Confederation and reported to the Continental Congress in September a new Constitution, which the Congress submitted to the states for ratification on September 17, 1787. Nine states—as required by the Constitution for its establishment—had ratified it by June 21, 1788, with eleven states ratifying by July 26, 1788.

The Continental Congress adopted a resolution on September 13, 1788, putting the new Constitution into effect.

The First Congress of the United States convened on March 4, 1789, and George Washington was inaugurated as the first president on April 30, 1789.

Appendix II

THE GETTYSBURG ADDRESS

GIVEN BY PRESIDENT ABRAHAM LINCOLN

November 19, 1863
Gettysburg, Pennsylvania

Four score and seven years ago our fathers brought forth on this continent a new nation, conceived in liberty and dedicated to the proposition that all men are created equal.

Now we are engaged in a great civil war, testing whether that nation or any nation so conceived and so dedicated can long endure. We are met on a great battle field of that war. We have come to dedicate a portion of that field as a final resting place for those who here gave their lives that that nation might live. It is altogether fitting and proper that we should do this.

But in a larger sense, we cannot dedicate, we cannot consecrate, we cannot hallow this ground. The brave men, living and dead who struggled here have consecrated it far above our power to add or detract. The world will little note nor long remember what we say here, but it can never forget what they did here. It is for us the living rather to be dedicated here to the unfinished work which they who fought here have thus far so nobly advanced. It is rather for us to be here dedicated to the great task remaining before us—that we here highly resolve that these dead shall not have died in vain, that this nation under God shall have a new birth of freedom, and that government of the people, by the people and for the people shall not perish from the earth.

UNIVERSAL DECLARATION
OF HUMAN RIGHTS

Adopted and Proclaimed by
General Assembly Resolution 217 A (III)
of 10 December 1948

On December 10, 1948, the General Assembly of the United Nations adopted and proclaimed the Universal Declaration of Human Rights, the full text of which appears in the following pages. Following this historic act the assembly called upon all member countries to publicize the text of the declaration and "to cause it to be disseminated, displayed, read and expounded principally in schools and other educational institutions, without distinction based on the political status of countries or territories."

PREAMBLE

Whereas recognition of the inherent dignity and of the equal and inalienable rights of all members of the human family is the foundation of freedom, justice and peace in the world,

Whereas disregard and contempt for human rights have resulted in barbarous acts which have outraged the conscience of mankind, and the advent of a world in which human beings shall enjoy freedom of speech and belief and freedom from fear and want has been proclaimed as the highest aspiration of the common people,

Whereas it is essential, if man is not to be compelled to have recourse, as a last resort, to rebellion against tyranny and oppression, that human rights should be protected by the rule of law,

Whereas it is essential to promote the development of friendly relations between nations,

Whereas the peoples of the United Nations have in the Charter reaffirmed their faith in fundamental human rights, in the dignity and worth of the human person and in the equal rights of men and women and have determined to promote social progress and better standards of life in larger freedom,

Whereas Member States have pledged themselves to achieve, in co-operation with the United Nations, the promotion of universal respect for and observance of human rights and fundamental freedoms,

Whereas a common understanding of these rights and freedoms is of the greatest importance for the full realization of this pledge,

Now, Therefore THE GENERAL ASSEMBLY proclaims THIS UNIVERSAL DECLARATION OF HUMAN RIGHTS as a common standard of achievement for all peoples and all nations, to the end that every individual and every organ of society, keeping this Declaration constantly in mind, shall strive by teaching and education to promote respect for these rights and freedoms and by progressive measures, national and international, to secure their universal and effective recognition and observance, both among the peoples of Member States themselves and among the peoples of territories under their jurisdiction.

ARTICLE 1.

All human beings are born free and equal in dignity and rights. They are endowed with reason and conscience and should act towards one another in a spirit of brotherhood.

ARTICLE 2.

Everyone is entitled to all the rights and freedoms set forth in this Declaration, without distinction of any kind, such as race, colour, sex, language, religion, political or other opinion, national or social origin, property, birth or other status. Furthermore, no distinction shall be made on the basis of the political, jurisdictional or international status of the country or territory to which a person belongs, whether it be independent, trust, non-self-governing or under any other limitation of sovereignty.

ARTICLE 3.

Everyone has the right to life, liberty and security of person.

ARTICLE 4.

No one shall be held in slavery or servitude; slavery and the slave trade shall be prohibited in all their forms.

ARTICLE 5.

No one shall be subjected to torture or to cruel, inhuman or degrading treatment or punishment.

ARTICLE 6.

Everyone has the right to recognition everywhere as a person before the law.

ARTICLE 7.

All are equal before the law and are entitled without any discrimination to equal protection of the law. All are entitled to equal protection against any discrimination in violation of this Declaration and against any incitement to such discrimination.

ARTICLE 8.

Everyone has the right to an effective remedy by the competent national tribunals for acts violating the fundamental rights granted him by the constitution or by law.

ARTICLE 9.

No one shall be subjected to arbitrary arrest, detention or exile.

ARTICLE 10.

Everyone is entitled in full equality to a fair and public hearing by an independent and impartial tribunal, in the determination of his rights and obligations and of any criminal charge against him.

ARTICLE 11.

(1) Everyone charged with a penal offence has the right to be presumed innocent until proved guilty according to law in a public trial at which he has had all the guarantees necessary for his defense.

(2) No one shall be held guilty of any penal offence on account of any act or omission which did not constitute a penal offence, under national or international law, at the time when it was committed. Nor shall a heavier penalty be imposed than the one that was applicable at the time the penal offence was committed.

ARTICLE 12.

No one shall be subjected to arbitrary interference with his privacy, family, home or correspondence, nor to attacks upon his honour and reputation. Everyone has the right to the protection of the law against such interference or attacks.

ARTICLE 13.

(1) Everyone has the right to freedom of movement and residence within the borders of each state.

(2) Everyone has the right to leave any country, including his own, and to return to his country.

ARTICLE 14.

(1) Everyone has the right to seek and to enjoy in other countries asylum from persecution.

(2) This right may not be invoked in the case of prosecutions genuinely arising from non-political crimes or from acts contrary to the purposes and principles of the United Nations.

ARTICLE 15.

(1) Everyone has the right to a nationality.

(2) No one shall be arbitrarily deprived of his nationality nor denied the right to change his nationality.

ARTICLE 16.

(1) Men and women of full age, without any limitation due to race, nationality or religion, have the right to marry and to found a family. They are entitled to equal rights as to marriage, during marriage and at its dissolution.

(2) Marriage shall be entered into only with the free and full consent of the intending spouses.

(3) The family is the natural and fundamental group unit of society and is entitled to protection by society and the State.

ARTICLE 17.

(1) Everyone has the right to own property alone as well as in association with others.

(2) No one shall be arbitrarily deprived of his property.

ARTICLE 18.

Everyone has the right to freedom of thought, conscience and religion; this right includes freedom to change his religion or belief, and freedom, either alone or in community with others and in public or private, to manifest his religion or belief in teaching, practice, worship and observance.

ARTICLE 19.

Everyone has the right to freedom of opinion and expression; this right includes freedom to hold opinions without interference and to seek, receive and impart information and ideas through any media and regardless of frontiers.

ARTICLE 20.

(1) Everyone has the right to freedom of peaceful assembly and association.

(2) No one may be compelled to belong to an association.

ARTICLE 21.

(1) Everyone has the right to take part in the government of his country, directly or through freely chosen representatives.

(2) Everyone has the right of equal access to public service in his country.

(3) The will of the people shall be the basis of the authority of government; this will shall be expressed in periodic and genuine elections which shall be by universal and equal suffrage and shall be held by secret vote or by equivalent free voting procedures.

ARTICLE 22.

Everyone, as a member of society, has the right to social security and is entitled to realization, through national effort and international co-operation and in accordance with the organization and resources of each State, of the economic, social and cultural rights indispensable for his dignity and the free development of his personality.

ARTICLE 23.

(1) Everyone has the right to work, to free choice of employment, to just and favourable conditions of work and to protection against unemployment.

(2) Everyone, without any discrimination, has the right to equal pay for equal work.

(3) Everyone who works has the right to just and favourable remuneration ensuring for himself and his family an existence worthy of human dignity, and supplemented, if necessary, by other means of social protection.

(4) Everyone has the right to form and to join trade unions for the protection of his interests.

ARTICLE 24.

Everyone has the right to rest and leisure, including reasonable limitation of working hours and periodic holidays with pay.

ARTICLE 25.

(1) Everyone has the right to a standard of living adequate for the health and well-being of himself and of his family, including food, clothing, housing and medical care and necessary social services, and the right to security in the event of unemployment, sickness, disability, widowhood, old age or other lack of livelihood in circumstances beyond his control.

(2) Motherhood and childhood are entitled to special care and assistance. All children, whether born in or out of wedlock, shall enjoy the same social protection.

ARTICLE 26.

(1) Everyone has the right to education. Education shall be free, at least in the elementary and fundamental stages. Elementary education shall be compulsory. Technical and professional education shall be made generally available and higher education shall be equally accessible to all on the basis of merit.

(2) Education shall be directed to the full development of the human personality and to the strengthening of respect for human rights and fundamental freedoms. It shall promote understanding, tolerance and friendship among all nations, racial or religious groups, and shall further the activities of the United Nations for the maintenance of peace.

(3) Parents have a prior right to choose the kind of education that shall be given to their children.

ARTICLE 27.

(1) Everyone has the right freely to participate in the cultural life of the community, to enjoy the arts and to share in scientific advancement and its benefits.

(2) Everyone has the right to the protection of the moral and material interests resulting from any scientific, literary or artistic production of which he is the author.

ARTICLE 28.

Everyone is entitled to a social and international order in which the rights and freedoms set forth in this Declaration can be fully realized.

ARTICLE 29.

(1) Everyone has duties to the community in which alone the free and full development of his personality is possible.

(2) In the exercise of his rights and freedoms, everyone shall be subject only to such limitations as are determined by law solely for the purpose of securing due recognition and respect for the rights and freedoms of others and of meeting the just requirements of morality, public order and the general welfare in a democratic society.

(3) These rights and freedoms may in no case be exercised contrary to the purposes and principles of the United Nations.

ARTICLE 30.

Nothing in this Declaration may be interpreted as implying for any State, group or person any right to engage in any activity or to perform any act aimed at the destruction of any of the rights and freedoms set forth herein.

THE EARTH CHARTER

March 2000

PREAMBLE

We stand at a critical moment in Earth's history, a time when humanity must choose its future. As the world becomes increasingly interdependent and fragile, the future at once holds great peril and great promise. To move forward we must recognize that in the midst of a magnificent diversity of cultures and life forms we are one human family and one Earth community with a common destiny. We must join together to bring forth a sustainable global society founded on respect for nature, universal human rights, economic justice, and a culture of peace. Towards this end, it is imperative that we, the peoples of Earth, declare our responsibility to one another, to the greater community of life, and to future generations.

EARTH, OUR HOME

Humanity is part of a vast evolving universe. Earth, our home, is alive with a unique community of life. The forces of nature make existence a demanding and uncertain adventure, but Earth has provided the conditions essential to life's evolution. The resilience of the community of life and the well-being of humanity depend upon preserving a healthy biosphere with all its ecological systems, a rich variety of plants and animals, fertile soils, pure waters, and clean air. The global environment with its finite resources is a common concern of all peoples. The protection of Earth's vitality, diversity, and beauty is a sacred trust.

THE GLOBAL SITUATION

The dominant patterns of production and consumption are causing environmental devastation, the depletion of resources, and a massive extinction of species. Communities are being undermined. The benefits of development are not shared equitably and the gap between rich and poor is widening. Injustice, poverty, ignorance, and violent conflict are widespread and the cause of great suffering. An unprecedented rise in human population has overburdened ecological and social systems. The foundations of global security are threatened. These trends are perilous—but not inevitable.

THE CHALLENGES AHEAD

The choice is ours: form a global partnership to care for Earth and one another or risk the destruction of ourselves and the diversity of life. Fundamental changes are needed in our values, institutions, and ways of living. We must realize that when basic needs have been met, human development is primarily about being more, not having more. We have the knowledge and technology to provide for all and to reduce our impacts on the environment.

The emergence of a global civil society is creating new opportunities to build a democratic and humane world. Our environmental, economic, political, social, and spiritual challenges are interconnected, and together we can forge inclusive solutions.

UNIVERSAL RESPONSIBILITY

To realize these aspirations, we must decide to live with a sense of universal responsibility, identifying ourselves with the whole Earth community as well as our local communities. We are at once citizens of different nations and of one world in which the local and global are linked. Everyone shares responsibility for the present and future well-being of the human family and the larger living world. The spirit of human solidarity and kinship with all life is strengthened when we live with reverence for the mystery of being, gratitude for the gift of life, and humility regarding the human place in nature.

We urgently need a shared vision of basic values to provide an ethical foundation for the emerging world community. Therefore, together in hope we affirm the following interdependent principles for a sustainable way of life as a common standard by which the conduct of all individuals, organizations, businesses, governments, and transnational institutions is to be guided and assessed.

PRINCIPLES

I. RESPECT AND CARE FOR THE COMMUNITY OF LIFE

1. Respect Earth and life in all its diversity.
   a. Recognize that all beings are interdependent and every form of life has value regardless of its worth to human beings.
   b. Affirm faith in the inherent dignity of all human beings and in the intellectual, artistic, ethical, and spiritual potential of humanity.

2. Care for the community of life with understanding, compassion, and love.
   a. Accept that with the right to own, manage, and use natural resources comes the duty to prevent environmental harm and to protect the rights of people.
   b. Affirm that with increased freedom, knowledge, and power comes increased responsibility to promote the common good.

3. Build democratic societies that are just, participatory, sustainable, and peaceful.
   a. Ensure that communities at all levels guarantee human rights and fundamental freedoms and provide everyone an opportunity to realize his or her full potential.
   b. Promote social and economic justice, enabling all to achieve a secure and meaningful livelihood that is ecologically responsible.

4. Secure Earth's bounty and beauty for present and future generations.
   a. Recognize that the freedom of action of each generation is qualified by the needs of future generations.
   b. Transmit to future generations values, traditions, and institutions that support the long-term flourishing of Earth's human and ecological communities.

In order to fulfill these four broad commitments, it is necessary to:

II. ECOLOGICAL INTEGRITY

5. Protect and restore the integrity of Earth's ecological systems, with special concern for biological diversity and the natural processes that sustain life.
   a. Adopt at all levels sustainable development plans and regulations that make environmental conservation and rehabilitation integral to all development initiatives.
   b. Establish and safeguard viable nature and biosphere reserves, including wild lands and marine areas, to protect Earth's life support systems, maintain biodiversity, and preserve our natural heritage.
   c. Promote the recovery of endangered species and ecosystems.
   d. Control and eradicate non-native or genetically modified organisms harmful to native species and the environment, and prevent introduction of such harmful organisms.
   e. Manage the use of renewable resources such as water, soil, forest products, and marine life in ways that do not exceed rates of regeneration and that protect the health of ecosystems.
   f. Manage the extraction and use of non-renewable resources such as minerals and fossil fuels in ways that minimize depletion and cause no serious environmental damage.

6. Prevent harm as the best method of environmental protection and, when knowledge is limited, apply a precautionary approach.
   a. Take action to avoid the possibility of serious or irreversible environmental harm even when scientific knowledge is incomplete or inconclusive.
   b. Place the burden of proof on those who argue that a proposed activity will not cause significant harm, and make the responsible parties liable for environmental harm.
   c. Ensure that decision making addresses the cumulative, long-term, indirect, long distance, and global consequences of human activities.
   d. Prevent pollution of any part of the environment and allow no build-up of radioactive, toxic, or other hazardous substances.
   e. Avoid military activities damaging to the environment.

7. Adopt patterns of production, consumption, and reproduction that safeguard Earth's regenerative capacities, human rights, and community well-being.
   a. Reduce, reuse, and recycle the materials used in production and consumption systems, and ensure that residual waste can be assimilated by ecological systems.
   b. Act with restraint and efficiency when using energy, and rely increasingly on renewable energy sources such as solar and wind.
   c. Promote the development, adoption, and equitable transfer of environmentally sound technologies.
   d. Internalize the full environmental and social costs of goods and services in the selling price, and enable consumers to identify products that meet the highest social and environmental standards.
   e. Ensure universal access to health care that fosters reproductive health and responsible reproduction.
   f. Adopt lifestyles that emphasize the quality of life and material sufficiency in a finite world.

8. Advance the study of ecological sustainability and promote the open exchange and wide application of the knowledge acquired.
    a. Support international scientific and technical cooperation on sustainability, with special attention to the needs of developing nations.
    b. Recognize and preserve the traditional knowledge and spiritual wisdom in all cultures that contribute to environmental protection and human well-being.
    c. Ensure that information of vital importance to human health and environmental protection, including genetic information, remains available in the public domain.

III. SOCIAL AND ECONOMIC JUSTICE

9. Eradicate poverty as an ethical, social, and environmental imperative.
    a. Guarantee the right to potable water, clean air, food security, uncontaminated soil, shelter, and safe sanitation, allocating the national and international resources required.
    b. Empower every human being with the education and resources to secure a sustainable livelihood, and provide social security and safety nets for those who are unable to support themselves.
    c. Recognize the ignored, protect the vulnerable, serve those who suffer, and enable them to develop their capacities and to pursue their aspirations.

10. Ensure that economic activities and institutions at all levels promote human development in an equitable and sustainable manner.
    a. Promote the equitable distribution of wealth within nations and among nations.
    b. Enhance the intellectual, financial, technical, and social resources of developing nations, and relieve them of onerous international debt.
    c. Ensure that all trade supports sustainable resource use, environmental protection, and progressive labor standards.
    d. Require multinational corporations and international financial organizations to act transparently in the public good, and hold them accountable for the consequences of their activities.

11. Affirm gender equality and equity as prerequisites to sustainable development and ensure universal access to education, health care, and economic opportunity.
    a. Secure the human rights of women and girls and end all violence against them.
    b. Promote the active participation of women in all aspects of economic, political, civil, social, and cultural life as full and equal partners, decision makers, leaders, and beneficiaries.
    c. Strengthen families and ensure the safety and loving nurture of all family members.

12. Uphold the right of all, without discrimination, to a natural and social environment supportive of human dignity, bodily health, and spiritual well-being, with special attention to the rights of indigenous peoples and minorities.
    a. Eliminate discrimination in all its forms, such as that based on race, color, sex, sexual orientation, religion, language, and national, ethnic or social origin.
    b. Affirm the right of indigenous peoples to their spirituality, knowledge, lands and resources and to their related practice of sustainable livelihoods.

    c. Honor and support the young people of our communities, enabling them to fulfill their essential role in creating sustainable societies.

    d. Protect and restore outstanding places of cultural and spiritual significance.

IV. DEMOCRACY, NONVIOLENCE, AND PEACE

13. Strengthen democratic institutions at all levels, and provide transparency and accountability in governance, inclusive participation in decision making, and access to justice.

    a. Uphold the right of everyone to receive clear and timely information on environmental matters and all development plans and activities which are likely to affect them or in which they have an interest.

    b. Support local, regional and global civil society, and promote the meaningful participation of all interested individuals and organizations in decision making.

    c. Protect the rights to freedom of opinion, expression, peaceful assembly, association, and dissent.

    d. Institute effective and efficient access to administrative and independent judicial procedures, including remedies and redress for environmental harm and the threat of such harm.

    e. Eliminate corruption in all public and private institutions.

    f. Strengthen local communities, enabling them to care for their environments, and assign environmental responsibilities to the levels of government where they can be carried out most effectively.

14. Integrate into formal education and life-long learning the knowledge, values, and skills needed for a sustainable way of life.

    a. Provide all, especially children and youth, with educational opportunities that empower them to contribute actively to sustainable development.

    b. Promote the contribution of the arts and humanities as well as the sciences in sustainability education.

    c. Enhance the role of the mass media in raising awareness of ecological and social challenges.

    d. Recognize the importance of moral and spiritual education for sustainable living.

15. Treat all living beings with respect and consideration.

    a. Prevent cruelty to animals kept in human societies and protect them from suffering.

    b. Protect wild animals from methods of hunting, trapping, and fishing that cause extreme, prolonged, or avoidable suffering.

    c. Avoid or eliminate to the full extent possible the taking or destruction of non-targeted species.

16. Promote a culture of tolerance, nonviolence, and peace.

    a. Encourage and support mutual understanding, solidarity, and cooperation among all peoples and within and among nations.

    b. Implement comprehensive strategies to prevent violent conflict and use collaborative problem solving to manage and resolve environmental conflicts and other disputes.

    c. Demilitarize national security systems to the level of a non-provocative defense posture, and convert military resources to peaceful purposes, including ecological restoration.

    d. Eliminate nuclear, biological, and toxic weapons and other weapons of mass destruction.

    e. Ensure that the use of orbital and outer space supports environmental protection and peace.

    f. Recognize that peace is the wholeness created by right relationships with oneself, other persons, other cultures, other life, Earth, and the larger whole of which all are a part.

THE WAY FORWARD

As never before in history, common destiny beckons us to seek a new beginning. Such renewal is the promise of these Earth Charter principles. To fulfill this promise, we must commit ourselves to adopt and promote the values and objectives of the Charter.

This requires a change of mind and heart. It requires a new sense of global interdependence and universal responsibility. We must imaginatively develop and apply the vision of a sustainable way of life locally, nationally, regionally, and globally. Our cultural diversity is a precious heritage and different cultures will find their own distinctive ways to realize the vision. We must deepen and expand the global dialogue that generated the Earth Charter, for we have much to learn from the ongoing collaborative search for truth and wisdom.

Life often involves tensions between important values. This can mean difficult choices. However, we must find ways to harmonize diversity with unity, the exercise of freedom with the common good, short-term objectives with long-term goals. Every individual, family, organization, and community has a vital role to play. The arts, sciences, religions, educational institutions, media, businesses, nongovernmental organizations, and governments are all called to offer creative leadership. The partnership of government, civil society, and business is essential for effective governance.

In order to build a sustainable global community, the nations of the world must renew their commitment to the United Nations, fulfill their obligations under existing international agreements, and support the implementation of Earth Charter principles with an international legally binding instrument on environment and development.

Let ours be a time remembered for the awakening of a new reverence for life, the firm resolve to achieve sustainability, the quickening of the struggle for justice and peace, and the joyful celebration of life.

FOREWORD

1. Clarence Page, "What America Wants to Forget," *Chicago Tribune*, June 13, 2001, p. A27.
2. Audre Lorde, *Sister Outsider* (Freedom, Calif.: Crossing Press, 1984), 115.

CHAPTER 1

1. Professor Pierre deVise's decennial listings of America's richest and poorest communities have been widely reported in national magazines and newspapers for 30 years.

CHAPTER 2

1. He never returned to finish his academic work. In 2000, however, the seminary's board voted to grant my father his master of divinity degree in honor of the totality of his public ministry since leaving CTS.
2. Martin Luther King, Jr., *Strength to Love* (New York: Harper & Row, 1963), p. 110.

CHAPTER 3

1. James M. McPherson, *Battle Cry of Freedom: The Civil War Era* (New York: Oxford University Press, 1988), pp. 149–150.
2. Ibid., p. 151.
3. Kenneth O'Reilly, *Nixon's Piano: Presidents and the Politics of Race from Washington to Clinton* (New York: Free Press, 1995), pp. 370–371.

CHAPTER 4

1. McPherson, *Battle Cry of Freedom*, p. 84.
2. Ibid., pp. 152–153.
3. Ibid., pp. 207–208.
4. Ibid., p. 342.
5. David B. Freeman, *Carved in Stone* (Macon, Ga.: Mercer University Press, 1997). I relied on this book to tell the general story of Stone Mountain. Only direct quotes, however, are footnoted.
6. Ibid., p. 52.
7. Ibid., p. 70
8. Ibid., p. 177.
9. Virginia M. Adams, *On the Altar of Freedom*, edited by Corporal James Henry Gooding (Amherst: University of Massachusetts Press, 1991), p. 118.
10. Ibid., p. 118.
11. John C. Waugh, *Reelecting Lincoln: The Battle for the 1864 Presidency* (New York: Crown Publishing, 1997), p. 5.
12. David Blight, "Healing and History: Battlefields and the Problem of Civil War Memory," Rally on the High Ground, Ford's Theatre, National Park Service Symposium, May 8, 2000.

CHAPTER 5

1. Catherine Drinker Bowen, *Miracle at Philadelphia: The Story of the Constitutional Convention May to September 1787*, The American Past (New York: Book-of-the-Month Club, 1966), p. 40.
2. Peter Applebome, *Dixie Rising: How the South Is Shaping American Values, Politics and Culture*, A Harvest Book (New York: Harcourt Brace, 1996), p. 8.
3. Kermit L. Hall, editor in chief, James W. Ely, Jr., Joel B. Grossman, and William M. Wiececk, editors, *The Oxford Companion to the Supreme Court* (New York: Oxford University Press, 1992), p. 278.
4. Bowen, *Miracle at Philadelphia*, p. 41.
5. Hall, et al., *Oxford Companion to the Supreme Court*, p. 279.
6. Ibid., p. 831.
7. Ibid., p. 830.
8. Ibid., p. 2.
9. Richard N. Current, editor in chief, Paul D. Escott, Lawrence N. Powell, James I. Robertson, Jr., and Emory M. Thomas, editors, *Encyclopedia of the Confederacy* (New York: Simon & Schuster, 1993), p. 1532.
10. Ibid., p. 1533.
11. Hall, et al., *Oxford Companion to the Supreme Court*, p. 862.
12. Ibid., p. 862.
13. Ibid., p. 862.
14. Ibid., p. 144.
15. Ibid., p. 590.
16. Ibid., p. 590.
17. Ibid., p. 49.
18. Ibid., p. 590.
19. Ibid., p. 590.
20. Ibid., p. 49.
21. Ibid., p. 531
22. Ibid., p. 715-716.
23. *Columbia State Newspaper*, August 26, 1999.
24. *Dallas Morning News*, August 26, 1999.
25. *Charleston Post and Courier*, August 26, 1999.

CHAPTER 6

1. Frederick Douglass July 4, 1841, Independence Day Speech at Rochester, New York. In Diane

Ravitch, editor, *The American Reader: Words That Moved a Nation* (New York: HarperCollins, 1990), pp. 115, 118.

2. Peter Kolchin, *American Slavery, 1619–1877* (New York: Hill and Wange, 1993, p. xi.

3. Ibid., p. 4.

4. Ibid., p. 4.

5. Ibid., p. 5.

6. Ibid., p. 22.

7. Ibid., p. 22.

8. Ibid., pp. 11–12.

9. Ibid., p. 17.

10. Ibid., p. 10.

11. Ibid., p. 17.

12. Kenneth Estell, editor, *Reference Library of Black America*, Volume I (Detroit: Gale Research, 1994), p. 5.

13. Ibid., p. 9.

14. Bowen, *Miracle at Philadelphia*, p. 202.

15. Ibid., p. 95.

16. Ibid., p. 95.

17. Ibid., pp. 201, 204.

18. Ibid., p. 201.

19. Ibid., p. 203.

20. Hall, et al., *Oxford Companion to the Supreme Court*, pp. 791–792.

21. Ibid., p. 792.

22. Estell, *Reference Library of Black America*, p. 12.

23. Ibid., p. 15.

24. Ibid., p. 13.

25. Ibid., p. 16.

26. Ibid., p. 18.

27. Ibid., p. 18.

28. O'Reilly, *Nixon's Piano*, p. 15.

29. Ibid., p. 15

30. Ibid., p. 18.

31. Ibid., p. 21.

32. Ibid., p. 31.

33. Kolchin, *American Slavery, 1619–1877*, pp. 184–185.

34. Ibid., p. 187.

35. Ibid., p. 188.

36. Ibid., p. 189.

37. O'Reilly, *Nixon's Piano*, p. 31.

38. Ibid., p. 33.

39. Ibid., pp. 34–35.

40. Eileen Shields-West, *The World Almanac of Presidential Campaigns: All the Facts, Anecdotes, Scandals, and Mudslinging in the History of the Race for the White House* (World Almanac, 1992), p. 58.

41. O'Reilly, *Nixon's Piano*, pp. 35–36.

42. McPherson, *Battle Cry of Freedom*, p. 57.

43. Ibid., p. 52.

44. O'Reilly, *Nixon's Piano*, p. 36.

45. McPherson, *Battle Cry of Freedom*, p. 57.

46. Shields-West, *The World Almanac of Presidential Campaigns*, p. 69.

47. McPherson, *Battle Cry of Freedom*, p. 62.

48. O'Reilly, *Nixon's Piano*, p. 37.

49. McPherson, *Battle Cry of Freedom*, p. 68.

50. Ibid., p. 66.

51. Ibid., p. 72.

52. Ibid., p. 72.

53. Ibid., p. 71.

54. Shields-West, *The World Almanac of Presidential Campaigns*, p. 76.

55. McPherson, *Battle Cry of Freedom*, p. 73.

56. Shields-West, *The World Almanac of Presidential Campaigns*, p. 76.

57. Ravitch, *The American Reader*, pp. 115, 118.

58. McPherson, *Battle Cry of Freedom*, p. 90.

59. Ibid., pp. 33–35.

60. Shields-West, *The World Almanac of Presidential Campaigns*, p. 77.

61. McPherson, *Battle Cry of Freedom*, p. 126.

62. Eric Foner and Olivia Mahoney, *A House Divided: America in the Age of Lincoln* (New York and London: Chicago Historical Society in association with W. W. Norton, 1990), p. 60.

63. Abraham Lincoln, Speeches and Writings, 1832–1858, Speeches, Letters, and Miscellaneous Writings, The Lincoln-Douglas Debates (Library of America, 1989), p. 426.

64. Foner and Mahoney, *A House Divided*, p. 63.

65. Ibid., p. 64.

CHAPTER 7

1. James M. McPherson, *Drawn with the Sword: Reflections on the American Civil War* (New York and Oxford: Oxford University Press, 1996), p. 37.

2. Abraham Lincoln, Speeches and Writings, 1859–1865, Speeches, Letters, and Miscellaneous Writings, Presidential Messages and Proclamations, "Address at Sanitary Fair," Baltimore, Maryland (Library of America, 1989), pp. 589–590.

3. Abraham Lincoln Research Site on the Internet, http://members.aol.com/RVSNorton/Lincoln2.html.

4. McPherson, *Battle Cry of Freedom*, p. 179.

5. Abraham Lincoln, Speeches and Writings, 1859–1865, pp. 122–126.

6. Ibid., p. 130.

7. McPherson, *Battle Cry of Freedom*, p. 259.

8. Ibid., p. 237.

9. Ibid., p, 241.

10. Ibid., p. 241.

11. Geoffrey C. Ward, with Ric Burns and Ken Burns, *The Civil War* (New York: Alfred A. Knopf, 1990), p. 30.

12. McPherson, *Battle Cry of Freedom*, p. 243.

13. Ibid., p. 248.
14. Bruce Catton, *The American Heritage New History of the Civil War* (New York: Viking Press, 1996), p. 41.
15. McPherson, *Battle Cry of Freedom*, p. 262.
16. Ibid., p. 273.
17. Ibid., p. 277.
18. Current, et al., *Encyclopedia of the Confederacy*, pp. 585–586.
19. Abraham Lincoln, Speeches and Writings, 1859–1865, p. 268.
20. McPherson, *Battle Cry of Freedom*, p. 479.
21. Ibid., p. 483.
22. Ibid., p. 500.
23. Abraham Lincoln, Speeches and Writings, 1859–1865, "Proclamation Suspending the Writ of Habeas Corpus," p. 371.
24. Ibid., p. 307.
25. Ibid., p. 358.
26. McPherson, *Battle Cry of Freedom*, p. 560.
27. Ibid., p. 559.
28. Abraham Lincoln, Speeches and Writings, 1859–1865, "Final Emancipation Proclamation," p. 425.
29. McPherson, *Battle Cry of Freedom*, p. 567.
30. Current, et al., *Encyclopedia of the Confederacy*, p. 532.
31. McPherson, *Battle Cry of Freedom*, p. 586.
32. Ibid., p. 502.
33. Iver Berstein, *The New York City Draft Riots: Their Significance for American Society and Politics in the Age of the Civil War* (New York and Oxford: Oxford University Press, 1990), p. 8.
34. Ward, Burns, and Burns, *The Civil War*, pp. 243–244.
35. McPherson, *Battle Cry of Freedom*, p. 622.
36. Ward, Burns, and Burns, *The Civil War*, p. 246.
37. Ibid., p. 247.
38. Ibid., p. 248.
39. Garry Wills, *Lincoln at Gettysburg: The Words That Remade America* (New York: Simon and Shuster, 1992), p. 25.
40. Ibid., p. 37.
41. Ibid., pp. 37-38.
42. Ibid., p. 39.
43. Ibid., p. 38.
44. Ibid., pp. 146-147.
45. McPherson, *Battle Cry of Freedom*, p. 675.
46. Ibid., p. 685.
47. Ward, Burns, and Burns, *The Civil War*, p. 248.
48. Ibid., p. 248.
49. Abraham Lincoln, Speeches and Writings, 1859–1865, "To James C. Conkling," pp. 495, 498.
50. Bruce Tap, *Over Lincoln's Shoulder: The Committee on the Conduct of the War* (University Press of Kansas, 1998), p. 216.
51. Ward, Burns, and Burns, *The Civil War*, p. 350.
52. Ibid., p. 351.
53. Abraham Lincoln, Speeches and Writings, 1859–1865, "Memorandum on Probable Failure of Re-election," p. 624.
54. Ward, Burns, and Burns, *The Civil War*, p. 347.
55. Ibid., p. 348.
56. McPherson, *Battle Cry of Freedom*, p. 835.
57. Ibid., p. 847.
58. Ward, Burns, and Burns, *The Civil War*, p. 378.
59. Abraham Lincoln, Speeches and Writings, 1859–1865, "Speech on Reconstruction, Washington, D.C.," p. 699.
60. Ibid., p. 699.
61. McPherson, *Drawn with the Sword*, p. 196.
62. Ibid., p. 196.
63. Ibid., p. 205.
64. Ibid., p. 207.

CHAPTER 8

1. Margaret Miner and Hugh Rawson, *Dictionary of American Quotations* (American Heritage, Selected and Annotated Penguin Reference, 1997), p. 116.
2. Ibid., p. 116.
3. Eric Foner, *Reconstruction: America's Unfinished Revolution, 1863–1877* (New York: Harper and Row, 1988), p. 31.
4. Ibid., pp. 26–27.
5. Ibid., p. 120.
6. Ibid., pp. 142–143.
7. Ibid., p. 150.
8. Ibid., p. 202.
9. Ibid., p. 231.
10. Ibid., p. 235.
11. Ibid., p. 236.
12. Ibid., p. 251.
13. Ibid., p. 283.
14. Ibid., p. 291.
15. Ibid., p. 340.
16. Ibid., p. 367.
17. Ibid., p. 369.
18. Ibid., p. 419.
19. Lou Falkner Williams, *The Great South Carolina, Ku Klux Klan Trials 1871-1872* (Athens and London: University of Georgia Press, 1996), p. 76.
20. Ibid., p. 84.
21. Ibid., p. 110.
22. Ibid., p. 113.
23. Ibid., p. 113.
24. Foner, *Reconstruction*, p. 455.
25. Ibid., p. 458.
26. Williams, *The Great South Carolina, Ku Klux Klan Trials*, p. 131.

27. Ibid., p. 131.

28. Ibid., p. 125.

29. Foner, *Reconstruction*, p. 446.

30. Ibid., p. 447.

31. Ibid., p. 454.

32. Ibid., p. 488.

33. Ibid., p. 489.

34. Ibid., p. 492.

35. Ibid., pp. 497–499.

36. Williams, *The Great South Carolina, Ku Klux Klan Trials*, pp. 133-134.

37. Ibid., p. 128.

38. Foner, *Reconstruction*, p. 583.

39. Ibid., p. 585.

40. Hall, et al., *Oxford Companion to the Supreme Court*, pp. 384–385.

41. Leon F. Litwack, *Trouble in Mind: Black Southerners in the Age of Jim Crow* (New York: Alfred A. Knopf, 1998), p. xiv.

42. Ibid., pp. xiv–xv.

43. Jacqueline Jones, *American Work: Four Centuries of Black and White Labor* (New York: W. W. Norton, 1998), p. 302.

44. Ravitch, *The American Reader*, pp. 186–188.

45. Jones, *American Work*, p. 297.

46. Ibid., p. 319.

47. Ibid., p. 108.

48. Tom Cowan and Jack MaGuire, *Timelines of African American History: 500 Years of Black Achievement* (New York: Berkley Publishing Group, 1994), p. 161.

49. Jones, *American Work*, p. 334.

50. Douglas Brinkley, *Rosa Parks* (New York: Viking, Published by the Penguin Group, 2000), p. 101.

51. Ibid., p. 172.

52. Henry Hampton and Steve Fayer, Voices of Freedom: An Oral History of the Civil Rights Movement from the 1950s through the 1980s (New York: Blackslide, A Bantam Book, 1990), p. 124.

53. Ibid., p. 124.

54. O'Reilly, *Nixon's Piano*, p. 50.

55. Ibid., p. 53.

56. Ibid., p. 65.

57. Ibid., p. 102.

58. David M. Kennedy, *Freedom from Fear: The American People in Depression and War, 1929–1949* (New York and Oxford: Oxford University Press, 1999), p. 340.

59. O'Reilly, *Nixon's Piano*, p. 145.

CHAPTER 9

1. Ravich, *The American Reader*, "Howard University Address," p. 340.

2. Borgna Brunner on the Learning Network Internet site, Timeline of Affirmative Action Milestones.

3. Hall, et al., *Oxford Companion to the Supreme Court*, p. 901.

CHAPTER 10

1. Thomas Jefferson, *The Jeffersonian Cyclopedia*, p. 726, #7015.

2. Chester Hartman, Housing Policy Debate, Volume 9, Number 2, 1998, "The Case for a Right to Housing" (Fannie Mae Foundation, 2000), p. 224.

3. Hall, et al., *Oxford Companion to the Supreme Court*, p. 590.

4. The Timetable of World Legal History Internet site (http://www.wwlia.org/hist.htm) provided the basic information for this history of law. It is part of the LAW Museum.

5. John Hope Franklin and Genna Rae McNeil, editors, *African Americans and the Living Constitution* (Washington and London: Smithsonian Institution Press 1995), p. 315.

CHAPTER 11

1. Miner and Rawson, *Dictionary of American Quotations*, p. 542.

2. Benjamin M. Friedman, *Day of Reckoning: The Consequences of American Economic Policy Under Reagan and After* (Robert V. Roosa, Partner, Brown Brothers Harriman and Company, 1988), p. 8.

3. Ibid., p. 8.

4. Ibid., p. 9.

5. Dean Baker, Jeff Faux, Edith Rasell, and Max Sawicky, "The Good-for-Nothing Budget: Clinton GOP Deal a Boon to the Wealthy, But Not the Economy," May 13, 1997.

6. Thomas I. Palley, *Plenty of Nothing: The Downsizing of the American Dream and the Case for Structural Keynesianism* (Princeton, N.J.: Princeton University Press, 1998), p. 38.

7. John Maynard Keynes, *The General Theory of Employment, Interest and Money* (Prometheus Books, 1997), p. 383.

8. Palley, *Plenty of Nothing*, p. 130.

9. Ibid., p. 62.

10. Ibid., p. 131.

11. William Greider, *One World, Ready or Not: The Manic Logic of Global Capitalism* (New York: Simon and Schuster, 1997), p. 23.

12. Palley, *Plenty of Nothing*, p. 187.

13. Ibid., p. 184.

14. Greider, *One World, Ready or Not*, p. 23.

15. Palley, Op. Cite., p. 75.

16. Donald L. Barlett & James B. Steel, America: Who Really Pays the Taxes?, A Touchstone

Book, Published by Simon and Schuster, New York, 1994, p. 14.

17. Palley, *Plenty of Nothing*, p. 100.

18. Ibid., p. 200.

19. Sheila D. Collins, Helen Lachs Ginsburg, Gertrude Schaffner Goldberg, *Jobs for All: A Plan for the Revitalization of America* (Apex Press, 1994), pp. 40–117.

CHAPTER 12

1. Roberto Suro and Eric Pianin, "Battle Cry for Free Health Care, Retired Veterans Push Congress to Restore 'Promised' Benefit," *Washington Post*, March 26, 2000.

2. Inci A. Bowman, Historic Medical Sites in the Washington, DC Area Celebrating the Bicentennial of the Nation's Capital, Internet site.

3. Children's Defense Fund Internet site, "Children in the States 2000," Introduction.

4. Children's Defense Fund Internet site, 1999 and 2000.

5. Robert Pear, "Poor Workers Lose Medicaid Coverage Despite Eligibility," *New York Times*, April 12, 1999.

6. Ibid.

7. Robert Kuttner, "Patchwork Health Care," *Washington Post*, op-ed, January 25, 2000.

8. Peter T. Kilborn, "Health Gap Grows, With Black Americans Trailing Whites, Studies Say," *New York Times*, January 26, 1998.

9. Ibid.

10. Ibid.

11. Kuttner, "Patchwork Health Care."

12. Robert Pear, "Medicare Panel, Sharply Divided, Submits No Plan," *New York Times*, March 17, 1999.

CHAPTER 13

1. President's Committee on Urban Housing, *A Decent Home* (Kaiser Report) (Washington: U.S. Government Printing Office, 1969), p. 2.

2. Michael Stegman, Roberty Quercia, and George McCarthy, "New Century Housing," *Center for Housing Policy* 1 no. 1 (June 2000), p. 1.

3. Marci McDonald, "Down and Out in Silicon Valley," *US News Online*, August 7, 1999; "Cisco Systems to Donate $800,000 to Housing Trust Fund," Cisco Systems Press Release, April 3, 2000. Silicon Valley dotcoms have begun investing in the Santa Clara County Housing Trust Fund—a broad-based collaborative, established in 1999, that provides funding for homelessness programs, affordable rental units, and first-time home buyer assistance programs.

4. Stegman, et al., "New Century Housing," p. 9.

5. *Affordability* is defined as paying no more than 30 percent of adjusted gross income in rent.

6. Peter Dreier, "Rebuilding Unions' Involvement in Federal Housing Policy," *Housing Policy Debate* 2 no. 2 (Fannie Mae Foundation; 2000), p. 352.

7. Ibid., p. 352.

8. Stegman, et al., "New Century Housing," p. 12.

9. Jennifer Daskal, "In Search of Shelter: The Growing Shortage of Affordable Rental Housing," Center on Budget and Policy Priorities, June 15, 1998, p. 31.

10. Dreier, "Rebuilding Unions' Involvement in Federal Housing Policy," p. 329.

11. Ibid., pp. 355–356.

12. Ibid., p. 328.

13. Chester Hartman, "The Case for a Right to Housing," *Housing Policy Debate* 9, no. 2 (1998), Fannie Mae Foundation, 2000, p. 224.

14. Ibid., pp. 224–225.

15. Ibid., p. 227.

16. Ibid., p. 228.

17. Ibid., p. 228.

18. Dreier, "Rebuilding Unions' Involvement in Federal Housing Policy," p. 351.

19. Alexander von Hoffman, "A Study In Contradictions: The Origins and Legacy of the Housing Act of 1949," *Housing Policy Debate* 11, no. 2 (Fannie Mae Foundation), p. 300.

20. More specific information on U.S. housing history can be found at http://www.cses.com, Rental Housing On Line. "Permission is granted to use information from our pages in rental housing association newsletters or Web sites, with email notification and provided the following notice is attached: 'This information was obtained from Rental Housing On Line, the Internet's most comprehensive landlord/tenant rental housing site, with information, law, forms, forums, live chat and vacancy listing service. Visit RHOL at: http//rhol.org.'" Also, information can be gained from "A Chronology of Housing Legislation and Selected Executive Actions, 1892–1992," December 1993.

21. Dreier, "Rebuilding Unions' Involvement in Federal Housing Policy," p. 340.

22. *United States v. Certain Lands in the City of Louisville*, 78 F. 2d 681 (6th Cir., 1935).

23. Soldiers and Sailors Relief Act of 1940, the Lanham Act of 1940, and the postwar Veterans' Emergency Housing Act.

24. Von Hoffman, "A Study In Contradictions: The Origins and Legacy of the Housing Act of 1949," p. 309.

25. Ibid., p. 305.

26. The Servicemen's Readjustment Act of 1944.

27. Von Hoffman, "A Study In Contradictions: The Origins and Legacy of the Housing Act of 1949," pp. 305–306.

28. Northern liberal supporters of civil rights joined segregationists to defeat the amendment, despite their support, so as not to jeopardize the passage of the bill and thus funding of the public housing program.

29. Von Hoffman, "A Study In Contradictions: The Origins and Legacy of the Housing Act of 1949," p. 309.

30. Ibid., p. 303.

31. Ibid., p. 301.

32. Ibid., p. 302.

33. Ibid., p. 303.

34. Ibid.

35. Ibid., p. 304.

36. Ibid., p. 311.

37. Lang and Sohmer, Fannie Mae Foundation, *Housing Policy Debate*, p. 293.

38. Through a series of changes to FHA mortgage insurance programs—Sections 220, 221, 207, 203(i), 222, 608, Title I, 701—it modified and expanded federal housing programs not just to eradicate existing slums, but to prevent them from developing.

39. Von Hoffman, "A Study In Contradictions: The Origins and Legacy of the Housing Act of 1949," p. 318.

40. Dreier, "Rebuilding Unions' Involvement in Federal Housing Policy," p. 350; Lang and Sohmer, p. 296.

41. Sections 231 and 202.

42. Sections 221(d) and 234.

43. Section 312.

44. The Public Works and Economic Development Act of 1965.

45. Sylvia Martinez, "The Housing Act of 1949: Its Place in the Realization of the American Dream of Homeownership," *Housing Policy Debate* 11 no. 2 (Fannie Mae Foundation), p. 471.

46. The act was amended in 1988 to expand the law's purview to protect families with children and the disabled. Fair Housing Amendments Act of 1988.

47. Kaiser Report, p. 2.

48. The Emergency Home Finance Act of 1970.

49. Charles J. Orlebeke, "The Evolution of Low Income Policy, 1949 to 1999," *Housing Policy Debate* 11 no. 2 (Fannie Mae Foundation), pp. 495, 500–501.

50. Ibid., p. 502.

51. Ibid., p. 505.

52. The Financial Services Modernization Act passed the House on July 1, 1999, as H.R. 10; it passed the Senate on November 4, 1999, as S. 900; and it became Public Law 106-102 on November 12, 1999, when the president signed it. The new law weakened the CRA in several ways. Communities, consumers, and public interest organizations are now more limited in their opportunities for public comment. They also will not have a chance to comment on mergers when banks that have received a satisfactory CRA rating are applying to become financial holding companies. Smaller banks that receive a satisfactory CRA rating will be reviewed every four years instead of every two. Smaller banks that receive an excellent CRA rating will be reviewed every five years. Since an estimated 97 percent of all small banks currently receive a satisfactory or better CRA rating, it essentially removes the majority of banks from a timely regular CRA review process. There are a number of reasons why banks are reviewed by regulators, but the law only cut back on the requirements for review of CRA.

53. Orlebeke, "The Evolution of Low Income Policy, 1949 to 1999," pp. 511, 514.

54. Ibid.

55. Ibid., p. 513.

56. Dreier, "Rebuilding Unions' Involvement in Federal Housing Policy," p. 361.

57. Orlebeke, "The Evolution of Low Income Policy, 1949 to 1999," p. 515.

58. Ibid., p. 516.

59. Dreier, "Rebuilding Unions' Involvement in Federal Housing Policy," p. 351.

60. H.R. 1176, the State Occupancy Standards Affirmative Act, which affirmed the role of states to set reasonable occupancy standards, and H.R. 190, the Credit Opportunity Amendments Act.

61. J. Michael Collins, Eric Belsky, and Nicolas P. Retsinas, "Toward a Targeted Homeownership Tax Credit," Joint Center for Housing Studies, Harvard University, November 1998.

62. Dreier, "Rebuilding Unions' Involvement in Federal Housing Policy," p. 359.

63. Ibid., p. 361.

64. Ibid., p. 352.

65. U.S. Department of Housing and Urban Development, Office of Policy Development and Research, "A Report on Worst Case Housing Needs in 1999: New Opportunity Amid Continuing Challenges," January 2001, p. 1.

66. "National Advocates Call for White House Commission to Address Homeless," press release, July 22, 1997. The six organizations were the National Alliance to End Homelessness, the National Coalition for Homeless Veterans, the

National Coalition for the Homeless, the National Health Care for the Homeless Council, the National Law Center on Homelessness and Poverty, and the Stewart B. McKinney Foundation.

67. National Coalition for the Homeless, Fact Sheet 1, "Why Are People Homeless?" June 1999.

68. Dreier, "Rebuilding Unions' Involvement in Federal Housing Policy," p. 353.

69. Koegel, et al., 1996, National Coalition for the Homeless Internet homepage.

70. Greenberg and Baumohl, 1996, Center on Budget and Policy Priorities Internet homepage.

71. Ibid., CBPP.

72. Dreier, "Rebuilding Unions' Involvement in Federal Housing Policy," p. 351–352.

73. Ibid., p. 354.

74. "1999 State of the Nation's Housing: Report from the Joint Center for Housing Studies at Harvard University. The study can be found on the Harvard University Internet site at: http://www.gsd.harvard.edu/jcenter/Publications/State%20of%20the%20Nation%27s%20Housing%201999/index.html.

75. Ibid., p. 368.

76. Stegman, et al., "New Century Housing," p. 6.

77. Ibid., p. 24.

78. Dreier, "Rebuilding Unions' Involvement in Federal Housing Policy," p. 375.

79. Ibid.

80. U.S. Department of Commerce, Economics and Statistics Administration, Census Bureau, Housing Starts, March 2000 (issued in May 2000).

CHAPTER 14

1. Miner and Rawson, *Dictionary of American Quotations*, p. 160.

2. Ibid., p. 160.

3. *Education Week*, January 26, 1994.

4. National Center for Education Statistics, http://nces.ed.gov.

5. Ibid.

6. Miner and Rawson, *Dictionary of American Quotations*, p. 160.

7. U.S. Supreme Court, *Plessy v. Ferguson*, 163 U.S. 537 (1896), 163 U.S. 537, No. 210.

8. U.S. Census Bureau.

CHAPTER 15

1. National Organization for Women (NOW) Internet homepage.

2. U.S. Department of Labor, "Good for Business: Making Full Use of the Nation's Human Capital," *Environmental Scan: A Fact-Finding Report of the Federal Glass Ceiling Commission*, Washington, D.C., March 1995.

3. Darlene Clark Hine, editor, *Black Women in America: An Historical Encyclopedia* (1994), p. 1157.

4. John Stuart Mill, "The Subject of Women," *The Feminist Papers*, edited by Alice S. Rossi (1988), p. 215.

5. Rev. T. H. Harrison, Adams Presbyterian Church, Nashville, Tennessee, A. Elizabeth Taylor, *The Woman Suffrage Movement in Tennessee*, p. 79.

6. Anti-suffrage leaflet titled "Beware," in ibid.

7. John R. Dos Passos, "Equality of Suffrage Means the Debasement Not Only of Women But of Men," *The Women's Protext*, January, 1913, p. 5.

8. Congressional Research Service, Women in the U.S. Congress, 1917–2001.

9. *The World's Women 2000: Trends and Statistics, Main Findings and Future Directions*, p. 1.

CHAPTER 16

1. The Earth Charter Campaign. More information can be found on their Internet homepage at http://www.earthcharter.org.

2. Miner and Rawson, *Dictionary of American Quotations*, p. 167.

3. Much of the basic framework and timelines for the latter part of this chapter come from the "Earth Charter Campaign" (http://www.earthcharter.org), the International Institute for Sustainable Development (http://iisd.ca/timeline/), and the U.S. Environmental Agency (EPA) (http://www.epa.gov/epahome/lawreg.htm). Generally, only direct quotes are attributed.

4. EPA Web page, http:..www.epa.gov/epahome/lawreg.htm.

5. International Institute for Sustainable Development, http://iisd.ca/timeline/.

6. Earth Charter.

7. Ibid.

8. Ibid.

9. Ibid.

10. Ibid.

11. Ibid.

12. Ibid.

CHAPTER 17

1. Miner and Rawson, *Dictionary of American Quotations*, p. 484.

2. Adam Smith, *An Inquiry into the Nature and Causes of the Wealth of Nations* (William Benton, publisher, Encyclopedia Britannica, 1952), p. 361.

3. Miner and Rawson, *Dictionary of American Quotations*, p. 485.

4. I relied on and referred to the Citizens for Tax

Justice (http://www.ctj.org) and the Center on Budget and Policy Priorities (http://www.cbpp.org) homepages for much of the information in this chapter. Generally, only direct quotes are attributed.

5. David Cay Johnston, "Corporate Taxes Fall, But Citizens Are Paying More," *New York Times*, February 13, 2000.

6. Office of Management and Budget, Budget of the United States Government, FY1998, Historical Tables.

6. Citizens for Tax Justice Web site, "Who Pays," June 26, 1996, study.

CHAPTER 18

1. Applebome, *Dixie Rising*, pp. 45–46.

2. The Religious Working Group on the World Bank and the IMF, "Moral Imperatives for Addressing Structural Adjustment and Economic Reform Measures," May 1997.

3. Ibid.

4. Ibid.

5. Ibid.

6. Ibid.

7. Ibid.

8. Ibid.

9. Douglas Farah, "'We've Not Been Honest'; '68 Memo Assails U.S. Role in Guatemalan War," *Washington Post Foreign Service*, March 12, 1999.

10. Frank Clemente with Frank E. Watkins, editors, *Keep Hope Alive: Jesse Jackson's 1988 Presidential Campaign* (A Publication of the Keep Hope Alive PAC and South End Press, 1989), p. 109.

11. Ibid., p. 190.

CHAPTER 19

1. Jesse L. Jackson, *Straight from the Heart*, edited by Roger D. Hatch and Frank E. Watkins (Fortress Press, 1987), p. 5.

2. Ralph Reed, *Politically Incorrect: The Emerging Faith Factor in American Politics* (Word Publishing, 1994), p. 245.

3. Ibid., p. 244.

4. David Firestone, "For Gore, Battle for South Begins Within Ranks of His Own Party," *New York Times*, August 21, 2000.

5. David Firestone, "The South Comes of Age on Religion and Politics," *New York Times*, August 10, 2000.

6. In the arguments ahead, while there will be many references to the Jesse Jackson presidential campaigns of 1984 and 1988, references to him or his campaigns are not designed to argue for him being on a Democratic ticket. I refer to his campaigns simply because his were the only serious national presidential campaigns that an African American has run. The general underlying factual and rational political arguments I will make should stand or fall on their own merit, apart from any particular political personalities.

7. Most of this information came in a memo from political consultant Steve Cobble.

8. Clemente and Watkins, *Keep Hope Alive*, p. 22.

9. Ibid., p. 24.

10. The first chart is from Bureau of Economic Analysis, U.S. Department of Commerce. I created the three additional charts from it.

11. U.S. Census Bureau.

12. Registration and turnout statistics courtesy of State Election Offices and the Congressional Research Service (Government Division), with data provided by Election Data Services Inc., Washington, D.C.

13. Ibid.

14. Ibid.

CHAPTER 20

1. Greider, *One World, Ready or Not*, p. 23.

2. Samuel DeWitt Proctor, *The Substance of Things Hoped For: A Memoir of African-American Faith* (New York: G. P. Putnam's Sons, 1995), p. xxiv.

3. Americans United for Separation of Church and State Web page (http://www.au.org) on church and state issues.

4. Hall, et al., *Oxford Companion to the Supreme Court*, pp. 278, 759.

5. Ibid., p. 1.

6. Americans United for Separation of Church and State Web page (http://www.au.org) on church and state issues.

7. Ibid.

8. Ibid.

9. Ibid.

10. Ibid.

11. King, *Strength to Love*, p. 130.

BIBLIOGRAPHY

Ackerman, Bruce. *We the People: Foundations.* Cambridge, Mass., and London: The Belknap Press of Harvard University Press, 1991.

———. *We the People: Transformations.* Cambridge, Mass., and London: The Belknap Press of Harvard University Press, 1998.

Allport, Gordon W. *The Nature of Prejudice: A Comprehensive and Penetrating Study of the Origin and Nature of Prejudice.* Addison-Wesley, 1958.

Ambrose, Stephen E. *Undaunted Courage: Meriwether Lewis, Thomas Jefferson and the Opening of the American West.* New York: Simon and Schuster, 1996.

Applebome, Peter. *Dixie Rising: How the South Is Shaping American Values, Politics and Culture.* New York: Harcourt Brace, 1996.

Avery, Michael J. *The Demobilization of American Voters: A Comprehensive Theory of Voter Turnout.* Greenwood Press, 1989.

Bailyn, Bernard. *The Debate on the Constitution: Federalist and Antifederalist Speeches, Articles, and Letters During the Struggle Over Ratification, Part One: September 1787 to February 1788; Part Two: January to August 1788.* Literary Classics of the United States, 1993.

Barlett, Donald L., and James B. Steele. *America: What Went Wrong?* Kansas City: Andrews and McMeel, 1992.

———. *America: Who Really Pays The Taxes?* New York: Simon and Schuster, 1994.

Berlin, Ira, Barbara J. Fields, Steven F. Miler, Joseph P. Reidy, and Leslie S. Rowland, editors. *Free at Last: A Documentary History of Slavery, Freedom, and the Civil War.* New York: New Press, 1992.

Berstein, Iver. *The New York City Draft Riots: Their Significance for American Society and Politics in the Age of the Civil War.* New York and Oxford: Oxford University Press, 1990.

Bowen, Catherine Drinker. *Miracle at Philadelphia: The Story of the Constitutional Convention, May to September 1787, The American Past.* Book-of-the-Month Club, 1986.

Boyer, Richard O., and Herbert M. Morais. *Labor's Untold Story.* Cameron Associates, 1955.

Brinkley, Douglas. *Rosa Parks.* New York: Viking, published by the Penguin Group, 2000.

Branch, Taylor. *Pillar of Fire: America in the King Years, 1963–65.* New York: Simon and Schuster, 1998.

———. *Parting the Waters: America in the King Years, 1954–63.* New York: Simon and Schuster, 1998.

Brandt, Nat. *The Town That Started the Civil War.* Syracuse, N.Y.: Syracuse University Press, 1990.

Brown, Peter. *Minority Party: Why Democrats Face Defeat in 1992 and Beyond.* Regnery Gateway, 1991.

Catton, Bruce. *America Goes to War: The Civil War and Its Meaning in American Culture.* Wesleyan University Press, 1958, 1986.

———. *The American Heritage New History of the Civil War.* New York: Viking Press, 1996.

Clay, William L. *Just Permanent Interests: Black Americans in Congress, 1870–1991.* Amistad Press, 1992.

Christian, Charles M. *Black Saga: The African American Experience, A Chronology.* New York: Houghton Mifflin, 1995.

Colbert, David. *Eyewitness to America: 500 Years of America in the Words of Those Who Saw It Happen.* New York: Pantheon Books, a division of Random House, 1997.

Conniff, Michael L., and Thomas J. Davis. *Africans in the Americas: A History of the Black Diaspora.* New York: St. Martin's Press, 1994.

Cowan, Tom, and Jack Maguire. *Timelines of African-American History: 500 Years of Black Achievement.* New York: Berkley Publishing Group, 1994.

Clemente, Frank, and Frank Watkins. *Keep Hope Alive: Jesse Jackson's 1988 Presidential Campaign.* South End Press, 1989.

Current, Richard N., editor in chief. *Encyclopedia of the Confederacy* (4 volumes). New York: Simon and Schuster, 1993.

Davis, Kenneth C. *Don't Know Much About History: Everything You Need to Know About American History But Never Learned.* New York: Crown Publishers, 1990.

Dawley, Alan. *Struggles for Justice: Social Responsibility and the Liberal State.* Cambridge, Mass., and London: The Belknap Press of Harvard University Press, 1991.

Dees, Morris, with Steve Fiffer. *A Season for Justice: The Life and Times of Civil Rights Lawyer Morris Dees.* New York: Charles Scribner's Sons, 1991.

Dionne, E. J. *Why American Hate Politics.* New York: Simon and Schuster, 1991.

Donald, David Herbert. *Lincoln.* Random House, 1995.

DuBois, Ellen Carol. *Harriot Stanton Blatch and the Winning of Woman Suffrage.* New Haven, Conn.: Yale University Press, 1997.

Fehrenbacher, Don E., editor and annotator. *Lincoln: Speeches and Writings, 1832–1858 and 1859–1865, Speeches, Letters, Miscellaneous Writings, Presidential Messages and Proclamations.* The Library of America, 1989.

Foner, Eric, and Olivia Mahoney. *A House Divided: America in the Age of Lincoln.* New York and London: Chicago Historical Society in association with W. W. Norton, 1990.

Franklin, John Hope. *From Slavery to Freedom: A History of Negro Americans.* New York: Alfred A. Knopf, 1947.

———. *Race and History: Selected Essays, 1938–1988.* Louisiana University Press, 1989.

Freeman, David B. *Carved in Stone: The History of Stone Mountain.* Macon, Ga.: Mercer University Press, 1997.

Gallagher, Gary W. *The Confederate War: How Popular Will, Nationalism and Military Strategy Could Not Stave Off Defeat.* Cambridge, Mass.: Harvard University Press, 1997.

Glatthaar, Joseph T. *Forged in Battle: The Civil War Alliance of Black Soldiers and White Officers.* New York: Free Press, 1990.

Germond, Jack W., and Jules Witcover. *Mad as Hell: Revolt at the Ballot Box, 1992.* New York: Warner Books, 1993.

Gooding, James Henry, edited by Virginia M. Adams. *On the Altar of Freedom: A Black Soldier's Civil War Letters from the Front.* Amherst: University of Massachusetts Press, 1991.

Gordon-Reed, Annette. *Thomas Jefferson and Sally Hemings: An American Controversy.* University Press of Virginia, 1997.

Gray, Ed. *Chief Justice: A Biography of Earl Warren.* New York: Simon and Schuster, 1997.

Greider, William. *One World, Ready or Not: The Manic Logic of Global Capitalism.* New York: Simon and Schuster, 1997.

Guinier, Lani. *The Tyranny of the Majority: Fundamental Fairness in Representative Democracy.* New York: Free Press, 1994.

Hall, Kermit L., editor in chief. *The Oxford Companion to the Supreme Court of the United States.* New York and Oxford: Oxford University Press, 1992.

Hampton, Henry, and Steve Fayer. *Voices of Freedom: An Oral History of the Civil Rights Movement from the 1950s Through the 1980s.* Blackslide, Inc., a Bantam Book, 1990.

Harrington, Walt. *Crossings: A White Man's Journey into Black America.* New York: HarperCollins, 1992.

Hatch, Roger D. *Beyond Opportunity: Jesse Jackson's Vision for America.* Fortress Press, 1988.

Hicken, Victor. *Illinois in the Civil War.* University of Illinois Press, 1991.

Hill, Anita. *Speaking Truth to Power.* New York: Doubleday, 1997.

History Book Club. *The Spark of Independence.* Book-of-the-Month Club, 1997.

Horwitz, Tony. *Confederates in the Attic: Dispatches from the Unfinished Civil War.* New York: Pantheon Books, 1998.

Isichei, Elizabeth. *A History of Christianity in Africa.* William B. Eerdmans Publishing, 1995.

Jackson, Jesse L., edited by Roger D. Hatch and Frank E. Watkins. *Straight from the Heart.* Fortress Press, 1987.

Johnson, Paul. *A History of the American People.* New York: HarperCollins, 1997.

Jones, Jacqueline. *American Work: Four Centuries of Black and White Labor.* New York: W. W. Norton, 1998.

Joseph, Alvin M. *500 Nations: An Illustrated History of North American Indians.* New York: Alfred A. Knopf, 1994.

Kanellos, Nicolas, editor. *Reference Library of Hispanic America* (4 volumes). Gale Research, 1993.

Karamanski, Theodore J. *Rally 'Round the Flag: Chicago and the Civil War.* Nelson-Hall Publishers, 1993.

Kennedy, David M. *Freedom from Fear: The American People in Depression and War, 1929–1945.* New York and Oxford: Oxford University Press, 1999.

Kimball, Penn. *Keep Hope Alive: Super Tuesday and Jesse Jackson's 1988 Campaign for the Presidency.* National Book Network, 1992.

King, Martin Luther, Jr. *Strength to Love.* Philadelphia: Fortress Press, 1963 (Fortress Press edition, 1981).

Kolchin, Peter. *American Slavery: 1619–1877.* New York: Hill and Wang, 1993.

Korten, David D. *When Corporations Rule the World.* Berrett-Koehler Publishers, Kumarian Press, 1995.

Kunhardt, Philip B., Jr., Philip B. Kunhardt, III, and Peter W. Kunhardt. *The American President.* New York: Penguin Putnam, 1999.

Kuttner, Robert. *Everything for Sale: The Virtues and Limits of Markets.* Alfred A. Knopf, 1998.

Lazarus, Edward. *Black Hills White Justice: The Sioux Nation Versus the United States, 1775 to the Present.* New York: HarperCollins, 1991.

Leckie, William H. *The Buffalo Soldiers: A Narrative of the Negro Cavalry in the West.* University of Oklahoma Press, 1967.

Lemann, Nicholas. *The Promised Land: The Great Black Migration and How It Changed America.* New York: Alfred A. Knopf, 1991.

Levy, George. *To Die in Chicago: Confederate Prisoners at Camp Douglas, 1862–1865.* Evanston Publishing, 1994.

Levy, Leonard W. *Origins of the Bill of Rights.* New Haven, Conn.: Yale University Press, 1999.

Lewis, David Levering. *W. E. B. DuBois: Biography of a Race, 1868–1919.* Henry Holt and Company, 1993.

Lind, Michael. *Up from Conservatism: Why the Right Is Wrong for America.* New York: Free Press Paperbacks, published by Simon and Schuster, 1996.

Litwack, Leon F. *Trouble in Mind: Black Southerners in the Age of Jim Crow.* New York: Alfred A. Knopf, 1998.

Loewen, James W. *Lies Across America: What Our Historic Sites Get Wrong.* New York: Simon and Schuster, 1999.

Long, E. B., with Barbara Long. *The Civil War Day by Day: An Almanac 1861–1865.* Da Capo Press, 1971.

Lowith, Karl. *Meaning in History.* Chicago: University of Chicago Press, 1949.

MacInnes, Gordon. *Wrong for All the Right Reasons: How White Liberals Have Been Undone by Race.* New York: New York University Press, 1996.

McFeely, William W. *Frederick Douglass.* New York: W. W. Norton, 1991.

McKelvey, Charles. *The African American Movement: From Pan-Africanism to the Rainbow Coalition.* General Hall, 1994.

McPherson, James M. *Drawn with the Sword: Reflections on the American Civil War.* New York and Oxford: Oxford University Press, 1996.

———. *For Cause and Comrades: Why Men Fought in the Civil War.* New York and Oxford: Oxford University Press, 1997.

———. *Marching Toward Freedom: Blacks in the Civil War, 1861–1865.* New York: Alfred A. Knopf, 1967.

Mandela, Nelson. *Long Walk to Freedom: The Autobiography of Nelson Mandela.* Little, Brown, 1994.

Morgan, Ted. *FDR: A Biography.* New York: Simon and Schuster, 1985.

———. *Wilderness at Dawn: The Settling of the North American Continent.* New York: Simon and Schuster, 1993.

Mostert, Noel. *Frontiers: The Epic of South Africa's Creation and the Tragedy of the Xhosa People.* New York: Alfred A. Knopf, 1992.

Nader, Ralph, and Wesley J. Smith. *No Contest: Corporate Lawyers and the Perversion of Justice in America.* New York: Random House, 1996.

Norrander, Barbara. *Super Tuesday: Regional Politics and Presidential Primaries.* University Press of Kentucky, 1992.

O'Reilly, Kenneth. *Nixon's Piano: Presidents and Racial Politics from Washington to Clinton.* New York: Free Press, 1995.

Painter, Nell Irvin. *Standing at Armageddon: The United States, 1877–1919.* New York: W. W. Norton, 1987.

Parker, Frank R. *Black Votes Count: Potential Empowerment in Mississippi After 1965.* University of North Carolina Press, 1990.

Patterson, James T. *Brown v. Board of Education: A Civil Rights Milestone and Its Troubled Legacy.* New York and Oxford: Oxford University Press, 2001.

Patterson, Thomas E. *Out of Order: How the Decline of the Political Parties and the Growing Power of the News Media Undermine the American Way of Electing Presidents.* New York: Alfred A. Knopf, 1993.

Piven, Frances Fox, and Richard A. Cloward. *Why Americans Don't Vote.* New York: Pantheon Books, 1988.

Polsby, Nelson W., and Aaron Wildavsky. *Presidential Elections: Contemporary Strategies of American Electoral Politics.* New York: Free Press, 1980.

Powe, Lucas A., Jr. *The Warren Court and American Politics.* Cambridge, Mass., and London: The Belknap Press of Harvard University Press, 2000.

Proctor, Samuel D., and William D. Watley. *Sermons from the Black Pulpit.* Judson Press, 1984.

Rakove, Jack N., editor and annotator. *Madison: Writings.* The Library of America, 1999.

Ravitch, Diane, editor. *The American Reader: Words That Moved a Nation.* New York: HarperCollins, 1990.

Reed, Ralph. *Politically Correct: The Emerging Faith Factor in American Politics.* Word Publishing, 1994.

Rossiter, Clinton, introduction. *The Federalist Papers: Hamilton, Madison, Jay.* New American Library of World Literature, 1961.

Schomburg Center for Research in Black Culture. *African American Desk Reference.* The New York Public Library, a Stonesong Press book, John Wiley and Sons, 1999.

Schwarz, John E., and Thomas J. Volgy. *The Forgotten Americans: Thirty Million Working Poor in the Land of Opportunity.* New York: W. W. Norton, 1992.

Shields-West, Eileen. *The World Almanac of Presidential Campaigns: All the Facts, Anecdotes, Scandals, and Mudslinging in the History of the Race for the White House.* World Almanac, 1992.

Sklar, Holly. *Chaos or Community? Seeking Solutions, Not Scapegoats for Bad Economics.* South End Press, 1995.

Skowronek, Stephen. *The Politics Presidents Make: Leadership from John Adams to George Bush.* Cambridge, Mass., and London: The Belknap Press of Harvard University Press, 1993.

Stock, Catherine McNicol. *Rural Radicals: Righteous Rage in the American Grain.* Ithaca, N.Y.: Cornell University Press, 1996.

Stockman, David A. *The Triumph of Politics: Why the Reagan Revolution Failed.* New York: Harper and Row, 1986.

Suriano, Gregory R., editor. *Great American Speeches.* Outlook Book Company, 1993.

Tap, Bruce. *Over Lincoln's Shoulder: The Committee on the Conduct of the War.* University Press of Kansas, 1998.

Taylor, Colin F., editorial consultant, and William C. Sturtevant. *The Native Americans: The Indigenous People of North America.* Salamander Books, 1991.

Terkel, Studs. *Race: How Blacks and Whites Think and Feel About the American Obsession.* New York: New Press, 1992.

Thomas, Hugh. *The Slave Trade.* New York: Simon and Schuster, 1997.

Tushnet, Mark V. *Making Constitutional Law: Thurgood Marshall and the Supreme Court, 1961–1991.* New York and Oxford: Oxford University Press, 1997.

Walters, Ronald W. *Black Presidential Politics in America: A Strategic Approach.* State University of New York Press, 1988.

Ward, Geoffrey C., with Ric Burns and Ken Burns. *The Civil War.* New York: Alfred A. Knopf, 1990.

Watkins, T. H. *The Great Depression: America in the 1930s.* Little, Brown, 1993.

Watley, William D. *Roots of Resistance: The Nonviolent Ethic of Martin Luther King, Jr.* Judson Press, 1985.

Waugh, John C. *Reelecting Lincoln: The Battle for the 1864 Presidency.* New York: Crown Publishers, 1997.

West, Cornel. *Race Matters.* Beacon Press, 1993.

Wicker, Tom. *Tragic Failure: Racial Integration in America.* New York: William Morrow, 1996.

Williams, Juan. *Eyes on the Prize: America's Civil Rights Years, 1954–1965.* New York: Viking Penguin, Blackside, Inc., 1987.

Wills, Garry. *Lincoln at Gettysburg: The Words That Remade America.* New York: Simon and Schuster, 1992.

Wilson, Douglas L. *Honor's Voice: The Transformation of Abraham Lincoln.* New York: Alfred A. Knopf, 1998.

Wright, Ronald. *Stolen Continents: The Americas Through Indian Eyes Since 1492.* A Peter Davison book, 1992.

Yergin, Daniel. *The Commanding Heights: The Battle Between Government and the Marketplace That Is Remaking the Modern World.* New York: Simon and Schuster, 1998.